BRAHMS AMONG FRIENDS

AMS Studies in Music

CHRISTOPHER REYNOLDS, *General Editor*

Conceptualizing Music:
Cognitive Structure, Theory, and Analysis
Lawrence Zbikowski

Inventing the Business of Opera:
The Impresario and His World in Seventeenth-Century Venice
Beth L. Glixon and Jonathan Glixon

Lateness and Brahms:
Music and Culture in the Twilight of Viennese Liberalism
Margaret Notley

The Critical Nexus:
Tone-System, Mode, and Notation in Early Medieval Music
Charles M. Atkinson

Music, Criticism, and the Challenge of History:
Shaping Modern Musical Thought in Late Nineteenth-Century Vienna
Kevin C. Karnes

Jewish Music and Modernity
Philip V. Bohlman

Changing the Score:
Arias, Prima Donnas, and the Authority of Performance
Hilary Poriss

Rasa:
Affect and Intuition in Javanese Musical Aesthetics
Marc Benamou

Josquin's Rome:
Hearing and Composing in the Sistine Chapel
Jesse Rodin

Details of Consequence:
Ornament, Music, and Art in Paris
Gurminder Kaur Bhogal

Sounding Authentic:
The Rural Miniature and Musical Modernism
Joshua S. Walden

Brahms Among Friends:
Listening, Performance, and the Rhetoric of Allusion
Paul Berry

BRAHMS AMONG FRIENDS

Listening, Performance, and the Rhetoric of Allusion

Paul Berry

OXFORD
UNIVERSITY PRESS

OXFORD
UNIVERSITY PRESS

Oxford University Press is a department of the
University of Oxford. It furthers the University's objective
of excellence in research, scholarship, and education
by publishing worldwide

Oxford   New York
Auckland   Cape Town   Dar es Salaam   Hong Kong   Karachi
Kuala Lumpur   Madrid   Melbourne   Mexico City   Nairobi
New Delhi   Shanghai   Taipei   Toronto

With offices in
Argentina   Austria   Brazil   Chile   Czech Republic   France   Greece
Guatemala   Hungary   Italy   Japan   Poland   Portugal   Singapore
South Korea   Switzerland   Thailand   Turkey   Ukraine   Vietnam

Oxford is a registered trade mark of Oxford University Press
in the UK and certain other countries

Published in the United States of America by
Oxford University Press
198 Madison Avenue, New York, NY 10016

.   © Oxford University Press 2014

Library of Congress Cataloging-in-Publication Data
Berry, Paul, 1977- author.
Brahms among friends : listening, performance, and
the rhetoric of allusion / Paul Berry.
pages   cm.— (AMS studies in music)
Includes bibliographical references and index.
ISBN 978-0-19-998264-6 (hardback : alk. paper)
1. Brahms, Johannes, 1833-1897—Criticism and interpretation.   I. Title.
ML410.B8B425 2014
780.92—dc23
2013031618

1 3 5 7 9 8 6 4 2
Printed in the United States of America
on acid-free paper

For friends past and present

ACKNOWLEDGMENTS

To fully recount the kindness of those who have made this volume possible, I would need to write another book. During the final months, Suzanne Ryan, Adam Cohen, Jessen O'Brien, Erica Woods-Tucker, Mary Sutherland, and the staff at Oxford University Press guided the project to fruition smoothly and graciously. Paul Kerekes and Benjamin Wallace created reams of meticulous musical examples with unflappable good cheer. Most of all, Christopher Reynolds read and reread each chapter with extraordinary precision and sympathy. For myriad improvements of style and substance, for stimulating interchange, and for unfailing encouragement, I remain deeply in his debt.

Throughout a decade of work on the book, crucial funding has come from several institutions, including a Fellowship from the National Endowment for the Humanities and research grants and fellowships from Yale University, the Yale School of Music, the University of North Texas, and the American Brahms Society. I am grateful to administrators and staff at Yale and the University of North Texas, especially Robert Blocker of the Yale School of Music and James Scott of the UNT College of Music. Without their support, the book would not exist. Likewise, I could never have completed it without assistance and generous permissions from archives, libraries, and publishing houses on two continents. In particular, I thank Dr. Prof. Otto Biba, Suzanne Lovejoy, Amy Hague, Dr. Prof. Wolfgang Sandberger, Richard Saunders, Dr. Roland Schmidt-Hensel, Dr. Wolf-Dieter Seiffert, Dr. Michael Struck, Dr. Thomas Synofzik, Dr. Silvia Uhlemann, Anita Wilke, and the caring staff at the Brahms-Institut an der Musikhochschule Lübeck, the Gesellschaft der Musikfreunde in Vienna, the Österreichische Nationalbibliothek, the Smith College Library, the Staatsbibliothek in Berlin, the Staats- und Universitätsbibliothek in Hamburg, the Universitätsbibliothek in Basel, the Universitäts- und Landesbibliothek in Darmstadt, the Wienbibliothek im Rathaus, the Yale University Music Library, and the Beinecke Rare Book and Manuscript Library at Yale University.

At every stage of the project, colleagues and friends have given unstintingly of their time and expertise. Floyd Grave provided detailed editorial assistance with my article, "Old Love: Johannes Brahms, Clara Schumann, and the Poetics of Musical Memory" (*Journal of Musicology*, 2007), which now forms the basis for chapter 6. Kristina Muxfeldt, Michael Friedmann, and Leon Plantinga have each continued to offer invaluable comments throughout the years since they served as readers for my dissertation, parts of which have worked their way into several chapters of the present volume. In addition to the readers and editors named above, I have benefited enormously from conversation and music making with Styra Avins, Daniel Beller-McKenna, Eric Bianchi, Benjamin Brand, David Brodbeck, David Clampitt, Richard Cohn, Dane Gordon, Virginia Hancock, Joel Haney, James Hepokoski, Robert Holzer, Evan Horowitz, Patrick McCreless, Margaret Notley, Ellen Rosand, Charles Rosen, Karl Schrom, Sarah Waltz, and the wonderful graduate students who challenged me each week in seminars on Brahms and Schubert at the UNT College of Music and the Yale School of Music. Because of them, and many others, each of the pages that follow will always bear the imprint of fond memories.

My gratitude goes last to those dearest to me. To my father, Paul, forever my favorite singer, and my mother, Elvera, the most dedicated rhetorician I know, for nurturing the confluence of interests that sustains my work; to my sons, Quinby and Benjamin, for long patience with a parent distracted by music and history; and above all to my wife, Holly, my truest friend, for all that we are and will be together—my thanks and love.

CONTENTS

BRAHMS AMONG FRIENDS

HISTORIOGRAPHIES OF ALLUSION

Among the remnants of Johannes Brahms's library in Vienna is a collection of children's folk songs arranged by his friend Elisabeth von Herzogenberg. The collection was not published until 1888, but Brahms's version was a copyist's manuscript from August 1881. It was annotated by Elisabeth herself and dedicated in pencil to her "honored and dear teacher and friend Heini von Steyer."[1] In place of Brahms's name Elisabeth invoked the refrain from "Dörpertanzweise" (Peasant Dance Tune), perhaps the most famous poem in Joseph Victor von Scheffel's 1863 collection *Frau Aventiure*, which Brahms owned. As Scheffel's text unfolds, a growing chorus of birds, beasts, and citizens celebrates a heroic musician's return after a long absence by closing each stanza with the same line: "Heini von Steier is home once again!" Against a steady drumbeat of communal good cheer, the last two stanzas then deepen and complicate the emotional implications of homecoming, at least for the hero and those closest to him.

Der aber hebt schweigend der Fiedel zur Brust...	But he, without speaking, holds fiddle to chest...
Halb brütend, halb geigend—des Volks unbewußt.	Half brooding, half playing—ignoring the folk.
Leis knisternd strömt Feuer um Saiten und Hand...	Soft crackling fire engulfs strings and hand...
Der Heini von Steier ist wieder im Land!	Heini von Steier is home once again!

[1] The copy survives in the archives of the Gesellschaft der Musikfreunde in Vienna, catalogued as VI 36483. Other samples of Elisabeth's handwriting appear on the cover of Antje Ruhbaum, *Elisabeth von Herzogenberg: Salon–Mäzenatentum–Musikförderung* (Kenzingen: Centaurus, 2009). Concerning the inception of Elisabeth's folk-song arrangements, see Johannes Brahms and Elisabeth and Heinrich von Herzogenberg, *Johannes Brahms im Briefwechsel mit Heinrich und Elisabeth von Herzogenberg*, ed. Max Kalbeck, 1:viii–ix (Berlin: Deutsche Brahms-Gesellschaft, 1912).

...Im Gärtlein der Nonnen auf blumiger Höh	...In the nuns' little garden on the flowery hill
Lehnt Eine am Bronnen und weint in den Klee:	One leans on the well and weeps in the clover:
"O Gürtel und Schleier...o schwarzes Gewand.	"O girdle and veil...o vestments of black...
Der Heini von Steier ist wieder im Land!"[2]	Heini von Steier is home once again!"

Brahms's professional itinerary for 1881 made the reference to Scheffel's poem both timely and flattering. Just one month before receiving Elisabeth's folk-song arrangements, he had renewed contact with her and her husband after a long silence and a six-week sojourn in Italy. Alongside tantalizing accounts of his vacation, his letters also included teasers for a brand-new orchestral piece, the Piano Concerto in B♭ major, which would soon be released as his Op. 83. As the Herzogenbergs knew, the latest concerto capped a period of unusual productivity for the typically methodical composer. In just five years, he had completed two symphonies, two concert overtures, two concerti, a string quartet, a violin sonata, ten piano pieces, three choral works, and nearly two dozen songs and duets.[3] The return to German-speaking soil of one of Germany's most prominent composers, bearing the latest in a formidable series of large-scale works, provided a ready parallel for the triumphant musical homecoming celebrated by Scheffel's multitudes, linking the dedication unmistakably to its recipient. Moreover, in the wake of Brahms's arrival in Austria, the Herzogenbergs had already begun campaigning for a face-to-face visit with their increasingly famous acquaintance, whose friendship with them was then at its height. For a reader familiar with the end of Scheffel's text, Elisabeth's dedication implicitly refigured their excitement as the anxiety of secret lovers, lending a playful urgency to their request.

Once Brahms proceeded past the title page, Elisabeth's music itself drew him close as well, this time in a manner so subtle that she apparently did not trust him to notice it on his own. At the beginning of her third song, *Wiegenlied* (Lullaby), she added a pair of revealing annotations to the copyist's score. A pencil bracket and ink quotation marks highlighted an accompanimental figure borrowed from one of Brahms's own arrangements of children's folksongs:

[2] Joseph Victor von Scheffel, *Frau Aventiure: Lieder aus Heinrich von Osterdingens Zeit* (Stuttgart: J. B. Metzler, 1863), 173. For details concerning Brahms's own copy of *Frau Aventiure*, see Kurt Hofmann, *Die Bibliothek von Johannes Brahms* (Hamburg: Karl Dieter Wagner, 1974), 98.

[3] The standard reference guides concerning Brahms's movements and the timing of his compositions are Renate and Kurt Hofmann, *Johannes Brahms, Zeittafel zu Leben und Werk* (Tutzing: Hans Schneider, 1983), and Margit McCorkle, *Johannes Brahms: Thematisch-bibliographisches Werkverzeichnis*, ed. in collaboration with Donald M. McCorkle† (München: Henle, 1984).

Sandmännchen (Little Sandman), the fourth of the fifteen *Volkskinderlieder*, WoO 31 (indicates works without opus number). Initially published anonymously in 1858, *Sandmännchen* had swiftly emerged as the most popular of the *Volkskinderlieder* once Brahms's authorship became known in the early 1870s.[4] Examples I.1a and b compare the opening measures of the two arrangements. Although resemblances are most apparent in the right hand of a sensitive pianist, they extended to every strand in the polyphonic fabric, from the singer's melody to the register and scale-degree content of the bass line. The similarity was brief, confined largely to the first four beats. Without the chance survival of the copy in Brahms's library, one would be hard pressed to identify Elisabeth's borrowing in the first place, let alone to argue convincingly that it was intended for anyone else's apprehension. Discovered in tandem with the dedication, however, her music-analytic annotations hint at a wealth of resonances both musical and personal.

EXAMPLE I.1a   Elisabeth von Herzogenberg, *Wiegenlied*, mm. 1–2. From an unidentified copyist's manuscript with autograph annotations (Gesellschaft der Musikfreunde, Vienna).

EXAMPLE I.1b   Brahms, *Sandmännchen*, WoO 31 No. 4, mm. 1–2

Elisabeth's score thus bears witness to a culture of mingled social and compositional interchange among Brahms and his associates. It also provides an opportunity

---

[4] In 1872, Rieter-Biedermann released a second edition of the *Volkskinderlieder*, now with English texts, and placed Brahms's name on the title page for the first time; a flood of transcriptions and arrangements greeted *Sandmännchen* within two years (see McCorkle, *Werkverzeichnis*, 581–83).

to reflect on the complementary roles of music-analytic judgment and primary documents in exploring that culture. Both topics are central to this book.

In the historiography of nineteenth-century music, public spheres have long overshadowed the more intimate contexts in which many new works were composed and performed. The wider availability of primary documents related to concert life, the continued dominance of large-scale genres in the Western European canon, and a marked emphasis on political and other broader contexts in recent musicological discourse have all partially obscured our view of the private music making that characterized the daily activities of many composers. Brahms's case is typical. His four symphonies and a handful of choral and orchestral works have remained central to musicological literature for over a century. His more extensive output in the small-scale genres of song, part-song, sonata, piano trio, and piano miniature has hardly been ignored; still, relative to its sheer preponderance within his oeuvre, this repertoire has received less consistent and concentrated attention, particularly with respect to its reception within the composer's circles. Throughout his career, Brahms crafted works in intimate genres and, like Elisabeth von Herzogenberg, shared them with friends prior to publication, inviting suggestions and discussing both the impressions his music had made and the personal contexts for which some of it was explicitly designed. Much of his correspondence was published early in the twentieth century, leading scholars beginning with Max Kalbeck and Karl Geiringer to posit connections between compositional activity and personal biography in his music.[5] Yet over the decades it has proven difficult and, at times, unfashionable to investigate how his compositional choices might be linked to specific aspects of his life and social milieu. While current studies of his songs and chamber works invariably acknowledge the potential for interplay between Brahms's compositional practice and the initial private audiences for his music, relatively few investigate the practical consequences of that interplay in detail.

Particularly in English-language literature, the main exceptions have occurred in scholarship concerning allusion, an intriguing but vexed topic in its own right. Given basic chronological plausibility, the tendency in Brahms studies has been to understand close musical resemblances among his works, or between them and those of other composers, allusively—that is, to interpret them, like Elisabeth's annotated borrowing, as deliberately referential gestures. One can understand why. Brahms's knowledge of music by his predecessors was famously

---

[5] Max Kalbeck, *Johannes Brahms*, 4 vols. (Berlin: Deutsche Brahms-Gesellschaft, 1915–27); Karl Geiringer, *Johannes Brahms: Leben und Schaffen eines deutschen Meisters* (Vienna: Rohrer, 1935).

wide ranging, and his own style often strikes modern listeners as nostalgic or evocative.[6] Moreover, despite a deep and abiding reticence concerning his own compositional process, Brahms himself occasionally admitted employing allusive strategies in the strictly intentional sense defined here, lending authorial sanction to what has since become a long-standing critical tradition. First and foremost, then, imputed allusions have figured prominently in Brahms scholarship precisely because their presumed intentionality opens a back door to a notoriously shuttered compositional workshop. Indeed, for some specialists they have arguably taken on many of the roles that sketches and drafts usually fill in studies of composers less prone to the destruction of unpublished materials. But all the while, they have also formed the basis for stimulating claims regarding his biography and interpersonal relationships. The most prominent of these claims involve music completed during the tumultuous beginnings of Brahms's acquaintance with Clara Schumann. In foundational studies of the Piano Trio, Op. 8, the Variations on a Theme of Robert Schumann, Op. 9, and the first Piano Concerto, Op. 15, purported allusive gestures have played pivotal roles in the retrospective evaluation of Brahms's feelings, romantic and otherwise.[7]

Small wonder, then, that scholars have continually sought for ways to tease instances and theories of allusion out of Brahms's music, from his symphonies to his small-scale works.[8] This book will do so as well, starting from a straightforward definition consonant with decades of previous discourse

[6] Recent literature on the topic of nostalgia or pastness in Brahms's music includes Daniel Beller-McKenna, "Distance and Disembodiment: Harps, Horns, and the Requiem Idea in Schumann and Brahms," *Journal of Musicology* 22 (2005): 47–89; Karen Bottge, "Brahms's 'Wiegenlied' and the Maternal Voice," *19th-Century Music* 28 (2005): 185–213; Elmar Budde, "Brahms oder der Versuch, das Ende zu denken," in *Abschied in die Gegenwart: Teleologie und Zustand in der Musik*, ed. Otto Kolleritsch, 267–78 (Vienna: Universal, 1998); Marjorie Hirsch, "The Spiral Journey Back Home: Brahms's 'Heimweh' Lieder," *Journal of Musicology* 22 (2005): 454–89; Margaret Notley, *Lateness and Brahms: Music and Culture in the Twilight of Viennese Liberalism* (Oxford: Oxford University Press, 2006); and Reinhold Brinkmann, *Late Idyll: The Second Symphony of Johannes Brahms*, trans. Peter Palmer (Cambridge. MA: Harvard University Press, 1995).

[7] Dillon Parmer, "Brahms, Song Quotation, and Secret Programs," *19th-Century Music* 19 (1995): 161–90; and Kenneth Hull, "Brahms the Allusive: Extra-Compositional Reference in the Instrumental Music of Johannes Brahms" (PhD diss., Princeton University, 1989); John Daverio, *Crossing Paths: Schubert, Schumann, and Brahms* (Oxford: Oxford University Press, 2002); 143–52; and Christopher Reynolds, "A Choral Symphony by Brahms?" *19th-Century Music* 9 (1985): 3–25.

[8] Symphonic repertoire provided especially fertile ground in the 1990s. Among the most prominent examples are David Brodbeck, *Brahms: Symphony No. 1* (Cambridge: Cambridge University Press, 1997); Kenneth Hull, "Allusive Irony in Brahms's Fourth Symphony," in *Brahms Studies 2*, ed. David Brodbeck, 135–68 (Lincoln: University of Nebraska 1998); and Raymond Knapp, *Brahms and the Challenge of the Symphony* (Hillsdale, NY: Pendragon Press, 1997). Recent studies involving chamber music and song include David Clampitt, "In Brahms's Workshop: Compositional Modeling in Op. 40, *Adagio mesto*" (paper presented at the Society for Music Theory annual meeting in Seattle, WA, 2004); Parmer, "Song Quotation" and "Brahms and the Poetic Motto: A Hermeneutic Aid?" *Journal of Musicology* 15 (1997): 353–89; and, above all, Christopher Reynolds, *Motives for Allusion: Context and Content in Nineteenth-Century Music* (Cambridge. MA: Harvard University Press, 2003).

on the subject: an allusive gesture entails a composer's deliberate incorporation into a new work of musical material that is designed to be perceived as
a reference to a specific preexisting work by some intended audience.[9] Yet in
recent years the hunt for new and ever-more-abstruse allusions has also provoked well-warranted skepticism from those who question the reliability of
music-analytic comparison in identifying the motivations behind seemingly
referential gestures.[10] Brahms's peculiar blend of evasiveness and ironic detachment regarding his working methods has exacerbated the problem. In
the absence of documentary evidence regarding his attitudes toward a given
musical resemblance, his assimilative style and encyclopedic mind can quickly
become blanks on which modern listeners inadvertently imprint their own
priorities. It is simply too easy to hear what one wants to hear or, more
subtly, to assume that whatever musical similarity one has discovered must
have been placed there deliberately in order to attract one's attention.

A thorough investigation of Brahms's musical friendships must therefore
begin by resituating the practice of allusion, first compositionally, within a
broader continuum of possible motivations for his borrowings, and then historically, within a deeper investigation of the social contexts of his music
making. As a point of departure, table I.1 provides a chronologically ordered
list of every allusive gesture for which solid documentary evidence of Brahms's
conscious awareness survives today. For eight of the thirteen examples, he revealed his compositional procedure unequivocally in extant correspondence,
most famously for the *Wiegenlied* and the finale of the first Violin Sonata.[11] Two
more referential gestures (in the *Geistliches Wiegenlied* and *Unüberwindlich*) were
also labeled explicitly in the published score in ways analogous to Elisabeth's
borrowing. For the remaining three examples (the *Triumphlied*, *Auf dem Kirch-*

---

[9] For the most influential precedent for this definition and a brief history of previous attempts, see Reynolds, *Motives for Allusion*, 1–6.

[10] Perhaps the most resounding call for reform in recent scholarly approaches to Brahms's allusive proce-
dures is John Daverio's thorough critique of Eric Sams's "Clara cipher" in *Crossing Paths*, 65–87. Although
Daverio's dismissal is directed toward a special subset of allusive techniques, it has also stimulated and
resonated with broader criticisms of allusion hunting in general. See James Hepokoski, "Beethoven
Reception: The Symphonic Tradition," in *The Cambridge History of Nineteenth-Century Music*, ed. Jim
Samson, 424–59 (Cambridge: Cambridge University Press, 2002); and Virginia Hancock's review of *The
Cambridge Companion to Brahms*, ed. Michael Musgrave, in *Music & Letters* 83 (2002): 131–33.

[11] Johannes Brahms and Joseph Joachim, *Johannes Brahms im Briefwechsel mit Joseph Joachim*, ed. Andreas
Moser, 1:56 (Berlin: Deutsche Brahms-Gesellschaft, 1908); Kalbeck, *Brahms* 2: 326–27; Julia Wirth (née
Stockhausen), *Julius Stockhausen, der Sänger des deutschen Liedes: Nach Dokumenten seiner Zeit* (Frankfurt
am Main: Englert und Schlosser, 1927), 482; Johannes Brahms and Julius Stockhausen, *Johannes Brahms
im Briefwechsel mit Julius Stockhausen*, ed. Renate Hofmann, 130 (Tutzing: Schneider, 1993); Brahms/
Herzogenberg, *Briefwechsel* 1:35–36; Theodor Billroth and Johannes Brahms, *Billroth und Brahms im Brief-
wechsel: Mit Einleitung, Anmerkungen und 4 Bildtafeln*, ed. Otto Gottlieb-Billroth, 283 (Berlin and Vienna:
Urban & Schwarzenberg, 1935); Johannes Brahms, *Briefe an P. J. und Fritz Simrock*, ed. Max Kalbeck, 2:155
(Berlin: Deutsche Brahms-Gesellschaft, 1917–19); and Billroth/Brahms, *Briefwechsel*, 398.

TABLE I.I Brahms's Acknowledged Allusive Gestures

Date	New composition	Source of borrowing
1854	Variations, Op. 9	Clara Schumann, Romance variée
1864	Geistliches Wiegenlied, Op. 91 No. 2	Josef, lieber Josef mein (medieval cantio)
1868	Wiegenlied, Op. 49 No. 4	Alexander Baumann, S'is Anderscht
1871	Triumphlied, Op. 55	Nun danket alle Gott (chorale tune)
1871	Dämmrung senkte sich von oben, Op. 59 No. 1	Hermann Levi, Dämmrung senkte sich von oben
1876	Symphony No. 1, Op. 68 / IV	Beethoven, Symphony No. 9, Op. 125 / IV
1876	Unüberwindlich, Op. 72 No. 5	Domenico Scarlatti, Sonata in D, K. 233
1877	Es liebt sich so lieblich im Lenze, Op. 71 No. 1	Julius Stockhausen, Die Wellen blinken
1877	O schöne Nacht, Op. 92 No. 1	Heinrich von Herzogenberg, Notturno II, Op. 22 No. 2
1879	Violin Sonata, Op. 78 / III	Brahms, Regenlied and Nachklang, Op. 59 Nos. 3 and 4
1880	Academic Festival Overture, Op. 80	Student songs (including Gaudeamus igitur)
1886	Violin Sonata, Op. 100 / I	Brahms, Wie Melodien zieht es mir, Op. 105 No. 2
1887	Auf dem Kirchhofe, Op. 105 No. 4	J. S. Bach, chorale from the Saint Matthew Passion

hofe, and the finale from the First Symphony), one must rely upon the accounts of Joseph Victor Widmann and Max Kalbeck, both of whom are generally deemed reliable witnesses concerning their personal interactions with Brahms.[12]

Kalbeck's anecdote concerning the finale to the First Symphony is perhaps better known than any of Brahms's own direct acknowledgments of allusive intent. When a musically educated noblewoman drew his attention to the "remarkable" similarity between his primary theme and that of Beethoven's Ode to Joy, Brahms reportedly responded "Certainly, and what's even more remarkable is that every jackass hears it right away." The story has been widely circulated in print and by word of mouth because it encapsulates the prickliness, plain speaking, and occasional misogyny that formed crucial aspects of the composer's character, at least as presented in countless biographical sketches. At the same time, the quotation reinforces the commonly held conviction that his allusive gestures served primarily to position his works relative to the emerging

[12] Joseph Victor Widmann, Johannes Brahms in Erinnerungen (Berlin: Gebrüder Paetel, 1898), 117; Kalbeck, Brahms 4:134; and ibid. 3:109n.

musical canon in the ears of a large and diverse musical public. Generations of scholars have rightly interpreted Brahms's remark as an oblique admission that his finale demands to be understood in relation to Beethoven's, notwithstanding his evident chagrin as to the misguided conclusions that dilettantish audiences might draw from that relationship.[13] To what extent the character traits and allusive motivations highlighted by Kalbeck's account held true in more private circumstances and less monumental musical genres has remained a more open question.

The existence of particular letters in Brahms's hand and the decisions of acquaintances to include specific anecdotes in their published reminiscences of the composer are, of course, accidents of history. Brahms clearly employed allusive techniques in works for which no explicit documentary confirmation of his intentions survives. The theme from the slow movement of the String Sextet, Op. 36, and the Alphorn theme from the introduction to the finale of the First Symphony provide clear examples; both were borrowed directly from musical excerpts that Brahms had interpolated into correspondence nearly ten years prior to the completion of the new works.[14] At the same time, a handful of compositions from early in his career include apparent musical ciphers, most notably the acronym for Joseph Joachim's self-proclaimed motto, *Frei aber einsam*, in the scherzo to the so-called FAE sonata, WoO 2, and Agathe von Siebold's first name (AGAHE) in both the women's part-song *Und gehst du über den Kirchhof*, Op. 44 No. 10, and the opening movement of the String Sextet, Op. 36. These are not included in table I.1 because ciphers constitute an exceptional situation: each putative instance refers to an abstract musical object rather than a preexisting musical work.

Nevertheless, even construed narrowly and limited by the chance survival of existing documents, the list of definitively acknowledged allusive gestures permits important generalizations regarding Brahms's preferred allusive strategies and the audiences for which they were designed.[15] As a group, the thirteen examples span from the earliest stages of Brahms's career to the last and run the gamut of genres across his entire output. Symphonies, accompanied choruses, songs, part-songs, and works for solo piano and chamber ensemble are all

---

[13] See Charles Rosen, "Brahms: Classicism and the Inspiration of Awkwardness," in *Critical Entertainments: Music Old and New* (Cambridge, MA: Harvard University Press, 2000), 162–97; and Brodbeck, *Brahms: Symphony No. 1*, 64–65. The allusion to Beethoven's finale was already an important strand in the reception of Brahms's symphony during the nineteenth century; see Brodbeck, 86, and Walter Frisch, *Brahms: The Four Symphonies* (New Haven, CT: Yale University Press, 2003), 146.

[14] Johannes Brahms and Clara Schumann, *Briefe aus den Jahren 1853–1896*, ed. Berthold Litzmann, 1:75 and 597 (Leipzig: Breitkopf & Härtel, 1927). Brahms also kept his own copy of the Sextet's theme in a small notebook that Clara had given him on Christmas Eve, 1854; that notebook is now preserved in the Wienbibliothek im Rathaus, Vienna.

[15] For a more general set of music-analytic criteria supposedly common to allusive gestures in Brahms's works, see Hull, "Brahms the Allusive."

represented as sources and hosts for musical borrowing. Yet despite their diverse generic contexts, the borrowings all share a remarkable musical precision relative to their sources. That precision can be described in at least three ways. First, like the initial gesture in Elisabeth's folk-song arrangement, every acknowledged allusion is concise, confined to a few short measures. Without exception, they stimulate brief flashes of insight in the mind of an informed listener rather than long-range structural comparisons. In other words, they differ markedly from the venerable technique of compositional modeling. This is not to say that Brahms never relied on previous music in constructing the large-scale framework of new compositions. To the contrary, he arguably based whole movements or even entire works on the tonal and formal outlines of specific models, especially early in his career. Examples include the third movement of the first piano concerto, Op. 15, the slow movement of the Horn Trio, Op. 40, and numerous solo songs.[16] Yet in documents that survive, he never implied that anyone was meant to notice his models. His acknowledged allusions, by contrast, were all condensed enough to attract attention as discrete references to previously existing music.

Second, whenever the sources for Brahms's borrowings were polyphonic, his allusive gestures incorporated elements of the full polyphonic textures of those sources. As in Elisabeth's folk-song setting, references to preexisting melodic lines brought with them the particular harmonies and voice-leading complexes that originally accompanied those melodic lines. Especially given the overwhelming emphasis on melodic resemblance in recent studies of allusion in nineteenth-century music, this aspect of Brahms's practice cries out for recognition: his acknowledged allusions were never merely borrowed patterns of melodic pitches. Even in the *Geistliches Wiegenlied*, the *Triumphlied*, and the Academic Festival Overture, for which the sources for his borrowings were simple, unaccompanied tunes, he invariably placed those tunes into a harmonic context that confirmed the unique scale-degree identity of each of their pitches. Moreover, he also duplicated precisely the relative rhythmic value of each pitch, making these melodic allusions arguably more literal in their presentation of borrowed material than any of his admitted references to polyphonic music. Indeed, one might provisionally conclude from the examples in table I.1 that the fewer musical parameters Brahms had at his disposal in creating a given allusive relationship, the more rigorous the remaining resemblances were between his new music and its source.

---

[16] Charles Rosen has described the first instance in "Brahms: Influence, Plagiarism, and Inspiration," in *Critical Entertainments*, 132–34, while David Clampitt has provided the most detailed account of the second in "In Brahms's Workshop." Songs unmistakably modeled on historical precedents include *Trost in Tränen*, Op. 48 No. 5, *In der Fremde*, Op. 3 No. 5, and *Mondnacht*, WoO 21, each of which sets a text for which Schubert or Schumann had already published a compelling setting.

Finally, in every case, Brahms's acknowledged allusions also involved musical characteristics that are most easily apprehended aurally and kinesthetically, in the moment of listening or performance, rather than through the pitch-specific parameters that have come to dominate music-theoretic and music-analytic discourse in academic circles since his death. Dynamics, articulation, register, tempo and affect, melodic and harmonic rhythm, and the many interrelated features associated with musical texture all provided critical opportunities to reinforce a referential relationship between new music and its preexisting source. By the same token, the placement of borrowed material invariably aligned its appearance with an important formal juncture in the unfolding of the new piece: the beginning of a movement, the coalescing of a new thematic area, the achievement of tonal closure for the whole. In these regards as well, Elisabeth's annotated borrowing emulated its recipient's allusive preferences exactly (ex. I.1). Register, meter, and harmonic rhythm all coincided precisely, and the reference drew together the initial melodic gestures of each song.

If Elisabeth's strategy in her *Wiegenlied* is any indication, the combination of conciseness, polyphonic density, and instantiation across aural and kinesthetic parameters may already have been understood as identifying features of Brahms's allusive practice during his lifetime, at least among some members of his circles. Yet the mere presence of these features is by no means a reliable indication of Brahms's allusive intent. They are also characteristic of myriad musical resemblances for which a far broader spectrum of explanations might obtain instead. Examples I.2a and b present the final vocal cadences of *In Waldeseinsamkeit* (In Forest Solitude), Op. 85 No. 6, and *Es schauen die Blumen* (The Flowers Gaze), Op. 96 No. 3, solo songs completed in 1878 and 1884 during the height of Brahms's craft and influence. Both vocal lines end by leaping upward from downbeat to upbeat and from scale degree 3 to 5 in B major. Brahms used this scale-degree pattern as a closing cadential formula in less than 3 percent of his solo songs; that two of these should be set in the same key suggests a special connection between register and melodic contour. Moreover, in both songs the accompaniment to the final cadence begins at its apex, then systematically retreats below the singer in both dynamic and registral space. Even for a male vocalist, the final f♯' is the highest sounding pitch at the end of both songs, leaving the singer free to employ a soft falsetto rather than his full voice. Perhaps the unique sonority of falsetto singing was part of what motivated Brahms's choice of key and cadential pattern in the first place. Finally, the vocal line's straightforward major-mode ending is inflected in both songs by a plagal cadence and modally ambiguous G♮s in the accompaniment.

EXAMPLE I.2a   Brahms, *In Waldeseinsamkeit*, Op. 85 No. 6, mm. 30–33

EXAMPLE I.2b   Brahms, *Es schauen die Blumen*, Op. 96 No. 3, mm. 28–31

In both passages, vocal tessitura, dynamics, texture, and minor-tinged harmonies create the same rare and striking sonic quality, at once plangent and
opulent. Such a sonic quality is textually appropriate at the conclusion of both
songs, though for slightly different reasons. The lyric subject in Karl Lemcke's
poem "In Waldeseinsamkeit" speaks directly to his beloved, recalling a shared
moment of physical intimacy and unspecified emotional import: "In mute
struggle I sank / my head into your lap, / and in my trembling hands / I clasped
your knee." One cannot tell whether the remembered moment represents the
first consummation of his love, the beginnings of a painful break with his beloved, or both. Rather than reveal the significance of his memories, the speaker
closes by invoking the sound of a distant nightingale, an image for which
Brahms's cadence facilitates an appropriately quiet and modally enigmatic
sonic analogue. The poetic speaker in Heinrich Heine's "Es schauen die
Blumen" also traces an ambivalent emotional trajectory, but this time with respect to a physically absent beloved who can be reached only in song. The
upward leap and quiet dynamics of Brahms's vocal cadence register the imminent departure of the music that "flutters" toward the beloved, while the modal
mixture in the piano underscores an ironic truth: the speaker's songs themselves are "melancholy and sad," bearers of tears and sighs instead of cheerful
greetings.

In these songs, then, the same distinctive vocal gesture and characteristic accompanimental strategy provided satisfying closure to independent but commensurate affective trajectories. Such a situation could have come about in at least two ways. On the one hand, Brahms might have composed the two passages almost automatically, with little effort and no conscious aware-ness of their similarity. After all, by the 1880s he had spent thirty years and literally hundreds of vocal compositions honing a stockpile of text-setting devices. When confronted by vaguely analogous tasks, he was bound to reach highly similar solutions from time to time, especially when working in the same key or for the same ensemble. According to such a scenario, the resem-blance at hand would best be understood not as a conscious reference but simply as a particularly striking manifestation of a fundamentally consistent musical style and manner of interpreting poetic texts. On the other hand, some compositional problems obviously demanded purposeful considera-tion. Brahms might have knowingly called *In Waldeseinsamkeit* to mind during his engagement with Heine's poem and borrowed from it deliber-ately, having recognized a convenient congruence between his old cadence

EMAMPLE I.3a   Brahms, *In der Ferne*, Op. 19 No. 3, mm. 58–72. Annotated.

and his new project. But in neither case does he seem likely to have expected anyone else to retrace his steps, nor would doing so seem likely to have altered anyone's interpretation of either song. With no documentary confirmation that he was aware of the similarity in the first place and no sense of an audience toward whom it might have been directed, one cannot justify a claim of allusive intent.

The situation was similar for the unaccompanied part-song *O süßer Mai* (O Sweet May), Op. 93a No. 3, in which an unnamed disquiet prevents Achim von Arnim's poetic speaker from enjoying the springtime. After twenty-eight measures of strict textural disjunction between the soprano and the rest of the

EXAMPLE I.3b   Brahms, *O süßer Mai*, Op. 93a No. 3, mm. 28–38. Annotated.

voices, a newly homogenous and lightly polyphonic texture emerges above a tonic pedal at the close of the song as the speaker asks to be set free "like song / along the dark hedgerows."[17] In the voice-leading patterns associated with this texture are unmistakable traces of the closing phrase of *In der Ferne* (In the Distance), Op. 19 No. 3, a solo setting of a poem by Ludwig Uhland. Examples I.3a and b compare annotated scores of the final phrases of the two works, in which bracketed voice-leading strands are labeled to reflect shared scale-degree content. The most obvious shared material occurs in the vocal line of *In der Ferne*, from which two four-measure phrase segments are borrowed almost verbatim in *O süßer Mai*—the first in the part-song's soprano line (labeled S1) and the second divided successively among its soprano, alto, and tenor lines (S2). Although a newly composed tonic pedal accompanies the first phrase segment in the part-song, the solo song's stepwise bass descent from scale degree 2 to 7 (B1) is preserved in the alto and baritone lines, while the inner voice of the piano accompaniment of *In der Ferne* (I1) reappears in the tenor line. The second phrase segment acquires a tonic pedal in both works (B2), and the part-song concludes with an ascending horn-fifth gesture in its soprano and alto parts, just like the close of the solo song's piano postlude (S3).

The ordered combination of these voice-leading strands leaves little doubt that memories of *In der Ferne* played a substantial role, whether consciously or reflexively, in the composition of *O süßer Mai*. As in the two solo songs, textual congruencies may help account for how the one came to mind during the making of the other, even at a distance of nearly twenty-five years. Like von Arnim's poem, Uhland's places its poetic speaker alone amid springtime surroundings to which the speaker eventually addresses his inner thoughts. But most of the borrowed voice-leading strands are woven subtly into the part-song's polyphonic texture, while the half-diminished supertonic seventh that harmonizes the chromatic inner voice from *In der Ferne* has already marked two previous half cadences in *O süßer Mai*, providing clear antecedents in light of which the closing cadence functions as a natural consequent. In short, the borrowings sound so unremarkable, so at home in their new context, that it seems most plausible for Brahms to have used them purely as a means of generating the closing measures of his part-song without ever intending anyone to notice what he had done. In purely musical terms, the result was as concise and polyphonically imbricated as any of his acknowledged allusive gestures, but it also concealed its effects from listeners familiar with its source.

---

[17] Daniel Beller-McKenna has discussed these textural features in "*Verlorene Jugend*: the Backwards Glance in Brahms's Late Choral Lieder" (paper delivered at the American Musicological Society annual meeting, Washington DC, 2005).

Even blatant borrowings could remain hidden from Brahms's contemporaries if either the source or the borrowing itself was unpublished. Perhaps the simplest such instance occurred in five settings of Ophelia's songs from Shakespeare's *Hamlet*, WoO 22, which Brahms composed for the actress Olga Precheisen in November 1873.[18] Examples I.4a and b compare the initial measures of the first setting, *Wie erkenn' ich dein Treulieb?* (How should I know your true love?), to the beginning of *Vom verwundeten Knaben* (Of the Injured Boy), Op. 14 No. 2, which Brahms had published more than a decade prior. Aside from a small transposition, an aurally insignificant shift in meter, and a slight adjustment in the placement of nonharmonic tones, the first six beats of the two songs are virtually identical in both vocal line and accompaniment. As usual, one can understand why *Vom verwundeten Knabe* might have come to mind during the setting of Shakespeare's poem, since both songs set texts in which young maidens learn that their sweethearts have died. Nevertheless, Brahms could hardly have expected anyone but Olga Precheisen herself to apprehend his borrowing at all, let alone perceive it as an allusive gesture. He never chose to publish *Wie erkenn' ich dein Treulieb*, which survived only because the actress happened to retain her manuscript. Furthermore, the piano

EXAMPLE I.4a   Brahms, *Wie erkenn' ich dein Treulieb?*, WoO 22 No. 1, mm. 1–2

EXAMPLE I.4b   Brahms, *Vom verwundeten Knaben*, Op. 14 No. 2, mm. 1–4

[18] Brahms's reasons for composing the Ophelia songs are addressed in Karl Geiringer's preface to his edition of the songs, upon which example I.4a is based. See Geiringer, ed., *Johannes Brahms: Fünf Ophelia-Lieder für eine Sopranstimme und Klavierbegleitung* (Vienna: Schönborn, 1960), 3–4.

part, whose voice-leading patterns preserve the most convincing evidence of deliberate borrowing, was meant only as a rehearsal guide, to be omitted in any dramatic performance of the song. One can only conclude that Brahms borrowed from his own song for purely pragmatic reasons: the passage apparently accomplished the compositional goals he had assigned himself in the setting of Shakespeare's text, while saving him the trouble of inventing a new melody and accompaniment.

Related factors surely motivated other instances of deliberate but covert self-borrowing, which persisted throughout Brahms's career in both vocal and instrumental music. In the first three movements of the motet *Warum ist das Licht gegeben?*, Op. 74 No. 1, he pilfered wholesale from the "Missa Canonica," WoO 18, which he had composed as part of a series of counterpoint exercises in the 1850s but never released in print. Likewise culled from the unpublished trove of the 1850s, themes from a harmonically enigmatic Sarabande, WoO 5 No. 1, and lively Gavotte, WoO 3 No. 2, each found their way into the slow movement from the String Quintet, Op. 88.[19] And one such borrowing remained completely unnoticed until well into the twenty-first century. As

EXAMPLE I.5a   Brahms, *Allegro con espressione* (1853), mm. 1–8. From the autograph.

EXAMPLE I.5b   Brahms, Horn Trio, Op. 40 / II, mm. 287–94

[19] Robert Pascall has provided foundational studies of Brahms's borrowings in both the Op. 88 String Quintet and *Warum ist das Licht gegeben?*; see "Unknown Gavottes by Brahms," *Music & Letters* 57 (1976): 404–11; and "Brahms's *Missa Canonica* and its Recomposition in his 'Warum' Op. 74 No. 1," in *Brahms 2: Biographical, Documentary, and Analytical Studies*, ed. Michael Musgrave, 111–36 (Cambridge: Cambridge University Press, 1987).

shown in examples I.5a and b, the principal theme of the central trio section in the second movement of the Horn Trio, Op. 40, was adapted almost without change from the initial motives in a short but self-standing piano piece that Brahms had inscribed more than a decade prior in the scrapbook of Arnold Wehner, music director at the University of Göttingen. Until the scrapbook was sold at auction more 150 years later, the piano piece seems to have been forgotten by everyone but its composer. Its composition clearly predated all of the lasting friendships that Brahms formed after his introduction to Joseph Joachim and the Schumann circle, and no evidence hints that any of his acquaintances were aware of its existence.[20]

————

From the perspective of Brahms's compositional process, each of the similarities addressed thus far in his songs, choral works, and chamber music is as richly suggestive as any of his acknowledged allusions. Nevertheless, in the absence of documents concerning his intentions or evidence as to the reception of those similarities by any contemporary listeners, it would be irresponsible to interpret them as allusive gestures when other, more plausible explanations for their presence lie ready to hand. Instead, against a variegated background of compositional strategies ranging from stylistic reflex to surreptitious borrowing, the phenomenon of allusion was clearly only one among many possible motivations for close and music-analytically compelling resemblances in Brahms's oeuvre. Music-analytic characteristics alone are therefore necessary—but categorically insufficient—for the identification and assessment of his allusive gestures.

Fortunately, Brahms's acknowledged allusions also share generic and contextual characteristics. The overwhelming majority, ten out of thirteen, occurred in small-scale genres. Of those ten small-scale works, Brahms shared literally every one with a specific friend, in manuscript form, prior to publication. Furthermore, in at least nine of the ten cases, he was demonstrably aware that the source for his allusive borrowing had already acquired its own private connotations for that friend before his new manuscript arrived. And for all ten manuscripts, he not only suggested concrete ways in which his borrowing might be interpreted, but also indicated his interest in the response it would provoke from the person who had received it. In other words, in the intimate genres of song, part-song, sonata, and piano miniature, each of Brahms's acknowledged allusions was oriented, at least initially, toward a small and highly specialized audience—a particular acquaintance with whose manner of performance and

———

[20]At the behest of Doyle Auction Galleries in New York, Michael Struck first identified Brahms's piano piece and dated its inscription to January 1853 in an online catalogue dated April 20, 2011; the catalogue includes a facsimile of the entire autograph, on which example I.5a is based.

prior musical experiences he was deeply familiar and whose musical memories he could willfully reopen through the technique of musical borrowing.

These acquaintances are the central figures in this book. From the moment of his forced emergence into the forefront of European musical consciousness in 1853, Brahms found quiet sustenance in mutually rewarding relationships with multiple, overlapping, and constantly evolving groups of friends. Not surprisingly, many of his closest confidantes were professional musicians themselves. Joseph Joachim, Julius Stockhausen, and Clara Schumann were acknowledged as preeminent performers in their respective fields of violin, voice, and piano. Hermann Levi was one of Germany's most successful conductors, Julius Otto Grimm and Heinrich von Herzogenberg were published composers and teachers of music, and the singers Georg Henschel, Amalie Joachim, and Hermine Spies enjoyed international careers as well. Other close friends played or sang at a professional level despite not appearing on the concert stage. Marriage effectively ended the public careers of pianists such as Elisabeth von Herzogenberg and Emma Engelmann, and singers such as Bertha Faber and Ottilie Ebner, but all four women maintained their techniques through private performances. Of course, Brahms also maintained close connections with men and women in other professions (poet friends included Klaus Groth and Joseph Viktor Widmann, and scientists included Theodor Billroth and Theodor Wilhelm Engelmann), but many of these were also avid amateur musicians themselves. Despite wide differences in training and temperament, all were shaped by participation in a musical culture increasingly remote from our own era of digitally reproduced and manipulated sound. To a degree then accustomed but now extraordinary, they experienced music either by playing and singing it themselves from score or by deliberately recalling specific performances they had heard or taken part in.

Among friends so musically inclined, it is hardly surprising that Brahms tended to circulate new pieces in manuscript prior to publication. Small-scale works could be read from score at the piano and performed on short notice at private gatherings; four-hand piano arrangements brought symphonies and other orchestral repertoire into the homes of close acquaintances as well. Brahms himself attended and participated in many of these intimate performances, but, more often than not, manuscripts passed from person to person through the mail before returning to the composer or his publisher. Especially after Brahms settled permanently in Vienna in the early 1870s, his friends were scattered across Western Europe, from Germany to England to the Netherlands; the more successful performers among his acquaintances were also on tour for large portions of the year. Along with written correspondence, mailed musical manuscripts provided important opportunities to keep in touch with people for whom actual visits were infrequent. Contact with Brahms's new music became an emotionally meaningful activity in ways that are difficult to recapture today, when telephone conversations and videoconferences permit daily, personal contact with far-off acquaintances, and mechanical reproduction has largely replaced live performance in private contexts. Even Clara Schumann, arguably Brahms's firmest friend, felt snubbed when he neglected to send her his unpublished work. One could ask for no clearer evidence of the centrality of music to their relationship than her accusatory letters from 1886, in which access to his compositions is directly equated with personal intimacy: "Do you want to put your old friend utterly last—that you send her absolutely nothing? That would be a crying shame, and I ask you urgently, send what you can spare for a short time."[21]

Two of Clara's perceived rivals for Brahms's musical attention during the 1880s were Heinrich and Elisabeth von Herzogenberg. When Heinrich became bedridden with acute rheumatoid arthritis in 1887, Elisabeth immediately arranged a performance of Brahms's second violin sonata, Op. 100, in her home, and asked Brahms to send the manuscript of the unaccompanied part-song *Im Herbst*, Op. 104 No. 5, to comfort her husband during his long convalescence: "Now, dear honored one, when my Heinz is doing so poorly and in such need of encouragement, truly, will you send him the piece now? We will then write you a long, excellent letter about it, singing your praises and your kindness—ah, please, send us something!" After Brahms complied, Elisabeth frequently reminded him of how much pleasure the invalided Heinrich found in his new music, and a bevy of prepublication manuscripts soon found their way to the couple.[22] For the Herzogenbergs, these compositions were not simply opportunities for entertainment but also a means of feeling the presence of a friend during a difficult time. Faced with chronic sickness and continuous pain, the couple seems to have wanted to surround themselves with Brahms's music just as one might decorate one's hospital room with pictures of distant loved ones. Likewise, others in the composer's circles drew upon his music for comfort in times of illness or sorrow. Upon hearing that the Vienna-based soprano Ottilie Ebner, to whom he had nearly become engaged on Christmas 1863, had lost her eldest son to an infection in 1870, Brahms visited almost daily in order to play for her and revive her interest in the world around her.[23]

Circulated autographs were almost always returned to the composer, but careful study of his compositions and keen memories of performances could keep their contents in mind long after the manuscripts themselves had gone. Some friends possessed a particular facility with new music. Having received an autograph of the third violin sonata, Op. 108, at breakfast on October 30, 1888,

[21] Brahms/Schumann, *Briefe* 2:308.

[22] Brahms/Herzogenberg, *Briefewechsel* 2:157; see also 169 and 182.

[23] Ottilie von Balassa, *Die Brahmsfreundin Ottilie Ebner und ihr Kreis* (Vienna: Franz Bondy, 1933), 55.

Elisabeth von Herzogenberg composed a detailed, 750-word critique of the formal, melodic, and harmonic properties of all three of its movements on the same evening.[24] Elisabeth was also able to retain complex contrapuntal textures with remarkable accuracy simply by ear. Sometime between September 8 and September 10, 1878, Brahms played three piano miniatures from the *Klavierstücke*, Op. 76, for the Herzogenbergs during a brief visit in Arnoldstein; among them was the A-minor *Intermezzo*, Op. 76 No. 7.[25] Having subtly and unsuccessfully requested a copy of the piano miniatures within days of Brahms's visit by claiming to suffer from "an alternating fever in B, F♯, and A minor," Elisabeth resorted to more explicit tactics on November 17. Instead of a letter, she mailed to Brahms a slightly misremembered version of a passage from the A-minor *Intermezzo* and appended to it a newly composed text: "Ah! Have pity for once on poor me, and finally send me the longed-for Intermezzi!"[26] Examples I.6a and b compare the beginning of her musical excerpt to the relevant measures of the *Intermezzo*. Her choice of time signature and her rhythmic proportions for the primary melody demonstrate that she had never laid eyes on a score of the piece, which makes her complete command of its melodic contour and harmonic structure all the more impressive. One wonders, indeed, whether her excerpt preserves memories of rhythmic flexibility in Brahms's performance. Her version projects a halting quality quite different from most modern renditions: might the composer himself have lingered on the longer, higher pitches when playing his own music?

EXAMPLE I.6a   Elisabeth von Herzogenberg to Johannes Brahms, November 17, 1878. From Max Kalbeck's transcription (1912).

EXAMPLE I.6b   Brahms, *Intermezzo*, Op. 76 No. 7, mm. 8–12

[24] Brahms/Herzogenberg, *Briefwechsel* 2:210–13, 215.
[25] For details on Brahms's movements, see Hofmann, *Zeittafel*, 142.
[26] Brahms/Herzogenberg, *Briefwechsel* 1:74, 79–80.

Elisabeth's memory may have been especially acute, but it was hardly unique among Brahms's acquaintances. A lifetime of practical musical experience, coupled with a stronger appreciation for live performance than remains today in an era of recorded alternatives, seems to have given even his amateur friends the ability to recall specific passages of music across large spans of time. The result was an interpenetration of oral and written musical culture that today's scholars are perhaps most accustomed to encountering in medieval and early modern contexts.[27] In 1883, for instance, the surgeon and medical professor Theodor Billroth wrote to Brahms concerning his efforts to maintain a side interest in music amid the cares of fatherhood and the demands of his career: "Well, even now it is not so bad, even if life's beautiful, pure moments occur less often. I sit very, very rarely at the piano; but often enough within me there sounds—." Here he inserted the first measure and a half of the primary theme from the slow movement of Brahms's string quartet Op. 51 No. 2, a piece the composer had dedicated to him a decade before. As shown in example I.7, Theodor's version of the theme is scored for piano and does not correspond precisely to any individual excerpt from the quartet movement, but it accompanies its melody with a basic harmonic pattern and steadily moving bass line characteristic of many of the theme's appearances. As the doctor explained: "It may not be written correctly, but you will know what I mean."[28] Here, as in countless instances discernible in surviving correspondence, remembered music provided a means of reinforcing mutual recollections of the shared past on which friendship was based.

EXAMPLE I.7   Theodor Billroth to Johannes Brahms, July 27, 1883. From the autograph.

Such experiences were by no means limited to Brahms's music alone. In exchanges with professional and amateur musicians alike, snatches of musical notation and citations of song texts spanned more than a century's worth of repertoire and facilitated all manner of dialogue: playful, resentful, reassuring, traumatic. Some examples took root across multiple phases in a friendship, as in the case of the great baritone Julius Stockhausen. In February 1877, Julius asked

[27]The *locus classicus* among studies of musical memory in the Middle Ages remains Anna Maria Busse Berger's *Medieval Music and the Art of Memory* (Berkeley: University of California Press, 2005).
[28]Brahms/Billroth, *Briefwechsel*, 352. The edition includes a facsimile of Theodor's entire interpolated excerpt, on which example I.7 is based.

Brahms to stand as godfather for his third son. His request concluded with a gentle plea: "Aber sag ein Wörtchen, das eine, eine Wörtchen 'Ja' & du machst uns glücklich" ("But say one little word, that one, one little word 'Yes,' and you will make us happy").[29] Here were direct echoes of the plaintive words of the miller lad in *Der Neugierige* (The Inquiring One), the sixth song in Schubert's *Die schöne Müllerin*, D. 795. As printed in the first edition of Schubert's cycle, the final three stanzas of Wilhelm Müller's poem read:

O Bächlein meiner Liebe	O brook of my beloved,
Wie bist du heut so stumm	How mute you are today.
Will ja nur Eines wissen	I only want to know one thing,
Ein Wörtchen um und um	One little word is all.
Ja, heisst das eine Wörtchen	"Yes" is that one little word,
Das andre heisset Nein	The alternative is "No."
Die beiden Wörtchen schliessen	Those two little words comprise
Die ganze Welt mir ein.	The entire world for me.
O Bächlein meiner Liebe	O brook of my beloved,
Was bist du wunderlich.	How strange you are to me.
Will's ja nicht weiter sagen	I certainly won't repeat it,
Sag Bächlein, liebt sie mich!	Tell me, brooklet, does she love me!

Without quoting the poem directly, Julius clarified the source of his textual allusion by setting the word *Ja* apart in quotation marks and by repeating the word *Wörtchen*, preceded first by the article *ein* and then by the words *das eine*. The miller lad's bashful awkwardness—he is, after all, asking a brook whether the object of his infatuation returns his love, rather than simply asking her directly—resonated perfectly with the overall tone of Julius's letter, which couched the request that Brahms become an extended family member in hesitantly flattering terms throughout: "Whoever, like you, has given the world so much beauty, to him one must show that one thinks of him on such occasions."[30]

More than a decade later, Brahms returned to the same portion of Müller's poem in a letter to Julius. Vacationing in Switzerland during the summer of 1888, he received word that the baritone planned to visit him there for the first time in several years. In reply, Brahms described the attractions of the prospective rendezvous: "Ungrische u. andre Lieder sind das Geringste, daß dich hier erfreuen kann. 'Der Andre aber hieß J. Br.'" ("Hungarian and other songs are the least that can delight you here, 'but the alternative would be J. Br.'") The phrase Brahms set off in quotation marks was taken almost verbatim from

---

[29] Brahms/Stockhausen, *Briefe*, 124.
[30] Ibid.

Müller's penultimate stanza, where it directly followed Julius's own allusion. Now, on the heels of a teaser for new songs that would greet the singer upon his arrival, Brahms's near-quotation flavored his words with a coy excitement amusingly appropriate for two old friends who had not seen each other, or made music together, for a long while. At the same time, for a singer of Julius's expertise, Brahms's textual parody could hardly help but recall the music that accompanied it, especially since that music is so extraordinary from the perspectives of both composer and performer. Example I.8 presents the relevant portion of *Der Neugierige* as it appeared in the first edition. To parallel the poetic speaker's combined excitement and agitation, Schubert had replaced the brook's previously continuous accompanimental figuration with a recitative-like texture and composed a marvelous modulation that hints at C major without ever quite reaching it. The modulation pivots on the word *Nein* or, when imagined as the accompaniment to the text of Brahms's letter, the initials *J. Br.* In the act of performance, this moment creates one of the song's central problems for both singer and pianist, who must work together to coordinate the demands of textual declamation, dynamic control, and vocal support with the timing and voicing of block chords in the accompaniment. Brahms's letter disingenuously presented his own name as the locus of all this compositional and interpretive activity just as it compared his own company favorably to that of his music. The result was absurd, and absurdly charming.

What else might Julius have experienced in reading Brahms's note and remembering *Der Neugierige*? The composer's excitement at a coming reunion and the singer's invitation to become his son's godfather merely hint at the

EXAMPLE I.8   Schubert, *Der Neugierige*, D. 795 No. 6, mm. 30–38

connotations Schubert's song might have acquired over the years for two friends who were still young men when they first performed that song together. Collaborative engagement with *Die Schöne Müllerin* was a feature of their relationship from the very beginning. Within three weeks of first meeting Stockhausen at the Lower Rheinland music festival in May 1856, Brahms had accompanied him in a performance of three songs from the cycle; the pair had then presented the entire *Schöne Müllerin* three times in 1861 and selections, including *Der Neugierige*, in 1868.[31] Perhaps one rehearsal or one performance in particular was the source of shared reminiscences by virtue of which the song entered the interpersonal vocabulary of their friendship. Unless some new evidence surfaces, no one will ever know. But the echoes of Müller's text in their correspondence show that this song was part of what drew singer and accompanist together—became, in fact, a part of how they communicated with each other. For either of them, the act of listening to or performing such a song in later years could easily have been charged with the retrospective knowledge of its roles in their earlier friendship.

It was these kinds of personal resonances, each specific to a particular piece of music and an individual member of his circles, that Brahms could then exploit in new compositions through the technique of allusive borrowing. Subsequent chapters in this book will return at length to many of Brahms's acknowledged allusive gestures and the interpersonal circumstances into which he introduced them. In the meantime, however, the general characteristics of his social milieu suggest a larger method for the investigation of other potentially allusive borrowings in small-scale genres. Rather than approach such borrowings exclusively via music-analytic criteria or from the neutral standpoint of an omniscient consumer to whom all of Brahms's music is equally accessible, one can begin, instead, by asking how each gesture might have addressed and manipulated the musical experiences and interpretive attitudes characteristic of specific, historically situated listeners. Where sufficient evidence survives regarding the prior associations that a certain passage of music most likely carried for a particular friend of the composer, one can then plausibly reconstruct a range of possible implications for its reanimation in a new musical and interpersonal situation. In doing so, one can explore the rhetorical potential of a specific musical gesture within a precise sector of Brahms's social sphere and thereby recover glimpses of the communicative landscapes peculiar to each of his musical friendships.

---

[31] Renate and Kurt Hofmann, *Johannes Brahms als Pianist und Dirigent: Chronologie seines Wirkens als Interpret* (Tutzing: Schneider, 2006), 40, 65–67, and 107.

Such work can only be done piecemeal, by means of detailed and fundamentally independent case studies. No two friendships are alike or even precisely analogous. Moreover, by virtue of his manifold activities as composer, pianist, conductor, and scholar, Brahms arguably came in contact with a wider array of individuals than many of his contemporaries, and his own friendships were correspondingly heterogeneous. Furthermore, as relationships shift over time, sometimes swiftly and decisively, so too does the interpersonal backdrop against which a given musical structure may be understood to have taken on significance. The historiography of Brahms's potentially allusive borrowings must therefore be predicated on comprehensive immersion in the primary documents surrounding each example. Only when each analysis responds adequately and intimately to the idiosyncrasies of its own historical and interpersonal moment can the aggregate mosaic yield an integrated vision of compositional and social praxis.

Close cognates for the outlines of this method can be found in rhetorical studies. For the most part, musicological appeals to formal rhetoric remain confined to accounts of treatises and compositions from the seventeenth and eighteenth centuries, when musicians were explicitly trained in the figures, topics, and formulae of classical oratory. Since Brahms's cognizance of these formulae was limited at best, few scholars have applied them to the analysis of his music.[32] However, the discipline of rhetorical studies has long been more broadly conceived than is typically acknowledged in music-historical inquiry. In particular, mid-twentieth-century developments in the work of sociologically oriented literary critics such as Kenneth Burke have drastically expanded the scope of rhetorical investigation to encompass a comprehensive array of cultural phenomena, from print propaganda to poetry to visual imagery. As Burke put it in his cheerfully polemical text, *A Rhetoric of Motives*, "Wherever there is persuasion, there is rhetoric. And wherever there is 'meaning,' there is persuasion."[33] In the wake of Burke's pivotal reorientation, the field has come to share many underlying concerns with cultural anthropology, identity politics, and poststructural criticism, while still maintaining its own traditional emphasis on the technical side of cultural production. At the most basic level, it now seeks to identify the unacknowledged interests at stake in cultural exchanges of all kinds and to explore the specific discursive or aesthetic means by which those interests are advocated.

Elements of recent rhetorical priorities have filtered slowly into musicological discourse, mainly through their influence on more fashionable sister disci-

---

[32]The main exception in English-language scholarship is the work of Ira Braus: "Poetic-Musical Rhetoric in Brahms's *Auf dem Kirchhofe*," *Theory and Practice* 13 (1988): 15–30; and "Textual Rhetoric and Harmonic Anomaly in Selected Lieder of Johannes Brahms," (PhD diss., Harvard University, 1988).

[33]Kenneth Burke, *A Rhetoric of Motives* (Berkeley: University of California Press, 1967), 172.

plines, but the full potential for interdisciplinary collaboration has not yet been realized, especially with respect to nineteenth-century European art music.[34] It is in the broadest sense of rhetoric—conceived as a mode of interpretation that foregrounds how artifacts and utterances influence the attitudes and assumptions of specific audiences—that this book borrows the term and incorporates it into its title. Construed as rhetorically charged constructs rather than abstract musical structures, Brahms's allusive borrowings can be said to operate persuasively insofar as they revise the potential meanings that his music might convey and the interpretive strategies that it might invite, especially from the specific listeners with whose habits of mind and music making he was most familiar. Thus, for the historian confronted by Brahms's intricate small-scale compositions, the poetic texts that often accompany them, and the voluminous correspondence, reminiscences, and diary entries that describe them, the flexible interplay between artifice and audience characteristic of modern rhetorical studies may provide a sympathetic model of engagement.

Readers for whom rhetorical analogies do not resonate productively may choose, instead, to view the method in ethnographic terms. Indeed, this book can be understood as an essay in historical ethnography, since it aims not to proscribe uniquely valid interpretations of musical works but to preserve—and thus to help the reader vicariously inhabit—alternative modes of listening, music making, and social interaction. And just as an ethnographer must often foreground the limitations inherent in his or her status as an outsider to the cultural practices under consideration, so, too, this narrative must frequently acknowledge the inevitable incompleteness of surviving evidence. As a final, cautionary example, consider the closing strophe of *Von ewiger Liebe* (Of Endless Love), Op. 43 No. 1, one of Brahms's most frequently performed solo songs. Completed in 1864, *Von ewiger Liebe* sets a folk-inspired text by Joseph Wenzig in which two lovers discuss their future.[35] After describing the quiet landscape through which the young man walks the maiden to her house, the poem presents their exchange as directly quoted speech. The lad worries that gossip and societal pressure will drive them apart, but the maiden assures him that their love will endure forever. Here is the text as it appeared in the first edition of the song in 1868; the title was Brahms's own.

---

[34] Burke's work may, itself, serve as a representative example. It is cited only occasionally in contemporary musicological or music-theoretic discourse. Exceptions include Kevin Korsyn, *Decentering Music: A Critique of Contemporary Musical Research* (Oxford: Oxford University Press, 2003), 45 and 110; and Ruth Solie, "Whose Life? The Gendered Self in Schumann's Frauenliebe Songs," in *Music and Text: Critical Inquiries*, ed. Steven Paul Scher, 222 (New York: Cambridge University Press, 1992). Yet Burke's influence is felt indirectly, among other ways through musicological borrowings from cultural anthropologists like Clifford Geertz, whose theory of "symbolic action" is explicitly based on Burke's. See Gary Tomlinson, "The Web of Culture: A Context for Musicology," *19th-Century Music* 7 (1984): 350–62.

[35] McCorkle, *Werkverzeichnis*, 155; Kalbeck, *Brahms* 2:129.

Von ewiger Liebe

Dunkel, wie dunkel in Wald und in
  Feld!
Abend schon ist es, nun schweiget die
  Welt.
Nirgend noch Licht und nirgend noch
  Rauch,
Ja, und die Lerche sie schweiget nun auch.

Kommt aus dem Dorfe der Bursche
  heraus,
Gibt das Geleit der Geliebten nach Haus,
Führt sie am Weidengebüsche vorbei,
Redet so viel und so mancherlei:

"Leidest du Schmach und betrübest du
  dich,
Leidest du Schmach von Andern um
  mich,
Werde die Liebe getrennt so geschwind,
Schnell wie wir früher vereiniget sind.
Scheide mit Regen und scheide mit
  Wind,
Schnell wie wir früher vereiniget sind."

Spricht das Mägdelein, Mägdelein
  spricht:
"Unsere Liebe, sie trennet sich nicht!
Fest ist der Stahl und das Eisen gar sehr,
Unsere Liebe ist fester noch mehr.

Eisen und Stahl, man schmiedet sie
  um,
Unsere Liebe, wer wandelt sie um?
Eisen und Stahl, sie können zergehn,
Unsere Liebe muss ewig bestehn!"

Of Endless Love

Dark, how dark in the woods and the
  fields!
It is already evening, the world is quiet.

Nowhere do light or smoke still appear,

Yes, and the lark is quiet now too.

The young man comes out of the
  village,
Accompanying his beloved to her home,
Leads her past the meadow's thickets,
Speaks of many and various things:

"If you suffer insults and worry about
  it,
If you suffer insults on my account,

Then our love will be parted so quickly,
As speedily as we once were united.
Depart with the rain and depart with the
  wind,
As speedily as we once were united."

The maiden speaks, the maiden speaks:

"Our love, it will not be parted!
Steel is strong and iron is too,
Our love is stronger yet.

Iron and steel, one can melt them
  down,
Our love, who can change it?
Iron and steel, they can fall to pieces,
Our love must last forever!"

Brahms's song aligns successive shifts in the poetic speaker's identity with clear sectional divisions through the juxtaposition of distinct melodic motives. The initial stanzas of scenic description receive two nearly identical musical strophes, both of them registrally confined and securely based in the tonic minor. Then, as the young man begins to speak in stanza 3, brashly contrasting melodic material intrudes, along with altered and accelerated accompanimental figuration. Finally, after a calming piano interlude during which the tempo gradually relaxes and the meter shifts from $\frac{3}{4}$ to $\frac{6}{8}$, the maiden's two stanzas of reassurance are set to two closely related strophes in

EXAMPLE I.9a   Brahms, *Von ewiger Liebe*, Op. 43 No. 1, mm. 99–110. Annotated.

the parallel major. As if to underscore her unshaken confidence, these final strophes completely avoid the motives associated with the song's shadowy beginning or the lad's agitated response. Instead, the maiden's section is based upon almost ostentatiously unrelated material: a lilting, gently acrobatic, and delicately ornamented melodic line above a slow-moving harmonic progression that pauses on a half cadence at the end of stanza 4, then proceeds toward a rousing authentic cadence at the close of the song. Example I.9a illustrates these features as they appear at the beginning of the final poetic stanza.

For Brahms, however, the maiden's melody and important aspects of its harmonic underpinning were not new at all. They were borrowed almost unchanged from his own *Brautgesang* (Bridal Song), an unpublished work for women's voices and orchestral accompaniment that he had completed in the autumn of 1858 and suppressed shortly thereafter. Ludwig Uhland's text reads "That house I bless and praise aloud / that has welcomed in a lovely bride; / it must bloom into a garden." Only the vocal parts to the *Brautgesang* survive today, preserved in handwritten partbooks copied by members of the women's chorus that Brahms directed in Hamburg from 1859 through 1862. The piece began with an introductory section, labeled *Andante* and consisting of a soprano solo and a tutti response. Example I.9b presents the vocal parts from the beginning and the end of this introductory section, assembled from partbooks belonging to Bertha Porubsky (later Bertha Faber), Marie Völckers,

EXAMPLE I.9b   Brahms, *Brautgesang* (1858), mm. 1–16 and 28–38. Vocal parts, from manuscript partbooks. Annotated.

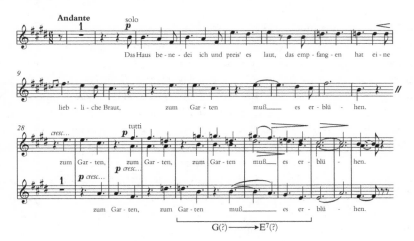

and two anonymous choir members.[36] The clearest evidence of musical borrowing is preserved in the first dozen measures of the solo soprano line, which anticipate every characteristic swerve from the final strophes of *Von ewiger Liebe*, including the placement of the initial crescendo. Mode and meter are aligned as well. Without the orchestral accompaniment to the *Brautgesang*, it is impossible to compare the harmonic underpinning or voice-leading structure of the two passages until the entrance of the chorus, by which time the shared melodic material has already begun to fade. Nevertheless, one might reasonably conjecture that mm. 31–32 of the *Brautgesang* were harmonized with a G-major triad and mm. 33–34 with a dominant seventh built on E. This pungent, sharpwards progression transforms a common tone, d♯″, from the stable fifth of one chord to the dissonant seventh of the next. As pointed out in example I.9a, the moment finds a direct analogue in the final strophe of *Von ewiger Liebe*.[37]

[36] All dynamics, slurs, and other performance indications were written in ink in the original partbooks; bracketed accidentals are my own additions. Penciled dynamics, which often duplicate the ink indications, are omitted. Bertha Faber's partbook is currently in the Brahms archive of the Staats- und Universitätsbibliothek in Hamburg. Marie Völckers's partbook is in private hands, and the two anonymous partbooks survive only in photostats in the Sophia Smith Collection at Smith College (Northhampton, MA), where they remain among the papers of Sophie Drinker. A photostat of Marie Völckers's partbook is also included in the Sophia Smith Collection at Smith College. (See McCorkle, *Werkverzeichnis*, 573 and 576–78.)

[37] Kalbeck first identified Brahms's borrowing from the *Brautgesang* shortly after the composer's death in *Brahms* 1:375–78 and 2:129. Since he had access only to Bertha Faber's partbook, however, Kalbeck's analysis is entirely melodic in orientation, as are all subsequent interpretations of the resemblance.

Intriguingly, Brahms seems to have reserved borrowed material for the maiden's words alone. Wenzig's final stanza, all of which is spoken directly by the girl, provoked a practically literal quotation from the first two phrases of the *Brautgesang*'s solo soprano line. By contrast, the previous poetic stanza begins with an introductory clause ("The maiden said"). As shown in example I.9c, Brahms avoided any melodic hint of the *Brautgesang* during these neutral words, only to return immediately to the second phrase of the soprano solo as soon as Wenzig's girl begins to speak. Confining borrowed material to the maiden's voice almost certainly entailed a conscious compositional decision, especially since the beginnings of the two strophes are harmonized identically and would just as easily have accommodated the same melody both times. Had the *Brautgesang* been published and popular by 1864, then, one could easily interpret Brahms's borrowing as a publically oriented allusive gesture designed to reinforce the maiden's claim of faithfulness to her beloved in the minds of knowledgeable listeners. Uhland's celebration of marriage certainly provides a harmonious counterpoint to Wenzig's reassuring peroration. Aside from the Hamburg women's chorus and a few friends of the composer, however, no surviving evidence suggests that anyone had ever seen or even heard of the *Brautgesang*. But for the composer himself and a few of those privileged friends, its echoes might have carried specific and highly personal connotations, for work was initially crafted during the height of his infatuation with the Göttingen soprano Agathe von Siebold.

EXAMPLE I.9c   Brahms, *Von ewiger Liebe*, Op. 43 No. 1, mm. 79–86. Vocal part.

From the beginnings of their relationship in the summer of 1858 until its unraveling early the following year, Brahms's connection with Agathe von Siebold is widely assumed to have motivated and influenced many compositional projects, including at least a dozen solo songs and several larger-scale works for voices and instruments.[38] The *Brautgesang* was one of these. Immediately upon completing it in October or early November 1858, Brahms had sent a copy to his close friend and primary contact in Göt-

---

[38] For evidence and assessments of Agathe's influence on Brahms's compositional output in the autumn of 1858, see Johannes Brahms and Julius Otto Grimm, *Johannes Brahms im Briefwechsel mit J. O. Grimm*, ed. Richard Barth, 68, 70, and 76 (Berlin: Deutsche Brahms-Gesellschaft, 1908); Kalbeck, *Brahms* 1:332–38; Hans Küntzel, *"Aber Fesseln tragen kann ich nicht": Johannes Brahms und Agathe von Siebold* (Göttingen: Steidl, 2003), 90–102; and Emil Michelmann, *Agathe von Siebold, Johannes Brahms' Jugendliebe* (Göttingen: Dr. L. Hützchel & Co., 1930), 189–90.

tingen, Julius Otto Grimm, who immediately played it for Agathe.[39] As the best singer and the only soprano associated with the Grimm household, she presumably sang the introductory solo during their impromptu performance. In turn, the piece may well have come to carry special interpretive weight for Brahms and Agathe during the ensuing months. Soon Brahms was commenting flirtatiously about having set Uhland's text to music.[40] He then circulated the piece privately to his closest confidantes outside of Göttingen, Joseph Joachim and Clara Schumann, just before he and Agathe secretly exchanged engagement rings in early January.[41] Within a few short weeks, however, the relationship had ended painfully, Brahms's friendship with the Grimms was nearly severed, and he never mentioned the *Brautgesang* again in surviving correspondence.

Having long since put the affair behind him, Brahms found himself brooding on it once again in 1864, the year in which he completed *Von ewiger Liebe*. His longtime bachelor friend Joseph Joachim had suddenly married in 1863 and announced his wife's pregnancy in February 1864; Brahms himself had considered proposing to Ottilie von Hauer at Christmas, 1863, only to be anticipated by her future husband, Eduard Ebner; and his parents had finally acknowledged the failure of their own marriage and agreed to a separation, the terms of which Brahms had helped to broker through a trip to Hamburg in June 1864. On its own, any of these events might have been enough to catalyze some reminiscences about the composer's own ill-fated romance with Agathe. In combination, they seem to have stimulated a prolonged bout of soul-searching. In mid-July he wrote to Julius Otto, with whom he was back on friendly footing, asking for news of Göttingen and, for the first time since 1859, news of Agathe in particular; at the end of the month he visited Göttingen himself, with Joseph and Julius Otto in tow.[42] By year's end he had completed an initial version of his second String Sextet, Op. 36. In one of his few documented uses of musical ciphers, the Sextet's first movement incorporated a musical version of Agathe's first name as repeated cadential material near the end of its exposition. Generations of scholars have interpreted this feature as a reflection of Brahms's

---

[39] Brahms/Grimm, *Briefe*, 67 and 76. Styra Avins has cleared up several mysteries concerning the chronology of the Grimm correspondence from this period in *Johannes Brahms: Life and Letters* (Oxford: Oxford University Press, 1997), 177 and 748.

[40] Brahms/Grimm, *Briefe*, 78.

[41] Clara Schumann first saw the *Brautgesang* in December 1858. She offered Brahms some focused criticism of the piece, particularly its melodic construction (Brahms/Schumann, *Briefe*, 234–35). Within a few weeks, Joseph Joachim had also encountered the work and found fault with it; his opinion survives in a letter to Clara dated January 16, 1859. See Johannes Joachim and Andreas Moser, eds., *Briefe von und an Joachim* (Berlin: Julius Bard, 1912) 2:46.

[42] Brahms/Grimm, *Briefe*, 111; Avins, *Life and Letters*, 298; Hofmann, *Zeittafel*, 64; and Joachim and Moser, *Briefe von und an Joachim* 2:342.

purported description of the piece: "There I freed myself from my last love!"[43] Certainly Joseph, at least, perceived Agathe's spectral presence in the Sextet. Thirty years later, he would substitute a score of the cadential figure for her name in a letter to Brahms.[44]

Especially in the context of Brahms's other compositional projects and personal preoccupations in 1864, the choice of borrowed material for *Von ewiger Liebe* and the deliberate alignment of that material with the words of the maiden in Wenzig's poem seem laden with rhetorical potential. In many respects, the tension between the lovers in the song recapitulated the conflict that had arisen between Brahms and Agathe in 1859: public gossip had forced him to into a swift evaluation his feelings, which were never as strong as hers to begin with.[45] Text and music thus reinforced the possibility of a deliberate parallel between compositional strategy and biographical circumstance. Furthermore, at least four people—Julius Otto, Joseph, Clara, and Agathe herself—had the requisite musical memories and knowledge of Brahms's past to identify his borrowing and speculate regarding his intentions. For these individuals in particular, recognizing the origins of the final stanzas in *Von ewiger Liebe* would arguably have facilitated a fluid mixture of musical analysis and personal assessment, encouraging a variety of interpretations as to Brahms's current mood and his long-term emotional allegiances. Perhaps he intended one or all of these friends to engage in such interpretations. On the other hand, perhaps the borrowing from the *Brautgesang* was attractive to Brahms for his own reasons but never meant for apprehension by any audience, large or small. Perhaps the private compositional challenge of accommodating a familiar melody into the context of his new song gave him an opportunity to inhabit and examine his own emotional past—to place words of reassurance in the voice of a woman he had irrevocably rejected and hear what they sounded like there.

Either reading of Brahms's music and motivations is inherently speculative. Both rely upon estimations of his compositional decision making and upon conjectures regarding the resonances that particular musical gestures may have carried years after the fact. Moreover, it is ultimately impossible to eliminate either reading conclusively in favor of the other. Brahms delayed publishing *Von ewiger Liebe* until 1868, and no evidence suggests that he circulated it in manu-

---

[43] Kalbeck, *Brahms* 2:157n. Brahms's remark was supposedly addressed to Joseph Gänsbacher. The cipher for Agathe's name consisted of the pitch-specific sequence A–G–A–B–E. Because in German B♭ is called H, these pitches come as close as one can get to Agathe's name using conventional note names (A–G–A–H–E). Brahms had already used this cipher in 1859 or 1860 as the ostinato bass line of *Und gehst du über den Kirchhof*, Op. 44 No. 10, an unaccompanied part-song for women's voices whose text describes the devastating impact of ill-fated love.

[44] Brahms/Joachim, *Briefe* 2:273.

[45] For a concise account of Brahms's relationship with Agathe, see Malcolm MacDonald, *Brahms* (Oxford: Oxford University Press, 2001), 51–53.

script during the intervening years to anyone who was in a position to reconstruct his compositional process. But the lack of such evidence may be due simply to the chance destruction of relevant documents. Unlikely as it seems, Brahms could have mailed a copy of his new song to Agathe von Siebold immediately upon completing it. And even if one were to recover hitherto unknown correspondence that established a clear intended audience for Brahms's allusion to the *Brautgesang*, his borrowing may still have fulfilled some purposes of which only he was aware. At the roots of this tension lies another historiographic principle concerning Brahms's borrowings: rhetorical potential need not imply communicative function. A borrowing from a source whose recognition would have been rhetorically charged for a given listener need not inevitably have been designed for that listener to apprehend allusively; instead, the rhetorical potential latent in the mere act of conjuring up remembered music may have served the composer's own private ends, regardless of its later reception.

Elusive in practice but heuristically revealing nonetheless, the distinction between social and psychological motivations for compositional borrowing informs the placement and ordering of the case studies in the remainder of this book. Parts 1–3 all approach their respective musical borrowings as instances of allusion in the strict sense. Each of the seven chapters situates borrowed gestures in the context of friendships within which the source of the borrowing carried strong and identifiable associations. In each case, surviving documents support the inference that Brahms explicitly intended the gesture to be apprehended and thus clarify its potential connotations for his target audience. Together, these examples reveal Brahms's compositional strategies to have been tightly woven into the fabric of his social life. Through the technique of allusive borrowing, the fashioning of new music served a variety of interpersonal purposes, from pedagogy and political solidarity to condolence, nostalgia, and amusement.

At the same time, parts 1–3 bear witness to the importance of performative parameters in the interpretation of allusive gestures within Brahms's circles. In each chapter I imagine how specific musical structures might have felt in the voices of singers or the hands of pianists and string players.[46] Whether by virtue

---

[46] Kinesthetic concerns are commonplace in recent musicological engagements with non-Western musics and with European repertoire outside the mainstream of the Austro-German canon; a foundational example of the latter can be found in Elisabeth Le Guin's *Boccherini's Body: An Essay in Carnal Musicology* (Berkeley: University of California Press, 2006). However, such issues have received only sporadic attention in scholarship devoted to Brahms's music. Exceptions include Daverio, *Crossing Paths*, 231–32; Rosen, "Classicism and the Inspiration of Awkwardness"; and Steven Rings, "The Learned Self: Artifice in Brahms's Late Intermezzi," in *Expressive Intersections in Brahms: Essays in Analysis and Meaning*, ed. Heather Platt and Peter H. Smith, 19–50 (Bloomington: Indiana University Press, 2012).

of tactile similarity to the sources from which they were taken or through striking kinesthetic divergences from those sources, Brahms's borrowings provide
suggestive evidence as to the centrality of physical sensation in his contemporaries' approach to new music. Perhaps unsurprisingly, given her overwhelming
musicianship and her long, complex relationship with Brahms, Clara Schumann
emerges as a pivotal audience for his allusive gestures, and her perspective dom-
inates part three. By contrast, part one engages a diverse collection of consummate performers and their spouses—Amalie and Joseph Joachim, Bertha and
Arthur Faber, and Julius and Clara Stockhausen—while part two charts the ups
and downs of Brahms's interchange with Heinrich von Herzogenberg, one of
the few professional composers to maintain a central position within his famous
colleague's orbit. All the while, these chapters also highlight the role of peripheral figures in mediating the experiences of each primary character, providing
a richly composite image of Brahms's musical and interpersonal commitments.

Finally, part four turns inward. Revisiting three of the friendships engaged in
earlier chapters, chapters 8–10 all describe the introspective redirection of the
allusive potential inherent in remembered music that was central to those
friendships. Each chapter identifies a borrowing whose recognition would
almost certainly have been explosively charged for a specific listener, but argues
that Brahms himself concealed his borrowing from the listener in question.
Like letters drafted but never quite sent, such works illuminate the topography
of Brahms's social landscape from oblique and unexpected angles. Given the
fragmentary nature of surviving evidence, the process of differentiating these
examples from purposefully allusive borrowings inevitably involves educated
guesswork. In return, however, the case studies in part four carve out a crucial
space within which to explore historically grounded alternatives to the traditional concept of allusion, while hinting at the psychological efficacy of some
of Brahms's musical borrowings—their capacity to explore in tones the potential solutions to matters of his own conscience.

As a whole, the book traces a double path. Its chapters move through Brahms's
adult life and his mature compositions in roughly chronological order, while, at
the same time, the overt rhetoric of address gradually gives way to the covert
rhetoric of self-analysis and self-control. In the end, some features of the private
emotional topography addressed in part four directly anticipate the psychoanalytic landscape mapped by Sigmund Freud and his later interpreters, providing
another interdisciplinary correlate for the argument as a whole. Such correlates,
however, receive little sustained attention in the body of the text. Likewise,
specialists intent upon positioning each chapter relative to current debates in
Brahms studies will be able to do so, but only by perusing the footnotes. Whatever its other contributions, this book is first and foremost about the power and
limits of the historical imagination. It seeks to define and expand the boundaries of what can be known about a culture already foreign to us, to retrace the

tangled and mutually dependent perspectives of historically situated agents, to plausibly and persuasively reconstruct their habits of mind and body, and therefore to avoid as best it can the imposition of overarching critical paradigms that enshrine the disciplinary claims of our own historical moment. It proceeds from the conviction that old music and old documents, no matter how fragmentary, are still rich enough to reward the undivided attention of scholars and performers alike.

This conviction shapes the musical examples and the excerpts from primary documents that appear in every chapter. All musical examples are drawn from sources known to Brahms and available among his circles, primarily autograph manuscripts, handwritten copies, and early published scores. Examples based on handwritten materials are labeled as such. All other examples are based on first editions unless otherwise indicated in their titles or the surrounding prose.[47] For Brahms's music, Breitkopf and Härtel's *Sämtliche Werke* of 1926–27 is avoided entirely, and later critical editions such as Henle's ongoing *Gesamtausgabe* are used only sparingly and cited as such. Likewise, excerpts from poetic texts are based upon publications or handwritten copies to which Brahms and his contemporaries had access, and specific editions are always cited. All translations are my own. In translating verse, I have sought to preserve for English-speaking readers the poetic parameters that I take to be most central to Brahms's aesthetic as a composer of texted music: meaning, meter, and tone. Casualties of this approach include rhyme and, on occasion, word-for-word congruence. For all poetic texts, the original German appears beside the English version. For prose and correspondence, English translations are accompanied by citations of the German sources on which they are based unless the specific diction of the original is itself at issue, in which case both German and English versions are provided.

---

[47]The Brahms-Institut at the Musikhochschule in Lübeck has recently made digital scans available for first editions of virtually every work that Brahms published.

PART I

OCCASIONAL LULLABIES

CHAPTER ONE

OLD MELODIES, NEW IDENTITIES

The child Marie grew up and became the young matron of the house who saw to it that friends, whenever they came to us, lacked nothing and always found a deliciously prepared meal. And so, in an attractively illustrated "Cook's Notebook for Good Housewives" there appears in Brahms's hand:

> For friendly use
> for Marie Schumann
> in thankful memory of the summer of 1864
> and in happy hopes of the one to come
>
> —J. B.

This book was the delight of my childhood years, and the pretty verses therein made themselves so at home within us that they were heard at every opportunity....

One always noticed with Brahms's presents that he gave them not for the sake of giving, but in order to give the other person pleasure, to which end he naturally had to take into account their inclination and taste. But what should one make of the birthday present that he gave me many years later? He was at our home in Frankfurt and discovered in the morning that it was my birthday. When I come to dinner at midday, I find at my place a charming, finely molded donkey in silver-bronze, and upon its back it carried—hear it and marvel!—a little cask of liquor; on both sides hung the necessary little glasses. Had he taken my inclinations into account then as well? Now then, who knows! Of course one laughed a lot over it; I was heartily teased but nonetheless perfectly content, for in any case Brahms had chosen for me something that had pleased himself.

—Eugenie Schumann

In neighboring passages from her memoirs, Eugenie Schumann juxtaposed complementary perspectives on Brahms's persona as giver of gifts.[1] In 1864 her oldest sister, Marie, was twenty-two years old and already the de facto administrator of the Schumann household. On the basis of a cookbook carefully chosen and kindly dedicated, Eugenie characterized the composer as a sensitive friend who understood presents as tokens of empathy and tailored his offerings to their recipients as a rhetor calibrates his utterance to its audience. Turning then to her own experience as a grown woman, she underscored his seemingly paradoxical delight in puckishly subverting the preferences of others. The second occasion she described was almost certainly her thirtieth birthday on December 1, 1881. Brahms had departed from Meiningen the previous day on his way to Zürich, where he arrived on December 4; although his intervening movements have not been definitively traced, Frankfurt am Main was directly en route by train, and correspondence from Clara Schumann in preceding weeks anticipated a brief visit with her family whenever he could "come through here."[2] His impromptu appearance in the midst of a longer trip could provide alternative explanations for what Eugenie perceived as a wholly unprovoked practical joke. Confronted by a birthday he had forgotten and a celebration for which he had not planned, it was surely easier to confound his recipient's expectations amusingly than to fulfill them meaningfully. In turn, perhaps the little donkey was meant to convey a shamefaced apology along with its liquid cargo. To those aware of the composer's hectic travel itinerary and propensity for coarse self-deprecation, a booze-toting ass might well have seemed amusingly appropriate to the awkward situation in which he had landed, directing their laughter away from Eugenie and toward his own bungled attempt to extricate himself.

For different dinner guests, then, even a present that appeared unambiguously frivolous could be made to support multiple, overlapping views of the composer's motivations, ranging from egoism and laziness to embarrassment and self-reproach. The interpretive extremes of empathy and mockery articulated in Eugenie's memoirs establish merely the outer boundaries of the complex social landscape that virtually all of Brahms's acquaintances were forced to navigate at one time or another as recipients of his gifts. When the gift in question was a piece of new music, underlying tensions between intimacy and humor often shaped both composition and reception in revealing ways. Such was the case with three lullabies designed to commemorate the births of sons to close friends. Completed during the decisive expansion of Brahms's public reputation in the 1860s and 1870s, these songs constituted a miniature tradition

---

[1] Eugenie Schumann, *Erinnerungen* (Stuttgart: J. Engelhorns Nachf., 1925), 240, 242–43.
[2] Hofmann, *Zeittafel*, 162; Brahms/Schumann, *Briefe* 2:247. Brahms was not in or near Frankfurt for any of the other birthdays that Eugenie spent there.

of occasional music that was well known among the composer's circles but invariably ignored as such in later studies of his works. Disparate in style and structure, all three lullabies incorporated acknowledged borrowings from sources that carried rich and specific prior associations for their recipients. Reconstructing the potential reactions of those recipients illuminates the conflicting self-images that Brahms projected through his music and opens new vistas on the religious, political, and interpersonal terrain upon which his gift-giving took place, and which it was sometimes intended to reshape.

The *Geistliches Wiegenlied* (Sacred Lullaby) first appeared to the general public in December 1884 as the second of Brahms's *Zwei Gesänge* for alto, viola, and piano, Op. 91. By then, the song was more than two decades old. From its inception in 1864, it had been closely connected to the domestic circumstances of Joseph Joachim, one of Brahms's earliest supporters and firmest friends. The work's unusual scoring facilitated performance, real or imagined, in the Joachim household: Joseph was a sensitive violist as well as a virtuosic violinist, and his wife, Amalie, had maintained a burgeoning career as an operatic contralto until their marriage the previous spring. The text—Emmanuel Geibel's translation and understated updating of Garcia Lope de Vega's sixteenth-century lyric—pictures the Virgin Mary cradling the infant Jesus and renders her concerns in first-person speech. Here is the poem as Brahms encountered it in Geibel and Paul Heyse's *Spanisches Liederbuch* of 1852:

Die ihr schwebet	You who hover
Um diese Palmen	Around these palm trees
In Nacht und Wind,	In nighttime and wind,
Ihr heil'gen Engel,	You holy angels,
Stillet die Wipfel!	Calm the treetops!
Es schlummert mein Kind.	My child is sleeping.
Ihr Palmen von Bethlehem	You palm trees of Bethlehem
Im Windesbrausen,	In the roaring gale,
Wie mögt ihr heute	How you like to howl
So zornig sausen!	So angrily today!
O rauscht nicht also!	O do not rustle so!
Schweiget, neiget	Be quiet, bend yourselves
Euch leis' und lind;	Softly and tenderly;
Stillet die Wipfel!	Calm the treetops!
Es schlummert mein Kind.	My child is sleeping.
Der Himmelsknabe	The heavenly boy
Duldet Beschwerde,	Patiently bears discomfort,
Ach, wie so müd er ward	Alas, how tired he became
Vom Leid der Erde.	Of the earth's suffering.

Ach nun im Schlaf ihm	Ah, now in sleep,
Leise gesänftigt	Softly mitigated,
Die Qual zerrinnt,	His torment dissolves;
Stillet die Wipfel!	Calm the treetops!
Es schlummert mein Kind.	My child is sleeping.
Grimmige Kälte	Bitter cold
Sauset hernieder,	Howls down from above,
Womit nur deck' ich	With what will I cover
Des Kindleins Glieder!	The little child's limbs!
O all ihr Engel,	O all you angels,
Die ihr geflügelt	You who, wing-borne,
Wandelt im Wind,	Walk in the wind,
Stillet die Wipfel!	Calm the treetops!
Es schlummert mein Kind.[3]	My child is sleeping.

Beset by chill winds that threaten the baby's slumber and stir premonitions of his future suffering, the Madonna calls both nature and angels to her aid, concluding each of her four stanzas with the same entreaty: "Calm the treetops! / My child is sleeping." Brahms's setting aligns the final couplet of each poetic stanza with a musical refrain, reproduced in example 1.1, that underscores the subjectivity of Mary's perceptions. Her plea for calm spurs a rising harmonic sequence and, in every stanza but the first, an immediate repetition of a single poetic line; this is one of only two lines so repeated in the song, making locally apparent the urgency latent in the refrain structure of the poem. Then her gaze shifts downward from the cold treetops to the still-slumbering infant in her arms, and the music is transformed. The singer encounters a second line repetition, markedly slower text declamation, the only lengthy melismas in the piece, and the stepwise descent of a ninth from the apex of the vocal part, while piano and viola share lilting figuration, a long diminuendo, and a single, slow, authentic cadence. The result is an aural image of gradual relaxation and returning warmth.

Placing this pivotal image earlier in each stanza might have affirmed the capacity of nature, divine intervention, or active self-assertion to mitigate Mary's plight. Instead, filtered through the tones of Brahms's refrain, the very act of focusing her attention exclusively on the child and away from her own anxiety provides the reassurance she seeks. Although the *Geistliches Wiegenlied* borrows the backdrop of first-century Judea and the stock imagery of pre-Reformation Christianity, its musical trajectory thus foregrounds a central dynamic of mid-nineteenth-century domesticity for middle-class women in German-speaking urban centers, for whom motherhood almost inevitably entailed solitary adjustments to the role of caregiver. At once compelling and potentially disconcerting to twenty-first-century listeners, Brahms's strikingly contemporary reading of

---

[3] Emmanuel Geibel and Paul Heyse, *Spanisches Liederbuch* (Berlin: Wilhelm Gertz, 1852), 8–9.

EXAMPLE 1.1   Brahms, *Geistliches Wiegenlied*, Op. 91 No. 2, mm. 58–68

Mary's situation would have been especially charged for the Joachims at the time of the song's completion. The earliest surviving autograph explicitly presented the piece as a gift for the couple's own firstborn son, who arrived on September 12, 1864. Initially owned by the Joachims and now untraceable in private hands, the manuscript was labeled "For the 12th of September for . . . Joachim with affectionate greetings from Johannes Br."[4] Since Brahms left a blank space before the boy's surname, he must have inscribed the autograph before the end of December 1864, when the hesitant parents finally selected a given name—Johannes, after the composer himself.

By then, however, the lullaby was already a prominent topic in correspondence among mutual friends, beginning with Joseph himself, who described it to Clara Schumann in a letter dated October 13: "How delightful is Johannes's lullaby, how beautiful the old, intertwined melody. When you come we must hear it; my wife's voice seems unchanged."[5] Along with appreciation for the song and thankfulness that neither pregnancy nor childbirth had altered Amalie's singing, Joseph's letter registered his awareness of borrowed material in Brahms's new lullaby. The "old, intertwined melody" is that of the late medieval *cantio*

---

[4] McCorkle, *Werkverzeichnis*, 375.

[5] Joachim and Moser, *Briefe von und an Joachim* 2:352. Joseph expressed his approval of the *Geistliches Wiegenlied* to Clara again before the end of 1864, but his letter is lost; see Brahms/Schumann, *Briefe* 1:489.

EXAMPLE 1.2   Brahms, *Geistliches Wiegenlied*, Op. 91 No. 2, mm. 1–10

"Resonet in laudibus," associated for centuries in German-language sources with the text "Joseph, lieber Joseph mein" (Joseph, my dear Joseph). In perhaps the longest and most explicit allusive borrowing in his entire oeuvre, Brahms's introduction presents the first three phrases of the ancient tune unadulterated, as a lightly accompanied solo for obbligato viola. As shown in example 1.2, rhythmic values and scale-degree content are so rigorously retained that the text could be printed directly below the viola line when the song was published in 1884. While one cannot tell whether such an explicit arrangement existed in earlier autographs, all of which are now lost or privately owned, a copyist's manuscript annotated in Brahms's hand confirms the composer's approval of the inserted text in the published versions of both piano score and viola part.[6]

Because of the obviousness of his melodic borrowing and the inclusion of the ancient text in the published score, Brahms's allusion is well known to performers and constitutes a perennial topic of program notes and other short prose devoted to the *Geistliches Wiegenlied*. Paradoxically, however, the manner in which Brahms integrated material derived from the *cantio* into the motivic structure of his song has rarely provided the focus for extended scholarly discussion.[7] The

---

[6] Copied by William Kupfer and annotated by Brahms in his customary blue pencil, the manuscript was a *Stichvorlage* (a model from which the engraver worked) presumably completed shortly before publication. A digital scan of the manuscript has been made available online, along with a vast trove of hitherto inaccessible *Stichvorlagen*, by the Brahms-Institut at the Musikhochschule in Lübeck. Among other requests for the engraver, Brahms indicated that the quotation beneath the viola line be placed in parentheses and rendered in a smaller font than the text of the song itself in both the score and the viola part.

[7] Max Kalbeck's seminal biography addressed Brahms's borrowing in some depth, but his error in aligning the work's inception with the date of its publication renders his account of the work's interpersonal

EXAMPLE 1.3　Brahms, *Geistliches Wiegenlied*, Op. 91 No. 2, mm. 48–59. Annotated.

three-phrase melody returns in full as an instrumental postlude, and its repeated seven-note incipit appears three times as a tonic-centered interlude between poetic stanzas. Meanwhile, motives derived from the incipit function in both vocal line and instrumental accompaniment as agents of stability and signals of return throughout the work's unfolding, most prominently in the initial vocal entrance and the measures immediately preceding the four refrains. Example 1.3 highlights these motives as they appear, along with a tiered modulation back toward the tonic, just before the final couplet in the second poetic stanza.

<hr />

associations extremely problematic; see *Brahms* 3:301–2. Florence May's early biography anticipated Kalbeck's in pointing out Brahms's borrowing, and her chronology accords far more comfortably with documentary evidence, but she devoted virtually no effort to music-analytic explication; see *The Life of Johannes Brahms* (London: E. Arnold, 1905), 2:33. The matter then became a commonplace in later biographies and surveys of Brahms's vocal music, none of which include close investigation of the song's motivic structure. For by far the most detailed interpretation of the interpenetation of borrowed music into the unfolding of the song, see Daniel Beller-McKenna, *Brahms and the German Spirit* (Cambridge, MA: Harvard University Press, 2004), 18–29. Beller-McKenna's overriding emphasis is on the broader Germanic resonances of Brahms's borrowing rather than its potential implications for the Joachims in particular. The closest equivalent in level of detail occurs in Georges Starobinsky, "Brahms et la nostalgie de l'enfance: 'Volks-Kinderlieder,' berceuses et 'Klaus-Groth-Lieder,'" *Acta Musicologica* 74 (2002): 157–61.

Securely framing Lope de Vega's poem and strategically buttressing its most important structural divisions, Brahms's borrowing implicitly reinforces the poetic speaker's self-assurance, in part by emphasizing her place within a larger social sphere. Mary's husband, conspicuously missing from the sung text, is the direct addressee of the German poem associated with the borrowed *cantio*, presented here in the syntactically convoluted version that Brahms appended to the song upon its publication:

Josef, lieber Josef mein,	Joseph, my dear Joseph,
Hilf mir wieg'n mein Kindlein fein,	Help me rock my beautiful little child,
Gott der wird dein Lohner sein,	God will be your rewarder
Im Himmelreich der Jungfrau Sohn,	In the heavenly kingdom, the son of the
Maria.	Virgin Maria.

To listeners familiar with it, this subtext opens a variety of perspectives on Mary's emotional stance. Most obviously, if one understands the repeated evocations of the *cantio*'s incipit as muted invocations of Joseph's presence, their consistent placement directly adjacent to the song's moments of relaxation would hint at a comforting role for the husband in the domestic drama. Whether one perceives that role as concretely inhabited or only wistfully desired is left ambiguous, dependent upon the listener's present inclination and the musicians' approach to the work in a given performance.

Since Amalie's husband, too, was named Joseph, Brahms's borrowing also established a unique and timely connection to the song's recipients. The mere appearance of the familiar name marked the lullaby as their private property and lent it the character of a carefully chosen gift, while the manner in which the borrowing was integrated into the structure of the song seems likely to have resonated provocatively against a wide range of possible experiences in the months following their child's birth. By inserting a soothing emblem of an otherwise absent husband into his setting of Lope de Vega's poem, Brahms created a versatile interpretive arena within which the young couple might search, both individually and collectively, for new senses of identity in the wake of momentous personal transformation.

───────────

Compared with Joseph's potential reception of the *Geistliches Wiegenlied*, Amalie's impressions lend themselves more easily to plausible reconstruction from surviving documents. Like most contracts for female opera singers, hers required her director's permission to marry. Just as important, Joseph's parents and siblings were deeply and unanimously suspicious of the supposedly loose morals associated with Amalie's background on the stage, and the violinist felt forced to defend her honor even in letters to Brahms and other friends.[8] Retirement from opera was the only socially acceptable option. Amalie's later correspondence bears frequent witness to the difficulty of re-orienting a professional singer's ambitions around the expectations of both her husband and the surrounding society, particularly after childbirth.[9] Brahms was not privy in advance to the details of her struggle, but neither was he ig-norant of the basic parameters to which she would inevitably have to adapt: primary responsibility for childcare, exponentially multiplied duties in the home, and a complete renunciation of the operatic stage in favor of limited concert appearances in oratorio and song. In accustoming herself to new boundaries between self and family, public and private, the various Marian perspectives inscribed in the *Geistliches Wiegenlied* were flexible enough to support Amalie's ongoing experimentation with a wide range of attitudes.

Indirect but tantalizing evidence of such role-play is preserved in two letters from Amalie to Joseph. The first, dated March 20, 1865, conveys the bustle and excitement that attended her return to the concert stage after Johannes's birth. Fresh from well-received performances in and around Hamburg, and preparing for her first major tour as a mother, Amalie was bursting with good news, both of her own singing and of the child's physical development during her short absence. By way of contrast to her own happily divided priorities and as if to gently underscore the importance of Joseph's continued engagement in their domestic affairs despite far-flung professional commitments, she presented the case of the baritone Julius Stockhausen and his wife, Clara:

> On the day when *she was expecting* their child, Stockhausen was in Schwerin and sang a recital. *She* was happy that he was not at home. Which of them amazes you more? I would have died if I could not have seen you at the moment when our third I [*drittes Ich*] came into the world.[10]

Complete with telling counterexample, her headlong letter of more than four hundred words encapsulated an exhilaratingly optimistic approach to balancing the demands associated with music, marriage, and parenthood. It was addressed to "Joseph lieber Joseph mein!"

The same musical citation appeared again barely a year later, this time as part of a stark reversal in attitude and circumstance. On March 24, 1866, two months

---

[8] Beatrix Borchard, *Stimme und Geige, Amalie and Joseph Joachim: Biographie und Interpretationsgeschichte* (Vienna: Böhlau, 2005), 234–37; and Brahms/Joachim, *Briefwechsel* 2:1–2, 10.

[9] Myriad examples can be found in Borchard's indispensible *Stimme und Geige*; see especially 319–25 and 253–82.

[10] The letter is transcribed for the first time, along with dozens of others in Amalie's hand, in Borchard, *Stimme und Geige*, 253–54 (emphases in original). In future years, Amalie would continue to compare her warm relationship to her children with what she considered the "somewhat short and cold" manner in which Clara Stockhausen approached hers (ibid., 267). For a glimpse of Julius Stockhausen's impressions of the Joachims' relationships to their children, see Wirth, *Julius Stockhausen*, 280–81.

after the birth of a second son, Amalie was snowed in and still bedridden at their home in Hannover. She wrote to her husband, then on an extended tour in England, to describe events that she wished he had witnessed in person:

> Nasty weather; first flooding, then ice and ice-skaters around our house....A darling little story of Putz which you should have seen first hand. Yesterday evening he was brought, already in his nightdress, to say "goodnight," and I began to sing "Joseph lieber Joseph mein" *sotto voce*—you should have seen the child's delight—and he pointed at me, "Mama, Mama," as if he wanted to say it was still the Mama from the old days, and then he sang along and even further with his sweet little voice.[11]

Here the familiar melody carried dim but affecting echoes of the singer's former confidence. In Amalie's ruined voice and between her bedroom walls, its hollow tones functioned as vessels for nostalgia and catalysts for retrenchment: buffeted, Mary-like, by cold, solitude, and forced inactivity, she turned inward toward her child, who became, for a time, the unrivaled center of attention and source of anecdote.

That music ostensibly intended simply to commemorate the child's birth found its way into such disparate letters testifies to the depth of its impact and the malleability of its metaphorical associations. At the same time, the implicit poly-textuality of the *Geistliches Wiegenlied* complicates interpretation of Amalie's references. On the one hand, since the violist neither sings Lope de Vega's text nor plays the head motive associated with it but instead spends nearly a third of the song playing literal or transposed versions of phrases from "Joseph, lieber Joseph mein," the latter appellation was surely the most efficient way of calling Brahms's lullaby to the mind's ear of a string player like Joseph. On the other hand, Brahms's song is vocally demanding, harmonically adventurous, and tex-turally complex, rendering it an improbable choice for practical use as an *a capella* lullaby under the best of circumstances, let alone for an ailing singer and precocious toddler. Although the *Geistliches Wiegenlied* seems likely to have altered the *cantio*'s connotations decisively for the Joachims and therefore to have been among a cluster of resonances inevitably called up by Amalie's cita-tions, the intimate singing described in her second letter almost certainly in-volved the medieval melody itself. Her access to that melody may have predated her first encounter with its reverberations in Brahms's lullaby.

Such was undeniably the case for her husband. On April 13, 1863, nearly two months before the Joachims' wedding in Hannover and three weeks before meeting Amalie for the first time, Brahms mailed Joseph a teaser consisting of the music and text for the first two phrases of "Joseph, lieber Joseph mein," along with a playful reference to the anticipated activities of the affianced: "At the proper time I will send you a wonderful old Catholic song for domestic use;

---

[11] Borchard, *Stimme und Geige*, 261. "Putz" was one of several pet names for Johannes Joachim.

you will dig up no more beautiful lullaby!"[12] The diction in his second clause was no accident. During the preceding months, Brahms had painstakingly unearthed the *cantio* in two rare sources: an early seventeenth-century collection of German-language Catholic music, which he discovered in the Hofbibliothek in Vienna, and a brand-new scholarly tome on German Catholic liturgical song by Karl Severin Meister, acquired as a present from Theodor Avé-Lallemant. Having compared editions meticulously, he had then copied multiple versions of both tune and text into his own growing manuscript collection of early music.[13] That he retained an interest in ancient polyphonic settings as well as the melody itself is evident from the initial entrance of the piano accompaniment in the *Geistliches Wiegenlied*, which parodies Johann Walter's harmonization of the corresponding phrase from the *cantio* at pitch and almost note for note. Examples 1.4a and b compare Brahms's introduction to a repeated, three-voice passage from Walter's five-voice *cantus firmus* song of 1544, which he had found in an appendix to Meister's volume.[14] Walter's three voices become

EXAMPLE 1.4a Walter, *Joseph, lieber Joseph mein*, mm. 13–16. From Karl Severin Meister's transcription (1862).

EXAMPLE 1.4b Brahms, *Geistliches Wiegenlied*, Op. 91 No. 2, mm. 3–4

[12] Brahms/Joachim, *Briefe* 2:7.

[13] Brahms's sources were David Gregor Corner's *Groß-Catolisch Gesangbuch* (Nürnberg: Georg Enders der Jüngere, 1631); and Karl Severin Meister's *Das katholische deutsche Kirchenlied in seinen Singweisen von den frühesten Zeiten bis gegen Ende des siebzehnten Jahrhunderts* (Freiburg im Breisgau: Herder'sche Verlagshandlung, 1862). George Bozarth has traced Brahms's engagement with these sources, along with the construction of his manuscript collection, in "Johannes Brahms und die Liedersammlungen von David Gregor Corner, Karl Severin Meister und Friedrich Wilhelm Arnold," *Die Musikforschung* 36 (1983): 177–99.

[14] For evidence of Brahms's exposure to Walter's harmonization, which appears (without page numbers) on 570–75 of Meister's *Das katholische deutsche Kirchenlied*, see Bozarth, "Liedersammlungen," 180.

the three primary voice-leading strands projected by the viola part and the two hands of the piano part; the characteristic positioning of the tune between bass line and descant a tenth apart is carefully preserved, as is the physical placement of the voices on the page (particularly striking given the clefs in Meister's transcription). Meanwhile, small adjustments in the piano's pitches fill in triads, maintain arpeggiated motion idiomatic for the instrument, and transform Walter's homophony into the lightly contrapuntal texture that marks the song's accompaniment throughout.

Given the obscurity of its model, Brahms's brief borrowing from Walter seems most likely to have reflected thoroughly private and composerly motivations, ranging from surreptitious theft of a pleasing progression to tacit acknowledgment of the peculiar, transhistorical camaraderie shared by harmonizers of the same tune. By contrast, his letter of April 1863 prepared Joseph Joachim to recognize the first two phrases of the *cantio* itself in the *Geistliches Wiegenlied* and to interpret them rhetorically, as allusive gestures. Moreover, subsequent correspondence suggests that the violinist encountered more of the *cantio* during the ensuing months. In early September 1864, in the midst of final preparations for Amalie's delivery, Joseph wrote from Hannover to Baden-Baden, where Brahms was staying with the Schumanns: "When are you going to Vienna? Please, write me that, and before then send from Baden the lullaby that you stole back from me; I will need it very soon now."[15] Beginning with Andreas Moser, who edited the Brahms/Joachim correspondence and appended an explanatory footnote to Joseph's letter, previous commentators have unanimously understood the passage as denoting a copy of an earlier version of the *Geistliches Wiegenlied*, which Brahms presumably retracted in order to improve the piece.[16] Yet no other evidence hints that the song was released in any version prior to the baby's birth, and Joseph's enthusiastic missive to Clara Schumann in mid-October reads more like an excited first impression than a sober appraisal of revisions. In fact, given his travel itinerary, Brahms might just as easily have stolen a copy of "Joseph, lieber Joseph mein," which would imply that he had delivered a complete version of the *cantio*, as promised, sometime after learning of Amalie's pregnancy in February.

The theft, whatever its target, must have occurred in late July 1864, when Brahms visited the Joachims in Hannover for the first time in fourteen months.

---

[15] Brahms/Joachim, *Briefe* 2:35.

[16] In 1983, George Bozarth provided the most comprehensive and influential attempt at dating the composition of the *Geistliches Wiegenlied*, along with a convenient summary of past efforts, which, though they differ in details, all follow Moser's interpretation of Joseph's letter of September 1864 ("Liedersammlungen," 188–92). Confusion persists until the present day, even in standard reference guides. Margit McCorkle's *Werkverzeichnis* dates the work to "1863/4?" (374), while Peter Jost flatly assigns its composition to 1863; see "Lieder und Gesänge," in *Brahms Handbuch*, ed. Wolfgang Sandberger, 248, Brahms-Institut an der Musikhochschule Lübeck (Kassel: Bärenreiter, 2009).

He then accompanied the violinist to Göttingen before continuing south, alone, to Baden-Baden, where he had long planned to spend August and September.[17] If he had lately begun to consider constructing a song around the *cantio* but had understandably left Meister's 620-page book and his own manuscript copies in Vienna or Hamburg along with the rest of his library, any copy he had previously mailed to the Joachims would have offered a precious chance to confirm his memory of the tune and ensure that his echoes matched Joseph's source precisely. Even if one or more of his own sources happened to be ready to hand, Joseph's copy offered another unique opportunity: returning the stolen manuscript along with his new composition would throw his allusive practice into stronger and more personal relief. While a dramatically paired delivery of allusively related manuscripts is purely hypothetical in this case, the scenario is eminently plausible: a few years later, having pilfered a handwritten copy of a song from Hermann Levi, Brahms subsequently returned it along with a new setting of the same text, which borrowed a vocal phrase from Levi's original.[18]

In any case, exposure to a short excerpt in 1863 and another, larger manuscript of some sort during the following year ensured that Joseph Joachim was familiar with at least three phrases of the *cantio*'s melody and two phrases of its text well before encountering them in the final manuscript version of the *Geistliches Wiegenlied*. Although Joseph's surviving correspondence preserves no record of his reception of the medieval melody until October 1864 and no citations whatsoever of its text, the timing and circumstances of his successively longer and more complex engagements with "Joseph, lieber Joseph mein" hint that Brahms was able to predict in detail how his friend would respond to its reanimation in a newly composed lullaby.

In the first place, the composer had probably assumed that his initial citation of the tune in April 1863 would be perceived as a well-timed joke. The humor is easy to miss if one views the eight-measure teaser in hindsight as evidence regarding the genesis of Brahms's later compositional efforts, rather than in its own context as a self-sufficient piece of an ongoing conversation. In his most recent letter to Brahms, dated April 7, Joseph had explained what had forced him to postpone his wedding, which he had originally hoped to schedule in late March: unexpectedly constrained by Amalie's operatic contract, the couple would be unable to marry until May at the earliest.[19] On the heels of this setback

---

[17] For evidence of Brahms's movements, see Hofmann, *Zeittafel*, 64–66; Joachim and Moser, *Briefe von und an Joachim* 2:342 and 344; and Brahms/Joachim, *Briefe* 2:30.
[18] Levi described the circumstance decades later in a letter to Julius Stockhausen; for a transcription, see Wirth, *Julius Stockhausen*, 482.
[19] Compare Brahms/Joachim, *Briefe* 2:2 and 6. In fact, the wedding was ultimately postponed until June.

for the eager violinist, the opening measures of the *cantio* were provocative in themselves. The genre of the lullaby hinted openly at the coming consummation of his nuptials, while its sacred subject matter placed that consummation at a comically exaggerated remove.[20] Indeed, Joseph's current predicament facilitated an impious but humorously precise parallel with the biblical holy family invoked by the ancient text: in his namesake's forbearance in the face of Mary's virginal conception, the violinist could find a venerable model against which to measure his own frustration as he waited for what Brahms coyly called "the proper time."

In addition to their given name and unexpectedly stymied physical intimacy with their betrothed, the two Josephs also shared a shifting religious and cultural affiliation. The biblical Joseph's acceptance of Mary's pregnancy violated contemporary Jewish norms and, through the lens of Christian doctrine, made him an archetypal convert to the new religion. The modern Joseph, too, had rejected the Jewish religion and culture of his parents in favor of Christianity; he was privately baptized Joseph Georg Maria Joachim in May 1855 with his patrons, the king and queen of Hannover, as godparents.[21] His conversion to Lutheranism coincided with wide-ranging patterns of assimilation in German-speaking cities after the failed revolutions of 1848, as a patchwork of ancient discriminatory laws returned to force and middle-class German Jews overwhelmingly adopted Liberal politics as a path to equal rights. The family of Felix Mendelssohn, Joseph's teacher and the idol of his youth, provided a potentially influential prototype dating back to the wave of conversions among Jews in Berlin during the first two decades of the century.[22] Emulation aside, Joseph's own motives were undoubtedly complex. Among friends in the rarified circles of Weimar and Hannover, he had occasionally professed ambivalence toward aspects of his own heritage. At the same time, although he denied it vehemently and rightly perceived the suspicion as a kind

---

[20] Lightly veiled discussion of sexual matters was by no means unprecedented between the two friends. Among other exchanges, Marion Gerards points to Brahms's 1857 recommendation of a book on sexual diseases and sexual function. See *Frauenliebe—Männerleben: Die Musik von Johannes Brahms und der Geschlechterdiskurs im 19. Jahrhundert* (Vienna: Böhlau, 2010), 53–56.

[21] Borchard, *Stimme und Geige*, 101.

[22] For a concise summary of the complex effects of the revolutions upon German Jews and the legal discrimination to which they were subject between 1848 and 1870, see Amos Elon, *The Pity of It All: A History of Jews in Germany, 1742–1933* (New York: Metropolitan Books, 2002), 149–92. A methodologically complementary approach to the nature of Jewish assimilation in the nineteenth century appears in Till van Rahden, "Jews and the Ambivalences of Civil Society in Germany, 1800–1930: Assessment and Reassessment," *Journal of Modern History* 77 (2005): 1024–47. Jeffrey Sposato has recently provided a balanced and detailed exploration of the cultural forces and family decisions that shaped the young Felix Mendelssohn's baptism in 1816; see *Price of Assimilation: Felix Mendelssohn and the Nineteenth-Century Anti-Semitic Tradition* (Oxford: Oxford University Press, 2006), 14–23. A more general introduction to the wave of conversions in Prussia during the early decades of the century can be found in Elon, *Pity of It All*, 81–90.

of anti-Semitism, professional pressure probably played some role in the decision as well, since throughout the 1850s Jews were still barred from official service at the Hannover court.[23] Whatever his reasons, baptism had led to severe strains with his family, and his recent betrothal to the Catholic Amalie had reopened and compounded the fractures.[24] As if to escape the strain, he had long since adopted a deliberately lighthearted tone when discussing his conversion among trusted allies from his own generation. On the eve of his baptism, he had quipped to Brahms: "Think of me tomorrow afternoon...and I ask you not to be a doubting Thomas."[25] In similar vein, the appearance of "Joseph, lieber Joseph mein" just as religious and familial tensions reached another peak might well have provoked a knowing chuckle or rueful smile, especially since Brahms's letter specifically emphasized the Catholic origins of the tune.

In the wake of the Joachims' wedding the stress naturally dissipated. Writing to Avé-Lallemant in June, Joseph cast his relief in epic terms: "I feel like a man who, for the first time since childhood, gets to know the feeling of his homeland again after long wandering!"[26] Especially once Amalie became pregnant, the exigencies against which the cantio's text had resonated so sharply gave way to new challenges and new equilibria. For Joseph, then, encountering the familiar melody for a second time during the spring or summer of 1864 would almost surely have encouraged a softer, less jocular perspective on the poem that accompanied it. And by the time the healthy infant was delivered in September and a clean copy of Brahms's new song arrived during the ensuing weeks, the violinist was well positioned to interpret the allusive gesture as a kind of symbolic amelioration. Brahms's motivic alignment of the ancient tune with moments of reassurance vis-à-vis Lope de Vega's poetic speaker enacted a powerful reversal of its prior associations. What had been a sardonic emblem of a bachelor's anxiety was re-imagined as a husband's essential contribution to domestic harmony. The greater the emotional distance traversed over the preceding eighteen months, the more persuasive the sense of homecoming an informed listener might experience in Brahms's lullaby.

The song's instrumentation seems likely to have reinforced this connotative shift in several ways. Of course, for a violinist named Joseph, the selection of an upper string instrument to present the cantio's first and most complete appearance confirmed the parallel with his namesake by placing in his own hands the

---

[23] See, for instance, Joachim and Moser, Briefe von und an Joachim 1:113–14 and 283–84. These and other letters align Joseph's questioning of his own Jewish identity with crises in his confidence and reevaluations of his chosen career. For more on the professional pressures facing Joachim in the years before his conversion, see Borchard, Stimme und Geige, 105–6.

[24] For more on the Joachim family's attempts to disrupt the union, see Borchard, Stimme und Geige, 139–40.

[25] Brahms/Joachim, Briefe 1:104.

[26] Joachim and Moser, Briefe von und an Joachim 2:314.

musical material associated with his biblical counterpart. At the same time, the unmistakably soothing role of that material in the unfolding of the new song hinted at a continuum linking musicianship and fatherhood, as if an increasingly peripatetic virtuoso might vicariously remain a family man through the imagined performance of chamber music. Yet the viola was not Joseph's primary instrument. How might its appearance, to the exclusion of his accustomed violin, have influenced his reception of the *Geistliches Wiegenlied*? Certainly its mellower timbre and lower range de-emphasized overt technical display in favor of collaborative listening, while ensuring that his wife's contralto would not be overbalanced. Stylistic and acoustical constraints aside, however, one wonders if Brahms's choice was also meant to evoke Joseph's own compositions for the same instrument. In particular, the moderate tempo, introspective tone, and comparatively subdued figuration of Brahms's obbligato part recall Joseph's three *Hebräische Melodien Nach Eindrücken der Byron'schen Gesänge* (Hebrew Melodies, After Impressions of Byron's Songs), Op. 9, for viola and piano. Drafted before July 1854 but carefully guarded from musical friends during a lengthy editing process throughout the next several months, these meditations on Lord Byron's *Hebrew Melodies* were finally circulated in manuscript early in 1855, then offered to Breitkopf and Härtel in April.[27]

In relation to Joseph's reception of the *Geistliches Wiegenlied*, both the title and the timing of his *Hebräische Melodien* are intriguing. The title left pointedly unstated which (if any) of Byron's poems had specifically stimulated the composer's three pieces. First published in London in 1815, Byron's collection engages numerous subjects, including natural beauty and romantic love, but the vast majority of the twenty-four poems are explicitly presented as utterances of identifiably Jewish speakers. Many revisit biblically recorded circumstances, while a few appropriate the broader voice of Jewish diaspora across the ages. Among the latter is "Were my bosom as false as thou deem'st it to be," whose implied reader could as easily be a nineteenth-century Bürgermeister as a Babylonian king:

Were my bosom as false as thou deem'st it to be,
I need not have wandered from far Galilee;
It was but abjuring my creed to efface
The curse which, thou say'st, is the crime of my race.

If the bad never triumph, then God is with thee!
If the slave only sin, thou are spotless and free!

---

[27] Brahms began asking to see the *Hebräische Melodien* in July 1854, having heard of their existence from Clara Schumann, but he was turned down because Joseph was not yet satisfied (Brahms/Joachim, *Briefe* 1:50–53). At least some revisions occurred in early October, but Brahms was not permitted to see a copy until mid-February 1855 (see ibid., 85, and Joachim and Moser, *Briefe von und an Joachim* 1:215–16). Joseph's negotiations with Breitkopf and Härtel began on April 14 and extended for at least ten days (ibid., 277, 279–80).

If the Exile on earth is an Outcast on high,
Live on in thy faith, but in mine I will die.

I have lost for that faith more than thou canst bestow,
As the God who permits thee to prosper doth know;
In his hand is my heart and my hope—and in thine
The land and the life which for him I resign.[28]

Like Adelbert Chamisso's *Frauenliebe und -Leben* of 1831 or Harriet Beecher Stowe's *Uncle Tom's Cabin* of 1852, Byron's poems make for strange and uncomfortable reading. Intertwined with a fundamentally sympathetic stance toward the poetic speaker are stock images and stereotypes that provoke intense scrutiny today. Yet recent scholarship has revealed a widespread and complex interest in literary portrayals of the perspectives of subjugated or otherwise marginalized persons in German-language criticism from the early and middle decades of the nineteenth century.[29] In such a climate, Byron's *Hebrew Melodies* found an enthusiastic and varied audience. By the early 1820s, the collection was available in at least three German translations,[30] and prominent composers such as Carl Loewe, Felix Mendelssohn, Robert Schumann, and Ferdinand Hiller soon took up the challenge of setting the texts to music.

In an otherwise favorable review of Loewe's Op. 4—which set "Were my bosom as false" along with five other *Gesänge* in Franz Theremin's 1820 translation—a Berlin reviewer in 1827 faulted the composer for failing to "portray the frame of mind of this remarkable folk" with sufficient consistency and depth.[31] On the other end of the spectrum, Theremin himself, the prominent and highly educated scion of a long line of French reformed pastors, felt

---

[28] George Gordon Byron and Isaac Nathan, *A Selection of Hebrew Melodies*...(London, 1815), 2:89.

[29] Kristina Muxfeldt has illuminated this largely unexplored terrain through a penetrating study of Chamisso's controversial cycle (along with Schumann's musical adaptation thereof) in "*Frauenliebe und Leben* Now and Then," *19th-Century Music* 25 (2001): 27–48. While Muxfeldt's evidence primarily concerns the portrayal of feminine subjectivity in poetry and song of the first half of the nineteenth century, many of her conclusions arguably apply to other marginalized identities in contemporaneous German literature as well. Consider the enduring popularity of enigmatically deviant characters such as Mignon and the Harper from Goethe's *Wilhelm Meisters Lehrjahre*, not to mention the commercial success of imitation Persian and Magyar lyric in the works of Goethe, Rückert, and Daumer. Alongside these and other offerings, sympathetic appropriations of the voice and experiences of German Jews found a place as well. Barely a year after completing *Frauenliebe und -Leben*, Chamisso himself engaged the contemporary plight of Jews in German-speaking lands in a pair of lengthy poems, "Abba Glosk Leczeka" and "Baal Teschuba." For the first of these, he enlisted the help of the David Friedländer, Moses Mendelssohn's protégé in Berlin, to ensure the authenticity of his references to Jewish folklore and traditions of Talmudic interpretation. See Hermann Tardel, *Studien zur Lyrik Chamissos: Beilage zum Programm der Handelsschule (Oberrealschule) zu Bremen, Ostern 1902* (Bremen: A. Guthe, 1902), 44–50.

[30] Franz Theremin, *Hebräische Gesänge* (Berlin: Duncker und Humblot, 1820); Julius Körner, *Israelitisches Gesänge: Lord Byron's Poesien 1* (Zwickau: Schumann, 1821); and Andreas Kretschmer, *Hebräische Gesänge* (Berlin: Magazin für Kunst, Geographie, und Musik, 1822).

[31] Anonymous, *Berliner allgemeine musikalische Zeitung* 4, 20 (May 16, 1827): 157.

impelled to justify his interest in texts that so strongly encouraged identification with the Jewish *Volk*. The preface to his translations concludes:

> The Jew lives in so unparalleled a torpor that he does not sense the horror of his fate....Only the Christian, insofar as he observes the fate of this folk from his universal-historical standpoint, insofar as he builds up the Jew and loans him the feelings of patriotism that perished in him long ago, can be moved over his fate by a melancholy as deep as that which articulates itself in these songs. I therefore believe that in translating them I have engaged in nothing unchristian, and that I have not brought myself under suspicion of any sympathy for the Jews that would go beyond the bounds of due charity.[32]

That a man could write this paragraph just after completing two dozen sensitive and beautiful translations of Byron's poems is a testament to the paradoxical fascination that their cultural ventriloquism stimulated upon arrival in German-speaking territories. Theremin's tortured logic and overt bigotry stand in marked contrast to the matter-of-fact tone of Loewe's anonymous reviewer, but both responses presuppose an empathetic mode of engagement with the poetry, at least during the immediate act of reading.

Informed critics could trace such receptive tendencies back to the prose introduction to Byron's original collection, in which the poems themselves are presented as *post facto* glosses on preexisting liturgical melodies transcribed in synagogues by the poet's collaborator, Isaac Nathan. Like the German vocal settings of his predecessors, Joseph Joachim's instrumental *Melodien* bore no resemblance to Nathan's melodies, which were far less accessible than Byron's poems outside of England. Nevertheless, an array of marked compositional features facilitated parallels between musical sonority and poetic subject matter. Many of these features were immediately apparent in the opening measures of the three *Melodien*. Examples 1.5a, b, and c present the initial viola entrances from each. The harp-like textures and hints of modality in the first two *Melodien* and the unusual ornaments in the second *Melodie* establish an exoticist musical distance commensurate with a range of ancient and modern Jewish perspectives toward assimilation into surrounding cultures. Meanwhile, the bass line of the third *Melodie* hints that some of Byron's more sentimental topoi may also have resonated for the composer. Here Joseph's cryptographic motto, F–A–E ("frei aber einsam," or "free but alone"), is repeatedly juxtaposed with G♯–E–A, the motto of his erstwhile beloved, Gisela von Arnim (through a combination of German and Latin note names, G♯–E–A spells Gis–E–La).[33]

---

[32] Theremin, *Hebräische Gesänge*, vii–viii.

[33] In tandem, the two ciphers play prominent roles in several works completed in the years following the end of Joseph's engagement to Gisela in 1853. First came the *Drei Stücke* for violin and piano, Op. 5. In a letter to Robert Schumann which he mailed along with a copy of the piece, Joseph described his cipher technique and explained its biographical connotations; see Daverio, *Crossing Paths*, 110 and 272. Later, both mottos appeared in Joseph's contributions to his counterpoint exchange with Brahms in 1856–57.

EXAMPLE 1.5a   Joseph Joachim, *Hebräische Melodie*, Op. 9 No. 1, mm. 3–7

EXAMPLE 1.5b   Joseph Joachim, *Hebräische Melodie*, Op. 9 No. 2, mm. 1–6

Whatever Joseph's own attitude toward the collection whose title he borrowed, that title and the attitudes embodied in the poetry for which it stood must have caught the attention of close acquaintances, especially given the work's chronological proximity to his conversion: his baptism occurred barely two weeks after he offered Op. 9 for publication. The convergence is all the more striking because it can be interpreted fruitfully from so many different angles. Loving farewell to his heritage, cathartic rejection of his family, ambivalent commentary on a troubled relationship with his Gentile love interest—all are plausible and powerful ways of hearing the work. Moreover, the *Hebräische Melodien* capped a period of compositional activity unprecedented in Joseph's

For a detailed summary of the contrapuntal correspondence course, see David Brodbeck, "The Brahms-Joachim Counterpoint Exchange: or, Robert, Clara, and 'the Best Harmony between Jos. and Joh.,'" in *Brahms Studies 1*, ed. David Brodbeck, 1: 30–80 (Lincoln: University of Nebraska Press, 1994). In the interim, the *Hebräische Melodien* were not the only published opus to employ at least one of the ciphers in positions of motivic prominence: the melody to the chorale-like theme of the Op. 10 Variations for viola and piano begins with the pitches G♯–E–A, infusing the entire work with Gisela's motto.

EXAMPLE 1.5C   Joseph Joachim, *Hebräische Melodie*, Op. 9 No. 3, mm. 1–16

earlier career and unparalleled in his later years. Coming directly on the heels of the *Variations for viola and piano*, Op. 10, the *Drei Stücke* for violin and piano, Op. 5, and the overtures *Hamlet*, *Henry IV*, and *Demetrius*, the piece seemed to confirm an increased commitment to his own music. Yet aside from his famous but abortive exchanges of contrapuntal exercises with Brahms in 1856–57 and the phenomenally popular "Hungarian" violin concerto, Op. 11, in 1861, he subsequently and emphatically gave up composition in favor of performance. Spread thinly over several decades, his handful of later efforts were plainly exceptions to a general rule.

For his part, Brahms had reacted enthusiastically to the *Hebräische Melodien* immediately upon first seeing them in manuscript. In a letter to the violinist from February 1855, he compared them favorably to the Op. 10 *Variations*, which he had encountered simultaneously. Brahms cast the difference between the two works in terms of the authenticity and originality of their compositional voice and, hence, the depth of their emotional impact. His formulation suggests, obliquely but significantly, an especially strong connection between musical and personal identity in Joseph's latest project:

> The variations are perhaps not as entirely your own as the overtures. But surely no one has yet wielded Beethoven's pen so powerfully. The Hebrew Songs, however, are truly Joachim, wonderfully moving....I ask you, observe the powerful crescendo from your Op. 1 until now.[34]

Less than a year later, Brahms played the two works as a pair in a private performance with Ferdinand David at the Leipzig home of Woldemar and Livia Frege.

---

[34] Brahms/Joachim, *Briefe* 1:85.

As he complained to Clara Schumann, both pieces provoked only "outrage and boredom" from the assembled guests, but he predicted that their future reception would shift in tandem with Joachim's then-growing reputation as a composer. Intriguingly, he presented his friend's current compositional hesitancy in terms similar to those in which the violinist himself had often decried his own Jewishness in the years leading up to his recent conversion: "If J. develops as I think and wish, his brooding and self-torture will cease as soon as others torture him, and then in ten years everyone will adore these present works more than I do now or ever will."[35]

From the first, then, Joachim's works for viola and piano were implicitly associated with an ongoing process of transformation that encompassed both musical and extramusical aspects of his character. At the time, Brahms could hardly have foreseen that the next decade would bring only one more opus from his formerly prolific counterpart. By 1864, however, it was clear that the *Hebräische Melodien* had come at the apex of an avocation long since abandoned. To the eye of an old friend, the work thus occupied a marked point of inflection in both the personal and the professional curve of Joseph's history. Might Brahms have understood the instrumentation in the *Geistliches Wiegenlied* as a gentle acknowledgment of two self-images, Jew and composer, which his friend had ostensibly left behind during the intervening years—an assurance that the past, despite its twists and turns, was somehow necessary and sufficient preparation for the present moment?

Such a reading of Brahms's compositional choices gains its specificity at the price of some speculation. At best it is a plausible account of extant evidence; complementary accounts could also be devised. By the same token, the many interpretive possibilities proposed in these pages cannot have all reflected Amalie and Joseph's lived impressions of Brahms's song with equal accuracy or equivalent degrees of consciousness at any given moment. Nevertheless, the preponderance of surviving documents surrounding the work and its reception supports a single, kaleidoscopic conclusion: given the Joachims' prior musical experiences and interpersonal circumstances, the pitches, text, timbre, and structural placement of Brahms's allusion to "Joseph, lieber Joseph mein" would likely have been perceived as drawing together and manipulating aspects of their identities, both past and present. The *Geistliches Wiegenlied* thus established the potential contours of a shared emotional landscape that facilitated each person's realignment in the service of their new and growing family, providing space for positive reinterpretations of past decisions in light of current commitments.

To what extent the Joachims knowingly explored this landscape must remain an open question. At the very least, Brahms's treatment of the work after its completion suggests that he anticipated and valued the intimacy it could encourage between its initial recipients. During the final weeks of 1864, he asked repeatedly for Clara Schumann's advice regarding publication plans for

[35] Brahms/Schumann, *Briefe* 1:168–69.

the lullaby. His letters no longer survive, but, after some initial confusion, Clara's second response clarified her opinion and revealed the nature of his concerns: "What do you mean about the lullaby for Joachim? You asked me whether I would find it tactless if you published it, to which I responded that you should not do so *now!*"[36] The composer's worries about perceived indelicacy demonstrate clearly that he expected the Joachims to understand the *Geistliches Wiegenlied* in inherently personal terms. Brahms ultimately waited two decades before releasing the song in print. His timing was a final testament to the work's initial associations. The Joachims' marriage had foundered during the interim, destroyed by mounting professional demands and Joseph's groundless jealousies and suspicions. Brahms's long friendship with the violinist sustained irreparable damage in 1881 because of his support for Amalie, who introduced a sympathetic letter from the composer as evidence in divorce proceedings in order to counter her husband's attempt to cast her as the sole guilty party. The publication of the *Geistliches Wiegenlied* in December 1884 along with a new song for the same ensemble (the autumnal *Gestillte Sehnsucht*, Op. 91 No. 1) is often taken as an attempt to reunite the couple, but the assumption flies in the face of chronology and overwhelming evidence.[37] By August 1884, when Brahms offered the songs to his publisher, the irreconcilability of the split had been obvious to the Joachims and their friends alike for more than three years. Widespread knowledge of the acrimonious separation had figured prominently in the popular reception of Amalie's return to the Berlin concert stage the previous February, and the divorce was finalized just as Brahms's Op. 91 went on sale for the first time in December.[38]

Far from attempting to reawaken past feelings, then, the decision to publish the lullaby seems to have acknowledged their irretrievability. The song became a widely available commodity precisely at the moment when the interpersonal conditions to which it had first responded and the relationships it had been designed to foster had faded beyond recall. Divested of its private connotations, it was now free to serve new ends, both public and pecuniary.[39]

---

[36] Ibid., 489. Emphases in original.

[37] Among recent variants upon this interpretation are Beller-McKenna, *Brahms and the German Spirit*, 25; MacDonald, *Brahms*, 345; Heather Platt, "2 Gesänge, for Alto, Viola, and Piano, Opus 91," in *The Compleat Brahms*, ed. Leon Botstein, 276 (New York: Norton, 1999); and Jan Swafford, *Johannes Brahms: A Biography*, 2nd ed. (New York: Vintage Books, 1999), 469.

[38] Borchard presents a trove of relevant documents in *Stimme und Geige*, 368–91. For two of the many extant indications that Brahms perceived the breach as irreconcilable as early as 1882, see Brahms, *Briefe an Simrock* 2:206 and 216.

[39] A ready-made, marketable song with attractive and unusual scoring, the *Geistliches Wiegenlied* was ripe for publication in its own right, but Brahms's motivations may have involved Amalie's profit as well as his own. Many in Joseph's considerable network of professional acquaintances shunned his wife during the early years of their estrangement, complicating her efforts to refashion her career and rebuild her public reputation. In letters to his publisher from late summer and autumn 1884, Brahms described both

Long before the Joachims' separation, Brahms had already crafted an alternative solution to the problem of publication for a second allusive lullaby. In early July 1868, he received word that Bertha and Arthur Faber, among his closest friends in his adopted home city of Vienna, had become the parents of a second son and had named the boy Johannes. Vacationing in Bonn after a busy concert tour in March and the triumphant Bremen premiere of his *German Requiem* in April, Brahms took time to compose a musical response to the Fabers' news. On July 15 he sent them a signed autograph of a song for solo voice and piano, titled simply *Wiegenlied* (Lullaby) and labeled "for happy use at all times," which he claimed to have completed on the previous day.[40] Along with the manuscript Brahms included a letter addressed to Arthur but clearly intended for Bertha's eyes as well:

> Now Frau Bertha will see at once that I made the lullaby yesterday especially for her little one; she will also find it completely fitting, as I do, that while she sings Hans to sleep, her husband sings to *her* and murmurs a love song. Moreover Frau Bertha would do me a favor if at some point she obtained for me the music and text to said love song "Du meinst wohl, Du glaubst wohl." I have only a vague notion of it in my ears. You, on the other hand, must now make verses for it, appropriate ones. But my song is equally appropriate for girls as well as boys, and you don't need to order a new one every time.[41]

Brahms's letter drew the Fabers' attention to multivalent echoes of Alexander Baumann's *S'is Anderscht* (It's Different), a popular song in Austrian dialect and simulated folk style. As in the *Geistliches Wiegenlied*, the clearest evocations of preexisting music begin immediately, in the song's instrumental introduction. Examples 1.6a and b highlight shared melodic and harmonic progressions in the initial measures of the *Wiegenlied* and *S'is Anderscht*. Notwithstanding Brahms's claims of partial amnesia, material borrowed from Baumann infiltrates every strand in the polyphonic fabric of the piano accompaniment. The right hand's upper voice duplicates the contour and scale-degree content of Baumann's melody, and its lower voice mirrors an optional second vocal line from Baumann's song; meanwhile, atop a tonic pedal, the left hand articulates a simple harmonic pattern shared by both songs. Performed without the vocal line, Brahms's piano part is a veiled but identifiable parody.

Apparently mistrusting either the accuracy of his reference or the Fabers' ability to disentangle accompaniment from melody, the composer took rare pains to direct their listening. His letter openly acknowledged his borrowing and isolated its source

---

songs of Op. 91 as designed specifically for Amalie's voice and requested that copies be sent to her; see Brahms, *Briefe an Simrock* 3:66 and 85. Having arranged professional engagements for the cash-strapped singer during the previous spring (see ibid., 54–55, 57, and 64), he seems to have hoped that the anticipated popularity of his new opus would provide her with needed repertoire.

[40] For a description of the autograph, see McCorkle, *Werkverzeichnis*, 198–99.

[41] Kalbeck, *Brahms* 2:326–27. Emphasis in original. Hans was, and remains, a standard childhood nickname for boys named Johannes.

EXAMPLE I.6a   Alexander Baumann, *S'is Anderscht*, mm. 1–4. Annotated.

EXAMPLE I.6b   Brahms, *Wiegenlied*, Op. 49 No. 4, mm. 1–6. Annotated.

by citing the two most common phrases in Baumann's text. Such candor was unusual for a man already known to avoid scrutiny of his compositional methods. As Brahms's reticence emerged as a dominant trope in the reception of his music and the writing of his biography throughout the late nineteenth and early twentieth centuries, the letter to the Fabers came to stand out against the backdrop of his accustomed stance as a potentially meaningful anomaly, an amusing exception that could help to prove an increasingly significant rule. After Max Kalbeck included an excerpt in his monumental biography of the composer, the passage above was almost invariably quoted or paraphrased whenever the song was mentioned in later scholarship.[42] In turn, attachment to a revealing anecdote made the *Wiegenlied* a prominent

---

[42] As with the *Geistliches Wiegenlied*, Florence May anticipated Kalbeck in recounting the story of the *Wiegenlied*'s inception in detail and describing the manuscript of the song, but she did not include direct quotation from Brahms's letter; see May, *Johannes Brahms* 2:82. Max Friedländer's seminal study of Brahms's songs included Kalbeck's redacted version of the letter and cited his biography directly; see Friedländer, *Brahms' Lieder: Einführung in seine Gesänge für eine und zwei Stimmen* (Berlin: Simrock, 1922), 61. Later treatments of life and work that recount the anecdote without explicitly citing Brahms's letter include: Richard Specht, *Johannes Brahms*, trans. Eric Blom, 109–10 (London: J. M. Dent, 1930); Geiringer, *Johannes Brahms*, 245; Max Harrison, *The Lieder of Brahms* (New York: Praeger Publishers, 1972), 88; MacDonald, *Brahms*, 200; and Michael Musgrave, "Words for Music: the Songs for Solo Voice and Piano," in *The Cambridge Companion to Brahms*, ed. Michael Musgrave, 197 (Cambridge: Cambridge University Press, 1999).

fixture in virtually all surveys of Brahms's songs and most book-length studies of his music or biography. For decades to come, letter and lullaby would reinforce each other's place in narratives of the composer's life and works. But for the Fabers themselves, Brahms's description was surely attractive not by virtue of its implications regarding his general aesthetic outlook but because of what it revealed about the piece at hand: the appropriation of Baumann's love song was an overtly allusive gesture intended specifically for their ears and designed to encourage a particular interpretive schema.

Brahms sketched the outlines of this schema using an analogy between contrapuntal combination and familial connection. By weaving a musical and textual register of Arthur's love for Bertha into a song for their son, the lullaby created the sonic equivalent of a family portrait: two parents drawn together in their relationship to the infant. Like a softly burnished frame, the continuous tonic pedal in the bass line and unadulterated major-mode harmony throughout the piece set into relief a carefully balanced arrangement of figures within the image itself. Thus, in Brahms's imagined scenario, the allusion encouraged complementary and subtly gender-specific interpretive stances from Arthur and Bertha both before and during the moment of performance. As befit his lucrative career as a manufacturer, Arthur's role was primarily that of supportive husband rather than directly engaged father. He would first construct a love poem, reverse engineered to fit "appropriately" beneath the piano part; then, as the accompanist, his attention would be directed toward Bertha rather than the baby, whose care, after all, was mainly her responsibility. Meanwhile, the act of singing the song's simple melody would leave Bertha's hands free to cradle the child and her ear open to the contrapuntal support offered by her husband's accompaniment.[43] For a couple with ample means, in tune with the predominant domestic values of their time and culture, the song's gentle polyphony could come to embody the dynamics of harmonious matrimonial partnership.

Beyond the fact that the Fabers treasured Brahms's manuscript and described his allusive gesture to multiple biographers in the years following his death, no evidence survives regarding their reception of the *Wiegenlied*. Nevertheless, in comparison with the interpretive stance that Brahms's music had encouraged from the Joachims, certain features of the Fabers' probable experience stand out. Most important, the hermeneutic proposed in the composer's letter and facilitated by his song clearly foregrounds the implications of polyvalent musical structure over the specific connotations of either text. For his lullaby, Brahms selected a one-stanza poem titled "Gute Nacht, mein Kind!" and first published

[43] For complementary views of the role of motherly singing in the *Wiegenlied*, see Gerards, *Frauenliebe—Männerleben*, 158–65; and Bottge, "Brahms's 'Wiegenlied,'" 185–213. In Gerard's volume, the song takes pride of place in a larger account of Brahms's perspective on women as articulated in his vocal music. By contrast, Bottge downplays Brahms's own attitudes in favor of a broader investigation of motherhood and the domestic arts in midcentury Germany and Austria.

in an appendix to Achim von Arnim and Clemens Brentano's seminal collection, *Des Knaben Wunderhorn* (1808):

Guten Abend, gute Nacht,	Good evening, good night,
Mit Rosen bedacht,	Covered with roses,
Mit Näglein besteckt,	Decorated with carnations,
Schlupf' unter die Deck,	Slide under the covers,
Morgen früh, wenn's Gott will,	Tomorrow morning, if God wills it,
Wirst du wieder geweckt.[44]	You'll be awakened again.

At the urging of his publisher, Brahms appended a second stanza four years later;[45] punctuation is clarified and contractions added in all printed editions of the song. In recent years, scholars influenced by feminist, psychoanalytic, and poststructural criticism have drawn attention to a strange disjunction between the charged imagery of the text, which figures the child's sleep as an intimation of death, and the deliberately restrained style of the musical setting.[46] Perhaps the Fabers found the relationship between poem and song amusing rather than unsettling; perhaps the enigmatic gap between textual and musical rhetoric was part of what made the lullaby appealing to them. But whatever their impressions, Brahms's initial gloss offered a pragmatic explanation: by downplaying the compositional significance of individual poetic images and maintaining a consistent affect, he had enhanced the work's broad suitability as a lullaby for children of any gender, at any time.

Likewise, the composer presented his engagement with Baumann's text as generic rather than specific. While his memory of Baumann's music remained intact, his letter registered scant regard for the nuances of his predecessor's poem. The two phrases he cited in place of a title never occur in sequence in Baumann's text, and his spelling normalized pointedly Austrian dialect into standard High German—"Du moanst wol" became "Du meinst wohl."[47] Furthermore, his straightforward designation of *S'is Anderscht* as a "love song" obscures significant complications. The poetic speaker's underlying motivations and ultimate success remain coyly uncertain throughout repeated attempts to coax a cynically flirtatious woman into long-term commitment. The choice of *S'is Anderscht* as the embodiment of a husband's love is consonant with the gender of Baumann's poetic speaker but flies in the face of the specific emotional circumstances described in the poem, which may help to explain why Arthur was immediately encouraged to invent new verses. Rather than search

---

[44] Achim von Arnim and Clemens Brentano, *Kinderlieder: Anhang zum Wunderhorn* (Heidelberg: Mohr und Zimmer, 1808), 68.

[45] Friedländer, *Brahms' Lieder*, 63–64.

[46] For contrasting approaches of this kind, compare Bottge, "Brahms's 'Wiegenlied,'" 204–12, with Gerards, *Frauenliebe—Männerleben*, 158–59.

[47] For a full transcription of Baumann's song, including all three stanzas of its text, see Bottge, "Brahms's 'Wiegenlied,'" 193–95.

fruitlessly for detailed parallels between himself and Baumann's protagonist, he could invest the now-familiar melody with private significance of his own choosing.

Nevertheless, that significance was still mediated by a definite musical structure. Whether Arthur actually wrote a poem to sing along with the *Wiegenlied* or the Fabers simply imagined the borrowed music as a symbol of mute affection, the manner in which the allusion was integrated into its new setting was bound to affect the apprehension of its message. In particular, the avoidance of on-beat attacks in the piano's right hand rendered the tune persistently behind relative to its harmonic underpinning and interposed a narrow gap between source and borrowing, between expectation and experience. Once alerted to the presence of Baumann's melody, the Fabers were predisposed to hear its slightly blurred echoes in Brahms's lullaby as emerging from a distance, along with whatever associations they had chosen to attach to it. Bertha seems especially likely to have perceived such a gap in personal terms. She was herself a singer, and *S'is Anderscht* had been part of her performing repertoire for nearly a decade. Brahms had heard her sing it in Hamburg in September 1859, shortly after he first met her as a young soprano of just seventeen.[48] In alluding to Baumann's song nine years later through a haze of gentle syncopations, the composer could assume that he was conjuring up long-range musical memories and foregrounding their separation from the present. In turn, by aligning an identifiably old melody with her husband's affectionate sentiments, he encouraged a uniquely bifurcated interpretive stance from Bertha. For her alone, Arthur's love song could resound as if from long ago as well as in the present—from early in their marriage, from before the children, from whatever moment in their shared history would best serve her current emotional need. Singing Brahms's *Wiegenlied* to her husband's accompaniment therefore allowed her to vicariously inhabit two related imaginaries: the balanced poise of a well-ordered family and the afterglow of a romantic past. Exploring the intersection between these ideals might have provided welcome opportunities for self-assessment and renewal amid the disruption she was bound to encounter in adjusting her household to a new baby.

However Bertha and Arthur chose to understand Brahms's allusion, it appealed to categories of experience peculiar to themselves, including prior familiarity with Baumann's song and personal circumstances against which its tones could resonate meaningfully. So obviously private a gesture might have been expected to remain unpublished for the time being, as the *Geistliches Wiegenlied* had for the Joachims. Instead, within two months, Brahms had completed preparations

---

[48] Kalbeck, *Brahms* 1:366–67. For a concise account of Brahms's initial encounters and subsequent friendship with Bertha, see Kurt Hofmann and Renate Hofmann, "Frauen um Johannes Brahms, von einer Freundin im Adressen-Buch des Komponisten vermerkt," in *Festschrift Rudolf Elvers zum 60. Geburtstag* (Tutzing: Schneider, 1985), 257–70.

to release the *Wiegenlied* as the fourth of the Five Songs, Op. 49.[49] At the time, he could not have anticipated the flood of public performances that quickly made the song one of his most popular compositions and its vocal line his best-known melody, passed down in oral tradition the world over and sung today to the myriad harmonizations of music boxes and electronic toys. But he did anticipate that the decision to publish the piece could be construed as a slight. Having arranged for a rare dedication just beneath the song's title in the published version ("To B. F. in Vienna"), he sent an advance copy to Bertha on October 25, 1868, along with another letter:

> You will not take offense at the familiar letters in the enclosed volume?…For our little song I had thought of nothing less than a commemorative print, but my publisher saw it lying next to me, seized it, and asked the cuckoo what other beautiful and amusing and serious things might be added to it. Do you think Hanslick will perhaps sniff out the smuggled-in Austrian song?[50]

As an excuse for releasing the lullaby in print, Brahms's story was patently transparent. Having only recently taken over his father's publishing house, Fritz Simrock had barely begun the well-nigh impossible process of securing an exclusive relationship with the composer.[51] Ambitious and not afraid to press Brahms for completed compositions in later years, he was hardly in a position now to force an unwanted publication out of his new client, whose fame was just approaching its zenith as positive accounts of the *German Requiem* spread throughout German-language music journals. If the *Wiegenlied* went to press, Bertha could rest assured that Brahms had wanted it to. Embellished as it must have been, however, the purported exchange with Simrock was still revealing. By associating himself with the cuckoo, a brood parasite that famously lays its eggs in the nests of other birds, the composer implicitly broached with Bertha a question left unspoken in his earlier correspondence with Arthur: In ventriloquizing for her husband, was he guilty of an intrusion analogous to

[49] Brahms had received initial engraver's models of the songs in Opp. 46–49 by the beginning of September (Brahms, *Briefe an Simrock* 1:56–57). His letter of receipt can be dated to the first four days of September because a walking tour with his father then took the composer away from Bonn, where the letter was mailed. By September 15, he had completed his revisions. See ibid., 58, and Hofmann, *Zeittafel*, 92.

[50] Kalbeck, *Brahms* 1:327. Brahms's final sentence ("Ob denn etwa Hanslick das hineingeschmuggelte Österreichische wittert?") poses a special challenge for the translator. The original uses the present tense, but especially in a colloquial German question beginning with *ob*, the present tense often substitutes for the future; an analogous situation occurs in English in questions that employ the progressive form of the present tense ("Is he coming?") with reference either to present or to future actions depending on context. Since no evidence suggests that Hanslick knew of the *Wiegenlied* prior to its publication in November 1868, I have translated Brahms's question in the future tense.

[51] Brahms had no interest in such agreements and remained opposed in principle throughout his later career; despite releasing nearly all of his works with Simrock beginning in 1868, he continued to use other publishers sporadically during the 1870s and 1880s. See Fritz Simrock, *Johannes Brahms und Fritz Simrock: Weg einer Freundschaft. Briefe des Verlegers an den Komponisten. Veröffentlichungen aus der Hamburger Staats- und Universitäts-Bibliothek, VI*, ed. Kurt Stephenson, 2–7 (Hamburg: J. J. Augustin, 1961).

marital indiscretion? That he would characterize his compositional practice using an image so rich in sexual undertones suggested an acute sensitivity to his own role in the domestic drama embedded in the Fabers' expected reception of his lullaby. More than the substance of his story, his diction declared the Fabers' continued centrality to his own understanding of the piece.

In similar vein, Brahms's parting reference to Eduard Hanslick was not merely idle banter. Hanslick had been personally acquainted with Alexander Baumann since 1847, and his memoirs suggest repeated and intimate contact with the poet/composer in Viennese literary circles during the ensuing years.[52] Moreover, he had almost certainly encountered *S'is Anderscht* as well. The song was originally printed as the first offering in the second installment of Baumann's *Gebirgs-Bleamln*, a nine-volume collection of imitation folksong in Austrian dialect released between 1842 and 1855.[53] In his capacity as critic for the imperial *Wiener Zeitung*, Hanslick had characterized Baumann's collection in general terms in an 1851 essay on folk song from Kärnthen, then reviewed the collection itself as a whole in 1854.[54] His detailed and enthusiastic account referred specifically to songs from no fewer than six of the eight volumes then extant; while *S'is Anderscht* was not among them, there were only six songs per volume, making some contact with the piece almost inevitable.

Brahms seems unlikely to have read the relevant articles when they first appeared; an informal discussion of Baumann's music sometime in the mid-1860s is more plausible, given his close friendship with Hanslick after 1863 and his own abiding interest in folksong.[55] But definite knowledge of the critic's exposure to the *Gebirgs-Bleamln* was beside the point. Even if they had never met, Brahms would have had every reason to suspect that Hanslick—and with him many other listeners—might notice the parody of Baumann's love song. After all, it was hardly hidden. Only a modicum of musical training and a chance familiarity with the thriving Viennese market for local folksong were required to recognize the source of the borrowed material. Yet the composer's tone and diction characterized Hanslick's potential experience of the *Wiegenlied* in ways qualitatively different from the Fabers': in place of a private realm of emotional meaning

---

[52] For details of their earliest and subsequent contact, see Eduard Hanslick, *Aus meinem Leben* (Berlin: Allgemeine Verein für Deutsche Literatur, 1894), 1: 110–13 and 217–18. Of particular interest is Hanslick's insistence that Baumann's greatest strengths were manifest in conversational settings rather than published works, even though Hanslick took pains to review several of his dramas during the 1850s.

[53] For details of the song's publication, see Otto-Hans Kahler, "Brahms' Wiegenlied und die Gebirgs-Bleamln des Alexander Baumann," in *Brahms-Studien 6*, ed. Kurt Hofmann and Karl Dieter Wagner, 65–70 (Hamburg: Johannes-Brahms-Gesellschaft, 1985).

[54] See Eduard Hanslick, *Sämtliche Schriften: Historisch-kritische Ausgabe*, ed. Dietmar Strauß, 1:2, 171–74, and 373–75 (Vienna: Böhlau, 1994).

[55] Brahms and Hanslick were already on intimate terms by the time the critic dedicated the second edition of his treatise, *Vom Musikalisch-Schönen*, to the somewhat embarrassed composer in 1863. Brahms's tactful response reveals his appreciation of Hanslick's friendship along with his comfort using the familiar *Du*-form of address. See Kalbeck, *Brahms* 2:76–77.

came amusing detective-work for a nosy critic. For Bertha the inference was simple and reassuring, but its implications for the historian of allusive practice are profound and unsettling: if the same musical structure could carry categorically distinct associations for different listeners, then recognizing even a publically available gesture in a music-analytic sense is only the first step, and by no means the most important, in its interpretation.

Finally, Brahms's apology underscored the growing reputation of his allusive lullabies within his many overlapping circles. By October 1868, news of his borrowing from Baumann had already spread to at least three distinct geographical centers. In Vienna, the Fabers had received their autograph and letter of explanation in mid-July. At around the same time in Bonn, Brahms had discussed the allusion openly with the philologist and music critic Hermann Deiters. Deiters recounted the conversation many years later in a letter to Max Kalbeck, but as early as 1869, he published a review of Brahms's recent songs that hinted tactfully at the presence of borrowed material in the *Wiegenlied* by drawing attention to its "delicate accompaniment that proceeds along its own independent path."[56] Meanwhile, according to Deiters, Julius Stockhausen had also visited Bonn in July 1868 and assisted the composer in impromptu performances of several of his new, unpublished songs; although one cannot be sure the *Wiegenlied* was among them, Brahms may well have discussed his borrowing with Stockhausen at the time.[57] And by the end of August, the eager Simrock had taken a copy of the piece with him from Bonn to Berlin, pursuant to publication. Within eight months, he would request a similar lullaby for himself and his pregnant wife, Clara. Brahms rejected the solicitation in April 1869:

> Lastly now, I am delighted that your honored wife is realizing once again why you are married. Bit by bit, I have now provided the requested trifle often enough; actually, I would very much like to take part in that admittedly many-sided business in another way. That was a seriously long-breathed sigh. But I must also first find a facetious text if I should once again help to put other people's children to sleep.[58]

This letter turned out to be one of the composer's last expressions of interest, albeit cryptic and ambivalent, in establishing a family of his own. It also con-

---

[56] Deiters's 1902 letter recounted Brahms's explanation of the *Wiegenlied* as follows: "Brahms pointed out to me that he had adumbrated in the accompaniment the melody of a waltz that was known to the woman to whom the song was dedicated" (Kalbeck, *Brahms* 2:300n). Deiters's 1869 review appeared in the *Allgemeine musikalische Zeitung* 4, 14 (April 7, 1869): 106–8; the quotation is from 107. Excerpts from the review, including the description of the *Wiegenlied*, were later republished in his "Johannes Brahms," *Sammlung Musikalischer Vorträge* 23/24 (1880): 319–74; for the *Wiegenlied*, see 359.

[57] For Deiters's account of Stockhausen's visit and the private music making that ensued, see Kalbeck, *Brahms* 2:300n. The account is immediately followed by Deiters's explanation of Brahms's allusive gesture, encouraging but not necessitating the inference that Stockhausen's performances had stimulated Brahms's discussion of his borrowing. Renate and Kurt Hofmann pursue the inference in their account of the event (*Brahms als Pianist und Dirigent*, 110–11).

[58] Brahms, *Briefe an Simrock* 1:73–74.

firmed that, at least for Brahms and among certain friends, the *Wiegenlied* of 1868 was already firmly associated with the *Geistliches Wiegenlied* of 1864. In light of his response to Simrock, the close of his initial letter to Arthur Faber takes on added significance. "You don't need to order a new one each time": Had the Fabers themselves actually requested a commemorative song along the lines of the allusive lullaby Brahms had completed for the Joachims? If so, they had charmed their way into an exclusive and increasingly prestigious club. As Brahms's influence grew and his personal allegiances shifted throughout the late 1860s and 1870s, the *Wiegenlied*'s rising popularity with the concert-going public paralleled expanding interest in and exposure to the *Geistliches Wiegenlied* within the composer's private orbit.[59]

Correspondence from two acquaintances is especially illuminating. In February 1878, Hermann Levi's relationship with Brahms had all but completely unraveled due to conflicts with mutual friends and strengthening attachment to the Wagnerites.[60] Coming from a former confidant now out of favor, his penultimate letter offers rare insight into the symbolic importance of prepublication access to Brahms's music among their shared social sphere. Pointedly omitted from the customary circulation of autographs and copyist's manuscripts among favored friends, Levi confessed to having bartered his way back in through Elisabeth von Herzogenberg, whom he allowed to copy the *Geistliches Wiegenlied* in exchange for access to more recent unpublished compositions.[61] That a song written for the Joachims in Hannover had become a fraught form of currency linking musicians based in Munich and Leipzig shows how far the work had traveled in private hands by the 1870s. By contrast, Theodor Billroth was free to ask Brahms himself, directly and repeatedly, for the chance to make his own copy of the work during the height of their friendship. Billroth's final request for a score demonstrates that he had already encountered the song in the performances of

---

[59] For evidence of the widespread popularity of the *Wiegenlied* in the mid-1870s, see George Henschel, *Personal Recollections of Johannes Brahms* (Boston: Richard C. Badger, 1907), 23. As Henschel's diary attests, Brahms himself was surprised and bemused by the lullaby's prominence in contemporary evaluations of his works. See also Brahms, *Briefe an Simrock* 2:36; here Brahms mocked the work's popularity outright in June 1877.

[60] For contrasting views of the circumstances that led to their estrangement, see Avins, *Life and Letters*, 474–75; and Peter Clive, *Brahms and His World: A Biographical Dictionary* (Lanham, MD: Scarecrow Press, 2006), 286–89.

[61] Levi used the language of the Roman Catholic sacrament of penance to describe his remorse and tacitly blamed his weakness on Elisabeth's feminine charms, which probably did little to win Brahms's sympathy: "In Leipzig I was often with the Herzogenbergs, and I have something to confess....If that was very impudent, I beg your pardon—Frau H is completely enticing; why couldn't people like us find such a wife!" See Johannes Brahms et al., *Johannes Brahms im Briefwechsel mit Hermann Levi, Friedrich Gernsheim sowie den Familien Hecht und Fellinger*, ed. Leopold Schmidt, 199 (Berlin: Deutsche Brahms-Gesellschaft, 1910). For her part, Elisabeth was clearly familiar with the *Wiegenlied*'s private dedication before asking Levi for a copy of its counterpart. She been on intimate terms with Bertha's family for over a decade, and, in a letter to Brahms in 1876, she had playfully echoed the lullaby's title page by referring to Bertha as "B. F. aus Wien" (Brahms/Herzogenberg, *Briefwechsel* 1:ix and 5).

mutual friends and suggests that he was aware of its origins in material borrowed from an early source. His chosen descriptor connotes a historical span roughly encompassing the medieval and early Renaissance periods: "I repeat my plea to give me the Old German [*altdeutsche*] slumber song with viola; in my memory it is endlessly poetic and original."[62] The composer obliged in April 1882.

The letters from Levi and Billroth preserve traces of what was must have been fairly widespread familiarity with the *Geistliches Wiegenlied* among Brahms's acquaintances prior to 1884. In turn, the awareness common to these acquaintances delineates the boundaries of a shadowy but crucial intermediate zone in the contemporary reception of the Fabers' *Wiegenlied*. At the broadest edges of the song's concentric ripples were innumerable individuals in Western Europe and beyond who bought, sang, and played it in myriad editions and arrangements during the decades following its release.[63] Particularly in Austria and Bavaria (which share similar dialects), a smaller number of Hanslickian musicians were well placed to detect echoes of Baumann's imitation folksong in the *Wiegenlied* and to draw their own conclusions; that Brahms's dedication indicated a specifically Viennese residence for the mysterious "B. F." might have figured prominently in their listening. Among an increasing proportion of the composer's friends, however, the *Wiegenlied* invited interpretation as one of a pair—the second in an intimate series of musical offerings initiated by the *Geistliches Wiegenlied*, associated with newborns named Johannes, and marked by allusive instrumental accompaniments. And at the narrowest end of the spectrum, the Joachims and Fabers held unique perspectives on their respective lullabies.

To differentiate among the categories of experience available at various positions within such a model is not to commit oneself to any particular hierarchy among them, but simply to acknowledge that many listeners close to Brahms and nurtured in the unabashedly composer-centric climate of the later nineteenth century may well have done so, reveling in their exclusive insights and coveting access to intuitions not yet their own. Brahms's letter to Simrock can be read as a response to this inherently competitive dynamic. In explicitly discussing previous iterations of "the requested trifle," he implicitly unmasked his publisher's seemingly personal petition as a symptom of interpersonal rivalry. As chapter 2 reveals, the situation was ripe for parody. True to his word, Brahms would compose a third allusive lullaby only to a text so facetious, and amid circumstances so unexpected, that historians of his music have never situated the resulting work in its original context as the final exemplar in a small but vibrant tradition of private musical gifts.

---

[62] Billroth/Brahms, *Briefwechsel*, 326. This is Billroth's only surviving request for a copy of the song, but it was clearly the latest of several.
[63] For a partial list of editions and arrangements, see McCorkle, *Werkverzeichnis*, 201–2.

CHAPTER TWO

LESSONS IN POLITICS AND INNUENDO

Brahms ultimately waited nearly a decade before completing his third occasional lullaby. Shortly before February 20, 1877, he received word from Fritz Simrock that Clara Stockhausen had delivered a third son on February 11.[1] On February 21, Julius Stockhausen sent a printed announcement of the boy's birth and his given name, Johannes, along with a handwritten note asking Brahms to stand as godfather.[2] The composer immediately accepted the honor of godfatherhood to the son of the acclaimed singer with whom he had been on intimate terms for over fifteen years, but declined repeated requests to travel from Vienna to Berlin for the baptism of his namesake, which was scheduled for April 2, Easter Monday. Instead, on Easter Day, he sent Julius a brief letter and the autograph of a new song, *Es liebt sich so lieblich im Lenze* (So Lovely is Love in the Springtime). His letter read:

> Dear friend, tomorrow you all will undoubtedly be in a good mood, and you [Julius] will not take offense even at a bad joke. But I can find no lullaby for small children—and no melody to one for bigger children.—So I take what I can find, and you see that even your music keeps procreating! And in addition I say my best congratulations and my prettiest greetings to everyone. With all my heart, your J. Br.[3]

The manuscript Brahms sent is now lost, but the Stockhausens' youngest daughter described it and included a transcription of Brahms's letter in a sumptuous biography of her father, published in 1927. The title page of the autograph bore the words "Lullaby for small and big, freely based on H.H. and Jul. St.,"

---

[1] Brahms, *Briefe an Simrock* 2:23–24.
[2] Brahms/Stockhausen, *Briefwechsel*, 123–24.
[3] Ibid., 130. German uses distinct pronouns for the second-person plural (*ihr*), translated here as "you all," and the familiar second-person singular (*du*); Brahms could therefore differentiate from one another the various audiences referred to in his first sentence without recourse to convoluted punctuation or parentheticals.

while the phrase "On a happy Easter Monday 1877" accompanied Brahms's signature at the end of the song.[4]

As it turned out, Brahms's musical gift arrived seven weeks early. Overwhelmed by preparations for three performances of Beethoven's *Missa Solemnis* in which he directed Berlin's Stern'scher Gesangverein in March and April, Julius had delayed the baptismal ceremony until May 20 (Pentecost Sunday).[5] Perhaps professional responsibilities also prevented him from replying to Brahms's letter immediately; in any case, no response survives, and Julius never mentioned *Es liebt sich so lieblich im Lenze* directly in extant correspondence. Nevertheless, an array of documentary and musical evidence permits plausible reconstruction of some of the roles that Brahms's gift might have played in the interpersonal dynamic of their friendship. Brahms's letter and dedication preserve clues as to the intentions the baritone may have perceived behind the song, including hints of a connection to his own setting of the same text. The song itself also survives. Brahms published it four months later, with minimal changes, as the first of the *Fünf Gesänge*, Op. 71. Finally, engraver's models, handwritten collections of song texts, and a wealth of correspondence illuminate the associations that Brahms's compositional choices may have carried when Julius first encountered *Es liebt sich so lieblich im Lenze*. Together, the extant evidence defines the outer boundaries of a multilayered interpretive arena within which selection of text and manner of musical setting could function as rhetorical gestures, acts of persuasion grounded in a social context at once political and personal. Imagined as if from Julius's perspective, words and tones illuminate Brahms's ideological allegiances and provide new ways of unraveling his tangled motives as composer and friend.

Brahms's letter of April 1 and the comments on his musical manuscript strongly implied that he had composed *Es liebt sich so lieblich im Lenze* specifically for Johannes's baptism. His account of the song's genesis not only suggested a recent date of composition through its consistent use of the present tense but also hinted that his goal from the first had been to create a work appropriate for the newest member of the Stockhausen family. The autograph itself went a step farther by

[4] Wirth, *Julius Stockhausen*, 418.

[5] For the dates of the performances, see Wirth, *Julius Stockhausen*, 420; for the new baptism date, see ibid., 418; and Brahms/Stockhausen, *Briefwechsel*, 131n. Julius asked for Brahms's musicological advice several times during the six weeks leading up to the first performance of the *Missa Solemnis* on March 31. See ibid., 123, 126–27, and 129: on this last occasion, Julius's letter does not survive, but Brahms's response registers amused frustration with his friend's repeated and increasingly frantic inquiries about Beethoven's original scoring. Julius also faced frustrating logistical problems: for the third and final performance, the hired tenor arrived so late that Julius himself had to sing the tenor solos in both Kyrie and Gloria from the podium (Simrock, *Briefe*, 98).

explicitly identifying the song as a lullaby. This generic designation would surely
have reinforced Julius's sense of the song's appropriateness for the baptism, especially since, in a letter of congratulation upon receiving word of the birth, Brahms
himself had drawn attention to the "refined lullabies" to which an infant would
have to become accustomed in the home of a busy singer and conductor.[6] At the
same time, Julius had just encountered eighteen of Brahms's unpublished songs in
company with Theodor Billroth, Amalie Joachim, and Fritz Simrock. Billroth had
brought sixteen of the songs in manuscript from Vienna to Berlin, where he accompanied the three singers in impromptu readings; Julius received the other two
songs from Brahms in the mail and passed them along to Billroth at the composer's request.[7] Yet *Es liebt sich so lieblich im Lenze* was not among either group. He
could therefore safely assume that he was the first member of Brahms's Berlin
circle to hear the song and that Brahms had either composed it within days of the
baptism or deliberately kept it secret until then. Either possibility hinted at a purposeful connection between song and occasion.

Exclusive access to any of Brahms's unpublished compositions would presumably have piqued Julius's interest, but the timing, dedication, and genre of
Es liebt sich so lieblich im Lenze could have made such access especially meaningful. Having taken part in the usual swift exchanges of soon-to-be published
material in late March, he would have been particularly attuned in early April
to the privilege inherent in receiving his own autograph of an unknown song.
He also knew that Brahms dedicated his works sparingly. Almost a decade had
already passed since the completion of the *Magelone-Lieder*, Op. 33, which
turned out to be the only work Brahms publicly dedicated to Julius; in the interim, the composer had highlighted the infrequency of his dedications in
a letter of 1872: "My title pages, which rarely carry one, will show you that I
consider a dedication a beautiful gift under any circumstances."[8] That the song
in question was a lullaby for his child added to the honor implied by its dedication. The *Wiegenlied* Brahms had composed for Bertha and Arthur Faber in
1868 had already become one of the composer's most popular songs, thanks in
part to Julius's own public performances.[9] Moreover, the Fabers' lullaby had also
inspired private admiration among Brahms's friends in Berlin, including the
Joachims and Simrocks, for whom it was part an intimate tradition associated

---

[6] Brahms/Stockhausen, *Briefwechsel*, 125. As examples, Brahms included a musical excerpt from the Credo
of Beethoven's *Missa Solemnis* along with a verbal citation of his Ninth Symphony.

[7] Billroth departed Vienna, sixteen manuscripts in tow, for a conference trip to Berlin on March 19 or 20,
1877 (Billroth/Brahms, *Briefwechsel*, 234n). Brahms sent the two additional songs (most likely *Klage I* and
Klage II, Op. 69 Nos. 1 and 2) to Julius himself in late March, asking him to give them to Billroth as well
(Brahms/Stockhausen, *Briefwechsel*, 129). For accounts of the shared readings with Amalie Joachim and
Fritz Simrock, see Billroth/Brahms, *Briefwechsel*, 236; and Simrock, *Briefe*, 95. Simrock himself was a tenor
(ibid., 99–100).

[8] Brahms/Stockhausen, *Briefwechsel*, 78.

[9] Wirth, *Julius Stockhausen*, 365 and 491.

with children named Johannes and extending back to the still unpublished *Geistliches Wiegenlied* of 1864. Given frequent contact with the Joachims and Simrocks in both public and private settings,[10] Julius seems quite likely to have known that labeling *Es liebt sich so lieblich im Lenze* a lullaby had conferred upon it a rare and coveted status.

Before Julius even looked at the song itself, then, its dedication and the accompanying letter had prepared him in advance to interpret the composition as honoring his son's baptism in a manner exciting for their shared social circle. One assumes he understood such special attention from his old friend as a reciprocal gesture, a quintessentially Brahmsian expression of gratitude for having been symbolically included in the Stockhausen family. In addition, he may have sensed an oblique apology for the composer's absence from the baptismal ceremony. But Brahms's words also hinted at a far more specific and personally significant link between the song and its recipient. The composer's letter cryptically referred to Julius's fecund music as the compositional inspiration for *Es liebt sich so lieblich im Lenze,* and the manuscript's dedication confirmed a musical connection to the baritone by describing the song as "freely based on H.H. and Jul. St." A mere glance at the song would have allowed Julius to identify "H.H." as Heinrich Heine, the author of the song's text, because he was intimately familiar with that text. He had set it to music himself six years prior in a song titled *Die Wellen blinken* (The Ripples Sparkle) and published as the third of his *Vier Gesänge mit Begleitung des Pianoforte* (Vienna: J. P. Gotthard, 1871). As registers of deliberate engagement with a poem he had already set, Brahms's comments encouraged Julius to examine the musical features of the new song with particular care and warned him to be on the lookout for traces of his own setting of Heine's poem.

Although evidence hinting at the possibility of compositional borrowing thus survived in multiple documents, all of them transcribed in a published biography, few scholars of Brahms's music have since addressed the matter in detail. In fact, Julius's music is readily apparent at the very beginning of Brahms's song, which may explain why scholarly attention, once drawn to the works, has focused on music-analytic rather than biographical concerns.[11] Examples 2.1a and b compare

---

[10] Julius had first met Joseph Joachim in 1859 and responded enthusiastically to both his musicianship and his companionship (Brahms/Stockhausen, *Briefwechsel*, 15–16). But while Joseph's friendship with Julius began earlier, Amalie's was equally important. Having first met Julius in February 1863, she studied intensively with him in late 1866 as part of an attempt to improve features of her timing and declamation; at the time, she lived for several weeks in his home (see Wirth, *Julius Stockhausen*, 239, and Borchard, *Stimme und Geige*, 266–67, 269–70, and 322–23). The two collaborated in concerts on numerous occasions throughout the decades that followed, even as Julius's relationship with Joseph began to unravel in the later 1870s (Brahms/Stockhausen, *Briefwechsel*, 133–38). Extensive and intimate contact with the Simrocks blossomed after the Stockhausens' move to Berlin in 1874, as Julius's letters to Brahms bear witness (ibid., 107, 115).

[11] Surely timing was partly to blame for the slow accretion of literature on Brahms's borrowing. The first attempt to address the issue in either Anglo-American or German-language literature was Ernest Walker's

the opening measures of the two settings. They share the same key and mode (D major), the same meter (common time), and variants of the same tempo (Julius's song is marked *Con moto*, while Brahms's bears the German equivalent *bewegt*, modified in turn by the adverb *anmutig*). Even Brahms's expressive indication, *dolce*, finds its antecedent at the beginning of Julius's vocal line. Most important, their piano accompaniments begin with a nearly identical two-measure introduction. The first measure of each song presents precisely the same limpid, pentatonic descent from b″ to a′, doubled at the octave below and articulated under a single slur. For the first three beats of m. 2, both songs repeat the first measure's scale-degree content; Brahms's version simply transfers the right hand up an octave. Such overriding and simultaneous similarities across virtually every musical parameter constitute incontrovertible evidence of deliberate borrowing. From Julius's perspective, the borrowing must have seemed unmistakable, purposefully designed for immediate and conscious comprehension as an allusive gesture.

Recognizing an allusion to his own music could complicate the baritone's assessment of Brahms's motivations in composing *Es liebt sich so lieblich im Lenze*. On one hand, noticing the borrowing would likely have reinforced in several ways Julius's sense that the new song was meant as an intimate gesture of commemoration. First, the song's basis in *Die Wellen blinken* securely confirmed what the dedicated autograph and accompanying letter had already hinted: *Es liebt sich so lieblich im Lenze* was composed specifically for his ears. Second, Julius's setting of Heine's text was originally dedicated to Brahms; indeed, it was the singer's dedication of the *Vier Gesänge* six years prior that had prompted Brahms to remind his friend of how rarely he dedicated his own compositions. Encountering echoes of *Die Wellen blinken* in *Es liebt sich so lieblich im Lenze* could thus have underscored the honor implicit in receiving a dedicated manuscript. Finally, the placement of borrowed musical material in the initial measures of the piano part

---

"Brahms and Heine," *Monthly Musical Record* 63/745 (March–April 1933), 51–52. Published just as Hitler rose to power, this short essay was unlikely to attract the attention or sympathy of either British or German readers. Though the essay was reprinted in 1946 as the concluding offering in Walker's collection, *Free Thought and the Musician* (Oxford: Oxford University Press), the topic rested for nearly six decades, when William Horne followed Walker's lead with a more detailed investigation of the two songs in "Brahms' Heine-Lieder," in *Brahms als Liedkomponist: Studien zum Verhältnis von Text und Vertonung*, ed. Peter Jost (Stuttgart: Franz Steiner, 1992), 93–115. In redacted form, Horne's proposal found broader readership on both sides of the Atlantic in Virginia Hancock's review of *Brahms als Liedkomponist* in *Notes: Quarterly Journal of the Music Library Association* 50/1 (September 1993), 143–45; and in Hans-Dieter Wagner, *Johannes Brahms—das Liedschaffen: Ein Wegweiser zum Verständnis und zur Interpretation* (Mannheim: Palatium, 2001), 122–24. Finally, Johannes Behr reexamined the connection between the settings in *Johannes Brahms—Vom Ratgeber zum Kompositionslehrer: Eine Untersuchung in Fallstudien* (Kassel: Bärenreiter, 2007), 15–29. Aided in part by the intervening publication of Brahms's extant correspondence with the Stockhausen family (Brahms/Stockhausen, *Briefwechsel*, 1993), Behr went beyond Horne's example to ground his investigation in a wider array of documents concerning Brahms's pedagogical relationship to Julius, of which more below. He followed Walker and Horne by explicating the relationship between the two settings in primarily music-analytic rather than biographical terms.

EXAMPLE 2.1a   Julius Stockhausen, *Die Wellen blinken*, mm. 1–6

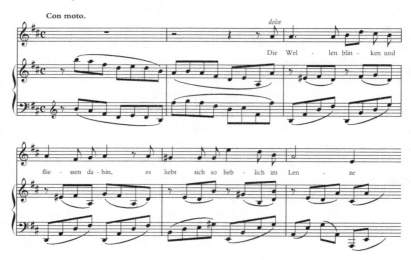

EXAMPLE 2.1b   Brahms, *Es liebt sich so lieblich im Lenze*, Op. 71 No. 1, mm. 1–6

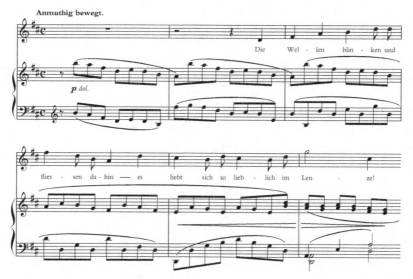

could easily be understood as situating Brahms's new song more firmly in the private tradition of the *Geistliches Wiegenlied* and the *Wiegenlied*, since those lullabies had begun with personally charged borrowings in their instrumental introductions.

On the other hand, while Brahms's borrowing may have enhanced the song's symbolic prestige among his circle, it also subverted the pattern established by his previous allusive lullabies by undermining the genre-designation suggested in his letter and confirmed in his autograph. Neither Julius's music nor Heine's poem was suitable for a lullaby of any kind, let alone a tender image of familial togetherness such as that implied by either of the *Wiegenlieder* from the 1860s. At the piano, Julius's chosen tempo and accompanimental figuration are far too animated, and his quick duple meter precludes all but the most aestheticized echoes of rocking motion. From the singer, his setting demands abrupt changes in affect and vocal lines marked by high tessitura and acrobatic leaps. Brahms emulated every one of these musical features in his own song, presumably because they all respond directly to Heine's text. If Julius had somehow forgotten the poem over the intervening years, Brahms's autograph would have reminded him that it was no more appropriate to a lullaby than the swift, fragmented tones of his old setting. Here is the text as it appeared in the published version of Brahms's setting:

Die Wellen blinken und fliessen dahin—	The ripples sparkle and flow away—
Es liebt sich so lieblich im Lenze!	So lovely is love in the springtime!
Am Flusse sitzet die Schäferin	The shepherdess sits on the riverbank
Und windet die zärtlichsten Kränze.	And weaves the tenderest garlands.
Das knospet und quillt und duftet und blüht—	It buds and swells and breathes and blooms—
Es liebt sich so lieblich im Lenze!	So lovely is love in the springtime!
Die Schäferin seufzt aus tiefer Brust:	The shepherdess sighs from deep in her heart:
"Wem geb ich meine Kränze?"	"To whom shall I give my garlands?"
Ein Reiter reitet den Fluss entlang,	A rider rides along the stream,
Er grüßet so blühenden Muthes!	He greets her with blossoming boldness!
Die Schäferin schaut ihm nach so bang,	The shepherdess timidly watches him go,
Fern flattert die Feder des Hutes.	His hat's feather waves in the distance.
Sie weint und wirft in den gleitenden Fluss	She weeps and throws in the gliding stream
Die schönen Blumenkränze.	The beautiful flower-garlands.
Die Nachtigall singt von Lieb und Kuss,	The nightingale sings of kisses and love,
Es liebt sich so lieblich im Lenze![12]	So lovely is love in the springtime!

Heine's poem closes in bitter but humorous irony. Having followed the shepherdess through a failed romantic awakening packed with stock figures and clichéd expressions of yearning and regret, the poetic speaker returns in the

---

[12] Heine's poem poses peculiar challenges for the translator because it contains no neuter nouns. The definite article "das" in line 5 is therefore grammatically ambiguous, linked to no particular antecedent but too specific to fit comfortably into a passive construction such as "*Es* knospet."

final line to the poem's refrain, "So lovely is love in the springtime," transforming its seeming optimism into sarcastic commentary on the banality of lived
experience. The speaker is so detached from the events the poem describes that
the precise reason for the shepherdess's unhappiness remains inaccessible, even
irrelevant. Does she simply project her amorous fantasies onto an innocent
passerby, or does the rider seduce her, callously adding a new feather to his cap
before leaving her to cope with the consequences? What actually occurs hardly
matters. In place of a complete series of events, the reader is left with the provocative interplay of hackneyed images and potential double entendres. Most
prominent among the latter are the shepherdess's flower-garlands: the word
"Kranz" also denotes a woman's maidenhead, making the distribution of garlands a thinly veiled metaphor for the deliberate attempt to lose one's virginity.
Whether the shepherdess truly undertakes such an attempt or only toys with
the idea, the poem leaves her frustrated and the poetic speaker smugly superior,
amused by her disillusionment.

Some readers might ultimately sympathize with the disappointed shepherdess while others might prefer to laugh knowingly along with the poetic
speaker. Whichever response one chooses, neither the risqué subject matter nor
the ironic tone of Heine's text is conventionally appropriate to the genre to
which Brahms assigned his new song. Heard against the decorous occasion of a
child's baptism, Heine's text and Julius's musical style seem utterly out of place.
Far from softening their impact, Brahms's letter compounded the incongruity
by casting *Es liebt sich so lieblich im Lenze* as an implicit tribute to the fifty-year-
old baritone's sexual prowess: "You see that even your music is still procreating."[13]
The metaphoric identification of compositional potential with sexual potency
found musical reinforcement in Brahms's manner of incorporating Julius's
opening accompanimental motive into its new context. The initial eight-note
motive of *Die Wellen blinken* is not Julius's primary melodic material: it occurs
literally just once and returns in attenuated form only briefly, at the song's close.
But the same eight-note accompanimental incipit provides the motivic basis for
Brahms's entire setting. Not only does the motive itself occur a full eleven times
in the piano at its original pitch and many times in modified transposition, but
the recurring head motive of Brahms's vocal line is derived from the piano's
incipit as well via a transparent combination of augmentation and retrograde
(ex. 2.1b). All told, nearly half of the song's fifty-two measures bear overt witness to Julius's thematic patrimony, including every important formal division
and point of harmonic arrival.[14]

---

[13] Johannes was the Stockhausens' fifth child in fewer than twelve years (the next youngest had already
died in infancy).

[14] For Johannes Behr, the motivic concision of Brahms's setting is one of its signal differences from
Julius's example. Behr therefore traces the integration of the borrowed accompanimental incipit into the

In combination, Brahms's letter and his motivic treatment of the borrowed incipit unavoidably introduced the mischievous sexual innuendo characteristic of Heine's poem into Julius's perception of his actions in writing *Es liebt sich so lieblich im Lenze*, referring to it as a lullaby, and using it to commemorate Johannes's baptism. Both words and music virtually ensured that the singer would understand the song as generically incongruous and unexpectedly explicit: in short, as a bawdy joke. By April 1877, Julius had long been familiar with *Unüberwindlich*, Op. 72 No. 5, another song that yokes a borrowed piano introduction (from a keyboard sonata of Domenico Scarlatti) to a facetious and risqué text (a poem by Goethe that concludes "Put your scissors in my hair, my beloved Delilah!"). Brahms had sent him a fair copy in May 1876 and proclaimed it well suited to his voice, and the piece had entered his active repertoire within a month.[15] Julius was therefore equipped to grasp his latest manuscript gift as the next in a characteristically Brahmsian series of wittily allusive *Lieder* and to perceive its affect as an ill-timed but incidental by-product of the composer's personality. Such an interpretation accords neatly with the image of the mature Brahms that has emerged in the past century's worth of scholarship on his character: brusquely independent, occasionally coarse, ambivalently misogynistic, chronically tactless in dealings with friends and statements about women, and perfectly willing to allow his own taste to outweigh the demands of decorum.[16] The composer certainly was all of these things at one time or another. Yet in this case, Julius's surviving correspondence suggests that the song's provocative humor may actually have been peculiarly appropriate to the occasion of young Johannes's baptism.

From the first, Brahms had greeted his own selection as the child's godfather with mischievous teasing. In letters to Stockhausen, he had sardonically displayed his qualifications for the responsibilities of godfatherhood—which traditionally centered on the child's religious upbringing—by providing mock-theological lessons on a variety of topics related to baptism. Based on obscure writings of Martin Luther and other figures of the early Reformation, his advice touched on proper timing and required materials for baptismal ceremonies: hot or cold water were both acceptable liquids, and even

---

thematic material of *Es liebt sich so lieblich im Lenze* in some detail (*Vom Ratgeber zum Kompositionslehrer*, 20), all the while ignoring the humorous side of this seminal motive.

[15] See Brahms/Stockhausen, *Briefwechsel*, 118 and 120.

[16] Michael Musgrave summarized many earlier characterizations of these aspects of Brahms's personality in *A Brahms Reader* (New Haven, CT: Yale University Press, 2000), 6–10 and 45–56, while Marion Gerards has more recently attempted to situate Brahms's attitudes within the larger context of gender construction in the later nineteenth century (*Frauenliebe—Männerleben*, especially 28–79).

beer was not rejected outright.[17] Stockhausen had joined in the fun, referring to Brahms as "man of God" and jokingly encouraging his research by soliciting a scholarly response to the baptismal invitation: "'Give us an answer,' but again a learned one, grounded in Bach and Luther's decrees."[18] The baritone's diction had played along as well. His sobriquet for Brahms, *Mann Gottes*, came directly from Luther's translation of 1 and 2 Kings, where it applies to the prophets Elijah and Elisha. The appellation was familiar to musicians across Germany by virtue of its five appearances in the libretto to Mendelssohn's oratorio *Elijah*, Op. 70, which also based an entire chorus around Julius's scare-quoted demand for a response, *Gib uns Antwort*.[19] Implicitly imagined as a twice unanswered, F♯-minor blast from full choir and orchestra at the culmination of the idolatrous people's vain appeals to an absent Baal, Julius's RSVP was hilariously overblown. In reply, Brahms had made light even of his preference not to attend the ceremony. Having exhaustively cited a sixteenth-century prohibition against "frivolous" and "unrepentant" godparents, he revealed his decision: "Now you will at least consider it a bit of luck that I myself cannot be *present*."[20]

Similarly ironic and overtly irreverent undertones pervaded pre-baptismal correspondence among mutual acquaintances. Theodor Avé-Lallemant was an old friend from Julius's years as director of the Hamburg Philharmonic from 1863 to 1867. In a letter of congratulation for the infant's birth, he interpreted the choice of the name Johannes as itself a consciously mock-religious gesture: "Many surely think 'he is pious and biblical,' but I know better. And in your way it is also an artistic piety to want to name him so, after a different Johannes from the one meant in the Bible."[21] The child's other godfather, the novelist Theodor

---

[17] Brahms/Stockhausen, *Briefwechsel*, 125 and 128.

[18] In this translation I have followed the version of the letter transcribed in Wirth, *Julius Stockhausen*, 416: "'Gib uns Antwort' aber wieder eine gelehrte, auf Bach und Luthers Sprüchen fußend." Renate Hofmann's 1993 edition interpolates an "e" into the word [so *Gieb*] and replaces the close quotation after *Antwort* with a semicolon, thus leaving the quotation unaccountably unclosed (Brahms/Stockhausen, *Briefwechsel*, 126).

[19] For instances of the phrase in Luther's Bible, see Martin Luther, *Die gantze Heilige Schrifft Deudsch*, ed. Hanz Volz in collaboration with Heinze Blanke and Friedrich Kur (Wittenberg, 1545; repr. in Munich: Rogner & Bernhard, 1972) 1:666–67, 682, and 688–89. Julius had served as title soloist in *Elijah* on scores of occasions, including at the Düsseldorff Niederrheinisches Musikfest in 1856 where he and Brahms had met for the first time, and had also directed the work in Berlin in November 1874. For details of the former occasion, see Wirth, *Julius Stockhausen*, 165–66; the latter performance, which featured Amalie Joachim as alto soloist, received a fair review in the *Leipziger allgemeine musikalische Zeitung* 9/49, (December 9, 1874): 779–80. The libretto for *Elijah*, though largely Mendelssohn's own creation, reflected a complex gestation involving detailed input from at least three other contributors; for an elegant account of the libretto's inception and textual history, see Sposato, *Price of Assimilation*, 115–28. The title *Mann Gottes* appears in numbers 8, 19, and 25, while the phrase *Gib uns Antwort* serves as the basis for the text of number 13.

[20] Brahms/Stockhausen, *Briefwechsel*, 128. Emphasis in original.

[21] Wirth, *Julius Stockhausen*, 414–45.

Fontane, approached even the ceremony itself with tongue in cheek. He and his wife, Emilie, had grown close to the Stockhausens, and particularly to Clara, since the singer's career had brought them to Berlin in 1874.[22] Asked to speak at the baptismal meal, Fontane composed a poem:

Ein alter Freund, schon lange tot,	An old friend of mine, already long dead,
Erzählte gerne Geschichten;	Used to enjoy telling stories;
Gestatten Sie mir, noch vor Butter und Brot,	Allow me, even before we break bread,
Eine davon zu berichten.	To tell one of them myself.
In Prag, ein alter Judenfrau	In Prague an old Jewish woman lay
Lag herzkrank im Spitale,	In the hospital with a weak heart,
Der Doktor behorchte ganz genau	The doctor listened quite carefully
Mit dem bekannte Pennale.	With his familiar instrument.
Er horchte und klopfte mit Ernst und mit Lust,—	Gladly and gravely he listened and tapped,—
Da begann ihm der Ernst zu weichen,	Then his gravity melted away:
Es lag halbversteckt auf der Alten Brust	Half-hidden upon the old woman's breast
Ein Kreuz, das christliche Zeichen.	Lay a cross, the Christian symbol.
Und er hielt der Alten das Kreuzchen vor;	And he showed the woman her little cross;
Die lächelte still auf dem Kissen	She quietly smiled on her pillow
Und raunte dann dem Doktor ins Ohr:	And whispered then in the doctor's ear:
"Man kann's doch am Ende nicht wissen."	"One never can tell in the end."
Mann kann es nicht wissen. Auch wir insgesamt,	One never can tell. We too, as a group,
Einem zweifelvollen Hoffen	To an ever-skeptical hope
Trotz Dr. Erich und Standesamt	(Despite Dr. Erich and the registry office)
Sind wir noch immer offen.	We still are always open.
Und möchten wir von der entkirchlichten Zeit	And while we'd prefer to avoid giving up
Auch nicht das Gute vermissen,	The good side of the secular age,
Doch, wenn ein Kind in der Wiege schreit,	Still, when a child in the cradle screams,
So heißt es: "man kann es nicht wissen."	As they say: "One never can tell."

---

[22] In close proximity in Berlin, they saw one another in person regularly and so left few documentary traces of their friendship before the summer of 1878, when the Stockhausens moved to Frankfurt. At this point the Fontanes, well known for letter-writing, began a warm and voluminous correspondence with Clara Stockhausen. For examples from the first few months of their separation, see Wirth, *Julius Stockhausen*, 447–51; and Regina Dieterle, ed., *Theodor Fontane und Martha Fontane: ein Familienbriefnetz*, *Schriften der Theodor-Fontane-Gesellschaft IV* (Berlin: de Gruyter, 2002), 53–59.

Und gesegnet, daß man nicht alles weiß,	And thank goodness one cannot know everything,
Daß Wunder und Rätsel bleiben;	That wonders and riddles remain;
Nicht unten liegt der höchste Preis,	The highest goal lies not below,
Nach oben muß es treiben.	One must strive forever upward.
Verloren, wer in des Lebens Drang	Whoever scuffles on the ground
Am Boden sich zerraufte,	In life's distress is lost;
Excelsior gehe Deinen Gang,	May your path lie toward Excelsior,
Johannes der Jüngstgetaufte![23]	Johannes the newly baptized!

Fontane's poem was obviously designed as light entertainment for the Stock-hausen family and assembled guests. It even mentioned one of the latter by name: in line 19, "Dr. Erich" probably referred to Erich von Hornbostel, a lawyer whose recent marriage to Stockhausen's student and confidante Helene Magnus, placed him in the singer's intimate circle.[24] While amusing a small community of friends, however, the poem also reinforced their sense of shared progressive values, particularly with respect to religious belief. The final four stanzas cautiously endorsed Johannes's baptism, not as a Christian sacrament but as a self-consciously humanistic acknowledgment of the continued importance of transcendent aspirations in an agnostic subculture. Such a stance resonated strongly with the tolerant, cosmopolitan, and ostensibly anti-sectarian tenets of midcentury political Liberalism in major German-speaking cities. A wealth of recent scholarship has illuminated the prevalence and influence of Liberal ide-ology among Brahms's close friends, as well as the critics and audiences that supported his music.[25] With good reason, these accounts have focused on the composer's later years in Vienna, when the values he shared were painfully superseded and therefore most clearly and urgently articulated. Yet well before

---

[23] Fontane's poem is reproduced in Wirth, *Julius Stockhausen*, 419.

[24] For a recent summary of available biographical information regarding Erich von Hornbostel and Helene Magnus, see Peter Clive, *Brahms and His World*, 229–31.

[25] The *locus classicus* of this important body of work is Margaret Notley's *Lateness and Brahms*, which built upon her own previous findings in (among other articles) "Brahms as Liberal: Genre, Style, and Politics in Late Nineteenth-Century Vienna," *19th-Century Music* 17 (1993): 107–23. Related scholarship includes Leon Botstein, "Brahms and Nineteenth-Century Painting," *19th-Century Music* 14 (1990): 154–68; Ryan Minor, "Occasions and Nations in Brahms's *Fest- und Gedenksprüche*," *19th-Century Music* 39 (2006): 261–88; and a wealth of literature that contextualizes Brahms's position relative to that of other compos-ers in fin-de-siècle Vienna. Prominent among the latter group are Leon Botstein, "Music and Ideology: Thoughts on Bruckner," *Musical Quarterly* 80 (1996): 1–11; David Brodbeck, "Dvořák's Reception in Liberal Vienna: Language Ordinances, National Property, and the Rhetoric of Deutschtum," *Journal of the American Musicological Society* 60 (2007): 71–132; and Margaret Notley, "Bruckner Problems in Perpe-tuity," *19th-Century Music* 30 (2006): 81–93.

Liberal parties lost their dominance in Vienna, their agendas were frustrated and their ideals compromised in myriad ways in urban centers throughout Austria and Germany. Furthermore, whatever the broader political situation at hand, individual members of Brahms's circle often confronted personal conflicts rooted in political and religious ideology.

Two such individuals were Julius Stockhausen and his free-spirited wife, Clara (née Toberentz), for whom Liberalism, agnosticism, and religious toler-ance were closely intertwined. Catholic Julius had married Protestant Clara in 1864 over the strenuous objections of Julius's parents and struggled, against his family's wishes, to raise their children according to exclusively humanistic prin-ciples.[26] As the conflict with the elder Stockhausens reached its height in May 1868, Clara proclaimed her own, secular credo in a remarkable letter to her husband:

> What would become of the tender spirits of our little ones if they grew up under the influence of extreme opinions? More and more I shy away from wanting to find hap-piness in any sort of faith; I "believe"—whatever one calls it—absolutely nothing anymore. I envision my duties to husband and children as very great, I have made for myself a powerful image of them; to fulfill them approximately already seems to me to be something meaningful, and thereupon my whole striving is directed. I naturally acknowledge universal human duties that impose themselves upon everyone who feels a member of human society. I seek to lead a humanly sound life, and whatever else there is I await in peace. To me it seems foolish to disavow a great law according to which the entire world takes its course. There is a coherence in everything that exists, that occurs. One cannot disturb it without paying the price. History and phi-losophy of history, natural science: it should be those with which our children are made great, rather than being taught unintelligible prayers that only place the germ of helplessness in their little souls. We will beware of this and both work so that our children become good, sound men who make themselves and others happy.[27]

Others in their circle of friends shared the same distaste for religious indoc-trination of the young. Barely a year earlier, Clara Schumann had expressed related sentiments in a letter to her then fifteen-year-old daughter Eugenie: "Now, for me, true piety consists primarily in working constantly on one's inner self, seeking to make it better and better, and living as much as possible for the good and advantage of others."[28] For Clara Stockhausen, self-assured in her views and nurtured by the mutual support of like-minded acquain-tances, the decision to have Johannes baptized at all must have represented an

---

[26] As Julius put it in a letter to Theodor Avé-Lallemant barely a month after the wedding: "Father has become a fanatic. They believe my soul is lost, and I feel how it receives ever more light, how it perceives the beautiful and the good ever more clearly through my beloved." Wirth, *Julius Stockhausen*, 276.

[27] Ibid., 314. As of yet the couple had only one child, Emanuel, born in 1865.

[28] Dated April 25, 1867, her letter is transcribed in Eugenie Schumann, *Erinnerungen*, 66–69.

uneasy compromise between personal inclination and tradition, between her own wishes and the assumptions of her husband's family. Fontane's non-doctrinal justification for baptism effected for the Stockhausens a clever reconciliation between potentially conflicting emotional demands, and articulated that reconciliation in language that resonated with the predominant political ideology of their social circle.

Liberal leanings found further and more complex expression in the novelist's choice of a secular Jewish woman as the central metaphorical figure of his first four stanzas. On the one hand, the woman's urban location, her Jewish heritage, and her pragmatically ecumenical religious stance all made her an apt representative of Liberal interests, which by the 1870s were strongly associated with the bourgeois Jewish electorate. On the other hand, read against the contemporary backdrop of a punishing economic depression and a rapidly rising tide of anti-Semitic sentiment in Berlin, the poet's depiction of a wager cleverly hedged carried undertones of mockery.[29] Less than two years later, Fontane would sketch out an essay, tentatively titled "Nobility and Jewry in Berlin Society," concerning the dominance of the Jewish middle class in Berlin's public life and the concomitant decline of the hereditary Christian aristocracy. Left unpublished in 1879 and only recently rediscovered, his draft cautiously endorsed the new social order on account of cosmopolitan benefits that extended throughout Prussia and Germany. Yet the physical appearance and moral character of bourgeois Jews could not compare to the memory of the Junker they had replaced:

> The sense of a pariah status barely shaken off does not relinquish them, and beside a six-foot-tall upstanding Arnim they still always strike an embarrassed attitude, even when the latter stands high upon the left-hand page of their books. The full measure of appearance is still lacking and in place of vigorous, reputable manners appears a quietly smiling vanity and narcissism and positive self-appraisal [*Schönfinderei*].[30]

Here the insidious stereotype of Jewish presumptuousness is cast in an image taken directly from the poem for little Johannes's baptism. The plucky old lady who "quietly smiled" (*lächelte still*) in the face of her doctor's questions becomes

---

[29] For a concise description of the economic downturn of 1873–80, its effects upon public opinion regarding Jews in Bismarck's Prussia, and the culmination of anti-Semitic sentiment in the so-called *Antisemitismusstreit* of 1879–80, see Amos Elon, *Pity of It All*, 210–20.

[30] Fontane's draft is transcribed in Jost Schillemeit, "Berlin und die Berliner: Neuaufgefundene Fontane-Manuskripte," *Jahrbuch der deutschen Schillergesellschaft* 30 (1986): 34–82 (the passage quoted here appears on 38). Fontane's choice of Achim von Arnim as his prototype of masculine nobility was surely no accident. Descended from Prussian nobility and dead now for nearly fifty years, Arnim had been a leading member of the Christlich-deutsche Tischgesellschaft (Christian-German eating club), a kind of anti-salon active in Berlin from 1811 to 1813 and deliberately closed to women and Jews. See Deborah Sadie Hertz, *Jewish High Society in Old Regime Berlin* (Syracuse, NY: Syracuse University Press, 2005), 271–73; and Amos Elon, *Pity of It All*, 99–100.

the "quietly smiling" (*still lächelnde*) financier, perpetually out of place and irredeemably self-centered.

Amid ostensible defenses of religious tolerance and Jewish influence, the interlocking language of poem and essay demonstrates the paradoxical power of anti-Semitism at the heart of the Liberal project. Fontane wisely kept the essay unpublished and preserved a high reputation with Jewish readers throughout the remainder of his career, despite expressing increasingly reactionary views in private.[31] But whether he already held such sentiments in 1877 or shared them directly with the Stockhausens is beside the point. What made the old woman's smile so compelling was its malleability, its enigmatic capacity to give shape to the hopes and the fears of all who encountered it. While the second half of the poem appealed to ideals that Clara and Julius had conceived through rational deliberation and articulated in prose, its first half conjured up a universe of associations less distinct, less controlled, but no less eloquent. The ambivalently fascinating Jew, simultaneously embraced and set apart as a punch line of a joke, provided an understated focal point around which a group of friends might orient their progressive politics in challenging times, each believing himself or herself in affective synchrony with the collective without having to adopt a consciously formulated position on the "Jewish question." In years to come, as Liberalism came under concerted and blatantly anti-Semitic assault in Vienna, maintaining the delicately poised dynamic embodied in Fontane's poem would pose problems for Brahms as well. Far more staunchly Liberal than his literary counterpart in Berlin but also far less tactful, the composer was publically known during the 1880s to express interest in humorous anecdotes regarding Jews and, in the context of a private dinner in 1893, verbally attacked the Jewish composer Karl Goldmark for setting one of Luther's texts.[32]

Brahms had not read Fontane's poem in April 1877, nor was he likely to have been cognizant of the author's fraught and evolving attitudes toward Jewish

---

[31] In correspondence with his family, Fontane would soon proclaim the outright failure of the secular values of the Enlightenment, which he called the "pseudowisdom" of the eighteenth century. In the same breath he lambasted Lessing's iconic "Nathan der Weise" and Schiller's "Ode to Joy" in a letter to his wife in 1883: "The harm that Lessing did with his story of the three rings, to pick just *one* point, is colossal. The 'Seid umschlungen Millionen' is nonsense." See Theodor Fontane, *Briefe I: Briefe an den Vater, die Mutter, und die Frau*, ed. Kurt Schreiner and Charlotte Jolles (Berlin: Propyläen, 1968), 239; the term "pseudowisdom" (*Afterweisheit*) appears here as well. Moreover, Fontane's scathing remarks about the Jews who bought his books and supported his career would earn him a posthumous reputation summarized in the title of Wolfgang Paulsen's seminal and controversial article, "Theodor Fontane: The Philosemitic Anti-Semite," *Leo Baeck Institute Yearbook* 26 (1981): 303–22.

[32] Margaret Notley has placed the nature and severity of Brahms's documented flirtations with anti-Semitism in a rich contemporary context in *Lateness and Brahms*, 18–21. For details of the two situations described here, see ibid., 20–21; Kalbeck, *Brahms* 4:175–76; Billroth/Brahms, *Briefwechsel*, 366; and Carl Goldmark, *Notes from the Life of a Viennese Composer*, trans. Alice Goldmark Brandeis (New York: Boni, 1927), 155–57.

Germans. But like Fontane, he was well aware of the irreparable damage that religious intolerance had inflicted on the Stockhausens' relationship with Julius's family. Just before Julius married Clara in June 1864, Brahms had commiserated wryly in a letter to his friend: "Hopefully filial love will have brought your parents' ideas into our fully respectable century."[33] Such hopes proved fruitless: Julius's parents pointedly skipped the wedding, and their relationship with their son never fully recovered. His disappointed mother was still living in Kolmar when the infant Johannes was baptized in 1877. Given the Stockhausens' history of family conflict over religion, greeting their child's baptism with letters marked by lightheartedly indecorous humor allowed Brahms, like Fontane and Avé-Lallemant, to indicate support for Julius and Clara's progressive stance by registering explicitly his own ambivalence toward religious propriety. In such a context, Julius could interpret Brahms's decision to base his baptismal lullaby on Heine's poem not as a tactlessly mistimed joke but simply as the most risqué of several symbolic proclamations of ideological solidarity from close friends. By projecting the opening accompanimental motive of *Die Wellen blinken* across his entire setting, Brahms enhanced his new song's bawdy humor and clarified his shared Liberal irreverence toward Christian orthodoxy.

At the same time, however, Brahms's sexually suggestive account of his allusion to Julius's music underscored the intimacy of the relationship between the two settings. Whether the singer was amused or annoyed by the new song on the specific occasion of his son's baptism, the pervasiveness of the borrowed incipit in *Es liebt sich so lieblich im Lenze* surely encouraged him, purely for the sake of musical curiosity, to search for further echoes of his own setting of Heine's text. To the eyes, ears, and voice of the man who had composed *Die Wellen blinken*, Brahms's entire song must have seemed strikingly familiar, and not simply by virtue of its seminal accompanimental motive.

The pace and pattern of text declamation is similar throughout the two settings. Both songs contain three authentic cadences, each shown in example 2.2, with Julius's on the left and Brahms's on the right. The piano part to every authentic cadence in Brahms's song returns, at pitch, to the characteristic scale-degree content and voice leading of a single prototype taken from Julius's second authentic cadence,[34] which completes an accompanimental interlude in the midst of his song and employs a distinctive combination of

----

[33] Brahms/Stockhausen, *Briefwechsel*, 38.

[34] Johannes Behr pointed out these cadential similarities for the first time in scholarly literature in 2007. He did so in passing, asserting simply that Brahms's cadences are "obviously based on" Julius's. See *Vom Ratgeber zum Kompositionslehrer*, 19.

passing seventh, 4–3 suspension, and melodic line that traces scale degrees 2–3–1. In addition, Brahms's third authentic cadence preserves Julius's precise configuration of hands and fingers for its last two chords, while the vocal line's plunge from scale degree 5 to 1 in Brahms's first and third cadences comes directly from the close of Julius's final vocal phrase. Finally, all three of Brahms's cadences are preceded by a pentatonic vocal descent and major supertonic harmony familiar from the half cadence that completes Julius's first vocal phrase (ex. 2.1a).[35] Between these pivotal cadences, the broad formal outlines of *Es liebt sich so lieblich im Lenze* recall those of Julius's setting as well. Both confine stanza 3 of Heine's text, in which the shepherdess encounters the rider, to a separate musical section with new triplet-based figuration, contrasting affect (marked *animato* in both), and distant key center related to the tonic by major third.[36]

In addition to large-scale correspondences, *Es liebt sich so lieblich im Lenze* also included a series of isolated points of contact with *Die Wellen blinken*, momentary but salient similarities of musical gesture or text-setting technique aligned with specific words or phrases in Heine's poem. Table 2.1 lists the most obvious of these small-scale congruencies, many of which are particularly noticeable during the act

[35] Brahms's intricate manipulation of borrowed material in these authentic cadences may have left its mark in an unlikely place. In his personal copy of the first edition of his Second Symphony, Op. 73, Brahms wrote the words "Es liebt sich so lieblich im Lenze—" directly below a *dolce* solo for doubled flute and oboe in the coda of the first movement. As Constantin Floros, Reinhold Brinkmann, and David Brodbeck have argued during the course of broader interpretations of the movement's affective trajectory, the melody here approximates the characteristic cadential figure of Brahms's song. Just as important, the underlying harmonic progression is identical: V/V–V–I in D major. These resemblances have led all three authors to propose the song as a kind of paratext for the close of the symphonic movement. See Floros, *Johannes Brahms: Sinfonie Nr. 2 D-Dur, op. 73* (Mainz: Goldmann/Schott, 1986), 205–7; Brinkmann, *Late Idyll*, 122–24; and Brodbeck, "Brahms," in *The Nineteenth-Century Symphony*, ed. D. Kern Holoman, 242 (New York: Schirmer, 1997). But the symphonic passage does not resemble all three authentic cadences with equal accuracy. Flute and oboe duplicate the pentatonic descent of a ninth, from e" down to d', that marks the song's first and third cadences but not its second. The subdued dynamic and expressive hairpins in both wind parts, along with the ascending approach to the high e", recall the song's first two cadences but not its third. Moreover, in Brahms's song, the words "Es liebt sich so lieblich im Lenze" actually occur only in conjunction with the third authentic cadence. Musical and textual resemblance thus diverge, prompting conflicting interpretations (Floros proposed the first cadence as the source of Brahms's paratext, Brodbeck the third, and Brinkmann all three at once.) Recognizing that the passage in question is actually a minute pastiche of Julius's cadences, however, allows one to suggest an alternative. Rather than take Brahms's annotation as acknowledging a deliberate allusion to one or another passage in his own song, we might instead understand it as rueful, retrospective commentary on his creative process: once adopted as one's own, the music of another composer may bear strange and unexpected fruit.

[36] In his 1992 account of the two settings, which stresses their shared characteristics rather than the differences that set them apart, Horne justifiably focused on the treatment of Heine's third stanza, which is arguably their most sustained and aurally apparent point of contact. See "Brahms' Heine-Lieder," 95–97. By comparison, Behr's account downplayed these stanza-specific connections, though their traces remain scattered throughout a general paragraph regarding similarities between the two songs; see *Vom Ratgeber zum Kompositionslehrer*, 19.

EXAMPLE 2.2   Authentic cadences in *Die Wellen blinken* and *Es liebst sich so lieblich im Lenze*

Stockhausen, mm. 21–22   Brahms, mm. 10–11

Stockhausen, mm. 25–26   Brahms, mm. 22–23

Stockhausen, mm. 61–62   Brahms, mm. 48–49

of singing Brahms's new song.[37] For instance, although Brahms's setting of Heine's third poetic stanza employs an entirely different key center from Julius's (F♯ as opposed to B♭), it preserves the vocal line's ascending leap of a major sixth to g″ or g♯″ for the word *blühenden*, its chromatic half-step from c″ (or b♯′) to c♯″ on the downbeat for the words *die Schäferin*, and its slow, descending octave leap for the word *Hutes*. Heard in isolation, few of these momentary points of contact are compelling enough to substantially alter one's perception of *Es liebt sich so lieblich im Lenze* or to support a vigorous claim of deliberate borrowing or allusive intent. But since

---

[37] Here I part company with Behr's analytic approach, which seeks melodic congruencies between the vocal lines of the two settings without regard for the placement of those congruencies relative to the text; see Behr, 19. Such an approach involves a level of abstraction far removed from a performer's typical experience of a new piece; furthermore, despite enormous flexibility, it yields few convincing insights in this case. (Of the ten examples listed in table 2.1, Behr notes only four.)

TABLE 2.1   Points of Contact in *Die Wellen blinken* and *Es liebt sich so lieblich im Lenze*

Line number and words in Heine's poem:	Location in Stockhausen and Brahms's songs, respectively:	Shared musical characteristics: (to avoid confusion, the vocal line is construed at its notated pitch rather than in the octave comfortable for male singers.)
[piano introduction]	mm. 1–2 of both	Piano introduction (quoted almost literally)
1: *Die Wellen blinken und fließen dahin*	mm. 3–4 of both	Harmonic motion from tonic to subdominant and back, above tonic pedal in accompaniment's left hand
9: *Es reitet* or *Ein Reiter*	mm. 32–34; 24–25	Affect change (*animato*), appearance of triplet figuration in piano, shift to chromatic mediant
10: *Er grüßet so blühenden*	mm. 36–37; 26–29	Ascending leap of major sixth from b♭' or b' to g'' or g♯'' (the highest pitch in either setting)
11: *Die Schäferin*	mm. 37–38; 30–31	Shift from major to minor mode and from triplets to quarters in left hand, voice moves from c'' (or b♯') to c♯'' on the downbeat
12: *Feder des Hutes*	mm. 42–44; 33–37	Voice traces stepwise descending minor third on *Feder* followed by slow octave descent on *Hutes*
13: *Sie weint und wirft in den gleitenden Fluß*	mm. 46–48; 37–39	Sudden appearance of minor mode, registered in the vocal line by the appearance of b♭' as upper neighbor to a'
16: *Es liebt sich so lieblich im Lenze*	mm. 53–62; 45–49	Aligned text repetition and harmonic trajectory (IV^6 through V^7 to vi, then back through V^7 to I);
16: *Lenze*	mm. 61–62; 49	Final vocal descent from a' to d'.
[piano postlude]	mm. 64–65; 49–52	Final, attenuated version of the initial accompanimental motive, missing portions of melody and metrically displaced by two beats.

Brahms's letter and his song's borrowed piano introduction had already brought to mind the singer's own earlier setting of Heine's text, Julius could hardly have missed its other connections with Brahms's new song, particular those involving pitch- or interval-specific echoes from the vocal line of *Die Wellen blinken*. The more he noticed, the more sensitized he would have become to further examples.

Taken as a group, Brahms's small- and large-scale borrowings do not simply confirm the presence of an allusive relationship between his song and Julius's; they also form a skeleton of continuously renewed references that facilitates direct and sustained comparison of the two settings. To a singer and composer with Julius's prior musical experience, *Es liebt sich so lieblich im Lenze* therefore offered rare insight into Brahms's compositional process. By quoting unmistakably from Julius's setting and then paralleling its overall form and its treatment of many small-scale poetic images, Brahms's baptismal gift implicitly invited investigation of the remaining differences between the two songs. Having noted those elements that his friend had taken directly from *Die Wellen blinken*, the baritone could then reconstruct in detail how he had deviated from that model and make educated guesses regarding his musical motivations for doing so. Heard from such a perspective, numerous features of Brahms's song present themselves as pointed adjustments rather than happenstance differences, and a few have been interpreted as such in previous literature.[38]

Many of these adjustments involve purely local details. For instance, Brahms's setting reorients the syllabic emphasis of the word *Nachtigall*: Julius's rhythm, ♩♪♪, conforms to the downbeat-oriented accents that predominate throughout his song, while Brahms's ♪. ♪ ♩ produces a more speech-like pattern of text-declamation specific to the word at hand. Likewise, while Brahms's authentic cadences borrow the piano part from Julius's second authentic cadence and the vocal line from his third, the first authentic cadence in *Die Wellen blinken* finds no analogue in *Es liebt sich so lieblich im Lenze*, presumably because it is marred by a blatant parallel resolution from leading tone to tonic in the vocal line and highest accompanimental voice (ex. 2.2). Small-scale alterations would have been particularly obvious when they affected the borrowed incipit itself. Brahms extended Julius's slur over the incipit's first measure to include the first eighth note of m. 2 in the pianist's right hand (ex. 2.1b), clarifying the ensuing motivic repetition by granting it an articulation identical to that of the motive's first iteration. Furthermore, as shown in examples 2.3a and b, Brahms's setting

---

[38]Walker's brief but foundational interpretation of *Es liebt sich so lieblich im Lenze* presented the work as an "unsolicited composition-lesson" ("Brahms and Heine," 52). The concept of marked difference between the settings received no sustained attention in Horne's treatment of their interrelationship in "Brahms's Heine-Lieder" but returned as a primary focus in Behr's case study in *Vom Ratgeber zum Kompositionslehrer*. Like that of all of his predecessors, Behr's fundamental interest lay in the abstractly music-analytic implications of Brahms's compositional decisions, as opposed to their rhetorical impact on specific listeners.

shares with Julius's the conceit of ending with an attenuated recollection of the accompanimental incipit, but decisively alters the manner of its attenuation. Whereas *Die Wellen blinken* simply removes the second half of the eight-note pentatonic motive, creating a truncated and seemingly accelerated close, *Es liebt sich so lieblich im Lenze* omits every other two pitches of the motive but fills in the gaps with rests and left-hand figuration, resulting in the illusion of deceleration and a far calmer and more ruminative conclusion.

EXAMPLE 2.3a   Julius Stockhausen, *Die Wellen blinken*, mm. 63–65

EXAMPLE 2.3b   Brahms, *Es liebt sich so lieblich im Lenze*, Op. 71 No. 1, mm. 49–52

Brahms's adoption of Julius's incipit as his setting's primary accompanimental motive and the basis of its initial vocal gesture could also be understood to rectify the earlier song's lack of any identifiably central melodic material.[39] Aside from the recollection of the introduction in its piano postlude, *Die Wellen blinken* contains only two sustained instances of melodic repetition: the vocal gesture that sets line 1 of Heine's poem returns almost immediately to set line 3, and once more in modally altered form to set line 13. By contrast, Brahms's pervasive repetition of the borrowed motive becomes a palpable musical image for the flowing water that forms an ever-present backdrop for the events recounted in Heine's text. After a few measures of absence at the beginning of the poem's third stanza, the surreptitious but pitch-specific recovery of the motive in the pianist's left hand, harmonized now in F♯ minor, subtly reinforces a reading of the text in which any liaison between the shepherdess and the rider is pure fantasy. Lost in self-delusion for the duration of stanza 3, the shepherdess returns to reality as the rider departs, gradually reawakening to the sound of the

[39] Such is Behr's view; see *Vom Ratgeber zum Kompositionslehrer*, 20.

river that had, one realizes in retrospect, been quietly rippling beside her all along. Example 2.4 presents the moment of this implied transformation in her relationship to the external world. At the same time, regardless of any text-interpretive implications, Brahms's continuous recycling of the simple motive provided a purely musical demonstration of his comparatively focused and thorough approach to melodic invention.

EXAMPLE 2.4   Brahms, *Es liebt sich so lieblich im Lenze*, Op. 71 No. 1, mm. 32–37

Brahms's treatment of his borrowed material likewise contributed to an increased formal clarity that is arguably his setting's most thoroughgoing break from Julius's precedent.[40] Both settings isolate stanza 3 of Heine's text as a contrasting section, and both foreground the ensuing return to comfortable tonalities and familiar musical material as a striking moment of retransition, Julius's through a pregnant fermata atop an augmented-sixth chord and Brahms's through the reharmonized return of the incipit in the final measures of stanza 3. But *Die Wellen blinken* is almost entirely through-composed. Its longest accompanimental interlude occurs between lines 5 and 6, directly in the middle of Heine's second stanza, and its settings of the four poetic stanzas each span a unique tonal trajectory (D to F♯, e to V/D, B♭ to V/d, and d to D). By contrast, *Es liebt sich so lieblich im Lenze* sets the first two poetic stanzas to nearly identical musical strophes and the fourth stanza to a closely related strophe. Furthermore, these strophes are framed by the two most obvious allusions to Julius's song: each of them begins with the borrowed incipit and closes with the borrowed authentic cadence. Particularly for a listener familiar with *Die Wellen blinken*, the formal boundaries of Brahms's setting clearly and deliberately reflected the basic structural division of Heine's poem into four stanzas. One need not assume that Brahms's musical structure was objectively more appropriate to Heine's text in order to realize that his deployment of Julius's material in *Es liebt sich so lieblich im Lenze* established a clearly defined alternative to his friend's compositional

---

[40] Behr concisely addresses this feature of Brahms's song in ibid., 19–20.

priorities and methods of text-setting. Heard from Julius's perspective, Brahms's song is a lesson in the craft of Brahmsian, modified strophic composition.

Presuming the baritone perused the published version of the song when it appeared in Berlin three months later, even the specific version of Heine's text that Brahms set could be understood as underscoring his personal priorities as a songwriter. Surviving documents permit detailed reconstruction of the composer's engagement with Heine's poem. A version appears in one of his *Taschen-bücher*, a notebook dating from 1869 in its earliest portions and containing a collection of hand-copied texts, many of which he ultimately set to music. Completed sometime after Brahms first encountered Julius's setting in 1871, this copy of the poem duplicates precisely all textual variants from the singer's publication, including the misreading of Heine's *duftender Lust* in line 5 as *Düften der Lust*, the substitutions of *Es reitet ein Reiter* for *Ein Reiter reitet* in line 9 and *Er grüßet* for *Er grüßt sie* in line 10, and numerous omissions of line-ending punctuation marks.[41] Having copied the poem from Julius's song in ink, however, Brahms consulted his own critical edition of Heine's poetry and edited his *Taschenbuch* accordingly, carefully noting every difference from Heine's original in pencil. His annotations also included a title, *Frühling* (Spring), and an alternate version of the end of line 5 (*duftet und blüht*) which he had found in a footnote to his edition.[42]

The painstaking process of text-critical editing to which the *Taschenbuch* bears witness was intimately bound up with Brahms's preparations to publish his new setting of Heine's poem. Engraver's models for *Es liebt sich so lieblich im Lenze* survive, copied by Franz Hlavaczek in the original key and Robert Keller in a B♭-major transposition for low voice; both are annotated in the composer's hand.[43] The transposed copy presents Heine's text precisely as it

[41]The copy of Heine's text appears on folio 8 verso of HIN 55731, Handschriftensammlung, Wienbibliothek im Rathaus, Vienna; for the problem of dating this particular *Taschenbuch*, see Horne, "Brahms' Heine-Lieder," 100–101. The four stanzas of the poem are crammed into an awkward, three-column format in the bottom quarter of a single page; the rest of the page contains a comfortable, one-column copy of Josef Wenzig's "Des Liebsten Schwur," which Brahms set to music in March 1877 (see McCorkle, *Werkverzeichnis*, 295). The contrasting visual formats of the two poems strongly imply that he copied Heine's text from *Die Wellen blinken* independently and well after Wenzig's, presumably in the immediate anticipation of setting it to music himself.

[42]Brahms's edition was the eighteen-volume *Heinrich Heine's Sämtliche Werke. Rechtmäßige Original-Ausgabe* (Hamburg: Hoffmann und Campe, 1861–63). The poem in question appears in vol. 16, *Dichtungen, Zweiter Theil, Tragödien und neue Gedichte* (1862), 288. Brahms's copy survives in the archives of the Gesellschaft der Musikfreunde in Vienna; the page bears no marks in pencil or ink, but Brahms did annotate the prologue, and the entire volume bears his characteristic signs of wear. William Horne noted Brahms's adoption of this edition as his primary textual source for *Es liebt sich so lieblich im Lenze* (see "Brahms' Heine-Lieder," 95), but did not address its traces in Brahms's *Taschenbuch*.

[43]The *Stichvorlage* in the original key was described, incompletely but intriguingly, by Max Friedländer in 1922 (*Brahms' Lieder*, 97–98). Thereafter it was presumed lost, but has recently resurfaced, along with engraver's models for the rest of Op. 71, in the holdings of the Brahms-Institut at the Musikhochschule in Lübeck. Those for *Es liebt sich so lieblich im Lenze* are catalogued as Bra: A2: 29 and Bra: A2: 30.

was eventually published in Op. 71, but the copy in the original key displays at least two layers of last-minute changes. In this copy, the text initially laid out by Hlavaczek conforms precisely to that of *Die Wellen blinken* in both wording and punctuation. Brahms then added Heine's original words above the vocal line wherever they diverged from Julius's version and inserted several missing punctuation marks, all taken from the amendments to his *Taschenbuch*, within Hlavaczek's text itself. Rejecting Julius's *Es reitet ein Reiter* in favor of Heine's *Ein Reiter reitet* in line 9 required the substitution of a single quarter note (*-ter*) for two eighth notes (*-tet ein*) in the vocal line; luckily, the second eighth had merely repeated the pitch of the first, so Brahms could rectify his text without compromising the pitch structure of his setting. The alternate version of line 5 also entered at this stage, while Heine's original title, *Frühling*, was crossed out in favor of the first line of the poem. Finally, Hlavaczek intervened once more. Presumably at Brahms's request, the copyist crossed out the composer's correction of line 10 (*Er grüßt sie*) in favor of Julius's original emendation, *Er grüßet*. As one would expect from a sensitive singer, Julius's alteration had broken up what would otherwise be an awkward consonant combination (ß–t–s), crammed onto the end of an eighth note in the midst of a swift-moving vocal line. Precisely the same constraints applied in Brahms's setting, exacerbated by higher tessitura. In fact, Brahms had already sanctioned a similar instance of performance-conscious text-editing himself: from the first, Hlavaczek's copy replaced Heine's *sitzt die* in line 3 with *sitzet die*, solving an even more egregious enunciation problem (t–z–t–d, again at the end of an eighth note) that had plagued Julius's setting as well.

Hlavaczek's models for the engraver are not dated, but one can trace their travels through a welter of correspondence. On April 18, 1877, Brahms wrote to Fritz Simrock in anticipation of a larger package to come: "So, in the coming days a few songs will drop in on you. We will reserve Op. 68 for the symphony, thus [they will be] 69–72. *In the meantime*, the songs are all labeled with opus and number."[44] Such was indeed the case with Hlavaczek's copy of *Es liebt sich so lieblich im Lenze*, which bears the designation "op. 71 nr. 1" in Brahms's hand, in the same dark gray pencil used to make some of his text-critical emendations. The package of songs departed for Berlin on April 23, stopping first with Heinrich and Elisabeth von Herzogenberg and then with Clara Schumann before arriving at Simrock's firm in early May.[45] Once the

---

[44] Brahms, *Briefe an Simrock* 2:26–27. Emphasis in original. Brahms's hurried letter was rife with abbreviation (e.g., "f. d. S." for "für die Symphonie"). The symphony in question was his first, which was published in October (McCorkle, *Werkverzeichnis*, 292–93).

[45] Brahms/Herzogenberg, *Briefwechsel* 1:19–27; Brahms/Schumann, *Briefe* 2:94–99; Simrock, *Briefe*, 99. Neither the Herzogenbergs nor Simrock specifically mentioned *Es liebt sich so lieblich im Lenze* in their responses to Brahms's package, but Clara Schumann praised it specifically (while criticizing the accompanimental figuration of its final strophe).

engraver's models had left his hands, Brahms seems to have had no access to them again. After belatedly deciding to change the tempo designation for *Geheimnis*, Op. 71 No. 3, at the Herzogenbergs' suggestion, he was forced to enlist Simrock's help.[46]

At the latest, then, Brahms discovered and rectified Julius's divergences from Heine's original poem less than a month after initially composing his own setting in late March. In fact, while Hlavaczek's copy indicates that *Es liebt sich so lieblich im Lenze* was originally conceived as a setting of the text as it appeared in *Die Wellen blinken,* one cannot rule out the possibility that Brahms had already corrected the text in the autograph that he sent to the baritone on April 1 and had simply neglected to transfer the changes to whatever fair copy he gave to Hlavaczek as the basis for the engraver's model. Julius surely was not privy to the multilayered decision making that Brahms's text-critical editing had entailed. Nevertheless, either the autograph itself or, at the very least, the published song that emerged in July 1877 could easily have alerted him to discrepancies between Heine's original text and the version of the poem to which his own setting had accustomed him. In retrospect, then, Brahms's dedication ("freely based on H.H.") could be understood to hold a sharper edge: along with an explicit admission that his new setting deviated from Heine's poem in certain singerly details came an implicit criticism of Julius's unacknowledged but far more substantial changes. Read with *Die Wellen blinken* in mind, the text of *Es liebt sich so lieblich im Lenze* was a case study in reconciling the demands of textual accuracy and musical sensitivity.

In sum, while Brahms's song borrowed heavily and obviously from Julius's, the singer would have been hard pressed to hear it as a straightforward homage. Instead, shared music and text brought the two settings into a peculiar interpretive proximity within which an informed listener would almost inevitably understand their differences in motivic construction, large-scale form, and treatment of Heine's poem as deliberate suggestions for improvement. *Es liebt sich so lieblich im Lenze* therefore put Brahms in the problematic position of criticizing Julius's composition on the occasion of his son's baptism. Why would the composer have willfully entered such potentially treacherous interpersonal territory? The question goes to the heart of the self-image that he projected toward his friends through the medium of commemorative gifts.

---

[46] Brahms/Herzogenberg, *Briefwechsel* 1:22–23 and 25; and Brahms, *Briefe an Simrock* 2:30. The tempo was corrected in the *Stichvorlage,* but in neither Brahms's nor Hlavaczek's hand.

Not surprisingly, the few scholars who have addressed how Julius might have received Brahms's setting have all begun from the assumption that its pedagogical implications must have offended him.[47] Yet no documentary evidence supports such a view. To the contrary, Brahms's only surviving reference to *Es liebt sich so lieblich im Lenze* after 1877 suggests that, if anything, both the setting and its close relationship to Julius's model remained dear to the Stockhausen family over the years that followed.[48] More important, while later documents offer few insights into the aftermath of the song's reception, earlier correspondence preserves plentiful evidence of preexisting interpersonal associations by virtue of which Brahms's allusion to *Die Wellen blinken* may have resonated for his friend. Just as the common ideology of Liberal agnosticism provided a social context within which bawdy humor could be construed as fitting for a baptism, so the privately fluctuating dynamic of the singer's long relationship with Brahms may have lent affirmative overtones to what has hitherto seemed a straightforwardly tactless composition lesson.

A series of letters dating from between 1869 and 1872 indicates that the detailed critique of *Die Wellen blinken,* which *Es liebt sich so lieblish im Lenze* offered in 1877, was not unsolicited after all but merely very tardy. Early in the spring of 1869, singer and composer had presented an extensive series of joint recitals in Vienna and Budapest. The concerts turned out to mark the beginning of Brahms's retreat from public appearances as a pianist except in performances of his own music, which was probably just as well, since Julius had begun complaining privately to Clara as early as the previous spring about his accompanist's technical limitations and reluctance to practice. He preferred to work with Theodor Kirchner, who "does not fancy himself capable of doing everything instantly like the arrogant Hamburg he-man."[49] Certainly in the wake of the *German Requiem* Brahms was devoting far less time to his instrument than

---

[47]Walker and Behr are the only previous scholars to address the issue. Both treat the jocular tone of Brahms's dedicatory letter as a symptom of a guilty conscience and extrapolate Julius's response accordingly. Walker actually invents a brief but decisive reception history out of whole cloth ("Stockhausen does not seem to have been particularly pleased"—how does one know?). See Walker, "Brahms and Heine," 52, and Behr, *Vom Ratgeber zum Kompositionslehrer,* 20–21.

[48] On April 28, 1880, Brahms gave to Julius and Clara's thirteen-year-old daughter, Margarethe, a scrap of paper containing the first eight notes of the right hand of *Die Wellen blinken.* Below the musical excerpt came the words "A wonderfully beautiful song by Papa, as a friendly memory, the copyist J. Brahms." At the time, Brahms was visiting the Schumanns in Frankfurt, where the Stockhausens had settled in 1878 (Hofmann, *Zeittafel,* 152). His miniature autograph for Margarethe would presumably have been presented to her directly, in the presence of her family; one assumes Brahms would not have done so without knowing that its reception would be positive. Johannes Behr interprets the autograph as a gesture of apology but offers no evidence in favor of his assertion (Behr, *Vom Ratgeber zum Kompositionslehrer,* 21).

[49]Wirth, *Julius Stockhausen,* 313. Hints of similar complaints can be found in an earlier letter to Clara Stockhausen (see ibid., 310) as well as in contemporaneous correspondence with Clara Schumann (see Litzmann, *Clara Schumann* 3:218).

he had in the days of their early collaborations in 1861, when the two men had
first become intimate friends through their shared delight in the performance
of song.[50] While their public music making began to falter, their friendship
continued to thrive, however, with the married baritone deriving vicarious but
unabashed enjoyment from his younger colleague's carousing and his escapades
with local women during their trip to Budapest in mid-March.[51] Julius also
brought along a composition project, a song for an unnamed woman, and asked
for Brahms's opinion of it. The song is now lost, but a letter to Clara from
March 17, 1869, preserves an account of Brahms's response, which was typical of
the composer both in its lightly sarcastic tone and in its emphasis on thorough
grounding in musical fundamentals:

> My song for Frau____came out so well that Brahms didn't change a bit of it or
> want to find fault with either the rests or the note-tails. At first, of course, he sat
> joking half-mockingly at the piano, but played ever more attentively and very pre-
> cisely. When it was over, he said "No, how can a man make a song like that, without
> having learned how?" That was just exactly his manner. He found it good, but
> wanted thereby to brand me as an instinctive composer [*Naturkompositor*] at the
> same time. But he was contented, and that was enough for me; for I have certainly
> learned, and very much, straight from Kirchner, and this little song took a great deal
> of effort.[52]

Although his letter made light of Brahms's remarks and presented them as
part of a series of entertaining anecdotes from their tour, Julius was obviously
bothered by the assumption that he lacked training, in part, one can only imagine, because it was unfounded. Perhaps he had also deduced that Brahms's
seemingly unqualified approval of his song was not entirely genuine. Whatever
his impressions at the time, the tenor and import of the exchange in Budapest
echoed throughout later discussions of his music. In August 1871, Julius sent
Brahms drafts of four new songs, including *Die Wellen blinken*. His approach had
shifted during the interim. This time he asked directly for technical criticism,
explaining that he would rather receive harsh editorial commentary than false
praise. As if in syntactic reflection of the awkwardness of the moment, his letter
began with an unprovoked conjunction:

> And if it were a young girl who handed over four songs to you today, she could not
> do it more fearfully than your already graying singer. However, it is not, as with ladies,
> the fear of rebuke that makes me tremble: *that* I do not fear, that I would like, so that
> I learn more than from those who call out "very pretty" to everyone. If you have time,

---

[50] For Brahms's own account of the importance of song in his early friendship with Julius, see Brahms/
Schumann, *Briefe* 1:362.
[51] Wirth, *Julius Stockhausen*, 329.
[52] Ibid.

then look through the songs until you can note each error so that I can correct it or, if it is too hard for me, do it yourself.[53]

Julius went on to solicit the composer's particular impressions of two of the songs, in the process describing his compositional priorities in exhaustive detail. In counterpoint with the explicitness and specificity of his request, his deliberately circuitous opening generated a sense of appeal carefully tailored to its reader. Brahms's dismissive attitude toward female musical dilettantes was well known among friends and acquaintances alike.[54] Julius's anonymous maiden therefore stood at the lower extreme in an implied social hierarchy defined by age, sex, degree of personal connection to the composer, and level and type of musical training. His second clause highlighted his own intermediate position within that hierarchy by referring to himself as "your already graying singer": a mature male friend and preeminent performer, he still lacked the creative master's craft. His overriding fear of superficial approval—and, hence, permanently inferior status—bore the rhetorical weight of the passage precisely because it remained outwardly unstated, concealed behind a list of superficial, supposedly womanly worries.

In the wake of Julius's request, Brahms must have known that he could no longer rely upon expressions of general admiration. A new strategy was essential, and he promptly chose evasion. He repeatedly put off responding to the new songs in writing, claiming instead that he preferred to address them in a face-to-face conversation and eventually sending the singer's manuscripts back unedited. Yet over the ensuing two months he never found time to travel seventy miles from Baden-Baden to Cannstadt for such a meeting, despite Julius's increasingly frantic pleas for assistance in the midst of professional obligations that precluded his own travel: "You know I would gladly do a better job, and if I had time in the summer to study with a master I would make progress."[55]

---

[53] Brahms/Stockhausen, *Briefwechsel*, 72. Emphases in original.

[54] Brahms's most famous putdown targeted an aristocratic but amateur female musician who drew his attention to the "remarkable resemblance" between the theme of the finale of his first symphony and that of Beethoven's Ode to Joy: "Yes, and what's even more remarkable is that every jackass hears it right away." (Kalbeck, *Brahms* 3:109n). Women who were neither first-rate performers nor long-standing associates of the composer frequently encountered this characteristic blend of coarseness and condescension. The topic is of central importance in Marion Gerards, *Frauenliebe—Männerleben*. Some prominent instances were recorded by Ethyl Smyth—English composer, suffragist, and erstwhile friend of the Herzogenbergs—in *Impressions that Remained: Memoirs* (New York: Knopf, 1946), 233–41. Another telling example found its way into the unpublished memoirs of Ellen Vetter-Brodbeck, stepdaughter of Joseph Viktor Widmann and wife of Ferdinand Vetter, during Brahms's vacations in Thun during the summers of 1886–88. Asked by a woman whether he always thought for a long time before composing, he responded: "Do you always think for a long time before you speak?" For a partial transcription of Ellen's memoirs and an account of the anecdote in question, see Kalbeck, *Brahms* 4:8–11.

[55] Brahms/Stockhausen, *Briefwechsel*, 74. For Brahms's repeated promises of face-to-face discussion and eventual return of the songs, see ibid., 73 and 75.

The two finally met on neutral territory in Karlsruhe on October 18, but circumstances left little time for leisurely discussion. Both men were heavily involved in a concert featuring Hermann Levi's Philharmonische Verein in the premiere of Brahms's still unpublished *Schicksalslied*, Op. 54. Brahms conducted his new opus along with arrangements of Schubert's *Geheimes* and *Greisen-Gesang* for solo voice and orchestra, while Julius sang the Schubert songs and the title role in his signature concert piece, Schumann's *Scenen aus Goethes Faust*.[56] Given the flurry of logistical preparations to which Brahms's correspondence with Levi bears witness, it seems unlikely that either he or Julius would have had much time to devote to matters of compositional style.[57] Detailed editorial assistance with respect to *Die Wellen blinken* can be almost definitively ruled out by the blatant parallel octaves that mar the first authentic cadence in the published version of the song. Given Brahms's documented sensitivity to infelicitous voice leading and his known emphasis on outer voices and cadential planning in the teaching of song composition, such an egregious problem would surely have caught his eye, let alone his ear.[58]

As Brahms immediately departed for Vienna, the brief meeting in Karlsruhe was Julius's last opportunity to obtain his advice in person. The set of four songs was published in December and dedicated to Brahms. Julius sent him an extravagantly apologetic letter on December 28, peppered with terms of mingled approbation and endearment, in which he belittled the quality of his songs and begged forgiveness for having taken the liberty of dedicating them without permission. His letter cited his exchange with Brahms in Budapest as the moment when he recognized his failings as a composer. His account of the exchange differed subtly but significantly from the rosier version he had sent to his wife in 1869; now, in hindsight, Brahms's snide comment registered preemptory skepticism rather than surprised approval after the fact, and its effects upon the singer's confidence were explicit and far-reaching:

---

[56] Kalbeck described the impact of the performance in *Brahms* 2:371. For a glowing but nevertheless detailed contemporary review, see the *Allgemeine musikalische Zeitung* 6/46 (November 15, 1871): 729–30.

[57] Brahms/Levi et al, *Briefwechsel*, 80–83. Behr is the only scholar to have previously assessed the likelihood of editorial discussions in Karlsruhe; though less detailed, his argument concurs with my own (Behr, *Vom Ratgeber zum Kompositionslehrer*, 16).

[58] Brahms's long fascination with problematic voice leading left its mark on his collection of parallel fifths and octaves in the works of previous composers. The collection is transcribed in Paul Mast, ed., "Brahms's study, *Octaven u. Quinten u. A.*, with Schenker's commentary translated," *Music Forum* 5 (1980): 1–196; for a broad and penetrating interpretation of Brahms's motivations in assembling the collection, see Notley, *Lateness and Brahms*, 107–43. Brahms's overriding focus on outer voices and cadential planning in compositional pedagogy, particularly that of song, is attested by virtually every musician who actually managed to obtain his advice. Prominent examples of his comments are recorded in Gustav Jenner, *Johannes Brahms als Mensch, Lehrer, und Künstler: Studien und Erlebnisse* (Marburg: N. C. Elevert, 1905), 38–40; and George Henschel, *Personal Recollections of Johannes Brahms*, 44.

I'll never forget your malicious remark in Pest when I showed you my first, weak attempt. "So, let's see how someone does it who's never learned how," you said, and so it became clear to me at your first word why writing down and composing music was so difficult—and still is. To be sure, I had studied harmony in 1848 with a student of Sechter named Nagiller (now M.D. in Innspruck), and already in my first year I had written a sonata and a string quartet, but I never progressed to fugue, to truly polyphonic development, and that was the great error. I never achieved facility in composition, and therefore every attempt to write things down remained tiresome and time-consuming. But as the years go by one understands ever better how it works and so again, with difficulty, perhaps something will be born, without your permission.[59]

Although securely patrolled by halting qualifiers, Julius's final sentence claimed the songs as his own artistic progeny, products of compositional training that, while curtailed, was nonetheless substantial. Rather than remind Brahms of his recent work with Kirchner, a mutual acquaintance and thus a potential rival in their claims of friendship, he traced his compositional pedigree back to Simon Sechter, the influential music theorist and teacher of Schubert and Bruckner whom Brahms himself had met in the early 1860s during his first visit to Vienna.[60] Julius's letter, his choice of dedicatee, and his recitation of a proper pedagogical lineage all constituted a final plea to take his music seriously.

This would have been the perfect chance for Brahms to respond with enthusiasm, affirm the quality of Julius's compositions, or, at the very least, comment substantively upon their style. Instead, for nearly two months he ignored his friend's letter and music entirely. As he finally explained in his next letter to Julius, dated February 16, 1872, his father's suddenly worsened illness and subsequent death had called him unexpectedly to Hamburg. Strategically omitted from his account was the timing of the trip: the frightening extent of the elder Brahms's cancer had not become apparent until late January, and the composer arrived in Hamburg only on February 1.[61] Arguably more important from Julius's perspective than the delayed arrival of Brahms's reply was the paucity of its engagement with his music. The composer avoided any assessment of the songs themselves and resorted transparently to complimenting the baritone's skills as a performer: "I do not want to praise at first, for in that I have a bad reputation and am always misunderstood. But with your songs one also always hears you singing them in one's mind—and then one is weak!"[62]

---

[59] Brahms/Stockhausen, *Briefwechsel*, 76–77. "M.D." stood for "Musik-Dirigent." In point of fact, Julius's training with Nagiller appears to have occurred in 1845, not 1848 (ibid., 77n).
[60] Kalbeck, *Brahms* 2:24.
[61] Brahms's letter is transcribed in Brahms/Stockhausen, *Briefwechsel*, 77–78. For details of his father's illness and his travel itinerary, see Kurt Stephenson, ed., *Johannes Brahms in seiner Familie: Der Briefwechsel* (Hamburg: Dr. Ernst Hauswedell & Co., 1973), 190–91; and Hofmann, *Zeittafel*, 106.
[62] Brahms/Stockhausen, *Briefwechsel*, 78.

Brahms cast his reticence to address Julius's opus as a purposeful response to previous experiences with music composed by friends. Assuming that he found the songs dull and inexpertly written, he was certainly in a tight spot. The bare truth would hurt Julius's feelings, but, as the singer's reference to his "malicious remark in Pest" reminded him, Brahms had never cultivated the tact or the finely tuned language required to lie convincingly. Rather than have his comments be misinterpreted or resented, he understandably preferred silence. Just as understandably, however, he received silence in return. Having asked so many times for help with the four songs he dedicated to Brahms, Julius never brought up the topic of his own compositions again in two-and-half-decades' worth of surviving correspondence. With the exception of singing exercises, he stopped writing music altogether after receiving Brahms's empty reply, explaining to Clara in a strongly worded letter from April 10, 1872, that composition was a dilettantish activity for which he no longer had time or interest: "Where I can be effective and have a definite profession, there I can persevere as well. Only dilettanting I can't do. To make a bit of music, to compose a bit, to snoop around in books, that is nothing for me."[63]

Insofar as one can reconstruct the larger curve of Julius's relationship with Brahms from extant documents, its extramusical side seems to have remained at least temporarily unaffected by his evolving attitude toward composition, in part because Brahms himself engaged in an atypically overt form of damage control. His letter of February 1872, so distant in its evaluation of Julius's songs, drew the singer close in other ways. The desolate image of the Stockhausens' former house in Hamburg, "the windows without curtains, without flowers," stood as an open question regarding their continued intimacy, and he closed by expressing a plaintive hope that "we will still hear from one another from time to time." In return, Julius thanked Brahms for his "dear letter and warm tone" and reassured the composer, with rare directness, on behalf of himself and Clara: "We are both very fond of you."[64] He and Brahms met amicably in Stuttgart at the end of April and again many times over the years that followed.[65] Just as when singer and accompanist had ceased their public song performances three years prior, all seemed well. Yet Julius had concealed his decision to abandon composing. In May 1876, Brahms inquired whether he was still writing music, but although he responded at length to Brahms's letter Julius never answered the question.[66] Perhaps the singer's continued avoidance of the topic, even

[63] Wirth, *Julius Stockhausen*, 356.
[64] Brahms/Stockhausen, *Briefwechsel*, 78, 80.
[65] For details of their rendezvous in April 1872, see Kalbeck, *Brahms* 2:399–400.
[66] Brahms/Stockhausen, *Briefwechsel*, 118 and 120–21.

when confronted directly, prompted Brahms to retrospectively reevaluate his strategy of avoiding compositional criticism. Perhaps he finally surmised that, in the case of Julius's four songs, his silence might have hurt his friend more deeply than any brash editorial comment.

Whatever ultimately induced Brahms to return to the music he had once ignored, his choice of borrowed material for his baptismal gift in 1877 was a profoundly rhetorical act. In the context of their former intimacy with regard to Julius's compositions and in the knowledge of how that intimacy had eroded since 1869, Brahms's allusion to *Die Wellen blinken* and his accompanying dedication carried the power to reopen old wounds and the potential to heal them in a new way. From Julius's perspective, Brahms's sexualized reference to musical procreation could have recalled and revised the singer's own 1871 description of his four songs as "born without your permission." Bastards they may have been, but now one, at least, had found legitimacy. The pervasiveness of the appropriated incipit in *Es liebt sich so lieblich im Lenze* was a ringing endorsement of Julius's former potential as a composer, implying a degree of approval for his melodic invention, which he certainly had never received in 1871. Most of all, a setting of Heine's text that facilitated interpretation as a composition lesson would have given Julius the chance to absorb the specific stylistic and editorial advice he had once craved with respect to *Die Wellen blinken*. Hearing and singing Brahms's song facilitated an imagined dialogue with its composer, an opportunity to tie up in music some of the loose ends that had accumulated in their friendship. In response to Julius's token of familial inclusion on the occasion of Johannes's baptism, *Es liebt sich so lieblich im Lenze* offered the possibility of long-overdue acknowledgment, apology, even reunion.

In assessing Brahms's birthday present of a liquor-laden donkey four years later, Eugenie Schumann ultimately juxtaposed the serious and the facetious sides of his gift-giving, presenting the two as mutually exclusive ethics espoused on distinct occasions by a complex and ultimately inscrutable personality. Contemporary biographical scholarship has largely followed suit, admitting the fundamental entanglement of caring and insensitivity at the core of Brahms's character but treating each individual anecdote as solely representative of one or the other extreme. Likewise, the broadly political and intimately personal contexts in which this chapter has sought to situate *Es liebt sich so lieblich im Lenze* may seem unrelated, even affectively at odds with each other. But like the competing interests of the stock figures and the poetic speaker in Heine's poem, these contexts and the rhetorical implications they carry are not inherently contradictory; they can be brought into interpretively fruitful contact through repeated acts of reading, listening, and performing. Through choice of text and manner of musical setting, Brahms's baptismal gift offered the Stockhausens a chance to vicariously inhabit and critique the contrasting perspectives of the rejected shepherdess who weeps for the loss of garlands lovingly made, the brash rider who callously ignores the garlands but perhaps, once out of sight, collects lost flowers to return to their owner when least expected, and the urbane poetic speaker, for whom the entire episode functions as a source of cynical but liberating amusement.

PART II

THEMES AND VARIATIONS

CHAPTER THREE

EMULATION AS EMPATHY

In August 1876, Heinrich von Herzogenberg published his *Variations on a Theme of Johannes Brahms*, Op. 23. The set of ten variations for four-hand piano took Brahms's early song, *Die Trauernde* (Girl in Mourning), Op. 7 No. 5, as its theme. Having received a copy in the mail, Brahms addressed the *Variations* in the initial paragraphs of his earliest surviving letter to Heinrich and his wife, Elisabeth, which he mailed on August 20. Although the letter dates from an early phase in his friendship with the Herzogenbergs, few passages in extant correspondence exemplify so concisely the interweaving of vicarious music making and personal interchange at the heart of Brahms's social imaginary:

> I thank you heartily for the joy you have given me by sending—I almost said by advertising—your Variations. But it is altogether too pleasant a thought to know that another person has been occupied with one's song in such an intimate way. One must be truly fond of a melody to repeat it so? And in your home surely two must harbor that love? Then forgive me, if my thanks begin more swiftly and my criticism ends sooner than you would like. I am too partial when I speak of the delight with which I place the volume before me and play four-handed in my mind, at my right side quite clearly a slim womanly figure in blue velvet and golden hair. If I wanted to say more, I would certainly anger either the husband or the wife.[1]

Late August found Brahms in the midst of final revisions to his long-anticipated First Symphony. He was also visiting Hamburg for the first time since his father's death four years prior, taking frequent walks and reminiscing in the hometown he had since forsaken for Vienna.[2] A new opus by one of the few full-time

---

[1] Brahms/Herzogenberg, *Briefwechsel* 1:6–7. The letter is undated, but Max Kalbeck assigned it to August 20 based, presumably, on the postmark (for his editorial practice, see ibid., xxx).

[2] Just before departing for Hamburg on August 10, 1876, Brahms wrote to Theodor Wilhelm Engelmann of his plans to "get my fill of sauntering about and reminiscing"; see *Johannes Brahms im Briefwechsel mit Th. Wilhelm Engelmann*, ed. Julius Röntgen, 50 (Berlin: Deutsche Brahms-Gesellschaft, 1918). Evidence of both activities survives in an undated letter mailed to Ottilie Ebner during the ensuing weeks. Here,

composers in his orbit offered the possibility of respite from work and self-imposed solitude, if only he could play it. The Leipzig firm of Rieter-Biedermann had followed standard practice by printing Heinrich's *Variations* with the parts separated on facing pages. As Brahms explained later in his letter, "nothing is harder to read than four-handed music that is at all complex." Confronted by a visually challenging score, he conjured up an image of the blonde, well-dressed Elisabeth to help him hear the piece. In the absence of another pianist, picturing a second pair of hands on the keyboard aligned the mind's eye and ear while drawing players and composer together in a simulated act of performance and listening. Of the two Herzogenbergs, Elisabeth was the natural choice for the *primo* part. As a pianist, she was far superior to Heinrich, and, as a woman, she provided the essential point of inflection in a characteristic rhetorical swerve from the professional to the personal. At the moment of her appearance as a physically attractive duet partner, Brahms's haltingly vague comments on the *Variations* gave way to surefooted teasing for their composer.

Just as in correspondence with the Stockhausens and Fabers, sexually charged humor released tensions that might otherwise have fueled deeper social conflict. In this case, the smooth conjunction of genre and gender in Brahms's four-hand scenario downplayed the real Elisabeth's pointed advocacy for her husband and his music. On August 1, each of the Herzogenbergs had sent a separate letter to accompany Brahms's copy of the *Variations*. Heinrich's was uniformly self-effacing. He praised Brahms's theme and presented his variations as an inferior curiosity accepted for publication only because the name "Brahms" on the title page allowed Rieter-Biedermann to perpetuate its rivalry with Fritz Simrock's firm. His letter closed with a plaintively indirect request for Brahms's impressions: "But when I consider that you will probably look through the volume, all my laughter dies away. Hopefully yours does not increase?" Elisabeth was less bashful. Having reminded Brahms that he had already expressed interest in the *Variations* in conversation with a mutual friend, she asked for substantive commentary: "Denn, wie der Hirsch lechzt nach frischem Wasser, so lechzt der Heinrich nach aufrichtigen Worten, möge ihr Inhalt verwunden oder streicheln" ("For, as the hart longs for fresh water, so longs the Heinrich for honest words, whether their substance wounds or caresses").[3] In German as in English, subject and object begin with the same pair of consonants in each half of the simile; Elisabeth's alliterative parody of Psalm 42 appealed directly to her reader's well-known sensibilities as wittily allusive correspondent and faux biblical scholar. From the first, then, husband and wife espoused divergent

---

Brahms compared the recent loss of Ottilie's father to his experience of his own father's death "in this room"; again, he promised to "take walks until I've had enough" (Ottilie von Balassa, *Die Brahmsfreundin Ottilie Ebner*, 87–88).

[3] Brahms/Herzogenberg, *Briefwechsel* 1:3–4.

approaches to the problem of soliciting concrete musical advice from their famous friend. Heinrich's caution, Elisabeth's candor, and Brahms's reticence would come to define the boundaries of mutual interchange throughout an ever-changing relationship that revolved, perhaps more exclusively than any of Brahms's other close friendships, around the exchange of new music.

Particularly in English-language scholarship, however, this fundamental dynamic remains partially obscured by speculation regarding Brahms's attraction to Elisabeth. The teenage Elisabeth Stockhausen had received a few piano lessons from Brahms while living in Vienna in 1863; contact was likely established through her father's close connections with the Viennese pastor Gustav Porubsky, whose daughter Bertha (later Bertha Faber) had been part of Brahms's Hamburger Frauenchor in the previous decade. In the introduction to his 1906 edition of the Herzogenbergs' correspondence, Max Kalbeck noted that Brahms soon stopped working with Elisabeth and returned her to the tutelage of Julius Epstein. At first, Kalbeck allowed readers to draw their own conclusions regarding the possible motivations of the "typically very quiet, unassertive, and shy teacher." But he then proposed his own explanation three years later in his massive biography of the composer: Brahms had withdrawn because he perceived that Elisabeth "could be dangerous to him," and when, in 1874, circumstances led to renewed contact with the Herzogenbergs, who were now married and living in Leipzig, he fell in love with her again, successfully concealing his feelings beneath a façade of "chivalrous gallantry, facetious irony, or cheerful sociability" until her death in 1892.[4] Although Kalbeck adduced not a shred of firsthand evidence in favor of his sweeping claims, Elisabeth nonetheless entered the Brahms lexicon as a signal constituent in arguments concerning the composer's avoidance of romantic entanglements, to which her husband and his music remained mere awkward footnotes.[5]

Yet Brahms had arguably taken at least as much interest in the talented young composer as in his future wife. Having met Heinrich in 1863 as well, Brahms had intervened on his behalf early the following year, urging Melchior

---

[4] Ibid., 1:xiii–xvi, and Kalbeck, *Brahms* 3:7–8. In formulating his explanation after the fact, Kalbeck was implicitly positioning himself vis-à-vis critical reception of the Brahms/Herzogenberg correspondence. Wilhelm Altmann was a (rare) partisan of Heinrich's music who had published a glowing précis of his life and work in 1903 ("Heinrich von Herzogenberg, sein Leben und Schaffen," *Die Musik* 2/19:28–47). In an otherwise positive review of Kalbeck's edition in May 1907, Altmann quipped: "I am surprised that Kalbeck, who has fabricated a novel between Clara Schumann and Brahms in his Brahms-biography, does not explain the swift abdication of piano lessons with Elisabeth von Stockhausen by means of Brahms's hopeless love for her!" See Altmann, "Brahms im Briefwechsel mit dem Ehepaar Herzogenberg," *Die Musik* 6/16 (1907): 229n. Perhaps Kalbeck did not perceive the sarcasm.

[5] Walter Frisch's otherwise excellent summary of Brahms's relationship with the Herzogenbergs provides a characteristic example of Kalbeck's outsized influence on English-language scholarship; see "Brahms and the Herzogenbergs," *American Brahms Society Newsletter* 4/1 (1986): 1–3.

Rieter-Biedermann to publish some of his songs and then following up two months later to see if an agreement had been reached. In 1865, the firm released collections of Heinrich's songs as Op. 1 and Op. 2.[6] The exchange represented an important early example of the professional assistance that Brahms more famously devoted to Antonin Dvořák during the following decade. Recent scholarship has therefore sought to refocus attention on Heinrich's compositions and their centrality to the Herzogenbergs' relationship with Brahms.[7] At the same time, Elisabeth's identity and influence have found new resonance in German-language literature, where Kalbeck's speculative reading of Brahms's feelings has been aggressively challenged for the first time. Relieved of her duties as secret muse for a repressed Hamburger, Elisabeth emerges as an independent agent in the musical life of Leipzig and Berlin: an incisive performer and critic, a talented organizer with broad contacts, and, above all, a formidable advocate who redirected the skills she had acquired as a diplomat's daughter toward the promotion of her husband's career and the honing of his craft. Such was the force of her personality that some acquaintances privately questioned her suitability as domestic partner for the instinctively diffident Heinrich.[8] In fact, the couple remained devoted to each other throughout the challenges of their marriage. Nevertheless, ongoing interplay between them affected their interactions with Brahms, provoking continuous adjustments and renegotiations which differed categorically from those that occurred as a matter of course in his friendships with single individuals.

Heinrich's *Variations on a Theme of Johannes Brahms* provides multiple points of entry into the mutually dependent relationships among these three musicians. The theme Heinrich chose, the flexibility of his variation procedure, and

[6] Brahms et al., *Johannes Brahms im Briefwechsel mit Breitkopf und Härtel, Bartolf Senff, J. Rieter-Biedermann, C. F. Peters, E. W. Fritzsch und Robert Lienau*, ed. Wilhelm Altmann, 96 and 100 (Berlin: Deutsche Brahms-Gesellschaft, 1920). The best resource regarding publication details for Heinrich's compositions remains Bernd Wiechert's *Heinrich von Herzogenberg (1843–1900) Studien zu Leben und Werk* (Göttingen: Vandenhoeck und Ruprecht, 1997); for Opp. 1 and 2, see 273.

[7] Two prominent exponents of this line of inquiry are Bernd Wiechert and Johannes Behr. Wiechert's foundational 1997 study, *Heinrich von Herzogenberg*, struck a delicate balance by acknowledging Brahms's strong influence upon his younger contemporary while simultaneously isolating idiosyncratic, non-Brahmsian features of Heinrich's style and tracing the reception of his works in unprecedented detail. Behr devoted a chapter to Brahms's relationship with the Herzogenbergs in his 2007 book, *Johannes Brahms—Vom Ratgeber zum Kompositionslehrer* (see 30–40); like Wiechert, he sought to differentiate Heinrich's musical and interpersonal perspective from Elisabeth's, and he foregrounded Brahms's reluctant role as compositional mentor.

[8] Central to the shift in German-language portrayals of Elisabeth is the scholarship of Antje Ruhbaum, especially her *Elisabeth von Herzogenberg* of 2009. Using a variety of methods grounded in the study of social networks, Ruhbaum has repositioned Elisabeth as a diplomatic counterbalance among the many prima donnas in her intimate circle (which included Clara Schumann and the English composer and suffragette Ethyl Smyth). She has also unearthed a trove of documents related to the Herzogenbergs' marriage, which prospered consistently despite the gossip that surrounded it. Among those occasionally discomfited by the differences between the pair were Eugenie Schumann, Clara Schumann, Marie Fillunger, and Brahms himself (Ruhbaum, 266–70).

the affective trajectory implied by his piece all permit plausible reconstruction of a complex nexus of influences and ambitions that informed the work's genesis and initial reception. Meanwhile, subsequent documents and compositions suggest that echoes of Heinrich's Op. 23 and the issues it raised continued to permeate Brahms's dialogue with the Herzogenbergs throughout the formative years of their friendship, as periods of warmth alternated with crises in communication. In particular, Brahms's accompanied part-song *O schöne Nacht*, Op. 92 No. 1; two of Heinrich's string quartets, Op. 42; the finale of Brahms's first string quintet, Op. 88; and slow movement of his second piano trio, Op. 87 preserve provocative evidence regarding both the power and the limits of musical interchange in sustaining and reforming interpersonal relationships.

Despite his avoidance of overt commentary on Heinrich's *Variations* in his letter of August 20, 1876, Brahms's response demonstrated that his initial impressions were mixed at best. Later in the same letter he proposed a list of conversation topics "if I again had the pleasure of chatting with you," including an informal taxonomy of variation sets:

> Then maybe I would babble even about variations, and I would wish that even in the title one would differentiate variations from something else, perhaps fantasy-variations, or whatever else one would want to call—nearly all recent variation works. I have a particular affection for variation form and believe that, with our talent and ability, we could probably still master this form. Beethoven treats it extraordinarily strictly, he can also rightfully translate: alterations [*Veränderungen*]. What comes after him, by Schumann, H., or Nottebohm, is something different. Naturally I have as little against the type as against the music. But I would wish that one would also differentiate through names what is distinct in type.[9]

Under cover of the subjunctive mode and a coy initial, Brahms took Heinrich and two generations' worth of contemporaries to task for generic carelessness. Whatever their musical quality, most recent *Variationen* simply were not "strict" enough to merit a title so steeped in tradition.

As expressed in 1876, Brahms's opinion resonated with other statements from the preceding two decades, most notably a letter he had mailed to Adolf Schubring in February 1869. Schubring was a jurist by profession, music critic by avocation, and father of yet another of Brahms's many godsons.[10] A self-proclaimed "Schuman-

---

[9] Brahms/Herzogenberg, *Briefwechsel* 1:7–8. As Kalbeck first pointed out in editing this letter, the term, *Veränderungen*, which Brahms associates with Beethoven's variation practice most likely refers to the Diabelli Variations, where it appears in the title in place of *Variationen*.

[10] Brahms stood as godfather for Max Johannes Schubring in January 1856; Johannes Brahms et al., *Johannes Brahms Briefe an Joseph Viktor Widmann, Ellen und Ferdinand Vetter, Adolf Schubring*, ed. Max Kalbeck, 168–69 (Berlin: Deutsche Brahms-Gesellschaft, 1915) (hereafter *Briefe an . . . Schubring*). For more on his relationship with Schubring, see Avins, *Life and Letters*, 139.

nian" unique among contributors to the *Neue Zeitschrift für Musik* during the years of Franz Brendel's editorship, Schubring had published close readings of each of Brahms's first eighteen opuses in an enthusiastic, five-part article in March and April, 1862. After revoking his affiliation with the *Neue Zeitschrift* in favor of the *Leipziger Allgemeine musikalische Zeitung*, he concluded his series on Brahms with two more substantial articles in February 1868 and January 1869. The letter he received the following month has become the central primary text in studies of Brahms's variation procedure because of its uncharacteristic detail.[11] Here the composer emphasized what he called the bass (*der Baß*) of any theme, which he described as "the fixed ground upon which I build my stories." The theme's melody, by comparison, was far less fruitful: "What I do with the melody is only fooling around or clever—fooling around." By means of a brief musical excerpt, he even attacked examples of melody-based variation his own *Variations on a Hungarian Song*, Op. 21 No. 2, of 1856. Finally, in language to which he would return seven years later in his letter to Heinrich, he inquired of Schubring: "Can't we make a distinction between variations and fantasies on a melody, a motive?"[12] The precise import of Brahms's retrospective self-criticism remains a matter of some debate. Nonetheless, it seems clear that by the late 1860s, he had become deeply suspicious of variation procedures that manipulated melodic motives at the expense of the harmonic progressions implied by the bass line.

In comparison to Schubring, Brahms shared with the Herzogenbergs only a fragmentary outline of his views on variation form. Yet the very fact that Heinrich's *Variations* stimulated a reprisal of his concerns opens important windows on Brahms's reception of the piece. First, as the theme for an ambitious and wide-ranging set of variations, *Die Trauernde* posed significant formal and affective

---

[11] Related concerns left traces on far earlier correspondence as well, especially an exchange with Joseph Joachim in 1856 (Brahms/Joachim, *Briefwechsel* 1:146–47 and 150–51). In 1984, Walter Frisch promoted the letter to Schubring as "one of the most penetrating glimpses available into Brahms's workshop" in *Brahms and the Principle of Developing Variation* (Berkeley: University of California Press, 1984), 32. It retained the same centrality in Elaine Sisman's seminal English-language article on Brahms's variation forms, "Brahms and the Variation Canon," *19th-Century Music* 14 (1990): 132–53. Also in 1990, Michael Struck formulated a complementary approach to Brahms's extant statements on variation form, emphasizing the shifts that had occurred over the course of Brahms's career; see "Dialog über die Variation—präzisiert: Joseph Joachims *Variationen über ein irisches Elfenlied* und Johannes Brahms' Variationenpaar op. 21 im Licht der gemeinsamen gattungstheoretischen Diskussion," in *Musikkulturgeschichte: Festschrift für Constantin Floros zum 60. Geburtstag*, ed. Peter Petersen, 105–54 (Wiesbaden: Breitkopf & Härtel, 1990). Based partially on Struck's concerns, William Horne proposed an alternative to Sisman's reading of the letter to Schubring in "Brahms Variations on a Hungarian Song, op. 21, no. 2: 'Betrachte dann die Beethovenschen und, wenn Du willst, meine,'" in *Brahms Studies 3*, ed. David Brodbeck, 47–127 (Lincoln: University of Nebraska Press, 2001). Even in studies that decisively privilege music-analytic concerns over historical source study, Brahms's comments to Schubring have since remained impossible to ignore; see, for instance, Julian Littlewood, *The Variations of Johannes Brahms* (London: Plumbago Books, 2004), 79–80.

[12] Brahms, *Briefe an . . . Schubring*, 217–18.

challenges. Brahms had composed the song in August 1852, but no autograph survives; example 3.1 presents the song as it was first published by Breitkopf and Härtel in November 1854. The text was adapted from Swabian sources by Wilhelm Hauff in 1824 and subsequently disseminated in multiple collections of regional folk poetry, among them the first volume of Brahms's beloved *Deutsche Volkslieder mit ihren Original-Weisen*, edited by Kretzschmer and Zuccalmaglio in 1838. The composer seems to have raided more than one edition in assembling his own transliteration of Swabian dialect.[13] For urbane consumers of folk literature, the poem's regional dialect, rural setting, and naïve tone interposed a sentimental distance between reader and poetic speaker.

Mei Mueter mag mi net,	My mother doesn't like me,
Und kei Schatz han i net,	And I don't have a sweetheart,
Ei warum sterb i net,	Ah, why don't I die,
Was thu i do?	What am I doing here?
Gestern isch Kirchweih g'wä,	The parish fair was yesterday,
Mi hot mer gwis net g'seh,	Surely no one saw me,
Denn mir ischs gar so weh,	For I'm in such pain,
I tanz ja net.	I never dance.
Lasst die drei Rose stehn,	Leave the three roses there,
Die an dem Kreuzle blühn:	That bloom on the little cross:
Hent ihr das Mädle kennt,	Did you recognize the girl,
Die drunter liegt?	You who lie below?

In Brahms's music, the sense of displacement inherent in the text found reinforcement in stylistic heterogeneity. Melody, phrase structure, harmony, and rhythmic profile evoked a wide array of popular and archaic idioms, ranging from the Middle Ages to the nineteenth-century present. The vocal line was short-breathed, syllabic, and repetitive in the manner of an extemporized folk song. Its ambitus remained confined within an octave, its tones constantly doubled by the uppermost voice of the piano accompaniment. Yet its structure was rigorously periodic: each poetic stanza received a vocal phrase of eight measures, neatly divided into two four-bar phrase groups and followed by a one-measure, accompanimental confirmation of the concluding cadence. Moreover, Brahms's literal repetition of the first phrase created an aurally apparent bar form (*Stollen*,

[13] For more on the date of the song's composition, which Brahms indicated retrospectively in his catalogue of his own works, see McCorkle, *Werkverzeichnis*, 21. For a detailed publication history of the poem, see Friedländer, *Brahms' Lieder*, 11–12. Friedländer asserts that Brahms encountered the text in Georg Scherer's *Deutsche Volkslieder* (Leipzig: Gustav Mayer, 1851), where it appears (184). However, the spelling and orthography used in Brahms's Op. 7 diverge from Scherer's version at least as much as from Kretzschmer and Zuccalmaglio's; see *Deutsche Volkslieder mit ihren Original-Weisen* (Berlin: Vereins-Buchhandlung, 1838), 193–94. It is therefore misguided to assume that Brahms borrowed such a widely disseminated poem from a single source alone.

EXAMPLE 3.1   Brahms, *Die Trauernde*, Op. 7 No. 5

Stollen, *Abgesang*, or AAB). Contrasting material in the first four measures of the *Abgesang* reflected the shift toward second-person address in the final stanza of the poem, whereupon the last five measures punctuated the whole with a gently varied return to the closing measures of the *Stollen*. Such a structure recalled that of the medieval *Minnelied*, a genre that had stimulated intense interest in German-speaking lands during the preceding decades.[14] Turning from melody to harmony, pure diatonic triads predominated over seventh chords as in sixteenth-century polyphony, but there were literally no nonharmonic tones. Furthermore, *Die Trauernde* completely avoided modulation. In place of harmonic dissonance and complex tonal unfolding came a thoroughly modern alternative: momen-

---

[14]At the heart of scholarly fascination with the genre lay Friedrich Heinrich von der Hagen's multivolume monument, *Minnesinger: Deutsche Liederdichter des zwölften, dreizehnten und vierzehnten Jahrhunderts* (Leipzig: Barth, 1838), which provided a detailed description of bar form as a poetic structure (see xxxii–xxxiv).

tary, coloristic tinges of the relative major in mm. 6 and 15 and the parallel major in mm. 11 and 13. Meanwhile, despite the poetic speaker's stated aversion to dance, an unmistakable two-measure stress pattern characteristic of the Baroque sarabande pervaded the piece from beginning to end.

Drawn from disparate repertoires and music-historical periods, these characteristics ultimately worked in tandem to complicate the song's position relative to its own genre and time. Contemporary critics acknowledged as much, if only inadvertently: even sympathetic reviews dismissed *Die Trauernde* as an unfinished draft and its text as unworthy of musical setting.[15] In selecting the song as his theme, then, Heinrich had taken on a mission of rehabilitation. But he had also set himself a compositional problem rooted in the affect and structure of the song—its retrospective and deliberately understated approach to large-scale climax and ebb. Given a theme marked by such uniformity, how to generate variety and maintain a sense of cumulative trajectory from variation to variation? A first step was to refashion the theme itself. Heinrich made telling alterations in transcribing the song for four-hand piano, as shown in example 3.2. One change involved pitch class: Brahms's c' became b on the third beat of m. 3, presumably for the sake of consistency vis-à-vis otherwise identical progressions in mm. 7 and 16. Registral doublings enhanced the texture throughout much of the theme, and Heinrich used doubled pitches to add a new attack in the *primo* part on the upbeat to m. 14, minimizing the break between the two phrase groups in the *Abgesang* and projecting a clearer sense of motion toward the final cadence. Most importantly, he deleted Brahms's repeat signs, rejecting the song's bar form in favor of a rounded binary with two halves of equal length, neither of them repeated. The result now bore outward proportions far more typical of the themes of variation movements spanning from Haydn through Schumann, but its internal tonal profile remained unusually static.

As if to compensate further for the stubborn regularity of his theme, Heinrich treated the process of variation with striking freedom.[16] Table 3.1 provides a graphic summary of Op. 23 in which each column represents an essential musical

---

[15] In a largely positive review of Op. 7 from February 1855, Louis Köhler criticized Brahms's choice of texts: "The selected poems, however, provide no room even for a keen invention, as it is called, for they are simple to the point of folksy naïveté. Some of them are indeed so crude that they have received an unearned honor through Herr Brahms's composition." See *Signale für die Musikalische Welt* 13 (1855): 65; the review appeared under Köhler's accustomed pseudonym, "Ker." Just as striking is Schubring's treatment of Op. 7, which appeared in April 1862 as part of his first essay on Brahms's music. For Schubring, the last four songs in Op. 7 were "mere mood paintings, gray painted in gray, or rather simple sketches, such as a brilliant artist jots down once—in order then to leave them unexecuted in his portfolio." See *Neue Zeitschrift für Musik* 56 (1862): 109. It was not until the twentieth century that commentators began to point out explicitly the music-historical precedents for specific features of *Die Trauernde*; the earliest and, still, most sensitive example of such analysis can be found in Friedländer, *Brahms' Lieder*, 10–11.

[16] The most detailed description of Heinrich's Op. 23 in previous literature can be found in Sisman, "Brahms and the Variation Canon," 137–38.

EXAMPLE 3.2   Heinrich von Herzogenberg, *Variations on a Theme of Johannes Brahms*,
Op. 23, mm. 1–18

parameter. Entries occur only when a given parameter shifts; an empty space
implies continuity from variation to variation. Read from top to bottom, the
table thus maps the degree of flux across the surface of the work. Over the

TABLE 3.1   Shifting Parameters in Heinrich von Herzogenberg's *Variations*, Op. 23

	Key	Meter	Tempo	Phrase Structure (durations in notated measures)
Theme	i	$\frac{3}{4}$	*Andante*	9 ; 9
Variation 1		$\frac{2}{4}$	*Adagio*	8 x 2 ; 9
Variation 2		$\frac{6}{8}$	*Con moto*	8 x 2 ; 10 x 2
Variation 3		**C**	*Allegro*	4 x 2 ; 6 x 2
Variation 4	[VI]			4 x 2 ; 8 x 2
Variation 5	[V]	$\frac{3}{4}$	*Poco meno mosso, ma agitato*	8 x 2 ; 8 x 2
Variation 6	I	$\frac{2}{4}$	*Allegretto*	10 x 2 ; 10 x 2
transition	I →V/♯iii		*Piu moderato*	12
Variation 7	♯iii	$\frac{9}{4}$	*Lento, appassionato*	8 x 2; 10
Variation 8	I	$\frac{3}{4}$	*Allegretto*	8 ; 15
transition	i → +6			13
Variation 9	i	$\frac{2}{4}$	*[Gleiche Viertel]*	8 x 2 ; 8 + 4 (+ last 4 cut off)
Variation 10		$\frac{3}{4}$ → **C**	*Meno mosso*	(first 4 cut off +) 4 ; 10
Coda	I			5

course of ten variations, the notated meter changes ten times, the tempo nine. The key signature shifts seven times across a spectrum that ranges from one flat in Variation 4 to four sharps in Variation 7. Not all variations are securely rooted in any tonic: Variation 4 circles around the submediant but never quite reaches it, while Variation 5 prolongs an active dominant for its entire duration. The mode changes five times, decisively forsaking the minor for the parallel major only at the close of the last variation. Amid harmonic variability, the melodic incipit of the theme remains a near constant presence, its contour readily identifiable beneath an array of motivic transformations and contrapuntal elaborations; examples 3.3a and b highlight some of these in the opening measures of Variations 4 and 5. Freely composed passages intervene between Variations 6 and 7, and again between Variations 8 and 9; beginning from material characteristic of the variation that precedes them, these passages provide seamless transitions in figuration, key, and/ or mode. Variations 9 and 10 are partly fused together, the latter taking over in the midst of the former's final phrase before giving way, in its turn, to a short coda.

EXAMPLE 3.3a   Heinrich von Herzogenberg, *Variations on a Theme of Johannes Brahms*, Op. 23, mm. 71–72

EXAMPLE 3.3b   Heinrich von Herzogenberg, *Variations on a Theme of Johannes Brahms*, Op. 23, mm. 85–88

Perhaps most remarkably, the lengths and relative proportions of phrases are constantly in flux. Not a single variation duplicates precisely the phrase structure of the theme, nor do any two variations share identical phrase structures or cumulative durations. Instead, successive changes in length and cadential profile create a complex shape, at once rounded and progressive, for the set

as a whole. The theme itself is devoid of internal repetition, while Variation
1 reprises the bar form of Brahms's original song. Variations 2–6 all employ
the double repeats conventionally associated with binary form. A gradual
increase in notated duration from twenty measures in Variation 3 to forty
measures in Variation 6 provides a sense of tiered expansion, which, in turn,
finds directional reinforcement in the harmonic progression traced by those
variations: i–VI–V–I. Variations 7 and 8, set apart as a pair by the transitional
passages on either side, provide the sharpest structural and affective contrast
of the set: a *lento* bar form in C♯ minor followed by an *allegretto* binary in A
major. The latter inverts the proportions of Brahms's original song. What had
began as a front-loaded structure (eighteen measures of *Stollen* followed by
nine measures of *Abgesang*) has now become end-weighted (eight measures
of *Stollen*-based material followed by fifteen measures derived from the *Abgesang*).
Finally, the last two variations together create a blurred mirror image of the
beginning of the set. Variation 9 unfolds as a straightforward bar form like
Variation 1 (albeit without its final four measures), whereupon Variation 10
recalls the theme once more by omitting internal repetition altogether.

According to the Beethovenian standards that Brahms vaguely invoked in 1876,
Heinrich's *Variations* were certainly "fantastic." In fact, in their continual refashion-
ing of the theme's proportions, they categorically exceeded Heinrich's only previous
variation set for chamber ensemble. Published in 1872, his Op. 13 had comprised
nine virtuosic variations on an original theme, scored for two pianos. Here,
Heinrich had occasionally omitted an internal repeat or delayed a cadence by a
measure or two, but the fundamental harmonic pattern and phrase structure of
the theme had remained aurally apparent in each and every variation. The same
was true of the more subdued, variation-form slow movement of his Piano Trio,
Op. 24, which he was still in the process of completing when Op. 23 went to
press.[17] For Heinrich, then, the very task of writing variations on a Brahmsian
theme seems to have called forth an uncharacteristically flexible approach. Given
Brahms's critical response, one might assume Heinrich had willfully selected his
procedures as declarations of independence from the prominent composer whose
song he had borrowed. Yet Brahms had hitherto attacked such procedures only in
correspondence with third parties as yet unattached to the Herzogenbergs.[18] In
mute defiance of his privately stated opinions, his own published works in variation
form actually furnished precedents for virtually every aspect of Heinrich's approach.

---

[17] For information on the genesis and publication of Heinrich's Op. 13 and Op. 24, see Wiechert, *Heinrich von Herzogenberg*, 275 and 277. As of August 1876, Brahms had almost certainly neither seen nor heard of Heinrich's still-unpublished piano trio; a copy of Op. 13 does survive in his *Nachlaß*, but the date of its acquisition is unclear.

[18] A brief postcard to Adolf Schubring written jointly by Brahms and Elisabeth in 1882 is the first and only evidence of direct contact between the Herzogenbergs and the critic himself, though they may have met at the 1877 Leipzig premiere of Brahms's Second Symphony (Brahms, *Briefe an . . . Schubring*, 231 and 234).

Three examples loomed especially large. First, Brahms's earliest published variation set provided a model in miniature for Heinrich's theme and for his progressive alteration of phrase lengths. The slow movement of the Piano Sonata, Op. 1, consisted of three variations on a theme that the published score proclaimed to be "based on an Old German Minnelied." As if to confirm its authenticity, Breitkopf and Härtel had printed a stanza of text beneath the theme's melody line in the first edition of December 1853. In actual fact, the source for both text and melody was not a *Minnelied* at all, but a Low Rhenish folk song titled *Verstohlen geht der Mond auf* (The Moon Arises Stealthily) and taken from the first volume of Kretzschmer and Zuccalmaglio's *Deutsche Volkslieder mit ihren Original-Weisen*. In scoring this song for piano, Brahms deleted or revised portions of the tune and interpolated both musical and textual repetitions for which his source provided no precedents. His tacit alterations transformed a freely composed, twofold alternation of soloist and group into a strict, three-part bar form precisely analogous to that of *Die Trauernde*.[19] Both songs consisted of three phrases of equal duration, each of which ended with an authentic cadence; both therefore threatened to stall the momentum of any variation-form movement before it began.

Unlike Heinrich, Brahms maintained the pseudo-archaic outlines of his theme in each of the ensuing variations. Yet his movement also brought about a gradual shift in the relative durations of *Stollen* and *Abgesang*, as shown in table 3.2. The theme allotted four measures of $\frac{2}{4}$ meter to each section, resulting in the proportions 4 + 4 + 4. Variation 1 slightly expanded the first *Stollen* and the *Abgesang* (5 + 4 + 5). Variation 2 further expanded all three sections, but the addition of evocative echoes in irregular meter focused the bulk of the expansion on the *Abgesang*; as expressed in $\frac{2}{4}$ measures, the new proportions were 8 + 7 + 10¼. Finally, regular meter and balanced phrase lengths returned for the last variation, but now material based on the *Abgesang* bore weight equal to that of the two *Stollen* put together (4 + 4 + 8). In tandem with the shift to the parallel major for the final variation, the expansion of the *Abgesang* generated a palpable sense of relaxation, of rosier vistas gradually opening to the mind's eye.[20] The movement thus

[19] Brahms had completed the slow movement of Op. 1 as an independent work in April 1852, nearly a year before the remainder of the sonata took shape. In retrospect, the movement's near-contemporaneity with *Die Trauernde* hints that the composer was already preoccupied with ancient musical genres well before his exposure to the Schumanns' library of early music in 1854. For details regarding Brahms's source for *Verstohlen geht der Mond auf* and the changes to which he subjected its tune and text, see George Bozarth, "Brahms's *Lieder ohne Worte*: The 'Poetic' Andantes of the Piano Sonatas," in *Brahms Studies: Analytical and Historical Perspectives. Papers delivered at the International Brahms Conference Washington, DC, 5–8 May 1983*, ed. George Bozarth, 348–50 (Oxford: Clarendon Press, 1990).

[20] Since one cannot know whether Heinrich von Herzogenberg had access to the later stanzas of the poem associated with *Verstohlen geht der Mond auf*, my reading of the Op. 1 Andante assumes no familiarity with those stanzas. For complementary interpretations that employ the full text as a hermeneutic window on the movement as a whole, see Bozarth, "'Poetic' Andantes," 348–53, and Parmer, "Song Quotation," 178–81.

TABLE 3.2   Shifting Parameters in Brahms's Piano Sonata, Op. 1 / II

	Key	Meter	Tempo	Phrase Structure (durations in 2/4 measures)
Theme	i	$\frac{2}{4}$	*Andante*	4 x 2 ; 4
Variation 1				5 + 4 ; 5
Variation 2		$\frac{2}{4}, \frac{4}{16}, \frac{3}{16}$		8 + 7 ; 10 ¼
Variation 3	I	$\frac{2}{4}$		4 x 2 ; 8
Coda			*a tempo → Adagio*	13

anticipated Heinrich's use of strategically altered proportions to bind multiple variations together into larger shapes.

Another potential model for Heinrich was Brahms's first independent variation set, the *Variations on a Theme of Robert Schumann* for solo piano, which was published as Op. 9 in November 1854. Here, as in Brahms's Op. 1, phrase length and relative proportions shifted often and conspicuously. As summarized in table 3.3, Schumann's twenty-four-measure theme begat sixteen variations that ranged from eleven to forty-three measures; only four of them duplicated the theme's structure precisely. Moreover, in terms of affect Op. 9 was the most kaleidoscopic variation set of Brahms's career, entailing fifteen notated shifts in tempo, eleven in meter, and six in key signature or tonal center. Like Heinrich's Op. 23, the result sounded more like a collection of related character pieces than a set of "strict" variations. Meanwhile, at the level of the individual variation, some of Heinrich's boldest strokes found detailed precedents in Brahms's Op. 9. Both sets subject the theme's melody to extensive contrapuntal manipulation, including strict canon and diminution relative to the overriding pulse. Most notably, Heinrich's *Variations* begin with an unusually forthright declaration of contrapuntal craft: the very first variation places the theme's tune in the bass line and constructs an independent melody above it (ex. 3.4a). As shown in example 3.4b, Brahms's Op. 9 began in precisely the same way. The parallel was strengthened by Heinrich's quiet dynamics and shift to duple meter. For the *secondo* player with whom Brahms seems to have vicariously identified, the passages in question were analogous even in their subdued figuration.

As it happens, Brahms was demonstrably aware of Heinrich's contrapuntal procedure in Variation 1 before drafting his response. On August 14, 1876, Clara Schumann had written from Switzerland regarding Heinrich's *Variations*, which

TABLE 3.3   Shifting Parameters in Brahms's *Variations on a Theme of Robert Schumann*, Op. 9

	Key	Meter	Tempo	Phrase Structure (durations in notated measures)
Theme	i	$\frac{2}{4}$	*Ziemlich langsam*	8 ; 16
Variation 1				
Variation 2		$\frac{6}{8}$	*Poco più moto*	(2 ; 4) x 2
Variation 3		$\frac{2}{4}$	*Tempo di tema*	8 ; 16
Variation 4			*Poco più moto*	
Variation 5			*Allegro capriccioso*	11 ; 32
Variation 6		$\frac{6}{8}$	*Allegro*	4 x 2 ; 18
Variation 7		$\mathbf{C}, \frac{3}{4}$	*Andante*	4 ; 7
Variation 8		$\frac{2}{4}$	*Andante (non troppo lento)*	8 ; 18
Variation 9	iv		*Schnell.*	4 x 2 ; 13
Variation 10	VI		*Poco Adagio*	8 x 2 ; 17
Variation 11	♭II → V	$\frac{4}{16}$	*Un poco più animato*	13 ; 14
Variation 12	i	$\frac{2}{4}$	*Allegretto, poco scherzando*	4 ; 18
Variation 13			*Non troppo Presto*	4 x 2 ; 16
Variation 14		$\frac{3}{8}$	*Andante*	12 ; 22
Variation 15	♮II	$\frac{6}{4}$	*Poco Adagio*	8 ; 18
Variation 16	I		*Adagio*	8 ; 16

she had recently played with Alfred Volkland.[21] Brahms subsequently closed his own letter to the Herzogenbergs by citing her enjoyment of the piece: "With what delight Frau Schumann plays your variations you have probably heard from her or from Herr Volkland."[22] Placing enthusiastic words in Clara's mouth allowed him to avoid searching for them himself. In actuality, her impressions, too, were mixed, though largely positive. As she explained to Brahms:

[21]Volkland probably brought Heinrich's *Variations* to Clara's attention in the first place; before moving to Basel in 1875, he had been an intimate friend of the Herzogenbergs and promoter of Heinrich's music in Leipzig (Wiechert, *Heinrich von Herzogenberg*, 35, 39–40). He may have introduced Clara to the piece in hopes of inducing her to perform it for the Herzogenbergs herself; by the end of August, Heinrich and Elisabeth had joined Clara and the Volklands for a visit of several days (Ruhbaum, *Elisabeth von Herzogenberg*, 318).

[22]Brahms/Herzogenberg, *Briefwechsel* 1:8.

EXAMPLE 3.4a   Heinrich von Herzogenberg, *Variations on a Theme of Johannes Brahms,* Op. 23, mm. 19–22

EXAMPLE 3.4b   Brahms, *Variations on a Theme of Robert Schumann,* Op. 9, mm. 25–28

I just played Herzogenberg's four-hand Variations on a theme by you, which actually surprised me with their ingenuity. To be sure, one notices your influence, but that doesn't hurt if it falls on fruitful ground—of course I would also have taken exception to various aspects of the Variations, for instance that the first immediately brings the certainly not easy theme into the bass before one has really become accustomed to it, etc.[23]

Perhaps Clara simply had not noticed the parallel with Brahms's Op. 9. Or perhaps she had, in which case her comment might represent a rare instance of humorous banter from a generally earnest correspondent. In either case, her letter alerted Brahms to Heinrich's unusual compositional decision before he had even heard the piece himself, making it all the more likely that he would perceive some resemblance to his own music.

Yet from Brahms's perspective, a third precedent was probably the most apparent. The *Variations on a Theme of Robert Schumann,* Op. 23, was conceived in 1861 for the private enjoyment of the Schumann family, then released in print two years later.[24] Like Heinrich's *Variations,* Brahms's were scored for four-hand piano. Compared to his Op. 1 or Op. 9, Brahms's Op. 23 hewed more closely to the phrase structure of the theme, but it, too, generated expressive flux via frequent changes in tempo, meter, and tonal affiliation, as shown in table 3.4. Indeed, with three minor-mode variations and four distinct key signatures ranging from six flats to five sharps, this variation set spent a greater

---

[23] Brahms/Schumann, *Briefe* 2:73–74.
[24] The original manuscript was dedicated to Julie Schumann (McCorkle, *Werkverzeichnis,* 79).

TABLE 3.4 Shifting Parameters in Brahms's *Variations on a Theme of Robert Schumann*, Op. 23

	Key	Meter	Tempo	Phrase Structure (durations in notated measures)
Theme	I	$\frac{2}{4}$	*Leise und innig*	16; 12 x 2
Variation 1			*L'istesso tempo.* *Andante molto moderato*	
Variation 2				16; 13 x 2
Variation 3				16; 12 x 2
Variation 4	i			16; 13 x 2
Variation 5	♭VI	$\frac{9}{8}$	*Poco più animato*	16; 12 x 2
Variation 6	I	$\frac{2}{4}$	*Allegro non troppo*	
Variation 7		$\frac{6}{8}$	*Con moto. L'istesso tempo*	
Variation 8	iii	$\frac{2}{4}$	*Poco più vivo*	
Variation 9	vi	**C**		
Variation 10	I		*Molto moderato, alla marcia*	8; 6 x 2
Coda				14

proportion of its length removed from the theme's original tonic than any other in Brahms's oeuvre. The two Op. 23s were also commensurate in scope and affective trajectory. Each consisted of ten variations followed by a coda. Each departed from its original key signature for the first time in Variation 4. In both sets, Variation 9 employed a stark combination of invertible counterpoint and minor-mode harmony; in both sets, the final variation and coda brought about a decrease in dynamic level and a decisive shift to the major mode. Each piece came to rest, slowly and quietly, in a common time gently at odds with the meter of the theme itself; each closed by reiterating and transforming melodic fragments taken from the theme, as if trailing off in midthought.

Finally, Brahms's Op. 23 bore the same opus number as Heinrich's *Variations*. Circumstantial evidence strongly suggests that the numeric affiliation was deliberate. Heinrich published four opuses in 1876: a piano quintet, Op. 17; a string quartet, Op. 18; four part-songs for mixed chorus and piano, Op. 22; and the *Variations*, Op. 23.[25] Like the six string quartets in Beethoven's Op. 18, Heinrich's quartet was his first published essay in the genre. There were thus not one but two precise convergences of opus number and generic model in the span of five works. Furthermore, opus numbers 19 through 21 remained permanently unused. Never again in his career did Heinrich neglect to fill

[25]Wiechert, *Heinrich von Herzogenberg*, 276–77.

an opus number; this singular divergence from his usual practice hints at a conscious alignment of publication data and musical content for one or more of the works published in 1876. Brahms was no stranger to such alignments; his first piano concerto, for instance, shares its opus number with Beethoven's.[26] Even Heinrich's choice of publisher for the *Variations* could be construed as referentially motivated. In returning to Rieter-Biedermann for first time since his Op. 2, Heinrich hearkened back not only to Brahms's crucial recommendation of his music in 1864 but also to the elder composer's own Op. 23, which, itself, had been published by Rieter-Biedermann in 1863.[27]

Taken in combination, Heinrich's archaic theme, flexible variation procedure, and choice of opus number seem deliberately designed to evoke a variety of specific Brahmsian precedents for his *Variations on a Theme of Johannes Brahms.* What might those precedents have meant to Heinrich, and why might he have sought to draw attention to them? One can securely retrace only the barest outlines of Heinrich's exposure to his predecessor's variation sets. At the very latest, he encountered the four-hand variations more than a year before writing his own. On January 31, 1874, Brahms's Op. 23 was performed in honor of its composer in Leipzig, the musically conservative city that had been the Herzogenbergs' home for the past sixteen months. The occasion was a concert celebrating the beginning of Brahms's first public tour in that city since the disastrous premiere of the first Piano Concerto in 1859.[28] Much had changed in the intervening years. With his reputation now firmly established in Germany by the success of the *German Requiem* in 1868 and the *Triumphlied* in 1872, Brahms did not fear the hisses that had once driven him from the Leipzig stage. Nevertheless, Heinrich and Elisabeth had each actively promoted his music to the local musical elite in the months leading up to his arrival. It seems inconceivable that either of them would have skipped the inaugural concert of his weeklong stay. Furthermore, Elisabeth's correspondence with Bertha Faber pinpoints Brahms's 1874 visit to Leipzig as the catalyst for renewed contact and increased respect among the three musicians after nearly a decade of mutual

---

[26] Christopher Reynolds has noted many similar congruencies and postulated a larger tradition within which composers deliberately assigned opus numbers to draw attention to generic precedents for their works. See *Motives for Allusion,* 144–45.

[27] Wiechert, *Heinrich von Herzogenberg,* 277, and McCorkle, *Werkverzeichnis,* 79–80.

[28] The house organ of the Leipzig publisher E. W. Fritzsch published a detailed account of the repertoire performed at this and other concerts during Brahms's visit; see the *Musikalisches Wochenblatt* 5/6 (February 6, 1874): 75. For instructive commentary concerning Brahms's difficulties in gaining a following in Leipzig, see Angelika Horstmann, *Untersuchungen zur Brahms-Rezeption der Jahre 1860–1880* (Hamburg: Karl Dieter Wagner, 1986), 316–27.

neglect.[29] One wonders if some of their conversations occurred in conjunction with the performance of Brahms's four-hand variations. If so, Heinrich's variations might themselves have been conceived as contributions to an ongoing discussion.

Unlike for Brahms's Op. 23, surviving correspondence provides no direct evidence concerning Heinrich's exposure to Op. 1 and Op. 9. The bulk of his contact with any of Brahms's keyboard works would surely have occurred through informal music making and private score study—activities that often leave no overt documentary traces at all. Yet contemporaneous critical opinion is also likely to have shaped his impressions of Brahms's variation practice and compositional aesthetic, the more so since he enjoyed little or no access to the composer's own views during the long hiatus in their relationship. Assuming that he perused the leading German music journals, Heinrich would have found particularly stimulating analyses of all three variation sets in the essays of Adolf Schubring. Schubring's gigantic 1862 article on Brahms in the *Neue Zeitschrift für Musik* included specific accounts of Op. 1 and Op. 9, while his 1868 debut for the *Leipziger Allgemeine musikalische Zeitung* was a lengthy review of Brahms's Op. 23. These essays blended biographical data and hermeneutic conjecture with detailed motivic analysis, copious score excerpts, and occasional music-analytic figures. Together they comprised by far the most penetrating and sympathetic investigation of Brahms's compositional style that had yet been undertaken in the popular press, and their stance with respect to variation form closely foreshadowed the approach Heinrich would eventually adopt in his own Op. 23. Moreover, they characterized the musical implications of Brahms's emotional life in ways that may well have influenced Heinrich's sense of large-scale affective trajectory and his choice of *Die Trauernde* as his theme.

To Brahms's later annoyance, Schubring understood the contrapuntal manipulation of motivic material as the primary engine of his variation technique. The first installment of the critic's 1862 article devoted a short paragraph to the slow movement of Op. 1. After apprising the reader of the theme's supposed origins in ancient *Minnesang*, a summary of the variations laid bare Schubring's modern priorities as an analyst:

> [The movement] is variations on the Old German Minnelied "Blau, blau Blümelein," the first of which is characterized by surprising harmonic progressions, while the second attracts us with a magnificent double counterpoint, the third with an earnest cantilena devised against the melody-carrying bass line, and the coda with an ingenious canonic progression.[30]

---

[29] For a transcription of Elisabeth's letter and an account of the Herzogenbergs' involvement in the weeklong visit, see Brahms/Herzogenberg, *Briefwechsel* 1:xix–xxii.

[30] Schubring's 1862 essay provided the lead article in five successive issues of the *Neue Zeitschrift*. See "Schumanniana Nr. 8. Die Schumann'sche Schule. IV: Johannes Brahms," *Neue Zeitschrift für Musik*

Accounts of contrapuntal structure also pervaded Schubring's more extensive treatment of Op. 9 in the third installment of the same article. Now, however, counterpoint was coupled with a fresh emphasis on flexibility in Brahms's approach to the theme. In this regard the critic's adjectives were as telling as his nouns: "The variations are written in the freest Schumannian manner, here upon the discant theme, there upon the bass theme . . . and with application of the most delicate counterpoint." Furthermore, in his sole criticism of Op. 9, Schubring attacked the "monotony" created by Variations 1 and 3.[31] As displayed in table 3.3, these were the only two variations in the entire set that shared identical meters, tempi, and cadential proportions. By implication, his commentary foregrounded and embraced the variegated affects projected by successive and proximate variations throughout the rest of Op. 9. To a listener like Schubring, the extreme heterogeneity of Heinrich's variations might well have seemed rigorously logical.

In any case, Schubring's 1862 portrayals of Op. 1 and Op. 9 offered a music-analytic discourse on variation form that construed contrapuntal nuance and "fantastic" manipulation of a theme's most basic parameters as inherently Brahmsian characteristics—the one a signal of his compositional skill, the other a legacy of his admiration for Schumann. That discourse found deeper resonance six years later in the critic's essay on Brahms's Op. 23. The essay was published in two installments, of which the second bore the weight of the music-analytic argument. Here Schubring isolated three motivic seeds in the opening and closing measures of Schumann's theme. The seeds themselves comprised just two or three notes each, taken either from the theme's melody or from its bass line. Next, Schubring explicitly derived the principal melodic figures of every variation from one or more of the three seeds, in the process pointing out more than a dozen examples of invertible counterpoint, canonic imitation, motivic diminution, and other indexes of contrapuntal craft. Having established a backdrop of motivic relationships that permeated the set as a whole, he then sought to unveil the individual "character" of each variation and to explain those "character images" as distinct points of inflection along an overriding affective trajectory that ended, like Heinrich's, in subdued reminiscence. His review closed by aligning each variation with a verbal phrase or quotation that suggested its semantic potential and clarified its position relative to the whole. His responses to the final four variations and coda illustrate the range and specificity of his interpretation:

56/12 (March 21, 1862): 93–96; 56/13 (March 28, 1862): 101–4; 56/14 (April 4, 1862): 109–12; 56/15 (April 11, 1862): 117–19; and 56/16 (April 18, 1862): 125–28. The portion addressing the slow movement of Op. 1 appeared on March 21 on 96.

[31] Ibid., 110, 111.

Var. 7. "Tears still tremble in your eyelashes, and behold, you are already smiling?"

Var. 8. Rapture of melancholy.

Var. 9. Pulling oneself together energetically, intermingled with outbursts of convulsive pain.

Var. 10. Funeral march:

"Alas, you have buried a good man,

(*coda*)—but to *me* he was more! *Requiescat in pace et lux perpetua luceat ei!*"[32]

As these phrases demonstrate, the extramusical implications of Schubring's essay were at least as striking as its music-analytic conclusions. In fact, through the prism of his review, Brahms's Op. 23 became a multifaceted *tombeau* in which each variation offered a distinctly shaded meditation upon the loss of a friend and compositional mentor. Schubring took pains to stress the inherent subjectivity of the autobiographical undertones that he perceived in the work. As he put it, "Others consider *my* impressions just as far from absolutely correct or authoritative as I theirs."[33] Yet the first installment of his essay had already introduced new documentary evidence that strongly supported his own perspective. Here Schubring claimed that Robert Schumann had composed the theme for Brahms's Op. 23 during the onset of his mental collapse in February 1854 and had completed his own set of variations upon it as well:

> In the last days before the catastrophe, the overwrought master had occupied himself with piano variations on a theme which, in his agitated state, he believed that Franz Schubert had sent him from the hereafter. I have seen Schumann's manuscript; they are modestly self-controlled variations, only one, the third or fourth, set in canon; the fifth variation develops a complex sixteenth figure in the middle voice. In the midst of this variation misfortune overtook him—and already on the next or the following day his martyred spirit is so far recovered that he can complete the interrupted closing variation with a firm hand![34]

The first half of Schubring's essay thus unmasked Schumann's own unpublished music as a potential model for Brahms's. It also plunged Schubring into the thick of then-current scholarship and popular gossip. In the first biography of Schumann, published a decade prior in 1858, Joseph Wilhelm von Wasielewski had revealed the existence of a theme from Schumann's final weeks in Düsseldorf; according to Wasielewski, the composer believed he had received this theme from the spirits of Schubert and Mendelssohn. Wasielewski did not describe the musical characteristics of the theme, but he did explain in a footnote that

---

[32] Schubring, "Schumanniana Nr. 11. Die Schumann'sche Schule. Schumann und Brahms. Brahms' vierhändige Schumann-Variationen," *Leipziger Allgemeine musikalische Zeitung* 3/6 (February 5, 1868): 41–42; and 3/7 (February 12, 1868): 49–51. The passage is taken from 51; the parentheses, the italics for Latin words, and the emphasis on "me" are all original.

[33] Ibid. Emphasis in original.

[34] Ibid., 42.

Schumann completed five variations on it before his removal to Endenich in early March, 1854.[35] Five years later, in a footnote to an 1863 review of Brahms's four-hand *Variations*, the editors of the *Allgemeine musikalische Zeitung* coyly suggested that Brahms's chosen theme "is said to be the master's *last idea*" but provided no source or evidence for their assertion.[36] Read in the context of contemporaneous music journalism, Schubring's review was nothing short of explosive. He not only positively identified Brahms's theme as that of Schumann's final composition, but also claimed to have seen the original autograph himself. He described Schumann's own variations in persuasive detail, outlining the progression of musical textures instantiated in the set and remarking upon the very appearance of the disturbed composer's handwriting. In short, his review lent an aura of firsthand knowledge to what must hitherto have seemed mere speculation.

Throughout the next several decades, myriad essays on Brahms and Schumann borrowed from Schubring's data and parroted his conclusions.[37] With the benefit of hindsight and the publication of relevant documents (including Schumann's manuscript in facsimile), scholars are now better positioned to assess Schubring's assertions instead of simply repeating them. Most were accurate. The theme of Brahms's Op. 23 was, indeed, the theme of Schumann's last composition.[38] Independent reports confirm that the composer believed he had received the theme from Schubert; Schumann's variations unfold roughly as Schubring described (the canonic one actually comes second); and, according to Clara

---

[35] Joseph Wilhelm von Wasielewski, *Robert Schumann: Eine Biographie* (Dresden: Rudolf Kunze, 1858), 288.
[36] *Allgemeine musikalische Zeitung* 1/42 (October 14, 1863): 709n. Emphasis in original. Angelika Horstmann has attributed the review itself, which was signed "D," to Hermann Deiters, one of Brahms's most consistent advocates in the press and a staff contributor to the journal; see *Untersuchungen zur Brahms-Rezeption*, 411. The editor(s) responsible for the footnote remained anonymous, but Brahms himself may have provided the information. He had discussed the origins of the theme directly with Melchior Rieter-Biedermann in November 1862, using a variant of the same phrase that found its way into the review of Op. 23 eleven months later: "You know that this theme was Schumann's last musical idea" (Brahms/Biedermann et al., *Briefwechsel*, 75–76).
[37] Prominent examples occured in two broad essays on Brahms's compositions, both published in 1880: Louis Ehlert's "Brahms," *Deutsche Rundschau* 23 (April–June 1880): 351; and Deiters's "Johannes Brahms," 46. Deiter's wholesale adoption of Schubring's hermeneutic is particularly revealing because his own 1863 review of Op. 23 had focused entirely on music-analytic issues. Philipp Spitta soon followed suit in an article on Schumann's life and works for the first edition of George Grove's *Dictionary of Music and Musicians* (London, 1883), 3:404. Spitta also released a German version of the same article in "Ein Lebensbild Robert Schumann's," *Sammlung Musikalischer Vorträge* 4 (1882): 57. Finally, the fourth edition of Wasielewski's own biography surreptitiously incorporated the dramatic compositional chronology that Schubring had unearthed for the fifth variation in Schumann's set; see Wilhlem Josef von Wasielewski, *Robert Schumann: Eine Biographie*, ed. Woldemar von Wasielewksi, 492, 4th ed. (Leipzig: Breitkopf & Härtel, 1906). Though left unpublished and in a somewhat unfinished state until its posthumous completion in 1905, this final edition was based on revisions undertaken by the author beginning in the 1880s (ibid., xiii–xiv).
[38] Brahms's four-hand arrangement of the theme reproduced Schumann's original almost note for note despite the change in instrumentation.

Schumann's diary, her husband began his fair copy of the variations before his suicide attempt but completed it on the following day.[39] It remains unclear how Schubring had learned so much about music that Clara herself kept carefully guarded as a private relic.[40] A surprised Brahms confronted him about his sources immediately upon reading the first installment of his essay: "Yesterday at a friend's house I saw the [*Leipziger Allgemeine musikalische Zeitung*]: with pleasure your DAS, with some shock the biographical description! That is now my special antipathy . . . And where did you get the stories?"[41] But for aspiring composers like Heinrich von Herzogenberg, the provenance of Schubring's revelations was surely of trivial importance compared with the insight they offered into the creative process of a modern master. Here was persuasive evidence, both documentary and music-analytic, that Brahms had drawn specific inspiration from the music and personal circumstances of his predecessor.

In fact, although Schubring's biographical hermeneutic yielded especially detailed results in his essay on Brahms's Op. 23, this was not the first time the critic had presented Schumann's descent into madness as a compositional stimulus for the young Brahms. His 1862 article on the early works had already assigned Opp. 7–10 to a "transitional period" marked by the tragedy of Schumann's breakdown. Thus, the contrapuntal Op. 9 *Variations* were "great, dismal, deep, and heavy music . . . the most worthy Nänie that ever was sung for a master by his

[39]To date, the most detailed investigation of the inception and convoluted textual history of Schumann's last composition is Wolf-Dieter Seiffert's "Robert Schumanns Thema mit Variationen Es-Dur, genannt 'Geistervariationen,'" in *Compositionswissenschaft. Festschrift Reinhold und Roswitha Schlötterer zum 70. Geburtstag*, ed. Bernd Edelmann and Sabine Kurth, 189–214 (Augsburg: Wißner, 1999). Seiffert cites the diary of Rupert Becker (first published in 1904) as confirmation for Schumann's hallucination of Schubert; Wasielewksi's addition of Mendelssohn finds no comparable support in contemporary documents (ibid., 191n). For a critical edition of both theme and variations, see Wolf-Dieter Seiffert, ed., *Robert Schumann. Thema mit Variationen "Geistervariationen"* (Munich: Henle, 1995).

[40]When Brahms first broached the possibility of publishing his four-hand variations in autumn 1862, Clara granted permission but stipulated that the theme be left unidentified in the printed score (Brahms/Schumann, *Briefe* 1:411). Brahms complied, but he also complained of her attitude in correspondence with Joseph Joachim (Brahms/Joachim, *Briefwechsel* 1:325). His matter-of-fact letter demonstrates that Schumann's last composition was already well known as such among intimate friends of his family.

[41]Brahms, *Briefe an . . . Schubring*, 211; DAS was Schubring's signature. Brahms's objections were somewhat disingenuous since, in one way or another, he himself was almost certainly one of Schubring's sources. It seems highly implausible that Clara would have allowed the critic to see Robert's manuscript itself; no record of any visit to the Schumann household survives in her diary or correspondence. Despite his claims of contact with the autograph, then, Schubring is far more likely to have seen a copyist's manuscript, which Brahms had possessed since 1855 (for details on this copy, which Robert seems to have annotated himself, see Seiffert, "Robert Schumanns Thema," 196–207). And Brahms's objections to Schubring's essay were far from unequivocal. In the same letter, he sweetened an invitation to the Bremen premiere of his *German Requiem* with a cryptic offer: "Whoever has such sympathetic ears for my music as you, to him I believe I can promise something!" (Brahms, *Briefe an . . . Schubring*, 212). Clara's correspondence reveals that Brahms then asked her in Bremen, and in Schubring's presence, whether the critic might make a copy of Schumann's variations! She denied the request and reproached Brahms for his tactlessness (Brahms/Schumann, *Briefe* 1:582).

pupil." This characterization juggled chronology: Schumann still lived for two years after the work was completed, and his friends harbored hopes of a recovery for much of that time. Still, especially given the paucity of accurate biographical information then available outside the Schumann circle, Schubring's interpretation of Op. 9 remained compelling for many years. Equally compelling—and, in retrospect, even less plausible—was his reading of the songs in Op. 7. Among these was *Die Trauernde*, the theme for Heinrich's own *Variations*. For Schubring, these songs reflected Brahms's state of mind when they were published, eight months after Schumann's removal to Endenich: texts and music were "a faithful mirror of the melancholy mood into which he had fallen by the end of 1854."[42] Neither Schubring nor Heinrich von Herzogenberg could have known that every song in Op. 7 was actually composed long before Brahms had even met Schumann. Instead, in Schubring's criticism *Die Trauernde* took its place alongside Op. 9 and Op. 23 as part of a series of musical reckonings with Schumann's breakdown. Erroneously but powerfully aligned with the tragic circumstances of the Schumann household in 1854, the generic lament of a "woman in mourning" could be understood in deeply personal terms, its restrained affect reinterpreted as the blank stare of a wife or daughter left behind in Düsseldorf.

Presuming Heinrich had read Schubring's essays or encountered his ideas through other sources, he may well have intended his own variations to conjure up a related aggregate of musical and interpersonal resonances. His opus number, his contrapuntal manipulation of melodic motives, and the deliberate flexibility of his variation procedure recalled Brahmsian precedents that Schubring had prominently associated with the aftermath of Schumann's mental collapse. His theme embodied an arcane familiarity with Brahms's most obscure and underestimated compositions, echoed the archaic form of Brahms's first published variation theme, and, through the lens of Schubring's hermeneutic, evoked once more the emotional landscape of the Schumann drama. Beginning with the ancient antecedent that Brahms had adopted in Op. 1 and ending with the quiet resignation that had concluded his Op. 23, Heinrich's variations appropriated and reimagined many of the compositional and biographical landmarks that had recently come to define Brahms's early compositions and formative personal experiences in the popular press. Against the backdrop of contemporaneous commentary, his new piece projected a keen sense of empathy with Brahms and thus, by implication, affirmed his own potential as a colleague and friend. In short, from Heinrich's perspective, the *Variations on a Theme of Johannes Brahms* may have been at once a public claim of pedigree and a private application for admission to an exclusive circle of informed musicians.[43]

---

[42] Schubring, "Schumanniana Nr. 8," 109, 111, and 109, respectively.
[43] Relying solely upon the precedent of Brahms's Op. 23, Johannes Behr hints at a similar conclusion in *Vom Ratgeber zum Kompositionslehrer*, 32.

The broader reception of Heinrich's *Variations* demonstrates widespread recognition of at least some of these ambitions. Upon the work's publication in 1876, critics specifically applauded its flexible treatment of the theme and its self-conscious references to Brahms's style.[44] Clara Schumann largely agreed with their assessment, as Brahms knew well. Yet his own perspective diverged strongly enough to warrant some criticism of Heinrich's Op. 23. Read as responses to Heinrich's perceived intentions rather than as articulations of abstract compositional principles, his comments on variation form seem likely to have been motivated by mingled musical and extramusical factors. Certainly Brahms harbored purely musical reservations regarding the structural freedom and melodic orientation typical of his own early variation sets. He had already explained his views to Schubring in 1869, less than a year after reading the latter's essay on the four-hand Schumann variations. If Brahms thought the same variation sets were now leading another musician astray, this was a chance to set Heinrich straight. But Schubring's review had also provoked a piquant rejection of composer biography, Brahms's "special antipathy." Perhaps by modeling new music so directly on works that were broadly perceived as privately meaningful compositions, Heinrich had prodded him into a similarly critical frame of mind. If so, Brahms's first letter to the Herzogenbergs bears rereading: "I place the volume before me and play four-handed in my mind, at my right side quite clearly a slim womanly figure in blue velvet and golden hair." While vicariously softening Elisabeth's hard-fought advocacy for Heinrich's compositions, this typecast duet might also have served a more pointed function by turning the tables on her husband—now he could experience first hand what it felt like to lose control of music for which he thought he had devised a stable network of associations.

[44] In an 1879 review, Hermann Kretzschmar praised the "free style" of the *Variations* and the "natural and efficacious" connections between them (*Musikalisches Wochenblatt* 10 (1879): 31), while an anonymous reviewer from 1877 pointed indirectly to the work's complex compositional lineage: "When I say that it reminds one of Brahms here and there, one should not thereby reproach the composer. One can very well attach oneself spiritually to another and yet go one's own way in the process; Brahms demonstrates this himself, in whom also, at the beginning, for instance, Schumann's influence could be detected" (*Allgemeine musikalische Zeitung* 12:539).

CHAPTER FOUR

CONSEQUENCES OF CRITICISM

Whatever Brahms's motivations, his response to Heinrich's Op. 23 was transparently equivocal. Despite its friendly tone, his letter vacillated between vague generic criticism and even vaguer expressions of approval. It provided neither the straightforward encouragement that Heinrich clearly craved in August 1876 nor the specific editorial advice that Elisabeth explicitly requested. Not surprisingly, the Herzogenbergs answered with silence. For more than three months, neither they nor Brahms renewed their correspondence, and Heinrich's *Variations on a Theme of Johannes Brahms* were never mentioned again in any extant letter. In the end, Brahms himself broke the stalemate in December 1876 by referring to a standing offer of hospitality that Elisabeth had made before Heinrich's music came between them. He thereby reopened communication with the pair and assured himself of an invitation to stay at their home, for the first time, during an upcoming trip to Leipzig in January 1877.[1] And during that visit or soon thereafter, he seems to have realized that continued interchange with the Herzogenbergs would inevitably involve frequent and extensive dialogue about new compositions—his own, at the very least, if not Heinrich's as well.

This realization may have coincided with a broader reexamination of the rhetorical strategies that Brahms had habitually applied to friends who wrote music. After all, it was precisely in the spring of 1877 that he reopened a long-dormant compositional exchange with Julius Stockhausen through the tones of *Es liebt sich so lieblich im Lenze*. Nevertheless, Heinrich differed in important ways from Julius, as well as from Joseph Joachim, Theodor Wilhelm Engelmann, Klaus Groth, Theodor Billroth, and most of Brahms's other close male friends in the 1870s. Unlike them, Heinrich was neither a career performer nor a musical dilettante

---

[1] Brahms/Herzogenberg, *Briefwechsel* 1:9–10. Both the content and the tone of Brahms's second letter demonstrate that no correspondence was exchanged between August and December 1876.

whose vocation lay elsewhere. Despite his attitude of profound veneration for Brahms, he, too, was a professional composer who might reasonably expect to talk shop with an established colleague; furthermore, as demonstrated in Elisabeth's very first letter to Brahms, his wife clearly hoped that he would do so. So, beginning in April 1877, Brahms began sending unpublished compositions to the Herzogenbergs and asking directly for their comments. The first installment comprised a keyboard étude and most of the songs that would soon be released in Opp. 69–72. As if to reinforce their sense of having entered a rarefied circle, he instructed them to forward the manuscripts directly to Clara Schumann, thereby revealing that they had received them before Brahms's oldest friend and closest confidante. Their responses, conveyed in separate letters, were characteristically distinct. Heinrich professed admiration for every song and catalogued some of his favorite moments using figured-bass notation; his only criticism was cast as a self-deprecating attack on his own powers of observation. Elisabeth praised most of the songs but took no trouble to hide her dislike for three of them, especially *Willst du, daß ich geh?* (Do you want me to go?), Op. 71 No. 4. For this, her least favorite, she even questioned Brahms's choice of text, opining that Karl Lemcke's heavy-handed and sexually suggestive poem was inappropriate in itself, independent of the musical setting. As she put it: "Such topics are really only acceptable when treated in a folk-like [*volkstümlicher*] style."[2]

Thus began a patterned interchange that lasted throughout the late 1870s and early 1880s. Between regular rendezvous in one another's cities or other convenient locations, written discussion of new music provided opportunities to deepen their acquaintance or, at times, to offer apologies when misunderstandings arose. Two examples of the latter situation are particularly instructive. First, Brahms wrote in mid-November 1877, hoping to obtain an invitation to stay with the Herzogenbergs in Leipzig during another concert tour the following January. Unfortunately, his letter concealed his wishes behind banter so cryptic that Elisabeth did not recognize his request in the first place. She concluded that he meant to stay in a hotel. Hurt by what seemed a deliberate slight, she responded two days later by proclaiming his letter "horrid." Brahms immediately apologized and plans for the visit were finalized, but Elisabeth still felt unsure of herself in dealing with his ironic epistolary style. As she put it on December 3: "My head has gone completely dumb because of this sudden surrender, and I feel myself strangely surrounded by ambiguous, sphinx-like storks."[3] In lieu of a second apology, Brahms's next letter offered exclusive access

---

[2] Ibid., 19–27. The quotation on 27.

[3] Ibid., 28–35. The two quotations are on 31 and 34. Elisabeth's reference to storks on December 3 recalled Brahms's previous letter, dated November 22. Here he had referred obliquely to Emma Engelmann's pregnancy and impending delivery using a quotation from the text of *Alte Liebe*, Op. 72 No. 1, one of the songs he had mailed to the Herzogenbergs in April: "Die frommen Störche kehren," or "the

to music both old and new. On December 12, 1877, he not only promised Elisabeth the autograph of the slow movement from his third piano quartet, Op. 60, but also sent along an unpublished piece to which he had first referred in November.[4] The work in question was an early version of *O schöne Nacht* (O beautiful night), a vocal quartet with piano accompaniment.

Brahms revised this part-song and published it seven years later as the first of the Four Quartets, Op. 92; his initial manuscript also survives, and the version it contains was published in its own right in 2008.[5] As far as the Herzogenbergs knew in December 1877, however, *O schöne Nacht* was available only to them. Brahms reinforced their special claim to the piece using techniques he had developed for his three allusive lullabies. First, his letter coyly drew attention to the possibility of musical borrowing: "To your astuteness I need not explain the enclosed bad joke, I need not say that I am very much in favor of the further exploitation of motivic invention!"[6] By the end of 1877, self-deprecating acknowledgment of his own allusive ingenuity had become a familiar trope between Brahms and close friends. Eight months prior he had downplayed his baptismal offering for the Stockhausens in almost precisely the same way, calling it, too, "a bad joke." Once more, the joke was easy to find. As shown in examples 4.1a and b, Brahms's piano introduction is taken almost literally from *Nacht ist wie ein stilles Meer* (Night is like a quiet sea), a part-song for the same ensemble that Heinrich had released the previous year through Breitkopf and Härtel as the second of his Four Notturnos, Op. 22.[7] In case either of the Herzogenbergs might miss the musical reference, Brahms also labeled his own piece "Nottorno II." No evidence suggests that he was at work on another nocturne at the time, and the label vanished

---

pious storks return" (ibid., 31). Brahms himself was not the first to associate the text of *Alte Liebe* with Emma's pregnancy; her husband, Theodor Wilhelm, had already made the same joke in a letter to Brahms dated November 7 (Brahms/Engelmann, *Briefwechsel*, 66).

[4] Brahms first mentioned the piece in his letter of November 13, calling it a "bad joke on manuscript paper" (Brahms/Herzogenberg, *Briefwechsel* 1:28), but the reference may well have gone overlooked given how frustrated Elisabeth became at the rest of that letter. He then quietly lent his autograph to Theodor Billroth in early December, explaining that he needed it back immediately. Billroth complied on December 11, which enabled Brahms to send the piece to the Herzogenbergs the following day (Billroth/Brahms, *Briefwechsel*, 254–55).

[5] Bernd Wiechert, ed., *Johannes Brahms: Neue Ausgabe sämtlicher Werke VI/2: Chorwerke und Vokalquartette mit Klavier oder Orgel. II* (Munich: Henle, 2008), 124–29.

[6] Brahms/Herzogenberg, *Briefwechsel* 1:35–36.

[7] For a borrowing to which Brahms freely admitted in published correspondence, his incorporation of Heinrich's music in *O schöne Nacht* has received surprisingly little attention. In a footnote to his edition of the Herzogenberg correspondence, Kalbeck informed his readers that Brahms had "used a motive of Heinrich von Herzogenberg in his composition" but provided no further details (ibid., 36n). Cursory and often inaccurate treatments of the relationship between the part-songs appear in Edwin Evans, *Handbook to the Vocal Works of Brahms* (London: W. Reeves, 1912), 405–6; Lucien Stark, *Brahms's Vocal Duets and Quartets with Piano: A Guide with Full Texts and Translations* (Bloomington: Indiana University Press, 1998), 113–14; and Avins, *Life and Letters*, 530–31. By far the most detailed and accurate investigation of the situation appears in Wiechert, *Chorwerke und Vokalquartette*, xix–xxi, xxiv–xxv, and 149. Wiechert confines his comparison to the piano introductions of the two works.

from the published version of the part-song in 1884. Instead, in his autograph alone, Brahms deliberately aligned title, number, and genre with his predecessor's music, just as Heinrich had in his Op. 23.

EXAMPLE 4.1a   Brahms, *O schöne Nacht*, Op. 92 No. 1, mm. 1–4. Autograph version (1877), as transcribed by Bernd Wiechert. Copyright 2008 by G. Henle Verlag. Printed by permission.

EXAMPLE 4.1b   Heinrich von Herzogenberg, *Nacht ist wie ein stilles Meer*, Op. 22 No. 2, mm. 1–4

Finally, through the music and text of his part-song, Brahms hinted at an intimate intertwining of borrowed music and interpersonal significance. Heinrich's *Notturno* had set an archly precise meditation on sleep and dreams by Joseph von Eichendorff. By contrast, Brahms's text was a two-stanza poem from the "Hungarian" section of Georg Friedrich Daumer's *Polydora*, an 1855 collection of notoriously sensual poetry modeled on a wide variety of national and archaic styles.

O schöne Nacht!	O beautiful night!
Am Himmel märchenhaft	Above as in a fairy tale
Erglänzt der Mond in seiner ganzen Pracht,	The moon shines down in all its splendid glow,
Um ihn der kleinen Sterne liebliche Genossenschaft.	Surrounded by the sweet companionship Of little stars.
Es schimmert hell der Thau	The dewdrops shimmer brightly
Am grünen Halm; mit Macht	On green stalks; the nightingale
Im Fliederbäume schlägt die Nachtigall;	Sings loudly in the lilac tree;
Der Knabe schleicht zu seiner Liebe sacht —	The boy steals quietly to his beloved —
O schöne Nacht!⁸	O beautiful night!

[8]The German text is presented here as it appeared in Brahms's source: Georg Friedrich Daumer, *Polydora, ein weltpoetisches Liederbuch* (Frankfurt am Main: Literarische Anstalt, 1855), 128–29.

Of Daumer's ten lines, nine imply a straightforward conflation of the aesthetic and the erotic. The speaker's attention shifts progressively from distant heavenly bodies (five lines) to the sights and sounds of nature close at hand (three lines) and, eventually, to a romantic tryst (one line). Just before the lovers meet, however, linear description gives way to sly double-entendre—"O beautiful night!" Set apart by the dash and implied pause that precede it, the final line can be understood simultaneously as an innocuous poetic refrain that recalls the poem's first line and as a teasing confirmation of the couple's physical intimacy.

The tension between these two readings was particularly charged in the context of recent correspondence with the Herzogenbergs. Given Elisabeth's rejection of an overtly sexual text in Brahms's previous packet of compositions, Daumer's final couplet offered an ideal opportunity for playful commentary on her priorities as reader and listener. In fact, Brahms made room for such commentary in his autograph. Having left a gap in the musical notation at a point corresponding to the dash between lines 9 and 10, he inserted a paratextual gloss that referred directly to Elisabeth's criticism of *Willst du, daß ich geh*:

> Stop, dear Johannes, what are you doing? At most one may discuss such things in "folk manner," which you have unfortunately forgotten *again*! Only a peasant may ask if he may stay or if he must go—you are, sadly, no peasant! Don't offend that lovely head, encircled with golden splendor—be quick, just say once more:. . .[9]

Here the part-song resumed and ushered in the poem's final line. Daumer's wittily ambiguous conclusion was thus reimagined as a concession to Elisabeth's taste.

Brahms's music played along, as shown in example 4.2a. After quietly circling around C major as the boy approached his lover, the harmony shifted, on a weak beat and with no preparation whatsoever, to an A♯ diminished-seventh chord on the word "O." Tessitura, texture, and dynamics reinforced the moment's unexpected intensity: the soprano leapt up a sixth from g' to e″, the piano's triplet eighths became sixteenths, and both voices and accompaniment were suddenly *forte*. Suspended for four beats on an ambivalent harmony, the performers gradually retreated to *piano*, at which point the words "schöne Nacht" provoked a reprise of the subdued, E-major music with which Brahms had originally set the poem's opening line. As if reassured, the soprano reversed her surprised exclamation, falling back from e″ down to g♯'. The gesture as a whole resolved Daumer's juxtaposition of sexual climax and modest formal return by placing the two options in an implied temporal continuum and

---

[9] Emphasis original. For a facsimile of this page of Brahms's autograph and a precise transcription of his gloss, see Wiechert, ed., *Chorwerke und Vokalquartette*, 221. The autograph was known to Kalbeck, who first transcribed Brahms's gloss in his edition of the Herzogenberg correspondence (Brahms/Herzogenberg, *Briefwechsel* 1:29n).

allowing the second to supersede the first. It also produced the effect of extreme harmonic disjunction. But, like the arpeggiated wash of E-major triads with which Brahms began *O schöne Nacht*, the progression here was actually familiar from Heinrich's own *Nacht ist wie ein stilles Meer* (ex. 4.2b). There, the same diminished-seventh chord, harmonically respelled, had ushered in an analogous return to a tonic-centered refrain from earlier in the piece. Brahms's jagged soprano line even matched the composite upper voice projected by the highest vocal pitches in Heinrich's part-song.

The implications were provocative and charming in equal measure: Brahms needed the respectable Heinrich's help to extricate himself from Daumer's poem, and the act of composition was itself a form of conversation with both the music and the extramusical opinions of the work's recipients. The conversation continued in the Herzogenbergs' responses to *O schöne Nacht*, which they mailed in tandem on December 16. Nettled by Brahms's implied accusation of prudery and his "atrociously good memory" of their exchange regarding *Willst du, das ich geh?* Elisabeth formulated a far more nuanced and cogent explanation of her objections to Lemcke than she had yet attempted. Meanwhile, her husband commented in detail upon the formal layout of Brahms's part-song and joked about how the master's allusion to a piece by his "most faithful disciple" would puzzle future music historians.[10] Heinrich had never yet been so at ease in written correspondence with his famous contemporary. Perhaps he had understood Brahms's borrowings as tokens of compensation for the composer's cursory response to his *Variations* the previous autumn. In any event, *O schöne Nacht* had done important social work by inviting the Herzogenbergs into an explicitly private arena of compositional and aesthetic criticism. As Brahms put it in the letter that accompanied his manuscript: "How profoundly and understandably one can write these days (for those in the know)."[11] Concrete discussion of new music temporarily dominated the correspondence, distracting both Elisabeth and Heinrich from the awkwardness of their recent interactions with Brahms. Tones and words were knit together into new, vicariously shared memories for the three musicians.

Such was the case as well in the spring and summer of the following year, after a second and more serious incident called Brahms's respect for Heinrich's

---

[10] Brahms/Herzogenberg, *Briefwechsel* 1:38–40. Heinrich regarded the diminished-seventh chord that Brahms had borrowed from *Nacht ist wie ein stilles Meer* as a non sequitur in its new context. Indeed, with no foreknowledge of Daumer's poem, he assumed that Brahms's interpolated gloss, like a censor's pen, had actually replaced an additional section of music and text that was left out of the manuscript entirely. Brahms never corrected Heinrich's error. His silence underscored a characteristic feature of his relationship with the Herzogenbergs: what made musical exchanges important was not the veracity of their analyses but that they had the chance to examine his new music in the first place.
[11] Ibid., 36.

EXAMPLE 4.2a   Brahms, *O schöne Nacht*, Op. 92 No. 1, mm. 59–64. Autograph version (1877), as transcribed by Bernd Wiechert. Copyright 2008 by G. Henle Verlag. Printed by permission.

music directly into question. Having visited the Herzogenbergs at their Leipzig home in January 1878, Brahms arranged to meet them again two months later, this time in Dresden, where he had traveled to hear a performance of his Second Symphony on March 6.[12] At some point they went out for a meal, accompanied by Elisabeth's brother Ernst von Stockhausen. Brahms was tipsy but good-humored until the discussion turned to music, at which point his characteristic sarcasm took over, and he loudly ridiculed a critic for denigrating his third and latest string quartet, Op. 67, in favor of Heinrich's first effort in the genre, his Op. 18.[13] Elisabeth reproached him for his tactlessness in a letter dated March 10. She cast her forthright criticism of Brahms's manner as

[12] Brahms had hoped to hear Clara Schumann play in Dresden as well, but she was forced to cancel her involvement at the last minute. The composer's trip is omitted from the standard reference guide to Brahms's location and activies (see Hofmann, *Zeittafel*, 140) but clearly documented in correspondence with the Herzogenbergs and Clara herself (Brahms/Herzogenberg, *Briefwechsel* 1:57 and Brahms/Schumann, *Briefe* 2:139).

[13] Kalbeck seems to have been unaware of the existence of Heinrich's Op. 18. His annotations to this and other letters erroneously identify the work as one of Heinrich's three quartets, Op. 42 (Brahms/Herzogenberg, *Briefwechsel* 1:58n and 62n).

EXAMPLE 4.2b   Heinrich von Herzogenberg, *Nacht ist wie ein stilles Meer,* Op. 22 No. 2, mm. 40–45

a testament to her newfound closeness with the composer. Yet her breathless prose and shifting tense, not to mention her thinly veiled mockery of the ambitious and peripatetic Joseph Joachim, belied her confidence and hinted at her sense of frustration:

> I believe and hope that we are on such terms that one may allow oneself not only pastry jokes, but also, once in a while, an honest word....On Schiller Street you were so endearing and good, and I truly can't describe the delight with which I listened as you sat in the little window corner and, after you had decanted so much liquor, so beautifully told off my good brother, who sometimes leads little paradoxes out to pasture, with the sun of your sense of justice.—Then the infamous ★ suddenly appears on the horizon of the conversation, and you actually tell us the well-known story of how he had praised Heinrich's quartet and disrespectfully dismissed your B-flat major in the same winter, you tell it, with that certain comfortable irony regarding the self-evident criticism to which ★ thereby subjected himself, not to an impartial third party, but to precisely him, of whom you well know that he is the first to call an ignoramus an ass, and you tell it not to a self-important man [i.e., Joachim] who wants to transfer the main focus of his occupation to England and whom it is worthwhile to cure of presumption, but instead to one [Heinrich] who does not feel worthy to untie your shoelace, a seeking, learning, submissive man who is a hundred times more

bothered by a foolish overestimation than by the most scathing criticism because he can learn absolutely nothing from the former![14]

Either Elisabeth herself did not name the person whose opinion had provoked Brahms's scorn or Max Kalbeck, in transcribing her letter, chose that asterisk to conceal his identity. The most likely candidate is Heinrich Ehrlich, a pianist and prolific music critic ten years Brahms's senior who had settled in Berlin in 1862. In December 1876, Ehrlich had published an account of Berlin concert life in *Die Gegenwart*, the Liberal literary weekly for which he served as music editor. His review juxtaposed the premieres of Brahms's Op. 67 and Heinrich von Herzogenberg's Op. 18 within a single paragraph:

> In the second Quartet Evening of Joachim and his associates a "manuscript" quartet by Brahms was performed which, if it were published under another name, *most likely* would not have been performed by the leader of the quartet and *certainly* would not have been regarded by public or critic as anything other than a failed work. The author of this review—a very enthusiastic admirer of Brahms from long ago, when no Brahms-community yet existed in Berlin—listened in vain to find ten measures that allowed him to recognize the composer of the B-flat Sextet, the A minor Quartet, the Trio for piano, violin, and horn, to find *one* movement that flowed from fresh springs of creativity and did not bear signs of brooding exhaustion—in vain! ... On the third evening the master [Joachim] performed a quartet by Herr von Herzogenberg, a composer who is still almost unknown here, who enjoys a good reputation in Leipzig and in the circles associated with that city, and who displays a very estimable talent this work (op. 18). The principal themes, particularly that of the first movement, are original, truly warm and melodically fluid; if the artist had chosen a clearer and more concise form for the development, this would have significantly enhanced his achievement. And the fugato at the beginning of the last movement demonstrates that he can handle fixed forms. Hopefully we will meet the composer again soon.[15]

Ehrlich's implication was clear: Heinrich's first quartet bespoke a burgeoning career, while Brahms's third emblemized a composer in decline, bereft of inventive craft, sustained only by means of well-placed contacts and a lingering reputation forged in earlier works. Like most of Brahms's new music in historically prestigious genres, the B-flat quartet had provoked a wide range of responses during the months after its premiere, but Ehrlich's unrelenting negativity, his direct comparison with a counterexample by a less prestigious composer, and

---

[14] Ibid., 57–58. Read in isolation, Elisabeth's characterization of Joachim seems harsh, perhaps even implicitly anti-Semitic. On the other hand, her views on his sense of ambition accorded with those of other mutual acquaintances in 1878. Within four months, the Stockhausens would forsake Berlin in protest of the violinist's jealousy and professional interference, and Brahms himself would express strong sympathy for their position (Brahms/Stockhausen, *Briefwechsel*, 135–38).

[15] Heinrich Ehrlich, "Von der Musiksaison," *Die Gegenwart: Wochenschrift für Literatur, Kunst und öffentliches Leben* 10/49 (December 2, 1876): 365–66. Parentheses and emphases original.

his accusations of professional cronyism were all unique.[16] Between the lines Brahms may also have perceived a covert attack on Joachim's programming decisions. Critic and violinist had once been on friendly, even intimate footing when they overlapped in service to the Hannover court in the 1850s, but the two had since become regular antagonists ever since Joseph's relocation to Berlin in 1868.[17] In reading Ehrlich's review, perhaps Brahms was piqued at least partially on an old friend's behalf as well as his own.

What Elisabeth might have known or guessed regarding the causes of Brahms's outburst remains unclear. In any event, she took care not to criticize his anger itself. Her target, instead, was the insensitivity that allowed him to lampoon Heinrich's music in public and in the presence of its composer. An apology was clearly in order, and she demanded one outright in her closing paragraph, having already hinted at the form it might take. Nestled within her elaborate description of her husband's humility was an echo of her very first letter to Brahms, complete with scriptural allusion and direct request for compositional advice. Thus, the hopeful Heinrich of the Op. 23 *Variations*, who had longed for honest commentary "as the hart longs for fresh water," had since become an admiring disciple "who does not feel worthy to untie your shoelace, a seeking, learning, submissive man who is a hundred times more bothered by a foolish overestimation than by the most scathing criticism because he can learn absolutely nothing from the former!" Brahms took the hint at once. His response to Elisabeth's accusation does not survive, but it was prompt: the date on her grateful reply shows that it arrived at most a mere three days later, on March 13, 1878. Furthermore, he had identified the appropriate penance. His next surviving letter to the Herzogenbergs thanked Heinrich for having mailed him the score of a string quartet, presumably

---

[16] For a summary and penetrating discussion of reviews that addressed Brahms's Op. 67 in prominent music periodicals, see Horstmann, *Untersuchungen zur Brahms-Rezeption*, 111–22 and 402–3. Ehrlich's review, however, is not mentioned there.

[17] Ehrlich seems to have sought to undermine Joachim as soon as his position at the new Berlin Conservatory was announced. Joachim's later references to the critic were invariably caustic—an 1878 letter to Ernst Rudorff refers to his "fish-like, ice-cold, flashily-conceited amphibianness" (Joachim and Moser, *Briefe von und an Joachim* 3:10–11 and 192–93). For his part, Ehrlich eventually published excerpts from cordial and detailed letters first that he had received from Joachim during their first acquaintance in 1853; see *Aus allen Tonarten. Studien über Musik* (Berlin: Brachvogel & Ranft, 1888), 74. Since these excerpts concerned the young Brahms's first impressions on the musicians of the Hannover court in 1853, Kalbeck republished them, along with Ehrlich's own description of Brahms's piano playing, in his biography of the composer (*Brahms* 1:74). Kalbeck's account, in turn, has led at least one contemporary scholar to the dubious conclusion that Ehrlich and Brahms themselves were on friendly footing; see Leon Botstein, "Time and Memory: Concert Life, Science, and Music in Brahms's Vienna," in *Brahms and His World*, ed. Walter Frisch and Kevin Karnes, 13 and 24n, rev. ed. (Princeton, NJ: Princeton University Press, 2009). To the contrary, although Ehrlich seems to have heard Brahms play the piano in 1853, no evidence hints at any lasting relationship between them, and his 1876 review of Op. 67 makes the possibility seem even more remote.

Op. 18 itself, a copy of which is preserved to this day in the remnants of his library.[18] Given what had transpired in Dresden, Heinrich would hardly have sent the piece unbidden. Brahms must have asked for it in his letter of apology, and now he promised to give it the attention it deserved: "Already upon quick review it gave me great pleasure—and this evening it will make a cozy hour for me."[19]

By sending this letter before examining the work closely—or, at least, by pretending to—Brahms avoided detailed commentary on Heinrich's Op. 18. Nevertheless, for the first time he had expressed interest in and unmitigated approval for Heinrich's music, and that seems to have been enough. Thereafter, correspondence with the Herzogenbergs remained warm for the rest of that spring and summer, and the three musicians enjoyed back-to-back, conflict-free visits to one another's vacation homes in August and early September. Indeed, during the second visit Brahms finally allowed himself to be drawn into conversation about Heinrich's own compositional process. Only dim echoes of the exchange survive. In a letter dated September 12, Elisabeth thanked Brahms profusely for sharing his insights with her husband.

> You were so good for my Heinz, and now he sits and reflects, bent over his quartet paper, and thinks to himself, as he forms new note-tails for theme and variations, that a word from the mouth of John the Baptist is worth more than a hundred essays on "the style in which we should compose," even if God himself wrote them.[20]

Elisabeth flattered Brahms with yet another scriptural reference and, for good measure, belittled the work of the prominent Wagnerite Richard Pohl.[21] But beneath a humorous surface her words reveal that her husband was at work on another string quartet and that, unlike Op. 18, this one included a movement in theme and variation form.[22] A new essay in the genre associated with the most recent strains in their relationship thus contained a new essay in the form in

[18] Brahms's copy of Heinrich's Op. 18 survives in the archives of the Gesellschaft der Musikfreunde in Vienna; it is catalogued as IX 36473.

[19] Brahms/Herzogenberg, *Briefwechsel* 1:60–62. The quotation occurs on 62. Based on his misreading of earlier correspondence and his apparent ignorance of Heinrich's Op. 18, Kalbeck erroneously assumed that Brahms was referring to a copy of one of Heinrich's later quartets, Op. 42, and annotated his letter accordingly (ibid., 62n). Subsequent literature has followed Kalbeck's assumption; see Behr, *Vom Ratgeber zum Kompositionslehrer*, 37.

[20] Brahms/Herzogenberg, *Briefwechsel* 1:74. Johannes Behr points to this instance as one of only two extant occasions on which live discussions of Heinrich's music left traces in surviving documents (*Vom Ratgeber zum Kompositionslehrer*, 38); the other occurred in December 1884 and involved Heinrich's Symphony Op. 50.

[21] "The style in which we should compose" referred to Pohl's gigantic series of articles, entitled "In welchem Stile sollen wir komponieren? Aesthetische Briefe an einen jungen Musiker," which appeared serially in the *Musikalisches Wochenblatt* between December 1877 and February 1879.

[22] For a convenient table listing the forms of each movement in Heinrich's output for orchestra and/or chamber ensemble, see Wiechert, *Heinrich von Herzogenberg*, 169.

which Heinrich's musical priorities had first provoked Brahms's disapproval nearly two years before. Detailed discussion involving such a piece could easily have drawn together multiple threads from the checkered history of their interchange. Well might Elisabeth frame the conversation as a form of baptism. At the time it represented a potential watershed in her husband's compositional development and his friendship with Brahms alike.

The advice Heinrich received in September 1878 proved slow to bear fruit, at least in public. No new string quartet appeared in print until 1884, when he released a set of three as his Op. 42 and dedicated them all "to his highly esteemed friend Johannes Brahms." Relegated to small print runs and routinely accused of epigonism, these quartets have garnered few performances and only minimal scholarly attention.[23] Yet as the potential repository for whatever Heinrich had discussed with Brahms in September 1878 and whatever he hoped to prove to him six years later, the Op. 42 quartets remain intriguing, particularly the first and third, which employ theme and variation form in their slow movements. Both of these slow movements are labeled *Andantino*. Heinrich's predilection for counterpoint remains evident in each of them, but the subjects of his contrapuntal manipulation are now quasi-independent melodies devised above the theme's harmonic progression rather than motives taken directly from the theme's own melody. Moreover, as shown in tables 4.1 and 4.2, each slow movement abandons the complex heterogeneity characteristic of Heinrich's Op. 23 in favor of transparent regularity. The cadential structures and phrase proportions of the themes are held absolutely invariant until the final variation or coda, and all variations are based securely in the tonic. Against the stable backdrop of phrase structure and key, minimal changes in meter, tempo, and/or mode articulate clear-cut gestures that define the shape of each movement. In the nine variations of Op. 42 No. 1, the overall effect is that of a circle gently closed. Concerted shifts in meter and tempo in Variation 5 are gradually reversed in Variations 8 and 9, leading to a return of the original theme's melody. The five variations of Op. 42 No. 3 are more open-ended. The short-lived shift

---

[23] In 1997, Bernd Wiechert used sensitively chosen excerpts from Op. 42 No. 3 as part of a broader investigation of Heinrich's approach to melody, harmony, and form in *Heinrich von Herzogenberg*, 161–201. The title of his chapter is telling: "Herzogenberg als Brahms-Epigone?" stands as the first serious attempt to problematize the caricature that has haunted Herzogenberg scholarship for decades in such essays as Hellmut Kühn, "Brahms und sein Epigone Heinrich von Herzogenberg. Zur Musik in der Grunderzeit und im Fin de siècle I," *Musica* 28 (1974): 517–21; Robert Pascall, "Brahms und die Kleinmeister," *Hamburger Jahrbuch für Musikwissenschaft* 7 (1984): 199–209; and Walter Frisch, "'The Brahms Fog': On Tracing Brahmsian Influences," *American Brahms Society Newsletter* 7/1 (1989): 1–3. More recently, Friedhelm Krummacher has provided the first survey of Heinrich's string quartets in *Das Streichquartett Teilband 2: Von Mendelssohn bis zur Gegenwart* (Laaber: Laaber-Verlag, 2003), 84–87. Krummacher identifies important characteristics of the opening movements of the three Op. 42 quartets, but his brief summaries of the remaining movements are deeply problematic, as they misconstrue formal schemes and misidentify tonic keys.

TABLE 4.1   Shifting Parameters in Heinrich von Herzogenberg's String Quartet, Op. 42 No. 1 / II

	Key	Meter	Tempo	Phrase Structure (durations in notated measures)
Theme	I	$\frac{6}{8}$	*Andantino*	4 x 2; 6 x 2
Variation 1				
Variation 2				
Variation 3				
Variation 4				
Variation 5		$\frac{2}{4}$	*Poco scherzando, gleiche Achtel*	
Variation 6				
Variation 7				
Variation 8		$\frac{6}{8}$	*Allegretto*	
Variation 9			*Tempo I*	4; 6
Coda				7

TABLE 4.2   Shifting Parameters in Heinrich von Herzogenberg's String Quartet, Op. 42 No. 3 / II

	Key	Meter	Tempo	Phrase Structure (durations in notated measures)
Theme	i	$\frac{2}{4}$	*Andantino*	8 x 2; 8 x 2
Variation 1				
Variation 2		$\frac{6}{8}$		
Variation 3		$\frac{2}{4}$		
Variation 4	I		*tranquillo*	
Variation 5			*Andante*	
Coda			*Più lento*	8

to compound duple meter in Variation 2 is merely the notational by-product of an underlying acceleration in surface figuration that encompasses the theme and initial variations; its furious apex achieved in the continuous sixteenth notes of Variation 3, the movement then shifts to the major mode and begins a long, discursive unwinding reflected in the ever-slower tempi of the ensuing variations and coda.

In their published form, Heinrich's two slow movements proclaimed a radical reorientation of his variation technique. Gone was the "fantastic" flexibility of his Op. 23 *Variations*, and in its place were new priorities closely aligned with the "strict" aesthetic for which Brahms had advocated privately since the late 1860s. For his part, Brahms could hardly have failed to notice a change so pronounced and so consonant with his own expressed opinions. He clearly approved of the final results. Upon receiving a copy of Op. 42 in March 1884, he declared the quartets Heinrich's best compositions to date. He reiterated the point on multiple occasions over the ensuing years, often pairing Op. 42 with his friend's two string trios, Op. 27, and praising them at the implied expense of other projects. For instance, having accused Heinrich's second symphony of unapproachability in 1885, he sought to excuse his criticism: "After the string trios and quartets I had hoped for more in this regard."[24] Even when the quality of the quartets was not explicitly at issue, Brahms articulated a peculiar interest in them. In a letter alerting Heinrich to the Vienna premiere of Op. 42 No. 1 in November 1884, he referred to the piece itself as a team effort, calling it "your-our quartet No. 1."[25] Brahms's status as dedicatee for Op. 42 surely helps to explain the sense of ownership reflected in his strangely blended pronouns. But perhaps his diction also conveyed an awareness that his own advice had influenced this particular piece in some way. Perhaps an early version of Op. 42 No. 1 had provided a topic for the shared conversation and compositional consultation that left their traces in correspondence from September 1878.

At best the scenario is plausible, not inevitable. Elisabeth's references to quartet paper and variation-writing are vague and circumstantial, and no other evidence hints that any of the Op. 42 quartets existed prior to 1883.[26] Nevertheless, imagined as a contribution to the hard-won détente that followed Brahms's mockery of Op. 18 in 1878, Heinrich's Op. 42 No. 1 might have carried special rhetorical potential. As illustrated in examples 4.3a and b, the theme of the slow movement bore a close and pervasive relationship to the theme of the variation-form finale to Brahms's B-flat major quartet, Op. 67—the very piece Ehrlich had attacked and Brahms himself had sought to defend by denigrating Heinrich's music. Beneath disparate meters, melodies, and accompanimental textures, the two themes were identical in phrase structure, cadential layout, and harmonic outline. Both were binaries with double repeats; both allotted four measures to the first section and six to the second. The first sections prolonged the tonic for two measures, then shifted suddenly toward the mediant. The second sections began with four measures of flux marked by prominent diminished-seventh chords; then, in a seeming non sequitur, diatonic melody and tonic harmony returned for the final two measures. Dynamics were analogous throughout the two themes. Even melodic contour displayed underlying congruencies despite different keys and contrasting motivic material. Presuming Heinrich had begun to work out a large-scale plan for his variations by the time he discussed them with Brahms, that plan, too, may have suggested a charged

---

[24] Brahms/Herzogenberg, *Briefwechsel* 2:23, 113 (quotation), and 136. Brahms paired the quartets and trios as late as 1891 in a letter to Clara Schumann (Brahms/Schumann, *Briefe* 2:450). In this instance, Berthold Litzmann erroneously transcribed "4tette" as "Oktette" (Behr, *Vom Ratgeber zum Kompositionslehrer*, 39).
[25] Brahms/Herzogenberg, *Briefwechsel* 2:40.
[26] See Wiechert, *Heinrich von Herzogenberg*, 282.

connection with the finale of Op. 67. At least in the published version, the two movements were commensurate in length and scope. They also employed precisely inverse metric strategies: while Brahms's eight variations shifted from $\frac{2}{4}$ to $\frac{6}{8}$ and back again, Heinrich's nine variations did exactly the opposite.

EXAMPLE 4.3a   Heinrich von Herzogenberg, String Quartet, Op. 42 No. 1 / II, mm. 1–10

EXAMPLE 4.3b   Brahms, String Quartet, Op. 67 / IV, mm. 1–10

Rather than borrow a specific melodic gesture and associated polyphonic complex, Heinrich appropriated the larger shape of Brahms's theme and, to a lesser extent, of his movement as a whole, echoing its proportions and mirroring some of its most striking turns.[27] Approached from the standpoint of Brahms's own allusive practice, the relationship between the two works remains diffuse and far less audible. Still, it is difficult to imagine that the possibility of deliberate compositional modeling could have escaped Brahms's ear and eye when he first encountered Op. 42 No. 1, especially if the piece had been the locus of detailed compositional interchange in September 1878. In the aftermath of a tactless insult and subsequent apology, the slow movement of the new quartet offered implicit confirmation that Brahms had lost neither Heinrich's friendship nor his admiration. The structure of the theme displayed elaborate respect for Brahms's Op. 67 in the face of Ehrlich's negative review. Meanwhile, more eloquently than any verbal assurance, the variation procedures that Heinrich ultimately applied to the theme demonstrated his willingness to learn from Brahms's criticism, be it kind or harsh, written or spoken. In view of his music's capacity to address and manipulate the interpersonal situation within which it was likely conceived, Heinrich's posthumous reputation as an unreflective Brahms epigone deserves reevaluation. In the initial drafts of one of the Op. 42 quartets, at least, imitation may have been a nuanced and highly effective form of flattery.

––––––––––

Despite a rocky beginning and occasional setbacks, the musical and personal exchanges of the late 1870s represented the apex of Brahms's friendship with the Herzogenbergs. Over the months that followed their informal lesson in September 1878, Brahms responded to Heinrich's compositional ideas with unprecedented frequency, while Elisabeth indefatigably encouraged and facilitated their exchanges. Among the works discussed in correspondence were Heinrich's two String Trios, Op. 27, and his twelve German Sacred Folk Songs for four-part mixed chorus, Op. 28. Elisabeth alerted Brahms to her husband's work on both opuses in April 1879, well before their publication, and presented them as potential topics for face-to-face conversation during a planned visit that summer.[28] Whether such conversation actually occurred when the three musicians met in August 1879 remains unclear, but Brahms took the pieces

––––––––––

[27] The boldest move in Brahms's finale, however, found no echo in Heinrich's slow movement: Brahms recast the theme of his first movement as a variation on the finale's theme, creating a cyclic connection across the Op. 67 quartet as a whole. For a detailed description of the finale's unfolding, see Friedhelm Krummacher, "Von 'allerlei Delikatessen': Überlegungen zum Streichquartett Op. 67 von Brahms," in *Johannes Brahms: Quellen—Text—Rezeption—Interpretation. Internationaler Brahms-Kongreß, Hamburg 1997*, ed. Friedhelm Krummacher and Michael Struck, with Constantin Floros and Peter Petersen, 133–35 (München: Henle, 1999).

[28] Brahms/Herzogenberg, *Briefwechsel* 1:93–94. Shortly before the visit itself, Heinrich mailed Brahms copies of the German Sacred Folk Songs and asked, with typical reticence, whether he might look them over while travelling, "if you have nothing better to do or to read and have also already grown tired of looking out at the green landscape" (ibid., 101).

seriously. Following the release of the String Trios in October, he proclaimed his approval in a letter to Elisabeth with a pithy and nearly untranslatable phrase: "In the new Trios it becomes entangled most charmingly." His verb, *wuzeln*, from Austrian and Bavarian dialect, evoked both the abstruse challenges of a then-neglected genre and the elaborate contrapuntal craft of Heinrich's offerings, which bristled with learned devices and extended points of imitation.[29]

Brahms then used the same word as a springboard for substantive critique of the German Sacred Folk Songs, which had not yet gone to press:

> But I think at the same time of the folksongs, in which entanglement [*die Wuzelei*] did not agree with me. Here I am admittedly not unbiased, I automatically and regretfully remember how I myself have entangled countless folksongs; unfortunately a small sample remains visible. We'll speak sometime about it. But I believe that later Herr Heinz, too, would not like to see them printed—and besides they seemed to me so especially difficult.[30]

By sending his comments through Elisabeth as an intermediary and by retrospectively attacking his own set of fourteen German Folk Songs for four-part mixed chorus, WoO 34 (published by Rieter-Biedermann in 1864), Brahms simultaneously softened and clarified his criticism of unnecessary complexity in Heinrich's Op. 28. The younger composer could now draw lessons from the music of his esteemed colleague while editing his own work in progress. Elisabeth gently defended the German Sacred Folk Songs in her next letter to Brahms, and Heinrich published them the following year.[31] Since his autographs no longer survive, one cannot assess whatever changes or simplifications he may have made, but the end result was perhaps beside the point. The mere chance to learn in private from a master was, in itself, part of what both Heinrich and Elisabeth had hoped for from the first in their friendship with Brahms.

The continued availability of such opportunities in turn reflected the general health of a friendship that, by any measure, was at its strongest during its initial phases. Beginning with Brahms's first visit to their home in January 1877, Heinrich and Elisabeth met the composer at least fourteen times over the next six years; over the same period, they mailed him sixty-three surviving letters. Then things began to change. Between 1883 and 1897, they saw Brahms only six more times, and the pace of their correspondence fell commensurately; from those fifteen years, only sixty-four of their letters to him survive.[32] Some face-to-face meetings

[29] Ibid., 106. Contemporary reviewers confirmed Brahms's positive impression of the Trios and expressed excitement at the release of new compositions in a genre that had been essentially dormant since Beethoven; for an example, see Eduard Hille, "Kritische Briefe an eine Dame. 24," *Allgemeine musikalische Zeitung* 14/42 (October 15, 1879): 666–68.

[30] Brahms/Herzogenberg, *Briefwechsel* 1:106.

[31] Ibid., 108; and Wiechert, *Heinrich von Herzogenberg*, 278.

[32] To date, Antje Ruhbaum has proposed the most detailed account of Brahms's evolving friendship with the Herzogenbergs in *Elisabeth von Herzogenberg*, 180–210. She identifies three phases: a "euphoric initial

were victims of unavoidable circumstance. The Herzogenbergs forsook Leipzig for Berlin in 1885, lured by Heinrich's appointment as professor of composition at the Hochschule für Musik. By then, Brahms's old friendship with Joachim had been largely destroyed in the wake of the latter's divorce from Amalie, and, as Heinrich and Elisabeth knew, he actively avoided Berlin for fear of stirring up trouble.[33] Nevertheless, Brahms was perfectly capable of sustaining stable, long-term friendships through correspondence alone, as demonstrated in his consist-ently warm interchange with the Engelmanns in Utrecht. Taken together, the decline in correspondence with the Herzogenbergs in the 1880s and the relative paucity of visits on neutral territory suggests a marked cooling in the relationship. The tone and content of surviving letters confirm the shift. Misunderstandings that Elisabeth might once have cleared up with a single question were now al-lowed to fester for months, and, while Brahms's music still served as the touch-stone for detailed commentary, Heinrich's faded from view, his proffered scores most often provoking nothing but silence.[34] The complex dynamic that linked the three musicians had clearly suffered some form of damage.

A variety of interlocking explanations might be reconciled with existing evidence. Beginning in 1883, Brahms's budding friendship with the young con-tralto Hermine Spies offered alternative opportunities for at least some types of interaction he had previously found in his relationship with the Herzogenbergs. Likewise, Heinrich's ever-deepening preoccupation with liturgical music made it more and more difficult for a skeptical Brahms to feign interest in his com-positions.[35] Brahms himself, however, did not address the issue directly until nearly a decade later, when Elisabeth was already suffering from what turned out to be terminal heart disease. In August 1891, Clara Schumann informed him that Elisabeth's prognosis had temporarily improved and speculated that the agitation aroused by her "dreadful ambition" might have exacerbated her symp-toms. In response to Clara's comment, Brahms provided a retrospective evalua-tion of his now-troubled friendship. He compared the Herzogenbergs to the composer Bernhard Scholz and his wife, Luise, and blamed his lack of contact

---

phase" in 1877 and 1878, a period of "cooling off and ambivalences" between 1879 and 1884, and a time of "crisis and change in the relationship" after 1885. She also provides statistical summaries of correspondence and face-to-face meetings (ibid., 184 and 317–21). Based in part on Ruhbaum's statistics, my own reading complements hers by pinpointing the years around 1882–83 as another pivotal moment in the relationship.

[33] Ibid., 78n.

[34] When Elisabeth was told, erroneously, that Brahms had visited Berlin in March 1886, she assumed he had deliberately neglected to inform her and refused to communicate with him for nearly a year (Ruhbaum, 191). Johannes Behr has documented Brahms's adoption of strategic silence as a means of deflecting ongoing conversations away from Heinrich's music in the 1880s and 1890s; see *Vom Ratgeber zum Kompositionslehrer*, 38–40.

[35] The potential disruptions caused by Hermine Spies receive pride of place in Ruhbaum's *Elisabeth von Herzogenberg*, 189–90, while the problems posed by Heinrich's later religious music take center stage in Behr's *Vom Ratgeber zum Kompositionslehrer* (38–39) and Wiechert's *Heinrich von Herzogenberg* (110–11).

with both couples on an increasingly jarring misalignment of music, gender, and social propriety:

> I'm delighted to hear that Frau von Herzogenberg is better; even indirectly I had found out nothing, and for myself I am growing accustomed to forgoing correspondence with them. Yes, ambition! With them it actually looks more and more like it does with the Scholzes. With both of them their otherwise so charming wives make communication impossible. Both wives are becoming ever more fanatical for their husbands' activities, and now even in many favorable situations one cannot speak to an artist about his work and perhaps dispute with him—when the wife listens—to say nothing of chiming in herself. I want to come to terms with the husbands alone and then so greatly enjoy the company of their wives![36]

When he wrote these words, Brahms was supremely confident in his once-precarious identity as independent bachelor. His letter to Clara underscored many of the values he had made his own in the final decades of his career, including a strong preference for one-on-one interaction with persons of either sex and a clear expectation of separate gender roles from even the most strong-willed and gifted of married women. Above all, he evinced a continued need for musical interaction in his friendships with fellow male professionals. Without the opportunity to exchange frank ideas about Heinrich's compositions, he implied, a meaningful relationship with either of the Herzogenbergs was impossible. Of course, Brahms's analysis told only part of the story, as Clara might have noticed when Elisabeth died in January 1892. Far from expanding after her death, Brahms's friendship with Heinrich and engagement with his music evaporated almost entirely, leaving behind mere sporadic contact and a scant thirteen letters in the final five years of their interaction. In hindsight, Elisabeth's diplomacy turns out to have been essential in maintaining even the fraught and flawed relationships that still existed among the three musicians in 1891. Nevertheless, Brahms's account illuminated a fundamental instability in his interchange with the Herzogenbergs during her lifetime. By forcing him to treat Heinrich's music seriously, Elisabeth's advocacy for her husband had laid essential groundwork for the kind of friendship Brahms craved, but that same advocacy then posed challenges of its own.

Ominous symptoms had already begun to appear in the early 1880s, before the Herzogenbergs moved to Berlin or Hermine Spies entered the picture. On July 27, 1882, Brahms forwarded the autograph of his String Quintet, Op. 88, to the Herzogenbergs for perusal and immediate return. Within days, Elisabeth

---

[36] Brahms/Schumann, *Briefe* 2:459–60. Here Berthold Litzmann's transcription replaced the Scholzes' name with an X, but the original text has recently come to light through the efforts of Michael Struck; see Behr, *Vom Ratgeber zum Kompositionslehrer*, 39 and 39n. Brahms had seen the Scholzes as recently as March 1890, by which point signs of strain in their relationship had already long been apparent to Clara herself; see Berthold Litzmann, *Clara Schumann: Ein Künstlerleben, nach Tagebüchern und Briefen* (Leipzig: Breitkopf & Härtel, 1923), 3:523.

could play the first movement of the still-unpublished piece from memory at the piano and had internalized the second movement as well. Having sent the manuscript back on August 2, she then followed it on August 6 with nine hundred words of commentary on the first two movements, complete with ten musical examples and detailed analyses of form and harmonic unfolding. Her critique was closely argued and overwhelmingly positive. Because she had recently injured her left thumb, however, the *Allegro energico* finale had proved too difficult for her to realize at the piano from score and in tempo. Rather than discuss the movement without having played it herself, she conveyed her husband's impressions instead:

> Heinz was amused that in structure and approach the movement has several similarities with his finale from the F-major Trio, which makes him very proud; not only the first theme but also the second, and how they intermingle, carry such traces as delighted my Heinz in the extreme.[37]

As if to jog Brahms's memory, she appended a musical excerpt comprising the initial thematic gesture from the finale of Heinrich's String Trio in F, Op. 27 No. 2.

Of course, Elisabeth was fully aware that Brahms already knew the Trio, having brought Heinrich's Op. 27 to his attention herself three years prior and received his favorable opinion of its artful "entanglement." Her thematic incipit was thus no mere mnemonic device. It also added urgency and specificity to the unspoken question raised by her husband's observations: How would Brahms respond to the implication that his own finale was related to Heinrich's? The question was freighted with interpersonal significance. Brahms had borrowed brief passages from Heinrich's music and implicitly discussed his compositional process in *O schöne Nacht*, but circumstances were qualitatively different now. The String Quintet was clearly a major work in the final stages of preparation for publication, not a private joke that relied on paratextual commentary in a presentation manuscript. Moreover, Brahms himself had not yet broached the possibility of musical borrowing in the Quintet. Perhaps most important, through his wife's letter Heinrich claimed to have identified not an isolated allusive gesture or two but a pervasive instance of compositional modeling involving multiple themes and their interaction across an entire movement. The fundamental originality of Brahms's latest opus for chamber ensemble was therefore at issue, quite apart from its rhetorical potential.

The stakes were especially high because Heinrich's claim was eminently plausible. To isolate the similarities that most likely stimulated his perception of a unique connection between the movements, one must first recognize that many shared features were actually broader generic hallmarks. In particular, both movements hearkened back to the same venerable tradition of fast, overtly

---

[37] Brahms/Herzogenberg, *Briefwechsel* 1:197–98.

contrapuntal finales in chamber works for unaccompanied strings.[38] The most prominent exponents of this tradition were the closing movements of Beethoven's C-major quartet, Op. 59 No. 3 (*Allegro molto*), and Mozart's G-major quartet, K. 387 (*Molto allegro*), inescapable repertoire well known to Brahms and Heinrich alike.[39] With these illustrious Viennese precursors, Brahms's *Allegro energico* and Heinrich's *Allegro vivace* shared an array of characteristics: close variants of the same headlong tempo and exuberant affect, unambiguous grounding in the major mode, large-scale trajectories that conform to the general expectations of sonata form, and, within the broad outlines of that form, primary thematic groups in which successive entries of each instrument invoke the unfolding of a fugal exposition. Other similarities between the two new finales could be traced back to one or another of their Classical predecessors. With Beethoven's Op. 59 No. 3, Brahms and Heinrich both shared a specific approach to sonata form in which the expositional repeat is omitted and commensurate weight thrown upon the development. With Mozart's K. 387, they both shared a special declaration of compositional craft: within the sonata-form exposition, the second theme is constructed such that it can be accompanied by the primary theme in invertible counterpoint.

Held in common across the decades, such features created a rich and stable backdrop against which new music might foreground its individual character and showcase its own motivic and contrapuntal innovations. It is all the more surprising, then, that so many of Brahms's most distinctive touches found clear antecedents in Heinrich's finale, and Heinrich's alone. Examples 4.4a, b, and c

---

[38]Warren Kirkendale's exhaustive *Fuge und Fugato in der Kammermusik des Rokoko und der Klassik* (Tutzing: Schneider, 1966) remains the indispensible compilation of examples of fugal and quasi-fugal procedure in chamber music of the eighteenth and nineteenth centuries.

[39]Beethoven's *Allegro molto* is frequently invoked in recent discussions of Brahms's finale; a typical instance occurs in Michael Musgrave, *The Music of Brahms* (London: Routledge & Kegan Paul, 1985), 202–3. Likewise, John Daverio has linked Brahms's Op. 88 to the broader tradition of fugal finales, including that of Mozart's K. 387, in his *Crossing Paths*, 172. Heinrich's familiarity with that tradition must be assumed given his training and temperament, but Brahms's can be more securely documented. He had actually arranged Beethoven's finale for solo piano and played it as a showpiece on at least four recitals in the 1860s and 1870s (Hofmann, *Brahms als Pianist und Dirigent*, 94, 96–98, and 157–58). Meanwhile, Mozart's finale was a fixture in contemporary evaluations of the composer, including Otto Jahn's definitive four-volume study of 1856–59, which Brahms, at least, had owned since the early 1860s. See Jahn, *W. A. Mozart*, vol. 4 (Leipzig: Breitkopf & Härtel, 1859): 88–89; Karl Geiringer, "Brahms as a Reader and Collector," *Musical Quarterly* 19 (1933): 161; and Musgrave, *Brahms Reader*, 155. By 1882, Brahms had already extolled the six "Haydn" quartets as pinnacles of their genre in correspondence with multiple friends. Pestered by an eager publisher for a new string quartet in June 1869, Brahms responded with a ringing endorsement of Mozart's famously slow and painstaking work in fashioning the "Haydn" quartets (Brahms, *Briefe an Simrock* 1:74–75). He also relied upon the finale from another of these quartets (K. 458) as a contrapuntal exemplar nearly a decade later, when confronted by accusations of illicit parallel fifths in his own compositions; see Brahms et al., *Johannes Brahms im Briefwechsel mit Philipp Spitta und Otto Dessoff*, ed. Carl Krebs, 199–200 (Berlin: Deutsche Brahms-Gesellschaft, 1920); and Notley, *Lateness and Brahms*, 129–31.

compare the primary contrapuntal subjects of both finales to that of Beethoven's *Allegro molto*. In its stepwise eighth notes and repeated three-note anacrusis, Brahms's subject evinced a generic similarity to Beethoven's. By contrast, its relationship to Heinrich's subject was far more specific. Linked by identical key signatures and registers, they also shared the same initial four pitches, the same unrelenting rhythmic profile, similar melodic contours, and analogous sentential structures (Heinrich's 2 + 2 + 4 became Brahms's 1 + 1 + 2). Brahms's subject certainly evoked Beethoven's, but it departed directly from Heinrich's model.

EXAMPLE 4.4a   Beethoven, String Quartet, Op. 59 No. 3 / IV, mm. 1–11

EXAMPLE 4.4b   Heinrich von Herzogenberg, String Trio, Op. 27 No. 2 / IV, mm. 1–8. Annotated.

EXAMPLE 4.4c   Brahms, String Quintet, Op. 88 / IV, mm. 1–5. Annotated.

The same was true of Brahms's second thematic group, as shown in examples 4.5a, b, and c; here, the relevant comparison is Mozart's *Molto allegro*. Angular leaps and irregular pauses marked the second themes of all three finales, but, just like his bustling primary theme, Brahms's lyrical second theme also shared nearly all of Heinrich's specific premises. Over a subdued alternation of dominant and tonic, the melody descended to scale degree 3 on the downbeat, then skipped up to scale degree 5 before articulating a larger ascending leap and corresponding descent; in turn, this basic gesture comprised the repeated initial phrase group in another sentential structure (again, 2 + 2 + 4 became 1 + 1 + 2). Meanwhile, like Mozart, Brahms juxtaposed the primary theme against the second theme as a countersubject, but, instead of first presenting the second theme in isolation, *forte*, he combined the two, *piano*, immediately upon the initiation of the second thematic group. The dynamics and formal placement of the counterpoint thus mimicked Heinrich's precisely, which was surely at least part of what the younger composer meant to emphasize by drawing Brahms's attention to the "intermingling" of the two themes.

EXAMPLE 4.5a   Mozart, String Quartet, K. 387 / IV, mm. 51–55 and 69–73

EXAMPLE 4.5b   Heinrich von Herzogenberg, String Trio, Op. 27 No. 2 / IV, mm. 64–73

EXAMPLE 4.5c   Brahms, String Quintet, Op. 88 / IV, mm. 34–38

As represented in his wife's letter, Heinrich's analysis was sensitive and convincing. His references to "traces" and "similarities" (as opposed to quotations or reminiscences) implied that Brahms had not simply borrowed passages of his music unchanged, as he had five years prior in *O schöne Nacht*. Instead, listeners familiar with Heinrich's Trio might easily have perceived the two themes in Brahms's Quintet as embodying a complex of related improvements on their models. For both themes the reconciliation with Brahms's $\frac{3}{4}$ meter entailed radically contracting the second measure in each of Heinrich's two-measure pairs; the result was a more concise and less foursquare version of the same basic phrase structure. Both of Brahms's themes replaced Heinrich's exact repetition of an initial two-measure gesture with a registrally expanded restatement, creating a more sharply etched profile in which three successive apexes traced out a single, coherent ascent across the phrase as a whole. In one respect, however, Brahms seems to have found Heinrich's original structure appealing enough to appropriate mostly intact. After a few measures of transitional material, the development section of Heinrich's finale began with a triplet-based transformation of the primary theme. The new version was derived from the original by strategically omitting some of its pitches, replacing its major scale with harmonic minor, and adding supplementary chromatic neighbors in later parts of the phrase. As shown in examples 4.6a and b, the beginning of Brahms's development duplicated every one of these procedures, including the precise omission of the second and seventh pitches from the theme's initial gesture. Having generated contrasting material in the same way, the two composers then put it to identical uses. After presenting two complete, *piano* iterations of the triplet-based theme (eight measures each for Heinrich, four each for Brahms), both subjected it to sequential elaboration during a gradual crescendo to *forte* (seventeen measures for Heinrich and, for Brahms, the closest proportional equivalent, or nine measures). At this point, both developments retained the minor mode but returned to the original, eighth-note version of the primary theme, setting it against itself in strict counterpoint (inversion for Heinrich, stretto for Brahms) while hurtling toward the retransitional dominant.

EXAMPLE 4.6a   Heinrich von Herzogenberg, String Trio, Op. 27 No. 2 / IV, mm. 124–28

EXAMPLE 4.6b   Brahms, String Quintet, Op. 88 / IV, mm. 63–65.

In combination with the thematic and contrapuntal resemblances to which the Herzogenbergs explicitly drew his attention, the motivic content and underlying structure of Brahms's development left little doubt that he had modeled at least some aspects of his Op. 88 finale exclusively and deliberately on the corresponding movement from Heinrich's Trio. At the very least, Heinrich's measured observations deserved to be taken seriously. Instead, in his next letter to Elisabeth, Brahms dismissed the possibility of an intentional connection out of hand with a single, sharply worded phrase all the more striking for its appearance in the midst of an otherwise friendly note:

> It really is too bad that I must write just now, when I really can't do it. I would so gladly have thanked you comfortably for your dear letter. So please simply believe that it really is a most agreeable and *necessary* pleasure to hear a truly cordially agreeable word about a new piece. Thus I owe the nicest thanks to you this time and to your Heinz, since he also inspected the last third [i.e., the finale]. So not merely on purpose, but also accidentally I am copying him!?[40]

Brahms's unease was suddenly palpable. His verb, *nachschreiben*, carried connotations of verbatim dictation, the menial work of children and maidservants in an epistolary age. In one stroke, he rejected Heinrich's claims and misconstrued them in such a way as to preclude further discussion.

Brahms's response has cast a long shadow over later commentaries on his letter, all of which have followed his lead and swiftly rejected any purposeful relationship between the two finales.[41] In the face of substantial music-analytic evidence, his denial seems likely to have been at least partly disingenuous, but its vehemence still demands interpretation. On the one hand, the Herzogenbergs might have inadvertently uncovered a genuine and embarrassingly derivative component of his mature compositional process. After all, it was Brahms who had first referred to the intertwining of musical material in Heinrich's "charmingly entangled" Trios. Perhaps his editorial eye had also discovered in Heinrich's counterpoint a surreptitious means of generating motivic and structural paradigms for his own work in progress. On the other hand, Heinrich may have noticed precisely what he was meant to notice but failed to grasp its intended implications. Brahms's finale might actually have been conceived as a private lesson along the lines of *Es liebt sich so lieblich im Lenze*, its subtler improvements designed for apprehension by a professional composer rather than a dilettante. If he had sent along the score in order to provide an intimate glimpse of the larger potential inherent in Heinrich's themes and formal patterning, Brahms might well have resented it when carefully constructed criticism was instead received as a simple compliment. In either case, Elisabeth's role as de facto intermediary surely contributed to the frustration that boiled over in Brahms's response. Her explicit investment in her husband's position left little room to maneuver. One could not address the issue without involving them both in the conversation. How to avoid Elisabeth becoming defensive on Heinrich's behalf, as she had on previous occasions? And if Heinrich had shared his theory with her, who else might hear of it soon?

---

[40] Brahms/Herzogenberg, *Briefwechsel* 1:199. Emphasis original.
[41] Examples span from Kalbeck's explanatory footnotes in the first edition of the Herzogenberg correspondence (ibid., 198n) to Wiechert's 1997 monograph on Heinrich's life and works (*Heinrich von Herzogenberg*, 108).

From Brahms's perspective in August 1882, an immediate end to the discussion probably seemed the best way of extricating himself from a potential minefield, especially if Heinrich's surmise contained a grain of truth. From either of the Herzogenbergs' perspectives, however, Brahms's preemptory denial must have been a disappointment on several levels. First, it bespoke a lack of trust. As aspiring friends of an artist both famous and famously private, they had taken pains to cultivate Brahms's confidence in their discretion throughout the initial years of their acquaintance. Despite the risks to Heinrich's career, they had shared their private and often critical opinions of mutual acquaintances and powerful musicians alike; Joseph Joachim, for one, would hardly have hired Heinrich at the Berlin conservatory in 1885 had he known that Elisabeth had dubbed him self-important and presumptuous in 1878. Yet now, given the chance to reciprocate in kind by acknowledging their unique and potentially compromising insight into his creative process, Brahms pointedly withdrew. His response to Heinrich's claims also suggested a continued lack of respect for his younger colleague's skill as an analyst and composer. Not only did he mischaracterize a delicate assertion of influence as a blatant accusation of plagiarism; his sarcasm also once again relegated Heinrich's music to an inherently inferior status. The Herzogenbergs had long known that Brahms thought highly of the Op. 27 String Trios, but now it turned out that even Heinrich's best efforts did not deserve a place in the tradition within which Brahms sought to situate his own works. Fodder for unpublished jokes like *O schöne Nacht*, Heinrich's music was apparently only worth appropriating in private, never in public. In short, when push came to shove and his own creative process was in question, Brahms had proven fundamentally self-interested, a taker of musical confidences rather than a giver.

The effects of the failed discussion concerning Op. 88 remain difficult to gauge from correspondence alone. Nevertheless, the episode coincided directly with the beginning of the lasting setback in Brahms's relationship with the Herzogenbergs. Elisabeth responded to his letter within a month, but her reply does not survive. The composer responded in turn with a short, undated note sometime between September 1 and September 8, 1882. His light, businesslike tone hints that Elisabeth had elected not to pursue serious matters in her own letter; instead, she seems to have simply requested the parts for Op. 88 on behalf of a friend, which Brahms explained could not occur given his copyist's schedule.[42] If any grievances were hashed out, the more likely venue was a face-to-face conversation in late September. The three musicians met in Venice sometime after September 17, along with Theodor Billroth, Alfred and Henriette Volkland, and Clara

---

[42] Brahms/Herzogenberg, *Briefwechsel* 2:1.

and Eugenie Schumann, for a long-planned rendezvous.[43] Presuming they could find opportunities for private discussion amid a crowd of mutual acquaintances, this shared vacation represented their only chance to address Brahms's String Quintet in person while the matter was still fresh in their minds. Relations deteriorated significantly soon after. No evidence suggests that Elisabeth renewed her correspondence with Brahms for at least six months. For his part, in another letter that is now lost, Heinrich invited Brahms to take part in a performance scheduled for January 1883, but Brahms turned him down. For the first time since their friendship had blossomed in 1876, there would be no January sojourn in Leipzig. Instead, Brahms seems to have visited briefly in mid-February as a side trip from professional engagements in nearby Meiningen.[44] And after that, the Herzogenbergs would meet him only five more times in their lives.

If Brahms's Op. 88 indeed played a role in the long-term cooling of the relationship, his next project likely made matters even worse. While drafting the String Quintet in late spring of 1882, Brahms had also cobbled together an initial version of his C-major Piano Trio, Op. 87, adding a new slow movement, scherzo, and finale to a preexisting first movement, which had lain dormant since 1880. He shared the results with Theodor Billroth and Clara Schumann in July 1882 just as he sent the score of Op. 88 to the Herzogenbergs, and arranged for a trial performance of the two new works in late August, shortly after responding to Heinrich's claims of influence in the Quintet. He then edited the Trio over the ensuing weeks and, having put it and the Quintet through a second test run on October 19, sent them both to his publisher two days later.[45] During their September rendezvous with Brahms in Venice, then, Heinrich and Elisabeth could have encountered an intermediate version of the Trio or at least heard the piece discussed, since three of the assembled party had already examined the score. Hard evidence of their exposure does not survive, however,

---

[43] For evidence as to the timing and cast of characters involved, see Ruhbaum, *Elisabeth von Herzogenberg*, 320. In vicarious tandem with Brahms, Elisabeth had been working on written excercises designed to improve her Italian since mid-July at the latest, before the autograph of Op. 88 arrived to complicate things (Brahms/Herzogenberg, *Briefwechsel* 1:190, 197).

[44] Brahms/Herzogenberg, *Briefwechsel* 2:1–2 and Brahms/Schumann, *Briefe* 2: 266–67. Here, in a letter dated March 26, 1883, Clara Schumann mentioned having heard from the Herzogenbergs that Brahms had visited them "recently." No record of such a visit survives in other correspondence, which may explain why the episode finds no mention in Kurt and Renate Hofmann's *Zeittafel* or Ruhbaum's otherwise reliable summary of meetings between Brahms and the Herzogenbergs (*Elisabeth von Herzogenberg*, 317). The only geographically feasible opportunity for a visit would have been during the week that Brahms spent in Meiningen between February 12 and February 19; since he was engaged in preparations for a soiree on February 16, any trip to Leipzig must have been short indeed (see Hofmann, *Zeittafel*, 172–74).

[45] McCorkle, *Werkverzeichnis*, 361–62, and Hofmann, *Brahms als Pianist und Dirigent*, 213–14. Evidence of Brahms's extensive editing is preserved in the manuscript of Op. 87, which has been available in facsimile since 1983 in George Bozarth, ed., *Johannes Brahms Autographs: Facsimiles of Eight Manuscripts in the Library of Congress* (New York: Garland, 1983).

until December 1882, when the published work was released in Berlin. In any case, confronted by the Trio mere months after the Quintet, the Herzogenbergs might easily have construed a second borrowing from Heinrich's oeuvre as yet another covert—and infuriatingly deniable—composition lesson. This time, in fact, Brahms's music hearkened back directly to the core of their very first exchange with him in August 1876.

The slow movement of Op. 87 was a variation-form movement labeled *Andante con moto*. Brahms's theme was remarkable in several ways. Comprising twenty-seven measures with no internal repetitions, it was the longest and weightiest theme he had yet composed for a variation movement.[46] Of his original variation themes to date, it was also the most evocative of musics from the periphery of the central Austro-German concert repertoire. A wide range of contemporaneous audiences immediately discerned an exotic flavor in the theme's angular melody, which featured repeated scotch snaps and uniquely declamatory scoring for *forte* violin and cello two octaves apart. In February 1883, the first British review of the piece located the theme's appeal in a combination of tune and texture:

> The second movement...has the form of an air with variations, the theme being distinctly Hungarian in character. It is most ingeniously treated, even at the outset, where the subject is announced in octaves by the strings, while the pianoforte accompanies with full syncopated chords in both hands. The effect is striking and charming—none the less because of the strange beauty distinguishing the melody.[47]

Scholars beginning with Kalbeck have largely followed this anonymous Englishman in emphasizing the theme's exoticist potential as a register for "Hungarian," "gypsy," or otherwise identifiably foreign undertones.[48] By comparison, Clara Schumann had approached similar music-analytic evidence from a related

---

[46] If one includes internal repetitions as part of a theme's length, Brahms had borrowed far longer themes from Schumann in the four-hand *Variations*, Op. 23, and Haydn (or so he thought) in the *Variations for Orchestra*, Op. 56; these themes comprise forty and fifty-eight measures, respectively. He had also composed a longer theme himself in the slow movement of his String Sextet, Op. 18, but that thirty-two-measure theme contained only sixteen measures of new material, with reorchestrated repetitions of each eight-measure phrase accounting for the rest.

[47] Anonymous, "Reviews," *Musical Times* 24 (February 1, 1883): 92.

[48] Kalbeck flatly proclaimed the theme a "Hungarian gypsy song" (*Brahms* 3:354). Among many others, Daverio and Musgrave have both followed Kalbeck in aligning the movement with other works in which Brahms deliberately evoked the *style hongroise* (*Crossing Paths*, 212–13 and *Music of Brahms*, 199). The most detailed analysis of exoticist elements in Brahms's theme and, indeed, the most extensive account of the entire movement in recent literature occurs in Littlewood's *The Variations of Johannes Brahms*, which interprets the large-scale trajectory of both the theme and the ensuing variations as a gradual "neutering" of gypsy-derived elements in favor of an assimilative, "gentrified" style (see 169–85). Finally, Siegfried Oechsle has recently advocated a broader approach to cultural and national identity in the Op. 87 slow movement, drawing on Scottish, Scandanavian, and even Ossianic precedents for its musical characteristics; see "Klaviertrios, Klavierquartette, Klavierquintett," in *Brahms Handbuch*, 412–13.

but subtly different standpoint when she encountered the score for the first time in late July 1882: "How attractive is the Scherzo, then the Andante with the charming theme, which must sound peculiar in the register of the doubled octaves, entirely folk-like [*volkstümlich*]."[49] For Clara, the theme's strangeness resounded less across geographical and cultural boundaries and more along an implied continuum of tradition and training. Her comments opened up the broader possibility of aligning Brahms's rough-edged rhythms and strident unisons with his abiding interest in folk music of all sorts.

In turn, for the Herzogenbergs, Brahms's artfully vernacular theme could easily have recalled a specific, rhetorically charged precedent. Beneath a boldly assertive veneer lay the understated melodic and harmonic outlines of *Die Trauernde* as Heinrich had transcribed them in his *Variations on a Theme of Johannes Brahms*. Examples 4.7a and b compare Heinrich's transcription to the first sixteen measures of Brahms's new slow movement. The old tune reappeared at pitch in mm. 1–8, its scale-degree content duplicated almost precisely despite radically altered meter and barlines. Every change in melodic contour lent itself to interpretation as a purposeful adaptation of preexisting material. The reordered dyads in mm. 1 and 3 coincided exactly with the introduction of the scotch snaps that gave the *Andante con moto* its distinct identity and most vivid associations in the public ear. The added a″ on the downbeat of m. 5 clarified the periodic organization of the song, which had also survived intact: the Trio presented direct analogues for the half cadence in m. 4 and the authentic cadence in m. 8 (both embellished using familiar 4–3 suspensions), as well as the brief excursion toward the relative major via its subdominant in m. 6 (now further compressed into the cadential gesture in mm. 7–8).

Meanwhile, essential features of Brahms's theme found antecedents not in the song itself, but in the changes that Heinrich had imposed when transcribing *Die Trauernde* for four-hand piano. The textural expansion of the song provided a straightforward model for the wide registral profile and strict octave doubling that so impressed contemporary audiences of Brahms's *Andante con moto*. Moreover, like Heinrich, Brahms avoided repeating the *Stollen* in favor of an immediate, eight-measure continuation based on the *Abgesang*. Here as in the original song, four measures of harmonic contrast in a narrower, densely packed register preceded a four-measure reprise of material from the *Stollen*. As in Heinrich's version, however, the melody anticipated the return to its upper tessitura and descended via slurred half step onto the downbeat of the reprise at m. 13, securely binding the two four-measure sections into a single larger gesture.

---

[49] Brahms/Schumann, *Briefe* 2:258. Clara's letter reveals that, as of July 1882, Brahms intended his slow movement to be performed after the *Scherzo*. His autograph preserves evidence of at least two changes of heart concerning the order of Op. 87's internal movements before the published version definitively placed the *Andante con moto* first.

EXAMPLE 4.7a   Heinrich von Herzogenberg, *Variations on a Theme of Johannes Brahms,*
Op. 23, mm. 1–18

EXAMPLE 4.7b   Brahms, Piano Trio, Op. 87 / II, mm. 1–16

Brahms could have ended his theme here simply by duplicating the cadence
from m. 8. For an informed listener, such a direct structural parallel between the
Trio and its two antecedents might presumably have implied an evenhanded
compositional exchange in which once-borrowed music returned to its creator,

enriched but fundamentally unchanged by its journey through another's mind. Instead, having established the possibility of balanced closure, Brahms wrenched the continuation open once more and expanded it to nineteen measures, drastically beyond the boundaries implied by either of its models. The result appears in example 4.8. Rising harmonic and melodic sequences generated a new and intensified climax in mm. 20–24, whereupon the very fabric of the theme began to unravel. Beginning in m. 21, the scotch snap vanished in favor of the slurred dotted eighth with sixteenth—its mellower retrograde—which permeated every remaining measure save the last. At the same moment, the stolid eighths and quarters that had dominated the melodic line gave way to flowing sixteenth notes. The sense of dissolution then redoubled in mm. 24–27. What seemed a culminating point of arrival on the downbeat of m. 24 was undermined at the last instant by an unexpected elision, and the theme's expressive apex collapsed into its own negative afterimage. The unison string texture faltered, dynamic levels quickly receded to *piano* for the first time in the piece, and both melody and bass line presented diatonic inversions of their climatic passages. The strings ascended to scale degree 5, a minor plagal cadence gave way at the last moment to a hazy parallel major, and the theme dissipated without really concluding, poised in uncertainty.

EXAMPLE 4.8   Brahms, Piano Trio, Op. 87 / II, mm. 15–27

This wide-ranging profile has elicited a variety of responses over the decades. Some commentators have identified the theme's extreme mutability as yet another manifestation of an impassioned exotic. Others have heard the contrapuntal complexity of its final measures as a gesture of assimilation whereby vernacular elements are systematically domesticated within the confines of art music.[50] More abstract interpretations might have resonated as well in the 1880s, particularly among listeners associated with the Leipzig conservatory, where the harmonic dualism of Moritz Hauptmann still exerted a strong influence more than a decade after his death. To ears attuned to Hauptmann's theories, the conjunction of modal mixture with pitch inversion and rhythmic retrograde may well have suggested an ambitious and unorthodox exploration of musical mirroring across multiple parameters, making the theme's end an erudite climax rather than a halting retreat. Although Brahms's own interactions with Hauptmann were minimal and unsatisfactory, many of his oldest friends and closest professional collaborators had studied with the theorist in the 1850s and 1860s, including Joseph Joachim, Julius Otto Grimm, Albert Dietrich, Otto Dessoff, and, at Dessoff's suggestion, Heinrich von Herzogenberg himself. In his own publications on harmony, Heinrich would later proclaim himself indebted to Hauptmann's ideas, which he had probably received from multiple sources over the years; he and Elisabeth had long since befriended Moritz's daughter, Helene, during their time in Leipzig.[51] In short, Heinrich's training and temperament left him well attuned to the more cerebral attractions of Brahms's theme.

But for the composer of ten variations on *Die Trauernde*, the scope and character of Brahms's new theme posed more than academic challenges. Within its suddenly enlarged boundaries, the theme itself enacted a process analogous to Heinrich's most "fantastic" variations, treating borrowed material as a melodic and contrapuntal point of departure rather than a structural determinant. Heard against the precedent set by Heinrich's Op. 23, Brahms's drastic phrase extension could easily have come to represent an aggressive reappropriation of his own music and, simultaneously, the first step in an uncompromising pedagogical demonstration. Expanding the theme and broadening its affective palette via techniques characteristic of Heinrich's variations paradoxically increased its

---

[50] For examples of these opposed approaches, see Musgrave, *Music of Brahms*, 199, and Littlewood, *Variations of Johannes Brahms*, 177–78.

[51] In conversation with Georg Henschel in 1876, Brahms described an 1853 encounter with Hauptmann in which the latter criticized his C-major piano sonata, Op. 1; this seems to have been the only time they met. For a compendium of Henschel's various accounts of the exchange, see George Bozarth, *Johannes Brahms and George Henschel: An Enduring Friendship* (Sterling Heights, MI: Harmonie Park Press, 2008), 41 and 263. For evidence as to Heinrich's early studies with Moritz Hauptmann and his later attachment to both Helene Hauptmann and her mother, Susette, see Wiechert, *Heinrich von Herzogenberg*, 21 and 91; and Brahms/Herzogenberg, *Briefwechsel* 1:xxviii–xxix and 2:265 and 272–73. Heinrich's main published work on harmony was a weighty essay, "Tonalität," *Vierteljahrsschrift für Musikwissenschaft* 6 (1890): 553–82; here he cited Hauptmann repeatedly and reverently (see especially 555, 569, and 582).

potential as the basis for a tutorial in Brahmsian approaches to variation form. Facilitated by a more diverse theme, the five variations in Brahms's *Andante con moto* explore nearly every texture and figuration familiar from Heinrich's far longer set. Their overarching trajectory is partially analogous as well: in each piece, the third variation begins and ends brashly *forte*, while the final variation closes quietly in a contrasting meter. Like *Es liebt sich so lieblich im Lenze*, then, Brahms's slow movement established a loose skeleton of resemblances with a preexisting model, encouraging informed listeners to interpret differences as deliberate suggestions for improvement.

Some of these implied suggestions would probably have been obvious to the Herzogenbergs, perhaps frustratingly so. After all, they knew Heinrich's piece intimately and had long since received some indications as to Brahms's opinion of it. They could easily recall, for instance, the melody-turned-bass-line that had proclaimed Heinrich's contrapuntal aspirations from the beginning of his first variation. Brahms, too, transposed part of his theme's tune into a bass line, as shown in example 4.9. However, he enhanced the effect in new and powerful ways by doubling the tune with its own contour inversion in the piano's right hand and simultaneously reversing the accustomed roles of string instruments and piano. He also delayed the pivotal moment until the beginning of the third variation, literally halfway through the movement; Clara Schumann would surely have approved. On a larger scale, once the theme itself was established, the remainder of the movement presented one of the "strictest" variation sets of Brahms's career. As displayed in table 4.3, tempo and phrase structure remained completely invariant until the end of the final variation. The mode flickered toward the parallel major in Variation 4 and back again to minor in Variation 5, but the tonal center never shifted; meanwhile, beginning in Variation 4, $\frac{6}{8}$ surreptitiously replaced $\frac{2}{4}$ without changing the larger pulse or disrupting the alternation of upbeat and downbeat. Here was blatant confirmation of Brahms's mature stance regarding "fantastic" variations, in case Heinrich had somehow missed the point in 1876 and again in 1878.

EXAMPLE 4.9   Brahms, Piano Trio, Op. 87 / II, mm. 82–85

TABLE 4.3   Shifting Parameters in Brahms's Piano Trio, Op. 87 / II

	Key	Meter	Tempo	Phrase Structure (durations in notated measures)
Theme	i	$\frac{2}{4}$	*Andante con moto*	8; 19
Variation 1				
Variation 2				
Variation 3				
Variation 4	I	$\frac{6}{8}$		
Variation 5 / Coda	i		*In Tempo,* then *più tranquillo poco a poco*	8; 27

Subtler but equally important improvements established mutually dependent relationships among the theme, the character of individual variations, and the overarching trajectory of the movement. Like many works in variation form, Heinrich's Op. 23 had treated its borrowed theme as a fairly neutral vessel for variation techniques whose ordered succession defined the larger shape of the set. This is hardly surprising since Heinrich seems to have intended the number, order, and structure of his variations to evoke preexisting works by Brahms that were based upon completely different themes. On its own, for instance, *Die Trauernde* provided no hint of his overtly contrapuntal ambitions, and the quiet dynamics that accompanied each of his major-mode variations actually cut against the grain of the song, which had consistently associated the parallel major with its only crescendos. Many of Heinrich's most striking compositional decisions therefore remained fundamentally external to the theme itself. By contrast, Brahms's expanded theme anticipated virtually the full repertoire of compositional parameters and affective associations that went on to define his slow movement as a whole. The combined motivic processes of inversion and fragmentation that first appeared in m. 24 returned, applied to new melodic material, at analogous points in every variation.

Most remarkably, the theme's conspicuously truncated narrative found both an echo and an answer in the large-scale progression of all the variations put together. Variation 1 employed reduced textures or *piano* dynamics for all but a few of its measures. Thereafter, a gradual increase in textural density and expressive intensity in Variation 2 mirrored the sequential buildup to the theme's climax. Like that climax, Variation 3 remained a full-throated *forte* throughout, reintroducing the scotch snap and eschewing the diminuendos that marked the final measures of every other variation. Variation 4 then revived unmistakable characteristics of the theme's suddenly ambiguous close—minimal dynamics, a shift toward the parallel major, and a softened rhythmic profile embodied in the metric shift from $\frac{2}{4}$ to $\frac{6}{8}$—but now those characteristics were prolonged across an entire variation. By fashioning an extended and delicately beautiful landscape from emblems of dissolution, Variation 4 reopened and intensified the conflict in affective identity that had first surfaced at the end of the theme. Brahms's fifth and final variation ultimately resolved the conflict. As shown in example 4.10, the lilting $^6_8$ and subdued dynamics of Variation 4 remained in place, but its modal mixture, chromatic saturation, and disjunct melodies receded in favor of the minor mode, folksy diatonicism, and stepwise melodic contour familiar from the theme itself. For the first time, long-breathed cantilenas in the strings and unobtrusively accompanimental arpeggios in the piano evoked the movement's prehistory in vocal music. Never had the borrowed outlines of *Die Trauernde* sounded so at home in their new context. As in every other variation, inversional complexity and modal mixture clouded the waters near the end, but at last an alternative intervened in the form of an elided coda shown in example 4.11. Here a strict canon in inversion gradually dissolved into the sweet parallel sixths of a lyrical duet just as the movement approached its first and only perfect authentic cadence in the minor tonic.

Heard in affective terms, Variation 5 and its coda completed a transformation left doubly unfinished by the theme and by the intervening variations. Alternating defiance and uncertainty had finally given way to calm self-assurance. Put more abstractly, Brahms had constructed a theme marked by internal contradictions, refracted those contradictions across the topography of four variations, and resolved them at the last possible moment. Such intricate coordination of multiple time-scales was extraordinary even by the standards of Brahms's own oeuvre to date. His *Andante con moto* was clearly an important essay designed to explore the outer limits of cohesion in variation form— which must have made it all the more galling for the Herzogenbergs when they encountered the movement in the autumn of 1882, still smarting from the rejection of Heinrich's cautious claims of influence in the String Quintet. After all, the expressive potential of Brahms's theme was predicated on a dramatized rejection of the short binary that Heinrich had selected and refined

EXAMPLE 4.10   Brahms, Piano Trio, Op. 87 / II, mm. 136–39

EXAMPLE 4.11   Brahms, Piano Trio, Op. 87 / II, mm. 164–70

for his own *Variations* six years prior, just as the tightknit fabric of the entire movement depended upon strict variation techniques directly at odds with Heinrich's own. "A little more creativity at the outset, a firmer grasp of large-scale form," the Trio seems to hint, "and look what can be accomplished with your material."

Considering his history of fraught compositional interchange with the Herzogenbergs and the prominent role that variation form had played in their exchanges from the very beginning, it is unlikely that Brahms could select and manipulate a model in such rhetorically potent ways without having in mind at least a plausible idea as to how the result might be received. If he was at all conscious of his borrowings in Op. 87, he must have known he was skirting dangerous territory. Yet he had drafted the slow movement of the Trio in the spring of 1882, months before the troubled conversation about the finale of the Op. 88 String Quintet had reopened latent questions regarding his attitude toward Heinrich's music. Perhaps he had simply overestimated the Herzogenbergs' tolerance for constructive criticism. Or perhaps he had misjudged his own abilities as a concealer of musical borrowing and had never meant the sources for either movement to be recognized at all in their new guise. But given what had since transpired with Op. 88, Brahms's original intentions for Op. 87 may not have mattered at all once the piece was published in December 1882. Among an audience of wounded friends already predisposed to question his compositional motivations, the implications of the *Andante con moto* could well have spun completely out of his control.

––––––––––––

No direct evidence survives as to the Herzogenbergs' impressions of Brahms's slow movement, but the Trio as a whole certainly found a chilly reception with them. Neither husband nor wife ever mentioned the piece in extant correspondence with Brahms. The omission was telling in and of itself because, in the years since their friendship had blossomed in 1876, literally every opus Brahms released had come up at least once in their letters to him. Moreover, in contrast to their usual practice at the time, both of them soon criticized Op. 87 in exchanges with third parties. In February 1883, Clara Schumann requested Elisabeth's advice as she selected repertoire for a chamber recital in Leipzig the following month. Clara had sought in vain to perform Brahms's latest piano Trio at an earlier venue, so Elisabeth included it among a number of possible programs for the Leipzig concert. Then, in an artfully winding paragraph worthy of her father's statecraft, she managed to subtly undermine the piece while enhancing her own dual position as a staunch advocate for its composer and ardent admirer of its performer:

> From the Röntgens we know that you proposed the new *Brahms* Trio and he declined it, the old fussbudget; it would please me if you were to return to it, although I don't believe that precisely this work will increase his band of friends in this place, but because I would not like to begrudge it to *Brahms*, who was intentionally treated disdainfully here this year, and because, if it does not find its way here under your name, it will never have a turn. (Besides you no one has ever played the G-major sonata here.) I only fear that with this piece, which would require more frequent rehearsals than a Beethoven or Schumann, you would strain yourself.[52]

More than three years later, Elisabeth offered Clara a specific musical reason for her opposition to the Trio. A letter from November 1886 compared Brahms's Op. 87 to his second Cello Sonata, Op. 99, and took both works to task for their lack of originality when compared to his earlier efforts in the same genres: "Brahms has already created a similar thing more meaningfully. In general we cannot resist feeling as if in [the cello sonata], as we perceive in the C major Trio, the *invention* is not exactly the strongest."[53] Elisabeth provided no specific examples of what she had in mind.[54] Still, her formulation could have carried

––––––––––––

[52] Elisabeth von Herzogenberg to Clara Schumann, February 28, 1883; cited in Ruhbaum, *Elisabeth von Herzogenberg*, 230–31. Emphases original. The "G-major sonata" was Brahms's first violin sonata, Op. 78.
[53] Elisabeth von Herzogenberg to Clara Schumann, November 17, 1886; cited in Ruhbaum, *Elisabeth von Herzogenberg*, 234. Emphasis original.
[54] One wonders if she knew that the *Adagio* of Op. 99, too, probably hearkened back to preexisting material (in this case, a discarded slow movement from the composer's first cello sonata, Op. 38). For details

special weight for listeners who understood the slow movement of Op. 87 to be based upon borrowed music.

The plural pronouns in Elisabeth's 1886 letter suggested that her husband shared related concerns regarding the Trio. For once, in fact, he was the more aggressive of the pair in articulating those concerns. Immediately upon the work's release, Heinrich had described his reactions in a remarkable letter to Philipp Spitta, a close confidant and soon-to-be colleague in Berlin:

> An entirely new style—recent Brahms! I suddenly understood why it has always bothered me when people railed against old folks who love the Eroica but not the late quartets!...The first movement of the C minor Symphony also brought enough newness; but there, however, how the approach adjusted itself to the ideas! And now the Trio! It lies next to me, and I cannot bring myself to open it again, it pained me so much as a whole (especially the first and fourth movements)! You can imagine into what confusion it throws the emotions of a composer colleague whose Pythia begins to speak Chinese![55]

This was the first time Heinrich had written negatively of Brahms's works in correspondence with Spitta, who, after all, was a mutual acquaintance of Brahms himself.[56] He couched his objections in strident but general stylistic terms and confined to parentheses the identification of the movements that had supposedly provoked him most. Nevertheless, the implied disjunction between "ideas" and "approach" in the Trio anticipated Elisabeth's indictment of the work's originality and resonated in sympathy with the perception of musical borrowing in its slow movement. Above all, Heinrich's decision to criticize the Trio in the first place hinted at a new and deliberately cultivated detachment in his broader stance toward Brahms, whom he presented as a reliable oracle suddenly turned inscrutable. A relationship hitherto characterized by one-sided devotion had been destabilized, perhaps by the very compositional interchange that had once helped to maintain its peculiar equilibrium.

For both of the Herzogenbergs, the ensuing disillusionment would prove irrevocable. Yet as contact with Brahms dwindled over the coming years, the memory of their short-lived intimacy remained a cherished ideal for Heinrich, particularly in times of stress and sadness. Elisabeth clearly perceived this and sought many times to broker short-term musical reunions with Brahms, most urgently during her husband's two-year struggle with acute rheumatoid arthritis in 1887–88. In turn, her own terminal illness provided the backdrop for one of Heinrich's most revealing assessments of his interactions with Brahms.

---

concerning this purported instance of self-borrowing, see Margaret Notley, "Brahms's Cello Sonata in F Major and Its Genesis: A Study in Half-Step Relations," in *Brahms Studies 1*, 139–40 and 148–52.

[55] Heinrich von Herzogenberg to Philipp Spitta, December 17, 1882; cited in Wiechert, *Heinrich von Herzogenberg*, 112.

[56] Ibid, 111–12.

In late December 1891, Elisabeth and her mother both lay dying, and Heinrich was splitting his hours between their bedsides, comforting each by concealing the other's condition. It is telling that at such an hour his old friend Spitta would write a letter conveying an enthusiastic description of Brahms's latest opuses, the Clarinet Trio and Quintet, Opp. 114 and 115. Heinrich clung to Spitta's favorable report as to a lifeline, a precious link to a former identity untouched by the ravages of disease:

> What you write to me about the two pieces by Brahms has truly edified me! After the latest volumes (from Peters) I had nothing good to say about him: always gypsies; I also could not see much in the canons, most of which we have already known for a long time, and certainly could not understand their ceremonious publication. I want so much to believe in Brahms still further despite many a disappointment in recent years; if I was displeased with him, that made me completely miserable! I can say that my relationship to his music is for me a vital question [*eine Lebensfrage*].[57]

"I want so much to believe in Brahms. . . ." Understood in the larger context of a musical and interpersonal dynamic that had long since stagnated, the penultimate sentence could apply to Brahms's compositions or, no less poignantly, to the man who wrote them. By the end, of course, with Brahms withdrawn and out of touch, only the music itself remained a vital question for Heinrich; only in tones could he seek an alternate source of selfhood *in extremis*. But within the remembered bonds of a friendship forged, for good and ill, around musical interchange, Brahms himself would always bear the imprint of his compositions.

---

[57] Heinrich von Herzogenberg to Philipp Spitta, December 27, 1891; cited in ibid., 113. The two volumes that Heinrich disparaged here were the six accompanied vocal quartets, Op. 112, and the thirteen canons, Op. 113.

PART III

CLARA AT THE KEYBOARD

CHAPTER FIVE

FAMILY RESEMBLANCES

Against the backdrop of Heinrich von Herzogenberg's Op. 23 *Variations* and the discussions that they had provoked over the years, Brahms's compositional choices in his String Quintet and Piano Trio resonate in specific and highly provocative ways. In combination, they suggest that he possessed a detailed awareness of how his music might have been received, and they hint at a plausible nexus of socially mediated motivations for his actions. Compared to his three occasional lullabies, most of the pieces associated with the Herzogenbergs therefore elicit a complementary method of exploring Brahms's allusive intentions. Rather than working outward from primary documents that purport to describe those intentions explicitly, one can spiral inward from broader contextual and music-analytic data.

The case studies in part three each fall somewhere between the two methodological extremes. Together, they consider the composer's long and tangled relationship with the Schumann family and, in particular, with Clara Schumann. Brahms's most important friendship began during Robert Schumann's breakdown and final decline, amid a profusion of impulses romantic and otherwise. Once the possibility of romantic attachment was rejected in the aftermath of Robert's death, periods of friction and readjustment were bound to occur with some frequency, especially between two strong-willed professionals with contrasting personalities. Small wonder, then, that scholars attempting to relate Brahms's music to his relationship with Clara have focused almost exclusively on moments of interpersonal tension. From the Op. 8 piano trio and Op. 9 Schumann Variations in the 1850s and the Alto Rhapsody and Alphorn greeting in the 1860s to the late piano pieces in the 1890s, Clara has cut a swath of conflict and crisis across the analysis of her friend's works. But there were also prolonged periods of rest and reconstruction in their relationship. In particular, the ten years beginning in 1870 provide manifold opportunities to explore the everyday functions of musical interchange in maintaining a deep and complex friendship in the face of geographical separation and the passage of time. A point of entry into this quiet but essential decade is *Meine Liebe ist grün* (My Love is Green), Op. 63 No. 5, one of Brahms's best-known and most frequently performed songs.

The earliest securely datable record of *Meine Liebe ist grün* is a letter that Brahms mailed to Clara Schumann, along with an autograph of the song itself, on December 24, 1873. The letter was short and to the point:

> Dear Cl., these verses just fell into my hands and head this morning, perhaps because I was annoyed with myself for never being able to think of or provide for a holiday. It can probably be a little holiday present for the sisters, since they will surely want to sing their brother's verses. To him or to his stern mother I naturally only *say* my holiday greetings. You all are passing the time quite happily, and you [Clara] are admitting no thoughts that modulate toward minor? Affectionate greetings then from me as well, and more soon! Your Johannes.[1]

Brahms claimed to have conceived the entire song that very morning as a Christmas present. As if to reinforce the claim, his autograph included a detailed date and time of completion, placed conspicuously just after the final bar line in lieu of his customary signature: "The 24th of Dec 73. Morning." In actual fact, a compositional process so fluid and concise was highly atypical of Brahms, and other documents hint that the rapid timeline implied by his letter and autograph may have been at least a slight exaggeration.[2] Still, the song was new to the Schumanns, who provided an ideal audience for its text: an unpublished poem by nineteen-year-old Felix Schumann, the youngest of Robert and Clara's children. As Brahms intended, his new song quickly found its place amid a lively family reunion. Clara had moved from Baden-Baden to Berlin during the preceding months, and Felix and several of his siblings were spending the Christmas holiday at her new home. Within a week, Clara had thanked Brahms for the gift and described the social circumstances of its premiere:

---

[1] Brahms/Schumann, *Briefe* 2:36. Emphasis original.
[2] Brahms's pocket calendar for 1873 preserves a note indicating that he may have at least contemplated setting Felix's text as early as November; the calendar is now in the Wienbibliothek im Rathaus, Vienna. See George Bozarth, "Brahms's Lieder Inventory of 1859–60 and Other Documents of His Life and Work," *Fontes Artis Musicae* 30 (1983): 105. Bozarth describes an entry mentioning *Meine Liebe ist grün* in Brahms's pocket calendar for November 1873 as well as January 1874. Margit McCorkle identifies what must be the same calendar entry as located on the page for December 1873/January 1874 (*Werkverzeichnis*, 269). Even leaving aside this discrepancy, it is not always possible to decide whether Brahms's calendar entries refer to the time at which he *completed* a work or the time at which he merely began *thinking* about a project. For instance, the pocket calendar also mentions a setting of "Wenn um den Holunder," a second poem by Felix Schumann, in the same month as *Meine Liebe ist grün* (either November or December 1873, depending on whether one follows Bozarth or McCorkle), but his calendar for 1874 also lists the same song in July. The surviving autograph of *Wenn um den Holunder* dates from July 1874 and still differs substantially from the published version.

The song was a lovely surprise, and even more especially for Felix, whom we had told nothing. And in the evening, when Joachim came, I showed it to him; we began to play, then Felix came and asked what kind of words they were, and became quite pale when he saw his own. And how beautiful is the song and the postlude—that alone I could just play forever for myself.—The G♯ returns back so wonderfully to the beginning![3]

At first glance, Clara's account might seem to imply that she understood Brahms's new song to be designed primarily for Felix. Certainly she arranged the first performance for her son's benefit, creating a dramatically staged surprise by concealing the identity of the text until the music had already piqued his interest. Contemporaneous events suggest a reason for such special attention. Already diagnosed with potentially life-threatening lung problems as early as 1868, Felix had suffered a serious infection beginning in September 1873. Since he would ultimately die of tuberculosis barely five years later, recent scholarly and popular accounts often imply that *Meine Liebe ist grün* was written out of pity for a doomed young man.[4] By mid-December 1873, however, Felix had recovered from his infection, and his long-term prognosis remained positive.[5] Brahms's song therefore seems likely to have been intended and received as a celebration of his recent recovery rather than a parting gift for someone on death's door. The text Brahms chose reinforced a sense of optimism through its references to ecstatic young love and teeming natural life. In the version of the poem preserved in the autograph of Brahms's song, the title he appended hinted directly at the future productivity of the young poet.

Junge Lieder. F. S. No. 1	*Youthful Songs. F. S. No. 1*
Meine Liebe ist grün wie der Fliederbusch,	My love is as green as the lilac bush,
Und mein Lieb ist schön wie die Sonne;	And my beloved is as fair as the sun
Die glänzt wohl herab auf den Fliederbusch	That shines down upon the lilac bush
Und füllt ihn mit Duft und mit Wonne.	And fills it with fragrance and bliss.

---

[3] Brahms/Schumann, *Briefe* 2:37.

[4] Examples include MacDonald, *Brahms*, 220; Lucien Stark, *A Guide to the Solo Songs of Johannes Brahms* (Bloomington: Indiana University Press, 1995), 195; and Eric Sams, *The Songs of Johannes Brahms* (New Haven, CT: Yale University Press, 2000), 203–4 and especially 206, where this maudlin streak is extended and elaborated with reference to Brahms's second setting of Felix's poetry, *Wenn um den Holunder*, Op. 63 No. 6. Earlier accounts, by contrast, did not connect the composition of *Meine Liebe ist grün* to Felix's impending demise at all. Max Kalbeck, for instance, proposed instead that the song was a thank-you gift to Clara in the wake of her Leipzig performance of Brahms's first piano concerto on December 4 (*Brahms* 2:482–83).

[5] During the autumn of 1873, Brahms kept himself informed of Felix's condition not only through correspondence with Clara, but also through contact with mutual friends (Brahms/Schumann, *Briefe* 1:578 and 2:25–33, and Brahms/Stockhausen, *Briefe*, 91).

Meine Seele hat Schwingen der	My soul has the wings of a nightingale
Nachtigall	
Und ruht sich in blühendem Flieder	And rests in the blossoming lilac
Und jauchzet und singet vom Duft	And, enchanted with fragrance, rejoices
berauscht	and sings
Viel liebestrunkene Lieder.	Many love-drunk songs.

In turn, Joachim and Clara's performance explicitly extended the circle of well-wishers beyond immediate family. Both Brahms and Joachim had stood as godfathers to Felix upon his baptism in 1854.[6] The recent convalescent thus experienced the joyful music of one godparent through the instrument of another, rounding out the happy community with which he might feel himself vicariously surrounded. Felix clearly appreciated the gesture. One can gauge his excitement by the fact that he soon undertook the challenge of learning to play *Meine Liebe ist grün* at the piano, no small task for one whose primary instrument was the violin.[7] Clara's carefully calibrated premiere had succeeded. Yet the remainder of her letter also hinted at more intimate encounters with the same music, repeated run-throughs at the piano for herself alone. She described her enthusiasm in overtly music-analytic terms, pointing out a climactic G♯ that linked the end of the postlude to the beginning of the second strophe. To a fellow performer and professional musician, her analysis carried an unavoidable subtext: Brahms's new song was not simply a familiar poetic text or a cheerful Christmas present, but also a complex and rewarding composition in its own right. Despite her elaborate efforts on her son's behalf and Felix's own attempts to learn the song, Clara knew that she was far better equipped than he, or any of her children, to perform such a composition and to apprehend its musical nuances.

One of these nuances was the presence of material borrowed from Robert Schumann's *Schöne Fremde* (Beautiful Unfamiliar), the sixth song in the *Liederkreis nach Joseph Freiherrn von Eichendorff*, Op. 39. Although *Schöne Fremde* was published in one of Robert's best-known song cycles in August 1842, and *Meine Liebe ist grün* has maintained a prominent position in the solo song repertoire ever since its release in November 1874, the connection between the two has been noted only once in print.[8] Both documentary and music-analytic factors have obscured

---

[6] Mathilde Hartmann served as a third godparent. Joachim's role was strictly unofficial in 1854 since he had not yet converted to Christianity, but the violinist remained deeply interested in Felix's development (Avins, *Life and Letters*, 760).

[7] Brahms/Schumann, *Briefe* 2:39.

[8] Eric Sams has identified what he called an "overt homage" and "deliberate allusion" to Schumann's *Schöne Fremde* in *Songs of Johannes Brahms* (204–5), his idiosyncratic survey of Brahms's solo song output. Many of the myriad motivic relationships that Sams posited in this and other publications are strained at best, which may account for other scholars' apparent lack of interest in his comments on *Meine Liebe ist grün*. My analysis of Brahms's compositional procedure in this song and my interpretation of its interpersonal implications differ substantially from his.

the relationship in earlier scholarship. Unlike the *Geistliches Wiegenlied*, the published version of *Meine Liebe ist grün* did not include an overt acknowledgment of musical borrowing, nor did Brahms mention any allusive procedure in surviving letters. Absent direct evidence of his decision making, one must argue partly by inference, working backward from the characteristics of his composition and the context for which it was initially designed. The autograph that Brahms sent to Clara has been privately owned and publically inaccessible since its completion. Questions about this manuscript can be laid to rest: I have examined the autograph, which replicates the vocal line and essential motivic content of the published version of the song while diverging in subtle accompanimental details during several short passages. Other complications remain, however, inherent in the words and music of the two songs. The text of *Schöne Fremde* contrasts sharply with that of *Meine Liebe ist grün*; Joseph von Eichendorff's affect is more subdued, his poetic speaker dramatically less self-assured. In the editions known to both Robert and Brahms himself,[9] the poem read:

Es rauschen die Wipfel und schauern,	The treetops murmur and quiver
Als machten zu dieser Stund'	As though at this very hour
Um die halbversunkenen Mauern	All around the half-ruined walls
Die alten Götter die Rund'.	The old gods were passing by.
Hier hinter den Myrthenbäumen	Here behind the myrtle-trees
In heimlich dämmernder Pracht,	In secretly twilit splendor,
Was sprichst du wirr wie in Träumen	What do you say to me wildly
Zu mir, phantastische Nacht?	As if dreaming, fantastical night?
Es funkeln auf mich alle Sterne	The stars all shine upon me
Mit glühendem Liebesblick,	With a glowing glance of love,
Es redet trunken die Ferne	The distance drunkenly speaks
Wie von künftigem, großem Glück! —	As if of some great future joy! —

The relevance of such a text to the interpretation of Felix's poem is not immediately apparent, especially when compared to the overt paratexts that Brahms associated with the *Wiegenlied*, the *Geistliches Wiegenlied*, and *O schöne Nacht*. Most of all, the manner in which Brahms's musical borrowings were integrated into their new environment was categorically more complex here than in his other allusive vocal music. Example 5.1a and b compare the initial measures of *Meine Liebe ist grün* and *Schöne Fremde*. As in Brahms's three occasional

---

[9] Brahms knew the poem from the second edition of Eichendorff's *Gedichte* (Berlin: M. Simion, 1843); he dog-eared the page on which "Schöne Fremde" appears in his personal copy. Robert Schumann almost certainly knew the poem from the first edition of the *Gedichte* (Berlin: Duncker & Humblot, 1837); for arguments concerning his likely source, see Helmut Schanze and Krischan Schulte, *Robert Schumann: Neue Ausgabe sämtlicher Werke. Supplemente. Literarische Vorlagen der ein- und mehrstimmigen Lieder, Gesängen und Deklamationen* (Mainz: Schott, 2002), 82 and 88.

lullabies, borrowed material played a determinative role in the pitch structure and contrapuntal texture of the initial accompanimental gesture. The first three beats of the piano's upper staff were identical in both songs except that Robert's sixteenth rests were expunged, as they would be by the sustain pedal on the more resonant pianos to which Clara and her family had since become accustomed. Taking all three staves into account, Brahms's opening measure also preserved Robert's time signature, his underlying root position D♯-minor harmony, the ascending melodic leap from the fifth to the root of the chord on beats 2 and 3 (now doubled by the vocal line), and the insistent eighth-note pulse in the pianist's left hand. Most strikingly, in both songs, the sonority of D♯ minor represented an off-tonic beginning whose claim to tonic status was immediately undermined by the appearance of a B♯ in the bass line on the downbeat of the second measure.[10] *Meine Liebe ist grün* thus retained both the opening harmony and the striking tonal instability of *Schöne Fremde*: the two songs departed from the same point, along the same unusual harmonic trajectory, and at the same pace.

EXAMPLE 5.1a   Robert Schumann, *Schöne Fremde*, Op. 39 No. 6, mm. 1–3

EXAMPLE 5.1b   Brahms, *Meine Liebe ist grün*, Op. 63 No. 5, mm. 1–4

[10] Sams confined his analysis of the musical relationship between *Meine Liebe ist grün* and *Schöne Fremde* to the first measure of the right hand of both piano accompaniments and, in a footnote, the "bass-line motion from D♯ to accidental B♯ in the opening bars" (Sams, *Songs of Johannes Brahms*, 204 and 205n). He hinted at the potential for other resemblances between the two songs but did not elaborate. His aim was to establish the possibility of an allusive relationship rather than to investigate that relationship in detail.

On the other hand, unlike the songs that Brahms composed in honor of his other godsons, this one pointedly eschewed a straightforward, one-to-one correspondence with the opening measures of its source. Instead, it presented parameters that actively precluded easy apprehension of its borrowing, at least on a first hearing. Brahms's dynamics and registral breadth far exceeded Robert's, resulting in a more extroverted affect. In place of his predecessor's static shimmering, Brahms's left hand ranged swiftly and ceaselessly across the keyboard in a distinctive pattern of interlocking upward and downward leaps that would remain unique in his entire output of solo songs. The only lasting similarity between the songs was the aggregate rhythmic and textural saturation produced by continuous attacks on every sixteenth pulse; all other initial resemblances faded immediately, replaced by conspicuous differences. The songs' true key-centers diverged, as did their methods of large-scale organization. *Meine Liebe ist grün* confirmed its F♯-major tonic as early as the downbeat of m. 4, while *Schöne Fremde* delayed the arrival of its B-major tonic until the final vocal cadence. Both songs set stanzaic poems, but they approached the task from opposite angles. Brahms's setting assigned each of Felix's stanzas to identical musical strophes, whereas Robert's elided all of Eichendorff's stanzas together into a delicately through-composed span that articulated a single authentic cadence.

Only toward the end of his song did Brahms return to procedures and specific pitches characteristic of Robert's model. In particular, the two piano postludes exhibited a cluster of similarities, as displayed in examples 5.2a and b; even a casual listener had two chances to perceive them because most of Brahms's postlude also doubled as an interlude between his strophes. First, *Meine Liebe ist grün* duplicated precisely Robert's spacing of the pianist's hands for the dominant-seventh chord that accompanies the singer's final vocal cadence. Both right hands sustained the chord's third and fifth with fingers 4 and 5 while repeating the seventh and root with the thumb and index finger, and both left hands played the root in a low register on beat 3, then filled in the root, third, and fifth in a middle register on the measure's three remaining eighth-note pulses. Next, both piano accompaniments presented and then repeated a two-measure phrase group that began on the tonic and ended on a modally ambiguous dominant substitute marked by the flatted-sixth scale degree. Both postludes thus comprised miniature AAB phrase structures, in which the A sections oscillated between tonic and dominant and the B section elaborated an unadulterated tonic triad. Such postludes were common in Robert's songs; indeed, the first six songs of the Eichendorff *Liederkreis* had contained no fewer than three unequivocal examples. Brahms himself had used the same technique before December 1873, including in at least two instances that involved modal mixture as well.[11] In the case of *Meine Liebe ist grün*, however, textural and kinesthetic resemblances hinted at a unique connection between Brahms's postlude and that of *Schöne Fremde*.

EXAMPLE 5.2a   Robert Schumann, *Schöne Fremde*, Op. 39 No. 6, mm. 23–30

EXAMPLE 5.2b   Brahms, *Meine Liebe ist grün*, Op. 63 No. 5, mm. 35–41

[11] Analogous examples from the first half of the Eichendorff *Liederkreis* included *Die Stille*, Op. 39 No. 4, and *Mondnacht*, Op. 39 No. 5. For Brahms's earlier adaptations, see *In meiner Nächte Sehnen*, Op. 57 No. 5, or, for a condensed version of the same phrase structure, *Vorüber*, Op. 58 No. 7.

Having presented his two-measure A section, Brahms did not simply repeat it unchanged the second time around. Instead, he relocated the upper voice to the bass line, producing an inverted repetition unprecedented among his uses of the AAB structure in piano postludes. While Robert's A sections contained no model for such a maneuver, his final tonic elaboration did: the four-note motive that began in the pianist's right hand in m. 28 was repeated two octaves down in the left hand one measure later. Reinforced by their formal placement in the post-lude, the two gestures were strikingly similar. Furthermore, for the pianist, the melody-turned-bass line in Brahms's second A section re-created a peculiar sensation familiar from Robert's postlude and aligned that sensation with the same characteristic harmony and voice leading. The left hand's ascending tritone leap from octave D♯s to octave G♯s on the fourth beat of m. 39 not only duplicated the scale-degree content of Robert's left-hand leap on the second beat of mm. 25 and 27; it also interjected the left thumb onto a black key in the midst of a diminished fifth spanning scale degrees ♯7 and 4 in the right hand, as did Robert's postlude. In both songs, thumb-crossing onto scale degree 2 coincided with the completion of the dominant substitute sonority that propelled the postlude toward its final resolution. Since the first five measures of Brahms's postlude provided the interlude between the two musical strophes of his song, the octave G♯s also directly preceded the return of the song's opening material. In turn, it was these very G♯s that provoked Clara Schumann's special admiration and encouraged her, quite literally, to play the song over and over.

Brahms may also have had a second Schumannian precedent in mind when constructing his postlude's registral inversion. The *Intermezzo* from Robert's *Faschingsschwank aus Wien*, Op. 26, was first published on its own in December 1839, well before the larger collection of solo piano pieces of which it subsequently became a part, and several months before work began on the Eichendorff *Liederkreis*.[12] Brahms knew the piece well. His own copy of Op. 26 testifies to frequent use: the bottom corners of pages in the midst of the fast-moving *Intermezzo* were worn and dog-eared for easy access during performance.[13] After the last page-turn, the *Intermezzo* punctuated the culminating arrival of its E♭-major tonic with a coda shown in example 5.3. Two melodic lines appear in

---

[12] Regarding the compositional history and publication date for the Eichendorff *Liederkreis*, see Margit McCorkle, *Thematisch-Bibliographisches Werkverzeichnis* (Düsseldorf: Robert-Schumann-Gesellschaft, 2003), 167–69; for the *Intermezzo*, see ibid., 113–14; and John Daverio, *Robert Schumann: Herald of a "New Poetic Age"* (Oxford: Oxford University Press, 1997), 179.

[13] Brahms's copy of *Faschingsschwank aus Wien* survives in the archives of the Gesellschaft der Musikfreunde in Vienna as part of a bound collection of various editions catalogued as VII 48826. Although it is impossible to know when he acquired the collection, multiple factors argue in favor of early ownership, including the elegant signature that Brahms inked into the title page of Op. 26; in later years, he rarely troubled himself with legibility in signing or annotating his own scores. In fact, Brahms may well have performed the *Intermezzo* on a recital program in Vienna on April 24, 1869. Surviving reviews mention an unspecified *Intermezzo* and *Romanze* by Robert Schumann (Hofmann, *Brahms als Pianist und Dirigent*, 121); the only opus in Robert's entire oeuvre that features both generic types is *Faschingsschwank aus Wien*.

loose canonic imitation over harmonies that produce yet another AAB pattern. After an initial two-measure A section, a second A section shifted these melodic lines into the left hand and allowed the lower of the two to assume the role of the bass. The textural and structural parallel with *Meine Liebe ist grün* was precise—more precise, in fact, than with *Schöne Fremde*. But in other respects, Robert himself seems to have returned to the *Intermezzo* for inspiration as well in his Eichendorff setting. The jagged melodic contour of the *Intermezzo*'s coda reappeared in the song's postlude, coupled with prominent flatted sixth scale degrees in the second measures of each A section. The opening measures of the two works also resonated sympathetically. Example 5.4 shows that the initial melodic ascent, the D♯/E♭ minor harmony, and the tonally unstable bass-line trajectory of the song's accompaniment all found direct antecedents in the *Intermezzo*. In other words, *Meine Liebe ist grün* borrowed from *Schöne Fremde* at precisely those points where Robert's own potential self-borrowings from the *Intermezzo* were already most apparent. It is almost as though Brahms's song sought to unearth—or to invent—a compositional prehistory for its source.

EXAMPLE 5.3   Robert Schumann, *Intermezzo*, Op. 26 No. 4, mm. 38–45

EXAMPLE 5.4   Robert Schumann, *Intermezzo*, Op. 26 No. 4, mm. 1–3

Finally, the closing vocal phrases of the two songs concealed an unexpected point of contact, a subtle but compelling conjunction of tessitura, text, and visual appearance in the score. Examples 5.5a and b compare the last four measures of both vocal lines. Although the final vocal cadences were entirely different in contour and scale-degree content, both were prepared by leaping upward to g#" on a strong beat, then descending stepwise down to c#" at the steady pace of one new pitch per beat. Of course, *Meine Liebe ist grün* was in F# instead of B: its vocal line descended through e#" rather than e♮". Nevertheless, on the written page, the two melodic spans were visually identical save for the placement of the barline. One would naturally dismiss such similarities as coincidences, were it not for their alignment with Felix's text. The second strophe of Brahms's setting placed the syllable *trunk* of the word *liebestrunkene* at the apex of the climactic upward leap to g#", just where *Schöne Fremde* had placed the first syllable of the word *trunken*. This textual alignment acquired special significance because, aside from words that any two German poems will inevitably share (pronouns, articles, conjunctions, prepositions, and the verbs *sein* and *haben*), the only words common to both poems are *liebes* (part of a compound adjective or noun in both cases) and *trunken*. The single vocal gesture common to both songs thus occurred at precisely the moment when their texts converged.

EXAMPLE 5.5a   Robert Schumann, *Schöne Fremde*, Op. 39 No. 6, mm. 21–24. Vocal part.

es   re - det trun - ken die   Fer   -   ne wie von künf - ti - gem gro - ssen Glück!

EXAMPLE 5.5b   Brahms, *Meine Liebe ist grün*, Op. 63 No. 5, mm. 33–36. Vocal part.

viel lie - bes - trun - ke - ne   Lie   -   der.

Given the opening measures, piano postlude, and closing vocal phrase of *Meine Liebe ist grün*, it seems undeniable that Brahms deliberately borrowed features of his song from *Schöne Fremde*. Yet his borrowings were brief, discontinuous, and confined primarily to the accompaniment. If he intended them to be understood as allusions—if he meant anyone to notice them at all—he must have had in mind a very special kind of audience for his song. To apprehend such fleeting and complex relationships would have required a deep and recent familiarity with *Schöne Fremde* and an expert pianist's engagement with *Meine Liebe ist grün*.

Clara Schumann had both. Her letter of thanks from January 1874 shows that the piano postlude in *Meine Liebe ist grün* drew her repeated attention and indicates her particular fondness for the very G♯ that made the passage so kinesthetically reminiscent of her late husband's music. More to the point, *Schöne Fremde* was already very much on her mind and in her fingers during the preceding months, and Brahms knew it. As early as May 1873, in response to a request from the French music publisher Flaxland, she had agreed to select thirty of Robert's songs and transcribe them for solo piano, to be published in Paris by Durand and Schönewerk. Among examples drawn from the Eichendorff *Liederkreis*, the *Myrthenlieder*, Op. 25, and other well-known collections, these transcriptions included *Schöne Fremde*. Clara's diary bore witness to her mounting interest in the project, which became a temporary obsession. An entry in June read: "The work has exhausted me like none ever has. For entire nights I heard the passages from the songs that I had considered and attempted, and I could not escape them, which exasperated me."[14] By mid-August, she had informed Brahms of the transcriptions and espoused a more measured view of their mingled frustrations and pleasures: "The work has cost me a lot of time, but has also incidentally brought me joy at the same time."[15] Upon the composer's visit to Baden-Baden later that month, she showed him her initial attempts and received some general advice on how to improve them.[16]

Clara then sent him copies of the transcriptions themselves on September 17, presumably in hopes of detailed comments and editorial corrections as she prepared her collection for publication. Brahms had therefore encountered Clara's version of *Schöne Fremde* barely three months before composing *Meine Liebe ist grün*. In addition, her package also contained reams of Felix's recent poetry, seemingly sent in response to a request from Brahms (no longer extant). As she explained, the demands of her upcoming move to Berlin had made it impossible for her to be selective; instead, she had simply enclosed all the poems to which she had access. "Some of them are quite pretty; he often has ingenious thoughts and humor. We are simply too busy right now, so I am sending them all, otherwise I would have copied the better ones for you."[17] Both the contents and the timing of Clara's literary offering are intriguing. Among the poems she had sent was "Meine Liebe ist grün." Perhaps Brahms's idea of incorporating Robert's music into a setting of

---

[14] Litzmann, *Clara Schumann* 3:293. Clara's diary also preserves details concerning her decision to become involved with the project in the first place (see ibid., 291–92). For more on the aesthetic of her song transcriptions, see Stefan Bromen, *Studien zu den Klaviertranskriptionen Schumannscher Lieder von Franz Liszt, Clara Schumann, und Carl Reinecke* (Sinzig: Studio, 1997), 106–36.

[15] Brahms/Schumann, *Briefe* 2:21.

[16] Ibid., 24–25. Brahms's visit occurred during August 21–27, directly after the Schumann-Fest in Bonn (for details of his movements, see Hofmann, *Zeittafel*, 112). Initially, he seems to have advised Clara to adopt a freer approach to her transcriptions instead of sticking as closely as possible to the original song, as was her wont (Litzmann, *Clara Schumann* 3:292).

[17] Brahms/Schumann, *Briefe* 2:26.

Felix's words was facilitated by the memory of this happenstance proximity between the son's poems and the mother's song transcriptions. In any case, Brahms replied to Clara's letter on October 15 with comments regarding both.

All but the first page of his letter is now missing. Of his impressions of his godson's poetry only an inscrutable fragment remains.[18] Fortunately, his response to the transcriptions survives intact. His commentary reveals that both texture and harmony played central roles in his and Clara's shared engagement with *Schöne Fremde* during the final months of 1873. Clara had evidently sent thirty-two transcriptions, exceeding the limit agreed upon with her publisher and prompting Brahms to search for some that might be cut:

> I found that they play themselves quite comfortably, some suitable ones truly delightfully, while others strongly resist translation for solo piano. I have not listed *Schöne Fremde* and *Schöne Wiege* on the reverse. I would put them aside for the time being, perhaps they will sound better later. (Besides, you still have to eliminate 2.) Especially in *Schöne Wiege*, I think, the manner of accompaniment would have to remain such that it still has its own allure for the player. The left hand should not have eighths (the middle section in that song is very good.)[19]

As exemplars of egregious resistance to transcription, Brahms settled on *Schöne Fremde* and the outer sections of *Schöne Wiege* (Beautiful Cradle), the fifth song in Robert's Heine *Liederkreis*, Op. 24. Like *Schöne Fremde*, the portions of *Schöne Wiege* that Brahms found problematic had originally featured a continuous alternation between on-beat pulses in the pianist's left hand and off-beat chords in the right hand. Brahms seems to have been concerned that adding a vocal line to the pianist's responsibilities disrupts the consistency of this delicate and idiomatically pianistic texture. Clara did not address the point again in any letter that survives. She apparently gave up on *Schöne Wiege* but included a transcription of *Schöne Fremde* in her publication the following year: even her final version forced the pianist out of the song's continuous hand-to-hand oscillation for a full six out of twenty-nine measures. Example 5.6 reproduces the first three measures of her published transcription and highlights missing eighth-note pulses.[20] Whether or not Clara ultimately agreed with Brahms's criticism of her draft, his comments

---

[18] Ibid., 28: "I would rather enclose Felix's poems right away, if I were not tempted to … everything until …" Brahms's verb was cut off along with the rest of his sentence, making it impossible to interpret his meaning.

[19] Ibid., 27.

[20] Most publicly available copies of Clara's transcriptions are reissues by Durand from the early twentieth century. However, comparison with Brahms's own copy of the original publication, currently housed in the Gesellschaft der Musikfreunde in Vienna, shows that Durand's reprint simply reused the old engraving plates, rendering it an accurate source for study. Clara had her own good reasons for ignoring Brahms's advice about *Schöne Fremde*'s texture. Her transcription creates a clear registral differentiation between the vocal line and the accompaniment by forcing melodic motives from the song's right hand down an octave into the transcription's left hand. In every case, it is these transposed motives that disrupt the song's accompanimental pattern.

show that her transcription project had alerted them both to *Schöne Fremde's* characteristic accompanimental texture. Brahms would soon employ precisely the same alternation between on-beat left hand pulses and off-beat right hand chords throughout *Meine Liebe ist grün*; his letter of October 15 suggests that he could confidently expect Clara to recognize its source.[21]

EXAMPLE 5.6   Clara Schumann, piano transcription of *Schöne Fremde*, mm. 1–3. Annotated.

Avec âme, animé (Innig bewegt)

missing left-hand pulses

The letter also hints that both musicians were explicitly attuned to *Schöne Fremde's* off-tonic beginning, another feature Brahms would soon mimic in the setting of Felix's text. The back of the page presented a list of Clara's acceptable transcriptions. Brahms omitted *Schöne Wiege*, as promised, but seems to have reconsidered his judgment of *Schöne Fremde*, which ultimately found a place despite his negative commentary. The list is no mere catalogue, however. It provides an order in which Clara could plausibly arrange her entire set of song transcriptions while maintaining a pleasingly varied succession of affects and performance techniques. The few songs in minor mode all occur between major-mode songs, and those most difficult to play are surrounded by easier ones. Brahms also seems to have intended his proposed order to organize the sequence of tonal areas established by successive transcriptions. His list included the key of each song alongside its title, thus clarifying for Clara the succession of keys created by the entire series. In turn, the order of those keys exhibits characteristics highly unlikely to occur by chance among thirty-one songs whose tonal centers span the entire chromatic. In twenty-nine out of thirty song-to-song transitions, the new tonic succeeds the old at comfortable distances of a fifth, third, or unison; the only remaining gap between songs is a whole step, which means the keys of successive songs are never related by half

---

[21] In later years, Clara's own execution of this characteristic texture would provoke admiration among other pianists in her circle. In 1874 or later, her daughter Eugenie witnessed an impromptu performance of the accompaniment to *Schöne Fremde*. The moment became the touchstone for a description of her mother's unique touch at the keyboard: "How the most perfectly legato melody hovered over the equally strictly legato bass, how the sixteenths fully subordinated themselves in rhythmic strictness and yet filled in so beautifully, and how all three—melody, bass, sixteenths—coalesced into poetry, poetry equal to that of the poet and the composer!" (Eugenie Schumann, *Erinnerungen*, 303).

step, tritone, or diminished fifth.[22] Within such a carefully planned sequence of song-to-song transitions, the placement of *Schöne Fremde* was striking indeed: the song's initial D♯-minor sonority follows *Lust der Sturmnacht*, Op. 35 No. 1, which ends in E♭ major. Brahms's proposed order thus provided a larger context in which *Schöne Fremde*'s off-tonic, D♯-minor beginning could be reinterpreted as part of a seamless modulation from the key of the previous song.

Brahms's list was copied hurriedly. At least as transcribed by Berthold Litzmann in 1927, it was inconsistent in its methods of differentiating between major and minor modes, inaccurate in its key designation for one song, and idiosyncratic in the titles it used for several—for instance, *Er, der Herrlichste von Allen* (Op. 42 No. 2) became *Er der Stockhausen*, playing on Clara's customary appellation of Julius as "der Herrlichste Sänger" (the Most Glorious Singer). Nevertheless, anyone intimately familiar with Robert Schumann's songs could easily make sense of Brahms's recommendations. Clara certainly did. With only one exception, her published transcriptions followed Brahms's order. Her fidelity to his proposed sequence is all the more remarkable because she ultimately rejected seven of the transcriptions she had sent to Brahms and replaced them with six more, which he had never seen. Rather than begin afresh, however, she simply interpolated the new additions into the remains of his framework, often directly in place of the songs she had decided to omit. With respect to *Schöne Fremde*, the results were especially telling. One casualty of her editing was *Lust der Sturmnacht*, which had preceded *Schöne Fremde* in Brahms's list, but Clara's published sequence still positioned *Schöne Fremde* immediately after another song that ended in E♭ major (*Freisinn*, Op. 25 No. 2). She thereby retained the sense of poised modulation from E♭ to B that had characterized Brahms's order and reinforced the player's appreciation for Robert's off-tonic beginning.

Taken together, Brahms's critical commentary on her transcriptions and his proposed sequence for their publication ensured that Clara would be playing *Schöne Fremde* and considering its peculiar textural and harmonic characteristics over the weeks that followed. After her move to Berlin was complete, she thanked him profusely for his help with the transcriptions on November 24. By the time she received the manuscript of *Meine Liebe ist grün* a month later, she was surely well equipped to notice borrowings from *Schöne Fremde*, especially those involving the piano accompaniment. And once the resemblances in their opening and closing measures had encouraged her to compare the songs, she

---

[22] Brahms's suggested order thus subjected Clara's transcriptions to the aesthetic of smooth song-to-song transitions so prevalent in nineteenth-century song publications. For more on the importance of such transitions in nineteenth-century song sets, particularly those of Robert Schumann, see Leon Plantinga, "Design and Unity in Schumann's *Liederkreis*, op. 39?" in *Word and Music Studies: Essays on the Song Cycle and on Defining the Field* (proceedings of the Second International Conference on Word and Music Studies at Ann Arbor, MI, 1999), ed. Walter Bernhart and Werner Wolf, 159–61 (Atlanta: Rodopi, 2001).

could identify and assess the many differences between them. Chief among these was the affective disparity between the two texts. Brought together by musical borrowings that Clara was uniquely positioned to apprehend, the poems themselves probably appeared surprisingly incompatible at first.

The treetops murmur and quiver
As though at this very hour
All around the half-ruined walls
The old gods were passing by.

Here behind the myrtle-trees
In secretly twilit splendor,
What do you say to me wildly
As if dreaming, fantastical night?

The stars all shine upon me
With a glowing glance of love,
The distance drunkenly speaks
As if of some great future joy! —

My love is as green as the lilac bush,
And my beloved is as fair as the sun
That shines down upon the lilac bush
And fills it with fragrance and bliss.

My soul has the wings of a nightingale
And rests in the blossoming lilac
And, enchanted with fragrance, rejoices
    and sings
Many love-drunk songs.

Eichendorff's text places its speaker in an exotic landscape suffused with starlight and indistinct sounds; Felix Schumann's speaker compares the beloved to the brilliant sunlight that causes plants to grow and birds to sing. Eichendorff's speaker knows that his nighttime vision is ephemeral and cannot even begin to explain its significance until his poem is almost over; Felix's speaker spends the entire poem carried away by a single proclamation of love, excitedly uncovering ever more extended ramifications of a single metaphor. The few characteristics common to the two texts occur in differing contexts and in the service of divergent ends. Both poems record the imprint of overwhelming happiness on the speaker's mind, but in Eichendorff's text that happiness is merely hinted at as a potential future condition, whereas in Felix's it is felt immediately in the present moment. Both poems share an image of ardent intoxication but permit different degrees of access to that image: whatever love-struck ecstasies Eichendorff's speaker glimpses in the pantheistic half-light of ruins and quiet distances, Felix's speaker has already experienced directly and expressed through song. In short, one poem waits in hopeful anticipation while the other celebrates joyous fulfillment.

To a musician familiar with both poems, Brahms's principles of large-scale organization in *Meine Liebe ist grün* would surely have underscored the characteristics that differentiated Felix's poem from Eichendorff's. The solid self-assurance of Felix's lyric persona resounded in Brahms's speedy cadence on the tonic in m. 4, whereas the single, long-delayed authentic cadence of Robert's song reflected his poetic speaker's more tentative attitude. Brahms's strophic form fit the static consistency of Felix's interrelated metaphors for the experience of love, while Robert's through-composed structure and gradual crescendo were appropriate to Eichendorff's expectant hesitation. So, too, with Brahms's choice of F♯ major for his tonic: the brighter key signature acknowledged Felix's overtly cheerful affect, especially set against the hushed confusion that surrounded the poetic speaker for much of Eichendorff's poem. Returning, then, to Brahms's initial measures (ex. 5.1b), one might assume that Clara would have interpreted small-scale divergences from Robert's model as further reflections of a straightforward contrast between the texts. After all, Brahms's louder dynamics, broader register, and busier left-hand figuration all accorded neatly with Felix's brasher affect. Yet unlike the form, key, and larger harmonic trajectory of his song, these local characteristics were not Brahms's inventions. All three found clear antecedents in a single passage from *Schöne Fremde*. Robert's piano postlude began at the apex of the song's long crescendo to *forte*; it also spanned more than three octaves and incorporated the distinctive, interlocking left-hand arpeggiation that pervades *Meine Liebe ist grün* (see ex. 5.2a). For a performer with Clara's recent and detailed experience of *Schöne Fremde*, Brahms's initial measures could establish two allusive relationships simultaneously, one to Robert's piano introduction and the other to his postlude. The overlapping musical references could then encourage such a performer to reevaluate the differences between the two songs in light of an imagined continuity between them.

As in many of Robert's mature *Lieder*, the piano postlude played a pivotal role in the musical and textual arc of *Schöne Fremde*.[23] After twenty-three measures of increasing tonal clarity and intensifying musical rhetoric, the tonic pedal, expansive range, *forte* dynamic, and animated figuration clearly marked the postlude as the musical goal of the entire song. That the expressive apex occurred as the singer fell silent was specifically appropriate to Eichendorff's text, which ends not in fulfillment but in the hope of happiness to come. Eichendorff's punctuation had originally reinforced this sense of expectancy, as Brahms and Robert both knew. In the editions with which they were familiar, the poem had closed with an enigmatic dash that was omitted from published versions of the song.[24] Like that dash, Robert's postlude gave shape to an emotional experience that waited just beyond the edges of language. The solo piano music that completed the song could thus be understood as an image in tones of the "great future joy"

---

[23] Other examples included *Widmung*, Op. 25 No. 1, *Nun hast du mir den ersten Schmerz getan*, Op. 42 No. 8, and many songs from *Dichterliebe*, Op. 48.

[24] Robert's autograph of *Schöne Fremde* does not survive, but the dash was absent from the first edition of the song. Perhaps, having created an instrumental equivalent for the dash, Robert feared that including the ambiguous punctuation in the score would undermine the singer's emphatic final cadence. At any rate, he did not correct the omission in his own copy of the first edition, in which he marked numerous other changes in preparation for a later edition. His copy survives today in the holdings of the Sibley Music Library at the Eastman School of Music in Rochester, New York.

that remained unreachable for the poetic speaker himself. By weaving musical features unique to *Schöne Fremde*'s piano postlude together with tonal and motivic material from its opening measures, then, Brahms ensured that his new song not only recalled Robert's model but also began where that model had left off—with a sonorous image of amorous happiness. Moreover, the registral breadth and expansive figuration that had taken *Schöne Fremde* its entire length to achieve permeated *Meine Liebe ist grün* from beginning to end, just as the joyful confidence Eichendorff's speaker foresaw permeated every line of Felix's poem. Brahms's treatment of his borrowed material therefore carried the potential to transform the simple contrast between two virtually unrelated texts into an implied musical and poetic progression, a single temporal span beginning with anticipation and ending in fulfillment. In short, for a pianist with the right prior musical experiences, *Meine Liebe ist grün* could satisfy precisely the kind of longing that Robert's *Schöne Fremde* had once articulated.

Brahms was intimately aware of Clara's aural and kinesthetic engagement with Robert's song when he composed the setting of her son's text. He had good reason to expect that his multilayered borrowings could lead her to perceive his own song as the realization of an ecstatic emotional state only adumbrated in *Schöne Fremde*. How might Clara have reacted to such a perception, and what might Brahms have predicted regarding her response? No surviving evidence can answer such questions definitively, yet correspondence allows one to reconstruct some contours of the broader interpersonal landscape within which composer and performer may have situated the song's implications in late December 1873. Depending upon aspects of her current relationships with family members and with Brahms himself, Clara might have interpreted her friend's compositional motivations from at least three interrelated standpoints. These interpretive perspectives were not mutually exclusive; one must assume, indeed, that both Clara's experience of *Meine Liebe ist grün* and Brahms's intentions relative to his song actually comprised complex amalgams of many potentially conflicting impressions, the majority of which left no trace in extant documents. The possibilities offered here are merely conjectural fragments of a larger whole that will remain forever incomplete.

First, Felix Schumann occupied a unique position among Clara's children in the early 1870s. Although he had never met his father (who was institutionalized before he was born), Clara had soon found that Felix resembled Robert more closely in talent and temperament than any of his older siblings. Brahms was aware of her perception. In 1868, a letter from Clara had described a visit with her youngest son during a recent vacation from his boarding school: "He reminded me every day in many ways of Robert, and I always felt blessed by those glimpses into his heart."[25] She had encouraged Felix's early interests in music and poetry and continued to support his changing educational needs throughout his adolescence and young adulthood. In 1872, he had passed his Gymnasium examinations, embarked upon a law degree at the University of Heidelberg, and filled his spare time with music and literature, just like his father before him.[26] But Felix's similarities to Robert had their drawbacks as well. Before his thirteenth birthday Clara had already begun to discourage his hopes of becoming a violinist.[27] She soon expressed disapproval of his poetic aspirations as well, warning that mediocre work would tarnish the family name. As she made clear in correspondence with Brahms, her concern stemmed from a direct comparison with Robert's artistry. In the letter that accompanied Felix's poems on their way to Brahms in September 1873, she demanded a candid assessment of their quality: "Tell me *openly* what you think of them—don't think that, as a weak mother, I believe he's a genius; to the contrary, I am so afraid of overestimating the talents of his children, that perhaps I sometimes demand too much of them."[28] That Clara's possessive pronoun required no explicit antecedent illustrates Brahms's shared awareness of Felix's problematic status within her family.

Insofar as *Meine Liebe ist grün* established an imagined temporal continuity in which Felix's poem fulfilled hopes articulated by *Schöne Fremde*, Brahms's song might have resonated with the double-edged connection that Clara already perceived between her youngest son and her late husband. With the aid of Brahms's allusions, she could find in Felix's words, as in Felix himself, a particular kind of joy that Robert had envisioned, even engendered, but never quite experienced. Beginning his new song where *Schöne Fremde* had left off therefore enabled Brahms to channel and redirect what he knew was already a strong current in Clara's relationship with her son. At the end of an autumn in which that relationship had survived the frightening threat of Felix's illness, he may well have intended her to perceive his compositional choices as private and

---

[25] Brahms/Schumann, *Briefe* 1:600. For a concise account of Clara's relationship with Felix, see Reich, *Clara Schumann: The Artist and the Woman*, rev. ed. (Ithaca, NY: Cornell University Press, 2001), 155–58; much of Reich's data is drawn from Eugenie Schumann's *Erinnerungen*.

[26] Eugenie Schumann, *Erinnerungen*, 134–35.

[27] Clara broached the subject with her son in writing on May 11, 1867, explaining bluntly that she considered him talented enough to be a competent amateur but incapable of the "high artistry" that the public would expect of Robert's son (Eugenie Schumann, *Erinnerungen*, 115). Shortly thereafter, she consulted Joseph Joachim regarding Felix's potential as a violinist. In a letter dated December 31, 1867, Joachim replied that he could not judge the boy's playing accurately unless he had taught him personally for a substantial period of time (Joachim and Moser, *Briefe von und an Joachim* 2:454–55). His apologetic tone and plea to give Felix a chance to prove himself both suggest that Clara had been hoping for a definitively negative judgment with which she might then have convinced her son to abandon his musical ambitions altogether.

[28] Brahms/Schumann, *Briefe* 2:25–26; emphasis in original.

very personal affirmations of her youngest child's potential. His title—"Youthful Songs. F. S. No. 1"—played along by hinting at more collaborations to come and offering an oblique reminder that Felix was, after all, only nineteen. Whether Clara actually agreed with his implied assessment of the poems is another question entirely. If Brahms's song effected any changes in her attitude, they were temporary at best. By 1877, Clara became worried that the publication of Felix's work would reflect badly upon the entire family. She turned to Brahms for advice once more and even sought to enlist his help in explaining her point of view to Felix, who was now a grown man and justifiably upset by his mother's interference.[29] Still, for at least a brief moment, *Meine Liebe ist grün* had offered an alternative vision of his place as the talented son of exceptional parents.

By the time Brahms composed his song, however, he knew that Felix's recent illness and artistic ambitions were not the only concerns disrupting Clara's holiday plans. Another cluster of potential implications for *Meine Liebe ist grün* involved the recent death of Clara's brilliant and domineering father, with whom she had maintained a tense but meaningful relationship ever since Robert's passing. Friedrich Wieck had died on October 6, but Clara's busy concert schedule and impending move had left little time to mourn him or attend to his affairs until early December, when she visited her stepmother in Dresden. Upon returning to her new home in Berlin, she confided her mingled feelings of grief and guilt in an anguished letter to Brahms, her "truest friend." His response does not survive, but on December 22 she sent him another letter, contrasting her children's excitement about the coming holiday with her own lingering sadness: "For me far too many sad thoughts are mixed in, and that cannot be otherwise when one has already buried so much that one loved!"[30] With these words Clara referred not only to her father but also to her mother and her daughter Julie, both of whom had also died within the past twenty-one months. Her grief compounded by temporary alienation from her new city and still-unfamiliar house, she was clearly in the midst of depression.

Clara's melancholic comments provoked Brahms's question of December 24: "You all [*Ihr*] are passing the time quite happily, and you [*Du*] are admitting no thoughts that modulate toward minor?" As in his baptismal letter to the Stockhausens three years later, Brahms's pronouns distinguished carefully between plural and singular addressees, ensuring that the last clause was directed, gently but specifically, to Clara alone. Surely it was no coincidence that Brahms cast his solicitous inquiry in the form of a musical metaphor. His diction encouraged her to receive his animated song as medicine appropriate to her current emotional state. In the context of their exchange, Clara could have

---

[29] Ibid., *Briefe* 2:109–10.

[30] Ibid., *Briefe* 2:32–33 and 35–36. For the timing of Clara's visit to Dresden, which occurred between concerts in Hamburg and Leipzig, see Litzmann, *Clara Schumann* 3:306n.

understood both Brahms's choice of preexistent material and his method of integrating that material into his new song as responses to her recent loss. By borrowing *Schöne Fremde*'s off-tonic beginning, *Meine Liebe ist grün* enacted literally the swift but permanent turn from minor to major that Brahms had advocated metaphorically for Clara's mood. At the same time, by implicitly affirming Felix's continuation of his father's artistic legacy, Brahms's layered allusions offered an alternative to Clara's currently gloomy view of the passage of time. Newly bereft of her father and painfully reminded of other recent losses, she might have found in Brahms's song an oblique but timely reminder that the unfulfilled potential of past generations could still be realized in her remaining children.

Finally, by facilitating for Clara certain patterns of thought regarding her family members, Brahms's compositional choices also encouraged from her a specific interpretation of his own place in that family. Insofar as his allusions to *Schöne Fremde* affirmed Felix's poetic talent as a worthy continuation of the Schumann legacy, reinforced Clara's appreciation of her son's unique resemblance to his father, or persuaded her to refocus her "sad thoughts" in the aftermath of her own father's death, she could perceive Brahms as tactfully but deliberately inserting himself into the interpersonal dynamics of her home. She might even interpret his song as part of an attempt to identify himself symbolically as a substitute for her absent husband. Brahms's compositional decisions allowed him to act, vicariously, as her partner in evaluating Felix's artistry and personality. At the same time, his selection and treatment of borrowed material in *Meine Liebe ist grün* could be understood as claiming the role of Robert's compositional surrogate.[31] Beginning a song where Robert had once ended one and completing in tones a triumphant emotional trajectory that that earlier song had left unfulfilled: if Clara perceived these actions as deliberate, she could easily have considered them evidence that Brahms saw his own composition as speaking for her late husband, finishing a task that Robert would presumably have taken on himself if he were alive to read his son's poetry.

Stepping into Robert's roles was by no means new to Brahms in 1873. He had first done so in March 1854, when he moved to Düsseldorf and took over myriad household tasks directly following the older composer's suicide attempt and subsequent institutionalization. For the next two years, Brahms managed the Schumanns' finances, organized their music library, and helped to

---

[31] Of the three interpretive perspectives that *Meine Liebe ist grün* likely encouraged from Clara, this one comes closest to Eric Sams's interpretation of the song's allusion to *Schöne Fremde*: "The song begins with an overt homage to the song-writing of Schumann senior at his most Romantic ... as if he had been reborn in his son's poetry and his disciple's music" (Sams, *Songs of Johannes Brahms*, 204). Because Sams treats Brahms's allusion as if it were intended for public consumption, however, he does not address what it might have meant to Clara in particular.

raise the children during the frequent concert tours that Clara undertook to support the family.[32] Beginning within a few weeks of his birth on June 11, Felix became one of his many responsibilities. Brahms bought his godson toys and kept both Clara and Robert informed of his growth throughout his babyhood and toddler years; Felix's first tooth and first mealtimes with the rest of the family figured prominently in correspondence with the absent parents.[33] On the one hand, memories of his time as surrogate caregiver clearly left a lasting and positive impression on the composer. Although many of his letters to Clara from the period of Felix's later childhood and adolescence no longer survive, the remnants show that Brahms retained a special fondness for the child and an active interest in his development that arguably surpassed his commitment to the other Schumann boys. Clara kept him informed of Felix's progress at boarding school and confided her difficulties when frustrated by her youngest son's "hard head" during his teenage years. For his part, Brahms responded enthusiastically to good reports, provided second-hand clothing from his own wardrobe during growth spurts, and expressed himself with unaccustomed warmth and directness in face-to-face conversations.[34] Eugenie Schumann recalled him exclaiming to her mother: "I don't know what I'd do for joy if I had a son like Felix."[35]

At the same time, however, Brahms's happy subjunctives belied the more ambivalent consequences of those formative years in Düsseldorf. While caring for the Schumann children, he had also found himself increasingly attracted to their mother. He had admitted his burgeoning feelings for what appears to have been the first time on June 19, 1854, in a letter to Joseph Joachim: "I believe I can really never again love a maiden, at least I have forgotten them completely; after all, they merely promise the heaven that Clara reveals to us opened."[36] Just eight days after Felix's birth, Brahms's metaphor of the open portal was exquisitely timed and extraordinarily flexible. Age, sexual experience, and maternity itself were all part of Clara's erotic allure. Over the ensuing months she became at least partially aware of his feelings

---

[32] An excellent summary of Brahms's role during this period can be found in Reich, *Clara Schumann*, 172–76. In addition, Avins has cogently addressed the nature of Brahms and Clara's relationship in the appendix to *Life and Letters*. She demonstrates persuasively that the couple's surviving correspondence does not support the conjecture of sexual intimacy between them. Instead, she argues, whether or not Brahms and Clara were ever lovers is far less interesting than "what, given their difference in background, character, and age, kept them bound to each other throughout their entire lives, in an alliance as close as any family tie" (Avins, 758).

[33] Brahms/Schumann, *Briefe* 1:143, 99, and 78.

[34] Ibid., 1:539, 566, 624, 577, and 580, and 2:9.

[35] Eugenie Schumann, *Erinnerungen*, 142–43.

[36] This passage was excised from Moser's edition of the Joachim correspondence. For a facsimile of the original letter, see Constantin Floros, *Johannes Brahms. "Frei aber einsam." Ein Leben für eine poetische Musik* (Hamburg: Arche, 1997), 93.

and relied ever more deeply on his emotional support as her husband's health worsened. Had events unfolded differently, Brahms might well have become a lasting substitute for Robert and a stepfather to Felix and the other children. Instead, three months after Robert's death in 1856, he and Clara made the pivotal decision to pursue separate lives.[37] For the next forty years, periods of intimacy would alternate with periods of awkwardness and realignment. Although both Brahms and Clara avoided broaching the topic directly whenever possible, nearly every documented conflict between them can be read as a reaction to the fundamental ambiguity of his continued place in her family.[38] One of their most serious quarrels had spanned much of 1868. Eventually, Clara had found herself forced to tell Brahms that his tactless and arrogant behavior toward her had alienated her children. With the breach only barely healed, he had further confused the entire family with his bitter reaction to Julie Schumann's engagement and marriage the following year.[39]

Following the tumult of the late 1860s, the early 1870s had brought a period of long-term rebuilding for Brahms and the Schumanns. Shared vacation time and mutual enjoyment of Brahms's newest music seem to have been particularly beneficial. Chapter 6 addresses the F#-minor *Capriccio*, Op. 76 No. 1, a compositional project that, along with some uncharacteristically charming behavior, helped renew Brahms's former closeness with Clara during the autumn of 1871. But by the end of 1872, communications had again become slightly strained. Brahms once more felt unduly left out of the Schumann circle; this time he had just cause to complain about not having been consulted earlier during preparations for the following year's Schumann Festival in Bonn. The situation was evidently serious enough that in December 1872 he overcame his usual reticence in order to reassure Clara of his continued feelings for her, and to address directly the already long history of awkwardness in their interactions: "There is nothing that could change or weaken my estimation of you and my reverence for you. As a sad joke, I have sometimes said you were looking at me

---

[37] Malcolm MacDonald has offered a concise and balanced description of this decision and its immediate effects in *Brahms*, 47–50.

[38] Brahms himself would not express this underlying concern in any surviving letter until an acrimonious exchange in 1892, when he finally drew an explicit connection between a then-current debate (regarding Clara's edition of her husband's complete works) and the long-standing tensions of their friendship. As he put it: "Unfortunately, I am an outsider to you more than any other. This I have perceived for a long time and painfully" (Brahms/Schumann, *Briefe* 2:476). For accounts of both the immediate and broader contexts in which this letter was written, see Reich, *Clara Schumann*, 179–80; and MacDonald, *Brahms*, 243–44.

[39] Regarding the breach in 1868, see Brahms/Schumann, *Briefe* 1:598–99. MacDonald has placed the argument in context and offered several possible explanations for its severity; see *Brahms*, 138. Brahms's apparently well-hidden infatuation with Julie could only have complicated his simultaneous feelings of involvement with and exclusion from the Schumann family in 1869. For Clara's own description of the situation, see Litzmann, *Clara Schumann* 3:229–30 and 232.

as the police look at someone who's already been punished three times."[40] The two musicians did not see each other during the first eight months of 1873 (Brahms spent the summer in Tutzing rather than with Clara in Baden-Baden), and, while they exchanged a few letters during the spring and summer, their correspondence regained its accustomed intimacy only after they had met at the Schumann Festival and played through Brahms's latest compositions, as well as the initial versions of Clara's song transcriptions, at the end of August.[41]

Both the occasion on which Brahms composed *Meine Liebe ist grün* in December 1873 and the source from which he derived its borrowings coincided closely with the latest in a recent series of rapprochements with Clara. In the context of their continually shifting friendship, beginning a song where Robert had once ended one and completing in tones a triumphant emotional trajectory that Robert had left unfinished were hardly neutral acts. Instead, the family resemblances embodied in Brahms's new song were potent rhetorical devices whose full effects were impossible to predict with any certainty, much less reconstruct in retrospect. Clara might have been wary of directly confronting echoes from her musical and personal past, or, at the same time, she might have perceived in those echoes a carefully timed confirmation of an old friend's continued devotion. But whether Brahms intended his allusions to *Schöne Fremde* as proclamations of her son's talent, gestures of reassurance in a time of grief, acknowledgments of the continued importance of their shared history, or something else altogether, he seems to have assumed they would not be ignored—not by the one listener he knew was prepared to apprehend their musical details and to grasp their potential textual and interpersonal ramifications. Moreover, the technique of layered allusion to multiple passages from a single source would soon find further applications in music designed specifically for Clara. From now on, however, the source would no longer be Robert's music, but Brahms's own.

---

[40] Brahms/Schumann, *Briefe* 2:13. This is the only letter that survived between May 1872 and March 1873. Using correspondence among mutual friends, however, Kalbeck identified Brahms's angry reaction to the Schumann Festival and contrasted his position with those of Clara and Joseph Joachim in *Brahms* 2:430–37. Kalbeck suggested that the dispute played a decisive role in Brahms's decision not to visit Baden-Baden in the summer of 1873.

[41] Brahms/Schumann, *Briefe* 2:22–23.

CHAPTER SIX

SHARED NOSTALGIA

The oldest surviving record of Brahms's *Capriccio* in F♯ minor for solo piano, Op. 76 No. 1, is an autograph manuscript completed for Clara Schumann on September 12, 1871. Brahms placed the date and a shorthand version of Clara's name, *Cl. Sch.*, at the top of the title page, along with an indication of tempo and affect, *Unruhig bewegt*, that remained unchanged in the *Capriccio*'s later, published version. He wrote in ink on ornately decorated music paper. His manuscript was virtually devoid of notational errors but replete with pedal indications, dynamic and expressive marks, and even specific fingerings.[1] Its legibility, the precision of its performance instructions, and the paper on which it was written all indicate that the autograph was a presentation copy of a finished composition. Brahms presumably presented his gift both in honor of Clara and Robert Schumann's thirty-first wedding anniversary on September 12, 1871, and to celebrate Clara's fifty-second birthday the following day. He almost certainly gave her the autograph in person. He had been visiting her home in Baden-Baden since May, and her diary places him among a group of friends who gathered at her house on the evening of September 13.[2]

Portions of this chapter were first published in Paul Berry, "Old Love: Johannes Brahms, Clara Schumann, and the Poetics of Musical Memory," *Journal of Musicology* 24 (2007): 72–111.

[1] The autograph is currently housed at the Yale University Music Library in New Haven, CT, where it is catalogued as Music Deposit 17, Special Collections. For a transcription of the autograph and a short introduction to the compositional history of the F♯-minor *Capriccio*, see Peter Petersen, ed., *Klavierstücke op. 76: mit der Urfassung des Capriccio fis-moll* (Vienna: Wiener Urtext Edition, Universal Edition, 1992).

[2] Litzmann, *Clara Schumann* 3:263. For details on Brahms's movements during 1871, see Hofmann, *Zeittafel*, 104–7. In perhaps the most influential account of the *Capriccio*'s genesis, Max Kalbeck flatly assumed that Clara's birthday was the occasion for which Brahms's manuscript was intended (*Brahms* 3:193). The birthday celebration on September 13 certainly figures prominently in the portions of Clara's diary and correspondence that Litzmann first published between 1902 and 1908 and to which Kalbeck had access, whereas her anniversary goes unmentioned. Since no direct evidence favors one occasion over the other, however, one must ultimately count both Clara's birthday and her anniversary as potentially important motivations for the manuscript's presentation. Petersen's introduction to his edition of Op. 76 steers such a middle course; see his *Klavierstücke*, 5 and 45.

Clara appears to have kept Brahms's new composition to herself. No evidence hints that anyone else was aware of the work's existence until the summer of 1878, when Brahms began assembling old solo piano pieces and composing new ones for publication in his *Klavierstücke*, Op. 76. In early July 1878, Theodor Billroth had access to most of the *Klavierstücke* through the copyist Franz Hlavaczek. In September, Brahms played three pieces from the set, including Clara's gift, for Heinrich and Elisabeth von Herzogenberg during a particularly close phase in his relationship with them.[3] At some point before November, the work preserved in Clara's manuscript had undergone significant revisions. By February 1879, when Brahms sent a final version to his publisher, it had also acquired its now familiar title, *Capriccio*.[4] Starting in the summer of 1878, then, the F♯-minor *Capriccio* circulated among the composer's musical friends in a manner typical of works he was about to publish, but until it began to find a place in Op. 76, the piece Brahms had presented to Clara in September 1871 seems to have remained a thoroughly private musical utterance.

Traces of her response to Brahms's gift survived in Clara's correspondence on three separate occasions. First, in a letter to Rosalie Leser from September 16, 1871, she displayed newfound warmth in her attitude toward Brahms, proclaiming him "charming as never before."[5] Perhaps her old friend's gift of an original, unpublished composition had helped color her impression of their time together at the birthday celebration three days prior. Next, in a letter to Brahms himself from July 1877, Clara confirmed that she still enjoyed playing from her manuscript long after its presentation and noted its date when she did so: "But I must still tell you that I take great pleasure in a piece in F♯ minor, 'Unruhig bewegt,' which you sent me on September 12th, 1871. It is dreadfully difficult, but so wonderful, so tender

---

[3] Brahms/Herzogenberg, *Briefwechsel* 1:72–75, and Billroth/Brahms, *Briefwechsel*, 267–75. Brahms informed Billroth that new music awaited him at Hlavaczek's in an undated letter from early July; by July 9, Billroth had seen all but Nos. 3 and 4 of Op. 76 and commented on them individually, including the F♯-minor *Capriccio*. At the Herzogenbergs' in September, Brahms played the works later published as Nos. 1, 2, and 7.

[4] Brahms, *Briefe an Simrock* 2:106. Because Brahms's autograph for the final version of the *Capriccio* does not survive and Hlavaczek's copy is in private hands, it is impossible to determine when the bulk of the revisions took place. Fortunately, George Bozarth has examined Hlavaczek's copies of Opp. 76 Nos. 1–4. In his edition of Brahms's correspondence with Robert Keller, Bozarth claims that "Brahms also made numerous small-scale compositional revisions in the Hlavaczek manuscript." Given this description, one might tentatively assume that Clara's *Capriccio* was revised in late June or early July 1878, just before it began to circulate among Brahms's other friends. See George Bozarth and Wiltrud Martin, eds., *The Brahms-Keller Correspondence* (Lincoln: University of Nebraska Press, 1996), 38. For the current location of Hlavaczek's copy, see McCorkle, *Werkverzeichnis*, 323.

[5] Litzmann, *Clara Schumann* 3:263. Clara used the same word (*liebenswürdig*, or charming) in a diary entry describing Brahms's behavior in the days surrounding her birthday: "Johannes's charming behavior had also contributed greatly to everyone's comfort" (262).

and melancholy, that when I play it, joy and sadness always surround my heart."[6] Among extant documents, this remains Clara's most detailed description of the *Capriccio* itself. The piece probably posed particular challenges in July 1877 because she had recently injured her right hand, as she had already explained to Brahms earlier in the same letter. Beyond the sheer difficulty of the work, however, her account also stressed its affective ambiguity and recorded how powerfully she experienced that ambiguity in the act of performance.

Finally, in November 1878, Clara addressed the newly revised *Capriccio* as part of a response to Brahms's request for her impressions of all eight piano pieces from Op. 76.[7] Her letter argued forcefully against Brahms's revisions, and her criticisms, in turn, revealed a deep prior engagement with her manuscript gift, both at the piano and in her musical memory. She presented two specific objections to Brahms's changes. The first involved the slow return of the work's opening flourish roughly halfway through the piece, a moment which Brahms had chosen to condense in his new version. Clara's letter appealed explicitly to her long familiarity with the original work, which had stretched the same material over four measures instead of two: "The earlier reading simply always delighted me so much. Why did you change it?"[8] Here was direct evidence that Clara felt significant personal attachment, at least in retrospect, to particular passages from the composition she had come to know. Perhaps the unapologetic directness of her question registered a hint of annoyance that Brahms was not only publishing a musical work she had long considered her own but also altering it significantly in the process. After all, when she had first received Brahms's gift in 1871, he seems not to have given her a signed autograph in ten years.[9] Whatever the actual substance of Brahms's revisions, the simple fact that he had deviated from her original manuscript may have removed some of what she perceived as the work's personal aura.

---

[6] Brahms/Schumann, *Briefe* 2:115.

[7] A letter from the composer, no longer extant, apparently prompted her to address the Op. 76 *Klavierstücke*. Brahms must have asked explicitly for comments about the individual pieces or at least mentioned some of his plans for the opus as a whole. Clara responded: "A favorite of mine is the C major, and you want to leave it out? Why that, exactly? If one should be left out, I am more for the one in A major" (Brahms/Schumann, *Briefe* 2:157). Brahms eventually retained the C-major *Capriccio* as the final piece in Op. 76.

[8] Brahms/Schumann, *Briefe* 2:159.

[9] Brahms had given Clara a choral score of the *German Requiem* on Christmas Day 1866, but most of that manuscript was in a copyist's hand. Curiously, the last two complete, signed autographs he made for her were also of solo piano pieces and also intended as birthday presents. In September 1861, Brahms gave Clara a signed autograph of his Handel Variations, Op. 24, apparently continuing a custom begun the previous year with a piano arrangement of the second movement of the string sextet, Op. 18 (McCorkle, *Werkverzeichnis*, 65 and 82). Clara's manuscript present of 1871 in turn became the first of another series of birthday autographs; see ibid., 197–99 and 251.

Supplementing Clara's proprietary claim of personal attachment was a point of focused music-analytic criticism. This time the target was a repeated, two-measure phrase group from a transitional section in the first half of the revised *Capriccio*. Although her comment was terse, she took care to include a musical example: "What used to be like this: [here she copied the relevant measures from the 1871 manuscript] now goes differently, in octaves, which sounds harsher, the second time as well."[10] Examples 6.1a and b compare the two versions of the passage. For Clara, Brahms's revised left hand created obtrusive parallel octaves against the bass on the third and sixth eighth-note partials of each measure. On the page, these octaves were buried amid cascading figuration; in singling them out Clara's letter hinted that her assessment of Brahms's compositions depended upon the constraints of performance as well as the analysis of musical structure. The new octaves were problematic partly because of their consistent metric placement, but mostly because of the fingering implied by the revised score, which placed the last two

EXAMPLE 6.1a   Brahms, *Capriccio*, Op. 76 No. 1, revised version (1878), mm. 28–29

EXAMPLE 6.1b   Brahms, *Capriccio*, Op. 76 No. 1, original version (1871), mm. 27–28. From the autograph.

EXAMPLE 6.1c   Clara Schumann to Johannes Brahms, November 7, 1878. From Berthold Litzmann's transcription (1927).

[10] Brahms/Schumann, *Briefe* 2:158–59. Clara's letter also applies the same criticism to mm. 32–33 of the revised *Capriccio*, which present a literal transposition of mm. 28–29.

sixteenths of each half-measure on the lower staff. This spatial arrangement would naturally lead a conscientious pianist to play each measure's third and sixth partials with the left thumb, inadvertently but almost inevitably creating the aural impression of an accentuated inner voice that progressed in parallel with the bass. In the broad marketplace of amateur music making, such an inner voice would become prominent only when played, but Clara might easily have identified it without sitting at the keyboard. For a musician of her caliber, simply looking at a score would surely have provided access to many of the sonic implications of the physical demands imposed by the music in the act of performance.

Most importantly, the musical excerpt Clara included in her letter illustrates how well she knew the original version of the *Capriccio*, ironically because the two did not correspond precisely. Example 6.1c provides her version below the passage it was meant to reproduce.[11] Of the twenty-four notes in Clara's excerpt, fully twelve diverged from her own copy of the piece owing to discrepancies in pitch, register, or scoring. The final three sixteenths presented rearranged or entirely different pitches. The sixteenths on the third eighth-note partial of the excerpt's second measure were transposed to the wrong octave with respect to the original; the fifth partial of the second measure acquired an upward stem. Finally, the excerpt scored the upper staff of its first measure in treble rather than bass clef, shifting the first three sixteenths of each beat into new positions on the page while leaving their pitches intact. The result preserved the essential melodic and harmonic features of the passage in question, and its departures prove negligible when heard in context. Nevertheless, it is inconceivable that Clara

---

[11] Like most of Clara's correspondence with Brahms, the original manuscript of this letter is lost, either destroyed or untraceable in private hands. Nevertheless, there are two good reasons to trust Litzmann's transcription of her interpolated musical example. First, he had already transcribed the same letter in *Clara Schumann* 3:391. His later transcription in the Brahms/Schumann *Briefe* was a new engraving, but it matched his earlier reading of the original letter except for the F♮ on the second beat of the second measure, which acquired a dot in the Brahms/Schumann correspondence. This change suggests that he may have returned to the original letter or at least scrutinized the earlier publication carefully before printing the excerpt a second time. Second, Litzmann took considerable pains to reproduce Clara's original as precisely as possible, even when it contravened standard notational practice. His two transcriptions were unanimous not only in the two successive upward stems on the second and third sixteenth notes in the last measure's second beat, but also in their substitution of paired eighth rests where Clara undoubtedly meant to place single sixteenth rests. In this regard Litzmann's zeal for precise replication seems to have led, ironically, to an error in transcription. Even in highly legible autographs written in her teenage years, the vertical stroke in Clara's sixteenth rests had always tilted significantly to the right. An 1836 autograph of her *Romanze*, Op. 5 No. 3, displays an early example in m. 11, as do mm. 10–11 of an 1838 autograph of the same work; for facsimiles, see Ingrid Bodsch and Gerd Nauhaus, *Clara Schumann 1819–1896 Katalog zur Ausstellung* (Bonn: Stadtmuseum Bonn, 1996), 29 and 118. The rightward tilt became even more pronounced in sixteenth rests from later years, as her musical handwriting became more fluid and confident; the autograph of an unpublished *Romanze* from 1856 provides prominent examples in mm. 1, 2, and 5 (ibid., 122). Litzmann's difficulties were compounded because the brief musical excerpts in Clara's letter of 1878 contain no legitimate eighth rests that he might have used as a basis for comparison; encountered in isolation, her unorthodox sixteenth rests might easily be mistaken for paired eighth rests.

Schumann could have so thoroughly miscopied a passage of music directly from her score. One can only conclude, instead, that she was quoting from memory.

Clara's misremembered musical excerpt, her explicit enthusiasm for the "earlier reading" preserved in her manuscript, and her stated admiration for the *Capriccio*'s affective ambiguity all suggest that the work remained important to her long after its presentation in 1871. Whereas the circumstances under which she first received Brahms's autograph and the personal connotations his gift might have evoked thereafter remain largely inaccessible, surviving documents show unequivocally that, by 1878, her memories of the *Capriccio* itself were emotionally powerful, musically specific, and intimately tied to the medium of performance at her instrument. Brahms seems to have anticipated the nature and depth of his friend's familiarity with his piano piece before she criticized his revisions. A wide array of evidence indicates that he had already used her familiarity as a compositional resource, purposefully designing a setting of Carl Candidus's poem "Alte Liebe" (Old Love) in order to stir her musical memories of the F♯-minor *Capriccio*. Correspondence, diary entries, and early compositional variants permit detailed investigation of Brahms's attitude with respect to his song and Clara's potential reception of its interwoven allusive gestures.

Brahms completed his setting of "Alte Liebe" on May 6, 1876, more than four years after he had given Clara her *Capriccio* but still two years before its revised version first surfaced among his broader circles. Three days later, on May 9, he finished a setting of Goethe's "Unüberwindlich" (Unconquerable). Fair copies of both songs survive today in Brahms's hand, the first in the Beinecke Rare Book and Manuscript Library at Yale University and the second in the Universitäts- und Landesbibliothek at Darmstadt.[12] Like the early version of Clara's *Capriccio*, the songs in both manuscripts differ from the readings Brahms eventually published. Most discrepancies are negligible, but each manuscript also preserves at least one musically significant variant. The autograph of *Alte Liebe* raises the third of the song's final triad, while the published version ends on the minor tonic. The autograph of *Unüberwindlich* scores its vocal line entirely in the bass clef, while the published version uses the more conventional treble; in addition, the published version brackets the piano's opening two-measure motive and attributes it to Domenico Scarlatti, but the manuscript neither brackets nor attributes the motive. Leaving aside the music itself, both autographs include another detail that the published versions omit: immediately following the closing double bar lines, Brahms appended his signature and the precise date on which he completed each song. All of these variants are useful in assessing the early reception of the songs.

---

[12] The autograph of *Alte Liebe* is catalogued as FRKF 870, Friedrich R. Koch Collection. The autograph of *Unüberwindlich* is catalogued as Mus. Ms. 1522.

In typical fashion, both songs circulated widely among Brahms's close friends immediately prior to their publication in August 1877 as the first and last of the Five Songs, Op. 72. In the spring of 1877, the composer sent them, along with many of the other songs from Opp. 69–72, to Theodor Billroth, and then to the Herzogenbergs and Clara herself, on their way to Fritz Simrock's publishing firm. Several acquaintances also encountered the songs secondhand, through mutual friends, during this flurry of prepublication activity.[13] Others, however, had already seen *Alte Liebe* and *Unüberwindlich* before Brahms released manuscripts widely within his circles—indeed, before he had written the bulk of the songs in Opp. 69–72. Independent and far narrower currents of reception had begun in 1876, just after Brahms completed the surviving autographs. Some of these currents left clear traces in extant documents. In late October 1876, for instance, Brahms gave the surviving autograph of *Unüberwindlich* and a copyist's manuscript of *Alte Liebe* to the baritone Josef Hauser in Karlsruhe.[14] Other currents, however, are more difficult to reconstruct in retrospect. Having gotten to know the songs of Opp. 69–72 in late April and early May 1877, Elisabeth von Herzogenberg wrote a letter to Brahms in which she referred to *Alte Liebe* as belonging to the baritone George Henschel. In actual fact she seems to have meant not the song itself but an autograph manuscript of it.[15] In November 1881, Henschel gave an autograph of *Alte Liebe* to Henry Lee Higginson, who had founded the Boston Symphony Orchestra and brought Henschel from Europe to be its first conductor that fall. Sold in 1982 to an unidentified American buyer by a small antiquarian company in upstate New York, Henschel's manuscript subsequently vanished from scholarly attention until it reappeared in the Beinecke Library in the early twenty-first century.[16]

[13] Billroth/Brahms, *Briefwechsel*, 234–36; Brahms/Herzogenberg, *Briefwechsel* 1:19–21 and 26–27; Brahms/Schumann, *Briefe* 2:96–98; and Simrock, *Briefe*, 99. Amalie Joachim and Julius Stockhausen heard many of the songs in Opp. 69–72 in late March or early April (see Billroth/Brahms, *Briefwechsel*, 236). Theodor Wilhelm Engelmann must have encountered at least some of them by early July 1877, since he referred playfully to the text of *Mädchenfluch*, Op. 69 No. 9, in a letter from July 10; see Brahms/Engelmann, *Briefwechsel*, 64. Moreover, a letter to Brahms from Simrock mentions a mid-July party at which both of the Engelmanns enjoyed performing from scores that incorporated Brahms's recent revisions to Opp. 69–72 (Simrock, *Briefe*, 107).

[14] Brahms was in Karlsruhe from October 28 through November 4, when his First Symphony was played under Dessoff's direction (Hofmann, *Zeittafel*, 134). Hauser probably received the autograph in late October rather than early November, since the copyist's manuscript of *Alte Liebe* is dated "Okt 76"; this manuscript is also preserved in Darmstadt's Universitäts- und Landesbibliothek (Mus. Ms. 1523).

[15] Elisabeth referred to the song by means of the opening line of its text and attributed its ownership to Henschel in parentheses, thus: "'die dunklen Schwalben' (von Henschel)." See Brahms/Herzogenberg, *Briefwechsel* 1:27. Labeling the song "Henschel's" allowed Elisabeth to remind Brahms tactfully of an old promise to send her an autograph manuscript of her own. Brahms had mentioned the promise in a letter to her husband from the previous month (ibid., 26) but did not fulfill it until November, when he sent a playfully annotated autograph of the allusive vocal quartet *O Schöne Nacht*, Op. 92 No. 1.

[16] I am indebted to Richard Saunders of the Hudson Rogue Company for providing a facsimile of the manuscript he sold in 1982. I have also traced its intermediary owners: an anonymous American who owned the manuscript from 1982 to 1985; Christie's King Street in London, which sold it on March 27, 1985; and a London art dealer who sold it to a representative of Friedrich Koch sometime before the

Elisabeth's letter shows that Henschel already owned this autograph in the spring of 1877. A clue as to when he acquired it remains in a little-known version of the diary that Henschel kept while visiting Brahms on the Baltic island of Rügen in July 1876. In 1901 and 1907, the baritone published English translations of his diary. The 1907 translation, which appeared as part of a small book, has since become a central primary source for Anglo-American scholars, not least because it purports to preserve Brahms's comments on his own compositional process in the famous song *Die Mainacht* (May Night), Op. 43 No. 2. But in 1898, before publishing either of his translations, Henschel allowed Max Kalbeck to print substantial portions of the diary in the original German. According to all three versions of the diary, the two musicians discussed some of the composer's latest songs on the afternoon of July 9, 1876. Henschel's English translations name only one specific song, *Unüberwindlich*.[17] By contrast, immediately after *Unüberwindlich*, another song appeared in the German version of the diary:"He gave me in manuscript an equally new, very beautiful song, 'Alte Liebe' of Candidus, so that I now already possess the manuscripts of four of his songs."[18] The autograph's later history itself provides a plausible reason for Henschel's omission of this sentence in his translations: by the time those translations were published, he had long since given his manuscript away, rendering irrelevant and inaccurate his enthusiastic claim of ownership.

Once Henschel acquired the autograph now in the Beinecke Library, it seems scarcely to have influenced the song's reception. Elisabeth's letter remains the sole evidence that anyone else in Brahms's circles was aware of his gift to Henschel, and nothing suggests that their mutual friends ever saw the manuscript again after July 1876. But Clara Schumann may already have encountered the autograph before Henschel acquired it. Prior to sending *Alte Liebe* and *Unüberwindlich* on the usual prepublication rounds or showing them to Henschel, Brahms ensured that his new songs, like the 1871 *Capriccio*, reached Clara's eyes

---

Koch Collection became part of the Beinecke Library's holdings. For earlier attempts to trace the later provenance of Henschel's manuscript, see McCorkle, *Werkverzeichnis*, 307, and George Bozarth, "The First Generation of Brahms Manuscript Collections," *Notes* 40 (1983): 260.

[17] Henschel, "Personal Recollections of Johannes Brahms," *Century Illustrated Magazine* 66/5, March 1901, 732; and *Personal Recollections*, 33.

[18] Kalbeck's version of Henschel's diary appeared in "Neues über Brahms, mitgetheilt von Max Kalbeck," *Neues Wiener Tagblatt* 32/91 and 32/94 (April 2 and 5, 1898). Both parts of the article appeared below the fold on 1–3 of their respective issues; the quotation regarding *Alte Liebe* appeared on 2 of the April 2 installment. In turn, Kalbeck himself relied upon this sentence when preparing his edition of the Brahms/Herzogenberg correspondence. There, Elisabeth's cryptic remark about *Alte Liebe* in 1877 received the following annotation:"The singer Georg Henschel (b. 1850) is meant, to whom Brahms gave the manuscript of"Alte Liebe"in the summer of 1876 during their shared vacation on Rügen" (Brahms/Herzogenberg, *Briefwechsel* 1:27n). For a fascinating attempt to reconcile the various published versions of Henschel's diary, see Bozarth, *Johannes Brahms and George Henschel*.

and ears first. He could not deliver them immediately in person, since he was still in Vienna during May 1876, far from her home in Berlin. Instead, sometime between May 9 and May 28, he sent manuscript copies to Julius Stockhausen, along with a note asking him to sing them to Clara: "Immediately before and after my birthday I wrote two songs that seem to me well suited for you. But go to Frau Schumann with them and sing them to her."[19] Stockhausen fulfilled Brahms's request for a performance immediately, singing *Alte Liebe* and *Unüberwindlich* for Clara on May 28, 1876. Circumstantial evidence suggests that he performed from the very autographs that survive today in New Haven and Darmstadt.

Brahms put off deciding where he would spend the summer of 1876 until late May or early June, after he had already sent Stockhausen copies of his new songs. Once he finally chose the island of Rügen, he quickly arranged to visit Clara in Berlin from June 8 to June 11 on his way north.[20] His time in Berlin gave him ample opportunity to retrieve the manuscripts he had sent to Stockhausen, and their unanticipated recovery might explain why he was carrying apparently expendable autographs when he encountered George Henschel in July and, while still on his way home to Vienna, Josef Hauser in October. Brahms's movements and correspondence thus support a plausible narrative that traces the surviving autographs from their creation, through Clara's hands, to their eventual dispersal and present locations, without requiring the existence of any more fair copies. Narratives involving multiple fair copies could also be derived from the same evidence, but by the mid-1870s Brahms was not in the habit of making multiple autographs of a single version of a solo song.[21]

[19] Brahms/Stockhausen, *Briefwechsel*, 118.
[20] Clara described his visit in her diary (see Litzmann, *Clara Schumann* 3:335). Brahms may have first begun considering the Baltic Sea as a potential summer retreat several months prior. Henschel's diary records that he and Brahms discussed possible vacation destinations on the evening of February 27 ("Personal Recollections," 731, and *Personal Recollections*, 26). In late April, however, Brahms was clearly still torn between various options: in a letter postmarked April 22, he asked Simrock whether he ought to return to Rüschlikon, near Zürich, where he had spent the summer of 1874 (Brahms, *Briefe an Simrock* 1:221). The first surviving evidence of his final decision to go to the island of Rügen dates from June 5, well after he had sent Stockhausen the manuscripts of *Alte Liebe* and *Unüberwindlich*; see Brahms/Engelmann, *Briefwechsel*, 45.
[21] While quite a few duplicate song autographs survive in Brahms's hand from the 1850s and early 1860s, the number drops precipitously after the premiere of the *German Requiem* in 1868. This trend is too marked to be blamed simply on chance losses of later autographs, especially as one would expect their owners to retain more of Brahms's manuscripts as his fame increased. One explanation might be that the composer's growing financial independence permitted him to rely more often on professional copyists instead of spending the time to make multiple fair copies himself. Indeed, the appearance and dates of the duplicate autographs that do survive from the 1870s suggest that Brahms understood the value of his manuscripts and created duplicates deliberately as formal presents. Many were clearly commemorative gifts, made on decorative paper for particular occasions long after the music they contained had already been published; see, for instance, the copies of *An ein Veilchen*, Op. 49 No. 2, and *Wiegenlied*, Op. 49 No. 4, that Brahms prepared for Clara Schumann in September 1872, almost four years after Op. 49 had been published (McCorkle, *Werkverzeichnis*, 197–99).

In this case, having drafted his new pair of songs and copied them cleanly by hand in early May, Brahms would had little reason to make a second set of fair copies within a week or two of the first. The work habits evident from his previous decade of song composition suggest, instead, that he simply sent to Stockhausen the autographs he had made (expecting him to return them by mail) and retained his own drafts, which, as usual, no longer survive.

It is therefore plausible to suppose that Clara had access to the song manuscripts in question. And even if she did not see the autographs themselves, she must have encountered both songs in the versions they preserve, complete with the Picardy third at the end of *Alte Liebe* and the bass clef and unattributed borrowing in *Unüberwindlich*. Brahms's letter refers to the songs as having been completed immediately before and after his birthday, May 7; the surviving autographs (dated May 6 and May 9) were therefore made as soon as the songs were finished, leaving no time for earlier versions that might have been sent to Berlin instead. At the same time, he did not consider altering any of the musical variants preserved in his autographs until several months after he mailed copies to Stockhausen.[22] In sum, documentary evidence shows that Brahms arranged a special premiere performance of his new songs for Clara shortly after completing them and significantly before releasing them among the rest of his circle; the versions of the songs he intended her to hear remain available today, as well as the manuscripts she probably saw. Finally, Brahms's letter to Stockhausen preserves an intriguing indication of the composer's attitude toward his new songs and their first audience. To his straightforward request for a performance of the songs, Brahms added a curious comment: "For as you are the best to sing them, yet she is the best to hear them."[23]

With regard to Stockhausen's voice, Brahms might have intended his comment to be understood in at least two distinct senses. Read as applying to the baritone's singing in general, the claim acknowledged his position among Brahms's friends as the preeminent male singer of Brahms's songs. By explicitly reminding Stockhausen of the authority of his vocal interpretations, Brahms implicitly reinforced

---

[22] Josef Hauser's dated copyist's manuscript of *Alte Liebe* shows that the song's original Picardy third persisted at least through October 1876. Later documents even cast some doubt on its eventual disappearance in the published version. Franz Hlavaczek's copy of the song, which served as the engraver's model for the first edition in 1877, maintains the Picardy third as well, but Robert Keller's, which served as the engraver's model for the transposed high-voice version during the same months, does not. Both are preserved in the collection of the Brahms-Institut at the Musikhochschule in Lübeck (Bra: A2:31 and Bra: A2:32). Brahms informed his publisher of his final decisions to rescore *Unüberwindlich*'s vocal line in treble clef and to attribute its opening motive to Scarlatti only in May 1877 (Brahms, *Briefe an Simrock* 2:31–32), although he had discussed possible ways of citing the source of his borrowed material with Henschel as early as July 1876 (Henschel, *Personal Recollections*, 33).

[23] Brahms/Stockhausen, *Briefwechsel*, 118: "Denn wie Du der Beste zum Singen, ist sie doch die Beste zum Hören!"

the baritone's sense of place within their shared social circle.[24] At the same time, however, *Alte Liebe* and *Unüberwindlich* seem particularly well suited to Stockhausen's voice, insofar as echoes of that voice remain in music Brahms clearly intended for it. For the sake of comparison one may take three examples from the 1860s, when Brahms formed his lasting impression of Stockhausen's singing during frequent collaborations in song recitals. He composed the baritone solos in movements 3 and 6 of the *German Requiem* (1865–66) and the orchestral arrangement of Schubert's *An Schwager Kronos* (1862) intending Stockhausen to perform them. All three movements employ similar overall ranges (A–f', B♯–f♯', and A–f♯') and treat either f' or f♯' as a carefully prepared climax; all three avoid prolonged passages between d' and f', but demand from a baritone the rare flexibility required to approach these high notes swiftly, both by step and by leap from the middle register. Unlike any of Brahms's other songs from the mid-1870s (the nine *Lieder und Gesänge*, Op. 63, from 1873–74, and *Abendregen*, Op. 70 No. 4, from 1875), *Alte Liebe* and *Unüberwindlich* employ virtually the same ambitus and the same climaxes as the examples from the 1860s (their ranges are c–f' and G♯–f♯'), and require the same agility in the upper tessitura. A man in whose voice the *Requiem* solos and Schubert arrangement rang true would be an ideal singer for the songs Brahms sent to Stockhausen in May 1876.

Brahms seems to have had ample motivation, both personal and musical, for his comment regarding Stockhausen's singing. What about Clara's listening? That Brahms respected her opinion of his unpublished compositions was certainly no secret among their mutual friends. But his formulation also indicates that he might have had musical reasons for considering these songs especially fitting for Clara to hear. "For as you are the best to sing them, yet she is the best to hear them": the letter's balanced syntax implied that *Alte Liebe* and *Unüberwindlich* fit Clara's ears just as precisely as they matched Stockhausen's voice, and the word "for" (*denn*) established her privileged listening as the reason for Brahms's wish that she hear the songs. He urged Stockhausen to perform them for her precisely because she was the best listener. Unfortunately, no immediate record of Clara's impressions of the new songs remains in her extant correspondence with Brahms, perhaps because his visit in early June gave her swift and ample opportunity to discuss them in person. When he asked her almost a year later for comments on all the songs he would soon publish in Opp. 69–72, she responded on May 2, 1877, with barely a sentence each of unqualified but vague praise for *Alte Liebe* and *Unüberwindlich*, explaining in both cases that she was already familiar with

---

[24]This is just one of many overt expressions of admiration preserved in Brahms's correspondence with Stockhausen. Conspicuously reinforcing their respect for one another's talent helped the pair maintain their friendship from its beginnings in 1861, despite distances later created by geographical separation and professional competition (for instance, the fact that Stockhausen was chosen over Brahms in 1862 to direct the concerts of the Hamburg Philharmonic; for a concise and balanced description of this circumstance and its effects on their friendship, see Renate Hofmann's introduction to Brahms/Stockhausen, *Briefwechsel*, 16–19).

the songs.[25] Even her diary entry from the day of Stockhausen's performance conveyed her opinion only in the most general terms: "The 28th [of May] at Stockhausen's home. Brahms had sent him two wonderfully beautiful new songs and asked him to sing them to 'the best listener' (me)."[26]

Nevertheless, while Clara's surviving writings reveal little about her response to Brahms's new songs, her diary still preserves a defining aspect of her encounter with them: whatever Brahms meant by proclaiming Clara the best person to listen, she was aware of his claim. Presumably on the day of the premiere, Stockhausen must have shown her Brahms's letter or told her exactly what he had read there. From the first, then, Clara's impression of *Alte Liebe* and *Unüberwindlich* was potentially charged with the awareness that, at least in their case, the composer privileged her ear above all others. Thus made conscious of the individuality of her own musical mind, attuned to the tendencies peculiar to her own experience, what *did* Clara hear when Stockhausen sang Brahms's new songs? *Alte Liebe*'s piano postlude conceals an intriguing possibility. Guided back by the final measures of the song into musical memories that only Brahms and Clara shared at the time, one may reconstruct a plausible scenario for the reception of *Alte Liebe* and *Unüberwindlich* in which allusive composition and informed listening drew together the texts Brahms set, the choices he made in setting them, and the musical knowledge unique to Clara's perspective.

Es kehrt die dunkle Schwalbe	The dark swallow returns
Aus fernem Land zurück,	Again from far-off lands,
Die frommen Störche kehren	The pious storks return
Und bringen neues Glück.	And bring new happiness.
An diesem Frühlingsmorgen	Upon this springtime morning
So trüb verhängt und warm	So cloudy, drear, and warm
Ist mir als fänd' ich wieder	I feel as if I've found
Den alten Liebesharm.	Love's old grief again.
Es ist also ob mich leise	I feel as if somebody
Wer auf die Schulter schlug,	Had gently touched my shoulder,
Als ob ich säuseln hörte	As if I heard a whisper
Wie einer Taube Flug.	As of a dove in flight.

----

[25] Brahms/Schumann, *Briefe* 2:98.

[26] Litzmann, *Clara Schumann* 3:335: "Den 28. bei Stockhausen. Brahms hatte ihm zwei wunderbar schöne neue Lieder geschickt mit der Bitte, sie 'der besten Zuhörerin' (mir) vorzusingen." Pressed for time amid her busy concert schedule and hampered by tiredness in her arms and hands, Clara occasionally completed her diary in retrospect, weeks or even months after the events it describes took place. Her entries for May 1876 were actually completed in August (Brahms/Schumann, *Briefe* 2:72–73), which may explain the vagueness of her account of Stockhausen's performance.

Es klopft an meine Thüre,	A knock comes at my door,
Und ist doch niemand draus;	But no one stands outside;
Ich atme Jasmindüfte,	I breathe the scent of jasmine
Und habe keinen Strauß.	But have no flowers here.
Es ruft mir aus der Ferne,	A voice calls in the distance,
Ein Auge sieht mich an,	An eye returns my gaze,
Ein alter Traum erfaßt mich	An old dream takes hold of me
Und führt mich seine Bahn.	And leads me along its path.

Such was the poem "Alte Liebe" as it appeared in Brahms's copy of Carl Candidus's *Vermischte Gedichte* of 1869.[27] To read it is to eavesdrop on the emotional workings of nostalgia. Initially apprized of the season and scene surrounding the poetic speaker, one then sinks ever deeper into mingled fantasy and reminiscence. The speaker cannot recover or even fully name the former intimacy hinted at in the glance of an eye or the call of a familiar voice, yet, once recalled, the past inevitably reasserts its own patterns of thought and emotion. Candidus's brand of nostalgia was inexorable but not consolatory. Springtime's warm weather and migratory birds initiate the process of recollection, but, unlike the returning seasons, the speaker's "old dream" is now lost forever. The cognitive dissonance between the speaker's unrecoverable memories and cyclically renewed natural surroundings likely resonated for contemporary readers in the uneasy relationship between the content of the poem and its title, which parodied a venerable and well-known proverb, "Alte Liebe rostet nicht" (lit., "old love never rusts").[28] Read in the context of its potential popular connotations, the title "Alte Liebe" may have suggested the possibility of reconciliation with the speaker's old love, but, within the poem itself, love has already faded entirely into self-conscious

---

[27] Candidus's original poem and the 1876 autograph of Brahms's setting omitted many of the internal and line-end commas that appear in printed editions of the song. Brahms's copy of the *Vermischte Gedichte* (Leipzig: S. Hirzel, 1869) survives in the archive of the Gesellschaft der Musikfreunde in Vienna; like the other texts he set from that volume, the poem "Alte Liebe" is dog-eared and clearly worn but bears no marks in pencil or ink.

[28] By the mid-nineteenth century in German-speaking countries, collections of folk proverbs (*Sprichwörter*) had become important corollaries of the popular and academic enthusiasm for folk stories and folk songs exemplified by the Grimms' *Märchen* or Arnim and Brentano's *Des Knaben Wunderhorn*. "Alte Liebe rostet nicht" found a place in nearly all collections of proverbs, including Karl Simrock's seminal 1846 collection, *Die deutschen Sprichwörter*, vol. 20 of *Die deutschen Volksbücher* (Frankfurt am Main: H. L. Brönner, 1846; repr. Stuttgart: Reclam, 1988) and its monumental successor, Karl Friedrich Wilhelm Wander's *Deutsche Sprichwörterlexikon* of 1867–80 (Leipzig: F. A. Brockhaus). The saying's popularity is also demonstrated by the fact that many collections contained variants on its basic form, such as "Alte Liebe rostet nicht, und wenn sie zehn Jahr in Schornstein hinge," which appeared in both Simrock's *Sprichwörter*, 331 (repr. ed.) and Wander's *Sprichwörterlexikon* 3 (1873): 129; Wander's lexicon included six other variants as well. For a concise history of these and other German collections, see Wolfgang Mieder's introduction to the Reclam reprint of Simrock's *Sprichwörter*, 10–15.

regret. The resulting disjunction between positive expectation and hopeless reality forces an informed reader to mimic the speaker's disturbing experience of half-forgotten memories.

Brahms's setting of Candidus's poem created an analogy in tones for the process by which those memories infiltrate and destabilize the poetic speaker's present mood. Against a through-composed structure that accommodates the affective turns of each poetic stanza, *Alte Liebe* overlaid strategic repetitions of the singer's initial motive. Example 6.2 presents this six-pitch vocal incipit and its recurrences throughout the song, in the manuscript version with which Clara was familiar. Following its initial appearance in mm. 2–3 (ex. 6.2a), the motive first recurs tentatively, buried in the accompaniment in mm. 11–12 (ex. 6.2b); it then disappears until mm. 34–35 and 38–39 (ex. 6.2c) where it returns to the vocal line, limited now to its first five pitches; it recurs in full six-note form in the vocal line in mm. 46–47 (ex. 6.2d) and finally in the piano postlude in mm. 55–57 (ex. 6.2e). Taken together, these repetitions allow *Alte Liebe* to link the gradual reappearance of the vocal incipit in its original form with the progressive resurgence of the speaker's past by engaging the listener's memory of the song's opening measures at moments carefully aligned with the speaker's various reactions to recollected intimacy.

EXAMPLE 6.2a   Brahms, *Alte Liebe*, Op. 72 No. 1, mm. 2–3. From the autograph.

EXAMPLE 6.2b   Brahms, *Alte Liebe*, Op. 72 No. 1, mm. 11–12. From the autograph.

The first repetition occurs just before the second stanza of the poem, in which the speaker begins to perceive echoes of lost love in natural phenomena. By rhythmically and texturally obscuring the singer's initial motive, mm. 11–12

reflect the hesitancy with which the speaker at first engages the past; by avoiding the vocal line in favor of the piano accompaniment, the tentative recurrence of the motive reinforces one's sense that the initial impetus behind the speaker's nostalgia comes from outside, in some chance configuration of season, climate, and natural surroundings. The next two repetitions (mm. 34–35 and 38–39) parallel the moments in stanza 4 when the speaker's reminiscences begin to produce sensory impressions that explicitly contradict empirical reality: "But no one stands outside / ...But have no flowers here." The song reverts suddenly to melodic material, accompanimental textures, and (in mm. 34–35) dynamic levels taken directly from the singer's opening measures, but the six-pitch vocal incipit is curtailed to five pitches in order to accommodate six syllables of text rather than seven. The abrupt reappearance and subsequent truncation of the motive make its familiar pitches sound out of place at this point in the song, registering in tones the speaker's increasingly agitated realization that resurgent memories cannot be reconciled with current reality. In the closing couplet, the speaker finally acknowledges that the past remains emotionally overwhelming despite being unrecoverable: "An old dream takes hold of me / And leads me along its path." At the moment of this pivotal admission, the six-pitch vocal incipit returns at last in full (mm. 46–47), complete with its original accompaniment from mm. 2–3.

EXAMPLE 6.2c   Brahms, *Alte Liebe*, Op. 72 No. 1, mm. 34–35 and 38–39. From the autograph.

EXAMPLE 6.2d   Brahms, *Alte Liebe*, Op. 72 No. 1, mm. 46–47. From the autograph.

Carried away from the reader and into private reminiscence, Candidus's speaker then falls silent and the poem ends, but Brahms's song accompanies the poet's silence with a musical image of the old dream the speaker has just reencountered. As the singer ceases in m. 55, the six-pitch motive emerges once more in the accompaniment, lifted momentarily into the highest register employed in the song by either voice or piano. Steady dotted half notes replace the halting rhythm characteristic of all five of the vocal incipit's previous appearances. The resulting agogic uniformity focuses the listener's attention fully on the motive's pitch content and simultaneously establishes a clear distinction in melodic and harmonic pace between the piano postlude and the rest of the song. The piano has never before played these six pitches on the beat, nor has the left hand been reduced to unobtrusive off-beat entrances. Range, rhythm, and relationship between tune and accompaniment all transform the motive into a lyrical melody of unprecedented clarity. Having already heard the motive itself five times, one naturally apprehends this final, augmented statement of its pitches as retrospectively evoking those previous occurrences. Measures 55–59 inevitably sound like a redaction of what preceded them—a final, distilled recollection of the song's most important melodic material. Yet the postlude's exceptional lyricism also tempts the listener to perceive its newly tuneful version of the motive as the song's true underlying theme. Indeed, for the space of five measures, one can almost let oneself be teased out of musical time into understanding *Alte Liebe*'s postlude as an echo from the past to which the poem refers, a heretofore elusive musical dream of which the motive's earlier manifestations were themselves only dim waking memories. Heard in the context of those earlier manifestations, the piano postlude is the goal of a consistent trajectory. From the vocal incipit's initial appearance, through stages of its partial and then full recovery, to its final lyric transformation, the song shapes the listener's progressive experiences of the motive in ways that model the speaker's nostalgic turn of mind.

EXAMPLE 6.2e   Brahms, *Alte Liebe*, Op. 72 No. 1, mm. 55–59. From the autograph.

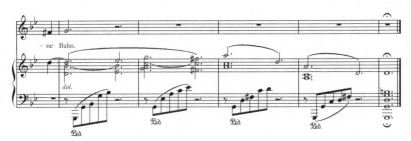

Some such interpretation of the relationship between Candidus's text and Brahms's setting probably informed the impressions of most trained musicians who encountered the song after it was published in 1877. Whatever personal idiosyncrasies one might bring to the task of listening, *Alte Liebe* clearly engaged in sophisticated and compelling play with musical memory. Its capacity to establish and then manipulate the hearer's apprehension of a specific and seemingly self-contained musical past probably accounted for much of the enthusiasm for the song among Brahms's friends before its publication, not to mention its subsequent public popularity.[29] The second lithograph in Max Klinger's *Brahmsphantasie* of 1894 was one testament to the song's prominence among aesthetic depictions of nostalgia during the years following its release. But in May 1876, for one listener only, *Alte Liebe* could unlock far older and more intimate musical memories because its piano postlude incorporated musical material hitherto unique to the still-unpublished *Capriccio* that Brahms had given Clara Schumann in September 1871.

Although the F♯-minor *Capriccio* resists interpretation according to any historically familiar formal outline, its theme was readily identifiable, whether understood as a scrap of music one can remember and hum to oneself later on, a polyphonic complex whose recurrences are aligned in a work's structure with moments of re-beginning, or a melodic and rhythmic profile that remains recognizable despite compositional manipulations such as fragmentation or inversion. Shown in upper-right corner of example 6.3 in the manuscript version Clara knew, the *Capriccio*'s theme began after an emphatic introductory half cadence, when a continuous melody separated itself from the texture and, for the first time, relegated the work's prevailing sixteenth-note figuration to an accompanimental role. This melody traced a slow, circuitous ascent from scale degree 5 to scale degree 9, then accelerated while dropping precipitously toward scale degree 3. Literal, transposed, and inverted repetitions of the first four pitches (scale degrees 5–6–8–♯7) pervaded the entire *Capriccio*, especially at structurally pivotal moments: transitions to and from fragmentary or developmental textures, sudden disappearances and reappearances of sixteenth-note figuration, and the final return to the tonic key (shown on the lower left of ex. 6.3).

The *Capriccio*'s theme was also the locus of Brahms's private allusion in *Alte Liebe*. From May 1876 until July 1878, only he and Clara could have recognized that the melody of the theme and the recurrent vocal incipit of the song were virtually identical. Both began by tracing scale degrees 5–6–8–♯7–9; both treated scale degree 9 as the apex of their melodic span and followed it with a downward leap. Not all of the song's presentations of this melodic material were equally evocative of the *Capriccio*'s theme. In contrast to earlier occurrences of the vocal incipit, the lyrical version in the piano postlude supplemented identical scale degree content with familiar rhythmic and registral strategies: it placed the tune in the same octave as the main theme of the piano piece and presented melodic pitches on successive downbeats and upbeats in a compound duple framework, just as they had appeared in the *Capriccio*. The center of

---

[29]The song's motivic organization is evidently compelling in its own right, even independent of Candidus's text. Michael Musgrave describes *Alte Liebe* as a paradigmatic example of Brahms's "instrumental type" of song composition (in contrast to the "declamatory type"). See "Words for Music," in Musgrave, *Cambridge Companion to Brahms*, 218, and Musgrave, *Music of Brahms*, 151–52.

example 6.3 reproduces *Alte Liebe*'s postlude, and the remainder of the figure illustrates its most salient parallels with Clara's piano piece in the original autograph version. On the upper right is the primary occurrence of the *Capriccio*'s theme, starting in m. 13. Aside from a semitone transposition and an aurally imperceptible metric shift from $\frac{6}{8}$ to $\frac{3}{4}$, the first five notes of its melody are the same as those of the postlude's tune.

Yet despite undeniable resemblances, the postlude did not constitute a straightforward quotation from the *Capriccio*. Instead, it accompanied its melodic reference with textural, harmonic, and kinesthetic characteristics taken from other specific moments in the piano piece. First, the postlude doubled its melody an octave below and placed a third voice in the middle, as did the *Capriccio*'s final return to a tonic pedal in m. 65, shown on the lower left of example 6.3. The tonic pedal itself also reappeared in the bottom pitches of the postlude's left hand. Second, the register and spacing of the pianist's hands in the first measure of the postlude duplicated precisely those characteristics of the *Capriccio*'s opening flourish (on the upper left of example 6.3). The right hand's rootless arpeggio became a rootless simultaneity, while the restless, fifth-less figuration in the left hand was translated into the unidirectional musical dialect of the song's accompaniment as a fifth-less arpeggio. Finally, *Alte Liebe*'s last chord is of special interest. Heard in relation to the *Capriccio*, the major triad preserved in the surviving autograph might have resonated strongly. Not only had the piano piece also ended with a major triad, as reproduced on the bottom right of example 6.3, but the major tonic had displaced its minor double throughout the last fifteen measures of the *Capriccio*, inflecting the work's mesmerizing conclusion with the affective ambiguity of modal mixture. For an ear steeped in the *Capriccio*, the final sonority in the version of *Alte Liebe* that Clara first encountered efficiently evoked the harmonic landscape in which the piano piece had slowly come to rest.

In addition to recalling the *Capriccio*'s theme, then, the last five measures of *Alte Liebe* conflated aurally identifiable moments and interpretively salient materials that together spanned the length of the piano piece, from first measure to last. As one might summarize a long conversation, the postlude encapsulated the essence of Clara's manuscript gift rather than literally quoting any single phrase. The resulting confluence of musical references was too powerful and too specific to have occurred by chance. Brahms must have woven these echoes of the *Capriccio* into the postlude deliberately, knowing where his new song might lead the mind of a musician intimately familiar with his old piano piece and knowing one listener whose mind was equipped to follow where it led. The hypothesis provides a detailed and plausible explanation for Brahms's actions—his compositional decision making in *Alte Liebe*, his efforts to arrange a timely performance especially for Clara, and his statement proclaiming her the song's "best listener"—insofar as those actions

EXAMPLE 6.3   Echoes of the *Capriccio* in the piano postlude of *Alte Liebe*

Capriccio, MS version, opening flourish (mm. 1–2)

Capriccio, MS version, theme (mm. 13–15)

Alte Liebe, piano postlude (mm. 55–59)

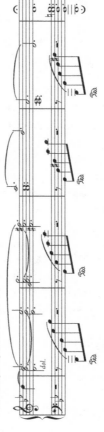

Capriccio, MS version, conclusion (mm. 85–86)

Capriccio, MS version, beginning of coda (mm. 65–68)

can be traced through the music and documents he left behind. In turn, exploring what it might have meant for Clara to recognize his multifaceted allusion can open new windows on Brahms's motivations, both compositional and personal.

At the very least, hearing echoes of music from nearly five years earlier in Brahms's new song would have enhanced Clara's experience of his text-setting. For any other audience, *Alte Liebe*'s strategic repetitions of the vocal incipit might have constituted a persuasive musical representation of long-term recollection. But for her, the piano postlude's basis in preexistent thematic material could insinuate the act of reminiscence itself into the apprehension and understanding of the song. By fashioning the poetic speaker's past in tones she could apprehend through the medium of her own memory, *Alte Liebe* created for Clara a uniquely compelling connection between words and music. By the same token, her prior memories of the *Capriccio* undoubtedly colored Clara's reception of *Alte Liebe* in ways that will never be recovered unless new evidence surfaces regarding her original impressions of the manuscript gift or the circumstances of its presentation. For instance, taking a cue from her stated admiration for the peculiar blend of tenderness and melancholy that she had found in the *Capriccio*, one might wonder if its evocation in *Alte Liebe* made the song sound more specifically bittersweet than either Candidus's poem or Brahms's setting could imply on its own terms.

Prior emotional connotations aside, however, simply recognizing the *Capriccio*'s theme in *Alte Liebe*'s postlude would have rendered Clara's encounter with the song a highly personal experience, for two reasons. First, realizing that Brahms had borrowed musical material known to her alone would have made *Alte Liebe* seem designed "for her ears only," lending the song the quality of a private utterance and urging her to interpret Brahms's intentions in interpersonal as well as aesthetic terms. Such a situation was clearly extraordinary. Although she and the composer were famously close, there is no reason to believe that Clara examined each of his new works for traces of private signification, despite occasional exceptions like the *Alto Rhapsody* and, perhaps, *Meine Liebe ist grün*. Yet *Alte Liebe*'s piano postlude would have all but compelled her to do so, especially given her awareness that he had characterized her as the song's best listener. Second, the *Capriccio* resurfaces just where the postlude presents a musical image of the poetic speaker's "old dream." By conjuring up her private musical past as the implicit object of the poem's nostalgia, *Alte Liebe* permitted Clara to participate vicariously in the speaker's unexpected encounter with neglected memories. Brahms's compositional choices thus allowed her to imagine herself as the poem's disquieted protagonist rather than as a detached reader. In combination, then, the intimacy of Brahms's allusion and its alignment with

Candidus's text facilitated a special way of interacting with vocal music, a perspective peculiarly attuned to the dual possibilities of private significance and empathetic identification with the poetic speaker.

Both the act of the playing *Alte Liebe* and the broader musical context in which Clara first encountered the song would have reinforced such an interpretive perspective. So far this study has approached her response to Brahms's music as a purely aural phenomenon, but surely the best pianist in the room on May 28, 1876, was not content simply to listen. One assumes she would rather have been at her instrument, accompanying Stockhausen's premiere of Brahms's new songs. In any case, a letter from the following spring shows that she later enjoyed playing the songs herself and even sang them to her own accompaniment if no other singer was available.[30] Given the kinds of physical engagement she brought to bear in assessing Brahms's revised *Capriccio* of 1878, the medium of performance would likely have colored her experience of Brahms's compositional choices in *Alte Liebe* in ways both overt and covert. Most obviously, the reference to the *Capriccio* occurred just as the singer fell silent and accompaniment became solo postlude. In the midst of performance, the song's textural organization focused the pianist's ear fully on her own music making precisely when Clara would have needed to listen and established the piano as the primary conduit through which the *Capriccio* entered the song. However Clara was meant to understand Brahms's allusive gesture, excluding the singer from its production could have helped underscore its intimacy by confining her private musical material to her instrument alone.

But there was a complication. Unlike *Meine Liebe ist grün* or any of Brahms's allusive lullabies, *Alte Liebe* was separated from the source of its borrowings by the gap of a semitone. Although the transposition was barely perceptible to the ear alone, it carried the potential to interpose a qualitatively new dimension of distance between remembered music and present music making at the piano. Since all systems of keyboard fingering, not to mention any individual's preferences, inevitably depend upon the relationships among black and white keys inherent in the instrument, one can roughly but systematically reconstruct and compare the physical constraints that a given melody or polyphonic complex placed upon the hand and fingers when played in different keys. Mapping musical gestures and their transpositions onto successions or simultaneities of black and white keys reveals a kinesthetic continuum of resemblance and difference capable of functioning independently from, or in productive tension with, more familiar pitch-based parameters. Within such a continuum, gesture and key can interact in ways both subtle and powerful. In this case, the G-minor tonic of *Alte Liebe* provided an ideal setting for the cultivation of underlying

---

[30] Brahms/Schumann, *Briefe* 2:96.

TABLE 6.1   Kinesthetic Maps of Borrowed Material in the Piano Postlude of *Alte Liebe*

	Initial tonic triad (i)	Theme: melodic incipit	Closing tonic triad (I)
F♯ minor (in *Capriccio*)	⊙○⊙⊙⊙○⊙○	⊙○⊙○⊙	⊙○⊙○⊙○
G minor (in *Alte Liebe*)	○○⊙○⊙○○○	○○⊙○○	○○○○○○

conflicts between sound and sense because it forced a pianist's hands into entirely new positions on the keyboard.

Table 6.1 demonstrates. The top row provides kinesthetic maps of three pitch collections that had played prominent roles in the *Capriccio*, using shaded circles to represent black keys and open circles to represent white. On the left appears the aggregate configuration of black and white keys implied by the root-position tonic triad as articulated in pitch space in the opening measure of the *Capriccio*; in the middle, the ordered pattern of keys implied by the melodic incipit of the *Capriccio*'s theme; and, on the right, the aggregate key configuration implied by the root-position major tonic with which the *Capriccio* ended. These collections correspond to salient material from the upper left, upper right, and lower right portions of example 6.3. As displayed in the central portion of example 6.3, each collection was also integral to Brahms's layered borrowings in the piano postlude of *Alte Liebe*. Accordingly, the bottom row in table 6.1 maps the same pitch collections in G minor.

For every note in every collection, the song's postlude inverts the original relationships among black and white keys. Furthermore, for these particular pitch collections, G minor is the only key in the entire chromatic that produces a complete kinesthetic reversal; at every other level of transposition, at least one pitch would have retained its original identification on the keyboard. In short, Brahms's choice of key gave his allusion to the F♯-minor *Capriccio* a unique combination of proximity in pitch space and difference in probable fingering.[31] Insofar as Clara identified the source from which Brahms borrowed his piano postlude in *Alte Liebe*, her hands could also be made to interfere with the full recovery of her musical memories, making the *Capriccio*'s theme feel strange just

---

[31] No evidence suggests that Brahms was consciously aware of this effect, yet he does seem to have explicitly considered the effects of key choice upon the performer's apprehension of musical structure, even in works that were realized on instruments tuned in equal temperament. Kalbeck recounted a debate from the mid-1880s in which Brahms initially sought to disavow any inherent relationship between musical material and the key in which it was composed, at least "insofar as the indifferent piano was concerned." Here the composer evinced a clear expectation of piano tuning that approached equal temperament and sought thereby to differentiate piano music from works composed for orchestral instruments. Yet when pressed with examples from his own oeuvre for piano, Brahms then seems to have admitted the possibility that his original key choice indeed encapsulated some essential qualities (albeit vague and ill-defined) associated with his treatment of theme and motive (Kalbeck, *Brahms* 3:442–43). It is perfectly plausible that his equivocation was motived, at least in part, by the importance of physical sensation on the part of the performer. For more on the role of half-step transposition in Brahms's music, see Notley, "Brahms's Cello Sonata in F major"; for an alternative view of transposed allusions, see Reynolds, *Motives for Allusion*, 136–37.

as it began to sound familiar. This built-in dissonance between aural and kinesthetic recollection could have instantiated for Clara the temporal distance that ultimately renders Candidus's old dream unrecoverable, adding a uniquely visceral impact to her identification with the poetic speaker. The very act of playing her instrument opened up a new and powerful way to experience firsthand the temporal disjunction inherent in the poem's disquieting nostalgia.

Clara's perspective on *Alte Liebe* may also have been contingent upon its pairing with *Unüberwindlich*, the second song Brahms urged Stockhausen to sing for her. Here is Goethe's text as it appeared in the autograph of Brahms's setting.[32]

Hab ich tausendmal geschworen	I must have sworn a thousand times
Dieser Flasche nicht zu trauen,	Never again to trust that bottle,
Bin ich doch wie neu geboren,	Still it's like I'm born anew
Läßt mein Schenke fern sie schauen.	When my innkeeper lets me see it.
Alles ist an ihr zu loben,	Everything about it beckons,
Glaskrystall und Purpurwein;	Crystal glass and purple wine;
Wird der Propf herausgehoben,	Once the cork's been popped, the bottle's
Sie ist leer und ich nicht mein.	Empty, and I'm not myself.
Hab ich tausendmal geschworen,	I must have sworn a thousand times
Dieser Falschen nicht zu trauen,	Never to trust that lying woman,
Und doch bin ich neugeboren,	And yet I'm still born anew
Läßt sie sich ins Auge schauen.	When she lets my eye meet hers.
Mag sie doch mit mir verfahren,	Even if she treats me falsely
Wies dem stärksten Mann geschah.	As befell the strongest man:
Deine Scheer' in meinen Haaren,	Put your scissors in my hair,
Allerliebste Delila!	My beloved Delilah!

Like Candidus's poetic speaker, Goethe's protagonist finds himself irresistibly reminded of an old romantic attachment, but his circumstances and attitude are entirely different. Rather than listening to the beating pinions of imaginary doves, he orders another drink. Instead of coyly confiding delicate memories of unrecoverable love, he roguishly submits to repeated seductions by a faithless lover. Brahms's settings of the two poems project opposite extremes with regard to nearly every compositional parameter, diverging markedly in mode, meter, tempo, affect, and overall form. To Stockhausen they probably seemed charmingly unrelated—two independent and distinctive lyrical utterances paired by chronological happenstance.

For Clara, however, a single shared compositional procedure could have brought Brahms's new songs into close interpretive proximity. Like *Alte*

---

[32] Goethe had used the word "pfropf" instead of "propf" in line 7, and his punctuation differed from Brahms's.

Liebe, Unüberwindlich borrowed musical material from a solo piano piece, in this case a keyboard sonata in D major by Domenico Scarlatti, K. 223. As of May 1876, however, Brahms had not yet decided to label his allusion explicitly in the score. Although Clara performed many of Scarlatti's works during solo recitals throughout her career, no mention of this particular sonata survives in her extant correspondence or diary entries, and no copy of the piece remains among the remnants of the Schumann library.[33] It is therefore impossible to determine for certain whether she could have recognized Brahms's reference, and whatever private associations the work might have carried for her are now lost. Nevertheless, it seems safe to assume that Brahms meant her to perceive the allusion in *Unüberwindlich* at least as easily as the one in *Alte Liebe*. Having constructed two new compositions around material borrowed from solo piano works, sent both to the same woman, and referred to her as their "best listener," he surely expected her to recognize what he had done. Even if she happened to miss his point at first, his bracketed attribution in the published version of *Unüberwindlich* soon ensured that any literate musician would notice his borrowing and provided sufficient information to identify its source.

Once Clara perceived the central compositional technique the two songs shared, she might have come to hear them as a related and deliberately complementary pair. This is not to deny the important differences between the two allusions. Instead of emerging near the end through a sublimated amalgam of musical references, the head motive of Scarlatti's sonata cheerfully commandeered the opening measures of *Unüberwindlich* with a texturally enhanced but nearly literal quotation. Examples 6.4a and b compare the song's piano introduction with the beginning of the sonata in the edition Brahms knew.[34] Yet even though the two references occurred at opposite ends of their

[33] Consistently programming a short piece by Bach or Scarlatti as a concert opener was one of many ways in which Clara decisively influenced the emerging spectacle of the public piano recital in the mid-nineteenth century; see Reich, *Clara Schumann*, 255–57. Unfortunately, contemporary concert reviewers rarely recorded the key or tempo marking of the Scarlatti sonatas that Clara played. The most accurate and comprehensive account of Clara's concerts and performing repertoire remains Claudia de Vries, *Die Pianistin Clara Wieck-Schumann: Interpretation im Spannungsfeld von Tradition und Individualität* (*Schumann-Forschungen V*), ed. Akio Meyer and Klaus Wolfgang Niemöller, 347–77, through the Robert-Schumann-Gesellschaft, Düsseldorf (Mainz: Schott Musik International, 1996). I am grateful to Dr. Thomas Synofzik, director of the Robert-Schumann-Haus in Zwickau, for information regarding Scarlatti-related materials formerly in the Schumann library.

[34] The placement of the trill in Brahms's quotation and the lack of alternative printed sources for K. 223 in the nineteenth century confirm that he knew the sonata from Carl Czerny's edition, *Sämmtliche Werke für das Piano-Forte von Dominic Scarlatti* (Vienna: Tobias Haslinger, 1839), where it appears as no. 133 on 402. Since Brahms did not acquire Czerny's publication until 1884, he must have encountered K. 223 in someone else's copy of the edition. Robert Schumann had reviewed the edition himself when it first appeared in 1839 (see "Ältere Claviermusik," *Neue Zeitschrift für Musik*, 10/39:153–54); one might reasonably assume that he had kept a copy, although no record of such a volume survives today. Brahms's quotation of K. 223 in a song intended for Clara would have seemed particularly appropriate if he had initially

EXAMPLE 6.4a   Domenico Scarlatti, Sonata in D major, K. 223, mm. 1–5. From Carl
Czerny's edition (1839).

EXAMPLE 6.4b   Brahms, *Unüberwindlich*, Op. 72 No. 5, mm. 1–4. From the autograph
(Universitäts- und Landesbibliothek, Darmstadt). With kind permission.

EXAMPLE 6.4c   Brahms, *Unüberwindlich*, Op. 72 No. 5, mm. 68–72. From the autograph
(Universitäts- und Landesbibliothek, Darmstadt). With kind permission.

respective songs, Brahms incorporated them into their new contexts in fundamentally similar ways. Scarlatti's melody vanished from the song's motivic
surface soon after the piano introduction, only to return triumphantly in the
vocal line to set lines 7 and 15 of the text, where Goethe's speaker finally gives
in to the dual temptations of wine and ill-advised lovemaking. The second of
these moments is reproduced in example 6.4c. In other words, both songs
aligned recurrences of borrowed melodies with the resurgence of latent amorous feelings. In light of this fundamental similarity, Brahms's contrasting
choices of borrowed material and divergent methods of large-scale musical

found the sonata in her library. For more on *Unüberwindlich*'s allusion to K. 223 and Brahms's copy of
Czerny's Scarlatti edition, see Joel Leonard Sheveloff, "The Keyboard Music of Domenico Scarlatti:
A Re-Evaluation of the Present State of Knowledge in the Light of the Sources" (PhD diss., Brandeis
University, 1970), 275–79; and Elizabeth McKay, "Brahms and Scarlatti," *Musical Times* 130 (1989): 586–88.

organization could be understood to register the contrasting origins of those feelings and the divergent emotional responses they elicit from the two poetic speakers. Obvious and immediate quotation of Scarlatti's melody paralleled Goethe's cavalier attitude toward past experience, whereas the subtle and delayed return of the *Capriccio* in *Alte Liebe* underscored Candidus's comparatively bashful stance.

By sending both songs at once, Brahms likely encouraged Clara to recognize their shared allusive strategy and to interpret their differing surfaces as opposite sides of a coin: one public and self-mockingly humorous, the other private and melancholically nostalgic.[35] In turn, perceiving the pair as complementary counterparts might have added a gender-specific dimension to her imagined identification with *Alte Liebe*'s protagonist. Unlike Candidus's poetic speaker, Goethe's was characterized unambiguously as a man, both by the explicitly feminine pronouns that describe his seducer and by his self-proclaimed association with Samson in the poem's final stanza. In the version of *Unüberwindlich* that Clara first encountered in May 1876, the musical setting reinforced the speaker's masculinity by scoring the vocal line in bass clef. Brahms's decision carried special weight for those familiar with his music. Although he had already published more than one hundred and twenty solo songs, many of them appropriate for baritone or bass voices, *Unüberwindlich* was the first for which even a draft survives that employs a clef other than treble.[36] Once Clara recognized Brahms's new songs as a contrasting but integrally related pair, his choice of text and vocal clef in *Unüberwindlich* might have encouraged her to place the two members of that pair on opposite sides of a prevailing gender binary—that is, to imagine the speaker in *Alte Liebe* as a woman, an introspective female alternative to the brash male protagonist of *Unüberwindlich*. Such imagining would have opened new ways in which Clara might empathize with the perspective of Candidus's speaker.

Gender-based identification with the poetic speaker in *Alte Liebe* was yet another level of engagement that Brahms seems to have reserved for the song's "best listener" alone. By the time the *Capriccio* began to circulate in 1878 (potentially allowing others to notice the shared allusive procedure that bound the two songs together), he had already changed the vocal clef of *Unüberwindlich*, undermining the musically heightened masculinity that had marked the song as

---

[35] Christopher Reynolds has explored a related notion of expressive doubling in "Brahms Rhapsodizing: The Alto Rhapsody and Its Expressive Double," *Journal of Musicology* 29 (2012): 191–238.

[36] Brahms had even avoided using the bass clef in *Dämmrung senkte sich von oben*, Op. 59 No. 1, whose vocal line spans G to e', a significantly lower tessitura than that of *Unüberwindlich* or, indeed, any other song Brahms composed prior to 1884.

an explicitly male counterpart to *Alte Liebe* in its manuscript version. For Clara, however, the gender-aligned contrast with *Unüberwindlich* could easily have reinforced aspects of the interpretive stance that *Alte Liebe* had already facilitated on its own. The musical structure of the song, the physical articulation of that structure during the act of performance, and the broader musical context in which she first encountered *Alte Liebe* all encouraged her to search for personal significance in Brahms's compositional decision making and, simultaneously, to identify empathetically with Candidus's poetic speaker. Why might Brahms have wanted Clara to adopt such an interpretive perspective toward his new song? What intentions might he have meant her to perceive as motivating his music?

At the very least, the deliberate privacy of *Alte Liebe*'s allusion and the subject matter of Candidus's text must have made it tempting for Clara to evaluate Brahms's compositional choices against the backdrop of his early relationship with her. After all, he had used the *Capriccio*, a work composed explicitly and exclusively for her, as his musical image for Candidus's dream of old love. By presenting echoes from "her" secret piano piece as nostalgic memories of an irrevocably lost romantic attachment, *Alte Liebe* established a metonymic equation that encouraged her to imagine herself as the poem's remembered beloved and, in turn, to align Brahms with the solitary poetic speaker who cannot escape his memories of her. Moreover, Clara was well aware that Brahms had written *Alte Liebe* in early May, either because she encountered the dated manuscript currently in the Beinecke Library or through contact with the letter he had sent to Stockhausen, which dates Brahms's new songs to "immediately before and after my birthday" and from which she quoted a passage in her diary. Knowing the song's date equipped her to perceive a connection between the season in which Brahms drew memories of the *Capriccio* into the making of new music and the returning springtime by which the speaker is reminded of his past and spurred to poetic utterance. The timing of *Alte Liebe*'s composition could therefore help her to perceive Brahms as further aligning himself with the poetic speaker's nostalgic perspective. Put together, the song's date and the origins of its borrowed material would have made it difficult for Clara to avoid interpreting the text of *Alte Liebe* as in some way retrospectively addressing the composer's old feelings for her.

At the same time, every compositional and contextual parameter that facilitated Clara's apprehension of private extramusical meaning also implicitly aligned her perspective with that of the poem's protagonist as well as its absent love interest, compelling her mind and body to reenact the poetic speaker's experiences and even encouraging her to imagine the speaker as a woman. For Clara, then, recognizing strains of the *Capriccio* in *Alte Liebe*'s postlude could lead to at least two seemingly distinct modes of reception: she might picture herself as a lost beloved whose memory was still a source of inspiration for the composer, or as a solitary musician suddenly caught, herself, in the throes of nostalgia. On its own, either mode could have profoundly affected her understanding of Brahms's attitudes and intentions. Since Candidus left the precise nature and extent of the poetic speaker's former relationship coyly undefined, his poem could accommodate a wide spectrum of memories and concerns that the topic of her shared history with Brahms might have elicited from Clara at two decades' remove. On the one hand, perceiving his allusion as an indication that Brahms still viewed her through the shaded lenses of failed romance might have brought the intense beginning of their relationship into current discourse with a forthrightness for which no precedent appears in written communications from the 1870s. If she found herself pulled in this direction, Candidus's careful avoidance of explicitly sexual imagery would have been particularly useful in maintaining a nonthreatening cognitive parallel between his poem and her past. On the other hand, experiencing *Alte Liebe* as a vicarious reenactment of the poetic speaker's confrontation with distant memories might have led her to imagine her friend's music as a creative muse in its own right, a source of continuing inspiration that remained, muted but subliminally powerful, even when the composer himself had moved on.

Changing circumstances would probably have inclined Clara toward one or the other reading of the same musical, textual, and contextual data. But in May 1876, a combination of both modes of reception seems likely to have resonated in tune with the concurrent dynamic of her friendship with Brahms. Having just returned to Berlin after completing her twelfth English concert tour during March and April of 1876, Clara sent Brahms an early birthday greeting on May 5, the day before he completed the surviving manuscript of *Alte Liebe*.[37] The first paragraph of her letter read:

> So I'm home again then, and my first letter is a greeting to you for the 7th of May—how long it's been already that I've had to commit such greetings to paper, which seems so cold compared to a real affectionate handclasp! I will not recount the many good wishes for you, but for us I wish that you may always be given renewed creative powers. How gladly I would like to know what you are working on now? I still keep thinking that a symphony is coming![38]

Brahms appears to have left this letter unanswered. Not only does no response survive, but Clara wrote again on May 23 with a second inquiry, more oblique but just as flattering, as to his current projects: "There is nothing musically interesting to report from here except what you've contributed, as to us new and beautiful things would come only from you!" Moreover, her final sentence echoed both the diction and tone of her birthday wish to greet Brahms in

---

[37] De Vries, *Die Pianistin*, 357.
[38] Brahms/Schumann, *Briefe* 2:67.

person: "And now yet another heartfelt handclasp from your old Clara."[39] From Clara's perspective, *Alte Liebe* itself must have seemed a fitting response to both letters when she first heard it five days later. She had asked for news of Brahms's compositional activities and alluded to his music's special importance for her. Here was a brand-new song, accompanied by a letter proclaiming her its best listener. She had longed for the chance to be with him on his birthday and lamented how long it had been since such a meeting last took place. Here, buried in the postlude of a song completed on the day before his birthday, were echoes from an older work completed on the day before *her* birthday. The postlude could even be heard as obliquely addressing Clara's rhetorical question "how long it's been already that I've had to commit such greetings to paper"; the occasion of the *Capriccio*'s presentation in 1871 appears to have been the last time she and Brahms were together on either of their birthdays.[40]

Brahms had surely composed *Alte Liebe* before receiving Clara's letter of May 5 (let alone her follow-up of May 23). Mail sent from Berlin would have taken at least a day to reach Vienna, by which time the fair copy was already signed and dated. But realizing that Brahms had already finished *Alte Liebe* before receiving her letter might actually have strengthened Clara's perception of a meaningful relationship between the two, because the song would then have anticipated and responded to hopes that she herself had just begun to express at the time of its composition. Encountering the dated autograph of *Alte Liebe* in the immediate aftermath of her unanswered birthday greeting hinted at the existence of an extraordinary communicative bond, a privately shared intuition, connecting Brahms's mind to hers. In the context of such communication, the two seemingly distinct modes of reception elicited by *Alte Liebe* could merge harmoniously. Understanding Candidus's poetic speaker as a surrogate for Brahms gave Clara a rare and intense glimpse of the composer's long-neglected feelings for her; vicariously enacting the speaker's nostalgia through the process of apprehending the allusion to her *Capriccio* enabled her to experience those neglected feelings as if they were her own. In the right context, both modes of reception reinforced the same conclusion: *Alte Liebe* was designed to reveal Brahms's private thoughts especially for her.

---

[39] Ibid., 70.

[40] The only possible exception was Clara's fifty-fifth birthday, September 13, 1874. She and Brahms were together in Zürich on September 15, but both were only passing through the city en route to different destinations. As late as September 10, Brahms was unsure if Clara was even going to travel through Zürich at all, which also argues against a longer visit. Most importantly, they certainly had not spent any of Brahms's birthdays together since the *Capriccio*'s presentation in 1871. For evidence of their geographical separation on either birthday during the years 1872–75, see (in chronological order): Brahms/ Schumann, *Briefe* 2:12; Hofmann, *Zeittafel*, 108; ibid., 112; Brahms/Schumann, *Briefe* 2:25; Brahms, *Briefe an Simrock* 1:173 and Simrock, *Briefe*, 67; Brahms, *Briefe an Simrock* 1:178–79; Litzmann, *Clara Schumann* 3:321–22; and ibid., 325–26.

In short, the interpretive tendencies that hearing or playing *Alte Liebe* encouraged from a listener familiar with the *Capriccio* confirmed precisely the type of personal, intuitive connection that Clara hoped for with Brahms during May of 1876 and, indeed, throughout much of their long relationship. Even simply recognizing the song's allusive gesture would have invited her into a uniquely intimate understanding of Brahms's music, creating a private exchange in which only he could reawaken her musical past and only she could retrace his compositional process. On any interpretive level, from the purely music-analytic to the broadly contextual, Brahms's compositional choices and his actions in sending her the song facilitated for Clara an imagined sharing of memories and emotions, a carefully constructed experience of mutual closeness between currently distant minds. Heard from Clara's perspective on May 28, 1876, *Alte Liebe*'s allusion summoned up her musical past and her shared history with Brahms not to mourn whatever they had lost over the years but to renew and deepen their current friendship. For her alone, Brahms's music could transform Candidus's nostalgia into a vehicle for personal reassurance.

CHAPTER SEVEN

GRIEF AND TRANSFORMATION

In *Alte Liebe* as in *Meine Liebe ist grün*, the apparent tenderness of Brahms's motivations cuts somewhat against the grain of recent biographical sketches. Scholars of his life and music have grown accustomed to thinking of the mature Brahms as tactless and fundamentally solitary, kind to strangers but prickly with friends, an introspective loner usually on the brink of alienating those around him. In the search for connections between his compositional choices and personal interactions, nostalgic aspects of his music are often interpreted as bearing witness to the consequences of his most antisocial character traits. Yet the imagined closeness and support that Clara could experience in Brahms's songs preserve traces of a man sensitive to her current mood and willing to shape his music so as to encourage positive changes in her outlook. The same was true of Brahms's first violin sonata, Op. 78, which wove together borrowings from both vocal and instrumental sources well known to Clara. Unlike the antecedents to the *Lieder* he had designed for her in the mid-1870s, each of several allusive strands in the violin sonata has been noted prominently in previous literature. Yet their cumulative impact on the listener best positioned to apprehend them remains underestimated, in part because most commentators have approached the sonata through the hindsight of published editions, as a single, uninterrupted whole. By contrast, Clara herself encountered the work piecemeal over the course of several months. Imagining the shifting contours of her perspective opens new windows on Brahms's allusive gestures and the emotional landscapes in which he situated them.

Like most of his instrumental chamber works, the first violin sonata began to circulate widely among Brahms's acquaintances only when all of its movements were essentially finished, and the process of publication was about to commence. According to his own handwritten inventory of his music, Brahms began work on Op. 78 during the summer of 1878, but he did not mention the sonata as such in any surviving correspondence until a year had gone by. Word of the project then spread quickly. Between late June and mid-August 1879, the

Billroths, the Joachims, the Simrocks, the Herzogenbergs, and Clara Schumann had each encountered the complete opus for the first time or heard news of its existence from mutual friends, whereupon Brahms sent a copy directly to Fritz Simrock and authorized him to publish the piece.[1] During the same period, he began to divulge aspects of his compositional process in the sonata to close acquaintances. Beginning in June, a series of puckish letters to Theodor Billroth, Fritz Simrock, and Otto Dessoff revealed that the finale incorporated material from his own *Regenlied* (Rain Song), Op. 59 No. 3, and *Nachklang* (Echo), Op. 59 No. 4; as news of the borrowing spread, the piece soon acquired its common moniker, the *Regenlied* Sonata.[2] Before releasing the complete work within his circles or discussing its structure with friends, however, Brahms had already made a carefully selected portion of it available to one listener alone. Sometime between February 3 and 18, 1879, he had mailed a single sheet of music paper to Clara. On one side was a response to her most recent letter; on the other were the first twenty-four measures of the slow movement in a fair copy, untitled but fully scored for piano and violin. Misplaced and mislabeled after her death, the combined letter and manuscript initiated an independent and intensely private current of reception that would subsequently remain completely unexplored for more than a century. Only since its rediscovery in 1988 have scholars begun to grapple with the possible implications of Brahms's small but potent musical offering.[3]

---

[1] Brahms allowed Theodor Billroth access to a copy of the sonata and told Joseph Joachim of its existence in late June 1879 (Billroth/Brahms, *Briefwechsel*, 282–86; Brahms/Joachim, *Briefwechsel* 2:154). Joseph immediately informed Fritz Simrock of Brahms's latest project, and publisher soon began to pester composer for more information (Simrock, *Briefe*, 144). Brahms also sent a complete copy of the work to Clara Schumann in late June, but she did not receive it until July 10 (Brahms/Schumann, *Briefe* 2:176–77). The Herzogenbergs and Joachims became acquainted with the sonata itself through direct contact with Brahms during a vacation rendezvous outside of Salzburg in mid-August (Brahms/Joachim, *Briefwechsel* 2:159–60; Brahms/Herzogenberg, *Briefwechsel* 1:100–104). Finally, Brahms mailed a copy to his publisher on August 31 (Brahms, *Briefe an Simrock* 2:128).

[2] Writing to Billroth in late June, Brahms suggested that the sonata required a "rainy evening hour" to complete its effect (Billroth/Brahms, *Briefwechsel*, 283). Two months later, his letter to Simrock was more practical: "I'm sending the sonata. But be careful, it can draw you into a piracy lawsuit! 2 measures have already appeared with Rieter" (Brahms, *Briefe an Simrock* 2:128). Brahms resumed a more poetic stance in September, explaining to Dessoff that rain "lends itself well to musical setting, which I've also tried to do this spring in a violin sonata" (Brahms, Spitta, and Dessoff, *Briefwechsel*, 218).

[3] Michael Struck rediscovered and described Brahms's letter and the attached autograph in "Revisionsbedürftig: Zur gedruckten Korrespondenz von Johannes Brahms und Clara Schumann," *Die Musikforschung* 41 (1988): 239–40. The relevant portion of Struck's article soon appeared in English, translated by George Bozarth and Ben Kohn, as "New Evidence on the Genesis of Brahms's G major Violin Sonata, Op. 78," *American Brahms Society Newsletter* 9/1 (1991): 5–6. Constantin Floros published the first facsimile of Brahms's letter and autograph in 1997 (*Frei, aber einsam*, 189), while in 2008, Wolfgang Sandberger included a facsimile of far higher quality in his "Vorwort" to Hans Otto Hinckel's edition of Op. 78; see *Johannes Brahms: Sonate für Klavier und Violine G-dur Opus 78* (Munich: G. Henle, 2008), vii–viii. Most recently, high-resolution color images have been made available online by the Brahms-Institut at the Musikhochschule in Lübeck, where the original is catalogued as Bra: A1:13.

As at Christmas 1873, Felix Schumann provided a focal point for the composer's interchange with Clara, but circumstances were entirely different five years later. Felix's tuberculosis had progressed to a critical point. Already by May 1878 Clara had confided to Brahms that she feared the worst, and in September she informed him that she had given up all hope for his godson's recovery: one lung was entirely useless and the other failing fast.[4] Felix moved back in with his mother and sisters in November 1878, and they cared for him throughout his final months, Clara keeping Brahms updated periodically as to his increasingly debilitated state. By early 1879, the end was clearly approaching. On February 2, 1879, she wrote to Brahms, pivoting in a single paragraph from questions regarding his unpublished violin concerto, of which she had hitherto encountered only the first movement, to a sobering account of recent events in her household:

> As soon as you've made a piano reduction of the concerto, I ask you for it, obviously I can't possibly get anyone to play it here since it is apparently so very difficult, but I can still get an idea for myself. Here it is very bad, Felix is fading noticeably, although he is still not bedridden; the poor man suffers indescribably, and we with him. I cannot tell you how sad I am at heart! I always see him only for a few minutes because it affects him too strongly, but my heart bleeds when I see him, and in the midst of every activity, whatever it may be, I always see him, the poor sufferer, and must truly pull together all the strength of my soul so that I do not succumb to the pain. This illness is surely the worst that can exist, in which one cannot alleviate anything in any way, only stand there always speechless. The suffering is so continuous that the poor sick man can be distracted by nothing even momentarily. Ah, I write you so much about it, but you can well imagine how this sadness now encompasses my entire existence.[5]

News of Felix's suffering appeared here, as in previous letters, alongside expressions of Clara's own feelings of helplessness and despair. As death approached, however, sickness and grief intermingled ever more closely in Clara's prose, aligning the experiences of mother and son in almost uncanny ways. His image shadowed her around the house; his breathlessness robbed her of words; his interminable pain became her inescapable preoccupation. In so charged an atmosphere her very presence had to be rationed like a toxic drug.

It was this letter that provoked Brahms's recently discovered response. His note began by professing sympathy for Clara and gratitude for her willingness to share continued news of Felix. His words were concise to the point of terseness, but he presented the attached musical excerpt as a more expansive corollary:

---

[4] Brahms/Schumann, *Briefe* 2:142 and 152–53.
[5] Ibid., 165–66. Clara had seen the first movement of the violin concerto and heard Joseph Joachim play the solo part during the previous fall (Litzmann, *Clara Schumann* 3:386) but had yet to encounter the rest of the piece, which at this point remained very much in flux due to Brahms's ongoing revisions and Joseph's editorial advice (McCorkle, *Werkverzeichnis*, 325).

Dear Clara,

If you play what is on the next page quite slowly, it will say to you, perhaps clearer than I otherwise could, how sincerely I am thinking of you and Felix—even of his violin, which, however, is surely at rest.

I thank you from my heart for your letter; I did not and do not like to ask for it, but I always want very much to hear from Felix.

Surviving correspondence preserves no record of Clara's response to Brahms's note or the musical offering that accompanied it. She may have addressed one or both in her next letter to the composer, which is now lost. Nevertheless, some aspects of her potential attitude were eminently predictable from Brahms's perspective and lend themselves to plausible reconstruction in retrospect. Like the rest of his friends in the winter of 1878–79, Clara appears to have been utterly unaware that Brahms was working on a violin sonata in the first place. Given her concurrent interest in his violin concerto and the wish she had just expressed to see a piano score of that work, she might at first have wondered whether the enclosed passage was taken from the concerto's slow movement. Yet the remainder of Brahms's letter forestalled such assumptions; he went on to explain that he would send her a piano arrangement of the concerto immediately, "if and when" he made one. In the absence of obvious sources from which it might have been excerpted, the passage she received in February 1879 therefore seems most likely to have struck Clara as an independent and newly created fragment, regardless of when Brahms had actually composed these measures or what purposes they would ultimately serve.

Heard as a musical response deliberately calibrated to her latest news, the fragment itself would have rewarded interpretation in deeply personal terms. Example 7.1 presents the entire passage as Clara received it. The initial tempo, mode, and affect certainly matched the exigencies of the moment, especially given Brahms's additional instruction to play "quite slowly." Emphasizing the *Adagio* in this *Adagio espressivo* would ensure a slow and luxuriant wash of purely diatonic major in the first five measures while providing room for expressive acceleration later on. The result was an expansive beginning whose warmth and spaciousness might well have provided a welcome escape from the grief and stress that pervaded the Schumann home. But Brahms's instrumentation also hinted at more thoroughgoing interplay between sound and situation. His letter explicitly associated the solo violin part with Felix's hard-won competence on his chosen instrument and recalled to Clara's mind the sound of her son's own violin, a Guarneri given to him a dozen years prior by his other godfather, Joseph Joachim.[6] The metonymic connection between instrument

---

[6] Joseph had made his Leipzig debut on his Guarneri and played it in public for several years before acquiring the first of many Stradivari in 1850. He initially offered the Guarneri to Felix via a letter to Clara in 1860, when the boy was just six years old, promising to deliver the instrument "as soon as his

EXAMPLE 7.1   Johannes Brahms to Clara Schumann, February 1879. From the autograph
(Brahms-Institut an der Musikhochschule Lübeck).

and player was potentially transformative. Even with the Guarneri now silent, its remembered timbre invoked the music making of its owner and thereby opened up the possibility of understanding Brahms's piano-violin duet as an empathetic landscape within which mother and son might vicariously collaborate, an arena in which to reassess their modes of interaction in the face of dire circumstances.

Within such an arena, the textural and thematic unfolding of the fragment presented intriguing affinities with the dynamic that had recently come to hold sway between Clara and Felix. Indeed, to one in whom the requisite sensibilities were already heightened, the excerpt as a whole might have felt like an idealized distillation of one of Clara's brief but intense visits with her son during his final month. The piano entered, alone, with five measures of quintessentially calming music: homophonic, melodically reiterative, and exclusively tonic-oriented. Yet the placid surface belied challenges for the player. On every downbeat but the first, the obvious accompaniment for the right hand was a root-position tonic triad, yet the left hand systematically thwarted the downbeat arrival of scale degree 1 in the bass, keeping melody and harmony out of alignment and, therefore, far more difficult to perform convincingly. Only when the phrase left the tonic for a chromatically tinged modulation in mm. 5–9 did the left hand emphasize the beat at all, and even the ensuing cadence on the dominant was undermined by an unorthodox, arpeggiated bass-line descent. As if to reinforce the subtle tensions inherent in the pitch structure of this initial phrase, dynamic levels remained surprisingly high throughout: too aggressive for mere sweetness, they, too, hinted at underlying strain. The overall impression—simultaneously sincere, emphatic, and halting—was consistent with Clara's self-description in her last letter: seeking to convey reassurance and comfort but forced to summon all her power to do so.[7]

In turn, the violin entered not with a repetition of the piano's theme nor with an accompanimental vamp, but with a full eight measures of its own unique material. Suddenly *piano*, tinged with the parallel minor, and delicately poised atop a prolonged dominant, mm. 9–17 immediately presented themselves in marked

---

fingers are not too short anymore." When Felix was thirteen, the time had come. On tour in mid-December 1867, Joseph wrote home to Amalie and asked her to pack the instrument, insure it, and send it to Felix, who presumably received it in time for Christmas (Joachim and Moser, *Briefe von und an Joachim* 2:124–25 and 454).

[7] Across the decades, musically sensitive commentaries on the opening measures of Brahms's slow movement can often be read as inadvertent glosses on the latent relationship between this music and the social context into which it was initially released. Shortly after the Vienna premiere of Op. 78, Eduard Hanslick commented wryly that "in the Adagio of the sonata the listener occasionally feels unsure where the downbeat falls"; see *Neue Freie Presse*, no. 5474, November 23, 1879, 2. More recently, Margaret Notley finds the beginning of the *Adagio* "austere" and "rather stiff"; see "Discourse and Allusion: The Chamber Music of Brahms," in *Nineteenth-Century Chamber Music*, ed. Stephen Hefling, 265 (New York: Routledge, 2004).

contrast to the beginning of the fragment, as if a second voice, tentative but distinct, had joined the musical conversation. Such direct and sustained contrast would remain unparalleled among initial entrances of the obbligato part in Brahms's entire output of slow movements for solo instrument and piano. Imagined in the dark tones of Felix's Guarneri, the phrase could resonate in tune with his current condition. The violin began as if trying to catch its breath, its quiet, two-note sigh figures accentuated by individual dynamic hairpins and separated by rests. Momentum gathered nonetheless: rests dissolved, volume and tessitura rose abruptly, and slurred melodic segments increased in length from two notes to four. The sudden urgency was itself short-lived, however, as slurs shortened once more and the register soon collapsed toward a subdued half cadence that ushered in the first and only general pause in the entire excerpt. Taken as a unit, the violin's arching phrase could easily be perceived as embodying the rapid and disruptive agitation that had forced Clara to strictly ration her time with Felix in recent weeks. Moreover, the accompaniment mirrored her response to that agitation. Just as her mind and body had adjusted themselves spontaneously in sympathy with her son's suffering, so the piano temporarily gave up its expansive articulation in favor of the violin's shorter slurs and more compact dynamic swings.

With the basic distinction between piano and violin established, the final phrase of Brahms's fragment reconfigured the relationship between them in provocative ways. Characteristics that had hitherto been presented as registers of difference between the entrances of the two instruments were now shared between them. For the first time, the violin found the tonic major and presented material recognizably based upon the piano's initial theme. Its slurs lengthened in accordance with its newfound melody, and it eventually reached the dynamic extreme of *forte*, which had so far been approached only in the piano's initial phrase. At the same time, rather than reverting to its original, diatonic harmonization of the melody, the piano retained the linear chromaticism and contrapuntal inner voices characteristic of the violin's first phrase, along with the steady eighth-note motion in the left hand that had first appeared to accompany the violin's anxious ascent in mm. 13–16. When heard, as Brahms had suggested, in dialogue with Clara's last letter, such synthesis between instruments may have seemed a logical outgrowth of the physiological and emotional dialectic she had described between herself and her son. In Brahms's duet, however, the blurring of instrumental identities coincided not with panic or paralysis but with the achievement of thematic and tonal closure for the passage as a whole, the rounding out and collaborative completion of its various impulses. The final authentic cadence may well have brought tears, but it also brought harmonious fulfillment. Approached from a certain angle, then, Brahms's music encouraged from Clara an alternate perspective on her remaining time with Felix. The deep affinity with his suffering that she described as a symptom of grief might be reclaimed as an emblem of togetherness.

This reading ultimately represents only one of many ways in which Clara might have reconciled Brahms's musical offering with the hermeneutic claims implicit in his letter. Related approaches involved potentially allusive resonances inherent in the excerpt, and particularly in its initial contrapuntal complex. Whatever Brahms's original intentions, the piano's opening motive could be perceived as borrowed from the primary themes of two of Robert Schumann's late works: the slow movement of his D-minor Violin Concerto, WoO 1, and his final variation set in E♭ major for solo piano (which Brahms had already elaborated in his own set of four-hand variations in 1861). The beginning of Brahms's fragment shared with both of these predecessors a characteristic rhythmic profile, a static bass line, and an inner voice that proceeded in parallel sixths with the melody, as shown in examples 7.2a and b.[8] Brahms's tune was different and its harmonic ambitus more compact, but the similarity was still close enough that recent commentators often assume the composer's intent in creating an allusive gesture.[9] Clara may have anticipated them in 1879. After all, she still possessed the autograph of the Variations and a copy of Robert's piano reduction of the concerto, and she herself had played a deciding role in suppressing both pieces in the years following Robert's institutionalization, ensuring that they remained known only to Brahms, the Joachims, and other close friends.[10] Because both works dated from the final months she had shared with her husband before his breakdown, encountering what she understood to be echoes of either one could only have enhanced her sense that Brahms's frag-

---

[8] Example 7.2a is based upon the transcription of Robert's piano arrangement in Reinhard Kapp, ed., *Robert Schumann. Konzert für Violine und Orchester d-Moll WoO 1, nach der Neuen Robert Schumann Gesamtausgabe* (Mainz: Schott, 2010), 66; figure 7.2b is transcribed from Schumann's autograph, a facsimile of which is provided in Walter Beck, *Robert Schumann und seine Geister-Variationen: Ein Lebensbericht mit Notenbild und neuen Dokumenten* (Tutzing: Schneider, 1992), 3–8.

[9] David Brodbeck, "Medium and Meaning: New Aspects of the Chamber Music," in Musgrave, *Cambridge Companion to Brahms*, 117–18; MacDonald, *Brahms*, 279; and Starobinski, "Brahms et la nostalgie de l'enfance," 188–94. To date, Michael Struck has presented the most compelling account of underlying similarities between Robert's two themes in *Robert Schumann. Violinkonzert D-Moll (WoO 23), Meisterwerke der Musik* 47, ed. Stefan Kunze, 50–51 (Munich: Wilhelm Fink, 1988), and *Die umstrittenen späten Instrumentalwerke Schumanns. Untersuchungen zur Entstehung, Struktur und Rezeption, Hamburger Beiträge zur Musikwissenschaft* 29, ed. Constantin Floros, 399–401 (Hamburg: Karl Dieter Wagner, 1984).

[10] For details concerning Clara's suppression of Robert's Variations, see ch. 3. The precise timing and justification for the suppression the Violin Concerto have been matters of debate ever since Eugenie Schumann publically objected to the work's publication in "Eugenie Schumann. Über das letzte Werk ihres Vaters Robert Schumann," *Schweizerische Musikzeitung* 78/1 (1938): 8–10. From her testimony alone derives the oft-repeated assumption that Brahms himself played an important role in the decision not to publish the concerto. In actual fact, Clara and Joseph Joachim may have reached that conclusion on their own, based on deliberations that spanned several years beginning in the mid-1850s. By 1873, Clara seems to have given Robert's autograph score, violin part, and piano arrangement to Joseph, retaining for herself only a corrected copy of the piano arrangement. For detailed descriptions of the debate concerning the concerto and Clara's own access to it after 1873, see Michael Struck, *Violinkonzert D-Moll*, 7–21, and *Die umstrittenen späten Instrumentalwerke Schumanns*, 314–16.

ment was deliberately designed as a personal response to Felix's ongoing decline. Indeed, once the violin itself picked up the theme, she might have perceived the allusive resonance as yet another musical index of her son's unique resemblance to the absent father whom he would soon join in death.

EXAMPLE 7.2a   Robert Schumann, Violin Concerto, WoO 1 / II, mm. 4–6. Piano arrangement.

EXAMPLE 7.2b   Robert Schumann, Theme and Variations, WoO 24, mm. 1–4. From the autograph.

In the scenarios explored here, Brahms's letter would have played a central role in Clara's impressions of his music. Presenting the fragment as an explicit reflection of his sympathetic thoughts allowed Brahms to shape his friend's perspective with unusual precision. This he could do regardless of the genesis of his musical offering. In actual fact, these measures had almost certainly been conceived and fully integrated into a larger movement before he received Clara's letter of February 2 and, quite possibly, before Felix's condition had reached a critical juncture in the first place. Evidence as to the timing of Brahms's initial work on the passage he sent to Clara can be gleaned by comparing the fragment to the surviving autograph of Op. 78 as a whole. Currently held in Vienna by the Wienbibliothek im Rathaus, this autograph is a collection of loose pages divided into two separately paginated sections. The first section contains movements 1 and 2 of the sonata on continuously numbered pages; the slow movement begins on a fresh sheet of paper, but a calligraphic flourish from the closing double bar line of the opening movement spills across the page break, making it clear that the two movements were notated in tandem. The second section contains the finale, to which Brahms assigned a new set of page numbers. Unlike the cleanly copied fragment that Clara received in the mail, both sections are working manuscripts, albeit of a type that reflects a late stage in the compositional process. All themes and phrase groups familiar from the published version are already present here, their order and formal functions fully established. An initial version in ink displays occasional revisions that encompass as much as a measure or two. Smaller but far more numerous changes and additions involving articulation, dynamics, tempo, and, occasionally, the pitches themselves were then added to all three movements in gray pencil.[11]

The final page of the autograph bears the date "June 79" in ink, just below the composer's signature. The date coincided with the end of Brahms's substantive engagement with the sonata, when he sent the work to his Vienna copyist and began publicizing it among his friends. The finale was clearly the last movement to be completed; Brahms would imply in later correspondence that he had been working on it "this spring."[12] The first two movements, by contrast, were demonstrably copied far earlier—earlier, in fact, than the fragment he sent to Clara in February 1879. Within the first twenty-four measures of the slow movement, the full autograph displays twelve editorial changes in Brahms's hand, one in ink and eleven in pencil. Clara's fragment incorporated all but two of these editorial changes.[13] Furthermore, the two manuscripts shared identical layouts: their line breaks occurred in precisely the same locations relative to the unfolding of the music. One was likely copied directly from the other. This is not to say that Clara's fair copy followed the full autograph in every respect; there are slight but numerous differences between them. Most of these could have emerged spontaneously during the combined processes of recopying a passage and inevitably reimagining its sound, while a few may have been consciously designed to maximize the fragment's expressive potential in view of Clara's recent letter. For instance, three slurs in the initial violin entrance were shortened or eliminated in her version and a slow crescendo replaced by multiple dynamic hairpins, contributing significantly to the sense of breathlessness for which her descriptions of Felix's suffering pro-

<hr>

[11] The autograph is catalogued in the music collection of the Wienbibliothek im Rathaus as MH 3908. The most detailed description remains Imogen Fellinger's "Brahms' Sonate für Pianoforte und Violine op. 78: Ein Beitrag zum Schaffensprozeß des Meisters," *Die Musikforschung* 18 (1965): 16–24. Fellinger's observations are individually illuminating but somewhat misleading in the aggregate: they present themselves as a comprehensive catalogue of alterations within the autograph, but in fact scores of emendations go unmentioned. Since most of these are additions made in pencil, one wonders whether she had access only to a photocopy of the manuscript, which would have made it difficult and sometimes impossible to recognize such changes for what they were.

[12] Brahms, Spitta, and Dessoff, *Briefwechsel*, 218.

[13] The alterations incorporated in Clara's fragment comprise five changes in pitch or duration and five changes in articulation or dynamics. The only alterations in the full autograph that found no analogue in the fragment were a cautionary accidental and a single added slur. These may have represented last-minute additions to the full autograph, which would explain why they did not appear in Clara's fair copy. Both were also added in an analogous passage later in the movement, and both pairs of additions were adopted in the published version of the work as well. Such rigorous consistency would certainly seem congruent with a later, more overtly editorial phase in the manuscript's history.

vided a concrete situational analogue. Nevertheless, if Brahms had truly composed this material independently, as a response to Clara's news, he surely would not have changed it in ten ways when integrating it into the sonata only to immediately overturn his changes in favor of the original version. Instead, the signs of editing in the full autograph must have preceded Clara's excerpt, or, at the very latest, they must have been conceived in conjunction with the project of copying the passage for her.

Brahms had therefore drafted the first two movements of Op. 78 in a complete, performance-ready form by February 1879, and perhaps far earlier.[14] Given that his inventory lists the sonata as dating partially from the summer of 1878, it is entirely plausible that one or both of these movements was composed then, before the end stages of Felix's illness. In any case, having already designed the two movements, Brahms was ideally positioned to anticipate how Clara might respond to their larger structures once he had encouraged her to perceive private and powerful emotional associations beneath the shorter excerpt he had sent her. He was also uniquely prepared to recall and redefine those associations in the tones of the finale he had not yet completed. In short, his musical offering of February 1879 had laid the groundwork for modes of persuasion unprecedented in his earlier allusive gifts.

––––––––––––

Precisely when Clara encountered the first two movements of Op. 78 is not clear. At the latest, Brahms mailed her a copy of all three movements at the end of June 1879, but he had already spent nearly a month with her in Frankfurt beginning in mid-March. During his visit, the two musicians seem to have continued the arduous process of editing Robert's piano music for the new *Gesamtausgabe* that Clara was assembling for Breitkopf and Härtel,[15] but they would surely have had manifold opportunities to play and discuss the completed portions of Brahms's current project as well, if he so desired. Naturally, no correspondence between them survives from the month in question, but later letters suggest at least some familiarity with the earlier movements of the sonata prior to the arrival of the entire piece. When Brahms mailed Clara her copy of Op. 78 in June, he lumped the

––––––––––––

[14]This view of the work's chronology is implied, though never fully worked out, in a few previous accounts (most notably Struck's "Revisionsbedürftig"). By contrast, other scholars have assumed that Brahms completed the finale of Op. 78 first, only later adding the other movements (Musgrave, *Music of Brahms*, 182–87). Finally, Wolfgang Sandberger splits the difference by assuming that the initial measures of the *Adagio* preceded the finale but casting doubt on the possibility that the entire *Adagio* was completed before Felix's death (see "Vorwort," v).

[15] For details on Brahms's movements, see Hofmann, *Zeittafel*, 144. For evidence of Clara's ensuing preoccupation with the *Gesamtausgabe* and echoes of Brahms's input, see Litzmann, *Clara Schumann* 3:400, and Brahms/Schumann, *Briefe* 2:168–70.

sonata together with edited copies of two of Robert's early piano works in a laundry list of apparently old business:

> Dear Clara,
>
> I'm sending here, besides the sonata, the Phantasie and the Novelletten. Send the former to Härtel and ask them, after corrections have been made, to prepare two sample copies for you.... The Novelletten I would advise you to send to Rudorf, so that a collaborative labor force can finally commence. The sonata—yes, it is enclosed as well, and just wait and see. I'm afraid it is boring. In the finale you can make a cut at "vi-de." A part is also enclosed—but if you *don't* like it, I ask very kindly that you don't try it out with Heermann.[16]

Even accounting for the composer's characteristically ironic self-deprecation, such words would have represented an extraordinarily cryptic and backhanded way of announcing a totally new opus for the first time. Instead, he had almost certainly provided Clara with news of the work, if not a preview of existing movements, during the preceding weeks.

Clara's reply also hints that the first two movements of the sonata may have been familiar to her already. In a letter dated July 10, she responded to the piece as a whole but focused almost exclusively on the finale, where she delighted in finding echoes of the *Regenlied*. The other movements received a combined total of barely a dozen words, all of them confined to relative clauses—a strange choice if she had never seen those movements before, but utterly justified if she had:

> I must send you word, tell you how I am deeply moved by your sonata. I received it today and naturally played it through immediately for myself and really had to have a good cry afterwards, for joy about it. After the first artful, delightful movement and the second you can imagine for yourself the bliss when I found again in the third my so enthusiastically beloved melody with the attractive eighth-note motion! I say *mine* because I don't believe that *one* person perceives that melody as blissfully and melancholically as I. After all the artful and delightful, that last movement too! My pen is poor, but my heart beats toward you, touched and thankful, and in my mind I press your hand. On Sunday I plan to be in Frankfurt; then I will play it immediately with H[eermann].[17]

Even before she first heard the work played on a violin, Clara's excitement at identifying Brahms's borrowing was palpable. In fact, her enthusiasm for the finale would soon become the central, determining factor in her reception of Op. 78, the predominant theme in literally every subsequent account of the piece that survives in her hand. In order to investigate its origins and implications, however, one must approach her attitude within the context in which it first manifested itself. For, whether she had actually encountered the other

---

[16] Brahms/Schumann, *Briefe* 2:174. Emphasis in original.
[17] Brahms/Schumann, *Briefe* 2:177–78. Emphases in original.

movements in March, April, or July, her diction makes it perfectly clear that she encountered them prior to the finale itself: upon receiving the piece, she "played it through," discovering the joys of the third movement only after she had already absorbed the artfulness of the first two. With the exception of the opening measures in the second movement, then, her perspective on the piece as a whole was fundamentally diachronic, predicated on the ordered unfolding of the work from beginning to end.

Within that unfolding, the first movement introduced motivic material and structural preoccupations integral to the entire opus. The initial thematic gesture, shown in example 7.3a, was built around three iterations of a single motivic cell: one pitch repeated three times to a dotted rhythm. This cell reappeared in differing guises throughout each movement. In the first movement, however, the broad outlines of sonata form provided a conventional backdrop against which recurrences of the cell could stand as straightforward registers of similarity or change. Primary, secondary, and closing thematic groups all incorporated the dotted rhythm, but only the primary theme literally began with it, highlighting its initial offbeat attack by placing it after a rest. The resulting lilt lent a sense of forward momentum to what was otherwise a strikingly placid beginning, even given Brahms's swift tempo indication. The theme itself was a study in textural clarity. The violin played the melody throughout, while the piano's steady pulse created agogic space for the tune's characteristic rhythm. The registers of the two instruments converged once but never crossed. Maximally differentiated texture found its analogue in minimized harmonic tension. In the absence of motion from dominant to tonic, plagal sonorities and plangent suspensions came to the fore. For the pianist, the complete lack of dominant triads also led to an exaggerated simplicity in performance: despite being firmly rooted in G major, the first four measures of the theme were played entirely on white keys. A host of challenges was subtly circumvented through the mere positioning of the passage on the surface of the keyboard, including simultaneity of chordal attacks, dynamic balance among the fingers, and uniformity of release time between repeated pitches under *portato* slurs.

EXAMPLE 7.3a   Brahms, Violin Sonata, Op. 78 / I, mm. 1–4

Aside from within the primary thematic area itself, these four measures returned only three times during the remainder of the movement: twice at the beginning of the development, shown in examples 7.3b and 7.3c, and once at the beginning of the recapitulation, shown in example 7.3d. Extended restatements of the primary theme at both of these critical junctures were commonplace in sonata-form movements. Nevertheless, in this case the position of the restatements set in special relief the larger topography of the movement, which juxtaposed a tuneful and overwhelmingly cheerful exposition and recapitulation against a contrapuntal and unrelentingly dark development. Successive modifications threw the theme increasingly out of joint as the development set in. At first the material could almost be mistaken for a repetition of the exposition, were it not for a textural exchange of melody and accompaniment that rendered it significantly more difficult for either musician to execute convincingly. Within a few measures, however, a swift modulation down the circle of fifths landed the same four-measure passage in A♭ major, a semitone removed from where it began. Half-step transposition played havoc with the kinesthetic constraints under which remembered material had first appeared. What had been all white keys for the pianist now became a volatile mixture that drew the hands ever farther from the body and into the thickets of the keyboard. Indeed, as the phrase progressed, white keys disappeared altogether for a measure and a half, precisely as both performers began their crescendo toward a thunderous A♭-minor attack that initiated the development proper with its cascading scales, pervasive sequences, and ubiquitous minor mode. Only forty-seven measures later did those characteristics gradually dissipate during the retransition. After several false starts, the primary theme finally recaptured its original texture and mode, reharmonized at first but soon buttressed with its familiar white-key accompaniment.

The overarching trajectory encapsulated a cycle of anxious departure and reassuring return: a nightmare shaken off, a weight suddenly eased, a lost happiness recovered. Alongside alterations to the primary theme itself, Brahms reinforced this trajectory through unusual performance indications in the published score. Just as the accompaniment completed its shift from white keys to

EXAMPLE 7.3b   Brahms, Violin Sonata, Op. 78 / I, mm. 82–85

EXAMPLE 7.3c   Brahms, Violin Sonata, Op. 78 / I, mm. 99–107

EXAMPLE 7.3d   Brahms, Violin Sonata, Op. 78 / I, mm. 148–58

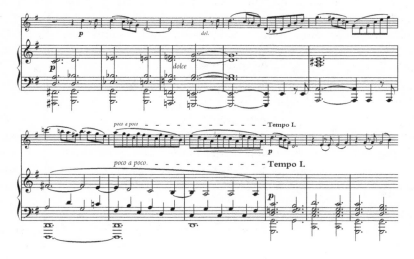

black at the beginning of the development, he notated a two-measure *ritard* that culminated in a new tempo, *più sostenuto*. The remainder of the development then avoided tempo indications altogether until the retransitional dominant, when a second two-measure tempo transition gradually brought back *Tempo I*. The implication of these balanced tempo shifts was clear, albeit counterintuitive:

all the intervening music was to be conceived within the rubric of a slightly slower tempo. Just as modal mixture and contrapuntal complexity darkened the color and thickened the texture of the development section as a whole, so the very pace of the music was to be bogged down as if by sleep or stagnant air. Such an impression is difficult to generate and even harder to maintain in performance. Goaded onward by sequential harmonic patterns and fragmented melodic motives, modern players almost always accelerate substantially rather than holding back during the development section. The problem can be exacerbated by the extreme resonance of today's concert grands and the continuous vibrato so pervasive in recent string pedagogy, both of which encourage such slow tempi for the initial primary theme that little space remains for deceleration later on.[18] For musicians who take them seriously, however, the struggle to execute Brahms's tempo indications can itself provide an expressive corollary to the larger shape of the movement, enhancing the feeling of recovery and renewal inherent in the motivic structure at the moment of recapitulation.

An array of documents preserves traces of a combined written and oral tradition, dating back at least to the 1880s, according to which the bulk of the development was actually performed *più sostenuto*. Writing in 1964, Joseph Szigeti recalled an account of Brahms's own preferences provided by his teacher, the Hungarian violinist Jenö Hubay, who had collaborated with Brahms in public performances of his later violin sonatas beginning in 1886. Hubay explained to Szigeti that Brahms "would insist that the *poco a poco più sostenuto* in the development section of the first movement of the G-major sonata should really be *più sostenuto* until the recapitulation which is in the (faster) tempo primo."[19] Four decades later, Donald Francis Tovey defended the composer's tempi against well-meaning practitioners by means of a music-analytic explanation: "In the first movement the development is the only stormy passage in the whole work, and room is made for its crowded incidents by slackening the tempo...a point not always understood by good players without special experience in Brahms."[20] Whether Clara Schumann could have anticipated this in-

---

[18] For complementary views on the complex effects of evolving piano construction and violin-playing, see Michael Musgrave and Bernard D. Sherman, eds., *Performing Brahms: Early Evidence of Performance Style* (Cambridge: Cambridge University Press, 2003), especially those chapters by Bernard D. Sherman, "How Different Was Brahms's Playing Style from Our Own" (1–10); Clive Brown, "Joachim's Violin Playing and the Performance of Brahms's String Music" (48–98); and Styra Avins, "Performing Brahms's Music: Clues from His Letters," (11–47).

[19] Joseph Szigeti, *A Violinist's Notebook. 200 Examples with Notes for Practice and Performance* (London: Gerald Duckworth, 1964), 152. Hubay had performed both the A-major Violin Sonata, Op. 100, and the D-minor Violin Sonata, Op. 108, with Brahms as his accompanist, but no record survives of any public collaboration involving Op. 78 (Hofmann, *Brahms als Pianist und Dirigent*, 262, 274, and 357).

[20] Donald Francis Tovey, "Brahms, Johannes" in *Cobbett's Cyclopedic Survey of Chamber Music*, ed. Walter Wilson Cobbett (London: Oxford University Press, 1929), 1:176.

terpretive tradition when she first encountered the piece must remain, to some degree, an open question. The surviving autograph of Op. 78 contains no tempo indications whatsoever during the first movement's development section. Yet Clara was clearly playing not from the autograph itself, but from a new fair copy made expressly for her.[21] This copy presumably contained the most recent version of the work available at the time and may well have included the *più sostenuto*. She may therefore have found herself compelled, like Hubay, Tovey, and countless other frustrated musicians, to slow down during the development, adding a visceral, agogic component to the section's discomfiting effect.

———————

Taken as a whole, then, the first movement aligned formal, motivic, and kinesthetic parameters to project an unusually straightforward tripartite structure in which a sunny status quo was established, called into question, and successfully regained. Pleasing and arresting in itself, this abstract shape could take on firmer implications as soon as Clara began to play the ensuing slow movement. Throughout the first twenty-four measures of the *Adagio*, she could not have failed to recognize the return of the music that Brahms had sent to her in February 1879. Notwithstanding occasional differences in orthography, articulation, and other details, the resemblance was absolutely overwhelming. Furthermore, Brahms's original decision to present the passage as an independent fragment now imbued his entire sonata with extraordinary rhetorical potential. From Clara's perspective, a fragment that Brahms had initially shared as a spontaneous and intimate expression of sympathy had suddenly made its way into a large-scale composition—had become, in effect, an allusive borrowing. The probable repercussions were profound. Whatever Op. 78 might mean to others, whatever Brahms's actual intentions might have been, for her the piece was secretly her own, drawn into her emotional orbit by means of an allusive gesture that only she could recognize in the first place. Such a realization could be expected to alter the very foundations of her attitude toward the entire work.

Clara never discussed Brahms's apparent allusion explicitly in extant correspondence. Perhaps she addressed it in person or in letters now lost, or perhaps she felt that words were beside the point. The barest hints of her response survive in a letter that she wrote to Brahms after first reading the sonata with a violinist in late July 1879: "Many may perhaps understand better how to speak of it, but no one can experience it more than I—the deepest, most tender strings of my

———————

[21] One can discern this from the letter that accompanied Op. 78 when it first arrived at Clara's doorstep. Brahms enclosed both score and part without asking for them to be returned, contrary to his usual practice with his own manuscripts of works approaching publication. Moreover, his letter also referred to an optional cut in the finale, which he had notated with the Latin "vide" (Brahms/Schumann, *Briefe* 2:174). No trace of such a mark appears in the surviving autograph.

soul vibrate to such music!"[22] The reappearance of the private musical fragment from five months prior could easily have contributed to her claim of
special insight into Op. 78. At the same time, however, intervening events
most likely complicated her assessment of Brahms's allusion. Felix Schumann
had succumbed to tuberculosis before dawn on February 16, just days after
Brahms's initial musical offering had arrived in the mail. In her diary, Clara
described his passing as "a death struggle in the fullest sense of the word."
In point of fact, she had slept through the decisive moment because Marie,
her eldest daughter, was determined to shield her from it.[23] Still, by the time
she first encountered the complete slow movement, whether in March,
April, or July, her son's death had already divided the borrowed passage irrevocably from its original extramusical correlates. Instead of intervening
directly in the interpersonal dynamic that preceded his passing, the familiar
strains of her fragment now conjured up the memory of that dynamic across
an insurmountable and ever-widening gap. The result was an exquisite dissonance between aural recollection and emotional memory: the source of
Brahms's allusion was easy to identify, yet its former connotations were no
longer congruent with current circumstances.

From Clara's perspective, the remainder of the slow movement might
have seemed expressly designed to prolong and then resolve the dissonance.
Certainly the various stages in the *Adagio*'s ternary form could be heard as
repositioning the musical registers of her final interactions with Felix within
a larger structure capable of reflecting, and reflecting upon, his passing. First
came the contrasting B section, of which example 7.4 provides the first fifteen measures. Simultaneous shifts in mode, motive, and tempo immediately announced the arrival of a new and darker affect. The piano's low
register, minor mode, persistent dotted rhythms, and repeating left-hand
ostinato all evoked the well-established *topos* of the funeral march. Decades
before Clara's manuscript fragment was rediscovered, commentators had
already begun to interpret these conventional markers as acknowledgments
of Felix's death.[24] It seems entirely plausible that Clara herself could have
done so as well in the spring and summer of 1879, for at least three reasons.
First, the march appeared in direct juxtaposition with the gentler passage

---

[22] Brahms/Schumann, *Briefe* 2:179.

[23] Litzmann, *Clara Schumann* 3:396.

[24] The leading exponents of this interpretive tradition were Max Kalbeck and Jürgen Beythien; see, respectively, *Brahms* 3:192 and "Die Violinsonate in G-Dur, Op. 78, von Johannes Brahms—Ein Beitrag
zum Verhältnis zwischen Formaler und Inhaltlicher Gestaltung," in *Bericht über den Internationalen Musikwissenschaftlichen Kongress Leipzig 1966*, ed. Carl Dahlhaus et al., 325–32 (Kassel: Bärenreiter, 1970). The
most detailed recent accounts of the slow movement, by Constantin Floros and Georges Starobinski,
have sought to reconcile the insights of these predecessors with Michael Struck's rediscovery of the fragment from February 1879; see *Frei, aber einsam*, 186–91 and "Brahms et la nostalgie de l'enfance," 189–93.

she had first received in February, as if posing an external threat to the precarious accord that had just been reached between the instruments. Second, contrasting material emerged first in the piano part, preserving the violin's metonymic identification with Felix. Third and most important, for ears already attuned to private, extramusical potential, the combined harmonic, motivic, and affective trajectory of the B section could provide a strikingly detailed musical cognate for the end stages of terminal illness.

EXAMPLE 7.4   Brahms, Violin Sonata, Op. 78 / II, mm. 24–38

The funeral march began quietly but soon became aggressive, scything across nearly five octaves of the keyboard with a swift and drastic crescendo. The violin then entered, *forte*, with a fanfare-like countermelody that hinted at resistance and the possibility of escape via modulation toward a half cadence in a new and distant key, B major.[25] Quieter and chromatically yearning music in

---

[25]The violin's *forte* indication in m. 29 is present in both the autograph and the first edition, but unaccountably omitted in Breitkopf & Härtel's *Gesamtausgabe* of 1926.

the major mode indeed ensued in m. 32, but the dotted rhythms of the funeral march persisted as an inexorable undercurrent, and the phrase remained open, poised on an active dominant. Before the dominant could resolve to B major, the minor-mode ostinato suddenly returned in m. 36 to initiate a second, more intense iteration of the same process—funeral march, countermelody and modulation, relapse. With resistance twice forestalled, a third iteration of the march then continued unopposed. Commandeering every strand in the texture, it gathered its own momentum toward a series of stabbing dissonances and a thunderous climax on the dominant of D minor, a tritone away from the movement's tonic. Example 7.5 begins there, literally *in extremis*, at the point of farthest harmonic remove and strongest thematic contrast in the entire movement. With the grim outcome of the struggle assured, the music quickly collapsed, its dynamic compass exhausted. Against the suspended backdrop of a chromatic bass-line ascent and attenuated echoes of the march in the piano, the violin reclaimed a fragile, halting independence by returning to the initial three-note gesture from the *Adagio*'s first theme. The gesture was rhythmically augmented, transposed down a minor third to begin on e', and reharmonized with shadowy double stops, but its intervallic content remained recognizable. Successively quieter transpositions follow, each a semitone higher than the one before. As the pitch level gradually approached that of the A section, the gesture was progressively truncated, as if even its short span were too much for the violinist's weak arms and labored breaths. Three notes became two, then one, until the instrument stalled on g♭', a half step below the g' with which the movement had begun. The harmonic progression likewise ground to a halt on an ambiguous diminished-seventh chord, and the phrase trailed off without actually ending.

EXAMPLE 7.5   Brahms, Violin Sonata, Op. 78 / II, mm. 56–67

Encountered in the spring or summer of 1879, the contours of the B section seem likely to have conjured up the imagined climax and ebb of Felix's death struggle, complete with a last, faltering attempt at dialogue with his caregivers. In the aftermath of such privately charged music, even the most conventional form could take on exceptional significance. A lightly varied reprise of the A section was entirely predictable at this point in the *Adagio* given the shape of the movement thus far. Yet for a listener marked by Clara's previous experiences and current circumstances, the recovered tones of her fragment could resound now as if from beyond the grave or within the heart of the bereaved. An array of changes to the compositional surface facilitated such interpretation and clarified that a fundamental shift had occurred in the theme's relationship to its original performer. As shown in example 7.6, the reprise began not with solo piano but with a full texture in which the violin took the lead from the start. Continuous double stops and *forte* dynamics lent the instrument unprecedented confidence and warmth, while the piano surrounded the tune with a shimmering haze of simultaneous sixteenths and sextuplets. In fact, the keyboard would never play the tune itself again in the entire movement. If the consolation of Brahms's melody had once seemed like Clara's to give, she now found herself cast primarily in the role of recipient. At the same time, the violin laid bare a series of horn fifths that had hitherto remained concealed among the theme's upper voices. Invoking what was by then a venerable tradition of musical works associated with leave-taking and memory, the altered voice leading enhanced the sudden sense of distance separating the reprise from its antecedents.[26] Across that dis-

EXAMPLE 7.6   Brahms, Violin Sonata, Op. 78 / II, mm. 67–70

[26] One of the most prominent examples in this tradition was the opening movement of Beethoven's "*Lebewohl*" Piano Sonata, Op. 81a, which, like Brahms's *Adagio*, was set in E♭ major. The most influential account of this sonata and the tradition of which it was a part remains Charles Rosen's *The Romantic Generation* (Cambridge, MA: Harvard University Press, 1995), 116–23 and 186. Ensuring that the horn fifths in his violin sonata emerged only at the reprise seems to have involved some labor on Brahms's part. In the surviving autograph of Op. 78, the first piano entrance in the *Adagio* originally used bare horn fifths as well in mm. 2–3, but then Brahms filled in the texture by adding several chord tones during a round of pencil revisions. Since these added chord tones also appear in the fragment that he mailed to Clara in February 1879, it is tempting (but purely speculative) to think that Brahms deliberately concealed the horn fifths from her at first in order to enhance their ultimate effect in the reprise.

tance, Clara's fragment could take on new connotations and facilitate new modes of imagined interaction with her departed son. In the realm of the aesthetic, at least, vicarious collaboration could recede in favor of elegiac recollection.

After the reprise of the A section, a lengthy coda reinforced and magnified the shift in attitude embodied in the rest of the movement. First, the funeral march returned in a piano solo reproduced in example 7.7a, but its effect was utterly different: the mode became major and the dynamics progressively quieter, the right-hand contour descended instead of ascending, and the formerly aggressive tempo was reduced to that of the main theme. Motives that had provoked the *Adagio*'s central crisis now laid the movement to rest, eventually establishing a tonic pedal that remained in place for a full fifteen measures, or well over a minute in performance.

Several in Brahms's circle gravitated toward the expressive weight of this affective reversal. In November 1879, Elisabeth von Herzogenberg used her admiration for the passage in the service of a social request: "When I play the last page of the E♭-major Adagio with the heavenly pedal point and become ever slower with it, so that it truly lasts a long time, then I always think that you still could only be a good man. Prove it by visiting us poor Leipzigers." For that matter, Clara herself expressed unspecified but warm appreciation for "several pedal points" in Op. 78 as a whole.[27] For her and for Brahms, pedal points had been a recurring preoccupation in musical exchanges dating back to 1854, when the composer declared that he could sense her presence in the pedal points of great fugues.[28] Now, however, the chance to initiate the *Adagio*'s slow unwinding in the unaccompanied tones of her own instrument could provide yet another measure of the emotional distance traveled since she had first encountered the A section in the midst of Felix's decline. In turn, following a brief but impassioned farewell to the main theme, the violin's horn fifths finally infiltrated the piano part for the first time, as shown in example 7.7b. The closing measures thus recapitulated once more the essential transformation enacted by the *Adagio* as a whole: in the aftermath of crisis, music initially associated with the here and now had instead come to reward apprehension through the tinted lenses of memory and fantasy.

EXAMPLE 7.7a   Brahms, Violin Sonata, Op. 78 / II, mm. 91–96

---

[27] Brahms/Herzogenberg, *Briefwechsel* 1:104; Brahms/Schumann, *Briefe* 2:179.
[28] Brahms/Schumann, *Briefe* 1:50.

EXAMPLE 7.7b   Brahms, Violin Sonata, Op. 78 / II, mm. 118–22

If the various echoes of her fragment indeed resonated for Clara in personally meaningful ways when she first encountered Brahms's slow movement, they may have stimulated her to reconsider her stance relative to the opening movement as well. To a larger extent than most contiguous pairs of movements, the two invited sustained comparison. In fact, their broad outlines were directly analogous. Both were tripartite; both set their contrasting central sections apart via a shift in mode and, most remarkably, a discrete tempo designation. Yet the specific impact of their structures was qualitatively disparate. Whereas the *Adagio* allowed the extremes of its B section to alter the main theme and to drastically revise its associations, the *Vivace ma non troppo* confined its anxieties to the development section and then recovered its primary thematic material intact. This tidily balanced trajectory must have seemed all the more striking once Clara had gone on to experience the complex and open-ended slow movement. In retrospect, the two movements together could have struck her as embodying a larger turn away from abstract optimism and toward a specific and intimate confrontation with pain and grief. Differing treatment of shared motivic cells could easily have reinforced such an impression. After all, the repeated dotted rhythm that had lent momentum to all three themes in the first movement became an emblem of death and disruption in the next. For the right kind of listener, then, form and content worked in tandem to bind the two movements into a tightly ordered succession rather than a mere juxtaposition of complementary units.

In turn, the finale continued that succession, knitting together threads from the previous movements and offering a comprehensive conclusion for the whole. Compositional chronology gave Brahms firm control over the end result, especially as far as Clara's impressions were concerned. Having completed the first two movements by February 1879 and sent the beginning of the slow movement to her then, he had four months to compose the last movement or to adjust it accordingly. Of course, many registers of the inter-movement continuity that he created were accessible to a wide range of listeners and not to Clara alone. Chief among these were motivic resemblance and self-quotation, each of which has provoked a broad array of commentary since the work's release. Both techniques mark the opening measures of the finale, shown in example 7.8. Motivic resemblance was the more pervasive and obvious of the two. The three-note cell with which the violin began the finale was essentially identical to the characteristic opening motive of the first movement. Only an aurally imperceptible change in notated meter distinguished them from each other; pitch level, scale-degree affiliation, and even articulation marks matched precisely. If anything, the motive was even more prevalent in the finale, where it appeared dozens of times at pitch and infiltrated the bass line as early as the first measure. For Elisabeth von Herzogenberg, saturation with a single motive drew the ear primarily toward the finale itself and generated a paradoxical sense of novelty in that movement alone, as if Brahms "had been the first to discover that one can dot an eighth note."[29] But for Clara Schumann and a long line of subsequent critics, the reappearance of the three-note cell established a cohesive atmosphere that enveloped the entire work.

Clara explained her impressions to Brahms in late July 1879. By then she had lived with the piece for several weeks and could use a concise rhythmic pattern as shorthand for the thematic incipit of the finale:

EXAMPLE 7.8   Brahms, Violin Sonata, Op. 78 / III, mm. 1–4

[29] Brahms/Herzogenberg, *Briefwechsel* 1:103–4.

How wonderfully the intimate affiliation of all the motives appeared to me again. How tenderly the rapturous accompaniment of the last motive ♩ 𝄾 ♪ | ♩. sounds already in the first motive, how one is already then as if breathed upon by the mood of the whole! The character of the whole sonata is refreshing for me, the grace and warmth of the melodies, the mastery in the treatment of all motives holds one captive, heart and soul, from the first until the last note. What heavenly places are therein, not the least blissful among them several pedal points, then the climax of the first melody in the last movement, where it comes back for the last time and rolls back and forth, melancholically, yearning! For such impressions there are only tones, not words.[30]

Clara's allusion to her beloved pedal points and her repeated references to the "whole" sonata imply that the motivic network she perceived had penetrated the slow movement as well as the first and last. Max Kalbeck made the connection explicit three decades later by identifying traces of the thematic incipit in the dotted "tread" of the funeral march, and the bulk of recent European scholarship has followed his lead.[31] Indeed, the sense of cohesion forged by the finale's opening motive was so strong that generations of analysts have flatly assumed the movement was completed in advance of the others, despite a total lack of documentary evidence supporting such a chronology.

EXAMPLE 7.9   Brahms, *Regenlied* and *Nachklang*, Op. 59 Nos. 3 and 4, vocal entrances

---

[30] Brahms/Schumann, *Briefe* 2:178–79.
[31] Kalbeck, *Brahms* 3:192. For recent echoes of Kalbeck's analysis in three distinct European traditions, see Constantin Floros, *Frei, aber einsam*, 186; MacDonald, *Brahms*, 279; and Georges Starobinski, "Brahms et la nostalgie de l'enfance," 189.

For acquaintances of Brahms, connoisseurs of his music, and avid readers of the musical press, a second factor contributed to the large-scale coherence of Op. 78: the rhythmic and melodic cell that tied the finale so
convincingly to the previous movements was itself part of a larger musical
borrowing. Example 7.9 provides the initial vocal entrance in Brahms's
Regenlied (Rain Song), Op. 59 No. 3. Particularly well-informed listeners
would have known that precisely the same music had also set the first vocal
phrase of the aptly named *Nachklang* (Echo), Op. 59 No. 4, whose text appears in brackets below that of the *Regenlied* in example 7.9.[32] The two
songs were initially conceived early in 1873 as bookends for a group of
four songs on the poetry of Klaus Groth and presented privately to the
poet and his wife, Doris, then inserted as a pair into the eight songs of Op.
59 later that year.[33] Now the melody, bass line, and pattering accompanimental figuration from their first four measures reappeared virtually unchanged in the finale to Op. 78. To friends and critics alike, knowledge of
the borrowing retrospectively colored the entire sonata. Once Brahms had
jokingly alerted him to its presence in June 1879 by associating the piece
with a "rainy evening hour," Theodor Billroth replied with a revealing pun
of his own: "To me the entire sonata is like an echo [*Nachklang*] of the
song, like a fantasy upon it." In turn, Billroth transmitted his comprehensive vision to Eduard Hanslick in October, while the work was still unpublished: "The sonata in three movements consists solely of the song's
motives."[34] The claim was exaggerated but provocative, especially coming
from one of the composer's most intimate associates, and it may well have
stimulated Hanslick's own thoughts when he reviewed the Vienna premiere of the work in November. His account publicly identified *Regenlied*
(but not *Nachklang*) as the source of motives in both the first and last
movements of the sonata and stressed the affective coherence of the piece
as a whole. Picked up within a month by the British musical press and

---

[32] The only surviving autograph of either song is an undated fair copy of *Regenlied* that was owned by Hermann
Levi and now resides in the Sibley Music Library at the Eastman School of Music in Rochester, New York (for
details of its provenance, see McCorkle, *Werkverzeichnis*, 252). For the measures in question, it matches the first
edition of the song in all details save for the addition of a "p" before the final entrance of the bass line. Since
Clara had no access to this particular manuscript, example 7.9 is based upon the published score.

[33] Brahms had a copyist prepare a clean copy of four songs for Klaus and Doris Groth in March 1873.
Regenlied and *Nachklang* occupied the first and last positions in this miniature cycle. For details con-
cerning the songs and their texts, along with a modern edition of the private offering of which they
initially formed a part, see Peter Russell, *Johannes Brahms and Klaus Groth: The Biography of a Friendship*
(Burlington, VT: Ashgate, 2006), 23–25, 51–54, and 57–68; and Michael Struck, ed., *Johannes Brahms: Vier
Lieder nach Gedichten von Klaus Groth* (Munich: Henle, 1997).

[34] Billroth/Brahms, *Briefwechsel*, 283–84 and 286.

reprinted in English translation, Hanslick's appraisal would soon provide the grist for subsequent reviews in multiple languages.[35]

By contrast, a second self-borrowing went unmentioned in Hanslick's review and, for that matter, in most contemporaneous accounts of Op. 78. The primary theme of the *Adagio* resurfaced during two extended sections in the finale, first at pitch in E♭ major near the middle of the movement and then again near the end in the prevailing tonic, G. Both returns were blatant, undisguised quotations, portentously introduced and directly aligned with important junctures in the form of the finale. Unlike the allusion to the paired *Lieder* from 1873, the reappearance of music from the slow movement demanded no prior familiarity with Brahms's oeuvre but could be identified aurally or from score by any careful listener or performer based solely on the piece at hand. There was therefore no cachet to be gained in pointing out so obvious a compositional device, which may explain why it garnered so little public attention in the years immediately following the work's release. Beginning in early 1900s, however, the effects of the *Adagio*'s returns began to interest scholars for their own sake. Some analytic traditions focused on the returns themselves as registers of Brahms's interest in musical memory, others on the changes to which the familiar theme was subjected in its new context.[36] As close readings of pitch structure and assumptions of organic unity provoked increasing skepticism at the end of the twentieth century, attention shifted again to encompass the larger allusive discourse within which material from the slow movement functioned.[37] In the process, recent scholarly literature has finally found itself recapitulating concerns that likely defined Clara Schumann's encounter with the piece in the first place. From her perspective in July 1879, the borrowings from both the songs and the *Adagio* were not neutral acts of compositional structuring,

---

[35] Hanslick's review appeared in its accustomed place, below the fold in the *Neue Freie Presse* on Sunday, November 23, 1879 (no. 5474). Brahms's violin sonata was addressed on p. 2. The review served as the basis for "Concerts in Vienna," *Musical World* 57/50 (December 13, 1879): 787; every essential element of Hanslick's analysis then reappeared in an anonymous review of the London premiere of Op. 78 in *Musical Times* 21/445 (March 1, 1880): 125. Meanwhile, the German-speaking critics also echoed Hanslick's emphasis on the *Regenlied*. For examples from both concert reviews and longer essays published in 1880, see Theodor Helm's review in the *Musikalisches Wochenblatt* 11/12 (March 12, 1880): 146–47; Deiters "Johannes Brahms," 342; and Louis Ehlert, "Brahms," 354.

[36] Kalbeck firmly established the first tradition in *Brahms* 3:192, where he glossed the return of the *Adagio* with a quotation from the poetry of Emanuel Geibel: "Like Snow White in the coffin of glass the beautiful past lies embedded in my heart." By contrast, Tovey emphasized the theme's new guise in the finale, proclaiming it "no mere ghost" ("Brahms, Johannes," 176). This second tradition finds its most forceful recent exponent in Musgrave, *Music of Brahms*, 187.

[37] Prominent examples may be found in Notley, "Discourse and Allusion," 265; MacDonald, *Brahms*, 282; Brodbeck, "Medium and Meaning," 117; and, above all, Parmer, "Song Quotation," 167–77.

but the latest in a series of appropriations and transformations of privately meaningful music. For her alone, the changing interaction between these borrowings over the course of the finale could open a world of rhetorical potential for the sonata as a whole.

Clara's first response to the finale is worth revisiting: "After the first artful, delightful movement and the second you can imagine for yourself the bliss when I found again in the third my so enthusiastically beloved melody with the attractive eighth-note motion." The diction in her letter to Brahms clarified that she had identified the dual vocal sources for the movement's initial allusion. By focusing purely on musical characteristics and refusing to assign a single title or poem to the familiar tune, she implicitly adopted the texts of both *Regenlied* and *Nachklang* as potential extramusical correlates for the finale's opening theme. Here are the poems as Brahms knew them, the first from Groth's 1854 collection, *Hundert Blätter: Paralipomena zum Quickborn*, and the second from a handwritten copy made for him by the poet himself in 1856.

Regenlied

Walle, Regen, walle nieder,
Wecke mir die Träume wieder,
Die ich in der Kindheit träumte,
Wenn das Naß im Sande schäumte!

Wenn die matte Sommerschwüle
Läßig stritt mit frischer Kühle,
Und die blanken Blätter thauten
Und die Saaten dunkler blauten.

Welche Wonne, in dem Fließen
Dann zu stehn mit nackten Füßen!
An dem Grase hinzustreifen
Und den Schaum mit Händen greifen,

Oder mit den heißen Wangen
Kalte Tropfen aufzufangen,
Und den neuerwachten Düften
Seine Kinderbrust zu lüften!

Wie die Kelche, die da troffen,
Stand die Seele athmend offen,
Wie die Blumen, düftetrunken

In den Himmelsthau versunken.

Rain Song

Billow, rain, billow down,
Wake again in me the dreams
That I dreamt in childhood
When the water foamed in sand!

When the humid heat of summer
Idly struggled with cool freshness,
And the bright leaves dripped with dew,
And the green crops darker blued.

What delight it was to stand
With naked feet in flowing water!
To stroll along upon the grass
And with one's hands to grasp
    the foam,

Or with overheated cheeks
To collect the cold droplets,
And to bare one's childhood breast
To the newly wakened fragrance!

Like the cups that trickled there,
The soul stood open, breathing,
Like the flowers, drunk with
    fragrance,
Immersed in the dew of heaven.

Schauernd kühlte jeder Tropfen	Every drop chilled shiveringly
Tief bis an des Herzens Klopfen,	Deep down to the beating heart,
Und der Schöpfung heilig Weben	And creation's sacred motion
Drang bis ins verborgne Leben.—	Pierced through to the life within.—
Walle, Regen, walle nieder,	Billow, rain, billow down,
Wecke meine alten Lieder,	Wake again my old songs
Die wir in der Thüre sangen,	That we sang inside the doorways
Wenn die Tropfen draußen klangen!	When the drops sounded outside!
Möchte ihnen wieder lauschen,	I'd like to listen to them again,
Ihrem süßen feuchten Rauschen,	To their sweet, damp murmuring,
Meine Seele sanft bethauen	Gently to bedew my soul
Mit dem frommen Kindergrauen.[38]	With the pious awe of childhood.

Nachklang	*Echo*
Regentropfen aus den Bäumen	Drops of rain from the trees
Fallen in das grüne Gras,	Fall into the green grass,
Thränen meiner trüben Augen	Tears from my melancholy eyes
Machen mir die Wange naß.	Are watering my cheeks for me.
Wenn die Sonne wieder scheinet	When the sunshine comes again
Wird der Rasen doppelt grün:	The grass will become doubly green:
Doppelt wird auf meinen Wangen	Doubly then upon my cheeks
Mir die heiße Thräne glühn.[39]	My ardent tears will glow.

The title *Nachklang* was Brahms's invention, not Groth's. By positioning the second poem as a reverberation of the first, it encouraged the listener to imagine them as continuous utterances of a single poetic speaker. Brought together by the title, by the shared theme of rain, and, above all, by closely related musical settings, the two songs reveal an intricate relationship. *Regenlied* places an adult poetic speaker amid falling raindrops that evoke memories of childhood. Filtered through a nostalgic lens, the cooling pleasure of a summer shower hints at a long-lost connection between the self and the natural world. After two poetic stanzas of detached reflection, the speaker becomes increasingly caught up in the attempt to recapture that connection; throughout stanzas 3–6, the present tense vanishes from the syntactic surface, replaced by the past in which remembered events occurred. Brahms's music follows suit, rejecting the song's initial material in

---

[38] Brahms's source was Groth's *Hundert Blätter: Paralipomena zum Quickborn* (Hamburg: Perthes-Besser & Mauke, 1854), 38–39. These pages in Brahms's own copy show heavy signs of wear.

[39] Transcribed from Groth's handwritten inscription on the title page of Brahms's copy of the *Hundert Blätter*. The first edition of Brahms's setting added a comma after line 5, as do subsequent editions of the song.

favor of contrasting sections in increasingly distant keys. The incipit reemerges, however, to set the last two poetic stanzas, which return abruptly to the present tense. Hopes of regained communion with nature are now tellingly confined to the subjunctive mood, and the speaker's poignant contrafactuals find musical reflection in modal mixture and a closing Picardy third. *Nachklang* picks up where *Regenlied* left off, surrounded by rain and pressingly aware of the gap between external conditions and internal emotion. Brahms's setting returns immediately to the familiar incipit, which now provides the motivic material for the entire song. Likewise, rather than retreat into memory or wishful thinking, the speaker explicitly acknowledges the bitter impact of nostalgia on lived experience—the brighter the memories, the starker the alienation from current reality. *Nachklang* thus provides an overtly disconsolate gloss on its longer and more understated counterpart. Through repeated echoes of the same music, the two songs clarify a single melancholic vision.[40]

Correspondence suggests that Clara had already internalized that vision years before encountering the violin sonata for the first time. Brahms himself had acquainted her with *Regenlied* and *Nachklang* at her summer home in late August 1873. His visit was filled with song; it was then that the two musicians began the reviewing her piano transcriptions of Robert's *Lieder*. Yet even amid the bustle of editorial collaboration, Brahms's new compositions left a distinct impression. Traces of Clara's response survive in a letter dated September 4:

> By the way, I had truly dismal days after your departure; the *Regenlied* would not leave my mind day or night, but for me the melody has something unutterably sorrowful and made me completely melancholy until I finally pulled myself out of it through proper work.[41]

Rarely had Clara attributed to Brahms's music such overwhelmingly negative consequences upon her own mood. Not that those consequences ultimately made the songs any less attractive to her; to the contrary, she thanked him enthusiastically two weeks later when autograph copies of both songs arrived as belated birthday presents, and her lack of surprise at receiving them indicates that she may have requested the copies herself.[42] In fact, the depressive tendencies she described had some basis in external circumstances. As she explained to Brahms at length in her letter of September 4, she was in the throes of a long and difficult decision to give up her house in Baden-Baden and settle in Berlin. In practical terms the move was inevitable, but Clara found herself plagued by

---

[40] For a complementary perspective on the relationship between the two songs, see Parmer, "Song Quotation," 173–77.

[41] Brahms/Schumann, *Briefe* 2:23.

[42] Ibid., 25. Clara also expressed approval of Brahms's latest songs in a contemporaneous letter to Joseph Joachim; see Litzmann, *Clara Schumann* 3:298.

sentimental attachment: "As soon as I have determined to give up Baden, then someone inevitably comes along who is enchanted by Baden and my little house!"[43] Context and content thus collided in late summer 1873. For a few days, Groth's texts and Brahms's music had brought nostalgic regret to the surface of her consciousness and sharpened its effects to the point of paralysis.

In July 1879, the time was ripe for another collision in the finale of Brahms's violin sonata. Especially when preceded by a slow movement so powerfully aligned with Felix's recent passing, the wandering and repetitive tones of *Regenlied* and *Nachklang* were perfectly calibrated to conjure up a mournfully obsessive atmosphere analogous to that with which Clara had initially associated them. The tonality and notated meter of Brahms's finale could only have deepened the shadows. As in *Alte Liebe*, material originally presented in F♯ minor now appeared a semitone higher, disrupting the pianist's kinesthetic memory and making familiar music feel strange. At the same time, old rhythmic patterns found expression in a new visual format. By halving note values and doubling the length of the measure, the sonata not only encouraged a slightly broader sense of phrase and gesture; it also created a pervasive graphic distinction between the borrowing and its sources. Clara herself found ways to collapse the distinction when discussing the passage in correspondence. She attributed to the songs the "attractive eighth-note motion" that was actually characteristic of the violin's melody, while notating the finale's initial rhythmic cell as it had appeared in the songs (♩ 𝅘𝅥𝅮 | ♩.). In performing the sonata from score, however, the underlying visual discrepancy might well have frustrated any attempt to immerse herself fully in remembered music. If Groth's poetry invoked an inaccessible past, Brahms's allusion highlighted the inaccessibility. Tone and technique recalled the development section of the first movement, but now the musical registers of melancholy had infiltrated the finale from the beginning, becoming the implied norm rather than a temporary exception. It was as though the elegiac conclusion of the *Adagio* had been undermined, and, in its wake, there could be no return to the optimistic trajectory that had held sway at the beginning of the piece.

During most of the finale, successive sections strengthened the impression that a new and bleaker mood had taken hold for good. First, material borrowed from the songs formed the basis for a twenty-two-measure primary theme that closed with an authentic cadence in G minor. Next, a brief, modulatory transition

---

[43] Brahms/Schumann, *Briefe* 2:23. A venerable scholarly tradition has associated Clara's depressive commentary on *Regenlied* and *Nachklang* with her concerns about Felix's health; for representative examples, see Beythien, "Die Violinsonate in G-Dur," and Starobinski, "Brahms et la nostalgie de l'enfance." The notion is attractive but extremely problematic. As discussed in ch. 5, Felix did contract a serious lung infection in the autumn of 1873, but later correspondence makes it clear that the infection did not manifest itself until September 9, nearly a week after Clara sent her commentary to Brahms in the first place (Brahms/Schumann, *Briefe* 2:25).

paved the way for a secondary thematic group that mirrored the first in length, content, and mode. Example 7.10 shows how the head motive of these twenty-four measures overtly proclaimed its derivation from the first theme's borrowed vocal incipit; the unusual choice of the minor dominant for a secondary key blurred the distinction between the two themes and reinforced the dark cast of the movement. A retransitional passage based on the primary theme then ushered in a full return of that theme in the tonic, creating the large-scale succession ABA. After eighty-two measures the finale was literally half over, and every one of those measures had introduced or prolonged a minor key. Whether Clara had parsed the movement thus far in sonata form or sonata-rondo form (or was still holding the two possibilities in tension), by now the lack of modal and affective contrast was striking and decidedly oppressive, a dull and interminable ache. Brahms himself seems to have wondered if so sustained a monotone could hold the attention of even the most sympathetic listener, which would explain why he expressed to Clara the worry that the sonata might be "boring" and why he indicated an optional cut in her manuscript copy of the finale. The precise location of the cut is unclear, but the prevalence of internal repetition in the first three sections of the movement makes these by far the most likely candidates for pruning. Moreover, Brahms's choice of the finale was itself revealing since, purely in terms of notated measures or duration in performance, the movement was by no means one of his longest. By implication, then, the problem must have involved its internal dynamic rather than its external dimensions. In tandem, the optional cut and associated commentary clarified the focus of his concerns and made it even more unlikely that Clara could have overlooked the affective uniformity of the finale's first half.

EXAMPLE 7.10   Brahms, Violin Sonata, Op. 78 / III, mm. 1–2 and 29–30. Violin part, annotated.

Against that uniformity the next section imposed a radical break. Without transition or preamble, the violin interrupted the characteristic pattering of the primary theme and ushered in an unabashed return of the main theme of the *Adagio*, shown in example 7.11. The melodic incipit occurred at pitch in E♭ along with its lagging bass line. Instrumentation and accompanimental figuration did not precisely match any one prior appearance of the theme, but the ethos clearly evoked the end of the slow movement rather than the beginning. The double stops in the violin, the confidence assumed by that instrument in seizing control of the musical discourse, and the shimmering string of horn fifths in the pianist's right hand all hearkened back to *Adagio*'s reprise and coda, as if picking up where the previous movement had left off. Related material dominated the next thirty measures, which eventually achieved an emphatic authentic cadence in E♭ using the loudest dynamics and highest register in the entire finale. For Clara, the potential implications of this climax were most likely ambiguous, at least initially. On the one hand, long-familiar music had attained the next and most overtly triumphant in a series of transformations dating back to the end stages of her son's illness. Amid the gray undertones of the song-inspired themes, this retrospective vision of the *Adagio* offered a bright, alternative model of interaction with the past. On the other hand, the very characteristics that made the passage so attractive also threatened to isolate it from its surroundings. Its distinct material, separate key signature, and closed harmonic trajectory clearly identified it as the central C section in a sonata-rondo structure. In the vast majority of Classical precedents, the themes presented in such sections produced little or no effect upon the larger course of the movements in which they occurred. They appeared once, for the sake of contrast, and then vanished, as elusive as the idealized past invoked by Groth's poems.

EXAMPLE 7.11   Brahms, Violin Sonata, Op. 78 / III, mm. 83–86

At first, Brahms's finale responded in accordance with convention. A retransitional passage appropriated the erstwhile tonic, E♭, as the bottom pitch in an augmented-sixth chord, retroactively shoehorning the key of the *Adagio* into an overarching progression in G minor. As shown in example 7.12, the primary theme then returned at pitch and in tempo, leading a trained ear to expect the straightforward recapitulation and rounded shape typical of sonata-rondo finales: ABACAB'A. Such a recapitulation would have dispelled any lingering confusion regarding the form of the movement and thus affirmed the ultimate irrelevance of the interruption. For a listener familiar with *Regenlied* and *Nachklang*, musical structure and poetic correlates would have reinforced one another to create an unequivocally depressive trajectory for the sonata as a whole. But then the primary theme itself began to change. The pianist's left hand fell behind immediately. Next, the right hand and the violin deviated from previous iterations of the theme. By the fourth measure, the harmonic progression itself

EXAMPLE 7.12   Brahms, Violin Sonata, Op. 78 / III, mm. 123–27

EXAMPLE 7.13   Brahms, Violin Sonata, Op. 78 / III, mm. 137–39, and II, mm. 114–17. Violin part.

shifted and, for a brief moment, actually increased the theme's resemblance to the songs from which it was borrowed. While the violin leaned into a dissonant suspension on scale degree 2, the piano's dominant pedal resolved deceptively to the flat submediant for the first time in the finale. Melody and harmony thus duplicateed the corresponding segment in both songs (ex. 7.9), throwing the movement's allusive source into sharp focus once more. From then on, however, the theme continued to diverge ever more sharply, both from the songs and from its own original form. By the end of the phrase, a tonic pedal supported an entirely new passage in which the violin's contour and scale-degree content hearkened back directly to the climactic cadence from the coda of the *Adagio*. Example 7.13 compares the two. As if in sympathy with the melodic resemblance, the mode of the accompaniment shifted as well, and the section came to rest on a G-major triad.

In combination, the changes to the primary theme suggested an identity in flux, straining to reassert itself intact but gradually yielding up its autonomy in deference to broader relationships among the movement's component parts. Those relationships coalesced rapidly in the ensuing measures.

The minor-mode secondary theme disappeared entirely, replaced by a major-mode coda in which motives from the A section and C section intermingled freely. Once again a change in affect found reinforcement in a relaxation of the tempo, in this case via the designation *Più moderato*, which remained in effect until the end of the piece. After two measures of introductory material drawn from the primary theme, the piano transposed the *Adagio's* familiar incipit from E♭ to G for the first time in the entire work, and the violin soon followed suit, as shown in example 7.14. As in the C section, texture and figuration recalled the end of the slow movement, but additional changes intervened as well for both performers, making the old motive feel unexpectedly at home in its new key. The violinist could at last take full advantage of open D and A strings in creating the theme's characteristic double stops, and the arpeggiated horn fifths in the pianist's right hand now glided easily across exclusively white keys. Meanwhile, the pianist's left hand finally relaxed into root position tonic triads on downbeats, consistently in synch with the melody for the first time in the entire work. The sense of easy, unforced collaboration between instruments was unprecedented in previous appearances of this theme. Their ongoing exchanges of material culminated in the closing measures of the coda, shown in example 7.15. Rising gradually above a haze of overlapping dotted figures and *tranquillo* arpeggios, the finale's primary theme appeared for the first time in the upper positions of the violin, recast in the tonic major and accompanied by a quiet plagal cadence in the piano. What had been bitter became, at the very least, bittersweet.

EXAMPLE 7.14   Brahms, Violin Sonata, Op. 78 / III, mm. 141–43 and 148–50

In short, throughout the diachronic unfolding of the finale, expectations consistent with the closed form of a standard sonata-rondo gave way to an open-ended experience in which initially contradictory themes were gradually integrated and their mutual implications redefined. One might summarize the resulting structure as ABACA'C'/A". This profile was specific to Op. 78 alone and carried overwhelming rhetorical potential for a listener

EXAMPLE 7.15   Brahms, Violin Sonata, Op. 78 / III, mm. 159–64

and performer in Clara's circumstances. A melody she had explicitly associated with paralyzing nostalgia was slowly repositioned as an emblem of quiet benediction. Within that painstaking process, the tones of Brahms's fragmentary musical offering emerged from the depths of Felix's illness as the leading advocates of progressive change. At the same time, the darker hues of *Regenlied* and *Nachklang* tempered the transcendent aspirations of the *Adagio*'s theme, rendering its triumph more subdued and gently undercutting its promise of continued contact with the departed. The finale thus brought the conflicting impulses of previous movements into a balanced alignment that spanned the sonata as a whole. First came the abstract optimism embodied in the blithe recovery of primary material in the first movement. Next, the seemingly borrowed theme of the slow movement facilitated an intensely personal confrontation with loss and grief in which elegiac memory temporarily supplanted present suffering. Last, the allusive finale laid bare the emotional consequences of long-term regret and presented the continual reimagining of the past as an imperfect but essential antidote.[44]

---

[44]With respect to the affective trajectory of Op. 78 as a whole, Clara therefore seems likely to have steered a middle course between interpretive extremes. The result would probably have been analogous to the admixture of assurance and skepticism espoused by Parmer in "Song Quotation," 176–67, rather than the more straightforward optimism articulated by Notley in "Discourse and Allusion," 265.

Correspondence shows that Brahms might well have considered the sonata's overarching trajectory a direct complement to his old friend's current mood. Two letters addressed to him survive from the months between Felix's death and the release of the complete work in manuscript form. Both conveyed clear evidence of ongoing sorrow, along with direct attempts to resist depression. May of 1879 found Clara guardedly optimistic, at least insofar as she was willing to admit to Brahms: "I often feel the clouds draw near my spirit, but they do not burst—I am constantly on the lookout." The following month brought a return to darker ruminations. The immediate trigger was a depressing report concerning her eldest son, Ludwig, whom she had committed to a mental institution nine years prior, but her youngest still weighed heavily on her mind as well. She compared the two explicitly in a letter dated June 21: "Such a poor, miserable man lives on now, and the other, the intellectually gifted, to whom life stood open with all its attractions, dies. Why?"[45] Within days of receiving Clara's brutally honest question, Brahms mailed her the complete version of the violin sonata. At the time, any new opus would surely have provided a welcome distraction regardless of genre, form, or mood. Given its allusive gestures and the curve of its unfolding, however, this particular work could also stir up and redirect the emotions of the moment in specific and positive ways. Like the allusive songs that Brahms had fashioned for Clara earlier in the 1870s, Op. 78 ultimately offered equipment for living as well as grist for performance or contemplation.[46] For a mind and body properly attuned to their appeal, musical structure and extramusical correlates could redirect the melancholic cast of present circumstances in the service of pleasure, closure, or—at the very least—change.

Such change might have touched Clara without her conscious effort or awareness. Particularly in a piece of instrumental music, the playing of her piano allowed her to imagine and enact complex adjustments in attitude without cataloguing their effects or relating them explicitly to the contours of her emotional life. By the same token, if she did perceive intentional connections between Brahms's music and her own recent bereavement, those connections may well have manifested themselves to her in ways incompatible with verbal description. Her initial written responses to the sonata stressed her own inability to explain how and why the piece had moved her so deeply. "My pen is poor,

---

[45] Brahms/Schumann, *Briefe* 2:172 and 173. In Berthold Litzmann's transcription, this sentence is surrounded by ellipses that probably represent an attempt to expunge detailed records of Ludwig's symptoms and mental state.

[46] Efforts to reclaim connections between aesthetic and social strategies were less common and more polemical when Kenneth Burke first articulated an approach to "literature as equipment for living" in the years leading up to the Second World War in *The Philosophy of Literary Form: Studies in Symbolic Action* (Baton Rouge: Louisiana State University Press, 1941), 293–304. The aims of the present study are commensurately less ambitious and more focused: not to demonstrate the broad applicability of such connections, but to explore in detail how they may have shaped the experiences of one historical agent.

but my heart beats toward you"—"Many may perhaps understand better how to speak of it, but no one can experience it more than I."Yet Clara's attempts to describe the ineffable also preserve hints that the finale had indeed struck her as transformative in relatively concrete ways. Not only did the last movement receive the lion's share of commentary in her letters; her descriptions of the borrowing from *Regenlied* and *Nachklang* signaled subtle but important shifts in her attitude toward the songs themselves.Already in her first response to Op. 78, she claimed: "I don't believe that *one* person perceives that melody as blissfully and melancholically [*wonnig und wehmutsvoll*] as I." In previous correspondence the songs had always been associated unequivocally with sadness, but now an alliteratively paired opposite softened her characterization, balancing the emotional toll of nostalgia against the rewards of imagined contact with the past.

One can only assume that the delicately uplifting close of the finale had helped to alter Clara's stance. Within a few weeks, she went on to single out these measures as the pinnacle of the work as a whole, the apex of its affective arc. Her second response to the piece was dominated by the final, major-mode version of the borrowed song incipit—"the climax of the first melody in the last movement, where it comes back for the last time and rolls back and forth, melancholically, yearning!" Her enthusiasm was not confined to July 1879. To the contrary, the passage remained the focal point for future interactions with the sonata. Perhaps the most tantalizing of these came more than a decade later. In a letter dated June 16, 1890, she told Brahms of a recent performance of Op. 78 at her home in Frankfurt: "Joachim was with us on the 8th (Robert's 80th birthday), for two days we played a great deal, once more the Rain Songs sonata, which I reveled in again—I always wish that last movement for myself at the passage from here to eternity."[47] In the aging pianist's imaginary, the end of the movement eventually became a bridge to the infinite, its plagal benediction and bittersweet thematic transformation carefully positioned as the final sensory experiences of her own life. Her letter therefore drew together and recombined a complex of extramusical connotations analogous to those Brahms might have planned or predicted when he first sent her the completed sonata: the approach of death, the memory of a departed male relative, and the gradual achievement of a broader perspective on loss and the passage of time.At least in retrospect, Op. 78 had fulfilled its potential as an agency of consolation and transformation.

---

[47] Brahms/Schumann, *Briefe* 2:415. Parentheses in original. Here Clara again called attention to the dual origins of the borrowed song incipit through a judicious plural: a work known to Hanslick and much of the general public as the *Regenlied-Sonate* remained, to her, the *Regenlieder-Sonate*.

PART IV

RHETORICS OF CLOSURE

CHAPTER EIGHT

FORESTS OF THE HEART

Incremental reorientations in a friend's perception of old music—and, thus, in his or her attitudes toward remembered events and emotions associated with that music—lay at the core of Brahms's rhetorical strategy in his allusive lullabies, his two songs for Clara, and many of his offerings for the Herzogenbergs. For the first violin sonata, however, the combination of a prestigious genre and a widely known source for at least one of his borrowings augmented the challenges inherent in allusive composition. Once apprehended by a broader audience, the finale's references to the *Regenlieder* and recycling of material from the *Adagio* might resonate in many ways, not all of them conducive to the work's aesthetic or commercial success. Devices originally designed for Clara as private gestures of amelioration might confuse or alienate listeners whose habits and circumstances differed substantially from hers. Perhaps for this reason, Brahms expressed concerns as to how Op. 78 might be received in larger venues. Responding to Joachim's excited hopes for a series of performances in August 1879, the composer hedged: "But my sonata is even less well-suited for the public than I!"[1] His acquaintances ultimately tended to agree, even when they themselves loved the work. Joachim himself echoed the composer's worries in private correspondence with Philipp Spitta once he had got to know the piece in September 1879, while Billroth did so as well in a letter to Hanslick in October. In turn, Hanslick gently broached the same concern with his Viennese readers in November, claiming that the sonata "seems to be created more for intimate enjoyment in private circles than for the effect in the concert hall."[2] Reviews from outside the composer's circles were less tactful. One of the harshest addressed the London premiere in February 1880: "The general impression produced by the Sonata is that of a mind striving to depict in musical language

---

[1] Brahms/Joachim, *Briefwechsel* 2:160.
[2] Joachim and Moser, *Briefe von und an Joachim* 3:214; Billroth/Brahms, *Briefwechsel*, 286; and Hanslick, *Neue Freie Presse*, no. 5474, November 23, 1879, 2.

an individual experience scarcely important enough to furnish the material for three movements."[3]

Having explored some contours of the deeply personal interpretive perspective that Op. 78 likely encouraged from Clara Schumann at the time of its completion, one can easily sympathize with the anonymous English critic who wrote these words. Many of us would prefer not to find ourselves cast in the role of eavesdroppers, whether to a composer's private ruminations or to his intimate exchanges with a fellow musician. Yet in the years since its release the first violin sonata has proven overwhelmingly popular in venues small and large. Performers and listeners with widely varying tastes and interests have clearly found their own ways to enjoy Brahms's allusive gestures and the affective trajectory they support. In reconstructing the rhetorical potential specific to the initial audience for this or any other piece, then, one does not proscribe the work's meaning. One merely describes a particular mode of interaction with the music and allows others to partake in it if they will. Many will not. After all, Brahms himself did not always conceive his compositional decisions in precisely the terms in which he sought to present them to any given recipient. The genesis and subsequent reception history of the Op. 78 *Adagio* provide a case in point. And there are some works for which the implications of borrowed music seem to have remained accessible primarily to the composer himself, hidden by happenstance or by design from the audiences to whom they might have mattered most. Such works provide the focus for the remaining chapters, beginning with muted echoes from one of Franz Schubert's lesser-known songs.

Sometime between January and May 1823, Schubert drafted a setting of an untitled poem by Friedrich Rückert, to which he attached his own title, *Greisen-Gesang* (Old Man's Song). The poem had appeared in 1822 in Rückert's *Oestliche Rosen: Drei Lesen*, a collection of poetry modeled on the Persian ghazels of Hafez, but Schubert may have encountered it through other avenues as early as 1821.[4] In any case, he did not release *Greisen-Gesang* until 1826, when he published a revised version as the first of two songs for bass voice with piano accompaniment, Op. 60. Now catalogued as D. 778, the published version displayed substantial changes from the initial draft, but Schubert's treatment of the text remained the same in one fundamental respect: in both versions, his setting omitted the poem's final two stanzas.[5]

[3] *Musical Times* 21/445 (March 1, 1880): 125.

[4] The title page of Rückert's *Oestliche Rosen* dates the volume to 1822, but copies seem to have begun circulating during the previous year; in addition, Schubert may have encountered some of the poems in the *Oestliche Rosen* in manuscript prior to the volume's publication. See Kristina Muxfeldt, "Schubert Song Studies" (PhD diss., State University of New York at Stonybrook, 1991), 72–73.

[5] For details concerning the date of Schubert's manuscript and the two versions of *Greisen-Gesang*, see Otto Erich Deutsch, *Franz Schubert: Thematisches Verzeichnis seiner Werke in chronologischer Folge*, rev. ed (Kassel: Bärenreiter, 1978), 466–67; and Robert Winter, "Paper Studies and the Future of Schubert

Here is Rückert's poem as it appeared in the *Oestliche Rosen*, with the stanzas Schubert omitted in italics.

Der Frost hat mir bereifet	The cold has frosted over
Des Hauses Dach;	My house's roof;
Doch warm ist mir's geblieben	Yet in my living chamber
Im Wohngemach.	I've still stayed warm.
Der Winter hat die Scheitel	The wintertime has covered
Mir weiß gedeckt.	My head with white.
Doch fließt das Blut, das rothe,	Yet still through my heart's chamber
Durch's Herzgemach.	The red blood flows.
Der Jugendflor der Wangen,	*From my cheeks' once youthful*
	colors
Die Rosen sind	The roses have
Gegangen, all' gegangen	Departed, all departed
Einander nach.	Each after each.
Wo sind sie hingegangen?	Whither have they departed?
In's Herz hinab.	Deep in the heart.
Da blühn sie nach Verlangen,	They bloom there when I wish it,
Wie vor so nach.	Just as before.
Sind alle Freudenströme	Have all the rivers of joy
Der Welt versiegt?	In the world dried up?
Noch fließt mir durch den Busen	A quiet stream is flowing
Ein stiller Bach.	Still through my breast.
Sind alle Nachtigallen	Have all the nightingales
Der Flur verstummt?	Of the field gone dumb?
Noch ist bei mir im Stillen	Here in the silence with me
Hier eine wach.	One is still awake.
Sie singet: Herr des Hauses!	She's singing to me: Master!
Verschleuß dein Thor,	Go close your door
Daß nicht die Welt, die kalte,	So that the cold world stays
Dring' in's Gemach.	Outside the room.
Schleuß aus den rauhen Odem	*Shut out the bitter breath*
Der Wirklichkeit,	*Of reality,*
Und nur dem Duft der Träume	*And only offer shelter*
Gib Dach und Fach.	*To the scent of dreams.*

Research," in *Schubert Studies: Problems of Style and Chronology*, ed. Eva Badura-Skoda and Peter Branscombe, 209–75 (Cambridge: Cambridge University Press, 1982). For a fascinating exploration of Schubert's revisions to *Greisen-Gesang* and their possible motivations, see Richard Kramer, *Distant Cycles: Schubert and the Conceiving of Song* (Chicago: University of Chicago Press, 1994), 47–52.

Ich habe Wein und Rosen	*I have both wine and roses*
In jedem Lied,	*In every song,*
Und habe solcher Lieder	*And of such songs I have still*
Noch tausendfach.	*A thousand more.*
Vom Abend bis zum Morgen	*From evening until morning*
Und Nächte durch	*And through the nights*
Will ich dir singen Jugend	*I'll sing to you of youth*
Und Liebesach.[6]	*And the pangs of love.*

As Rückert's poem unfolds, the speaker assembles a subdued but increasingly self-assured response to the passage of time. Faced with the inevitability of aging, he reclaims his dignity by methodically embracing the depth of remembered experience available only to the old. He weighs the external effects of time against the resilience of his imagination through a series of metaphorical comparisons. For the duration of the first eight stanzas, these metaphors all elaborate a single poetic motive: withdrawal into the self. Inward transit replaces cold with warmth, torpor with liquid motion, pallor with vibrant color, silence with birdsong, and bitter reality with fragrant dreams. At the same time, the speaker's embrace of memory entails a commensurate retreat from the present, isolating him from the outside world and completing a measured transition from social interaction to solitary rumination.

At this point, Schubert stopped setting the poem, which then proceeds to partially reverse the speaker's inward turn. In fact, in stanzas 9 and 10, Rückert's avoidance of quotation marks destabilizes the speaker's very identity. On one hand, the last eight lines might be sung by the nightingale who has just invited the old man to seal off his home and heart from external influence in stanzas 7 and 8. In this case, the poem's closing reference to the "pangs of love" would represent an uncharacteristically energetic manifestation of youthful memories that had thus far confined themselves to images of calm and soothing beauty. On the other hand, since every other first-person pronoun in the text refers to the old man himself, one might more convincingly read the final stanzas as a return to the initial speaker's own voice. In that case, the tone and content of the poem's close would represent an even more explicit departure from its first eight stanzas. Having discovered through his solitude turn a newly confident sense of self, the speaker would suddenly turn outward again to address a current beloved. The ambiguity of the last two stanzas retrospectively inflects the rest of the text.[7]

---

[6] Friedrich Rückert, *Oestliche Rosen. Drei Lesen* (Leipzig: F. A. Brockhaus, 1822), 272–74.

[7] Such ambiguity was by no means uncommon in Rückert's Persian-inspired verse. Although many of the more than three hundred poems in the *Oestliche Rosen* feature shifts in the identity of the poetic speaker, only five employ quotation marks to identify those shifts. Moreover, in every case, the quotation

Read in its entirety, Rückert's poem presents a complex and realistic response to old age: the speaker wavers between resignation and indignation, unable to fully differentiate the two even through the purposeful self-expression of poetic utterance. By the same token, however, the final lines significantly complicate the mental trajectory for which Schubert had to compose a musical analogue. Schubert's text-editing simplified the speaker's withdrawal and clarified his self-immersion in reminiscent fantasy, casting his attitude in a sharper light.

Truncating the poem also left Schubert with a balanced, eight-stanza structure that could be divided in half along the seam between stanzas 4 and 5. Stanzas 1 and 2 each articulate a self-contained comparison between the speaker's outward appearance, which is described in two lines, and his inner youthfulness, which also receives a two-line description. Similarly, stanzas 5 and 6 each pose negative, two-line questions about the speaker's continued hopefulness and answer those questions immediately with affirmative, two-line responses. The first and third lines of stanzas 1 and 2 begin with the same words (*Der...Doch, Der...Doch*); this syntactic structure is replicated in the first and third lines of stanzas 5 and 6 (*Sind...Noch, Sind...Noch*). Following these paired, single-stanza units of comparison, stanzas 3 and 4 and stanzas 7 and 8 articulate larger, two-stanza units of motion between the poetic speaker's external and internal worlds. His cheeks are pale now, but their colors still bloom if he withdraws into his heart; reality is cold and harsh, but his dreams remain sweet if he seals himself inside. Taken as a whole, each four-stanza segment behaves like a musical sentence, progressing from the twofold repetition of a small syntactic unit toward a single, expanded elaboration of the same unit.[8] Perhaps Schubert's decision to omit Rückert's final lines had as much to do with musical structure as textual affect. The succession of two four-stanza sections was certainly amenable to musical setting in two parallel strophes, which is exactly how he arranged them: his setting of stanzas 1 through 4 returns in full to set stanzas 5 through 8, adapted only through localized changes in vocal contour and accompanimental register and texture.

---

marks are aligned with exceptional poetic situations that do not apply in the case of *Der Frost hat mir bereifet*: direct address to the beloved by means of an intermediary, patterned dialogue between lovers in stanzaic or line-by-line alternation, or the interpolation of a supposedly preexisting maxim. For readers familiar with the *Oestliche Rosen*, however, experience with the other poems in the collection would tend to support the view that stanzas 9 and 10 represent the voice of the original poetic speaker. In lieu of quotation marks, Rückert often used stanza breaks as implicit markers of the end of interpolated dialogue; see, for instance, *Zünd', o Schenke! die Lampe, Schenk'! o bring' mir frische Rosen*, and *Du siehst nicht, wer hier steht* (269–71, 275–77, and 365–66).

[8]William Caplin has presented a detailed and influential account of this phrase structure in *Classical Form: A Theory of Formal Functions for the Instrumental Music of Haydn, Mozart, and Beethoven* (Oxford: Oxford University Press, 1998), 35–48.

Once Schubert's text-editing and strophic repetition had concentrated the most elaborate metaphors for the poetic speaker's inward turn toward the end of each four-stanza strophe, his compositional treatment of those metaphors made them the musical and emotional climax of the song. Although the entire length of *Greisen-Gesang* projects the poem's central tension between present and past through obvious contrasts in mode, texture, and vocal range, the song centers the listener's attention on the final stanzas of each strophe by means of drastically slowed text declamation, stretching stanzas 4 and 8 over more than twice as many measures as any other stanza. Furthermore, Schubert's setting of stanzas 4 and 8 conspicuously reanimates an already venerable and aurally recognizable musical emblem: the horn fifths characteristically associated with distance and farewell. His manner of incorporating this preexisting emblem into the setting of Rückert's poem repays detailed examination. Example 8.1a presents an annotated score of the opening measures of Ludwig van Beethoven's piano sonata in Eb major, Op. 81a, of 1809, arguably the *locus classicus* of the horn-fifths gesture. Here the words *Lebe wohl* (Farewell) are explicitly paired with simple, three-note horn fifths in the pianist's right hand. The upper voice descends stepwise from scale degree 3 to 1 while the lower voice traces scale degrees 8, 5, and 3. Meanwhile, the left hand poignantly harmonizes the downbeat of m. 2 with the minor submediant and a precipitous drop in register. Quiet dynamics, slow tempo, "expressive" affect, and measured rhythm all mark the moment as simultaneously intimate and extraordinary.

EXAMPLE 8.1a   Beethoven, Piano Sonata, Op. 81a / I, mm. 1–2. Annotated.

Schubert need not have drawn consciously upon Beethoven's model for his setting of Rückert's poem. His own varied and subtle use of similar gestures is well documented throughout his career as a composer of song.[9] Nonetheless, the opening measures of the *Lebewohl* sonata provide a compelling point of

---

[9] See Rosen, *Romantic Generation*, 116–23 and 186.

EXAMPLE 8.1b   Schubert, *Greisen-Gesang*, D. 778, mm. 30–40. Annotated.

comparison for Schubert's text-setting techniques in *Greisen-Gesang* because the song recalls and reorganizes nearly every salient feature of Beethoven's gesture at the pivotal moments in the fourth and eighth poetic stanzas. Example 8.1b presents Schubert's setting of the first three lines of stanza 4 with annotations indicating similarities to Beethoven's model; the score appears here as in the first edition of the song, published in Vienna by Cappi and Czerny in 1826. First, a chromatically ascending vocal line and the song's most complex harmonic progression propel the poetic speaker's anxious question toward a dissonant appoggiatura and a pregnant pause on the dominant. The singer and the pianist's right hand then respond with the three-note horn-fifth emblem, complete with Beethoven's steady pace, quiet dynamics, and submediant harmonization of the final sonority. Despite Schubert's rich doublings in mm. 34–36 and his added chord seventh and decorated suspension in m. 35, the preexisting associations of the horn fifths resonate clearly: the music of leave-taking accompanies the poetic speaker's retreat into the depths of his own heart.

Indeed, *Greisen-Gesang* invests the generic voice-leading pattern of the horn fifths with text-specific significance by assigning the higher of its two voices to the piano accompaniment. The singer, who has so far presented the song's primary melodic material, suddenly descends into an inner voice and remains there, encompassed above and below by the pianist's melody and bass, through the end of the strophe—and, in the case of the second strophe, through the end of the song.[10] Just as Schubert's text-editing eliminated Rückert's equivocation and guided the poetic speaker firmly into the self-imposed exile of private recollection, so his setting clarified the timing and underlined the finality of the speaker's inner trajectory. Heard against Beethoven's precedent, his textural presentation of the horn fifths aligned the singer's experience of the song with the speaker's experience of old age and isolated the final lines of stanzas 4 and 8 as pivotal moments in the poetic speaker's inward turn. It is precisely these moments that seem to have captured Brahms's imagination, particularly the end of the song's first strophe, where the first appearance of horn fifths coincides with the phrase *Im Herzen tief* (deep in the heart). Documentary evidence indicates that Brahms had ample opportunity to reconstruct in detail both the textual and the compositional means by which Schubert had pinpointed the speaker's retreat from the external world and rendered that retreat musically convincing.

At the latest, Brahms's interest in *Greisen-Gesang* began during the initial years of his friendship with Julius Stockhausen. As one of the very few songs that Schubert had scored explicitly for a low male voice, the setting was ideal for Julius, and it entered his performing repertoire as early as February 1862.[11] Whether the baritone introduced Brahms to the song or vice versa is impossible to tell. Both singer and composer were already avid Schubert enthusiasts before they met each other. Moreover, the pair immediately collaborated in multiple recitals featuring Schubert's music, including two complete performances of *Die Schöne Müllerin* in April 1861.[12] Regardless of who first discovered *Greisen-Gesang*, the song soon acquired a special place in their relationship. Brahms composed an orchestral arrangement of the song for Julius in April 1862, along with orchestrations of at least two other songs by Schubert, *An Schwager Kronos*, D. 369, and *Memnon*, D. 541. (He probably arranged *Geheimes*, D. 719, in April as well, but he did not date the surviving autograph). Perhaps

---

[10]This textural shift is even more pronounced in Schubert's initial draft of *Greisen-Gesang*, which omits the decorated vocal figuration that marks the final lines of stanzas 4 and 8 in the published version. The cadenza-like cascade of eighth notes draws the listener's attention away from the piano's melody and toward the singer. Again, see Kramer, *Distant Cycles*, 40–52.

[11]Julia Wirth's biography of her father includes a list of his performing repertoire and the years and cities in which he first performed individual works in public. According to Wirth, Julius first performed *Greisen-Gesang* in Bern sometime in 1862. In February, he and Clara Schumann gave a series of concerts in Zürich and the surrounding area, including Basel, Mulhouse, and Guebwiller (Litzmann, *Clara Schumann* 3:115n; and Wirth, *Julius Stockhausen*, 220). As Bern was also in the immediate vicinity, this seems the best opportunity for Julius to have given a recital there during the year in question.

[12]Ibid., 212, and Hofmann, *Brahms als Pianist und Dirigent*, 65–66.

the arrangements were meant as a response to Julius's public premiere of two of Brahms's own solo songs during the Hamburg Philharmonic's concert on April 4;[13] perhaps Julius had requested them as a means of expanding his concert repertoire and promoting Schubert's music. Whatever the case, orchestrating *Greisen-Gesang* gave Brahms an important opportunity to deepen his acquaintance with the song. Indeed, the project forced him to come to terms with literally every note in deciding how best to project Schubert's sonorities onto the fuller texture and broader register provided by a full complement of instruments.

Brahms's autograph remains in private hands. His arrangement, scored for low strings, trombones, bassoons, clarinets, and flutes, has only recently become available in a scholarly edition.[14] Close examination reveals three important features of his engagement with Schubert's song. First, he knew *Greisen-Gesang* from Cappi and Czerny's first edition. The hyphen in the title of his autograph of the arrangement, the placement or omission of dynamic indications and articulation marks, and numerous other notational details confirm his source beyond any doubt.[15] Second, he seems to have been particularly interested in the pivotal moments of introspection that close each musical strophe. One can discern which parts of the song attracted his attention because his arrangement was by no means a literal transcription of the original. At the words *Ins Herz hinab*, he doubled the two uppermost string parts with flutes an octave above, as shown in example 8.2a. This is the first time the flutes were heard in the entire arrangement and the first time any pitch higher than f♯' occurred. Reserving the instrument and its higher register until now lent a quality of difference and significance to the musical and poetic gesture they accompany.

Finally, having highlighted its first appearance using textural and registral parameters, Brahms then allowed elements of the gesture itself to infiltrate the remainder of his orchestration. The arrangement of *Greisen-Gesang* did not simply deploy orchestral doublings for the sake of textural contrast; it also exploited them in order to create new contrapuntal lines. Rather

---

[13] Hofmann, *Zeittafel*, 238.

[14] See Peter Jost, ed., *Schubert: Sechs Lieder für Singstimme und Orchester, bearbeitet von Johannes Brahms* (Leipzig: Breitkopf & Härtel, 2000), 22–28. Jost's edition draws upon two manuscript sources: Brahms's own autograph, currently in private ownership, and an anonymous copy made in 1904 for a student of Julius Stockhausen, currently in the Rare Book and Manuscript Library of the University of Pennsylvania (MS. Coll. 97); see ibid., Revisionsbericht, 52. Given the provenance of this second source, Julius also clearly possessed his own manuscript copy of the arrangement, but that copy is now lost.

[15] Compare with Jost, *Sechs Lieder*, 22–28 and Revisionsbericht. Jost's edition arrangement includes a facsimile of the first page of the privately owned autograph, on which the title appears as *Greisen-Gesang*. Subsequent editions of Schubert's song removed the hyphen and collapsed the two words into one, *Greisengesang*, which is how Jost also presents the title in his edition. Readers unable to access the first edition of Schubert's song may consult Walter Dürr, ed., *Franz Schubert: Neue Ausgabe sämtlicher Werke*, *Lieder* (Kassel: Bärenreiter, 1982) 3:283, which describes the print in detail.

EXAMPLE 8.2a   Brahms, orchestral arrangement of *Greisen-Gesang*, mm. 30–36. With kind permission from Breitkopf & Härtel, Wiesbaden.

than adding distinct pitch classes to those provided by Schubert, Brahms created new countermelodies by reinforcing linear progressions among successive pitches, which were individually present but only latently connected in his model. The technique was not limited to *Greisen-Gesang*. Indeed, it appeared in all four orchestrations of Schubert's songs from April 1862, usually confined primarily to the winds while the strings retain Schubert's original voice leading.[16] In the arrangement of *Greisen-Gesang*, however, Brahms's new contrapuntal lines shared a surprising characteristic: nearly every one of them presented a pitch-specific echo of the singer's half of the horn-fifth emblem. The echoes began at the end of the first strophe, immediately after the emblem appeared in the vocal line itself. Example 8.2b provides two instances. First, the second bassoon adopted the singer's gesture a mere five measures later, articulating the descending arpeggio at pitch. Here the motive's initial scale degree 8 was entirely

---

[16] Examples are particularly prevalent in *Memnon* and *An Schwager Kronos*. Nevertheless, even *Geheimes*, by far the smallest and simplest of the 1862 Schubert arrangements, uses the technique. These new countermelodies should prompt the reevaluation of Peter Jost's claim that Brahms left Schubert's models "practically unchanged," with only a single instance of "arrangement proper" in all of his song transcriptions. See *Sechs Lieder*, [iii] and [v].

Brahms's invention, since Schubert's version contained no new attack whatsoever on the second half of beat one. The second strophe then provided echoes in more aurally apparent registers. On two occasions the first flute played scale degrees 8, 5, and 3 in succession against a scalar descent from scale degree 3 to 1 in the first clarinet and vocal line, resulting in an inverted and accelerated version of the two-voice horn-fifth complex.

EXAMPLE 8.2b   Brahms, orchestral arrangement of *Greisen-Gesang*, mm. 41–44 and 59–61. Annotated. With kind permission from Breitkopf & Härtel, Wiesbaden.

Taken together, these newly fabricated echoes indicate that Brahms was particularly struck by Schubert's musical equivalent for the poetic speaker's inward turn. At the same time, the orchestral arrangement of *Greisen-Gesang* also hints at his knowledge of Rückert's poem. The Cappi and Czerny edition that served as his source for the song had mangled the text severely, omitting crucial punctuation (including a question mark in ex. 8.1b) and even altering words. The most egregious changes were three erroneous substitutions: *Ernst* for *Frost* in stanza 1, and *die* for *dein* and *alte* for *kalte* in stanza 7.[17] Brahms's arrangement followed the song's version of the text in the case of the word *alte*, but replaced the other two substitutions with Rückert's original words.[18] These corrections imply that he had consulted the poem itself, independent of Schubert's setting, and compared it at least cursorily to his copy of *Greisen-Gesang* at some point before or during the process of orchestration. No copy of the *Oestliche Rosen* survives in the remnants of his library, but Rückert reprinted the poem in 1837 in volume 4 of his *Gesammelte Gedichte*, a collection Brahms owned.[19] Rückert's reprint gave his previously untitled poem a title, *Vom künftigem Alter* (Of Approaching Old Age). Probably for reasons of space, the new edition also removed the original stanza breaks and consolidated each pair of lines into a single five-beat line. The twenty-line result fits easily on a single page instead of taking up three pages, as it had in the more sumptuous *Oestliche Rosen*. Aside from issues of presentation, the text itself remained unchanged.

Brahms's copy of the *Gesammelte Gedichte* survives, signed but undated, in the archives of the Gesellschaft der Musikfreunde in Vienna. The page bearing *Vom künftigem Alter* suggests yet another level to his engagement with Schubert's song. As he frequently did when he came across texts that his predecessors had set to music, Brahms dog-eared the poem. What makes the page remarkable, however, is a pencil annotation in the right margin. At the point where Schubert stopped setting Rückert's poem, Brahms drew a horizontal line, and above the line he wrote the word "Schubert." Comparison with other instances of the name in his handwriting (for instance, from his chronological catalogue of Schubert's works, currently in the Wienbibliothek im Rathaus in Vienna[20]) confirms that the annotation is his own. The mark is extraordinary because virtually all of Brahms's annotations in his volumes of poetry are text-critical: corrections of misprints, comparisons between editions, and occasional references to other poems or poets. Almost never did he mark a poem in such a way as to indicate how a previous composer had treated that poem. The decision to do so here bears witness to a peculiar fascination with Schubert's text-editing.

----

[17] Walter Dürr plausibly interprets these substitutions as accidents on the part of the composer rather than the publisher, arguing that Schubert misread his own handwriting when copying the song from his original draft (Dürr, *Lieder* 3:283).

[18] See Jost, *Sechs Lieder*, 22, 26, and Revisionsbericht. The changes are all the more interesting because the remainder of the arrangement transmits Rückert's text somewhat loosely. Brahms erroneously replaced the word *Stillen* with the word *Busen* in stanza 6 and, as he sometimes did in his own songs, modified or omitted punctuation in accordance with the implications of musical phraseology.

[19] Friedrich Rückert, *Gesammelte Gedichte* (Erlangen: Carl Heyder, 1837). The poem appears in 4:477.

[20] The Schubert catalogue occupies the final pages of one of Brahms's surviving collections of song texts, designated Ia 79564.

Brahms's interest in the music and text of *Greisen-Gesang* might be relegated to a footnote in the long history of his scholarly and music-historical pursuits were it not for his setting of Clemens Brentano's "O kühler Wald!" (O forest cool!). Completed almost fifteen years after the orchestration of *Greisen-Gesang, O Kühler Wald* was one of sixteen solo songs that Brahms finished in March 1877.[21] The first person to see the setting was Theodor Billroth, who received it in a packet of newly-completed song autographs in mid-March. In a letter from the beginning of April, Brahms begged Billroth to respond with his impressions and return the manuscripts, which he had brought with him to a conference in Berlin during the intervening weeks. The letter concluded with a gleeful postscript: "If you were to examine the Brentano, I believe you could see how one makes a beautiful poem out of a chatty one?!"[22] Thus Brahms drew attention to perhaps the most radical instance of text-editing in any of his solo songs. Of Brentano's original four-stanza poem, he set only the first and third stanzas to music, transforming both the tone and the substance of the text. Here is the complete poem as Brahms found it, with the stanzas he omitted in italics.

O kühler Wald!
Wo rauschest du,
In dem mein Liebchen geht,
O Wiederhall,
Wo lauschest du,
Der gern mein Lied versteht?

O Wiederhall!
O sängst du ihr
Die süßen Träume vor,
Die Lieder all,
O bring sie ihr,
Die ich so früh verlor! —

Im Herzen tief,
Da rauscht der Wald,
In dem mein Liebchen geht,
In Schmerzen schlief
Der Wiederhall,
Die Lieder sind verweht.

O forest cool!
In which my darling
Walks, where do you murmur?
O echo, you
Who gladly grasp
My song, where do you listen?

O echo!
If you'd only sing
To her of my sweet dreams,
O bring to her
All of the songs
That I so quickly lost! —

Deep in the heart
The forest murmurs,
In which my darling walks;
In pain the echo
Fell asleep,
The songs have blown away.

---

[21] Brahms's catalogue of his own works (currently in the Wienbibliothek im Rathaus in Vienna) lists all twenty-three of the songs published in Opp. 69–72 as composed in March 1877. However, at least seven of those songs can be securely dated to earlier or later periods based on dated autographs or other evidence (McCorkle, *Werkverzeichnis*, 295, 300, and 306).

[22] Billroth/Brahms, *Briefwechsel*, 235. The composer seems to have drawn attention to his reshaping of Brentano's poem during the following decade as well. According to the memoirs of Ellen Vetter-Brodbeck, Brahms discussed his treatment of an unnamed poem by Brentano during one of his summer vacations in Thun (1886–88), claiming to have "completely changed it" (Kalbeck, *Brahms* 4:10).

Im Walde bin	*In the forest I*
Ich so allein,	*Am so alone,*
O Liebchen wandre hier,	*O darling, wander here,*
Verschallet auch	*Though songs so pure*
Manch Lied so rein,	*Have died away,*
Ich singe andre dir![23]	*I'll sing some more to you!*

One would be hard-pressed to find a poem so amenable to modification according to the principles of text-editing that Schubert had applied in *Greisen-Gesang*. Brentano's final stanza relates to the entire poem in ways directly analogous to the last two stanzas of Rückert's text: having maintained the illusion of lyric self-address, the poetic speaker suddenly turns outward, speaking in the second person to his beloved. In both poems, this shift in the speaker's relationship to the reader mitigates what would otherwise have been a single-minded retreat away from the external world of interpersonal connection and into solitary memories. For both composers, therefore, shortening the text clarified the poetic speaker's inward trajectory. At the same time, prior to their unexpectedly extroverted endings, both poems encapsulate the speaker's progressive introspection by means of a three-word prepositional phrase describing a descent into the heart. *Ins Herz hinab—Im Herzen tief*: the motion is the same, from surface to depth, from absence to recollected presence. In Rückert's poem, however, this pivotal prepositional phrase is the answer to a question about location (Whither have they departed?). By deleting Brentano's second stanza, Brahms presented his poem's pivotal moment, too, as the response to a question about location (Where do you murmur?). Especially given his annotated copy of Rückert's poem, Brahms's treatment of "O kühler Wald" is strikingly familiar. In "making a beautiful poem out of a chatty one," he created an opportunity to imitate his predecessor's habits of reading and, in so doing, to assemble a poem that closely paralleled the text of *Greisen-Gesang*, especially during the speaker's crucial inward turn.

Having availed himself of Schubert's editorial procedure and poetic trajectory, Brahms could still have chosen to avoid any clear evocation of his music. The autograph that Billroth saw is lost now, but the song was released in August 1877 as the third of the *Fünf Gesänge*, Op. 72. For much of its length *O kühler Wald* bears few musical similarities to *Greisen-Gesang*. The modes, meters, tempi, and tonal outlines of the songs diverge, and, although Brahms's setting, like Schubert's, consists of two musical strophes of which the second is varied, Brahms's second strophe is far more radical in its transformations of the first strophe's material. Yet at the moment of closest intersection between the two poems, the musical gesture that attracted Brahms's attention when he orchestrated *Greisen-Gesang* found pervasive echoes in his setting of Brentano's text. Examples 8.3a and b

---

[23] Clemens Brentano, *Gedichte. In neuer Auswahl*, 2nd ed. (Frankfurt am Main: J. D. Sauerländer, 1861), 293–94.

compare mm. 9–14 of *O kühler Wald* to mm. 30–36 of *Greisen-Gesang*; the passages correspond in both poems to the end of the poetic speaker's questions and the beginning of his answers. The echoes begin in the vocal line. Brahms's setting duplicates Schubert's downward-resolving dissonance from scale degree 8 to 7, his two-measure pause above a dominant seventh chord, and his ascending leap from scale degree 5 to scale degree 8 on the downbeat for the syllables *Im Herz*. Then the piano accompaniment takes the lead. Understanding mm. 12–13 of *O kühler Wald* in the temporary key of F♭ major, the right hand traces the stepwise descent from scale degree 3 familiar from the upper voice of Schubert's horn-fifths gesture. The left hand provides the chord roots for Schubert's harmonization, while the *pianissimo* dynamic, rich doubling, slow pace, visually spare notation in whole notes, and specific voice leading in the right hand's lowest voice all recall mm. 34–35 of *Greisen-Gesang*.

In light of Brahms's extensive prior engagement with Schubert's song, these similarities are unlikely to have occurred by chance, particularly at the point where the diction and emotional trajectories of the two poems reach their closest intersection. They suggest a deliberate act of compositional borrowing that identifies the familiar sounds of *Greisen-Gesang* with the lost past for which

EXAMPLE 8.3a   Schubert, Schubert, *Greisen-Gesang*, D. 778, mm. 30–36. Annotated.

EXAMPLE 8.3b   Brahms, *O kühler Wald*, Op. 72 No. 3, mm. 9–14. Annotated.

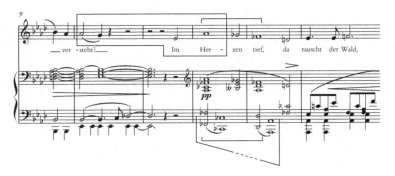

Brentano's poetic speaker longs. But *O kühler Wald* also alters Schubert's music in ways that obscure its origin and complicate its implications. Most obviously, instead of presenting the lower of the two voices in the horn-fifths complex, the vocal line doubles the piano's upper-voice melody. Brahms might have avoided Schubert's characteristic vocal descent for purely musical reasons: out of concern for the singer's range, in an effort to ensure a smooth, stepwise approach to the eb that initiates the song's second strophe in m. 14, or in order to mitigate the parallel octaves that the horn-fifth gesture creates between singer and accompanimental bass line in mm. 34–35 of *Greisen-Gesang*.[24] Whatever its musical impact, however, the omission also affects the projection of Brentano's poem. Although the descent through scale degrees 8, 5, and 3 is surreptitiously provided by the pianist's left hand (as indicated with slanted brackets in ex. 8.3), the characteristic texture of Schubert's farewell gesture remains compromised. No longer does the singer enact the poetic speaker's retreat into private recollection by plunging into the thick of the accompaniment.

More subtly, *O kühler Wald* reconfigures the harmonic underpinning of the borrowed gesture and weakens its continuity with the rest of the song. Schubert's horn fifths had coincided with a straightforward resolution to the major tonic. By contrast, just where the two poems literally converge, Brahms's version introduces a sudden shift toward the flat side of the circle of fifths, reharmonizing the singer's scale degree 8 as scale degree 3 in Fb major on the downbeat of m. 12. The timing of the shift preserves Schubert's ascending leap of a fourth, while seamlessly placing the voice on the first pitch of the upper voice of the horn-fifth gesture. But on the heels of the half cadence that marks the end of Brentano's first stanza, the flat submediant cannot help but seem completely unexpected, and its precipitous advent coincides with the disappearance of harmonic, melodic, and rhythmic characteristics that had consistently held sway since the beginning of Brahms's song. For the space of two measures, functional harmony and predominantly diatonic melody give way to a fragmentary harmonic sequence and a four-note whole-tone scale in the vocal line. The formerly continuous quarter note pulse ceases, replaced by an unsettlingly slow syncopation between the bass line and the rest of the texture. Presented in such a manner, familiar music emerges as if from another world, to which it then recedes just as swiftly and decisively. In fact, mm. 12–13 are completely unnecessary to the declamation of the song's text or the unfolding of its modified strophic structure. One need only replace the words *rauscht der Wald* in m. 14 with the words *Herzen tief* in order to skip directly from m. 11 to the beginning of the second strophe in m. 14, resolving the dominant conventionally and bypassing the horn fifths entirely.

[24] Brahms's own collection of parallel fifths and octaves included three examples of fifths from songs by Schubert, at least two of which Brahms considered so problematic that he experimented with recomposing them; see Mast, ed., "Octaven u. Quinten," 60–63 and 132–33.

Key center and context thus transform a gesture that had once functioned as a large-scale culmination into an unanticipated interruption, a deep and seemingly gratuitous rupture in an otherwise homogenous musical surface. Heard against Schubert's expansive setting of Rückert's inward turn, Brahms's brief and disjunct borrowing stirs up the darker undercurrents in the truncated poem produced by his own text-editing. Despite the manufactured similarities between Brahms's text and Schubert's, the emotional trajectories described by the two poems ultimately point in starkly different directions. Brentano's heart conceals a murmuring forest, not a cozy living room, and, in Brahms's version of the poem, even the self-imposed exile of private memory cannot bring back what the poetic speaker has lost. In the absence of the renewed social connections implied by Brentano's original final stanza, the speaker's songs have "blown away" beyond recall, and the poem closes far more pessimistically than Rückert's did in either its original or its edited version. Brahms's treatment of the borrowed material in mm. 12–13 confirms his text's comparatively hopeless stance: just as the poem permits no true immersion in positive memories, so the song provides no textural interior in which the voice might come to rest and no lasting parallel with Schubert's song.

Because of Brahms's textural reorganization, the cognitive dissonance between source and borrowing is particularly strong for an informed singer. By the same token, however, since virtually no vestige of Schubert's vocal contour reappears in O kühler Wald, even a vocalist intimately familiar with both works is unlikely to notice the relationship between them in the first place. In this regard a pianist's perspective on Brahms's borrowing will probably diverge, subtly but substantially, from a singer's. Although the plunge toward F♭ major separates mm. 12–13 from the rest of the song and obscures the vocal line's basis in Schubert's music, it also adds a physical dimension to a keyboard player's recollection of Greisen-Gesang. In B major and F♭ major, the accompanist's right hand follows the horn-fifth gesture and its rich harmonization along virtually the same path among the instrument's black and white keys. Remaining in A♭ major, by contrast, would have removed any kinesthetic similarity to Schubert's song during the act of performance. For the pianist alone, the situation is the inverse of that created by Brahms's allusive gestures in Alte Liebe or the finale of the first violin sonata: Schubert's music sounds strange but feels familiar.

In combination, Brahms's omission of the characteristic vocal descent into an inner voice and his tactile enhancement of similarities in the accompaniment create a marked disparity in the immediacy with which singers and keyboardists would be likely to recognize his borrowing and perceive its bearing on Brentano's text. If the momentary and problematized recovery of Schubert's culminating gesture provides the musical equivalent of fleeting contact with the poetic speaker's remembered past, the contact occurs primarily through the fingers rather than in the voice. This disparity, in turn, is merely part of a larger

EXAMPLE 8.4   Linear chromaticism in *O kühler Wald*

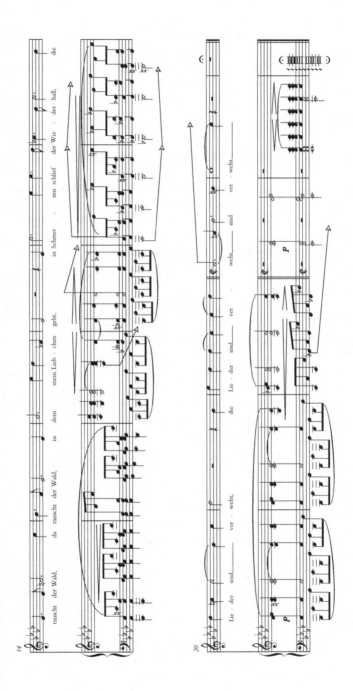

pattern that spans the entire song, for *O kühler Wald* also employs another compositional device familiar from *Greisen-Gesang*—that of unidirectional linear chromaticism. In Schubert's song, melodic lines comprising two or more successive half steps in the same direction occur at just one location in each strophe. The vocal line that sets the question "Whither have they departed?" (and, in the second strophe, the command "Shut out the bitter breath of reality") ascends by half step three times, doubled by the bass and accompanied by a chromatic descent in the middle voice of the pianist's right hand (ex. 8.1b). For both singers and players of Schubert's song, linear chromaticism immediately precedes the diatonically grounded horn-fifth gesture and is therefore powerfully associated with the anxiety that the prospect of aging provokes in the poetic speaker.

Brahms's song appropriates the same device while enhancing its affective associations. In *O kühler Wald*, unidirectional half-step motion occurs no fewer than nine times and generates the vast majority of non-diatonic harmonies. Leaving aside octave doublings, immediately repeated notes, and the borrowed material in mm. 12–13, the song contains twenty-six altered pitches, of which twelve belong to chromatic lines and an additional ten accompany them. Example 8.4 presents a full score in which chromatic ascents and descents are indicated with slanted arrows attached to the stems of their initial pitches. As in *Greisen-Gesang*, such lines are closely aligned with the poetic speaker's mood. In the first strophe of Brahms's song they coincide with the tail ends of the speaker's questions about location, once in mm. 4–5 and twice in mm. 8–9, adding an air of rising urgency to his queries. In the second strophe they intrude more frequently, twice in mm. 16–17 and then a full six times in conjunction with the closing tercet in mm. 18–24, where the speaker's pain finally overwhelms his memories and renders his lost songs unrecoverable.

The steady increase in chromatic saturation throughout *O kühler Wald* reinforces the fundamental pessimism of Brentano's poem in Brahms's version: the song's persistent repetition of what for Schubert was merely a momentary register of doubt underscores the speaker's realization that not even the willful solitude of reminiscence can bring him comfort. But if *O kühler Wald* borrows the connotations that half-step motion carried in *Greisen-Gesang*, it also subtly modifies the experience of those connotations for the two performers during the act of playing and singing the song. Unlike in Schubert's setting, chromatic lines initially appear in the accompaniment alone. Only after repeatedly disrupting the diatonic surface are they allowed to infiltrate the vocal line, first tentatively in mm. 16–17 and then brazenly in mm. 23–24. It is as if the pianist is already aware of the anxious undertones of Brahms's text but must struggle against the song's lush doublings, broad phrases, and plangent major mode in order to bring those undertones to the singer's ear. The vocalist, by contrast, begins swathed in fully diatonic melody and seemingly oblivious to the poetic speaker's pessimism, then is compelled to enter ever more challenging motivic and affective territory until, in mm. 23–24, he or she adopts the piano's chromaticism wholeheartedly, producing a striking musical analogue for the speaker's unfulfilled longing. The final vocal phrase ascends plaintively from scale degree 1 to 3 in the song's longest and most aurally apparent chromatic line, dashing any hope of a convincing perfect authentic cadence and relegating the piano to off-beat accompanimental support; in its wake, the song cannot end but merely dies away.[25] For the first time, the voice is the primary embodiment of the song's emotional content, the keystone of the music's relationship to the text.

Singing *O kühler Wald* therefore enacts a gradual process of coming to terms with the bleakness of the poetic speaker's perspective, a painstaking transformation in attitude begun at the instigation of the accompanist but later embraced and completed on one's own. By the same token, playing the song gives one the implicit responsibility of provoking that transformation in the singer. These bifurcated, instrument-specific interpretive stances are encouraged during the act of performance by the changing motivic relationship between the vocal line and the accompaniment. They are readily perceived, independent of the song's compositional roots in Schubert's setting. Nevertheless, recognizing Brahms's borrowing from *Greisen-Gesang* can enhance both performers' unique experiences of music and text in *O kühler Wald*. At the keyboard, the momentary recovery of physical sensations familiar from Schubert's horn-fifth gesture locates Brentano's lost songs firmly in the fleeting memories of the pianist's own musical past. For an informed singer, the implied contrast with Schubert's texturally and harmonically grounded climax renders Brahms's final vocal phrase an especially powerful emblem of open-endedness.

Unlike many of the works addressed in parts 1–3, *O kühler Wald* was not associated with any specific recipient in surviving documents from within Brahms's circles. Although he bragged to Theodor Billroth about the effects of his text-editing, Brahms's brief comment about Brentano's poem would hardly have warned the surgeon to be on the lookout for musical reminiscences from an old and little-known song. Moreover, among his many friends, Billroth does not seem to have been the best suited to the apprehension of subtle allusive gestures. When sharing the first violin sonata with him two years later, the composer provided explicit verbal clues as to the source of the head motive for the finale. If Brahms found it necessary to coach him in the apprehension of a thoroughly straightforward and obvious borrowing, Billroth seems unlikely to have been the target audience for so complex and attenuated a reference as the

---

[25] In one of the more evocative recent accounts of *O kühler Wald*, Inge van Rij has described this moment as the "uneasy negating of the very existence of song as it is actually being sung"; see *Brahms's Song Collections* (Cambridge: Cambridge University Press, 2006), 108.

horn-fifth gesture in *O kühler Wald*. At any rate, he did not respond to Brahms's comments about Brentano's poem, even in a lengthy letter that directly addressed the new songs he had encountered in March 1877. Aside from categorizing the setting among the composer's "lyrical" *Lieder* (as opposed to folk-inspired, impassioned, or graceful and humorous), he never mentioned *O kühler Wald* again in their surviving correspondence.[26]

With no clear-cut intended recipient confirmed by extant documents, a range of possible audiences remains for whom Brahms might have designed his muted echoes of *Greisen-Gesang*. On one end of the spectrum were numerous composers, performers, and other initiates in the tradition of the *Lied*. For listeners sufficiently familiar with Schubert's oeuvre and attuned to the intricacies of his voice leading, Brahms's borrowing could have functioned as a carefully calibrated register of admiration across a marked music-historical distance. Like the memories that the poetic speaker vainly tries to recapture, the vast majority of Schubert's compositions had faded from Viennese concert life shortly after publication—if, indeed, they had ever been released or publicly performed at all—and resurfaced only sporadically throughout the second half of the nineteenth century. Brahms participated in this revival in the decades leading up to the composition of *O kühler Wald*. Describing his first visit to Vienna in March 1863 in correspondence with Adolf Schubring, he had reveled in unexpected contact with Schubert's still-unknown works:

> The merry city, the beautiful surroundings, the sympathetic, lively public: how stimulating that all is for an artist! And particularly for us the blessed memory of the great musicians, of whose lives and works one is daily reminded here. There is especially Schubert, of whom one has the feeling that he is still alive! One meets ever more people who speak of him as a close acquaintance, and one sees ever new works of whose existence one knew nothing at all, and that are so untouched that one can scour away the sand.[27]

More recently, in the spring of 1876, Brahms prepared the first edition of an unpublished song, *Der Strom* (D. 565), directly from the original autograph.[28] In the context of his ongoing fascination with Schubert's lost songs, his text-editing and musical borrowing may have provided an opportunity to lament his predecessor's early death and the undeserved obscurity of many of his compositions.

If presented overtly to a broad musical public, however, such a lament would have been susceptible to interpretation as a manifesto. In the immediate aftermath of the comparisons to Beethoven that surrounded the successful

---

[26] Billroth/Brahms, *Briefwechsel*, 236–37.
[27] Brahms, *Briefe an ... Schubring*, 196–97.
[28] Brahms/Stockhausen, *Briefwechsel*, 118.

premiere of his first symphony in 1876,[29] Brahms must have been acutely aware that obvious musical homages to any of the central figures in the growing Austro-German canon might well be understood as polemical attempts to redefine his own relationship to that canon. Explicitly adopting Schubert as a distant muse could transform *O kühler Wald* into an elegy upon Brahms's temporal remove from his preferred compositional models, thematizing the historicist bent that had recently become a defining characteristic of his works in the eyes and ears of German-speaking musicians. Such a reading of his intentions may seem attractive from the perspective of music-historical scholarship, but Brahms's song did not facilitate its adoption by the general public, then or now. Due to the altered vocal line and reconfigured accompanimental harmonies, his borrowing from Schubert was far less audible than the private allusive gestures investigated thus far in this book, let alone the well-known allusions that he demonstrably designed for large audiences in such works as the First Symphony and the *Triumphlied*. Subsequent reception confirms the challenges of perceiving preexisting material in *O kühler Wald*. Although the sudden flat submediant in m. 12 has drawn the ear of virtually every commentator to the precise moment of Brahms's borrowing from *Greisen-Gesang*, neither early reviews nor recent musicological literature have ever acknowledged the borrowing itself.[30]

In short, Brahms's treatment of Schubert's horn fifths suggests that he was not interested in making them recognizable for either public or posterity—that he may have intended them, instead, for a more exclusive audience with whose prior musical experiences he was particularly familiar.[31] At the extreme end of the spectrum lay the composer himself, for whom echoes of *Greisen-Gesang* might have taken on all manner of personally symbolic importance as his career approached its zenith. By the same token, though, those echoes may also have been meant for apprehension by one or more of his acquaintances. In the absence of evidence to the contrary, the best candidate is surely his old friend and fellow Schubert enthusiast, Julius Stockhausen. The baritone had access to *O kühler Wald* before its publication, along with most of the other

---

[29] Brodbeck, *Brahms: Symphony No. 1*, 79–90.

[30] Among the many scholars to draw attention to the very moment of Brahms's borrowing without noting its origins are Peter Jost ("Brahms und das deutsche Lied," in *Brahms als Liedkomponist*, 25n, and "Lieder und Gesänge," 245–46), Michael Musgrave ("Words for Music," 223–25) and Heather Platt ("5 Gesänge, Opus 72," in Botstein, *Compleat Brahms*, 264–65).

[31] On the other hand, within recent memory it might have been fashionable to explain Brahms's treatment of his borrowed material according to antagonistic theories of influence in nineteenth-century music. The notion of poetic influence proposed in Harold Bloom's *The Anxiety of Influence* (Oxford: Oxford University Press, 1983) and *A Map of Misreading* (Oxford: Oxford University Press, 1985) cast a long shadow in North American musicological discourse toward the end of the twentieth century. Relevant publications concerning Brahms's works include Brodbeck, *Brahms: Symphony No. 1*, and Kevin Korsyn, "Towards a New Poetics of Musical Influence," *Music Analysis* 10 (1991): 3–72.

songs in Opp. 69–72.[32] Although no record of his initial impressions survives in written correspondence, he devoted significant time and energy to the task of learning the song: according to his student Max Friedländer, it became one of his favorites among Brahms's entire output of solo vocal music.[33] Most important, prior to the release of *O kühler Wald*, *Greisen-Gesang* was already part of his active performing repertory, particularly in Brahms's orchestrated version. He had sung the arrangement in public concerts at least five times between 1863 and 1872, twice with Brahms in attendance, and had performed Schubert's original song as well.[34] He was therefore as well equipped as any singer could possibly be to perceive the complex relationship between *Greisen-Gesang* and *O kühler Wald*.

Assuming for the moment that Brahms intended Julius to notice his borrowing and to interpret it allusively, one can speculate in various ways as to the resonances that it might have been designed to evoke in March 1877. Not only had the two musicians collaborated in countless performances of Schubert's music over the decades; Brahms had also enlisted the singer's aid in deciphering Schubert's autograph for his edition of *Der Strom* just seven months prior to the completion of *O kühler Wald*. He would thus have known that Julius was especially well prepared to perceive echoes of any of Schubert's songs as tokens of composerly appreciation and emblems of music-historical distance. At the same time, the selection and adjustment of borrowed material in *O kühler Wald* facilitated a more intimate cluster of associations. After all, the orchestral arrangement of *Greisen-Gesang* dated from the period of closest musical cooperation and budding friendship between singer and composer. Their remarkable series of joint performances in 1861 and 1862 was artistically stimulating and personally edifying for them both; as Brahms explained in correspondence with Clara Schumann, it was in working through song repertoire together that they came to be on intimate "du"-terms.[35]

But just seven months after Brahms arranged *Greisen-Gesang* for Julius, their professional closeness was suddenly cut short. In November 1862, before they had ever performed the arrangement together in public, Julius took up the directorship of the Hamburg Philharmonic, a position Brahms had erroneously assumed would be his. By the time their friendship regained its former firm

---

[32] Billroth/Brahms, *Briefwechsel*, 236.

[33] Friedländer, *Brahms' Lieder*, 101.

[34] The first performance of the arrangement occurred in February 1863 in Hannover; Julius informed Brahms of the premiere two months later (Brahms/Stockhausen, *Briefwechsel*, 33–34 and 35n). He revived the work in Hamburg in October 1867 and again in Breslau (now Wroclaw, Poland) the following year (Hofmann, *Zeittafel*, 275; Wirth, *Julius Stockhausen*, 496). Finally, he sang it twice in Karlsruhe, in 1871 and 1872 (Kalbeck, *Brahms* 2:371 and 398). Julius also performed the original song in Leipzig in January 1868; an anonymous review appeared in the *Leipziger Allgemeine musikalische Zeitung* 3/5 (January 29, 1868), 39.

[35] Brahms/Schumann, *Briefe* 1:362.

footing, Brahms had permanently forsaken Hamburg for Vienna. The two musicians never again lived in close proximity, and collaboration of any kind was necessarily sporadic. As explored in chapter 2, their relationship became strained once again in the early 1870s, this time due to Brahms's awkwardness in dealing with Julius's own attempts at songwriting. In fact, their final opportunity for face-to-face discussion of compositional technique occurred in conjunction with their only joint performance of the *Greisen-Gesang* arrangement—in Karlsruhe, with Brahms at the podium, on October 18, 1871.[36] One imagines that both men might have initially perceived the coincidence as a good omen, but far from heralding a new era of professional collaboration the concert proved to be the last time Brahms and Julius made music together in public at all until after the composition of *O kühler Wald*. Despite repeated efforts throughout the mid-1870s, Julius could not convince Brahms to join him on tour or on the concert stage in Berlin.[37] For his own part, the composer began performing actively with another baritone, Georg Henschel, whom he met in 1874.

By 1877, Brahms could most likely assume that Julius would associate his arrangement of *Greisen-Gesang* with memories of a collaborative intimacy that was long past, but had once strongly characterized their friendship and their music making alike. He could therefore predict that a perceived allusion to *Greisen-Gesang* at the pivotal moment of *O kühler Wald* would facilitate a powerful alignment of textual trajectory and personal circumstance. Through the fleeting echoes of Schubert's horn fifths, Brentano's lament on the passage of time could resonate in sympathy with Julius's memories of bygone musical partnership, laying bare the emotional consequences of the ruptures that had accumulated between him and Brahms over the intervening years. The conclusion of *O kühler Wald* implied a starkly realistic assessment of the present situation, as if to reiterate that no amount of solitary reminiscence on either man's part could recapture the cooperative excitement of their early friendship. Yet although the poetic speaker's remembered songs die away forever and Schubert's music is never fully recovered, Brahms's shifting textural deployment of linear chromaticism invited Julius to experience the poem's bleak realism as a shared perspective, a truth first perceived by the accompanist but ultimately accepted by the singer as well. In the realm of tones, two proud musicians could still find common ground, albeit only through the hindsight of regret.

In many ways, then, Julius was uniquely positioned to understand Brahms's compositional choices—the revisions to Brentano's poem, the adoption and adaptation of Schubert's horn-fifth gesture, and the affective trajectory articu-

---

[36]That Brahms conducted the *Greisen-Gesang* arrangement is documented in an anonymous review of the concert in the *Leipziger Allgemeine musikalische Zeitung* 6/46 (November 15, 1871), 730, as well as in the local musical press in Karlsruhe (Hofmann, *Brahms als Pianist und Dirigent*, 127).

[37]Brahms/Stockhausen, *Briefwechsel*, 112, 115–17, 121–23.

lated by the song—as manifestations of an underlying rhetorical act. But first he would have had to perceive those choices in the first place. The echoes of *Greisen-Gesang* were not aurally apparent, nor were they enhanced for any singer during performance. As Brahms well knew, Julius's responsibilities in Berlin afforded no time to maintain a professional keyboard technique, yet the altered horn-fifth gesture was nearly unrecognizable as a reference to Schubert's song except in the fingers of a sensitive pianist. Moreover, no documentary evidence indicates that Brahms ever alerted his friend in writing, even obliquely, to the special characteristics of his new song, despite frequent communications from March 1877 and the surrounding months.[38] Although he may have deliberately drawn musical inspiration from his shared history with Julius, one cannot assume that Brahms expected the baritone to perceive an allusion to *Greisen-Gesang* at all. Instead, the private connotations explored in this chapter are more likely to have remained completely obscure to the only audience musically and contextually equipped to receive them, leaving the rhetorical potential of Brahms's borrowing unrealized within his social sphere.

Yet even if it remained forever latent, that potential was not necessarily wasted. From Brahms's own perspective, *O kühler Wald* was arguably as rich and specific in its potential interpersonal implications as any of his overtly allusive songs or instrumental works. Like the explicitly referential gestures explored in earlier chapters, the concealed echoes of Schubert's horn fifths could still open interpretive arenas in which remembered music facilitated an imagined dialogue between old friends. Even if the borrowing from *Greisen-Gesang* was ultimately too subtle for Julius, Brahms himself could still participate in that dialogue as both songwriter and pianist. In turn, such imagining might have served a larger purpose, for this is not the only song in which the prospect of musical communication with Julius seems to have preoccupied the composer during the spring of 1877. Within two weeks, he would complete *Es liebt sich so lieblich im Lenze*, his bawdy baptismal offering for the Stockhausen family. Heard against the veiled borrowing and anxious conclusion of *O kühler Wald*, the latter song's forthright and humorous allusive strategy echoes the ebullient close of Brentano's poem in its original version: "Though songs so pure have died away, / I'll sing some more to you." Perhaps only after experimentally rejecting Brentano's final stanza could Brahms embrace its optimistic trajectory in a subsequent composition. As one might compose a letter one had no intention of mailing, simply in order to organize one's thoughts in preparation for a difficult conversation, so *O kühler Wald*'s unobtrusive borrowing might have allowed Brahms to chart a darkly realistic assessment of his friendship with Julius before undertaking in earnest the musical and interpersonal project of improving that

---

[38] Ibid., 126–29.

friendship. Without first brooding in private, maybe he would not have allowed *Es liebt sich so lieblich im Lenze* to argue so openly on behalf of renewed connections with the singer.

Whatever Brahms's motivations, ruminating on the clustered associations of regret and lost intimacy called forth by Brentano's text and Schubert's music clearly interested him more than producing an easily apprehensible allusive gesture. In other words, he seems to have been concerned not only with the song as completed product but also with the act of composition as psychological process. Independent of how or whether anyone else might have perceived Schubert's horn fifths in *O kühler Wald*, the self-assigned task of adapting those horn fifths to their new affective and musical context permitted Brahms to engage emotionally sensitive issues on the comparatively comfortable level of compositional craft. The phenomenon of musical borrowing thus provided an opportunity for personal reflection as well as interpersonal communication. Such opportunities were not confined to the cool depths of Brentano's forest. Although the borrowings addressed in parts 1–3 carried rich extramusical associations for their intended recipients and projected those associations far more unequivocally than *O kühler Wald* during the act of performance, they, too, can also be understood as registers of private self-examination. Just as Brahms's allusive compositions prodded and cajoled the Herzogenbergs, strengthened his complex friendship with Clara Schumann, and assisted the Joachims, Fabers, and Stockhausens in the forging of new parental identities, so the private process of composing those pieces may have fulfilled in various and unpredictable ways the demands of the composer's own conscience. Continuing along the same lines, chapter 9 explores how conscience and composition intertwined in a borrowing so well hidden that Brahms himself seems to have been its only conceivable audience.

CHAPTER NINE

COUNTERPOINT AND CATHARSIS

Shortly after its release in 1883, Brahms acquired a copy of *Adjutantenritte und andere Gedichte*, a new collection of poetry by Detlev von Liliencron. One of the shortest poems in the volume was "Auf dem Kirchhofe" (In the Grave-yard), which recalls a sudden, drastic transformation in the poetic speaker's attitude toward death. The poem reads:

Der Tag ging regenschwer und sturmbewegt,	The day passed, pouring rain and tossed by storm,
Ich war an manch vergessenem Grab gewesen.	At many a long-forgotten grave I'd been.
Verwittert Stein und Kreuz, die Kränze alt,	Headstone and cross were withered, wreathes were old,
Die Namen überwachsen, kaum zu lesen.	Names, overgrown, were near-illegible.
Der Tag ging sturmbewegt und regenschwer,	The day passed, tossed by storm and pouring rain,
Auf allen Gräbern fror das Wort: Gewesen.	On every grave there froze the words: *Has Been.*
Wie sturmestot die Särge schlummerten—	Calm as the end of storms the coffins slept—
Auf allen Gräbern taute still: Genesen.[1]	On every grave appeared still dewdrops: *Healed.*

Outside in bitter weather, the speaker confronts the moldering headstones of a deserted churchyard. He broods on the fate of the forgotten dead who lie around him and, by implication, on his own mortality. His anxiety grows apace, fanned by a gathering cloud of poetic devices. Line 5 chiastically rearranges the already ponderous epithetic compounds from line 1, stalling the poem's forward momentum

---

[1] Detlev von Liliencron, *Adjutantenritte und andere Gedichte* (Leipzig: Wilhelm Friedrich, 1883), 31.

under the combined weight of verbal repetition and rhetorical flourish.[2] By the end of line 6 a crisis comes. Syntactic stasis and semantic obsession merge in the jarring return to the word *gewesen* (past participle of the verb *sein*, to be) far too soon after its initial occurrence at the end of line 2. The speaker is trapped, forced to acknowledge the inevitable finality of death. Then, somehow, in the space between lines 6 and 7, he finds release from fear and assurance that the departed are at peace. The last couplet turns once more to the graves, but their formerly frozen surfaces have softened—blurred, perhaps, by the tears that accompany newfound vision. The final word, *genesen* (healed), refocuses the imagery of the entire poem. Juxtaposed through rhyme and metric placement with the dire *gewesen* from lines 2 and 6, the shift of a single letter simultaneously completes and encapsulates a sharp turn away from overt anxiety and toward an ambiguous calm.

The narrative past tense in which the entire poem takes place anticipates this crucial shift in perspective. The immediacy of the act of reading is tempered, its significance altered: instead of encouraging a visceral response to a linear series of events, the text as a whole facilitates the contemplation of a transformation already completed. For the poet himself, the sense of introspection rather than immediate experience was a hard-won achievement. After Liliencron died in the early twentieth century, his first biographer discovered that drafts of "Auf dem Kirchhofe" had initially begun as private reflections on the death of his own mother. The anonymous tombstones were originally "my mother's grave," their faded names her own. The final line had always ended with the word *genesen*, but, at first, far from finding comfort in the universal fact of human mortality, the poetic speaker had actually addressed the departed directly in a wrenching apostrophe: "Ah mother, if only I were like you—healed." By explicitly denying the possibility of closure for the bereaved, Liliencron's initial text had remained unequivocally melancholic, indeed almost voyeuristic in its intensity. The resigned detachment and cautious optimism characteristic of the published poem emerged only over the course of the next two months, through at least four rounds of painstaking revision.[3] In the published version, then, the word *genesen* actually served as the endpoint for two intertwined trajectories: the sudden, blatant shift embodied in the internal dynamics of the poem itself and the slow, secret process of self-consolation in which the writing and rewriting of the poem had functioned for the poet. Perceived

---

[2] In one of the few close readings of Liliencron's "Auf dem Kirchhofe," Ira Braus has emphasized the "anaphoral transformation" effected by the reversal of adverbs in lines 1 and 5 ("Poetic-Musical Rhetoric"). By contrast, I understand the poem's essential shift to occur only in its final two lines. Palindromic structures, whether musical or poetic, tend to impede forward momentum. Rather than setting the poem "in motion," as Braus proposes, lines 5 and 6 produce the impression of extreme stasis.

[3] Heinrich Spiero, *Detlev von Liliencron: Sein Leben und seine Werke* (Berlin: Schuster & Loeffler, 1913), 120–21.

in tandem, these dual trajectories enrich the experience of "Auf dem Kirch-hofe" by facilitating both detached and empathetic modes of reading.

Only the first trajectory, however, was available to Brahms in the mid-1880s when he encountered the poem, or to his audiences in October 1888 when he published a musical setting as the fourth of the Five Songs for Low Voice and Piano, Op. 105. Without a personal context or a longer temporal span in which to situate the poetic speaker's shift in attitude, the text presented a host of chal-lenges for composer and listener alike, most obviously the questions of how to generate and apprehend sufficient continuity in the face of extreme affective flux. Not everyone found Brahms's solutions convincing. Eduard Hanslick, for one, blamed Liliencron's "affected" poem for wrecking an otherwise effective song.[4] Nonetheless, *Auf dem Kirchhofe* soon gained a substantial following, first within Brahms's own circles and then among the broader communities of *Lied* enthusiasts across Western Europe. By the early 1910s, it was routinely numbered among the composer's best songs.[5] Its contemporaneous popularity may ex-plain why Max Kalbeck felt impelled to engage both text and music closely in the final volume of his monumental Brahms biography in 1914. His commen-tary echoed Hanslick's in attacking the inadequacies of Liliencron's published text, but it departed from previous accounts by retracing the compositional origins of the song. The result wove together literary and genetic criticism, beginning with a parallel to Brahms's *Meine Lieder*, Op. 106 No. 4:

> We wander in the shadow of the cypresses planted in "Meine Lieder," which would rather lead us to Italy than to the ancient graveyard of Scherzligen. There the music to Detlev von Liliencron's detestably abbreviated poem originated. It was not this af-fected, Goethe-imitating, corporeal terseness, but far more an overmastered poetic soul yearning for release that challenged the composer to produce his salvage opera-tion. The tormented body of the poem was removed from the torture chamber, the stanzas freed from Spanish clumsiness and refreshed with the balm of tones, until the life that had fled returned and the spirit of the poem reawakened, so that the beauty of its conception could reveal itself to everyone. Now the soul's portrait, incomparable in its concise tragedy, simple greatness, and sublime sorrow, appears for the first time as the poet may have intended. Through melodic expansion Brahms transformed the antithesis of outward wordplay between "Gewesen" and "Genesen" into the opposi-tion between concrete feelings. The "*word* Gewesen froze" no more; instead, the *man*

---

[4] Eduard Hanslick, *Musikalisches und Literarisches* (Berlin: Allgemeiner Verein für Deutsche Literatur, 1889), 144.
[5] As usual, Elisabeth von Herzogenberg provided one of the earliest extant responses to the song in cor-respondence with its composer (Brahms/Herzogenberg, *Briefwechsel* 2:205). Among the many biogra-phers, critics, and performers whose prose featured *Auf dem Kirchhofe* prominently in the ensuing decades were the pianist Florence May, the scholar John Alexander Fuller Maitland, and the baritone Harry Plunket Greene. See May, *Johannes Brahms* 2:238; Fuller Maitland, *Brahms* (New York: John Lane, 1911), 184; and Greene, *Interpretation in Song* (New York: MacMillan, 1912), 14–15.

who lamentingly uttered it trembled. But for the "Genesen" the soothing final cadence sufficed, after the music had dissolved the bitter consolation in a dew of tears with the Passion Chorale "O Haupt voll Blut und Wunden." With the reminiscence the major mode arrives, a sunny surprise after the overcast C minor.—Brahms asked me, when he showed me the song in manuscript, whether I had noticed the "joke" at the end, and also divulged to me the place of its genesis. It will not be easy to find a more fitting illustration for this psalm of transience than the overgrown churchyard surrounding the little gothic chapel on the left bank of the Aare, with its sunken burial mounds, withered monuments, and rust-eaten crosses.[6]

The passage represents Kalbeck at his worst and best, hagiographic but perceptive, opinionated but indispensible. Certainly it is difficult for a musician to read Liliencron's poem today without imagining it sung in Brahms's famous setting. The composer's large-scale structure allows the text much-needed time to unfold its images slowly and ruminatively, and his harmonic planning clarifies the timing and affective implications of the poem's central transformation. Yet Kalbeck's interpretation focused almost exclusively on the song's ability to succeed where the poet had failed, ignoring or downplaying those elements of verbal structure and syntax that must have appealed to Brahms in the first place. With respect to the relationship between music and text, then, many of Kalbeck's successors have provided far more balanced appraisals than he.[7] In other ways, however, later studies have remained uniformly indebted to his account because it appears to record Brahms's own comments about the song. A single, undated autograph survives today, bearing marks that confirm its use as the engraver's model. Whether it is the manuscript Kalbeck claimed to have encountered cannot be determined definitively, but it matches the first edition in every detail save the tempo indication and the punctuation of Liliencron's poem, which were altered at some point later in the publication process.[8] It is therefore entirely plausible that Kalbeck had access to the song in its final form before its release. Based upon the identification of the Scherzligen chapel as the inspiration for Brahms's setting, scholars have narrowed down the possible dates of composition to the summers of 1886–88, which the composer spent in Thun, Switzerland. No independent confirmation of a visit to the chapel survives in Brahms's correspondence, but the rooms he rented in Thun were directly across the Aare River from Scherzligen.[9] If he felt the need for atmospheric inspiration during those three summers, he did not have far to walk.

[6] Kalbeck, *Brahms* 4:133–34. Emphases original.
[7] For examples from both sides of the Atlantic, see Braus, "Poetic-Musical Rhetoric," and Hartmut Krones, "Harmonische Symbolik im Vokalschaffen von Johannes Brahms," in *Johannes Brahms: Quellen— Text—Rezeption—Interpretation*, 415–37.
[8] The autograph of *Auf dem Kirchhofe* is now preserved in Vienna in the Wienbibliothek im Rathaus as MH 5500/c.
[9] Widmann, *Johannes Brahms in Erinnerungen*, 54.

Most important to subsequent scholarship was Brahms's purported comment concerning his own compositional process. The reference to a "joke" near the end of the song would constitute one of only a few direct acknowledgments of musical borrowing in his oeuvre. Given Brahms's documented use of the same term, *Witz*, in reference to allusive gestures in at least two earlier vocal works (*Es liebt sich so lieblich im Lenze* and *O schöne Nacht*), Kalbeck's diction rings true. And from a music-analytic standpoint, the claim is plausible enough to be taken seriously. As shown in example 9.1a, immediately following the pivotal transformation in the poetic speaker's attitude, the first six notes in the vocal line present the melodic incipit of the Passion Chorale, so called because of its five appearances in J. S. Bach's *St. Matthew Passion*, BWV 244. Scale-degree content and metric placement are maintained precisely. If Kalbeck can be trusted, Brahms did not explain whether his borrowing was designed to evoke any particular prior arrangement of the chorale tune, but simply asked whether his friend had perceived something amusing in the final measures of his new piece. Both composer and biographer were well aware that the borrowed melody had a long history in sacred and secular song dating back to the early seventeenth century.[10] A wide variety of sources might therefore have come to mind for either of them. Nevertheless, the uniform texture and strict contrapuntal style of Brahms's piano accompaniment clearly recalled Bach's chorale harmonizations, which was presumably why Kalbeck identified the source of the borrowing as *O Haupt voll Blut und Wunden*, the best-known text and harmonization associated with the Passion Chorale.

Through Kalbeck's retelling, Brahms's joke found its way into virtually every subsequent commentary on *Auf dem Kirchhofe*. This does not mean that Kalbeck himself had thoroughly grasped the punch line. Beginning with Max Friedländer in 1922, dissenting scholars have proposed a more likely source for the borrowing: *Wenn ich einmal soll scheiden* (When once I must depart), the final harmonization in Bach's *St. Matthew Passion*.[11] Example 9.1b presents the first phrase of the latter harmonization as it appeared in the Bach-Gesellschaft

---

[10] In his copious handwritten extracts from early music and folk song, compiled mainly during the 1850s, Brahms notated the tune four times in versions that included its original source: Hans Leo Hassler's *Mein G'müth ist mir verwirret* (Nürnberg, 1601); see McCorkle, *Werkverzeichnis*, 735–36. Similarly, Kalbeck noted Hassler's role as the initial composer of the famous melody when discussing Brahms's Chorale Preludes for organ, Op. post. 122 (*Brahms* 4:476).

[11] Friedländer proposed his alternative gently, confining it to parentheses (*Brahms' Lieder*, 140). Sams has fleshed out a more aggressive and detailed argument for *Wenn ich einmal soll scheiden* in *Songs of Johannes Brahms*, 304n, whereas Braus and Musgrave have followed Kalbeck's original claims; see "Poetic-Musical Rhetoric," 26–29, and "Words for Music," 221. Finally, Hartmut Krones and Clemens Goldberg have each sought to establish a middle ground by refusing to favor any one of Bach's harmonizations as Brahms's probable source; see "Harmonische Symbolik," 424, and "Vergänglichkeit als ästhetische Kategorie und Erlebnis in Liedern von Johannes Brahms," in *Brahms als Liedkomponist*, 190–211.

EXAMPLE 9.1a   Brahms, *Auf dem Kirchhofe*, Op. 105 No. 4, mm. 26–28

EXAMPLE 9.1b   J. S. Bach, *Wenn ich einmal soll scheiden*, mm. 1–2

edition to which Brahms subscribed.[12] At least three features make it a better candidate for his source. First, only this harmonization shares the song's low tessitura and C-major tonality. When sung by a woman, *Auf dem Kirchhofe* presents the familiar melody at pitch. Second, aside from the unaccented passing tone in the pickup to the first measure of the chorale, Brahms's bass line also duplicates that of *Wenn ich einmal soll scheiden* note for note, including the F♯ on the downbeat of the second measure. That F♯ and the secondary dominant it creates are unique among Bach's many harmonizations of this tune. Last, Brahms's inner voices echo a peculiar quality of Bach's: both passages create the aural impression of parallel perfect intervals above the bass from beats three to four of the first measure. *Wenn ich einmal soll scheiden* resorts to unorthodox voice crossing in order to avoid parallel octaves between bass and alto and implied parallel fifths between bass and tenor; the accompaniment to *Auf dem Kirchhofe* interpolates a chordal skip in the tenor line to avoid parallel fifths. The two phrases produce the same characteristic ambiguity between the written page and its sonic realization. Brahms's acute sensitivity to such subtleties is well

---

[12] Brahms's copy of the St. Matthew Passion in the Bach-Gesellschaft edition, ed. Julius Rietz (Leipzig: 1854), survives in the archives of the Gesellschaft der Musikfreunde in Vienna. It bears copious markings in pencil, many of them clearly in Brahms's hand.

documented, most prominently in his sprawling collection of passages containing unorthodox voice leading in the works of other composers.[13]

Whether Kalbeck realized it or not, then, the transformation in attitude at the beginning of line 7 coincided with the emergence of melody, harmony, and voice leading intimately tied to the Passion Chorale as Bach had harmonized it in *Wenn ich einmal soll scheiden*. A borrowing from so venerable a source would naturally have functioned in different ways depending upon the prior experiences specific to a given listener or performer. Brahms's chance remark to Kalbeck—neither his closest confidant nor the most musically talented of his acquaintances—suggests that he expected his borrowing to be perceived as an allusive gesture by broad variety of musically literate audiences extending well beyond his intimate circles. After all, he had hardly bothered to hide it. The passage was preceded by a grand pause and aligned with a shift in mode and key signature, and it carried a performance instruction (*pp legato*) both striking and unprecedented in the rest of the song. Especially when prepared so precipitously, the contrapuntal texture, diatonic harmony, and steadily plodding melody must have evoked a chorale "topic" for even the most minimally knowledgeable of musicians, regardless of the specific identity of the chorale tune at hand. As the calm of the churchyard descended on Liliencron's speaker, so the music of the church echoed from the liturgical past, bestowing its vaguely Protestant unction upon a wide swath of German-speaking listeners.[14] Familiarity with the melody of the Passion Chorale itself would have allowed some such listeners to define more precisely the affective tone of Brahms's closing measures. Finally, those more discerning than Kalbeck might also have noted the specific harmonization alluded to and thereby recalled the stanza of Paul Gerhardt's text for which Bach had devised that harmonization.

Wenn ich einmal soll scheiden,	When once I must depart,
So scheide nicht von mir!	Do not depart from me!
Wenn ich den Tod soll leiden,	When I must suffer death,
So tritt du dann herfür!	Step forward then with me!
Wenn mir am allerbängsten	When my heart is surrounded
Wird um das Herze sein,	With utmost fearfulness,
So reiß mich aus den Ängsten	Remove me then from terror
Kraft deiner Angst und Pein.[15]	Through your own fear and pain.

[13] Brahms's famous collection includes thirty-nine examples from Bach's music alone. In a passage from Cantata 64 (*Sehet, welch eine Liebe hat uns der Vater erzeiget*) labeled "Avoided parallel fifths," the tenor crosses the bass line to avoid parallel fifths in a manner analogous to the inner voices in *Wenn ich einmal soll scheiden* (Mast, "Octaven u. Quinten," 138–39).

[14] Clemens Goldberg's reading departs from this assumption ("Vergänglichkeit als ästhetische Kategorie," 210).

[15] Text here as it appeared in the Bach-Gesellschaft edition of the St. Matthew Passion (218).

Especially in the second quatrain, Gerhardt's poem provided a potentially revelatory complement for Liliencron's: an explicit appeal for divinely inspired courage in the face of death. Precisely when Liliencron's poetic speaker leapt from crisis to calm, Gerhardt's prayer demonstrated how the crisis might be overcome. Moreover, in its original context in the *St. Matthew Passion*, the chorale *Wenn ich einmal soll scheiden* had appeared immediately after the death of Jesus, its uniquely low tessitura a hushed response to the climax of the crucifixion. For listeners so attuned, Bach's music and the scene it brought to mind placed Liliencron's solitary poetic speaker amid the solidarity of a Lutheran congregation at its darkest hour and offered the context of an explicitly Christian theology of redemptive suffering in which to place his anxiety and his altered attitude. Of course, to friends of the agnostic Brahms, such a doctrinal *deus ex machina* might well have seemed too glib for the composer to have summoned without at least a trace of self-consciousness or irony. Kalbeck was one of those friends. Despite his reverence for Brahms, his biography demonstrates a clear awareness of his subject's detached stance on matters of religious dogma.[16] Perhaps Brahms's lighthearted characterization of his allusive gesture as a *Witz* was intended to convey to a like-minded interlocutor some amusement or discomfort with the theological implications that that gesture could so easily evoke.

For along with quasi-liturgical gravity came purely technical display. Listeners less religiously inclined might, instead, have decided that part of what had motived Brahms to include so audible a borrowing from so prominent a source (let alone to talk about it afterwards) was the sheer challenge and craft of reconciling divergent affects, modes, meters, surface rhythms, and melodic material within a single song. Bach's strict four-part texture and steady text declamation produce a striking sense of stylistic disjunction when they first appear in *Auf dem Kirchhofe*, but, as shown in example 9.2, both strictness of texture and pace of declamation relax during the ensuing measures, retroactively smoothing over the most disruptive characteristics of the allusive gesture and thereby presenting the song as a single utterance, albeit one that chronicles a radical shift in the poetic speaker's perspective. At the same time, Brahms set Liliencron's final line to a diatonically transposed repetition of the melodic phrase he had taken from the chorale; in so doing, though, he stripped the tune bare of its original harmonic underpinning and allowed it to recede slowly into the motivic background of the song. Before the final chord dies away, *Auf dem Kirchhofe* has returned entirely to Brahms's own vocal and pianistic idiom: Bach's music has been assimilated but not dismissed outright. In its long-standing connotations

---

[16] Kalbeck's own stance emerges clearly in his discussions of Brahms's settings of scriptural texts, above all the *German Requiem* (*Brahms* 2:237–42).

of cleverness and esprit, the word *Witz* captures fittingly the intellectual pleasure that such a balanced reconciliation might have afforded the composer, a knowledgeable performer, and a musically informed audience alike.

EXAMPLE 9.2   Brahms, *Auf dem Kirchhofe*, Op. 105 No. 4, mm. 26–31

Hearsay or not, Kalbeck's account of Brahms's joke therefore remains highly valuable, both for what it purports to reveal about the compositional process and because it can be made to serve as the basis for imaginative reconstruction of the impact of that process on a wide variety of potential listeners. Yet one should not let Kalbeck's answers obscure the questions his account leaves unasked. There were other broadly circulated chorale melodies associated with texts that could be understood to complement Liliencron's poem, so why did Brahms choose this particular tune? Furthermore, especially as compared with the privately significant musical borrowings explored in parts 1–3, broadly accessible allusive gestures were by no means Brahms's usual practice in song and small-scale chamber music. Why was such easily identifiable preexisting material called for in *Auf dem Kirchhofe* in the first place? As it turns out, these questions are not merely philosophical. There are also concretely music-analytic reasons to ask them. Despite Kalbeck's well-warranted admiration for the affective potential of the borrowing and the skill with which it was woven into its new context, the transition from Bach's music back into Brahms's seems less seamless the more closely one listens to it.

Returning once more to example 9.2, the conclusion of Bach's first phrase would have been a poor fit for Liliencron's poem if left unchanged. The chorale melody came to rest too early, leaving only seven notes for Liliencron's ten syllables; at the same time, Bach's authentic cadence would have broken up Liliencron's final couplet, undermining its status as the culmination of the entire song. Brahms therefore extended the vocal line and replaced Bach's fermata with an elided half cadence that punctuated the middle of the phrase without stalling its momentum. Yet his solution created problems just as pervasive, if not as obvious. The new half cadence generates a powerful cross relation between the vocal line and bass at the arrival of the dominant in the middle of m. 28, adding a piquant dissonance just where the harmony seemed to be relaxing. The ensuing vocal line is awkward in ways unusual for Brahms's mature songs: after outlining a descending diminished triad, it fails to resolve the melodic dissonance in the same register, surging up a minor ninth instead.[17] And there is something unsettling about the mutual relationships among harmonic rhythm, phrase structure, and text declamation in m. 29. The F in the bass seems to occur slightly too early against the voice, creating a jarringly accented tritone that echoes and intensifies the dissonance already outlined by the singer. The result sounds subtly inappropriate on the unstressed final syllable of the word *schlummerten* (slept), particularly given Brahms's own comments on the placement and resolution of dissonances. In a characteristic remark from the previous decade, he had bluntly criticized a song by George Henschel: "No heavy dissonances on unstressed parts of the measure, that is weak! I love dissonances very much, but on stressed parts of the measure, and then to be resolved lightly and smoothly."[18] While the downbeat of m. 29 appears stressed on the page, its accented status is undermined both by the text underlay and by the arrival of dominant harmony two beats prior. In any case, the acrobatic vocal line that follows hardly provides the "light and smooth" resolution that Brahms himself had advocated.

None of these awkward features is likely to stick in the ear for long, especially on the heels of the total stylistic break that initiated the borrowing from the Passion Chorale. But mm. 28–30 are precisely the point at which, according to Kalbeck and most subsequent scholarship, Bach's chorale and its specific textual resonances should begin dissolving graciously into the overall meaning of

---

[17] This is not to say that Brahms had never experimented with melodic disjunction in vocal music. James Webster has pointed out that wide melodic leaps are common to both the C-major close of *Auf dem Kirchhofe* and the C-major close of the Alto Rhapsody, Op. 53, in "The *Alto Rhapsody*: Psychology, 'Intertextuality, and Brahms's Artistic Development," in *Brahms Studies 3*, 34–36. The fundamental issue, then, is why Brahms returned to an idiom so striking and intense in the final measures of *Auf dem Kirchhofe*.

[18] Kalbeck, "Neues über Brahms" 2:2 and *Brahms* 3:85. This passage occurs in every surviving version of Henschel's diary, but the baritone's English translations soften Brahms's tone.

the song and Brahms's compositional skill should be at its most understatedly brilliant. Instead, although the Passion Chorale does eventually recede from the forefront of the listener's consciousness, its departure is not easy, and the music that replaces it is audibly disconcerting. Whether or not one recognizes the borrowed material, Brahms's treatment of its disappearance adds a growing weight and sense of intensity to the last two lines of Liliencron's poem. Such a setting was by no means the only viable interpretive possibility implied by the text. Brahms could have positioned an unequivocal emotional climax at the entrance of Bach's melody and set the closing line as a quiet, unobtrusive postlude. He did not. Instead of completing the poem's motion from anxiety to release, then, Brahms's *Witz* in fact impels *Auf dem Kirchhofe* slowly but irresistibly toward its final word—and toward a place and time far removed from the Scherzligen churchyard.

This was not the first of Brahms's songs to end with the word *genesen*. Thirty years earlier, he had set a very different poem that did the same. "Ein Sonett" (A Sonnet) was a translation by Johann Gottfried Herder of a French courtly lyric attributed to Thibault of Champagne.[19] Brahms's setting originated in 1858 and was published in December 1860 or January 1861 as the fourth of the Eight Songs and Romances, Op. 14. The final cadence of *Auf dem Kirchhofe* borrows musical elements previously unique to *Ein Sonett*. The relationship between the two songs has completely escaped attention. No sudden shift in texture or affect proclaims its presence; no documentary evidence suggests that anyone in Brahms's circle was aware of its significance. Nevertheless, his compositional decision produced specific effects on the surface of *Auf dem Kirchhofe*, effects that span a far larger portion of the song than the borrowing from the Passion Chorale and that admit of at least as close a musical analysis. Approached in tandem with the publicly available allusion to Bach's chorale harmonization, this unacknowledged self-borrowing hints at complex intersections among Brahms's compositions and his conscience.

Brahms first encountered the text of *Ein Sonett* in a multivolume compendium of Herder's works, where it appeared under the title "Ein Sonnet aus dem 13ten Jahrhundert" (A Sonnet from the 13th century).[20] The composer's copy survives in the archives of the Gesellschaft der Musikfreunde in Vienna; the page

[19] The original French poem may not actually have been by Thibault at all. See Friedrich Gennrich, "Glossen zu Johannes Brahms' 'Sonnet' op. 14 Nr. 4: Ach könnt' ich, könnte vergessen sie!," *Zeitschrift für Musikwissenschaft* 10/3 (December 1927), 129–39.

[20] Herder, *Sämtliche Werke: zur Literatur und Kunst* (Stuttgart: Cotta, 1827–30) 7:205.

bearing this poem bears no marks in pencil or ink but was noticeably worn and dog-eared for easy access.

Ach könnt' ich, könnte vergessen Sie!	Ah! If only I could forget her!
Ihr schönes, liebes, liebliches Wesen,	Her beautiful, dear, and darling essence,
Den Blick, die freundliche Lippe, die!	The glance of her eyes and her smiling lips!
Vielleicht ich möchte genesen!	Perhaps I'd like to be healed!
Doch ach! mein Herz, mein Herz	But ah! My heart would never endure it!
kann es nie!	
Und doch ist's Wahnsinn, zu hoffen Sie!	And yet it's madness to hope for her!
Und um Sie schweben	And to hover around her
Gibt Mut und Leben,	Brings life, and the courage
Zu weichen nie! —	Never to yield! —
Und denn, wie kann ich vergessen Sie,	And then, how can I forget her,
Ihr schönes, liebes, liebliches Wesen,	Her beautiful, dear, and darling essence,
Den Blick, die freundliche Lippe, die!	The glance of her eyes and her smiling lips!
Viel lieber nimmer genesen!	Much better never to be healed!

The poem plays upon courtly conceits that were particularly amenable to appropriation in late eighteenth- and early nineteenth-century German lyric. The lover begins in the subjunctive, pretending hesitantly that he longs to forget his beloved since she is unattainable. By the fifth line he begins to doubt his resolve or, rather, to admit his doubt. After vacillating between the ecstasy and the agony of his courtly service, he ultimately espouses an unambiguous stance in the final quatrain: it is better to remain in love with no hope of consummation than to abandon the ideal vision of his beloved. At the same time, however, orthography introduced a complication, at least in the edition with which Brahms was familiar. Whereas the original French referred to the beloved unequivocally in the third person, Herder's translation consistently capitalized the pronoun *Sie* and the possessive determiner *Ihr*. Thus altered, these words can be interpreted in either the third person or the formal second person, making the poem a delicate amalgam of solitary musing and direct address to a woman who might actually be swayed by overwrought entreaty. Beginning with the first edition, all published editions of Brahms's setting resolved the ambiguity in favor of the third person by removing the capitalization, but the composer's own autograph retained Herder's original orthography. With the engraver's models lost, one cannot discern whether Brahms himself or the editors at Rieter-Biedermann were responsible for the change. In either case, the composer first encountered and copied the poem in a multivalent version with no single equivalent in English.

In Herder's translation, "Ein Sonett" diverges radically from "Auf dem Kirchhofe" in both tone and content, yet the two poems share sonic and structural characteristics that could easily have spurred Brahms's memory of his earlier song during the process of setting Liliencron's text. Not only are their final words identical and somewhat unusual; in each poem, the word *genesen* also completes and encapsulates a transformation in the poetic speaker's attitude. The word first appears in line 4 of Herder's translation as an image of the peace the speaker would find if he could only tear himself away from his amorous attachment. It then returns in the last line to confirm his newly declared fidelity through deliberate contrast with its first appearance. *Ich möchte genesen* ("I'd like to be healed") becomes *nimmer genesen* ("never to be healed"), just as *gewesen* becomes *genesen* in the second stanza of "Auf dem Kirchhofe." Both poems intensify the contrast by beginning the two opposing lines with the same syllable: *viel* for Herder, *auf* for Liliencron. At the same time, Herder's rhyme scheme pairs *genesen* with *Wesen* in both his first and last quatrain. Although few German words end with the syllables "*esen*," the similarity between Herder's *Wesen* and Liliencron's *gewesen* still increases the likelihood that "Auf dem Kirchhofe" could recall "Ein Sonett" when read aloud or recited silently to oneself, as was Brahms's wont when setting texts to music.

Whatever textual congruencies first reminded Brahms of his earlier song, the music of *Ein Sonett* seems to have worked its way into the composition of *Auf dem Kirchhofe*. Its effects were subtle but substantial, especially at the word *genesen*, where the texts of the two poems intersect most closely. As it turns out, finding a suitable setting for this word had already cost Brahms some effort the first time he attempted it, in 1858. The surviving autograph of *Ein Sonett* is a fairly clean copy in ink with occasional corrections in both ink and pencil.[21] Brahms initially notated the final vocal cadence as it appears in example 9.3a, where a simple scalar descent for the singer finds predominantly stepwise support from the inner voices during the piano accompaniment's authentic cadence. He then revised the passage and complicated both vocal line and accompaniment with alternative suggestions in pencil, all of which appeared in the published song two years later. Example 9.3b presents the result. The underlying harmonic motion remained the same, but the voice now carved out a sharper melodic profile, descending by leap from scale degree 5 to 7 in preparation for a final ascent to the tonic. The upper voice of the accompaniment was adjusted accordingly, presumably so as to avoid a doubled resolution of the leading tone.

As shown in example 9.3c, nearly every voice-leading strand that Brahms created in his revisions to *Ein Sonett* would find a direct analogue in the closing vocal cadence of *Auf dem Kirchhofe*. Bass line and vocal line offer the most

---

[21] Long in private ownerwhip, the autograph now resides at the Brahms-Institut of the Musikhochschule at Lübeck.

EXAMPLE 9.3a   Brahms, *Ein Sonett*, Op. 14 No. 4, original version, mm. 53–56. From the autograph (Brahms-Institut an der Musikhochschule Lübeck).

EXAMPLE 9.3b   Brahms, *Ein Sonett*, Op. 14 No. 4, published version, mm. 53–56

EXAMPLE 9.3c   Brahms, *Auf dem Kirchhofe*, Op. 105 No. 4, mm. 31–33. Annotated.

obvious resemblances but also the easiest to dismiss as coincidences. A perfect authentic cadence accompanies the singer's conclusion in the vast majority of Brahms's songs, and the lilting vocal line he eventually crafted to embody that cadence would appear frequently in his later output as well. Of the more than two hundred solo songs he published as *Lieder* (as opposed to folk-song settings), over 10 percent employ scale degrees 5–7–1 as their final three vocal pitches. The only three-note scale-degree pattern that occurs more frequently as a closing vocal cadence is the one he initially adopted and then rejected in 1858: 3–2–1. The melodic and harmonic characteristics shared by the two published settings of the word *genesen*, then, are actually quite common. Likewise, the upper voices of the piano accompaniment at first appear unremarkable, at least in the context of Brahms's earlier compositions. The lightly polyphonic texture created in *Ein Sonett* is so strong a stylistic tendency in works of a certain tone that one might even consider that texture to be part of a loosely defined topic to which he referred occasionally in the late 1850s and early 1860s. Certainly the interaction between vocal melody and accompanimental countermelody in *Ein Sonett* recalls other nearly contemporaneous triple- or compound-meter works in the major mode. Prominent examples include the four-part *Ruf zur Maria*, Op. 22 No. 5; the *Ave Maria* for women's voices, Op. 12; the slow movement of the first piano concerto, Op. 15; and the fourth movement of the *German Requiem*, "Wie lieblich sind deine Wohnungen."[22] Largely neglected by the 1880s, one might easily imagine that such a topic could have provided an appealing correlate for the end of Liliencron's poem, a vague source of affective contrast toward which Brahms could have groped unconsciously, with no need for specific precedents from among his own works.

Along with its broader stylistic affiliations, however, the countermelody in the right hand of the piano accompaniment presented a specific melodic profile in the published version of *Ein Sonett*, and the scale-degree pattern traced by its upper voice turned out to be remarkably rare in Brahms's vocal output. The scale-degree series 3–2–1–7–2–1 occasionally occurred in the midst of a phrase, but for three decades Brahms never employed it again at a cadence point, either in an inner voice or in the vocal melody. The closest cadential figure in a melody line was the melisma at the end of *Ich schell mein Horn ins Jammertal*, Op. 43 No. 3 (see ex. 9.4a). Yet this purposefully archaic song sounded nothing like *Ein Sonett*, since the accompaniment doubled the voice, and each note of the melody received individual support from a root-position triad. Because of the submediant-centered harmonies that accompanied them, the first five notes lost the clarity of their scale-degree identity, and the leading tone functioned as a neighboring elaboration to the tonics that directly surrounded it; it was resolved immediately, both harmonically and melodically, rather than departed by leap over the same harmony. A better aural and stylistic match for *Ein Sonett* occurred in *Erinnerung*, Op. 63 No. 2 (ex. 9.4b). Here the characteristic interaction between inner voices and vocal line—gentle po-

---

[22] *Ein Sonett's* similarity to the fifth of the Op. 22 *Marienlieder* is particularly striking. The two works were composed within eight months of each other; see McCorkle, *Werkverzeichnis*, 76, and Sophie Drinker, *Brahms and his Women's Choruses* (Merion, PA: author, under the auspices of Musurgia Publishers, A. G. Hess, 1952), 21 and 25–32. Although the text of *Ein Sonett* treats a distinctly secular subject, the courtly manner of its supplication finds distinct resonances in the text of *Ruf zur Maria*, and the two works present closely related approaches to rhythm and phrase structure.

lyphony entwining scale degrees 2 and 7 around the final tonic—reappeared, along with the same underlying harmonic pattern and triple meter. But the vocal line lacked the suspended scale degree 5 and the ensuing downward leap of *Ein Sonett*, and the inner voices presented none of the smooth, predominantly stepwise motion featured in the earlier song. Although the two cadential gestures were almost identical in tone and texture, nearly every specific melodic feature of *Ein Sonett* failed to appear in either the upper or the inner voices of *Erinnerung*.

EXAMPLE 9.4a   Brahms, *Ich schell mein Horn ins Jammertal*, Op. 43 No. 3, mm. 42–47

EXAMPLE 9.4b   Brahms, *Erinnerung*, Op. 63 No. 2, mm. 93–95

In fact, out of Brahms's entire output of songs for voice and piano, only *Auf dem Kirchhofe* employs a cadence that preserves both the texture and the particular countermelody familiar from *Ein Sonett*. Taking into account the transpositional distance between the two songs, the highest voice in the pianist's right hand is identical in each. In both songs that voice is doubled below at the sixth. Just as for every other borrowing investigated in this study, the result is not a literal quotation. Significant disparities remain between the two passages, but these disparities can themselves be understood as adjustments undertaken in order to accommodate old material in a new context. For instance, in the penultimate measure *Auf dem Kirchhofe* postpones the arrival of the chord's seventh in the right hand's lower voice until the final beat, perhaps because there is no hemiola in the vocal line against which the accompanimental downbeat demands added harmonic emphasis. Indeed, the song actually reproduces the right hand's countermelody in a completely different rhythmic context than *Ein Sonett*. Not only has the meter itself shifted from triple to duple, but the relationship between the pace of the right hand and the pulse of the song has also changed so that the accompanimental scale-degree pattern moves twice as fast with respect to the beat. Still, across thirty years, melody, bass, and counter-melody all survive intact.

An analogous situation obtains for the vocal line as well. The ascending leap from scale degree 3 to 5 that had preceded the final cadential descent in *Ein Sonett* vanishes from the corresponding point in *Auf dem Kirchhofe*. One reason for its absence might be the acceleration of the inner voices relative to the tactus. To remain in line with the countermelody in *Auf dem Kirchhofe*, a vocal line borrowed literally from *Ein Sonett* would have to strike scale degree 5 at what is now the middle of an off-beat. Brahms instead chose to omit scale degree 3 altogether from the singer's version of the word *genesen*, which enabled his new vocal melody to reach scale degree 5 on the downbeat and thereby stretched the poem's last stressed syllable into the song's longest note. Omitting the ascent from scale degree 3 also freed the singer to present a simpler, more unanimously descending cadential formula: 8–5–7–1. Brahms had used this formula once during the intervening years (at the conclusion of *Schwermut*, Op. 58 No. 5), but in *Auf dem Kirchhofe* it drew the song to an especially satisfying conclusion. As illustrated in example 9.5, the new pattern literally reversed, and thereby kinesthetically resolved, the singer's unsettling ascent at the end of the allusion to the Passion Chorale. At the same time, the singer's omission of the ascent from scale degree 3 to 5 may account for the insertion of precisely that ascent into the left hand of the piano accompaniment, highlighted with a circle in example 9.3c.

EXAMPLE 9.5   Brahms, *Auf dem Kirchhofe*, Op. 105 No. 4, mm. 28–29 and 31–33. Vocal part.

Beyond the vocal cadences themselves, additional similarities emerge in the remainder of the songs that surround them. As shown in examples 9.6a and b, the two piano postludes exhibit obvious parallels. Beneath a richer harmonic palette, the close of *Auf dem Kirchhofe* blends the plagal benediction and upper tonic pedal tone of its predecessor's last four measures with an expansive farewell to the cascading inner voices so typical of the earlier song throughout. More intensification than straightforward duplication, the later postlude still

EXAMPLE 9.6a Brahms, *Ein Sonett*, Op. 14 No. 4, mm. 56–59

EXAMPLE 9.6b Brahms, *Auf dem Kirchhofe*, Op. 105 No. 4, mm. 33–36

recalls its predecessor strongly when heard directly after the borrowed vocal cadence. More important, hypothesizing that Brahms held *Ein Sonett* deliberately in mind while setting Liliencron's poem also provides a plausible explanation for the otherwise baffling disruptions that emerge after his allusion to the Passion Chorale but before the final vocal cadence proper. As shown in examples 9.7a and b, the diminished triad in the vocal line of *Auf dem Kirchhofe* sounds strange on the heels of Bach's stepwise melody but perfectly at home in *Ein Sonett*, where it concludes the first and third lines of the opening and closing quatrains. The last of these four appearances directly precedes the high a♭" that initiates *Ein Sonett*'s climactic final phrase, forcing the singer into the unexpected leap of an ascending minor ninth—precisely the same interval spanned, between the same scale degrees, by *Auf dem Kirchhofe*'s acrobatic ascent in mm. 29–30. The struck tritone between singer and bass line that marks the downbeat of m. 29 in *Auf dem Kirchhofe* is just as metrically prominent on the downbeat of m. 51 in *Ein Sonett*, but the emphasized dissonance sounds far more appropriate in the earlier song because it accompanies the accented syllable *die* and its emphatic exclamation point.[23]

Finally, material characteristic of *Ein Sonett* not only supersedes the allusion to the Passion Chorale but also resounds across the formal articulation of *Auf dem Kirchhofe* as a whole. As indicated in example 9.8, Brahms set the end of the first poetic stanza to an altered version of the borrowed vocal cadence, transposed to

---

[23]Though unequivocal in Brahms's autograph, this exclamation point somehow became a question mark in the published version of the song.

EXAMPLE 9.7a   Brahms, *Auf dem Kirchhofe*, Op. 105 No. 4, mm. 27–30. Vocal part. Annotated.

EXAMPLE 9.7b   Brahms, *Ein Sonett*, Op. 14 No. 4, mm. 48–52. Vocal part. Annotated.

the dominant minor but with inner voices and underlying harmonic progression fully intact (compare to ex. 9.2). Here, in fact, the melodic ascent from scale degree 3 to 5 returns to its original register in the vocal line. Yet within their new context in the setting of Liliencron's poem, the two passages demand interpretation not as mere motivic corollaries but as flashpoints of contrast in a modified strophic song. The first is the anxious culmination of an anxious strophe: chromatic, crammed full of syllables, metrically ambiguous when heard without reference to the printed page, and immediately undermined by a crashing dominant-ninth chord. The second is its opposite according to every affectively relevant music-analytic criterion: overwhelmingly diatonic, long-breathed and self-assured, and ultimately grounded in the tonic major. In retrospect, the minor-mode prefiguration at the end of the first stanza establishes the backdrop against which the word *genesen* ultimately reveals its revisionary power. The juxtaposition between the two moments weaves the final vocal cadence of *Ein Sonett* all the more inextricably and unobtrusively into *Auf dem Kirchhofe*. Not only does no sudden stylistic break or pregnant caesura draw attention to the presence of borrowed material, but Brahms's new song actually proposes its own internal source from which its final vocal cadence seems to spring.

EXAMPLE 9.8   Brahms, *Auf dem Kirchhofe*, Op. 105 No. 4, mm. 12–14

Even for an informed audience, then, the effects of *Ein Sonett* in *Auf dem Kirchhofe* are categorically distinct from those of the Passion Chorale. On the one hand, once uncovered, the preponderance of evidence in favor of an intentional relationship between the two songs is compelling. The specificity with which a unique polyphonic complex returns; the detailed manner in which that complex is integrated with the allusion to the Passion Chorale; and the myriad and disparate compositional decisions that can be plausibly explained as the result of the accommodation of preexisting material within a new context: all the signs suggest that Brahms was fully aware of his borrowing in the final measures of *Auf dem Kirchhofe*. On the other hand, one cannot easily describe that borrowing as an allusive gesture, at least not in the sense explored in parts 1–3 of this book. To the contrary, in the moment of performance or the midst of listening, one cannot help but perceive the song's close as a transformation of the end of its first strophe, regardless of the order in which the passages were actually composed and whatever one's speculations about the source of the melodies and harmonies contained therein. The choice to interpolate music from *Ein Sonett* into *Auf dem Kirchhofe* was most likely not designed to be noticed at all, at least by the same sorts of audiences as might be expected to perceive the echoes of the Passion Chorale. Indeed, generations of singers and pianists have wandered deep into Brahms's musical past without ever realizing it.

What could have motivated a borrowing so purposeful and yet so private? The textual resonances that called the earlier song to mind during Brahms's engagement with Liliencron's poem were a necessary precondition for the composer's decisions, but they were not in themselves sufficient reasons for the musical result. Merely realizing that two texts shared a word did not obligate Brahms to borrow from his setting of the first when writing music for the second. After all, he had already set the word *genesen* to music during the intervening years, in the song *Todessehnen*, Op. 86 No. 6, without a trace of compositional modeling. The question, then, is not how *Ein Sonett* came to mind, but why it stayed in mind. The publically accessible allusion to the Passion Chorale provides a telling point of comparison. Whereas the poem with which Bach's harmonization was associated remained congruent with the affect and trajectory of Liliencron's poem, such was not the case for Thibault's lyric in Herder's translation. Structural analogies and shared vocabulary notwithstanding, the text to *Ein Sonett* actually projected an opposing transformation in the poetic speaker's attitude. Instead of achieving a quiet recovery from personal crisis, Herder's poem charted the willful decision to extend a painful infatuation. Brahms's borrowed vocal cadence might reflect textual similarities, but it also brought the two poems into antagonistic proximity. *Genesen* or *nimmer genesen*—words of redemption undercut by the melodies of suffering sweetly prolonged, or long-suffering music finally healed by association with a new text? The notes alone can only introduce the cognitive dissonance, not resolve it.

Given the depth and specificity of Brahms's renewed engagement with *Ein Sonett*, the textual mismatch exposed by his borrowing may have proven difficult for him to ignore. Indeed, once Liliencron's treatment of the word *genesen* had called Herder's to mind, the differences between the two poems could have become as important to Brahms's project as their similarities. Rather than emerging as the accidental byproduct of compositional decisions, the affective ambivalence produced by the juxtaposition of the texts might, in itself, have come to motivate those decisions in the first place. Surviving documents preserve brief but provocative glimpses of the interpersonal contexts within which the two songs were composed and the connotations that *Ein Sonett* had acquired in Brahms's circles during the intervening decades. To a composer attuned to these resonances, the peculiar conflict in tone embodied in the vocal cadence of *Auf dem Kirchhofe* could easily have taken on personal as well as musical urgency. More surprisingly, the same complex of impulses also provides a plausible explanation for Brahms's selection of the Passion Chorale as the source for a publically accessible allusive gesture.

The surviving autograph of *Ein Sonett* bears an abbreviated and dated signature immediately following the final barline: "Joh⁵ Brahms Sept. 58." The date places the song squarely at the center of Brahms's relationship with the Göttingen soprano Agathe von Siebold, which began in autumn 1858 and culminated in a secret engagement before ending precipitously early in 1859. This brief but intense infatuation is generally understood to have influenced Brahms's work on numerous compositional projects dating from the months in question, including the unpublished *Brautgesang* discussed in the introduction. *Ein Sonett* belonged to a special subset of those projects: it was one of six songs that Brahms completed while staying in Göttingen himself as a guest of the composer and teacher Julius Otto Grimm and his wife Phillipine in September 1858.[24] It was the Grimms who first introduced Brahms to Agathe and encouraged their relationship. During his visit Brahms had frequent contact with Agathe's singing, and both documentary and musical evidence indicates that he designed all six new songs especially for her voice. For one thing, Julius Otto described Agathe's informal performances of the songs in a letter to Joseph

---

[24] In addition to *Ein Sonett*, Brahms also completed *Vor dem Fenster* and *Ständchen*, Op. 14 Nos. 1 and 7; *Der Kuß* and *An eine Aeolsharfe*, Op. 19 Nos. 1 and 5; and *Die Liebende schreibt*, Op. 47 No. 5, in September 1858. For the dating of songs from Opp. 14 and 19, see Bozarth, "Brahms's Lieder Inventory," 99–100, and McCorkle, *Werkverzeichnis*, 44 and 67; for the dating of Op. 47 No. 5, see Avins, *Life and Letters*, 173.

Joachim dated September 23.[25] Just as important, when sung by a woman, all six of the songs require clarity and flexibility in high registers that Brahms had hitherto tended to reserve for powerful climaxes rather than sustained or quiet singing. Moreover, as a group they lie higher in the voice than any of his previous song sets, even the two sets of six songs "for Soprano or Tenor" which he had published five years prior as Op. 3 and Op. 6.

Precise comparison of the challenges created by vocal tessitura across distinct repertories is notoriously difficult. For the six songs Brahms composed in Göttingen, three related criteria are especially revealing: overall vocal range, average vocal pitch (weighted by duration and calculated in equal temperament), and time spent above fixed reference points. First, Brahms's new songs display a higher overall register than that of Opp. 3 and 6: although their lowest pitches are virtually identical, the vocal lines extend on average a full half-step higher. All six new songs reach at least g" and four reach at least a♭", compared to only eight and four of the twelve earlier songs, respectively. Second, the average pitch of their vocal lines is well above c", nearly a semitone higher than the average pitch of the songs in songs in Opp. 3 and 6. A half-step difference may seem small, but it significantly exceeds the gaps that separate Opp. 3 and 6 from each another and from the six songs of Op. 7. Even song sets that Brahms would later publish explicitly for "low voice" average less than four half steps lower than Opp. 3 and 6; if the difference between the average pitches of "high" and "low" songs amounted to less than a major third, the shift of a semitone surely represented an appreciable distinction as well.[26] Finally, for Brahms's new songs, the proportional duration spent in the upper tessitura is consistently larger than for any previous song set. The new songs exceed their average pitches 54 percent of the time (as opposed to 49 percent for the songs of Opp. 3 and 6) and reach or exceed f" and g" 13 percent and 4.2 percent of the time (compared to 9 percent and 1.6 percent).

In combination, these three factors argue strongly on behalf of a subtle but significant shift in Brahms's approach to vocal composition in the songs he composed in September 1858. His contact with Agathe seems the likeliest explanation for that shift. Certainly the vocal characteristics accentuated by his new songs match the capabilities of Agathe's soprano voice, insofar as echoes of her voice remain in the recollections of her family and can be reconstructed through examination of other song repertoire that she sang at the time. Her favorite song during her relationship with Brahms seems to have been Schubert's

---

[25] Küntzel, *Brahms in Göttingen. Mit Erinnrungen von Agathe Schütte, geb. von Siebold* (Göttingen: herodot, 1985), 54–56 and Avins, *Life and Letters*, 172–73; for corroboration and further description of these impromptu performances, see Michelmann, *Agathe von Siebold*, 158.

[26] See the six *Lieder für eine tiefere Stimme*, Op. 86, whose average vocal pitch approaches g♯'.

Rastlose Liebe, D. 138.[27] When sung at its original pitch, *Rastlose Liebe* demands precisely the high tessitura that Brahms employed in September 1858; indeed, its average vocal pitch exceeds d♯", and the singer spends more than 15 percent of the song at or above g". Even if Agathe transposed it down slightly, her interest in *Rastlose Liebe* indicates how appropriate Brahms's new songs would have been for her voice. *Ein Sonett* was no exception. Its vocal line was thoroughly typical of the songs that Brahms completed in Göttingen. Its highest notated pitch is a♭", and it spends nearly 6 percent of its duration at or above g", a proportion that exceeds any song from Opp. 3 or 6. Given the song's vocal characteristics and the timing and circumstances of its composition, one may well imagine that, even three decades later, its final cadence could still bring Agathe's voice to Brahms's ear.

No direct correspondence between singer and composer has ever been rediscovered if, indeed, any existed in the first place. During their romantic attachment and brief engagement they exchanged greetings and pleasantries in the margins of Brahms's epistolary exchanges with the Grimms, but none of the surviving correspondence refers to *Ein Sonett*. The only evidence that the song may have been special to Agathe is purely circumstantial: she once owned the surviving autograph. Although this was the only work completed during her connection with Brahms for which she demonstrably retained a manuscript in the composer's hand, it is highly probable that she once owned other autographs as well.[28] In any case, the circumstances under which Brahms gave her the autograph are entirely unknown, and nothing suggests that this song was any more or less meaningful to the pair than the other songs he composed in the autumn and winter of 1858. While its amorous text might have found reverberations amid the emotionally charged circumstances in which the setting was composed and first performed, the same was true of the texts of most of Brahms's new songs or, for that matter, the texts of many of the *Lieder* he had already published in the early 1850s or would soon compose in the months to come.[29] Evaluated against the few surviving documents that bear witness to the composer's time in Göttingen, then, any unique connections between Herder's translation and Brahms's infatuation with Agathe are purely speculative.

---

[27] Michelmann, *Agathe von Siebold*, 161.

[28] McCorkle, *Werkverzeichnis*, 45–46. In addition to the autograph of *Ein Sonett*, Agathe also owned a copy of *Das Lied vom Herrn von Falkenstein*, Op. 43 No. 4, which was composed prior to her relationship with Brahms (ibid., 155 and 157, and Bozarth, "Manuscript Collections," 261). In addition, Agathe's descendents recall that she had passed along multiple autographs to her family, all of which seem to have disappeared immediately following the Second World War (Avins, *Life and Letters*, 748).

[29] Hence, perhaps, the tendency of biographers to use fragments of the texts Brahms set in autumn and winter 1858 as chapter titles in their books regarding the composer's connection to Agathe (Küntzel, *Brahms in Göttingen* and *Johannes Brahms und Agathe von Siebold*, and Michelmann, *Agathe von Siebold*).

On the other hand, previous chapters have demonstrated on several occasions that, in the memory of any given musician, a change in circumstances could refocus or even supersede the extramusical connotations that a work had initially carried at the time of its completion. In the case of *Ein Sonett*, once Brahms's romantic relationship with Agathe had ended irrevocably in 1859, Herder's translation became peculiarly amenable to retrospective reinterpretation in light of the breakup. The texts of virtually every other song composed in Göttingen featured continuous and unequivocal amorous attachment; physical distance might intercede between poetic speaker and beloved, but their love remained pure and true. Herder's text stood alone in the explicit ambivalence of its attitude toward romantic entanglement.[30] Notwithstanding the poetic speaker's eventual resignation to the role of a faithful and forever rebuffed courtly lover, his initial plea for forgetfulness was strangely appropriate to the awkward situation in which Brahms and Agathe found themselves once their relationship had collapsed. At the same time, Herder's ambiguous capitalization facilitated such reinterpretation by allowing the intimacy of second-person address to dissolve smoothly into the detachment of third-person narration. Put simply, Herder's poem is the one text Brahms had set during his affair in which the altered vision of hindsight could conceivably discern traces of the coming break.

Brahms's retrospective attitude toward that break is well documented. As summarized in the introduction, the composer's own letters, the recollections of his friends, and the motivic construction of at least three of his works from the ensuing years all demonstrate that he was occasionally preoccupied with painful memories of the affair in Göttingen. Brahms himself never connected the music or text of *Ein Sonett* with these bouts of regretful rumination in any document that survives; in fact, the song is never mentioned in his extant letters. Nevertheless, the correspondence of his friends suggests that the memory of its tones may indeed have been capable of stimulating continued reevaluation of his failed romantic attachment to Agathe. In April 1862, toward the end of his initial flurry of professional collaborations with Brahms, Julius Stockhausen presented the public premiere of *Ein Sonett* with the composer at the piano during a concert of the Hamburg Philharmonic. At the time, Julius was deeply infatuated with a married woman whose identity is now unknown. Within a few months, however, he confided to his diary that love had turned

---

[30]Aside from *Ein Sonett*, the one possible exception was *Trost in Tränen*, Op. 48 No. 5, which Brahms completed sometime in the autumn of 1858 (McCorkle, *Werkverzeichnis*, 190). But Goethe's poem is far less straightforward than Herder's translation—the cause of the speaker's melancholy is left tantalizingly unspecified and cannot be traced directly to amorous issues in the first place.

to disillusionment.[31] On November 27, 1862, he wrote to Brahms in Vienna enclosing a photograph of the woman in question, along with a bitterly misogynistic comment: "She has eyes! Black as coals and so faithful (seemingly) for they are not, and I realize now, *a little too late*, that we are completely different fellows from that *weak* sex!" On the photograph itself, he inscribed a slightly misremembered version of the first line of Herder's translation: "Ach könnt' ich, könnt' ich vergessen Sie! Hamburg 1862."[32]

Julius's orthography was consistent with his diary, where he had capitalized the third-person pronoun *Sie* with reference to his love interest up until the moment of his disillusionment, but it also hints that he may have known Herder's translation himself independent of Brahms's setting. Whatever the case, the quotation exposed the darker undertones of the song the two musicians had just premiered by highlighting the ultimate futility of courtly love and its potentially devastating effects on the lover. Read in the context of his letter to Brahms, the baritone's inscription implicitly questioned the wisdom of the poem's final declaration of fidelity, while still acknowledging that the pain of romantic attachment did not heal easily. For Julius, at least, the text of *Ein Sonett* could be made to address the regrets of remembered amorous failure as well as the poignant pleasures of present love. Brahms may not have been in the mood to sympathize with his friend's lament when the photograph arrived, since he had only recently been informed of Stockhausen's selection for the conductorship of the Hamburg Philharmonic, the position he had hoped to acquire himself. Nevertheless, the singer's letter demonstrated the interpretive malleability of Herder's translation, its capacity for retrospective association with failed romance. Given that the first performer and initial recipient of Brahms's setting was a former love interest whose relationship with the composer had ended awkwardly, it seems reasonable to assume that Brahms himself might have perceived a similar association between his own attitude and that of the poetic speaker's initial utterance, especially once encouraged by Julius's example.

A cluster of possible connotations is emerging for *Ein Sonett*. Once recalled during the setting of Liliencron's text, the older song may have brought with it the potential to conjure up memories not only of Agathe von Siebold's voice and her relationship with Brahms, but also of the regret later associated with that episode. The question, then, is whether such memories might have played some role in the composition of *Auf dem Kirchhofe*. Aside from Kalbeck's account of the

---

[31] For details of the premiere, see Hofmann, *Brahms als Pianist und Dirigent*, 71–72. Julius seems to have begun keeping a diary only in October 1862 and never referred to the object of his affection by name. Significant portions of the diary are reprinted in Julia Wirth's biography of her father (*Julius Stockhausen*, 224–34). Wirth hinted that the woman's identity was known to Julius's family and indicated that the infatuation dated back to the 1850s.

[32] Brahms/Stockhausen, *Briefwechsel*, 32 and 33n; emphases original. Brahms had apparently asked for the photograph in a letter from July 22 (no longer extant).

churchyard in Scherzligen, no documentary evidence survives regarding Brahms's engagement with Liliencron's text. Since he lived within easy access of Scherzligen during the summers of 1886, 1887, and 1888, even the year of the song's composition remains uncertain, although circumstantial evidence points to 1887 as the likeliest year. In August 1886, Brahms sent to Theodor Billroth manuscripts of no fewer than nine unpublished works, the fruits of an entire summer's compositional activity. In a rare display of diligent record-keeping, he also recorded every one of those works in his pocket calendar for the month of August. Since his offering to Billroth comprised every work he is known to have composed during the summer of 1886, including four solo songs, one would imagine Brahms sending *Auf dem Kirchhofe* along if it were already complete at the time.[33] This leaves only a few remaining weeks in which the song could have been composed in 1886 before he returned to Vienna on October 6. Furthermore, assuming that Brahms's setting of Liliencron's poem truly coincided with a visit to Scherzligen, he would have had very little time for such a visit in 1888. He arrived in Thun, following his sixth Italian vacation with Joseph Viktor Widmann, on May 29. A mere two days later he wrote to Fritz Simrock offering both old and new solo songs for publication in what would become Opp. 105, 106, and 107; there is no reason to think that *Auf dem Kirchhofe* was not among these songs. By mid-July 1888, when he belatedly decided to add *Klage* to the songs of Op. 105, *Auf dem Kirchhofe* had already long been assumed to be part of that opus.[34]

Therefore, if one follows Kalbeck's account of the song's connection to Scherzligen, it seems most likely that Brahms composed *Auf dem Kirchhofe*

[33] Brahms's pocket calendar for August 1886 lists four songs (*An die Stolze*, Op. 107 No. 1, and *Wie Melodien zieht es mir*, *Immer leiser wird mein Schlummer*, and *Verrat*, Op. 105 Nos. 1, 2, and 5), a part-song for mixed vocal quartet (*Im Herbst*, Op. 104 No. 5), and four chamber works (the second cello sonata, Op. 99; two violin sonatas, Opp. 100 and 108; and the third piano trio, Op. 101). See Bozarth, "Brahms's Lieder Inventory," 105; the calendar itself confirms Bozarth's findings. Exactly which vocal music Brahms forwarded to Billroth bears the attention of specialists because, in editing and annotating his father-in-law's correspondence with Brahms, Otto Gottlieb-Billroth mistook the identity of some of the songs that Theodor received. Because the letters referred to most of the vocal works only by poet or key, and because Gottlieb-Billroth did not have access to Brahms's pocket calendars, he erroneously placed *Komm bald*, Op. 97 No. 5, and *Das Mädchen spricht*, Op. 107 No. 3, among them (Billroth/Brahms, *Briefwechsel*, 396–401). In turn, McCorkle's thematic catalogue based its dating of *Das Mädchen spricht* solely on Gottlieb-Billroth's spurious reasoning (McCorkle, *Werkverzeichnis*, 433).
[34] Brahms, *Briefe an Simrock* 3:184 and 192. One can tell that *Auf dem Kirchhofe* was already included in Op. 105 because, as Brahms explained to Simrock, the addition of *Klage* forced *Verrat* to the fifth and final position in the opus; *Verrat* would have been fourth if *Auf dem Kirchhofe* did not yet exist. Moreover, in the same letter Brahms asked Simrock whether he "still" had the English translation of Liliencron's poem. This strongly implies that the song had been familiar to both of them for a significant period of time already—else why would Simrock have already lost or discarded his translation of its text? In the absence of further evidence, then, it seems most likely that Brahms had already sent Simrock the song on May 31, which in turn implies that it was composed during the previous summer at the latest. Strangely, McCorkle refers to Brahms's mid-July letter as evidence in favor of a late date of composition for *Auf dem Kirchhof* as well as *Klage* (*Werkverzeichnis*, 426).

during the summer of 1887. In any case, however, the period encompassing all three of his summers in Thun was marked by certain trends against which the potential connotations of *Ein Sonett* might have stood out with special clarity. The most obvious of these trends was a shift away from flirtation in his relationship with the contralto Hermine Spies. Trained by Julius Stockhausen as a singer of *Lieder* and oratorio, and endowed with charming appearance and a winning style of repartee, Spies had met Brahms in 1883 when he was fifty and she just twenty-six. They had collaborated in concert performances of Brahms's music several times over the next eighteen months and engaged in increasingly flirtatious conversations and correspondence. In June 1885 Brahms had sent her an autograph of an unpublished song, *Komm bald*, Op. 97 No. 5, referring to it as a joint product of "two of your admirers" (the text, a plea for a far-off friend or lover's return, was by the poet Klaus Groth, who was equally smitten by Hermine's singing).[35] In autumn 1886 he had arranged for an idyllic private performance of two more unpublished songs for low voice, *Wie Melodien zieht es mir* and *Immer leiser wird mein Schlummer*, Op. 105 Nos. 1 and 2, and had assumed responsibility for arranging Hermine's debut in Vienna in November. But just as singer and composer had appeared to some of their friends to be moving toward romantic involvement, Brahms began to withdraw. He expressed pointed reservations about her singing to mutual acquaintances, and he deliberately ceased giving her privileged prepublication access to his songs, as Hermine herself noted wryly while trying to dampen the gossip surrounding their relationship.[36]

By December 1886, Hermine was under no illusions regarding Brahms's ultimate intentions, if indeed she had ever been. As she explained in a letter to Maria Fellinger: "Yes, he likes me just fine, because I sing his songs no worse than others and because I am a creature equipped with five healthy senses....But that he is mine? I must deny it."[37] Although she and Brahms collaborated again

---

[35] Hermine died in 1893 at age thirty-six. The following year her sister, Minna Spies, published a tribute, including excerpts from the singer's diary. After Brahms's death, Minna released an expanded version, which now included correspondence from Hermine, Brahms, Klaus Groth, and Maria Fellinger; see Spies, *Hermine Spies: ein Gedenkbuch für ihre Freunde*, 3rd ed. (Leipzig: G. J. Göschen, 1905). As transmitted in Minna's book, Hermine's diary recorded one of her early conversations with the composer, from September 1883 (ibid., 95). The earliest surviving letter from Brahms to Hermine was sent on December 8, 1884; the letter is undated but contains sufficient details of Brahms's current travel itinerary to enable a reliable estimate of its date. Already the composer was roguishly referring to her directly as a "pretty, merry Rheinland girl" (ibid., 308–9). Finally, the letter concerning *Komm bald* appears on ibid., 297.

[36] Ibid., 275–76. Prompted by a critical note from Elisabeth von Herzogenberg, Brahms responded on December 22, 1886, by agreeing with her concerns about Hermine's under-rehearsing and facile interpretative decisions. He also undermined the Vienna debut that he himself had faciliated for the singer: "In Vienna one hears little good singing, and her success is very natural and very useful" (Brahms/Herzogenberg, *Briefwechsel* 2:136).

[37] Spies, *Hermine Spies*, 274.

in private performances in Thun during the summers of 1887 and 1888 and maintained a cordial correspondence thereafter, Hermine's characterization of the situation was entirely accurate. The composer's attitude toward her had assumed a trajectory familiar from his previous connections with attractive and musically talented women: enchanted enthusiasm and overt flirtation gave way to a purposefully detached demeanor, and whatever ambiguity may have marked the beginnings of the relationship was replaced by warm but straightforward friendship. Whether by accident or design, the same pattern had marked his interactions with Bertha Faber and Ottilie Ebner in the 1860s, and, most importantly and problematically, Clara Schumann in the 1850s.[38] Indeed, the care and energy Brahms devoted to his friendship with Clara after their potential for romantic attachment had faded is generally understood to have provided the model on which he based his later relationships with women, while at the same time discouraging him from pursuing serious plans of marriage. However strange his continued bachelorhood may have seemed to some contemporaries, it was surely no more unorthodox than his ability to maintain close and rewarding friendships with so many former love interests.

Among Brahms's documented relationships with women, his break with Agathe von Siebold was the singular exception. Confronted by increasing gossip regarding their secret engagement and urged by the Grimms to declare his intentions, Brahms wrote to Agathe early in 1859 professing his love and physical attraction to her but backing out of any long-term commitment. As she remembered it, his note was short and to the point: "I love you! I must see you again! But I cannot bear fetters. Write to me whether I should come again to hold you in my arms, to kiss you, to tell you that I love you!" She responded with a letter that definitively ended the relationship, and the two never communicated directly or saw each other again.[39] At the time, their breakup and subsequent lack of contact may not have seemed extraordinary, though it

---

[38] Brahms evidently considered previous interactions with Bertha Porubsky to have been sufficiently ambiguous that he expressed relief to Joachim when discovering that she was engaged to Arthur Faber upon his arrival in Vienna in 1862 (Brahms/Joachim, *Briefwechsel* 1:320). Barely a year later, on Christmas Day 1863, he seems to have been on the point of proposing to the soprano Ottilie Hauer but was preempted by the timely appearance of her future husband, Edward Ebner (Ottilie von Balassa, *Die Brahmsfreundin Ottilie Ebner*, 45–46). Once more, Brahms's response was relief at not having become inextricably entangled. He wrote to Clara Schumann the following spring about a pretty girl, "with whom, God knows, I would have done stupid things, if someone hadn't quickly snagged her, luckily, on Christmas Eve" (Brahms/Schumann, *Briefe* 1:446). If there were any truth to Kalbeck's conjectures concerning Brahms's earliest encounters with Elizabeth von Stockhausen, that relationship, too, would fit the pattern perfectly.

[39] Although no correspondence between Brahms and Agathe survives, Agathe recorded the circumstances of the break after Brahms's death in a lightly fictionalized, handwritten document. Hans Küntzel has provided a transcriptions of her account in *Johannes Brahms und Agathe von Siebold*, 134–36, and a facsimile of the handwritten version in *Brahms in Göttingen*, 101–5. For the quotation above, see ibid., 100 and 103.

obviously wounded both of them deeply. But by the late 1880s, after preserving his friendship with Clara Schumann through countless strains and disagreements, and after finding ways to maintain cordial and close communications in the wake of his flirtations with Bertha Faber, Ottilie Ebner, and now Hermine Spies, Brahms might well have understood the acrimonious ending of his relationship with Agathe as a striking anomaly, a sharp break in the otherwise smooth and carefully maintained topography of his self-image. Encountered amid the predictably shifting dynamics of his friendship with Hermine, the echoes of Agathe's voice and the connotations of postrelationship regret potentially latent in the words and music of *Ein Sonett* could have struck a discordant note.

Further evidence suggests that Brahms was especially sensitive to such a cognitive dissonance around the time he composed *Auf dem Kirchhofe*. More and more throughout the 1880s he spoke openly about his continued bachelorhood, often in lightheartedly sarcastic tones but also with increasing seriousness.[40] His most famous recorded comments on the subject of marriage and family life were made to Joseph Viktor Widmann on the outskirts of Thun during one of the three summers of 1886–88; Widmann remembered the place but not the particular year of their conversation.

> I missed my chance. When I would have wanted to, I could not provide for a woman as would have been proper.... At the time when I would most like to have married, my things were booed in the concert halls or at best received with icy silence. I could bear that very well, for I knew precisely how good they were and how the page would yet turn. And when I entered my secluded room after such failures, I was not sad at heart. To the contrary! But if I had come home to a wife in such moments, saw her questioning eyes anxiously meet my own, and had had to say: "Once again nothing"—that I could not have borne! For even if a woman loves an artist who is her husband very much and also, as one calls it, believes in him—she cannot have the full certainty of eventual victory as it lies in his breast. And if she had wanted to comfort me...the pity of one's own wife at the failures of her husband...ugh! I don't want to think about what hell, at least as I perceive it, that would have been.[41]

Brahms's remarks have provoked a variety of responses over the years. Some scholars have interpreted them as an uncharacteristically candid self-analysis, while others more skeptical have sought to read them as defensive or deliberately

---

[40] Michelmann, *Agathe von Siebold*, 201–2, and Kalbeck, *Brahms* 1:331n. Kalbeck recorded two of the expressions to which Brahms resorted frequently during the 1880s when the topic of his continued bachelorhood came up in conversation: "Sadly, I was never married, and, thank God, I remain so still," and "I am doubly careful now, for I am now approaching the age in which one can easily make a dumb move." In January 1888, Brahms used a more private formulation of the same attitude in a letter to Joseph Viktor Widmann: "Haven't I spoken to you of my beautiful principles...? Among them: No more attempts at opera or marriage" (Widmann, *Johannes Brahms in Erinnerungen*, 45).

[41] Widmann, *Johannes Brahms in Erinnerungen*, 47–48. The last two ellipses are in the original as well.

misleading.[42] Regardless of what had actually motivated his youthful decisions, his mature distaste for feminine interference in what he understood as a masculine career resonates with his contemporaneous impressions of couples like the Herzogenbergs and Scholzes. And however one approaches his comments, Brahms's references to the poor reception of his music demonstrate that his relationship with Agathe, which coincided with the disastrous Leipzig premiere of the first piano concerto in January 1859, was foremost in his thoughts in the late 1880s.

At the same time, in the summer of 1887, when Brahms was most likely at work on *Auf dem Kirchhofe*, two independent events might well have further stimulated retrospective reconsideration of the Göttingen situation. First, he and Clara Schumann spent the late spring and summer of 1887 negotiating the exchange and destruction of their early correspondence. The possibility of returning each other's letters had arisen as early as May 1886, but negotiations began in earnest in May 1887 and lasted through August, after which they met in October to complete the exchange.[43] The discussion was prolonged in part because Clara took the opportunity to reread some of Brahms's old letters, provoking a wave of nostalgia that crested in July 1887: "I am living now entirely in your letters—a melancholy joy. Words cannot express what moves the soul when one buries oneself so completely in long departed times. In giving back these letters it is as if I am already taking leave of you!" In turn, Brahms gently chided his friend for having reopened the letters in the first place.[44] Nevertheless, even if he held true to his word and returned hers unread, the whole endeavor surely provoked some reminiscence on his part, as well, concerning his younger years—not to mention the pains he had taken to maintain a close friendship with Clara in the wake of their initial romantic attachment.

The second event was more precipitous. On March 11, 1887, Carl Schütte, the man Agathe had finally married nearly a decade after her failed romance with Brahms, died suddenly in Göttingen.[45] Brahms's extant correspondence does not mention Schütte's passing, but he might easily have learned about it once he arrived in Thun in May. Just before leaving for Italy in late April, he had renewed his long-neglected correspondence with

---

[42] Kalbeck presented Brahms's remarks as if they provide direct access to his feelings on the subject of marriage (*Brahms* 1:329–30). For Michelmann and Avins, however, Widmann's recollections preserve yet another rhetorical stance adopted by the composer in partial concealment of his true motivations for breaking off his relationship with Agathe (*Agathe von Siebold*, 188–89, and *Life and Letters*, 181, 183, and 188).

[43] Avins, *Life and Letters*, 761–62; Brahms/Schumann, *Briefe* 2:300, 315–16, 320–21, and 330.

[44] Brahms/Schumann, *Briefe* 2:320–21. Clara's nostalgic attitude may help explain her seemingly clandestine decision to preserve some of the correspondence in question.

[45] Michelmann, *Agathe von Siebold*, 264.

Julius Otto Grimm and invited his longtime friend to visit him in Thun later that summer in order to reminisce about old times together.[46] No reply survives, but this is hardly surprising since the composer did not retain any of Julius Otto's letters between 1881 and 1890. Prompted by Brahms's invitation to recall their shared friendship in Göttingen, Julius Otto may well have informed him of Schütte's death. He did try to broker a reconciliation between Agathe and Brahms during exactly this period by approaching the newly widowed woman and asking if she wanted him to convey greetings to her old flame.[47] The attempt seems to have failed spectacularly, but one wonders if Brahms knew or approved of his old friend's efforts on his behalf.

Whatever had actually provoked the persistent reminiscences of Göttingen to which Brahms's conversation with Widmann bears witness, those reminiscences were at least generally contemporaneous with his setting of *Auf dem Kirchhofe*. In such a context, even though the borrowing from *Ein Sonett* remained hidden beneath the rhetorical surface of his new song, Brahms's selection and treatment of borrowed material seem unlikely to have been purely coincidental. To the contrary, the latent tension between the sickness of willfully prolonged infatuation in Herder's closing quatrain and the healing promise of redemption in Liliencron's final couplet might have struck him with particular force during those three Thun summers as he struggled with the unique regrets associated with his failed relationship with Agathe. Bringing the two poems together by means of musical borrowing at precisely the point where the perspectives of their poetic speakers most clearly diverge would have given Brahms an opportunity to experiment in tones with the contrasting emotional implications of past and present. The compositional problem of matching Liliencron's closing line to a vocal gesture initially designed for Herder's poem would have opened a new arena in which he could wrangle yet again with his memories of Göttingen and reconsider the pattern of his relationships with musically talented women.

Such reconsideration could have affected other features of his new song as well. For instance, to ears and mind properly attuned, the contour of the singer's line might imply a subtle but telling revision of the perspective adopted by Herder's poetic speaker. Taken as a whole the vocal range of *Auf dem Kirchhofe* is generally quite low. Its average pitch is nearly a perfect fourth below that of *Ein Sonett*—and consistent, instead, with the two songs that Brahms had written for Hermine Spies in August 1886. Yet within this mellow span the borrowed vocal cadence pointedly revises its registral affiliation

[46] Brahms/Grimm, *Briefwechsel*, 148.
[47] Michelmann, *Agathe von Siebold*, 208.

over the course of the song. The lilting cadential pattern that Brahms had labored to compose for Agathe in 1858 appears first in G minor at the end of the first strophe, just a half step below its original placement in A♭ major. Only after eighteen more angst-ridden measures, or more than half of the work's total duration, does the gesture arrive at its permanent home at the end of the second strophe, transposed down a minor sixth to C major. The shifting register of the borrowed material finds reflection, in turn, in the trajectory of the vocal line as a whole, which reaches its apex within an eighth note of its beginning and reserves its two lowest pitches for singer's last two notes. Having surreptitiously conjured up the piercing tones of Agathe's soprano voice, *Auf dem Kirchhofe* could gradually transform that voice into something much closer to Hermine's warm contralto. From the perspective of form and contour, then, the entire song can be understood as a slow descent that draws the episode with Agathe into a larger pattern of reconciliation and release.

In short, during the summers of 1886–88, the musical challenge of adapting the final vocal cadence of *Ein Sonett* to its new context may have allowed Brahms to imagine and inhabit the act of composition as a process of self-examination. This nexus of musical and personal motivations provides a plausible means of accounting for his treatment of the cadence he borrowed from *Ein Sonett*, a hypothetical scenario in which psychological closure and compositional completion converged in the word *genesen*. Such a scenario is inherently speculative, as much if not more so than any other case study addressed in this book. It relies upon fragmentary reconstructions of patterns of thought that Brahms rarely revealed even to close friends and musical decisions to which he did not alert any member of his circles, even obliquely. Or did he? Strangely, the most provocative evidence that the act of composing *Auf dem Kirchhofe* was bound up with memories of Agathe von Siebold may lie not in Brahms's borrowing from *Ein Sonett* but in his allusion to the Passion Chorale.

In 1930 Emil Michelmann, Agathe's grandson by marriage, published an account of her life and her relationship with Brahms. Based in large part on his mother-in-law's descriptions of Agathe's own recollections, Michelmann's account includes a remarkably detailed anecdote concerning a composition assignment that Brahms had deliberately botched as a prank during his stay in Göttingen in September 1858. While the young composer was busily crafting *Ein Sonett* and other songs for her voice, Agathe herself was studying music theory with Julius Otto Grimm. She and her fellow student Phillipine Grimm had recently given their teacher a new nickname: Isegrimm, or Ise for short, after the stern and oft-aggrieved wolf in German-language versions of the fable *Reinecke Fuchs* (Renard the Fox). The sobriquet highlighted the sincerity and thoroughness of Julius Otto's pedagogy, which centered, like his compositions themselves, on canon and strict counterpoint.[48] His fabled namesake had, since the late Middle Ages, maintained a dogged determination to bring a wily antagonist to justice, but most recently and famously in Goethe's twelve-part verse adaptation of 1794, where the Isegrimm had proclaimed: "The right remains the right, and whoever is right will reveal itself in the end."[49] In wolf or composer, such single-minded seriousness was an open invitation to mockery, and, like the fox, Brahms eventually succumbed to the temptation. Michelmann's anecdote is worth quoting in full:

> The severe teacher himself was not treated with consideration by the high-spirited young people and had to endure many jokes. Once he had assigned Agathe to harmonize a chorale, each stanza in a different key. And "Befiel Du Deine Wege" [Commit your ways] had a terrible number of stanzas! She came with two. The master was not satisfied. Next time she had more, but again errors. Now Grimm became angry. She complained to Johannes. Ha, for once we'll amaze Ise! The artwork was soon completed, the melody harmonized differently twelve times. Agathe reported to her lesson, quite proud, the cleanly copied exercise under her arm—assured in advance of success. With raised eyebrows Ise looked over the botched piece of work and wrinkled his brow. "Who made this obscenity, then?" he cried in his righteous indignation. "Nothing will come of him, nothing, absolutely nothing!" Poor Agathe, utterly disappointed, then stammered: "But what if Johannes did it?"—"That would be even worse!"—Now it dawned on Grimm that Brahms had had the best of both of them with his piece of devilry. Not until evening were they reconciled; the drinks helped, and in the end Agathe overcame even Isegrimm with her Brahms songs.[50]

In the nineteenth century just as today, the melody overwhelmingly associated with the text "Befiehl Du Deine Wege" was that of the Passion Chorale. Tune and text were paired in Bach's *St. Matthew Passion*, as well as in numerous compositions published throughout the 1700s and 1800s.[51] The modal ambiguity of the Passion Chorale melody made it an ideal choice for Julius Otto's task of multiple harmonizations. The length of Paul Gerhardt's poem may well have been a factor, too: Michelmann's claim that Brahms harmonized the tune a dozen times might seem exaggerated, but Gerhardt's text had exactly twelve stanzas, rendering it perfect for the assignment at hand. At least some memory

---

[48] Brahms/Grimm, *Briefwechsel*, vii–viii and 66n; for the earliest appearances of the nickname Isegrimm in surviving correspondence, see ibid., 66.

[49] Johann Wolfgang von Goethe, *Reinecke Fuchs in zwölf Gesängen* (Berlin: Johann Friedrich Unger, 1794), 438. The quotation occurs just before the final, deadly confrontation between Isegrimm and Reinecke, the fox.

[50] Michelmann, *Agathe von Siebold*, 158–59.

[51] Examples include Christoph Graupner's 1727 chorale cantata (the autograph of which is preserved in the Darmstadt Universitäts- und Landesbibliothek as Mus. Ms. 435/24) and Jan Albert van Eyken's 1853 organ sonata, Op. 13 (for a modern edition, see Joachim Dorfmüller, ed., *Jan Albert van Eyken: Sonata Nr. 1 c-moll für die Orgel, op. 13, über den Choral Befiehl Du Deine Wege* [Bonn: Rob. Forberg, 1974]). Van Eyken counted Niels Gade, Moritz Hauptmann, and Felix Mendelssohn among his teachers.

of the episode seems to have remained with the composer, for two months later he wrote teasingly from Detmold to Agathe and Phillipine, asking if they could "already harmonize chorales or compose waltzes."[52] After his relationship with Agathe ended, might not Brahms have felt a twinge of conscience regarding a prank in which he had so brazenly taken advantage of her trust, not to mention her compositional naïveté? The presence of the Passion Chorale's melodic in-cipit in *Auf dem Kirchhofe*, newly and richly harmonized in five voices, hints at another layer of resonances with Brahms's time in Göttingen, especially given its proximity to and surreptitious intertwining with material taken from *Ein Sonett*. Though disparate in their sources and their impact on the rhetorical sur-face of his new song, the two borrowings ultimately shared the potential to facilitate for Brahms the reevaluation of a period in his life that had become charged, over the intervening years, with retrospective significance.

Interpretations of a composer's intentions are inevitably our own inventions. Incorporating borrowed material into *Auf dem Kirchhofe* may have given Brahms the opportunity for timely introspection regarding his relationship with Agathe von Siebold; then again, more prosaic arguments could also explain the music and documents that survive. Brahms himself certainly never mentioned any connection between Agathe and *Auf dem Kirchhofe* in extant correspondence. The song's many resemblances to *Ein Sonett* could conceivably have come about without his conscious awareness, however unlikely that may seem. Mi-chelmann's secondhand anecdote regarding the botched harmonizations of the Passion Chorale remains the sole surviving evidence that such an event ever occurred. Most important, other pivotal information has surely been lost over the years, rendering any account of Brahms's motivations incomplete at best. This last problem, of course, also haunts every other chapter in this book, but our fundamental limitations as historians seem especially insurmountable in the absence of an identifiable audience for whom Brahms's purported borrowings might have been designed and from whose perspective one can seek vicariously to experience his music.

Nevertheless, there is something compelling about the idea that Brahms might have understood the act of musical borrowing as a means of effecting personal catharsis. Nearly a decade before completing *Auf dem Kirchhofe*, he had written to Otto Dessoff regarding another of Herder's translations, this time of the Scottish ballad *Edward*, which he had just set to music for alto, tenor, and piano: "I hardly need mention how that beautiful poem simply never leaves

---

[52] Brahms/Grimm, *Briefwechsel*, 78. The letter can be securely dated to mid-November, given Brahms's report that his time in Detmold was already half over (see also Avins, *Life and Letters*, 748).

one's mind, how one must at some point, in a certain sense, get rid of it."[53] The implication was obvious. Brahms could clear his mind of Herder's text only by composing music for it, engaging it in detail through the medium of his own craft. The string of Agathe-related compositions from the 1860s suggests that he had already sought to apply a similar purgative strategy to the remembered melodies and bitter personal experiences associated with his time in Göttingen. Although he had broken off his relationship with Agathe precisely in order to avoid long-term commitment, persistent recollections of the affair had forced him to "free himself" from her again by writing her name into the G-major String Sextet and her voice into *Von ewiger Liebe*. In both of those works, interpolated musical material imbued with personal significance played a demonstrably conscious role in the construction of new music. If, in turn, Brahms did associate the blended echoes of *Ein Sonett* and the Passion Chorale with recollections of his time in Göttingen, *Auf dem Kirchhofe* would have been but the latest and the most complex iteration of a broader pattern, the next in a long series of attempts to achieve emotional closure by creating and then solving the compositional problems inherent in surreptitious musical borrowing.

Imagined in this way, Brahms's music can be said to anticipate techniques of free-associative self-examination that would find broader currency and more formalized expression in the early decades of the twentieth century through the psychoanalytic practices of Sigmund Freud and his various disciples and critics. Perhaps the most musically sensitive of Freud's students was Theodor Reik, who spent his childhood years in 1890s Vienna and emerged steeped in the works of Brahms, Bruckner, and Mahler. A lifelong agnostic raised in a secular Jewish household, Reik became troubled in 1925 when the chorale melody from the finale of Mahler's "Resurrection Symphony" lodged itself persistently in his mind's ear during the composition of a funeral oration for his analyst and benefactor, Karl Abraham. Mahler's tune, along with his own inability to explain its apparent psychological importance, continued to frustrate Reik over the ensuing decades until it became the central case study in his 1953 book *The Haunting Melody*, a wide-ranging self-analysis and exploration of involuntary musical memory. By reproducing and criticizing his early drafts within the text of the published volume, he presented the act of writing as itself a cathartic reevaluation of his youthful attitudes—his hunger for fame and his suppressed desire to destroy and replace his mentors, Abraham and Freud.[54] In form if not in content, the gesture might well have seemed familiar to Brahms, for whom the writing of *Auf dem Kirchhofe* could have facilitated an analogous process of self-evaluation.

---

[53] Brahms, Spitta, and Dessoff, *Briefwechsel*, 192.
[54] Theodor Reik, *The Haunting Melody: Psychoanalytic Experiences in Life and Music* (New York: Farrar, Straus, and Young, 1953); see especially 219–376.

If such a process actually occurred, the composer's means of self-analysis were supremely appropriate, both to his own profession and to the comparative reticence that marked his character over the decades. Instead of confessional autobiography, then, came the covert integration of disparate musical materials. Not unlike Reik, however, Brahms eventually found himself driven to overt expression. Even for a man who had long since claimed to speak in tones,[55] the exercise of solitary contrapuntal ingenuity ultimately seems to have proven unsatisfactory as a means of revisiting his relationship with Agathe. Six years after publishing *Auf dem Kirchhofe*, Brahms finally took the initiative to contact her personally. Using their mutual acquaintance Joseph Joachim as an intermediary, he sent her his greetings on the occasion of her fifty-ninth birthday on July 8, 1894. She apparently received his words graciously and with deep emotion. Later that summer in Göttingen, Agathe and Joseph collaborated in numerous informal performances of Brahms's latest published music: folksong arrangements from the forty-nine German Folksongs, WoO 33. For Agathe, the experience must have been rich with musical memories of her original relationship with Brahms. Not only did many of these folksong settings themselves originate in 1858, but during the affair Brahms had also given her a copy of Kretzschmer and Zuccalmaglio's *Deutsche Volkslieder mit ihren Original-Weisen*, his source for the majority of their tunes and texts, which she retained throughout her life.[56]

Agathe had to have known that Joseph might keep the composer apprised of her reception of this latest but long-familiar opus. Indeed, he did just that in a letter from late September 1894. Brahms replied by thanking Joseph for the "twofold memory of G"—that is, of Göttingen and Gathe, Agathe's nickname.[57] Such memories could only have come as a form of symbolic reconciliation. By allowing Brahms to know that she still sang his songs in the city where they had first met, Agathe had repaired at least a few of the intimate and unspoken connections that bound composer to performer within his orbit. Those bonds, at least, were fetters he would always remain content to bear.

---

[55] Brahms/Schumann, *Briefe* 1:595.

[56] Michelmann, *Agathe von Siebold*, 314–17 and 250.

[57] Brahms/Joachim, *Briefwechsel* 2:273–75. By interpolating "[öttingen]" after Brahms's unadorned "G" in his edition of the Brahms/Joachim correspondence, Andreas Moser obscured the "twofold" implications of Brahms's comment.

CHAPTER TEN

CONCEALMENT AS

SELF–RESTRAINT

In hindsight, at least, *Auf dem Kirchhofe* may well have served emotional needs similar to those fed by *O kühler Wald* a decade prior. Insofar as one can reconstruct Brahms's perspectives on his own music, the concealed borrowings in both songs seem likely to have facilitated detailed rumination on long-standing interpersonal conflicts. Within the larger trajectories of the composer's relationships with Julius Stockhausen and Agathe von Siebold, his work on both songs preceded more overt and definitive steps to mitigate those conflicts. Furthermore, Brahms hinted at aspects of both borrowings in exchanges with third parties unaffected by the rhetorical charges that those borrowings might release. His query as to whether Max Kalbeck had perceived a musical joke in *Auf dem Kirchhofe* found a direct equivalent in his cryptic remark to Theodor Billroth concerning changes to Brentano's poem in *O kühler Wald*.

These playful comments, in turn, drew the two songs into a gathering haze of tantalizing banter that obscured highly personalized allusions and privately meaningful borrowings throughout his oeuvre. Even at his most guarded, Brahms often found it hard to resist pointing out his own skill. His tendency was to disclose a small portion of his compositional strategy to persons safely removed from the emotional situation at hand—enough to pique their interest and demonstrate his craft, but not enough to permit a full accounting of his creative process and its potential ties to his social relationships. The most influential example was his suggestion that Theodor Billroth save the *Regenlied* sonata, Clara Schumann's elegiac and transformative gift, for a drizzly evening. Especially once the majority of Brahms's extant correspondence was published in the decades following his death, the paradoxical effect of these exchanges was to broaden awareness of his compositional borrowings while redirecting attention away from their more serious interpersonal resonances.

On one such occasion, however, Brahms himself seems to have realized that he had revealed too much to some acquaintances and sought, belatedly, to cover his tracks. His change of heart involved one of his darkest and strangest works, the *Intermezzo* in E♭ minor, Op. 118 No. 6. Fragments of evidence both musical and documentary hint that the *Intermezzo* began with a compositional borrowing whose recognition as an allusive gesture would have carried devastating implications for Clara Schumann; the same evidence suggests that Brahms then deliberately concealed his borrowing from her. The result stands as a final, tenuous witness to the interwoven compositional and emotional efforts demanded by his longest and most complex friendship.

Brahms's *Intermezzo* in E♭ minor has been characterized as an enigma almost since its publication. By turns oppressively melancholic and brusquely assertive, the work invites hermeneutic inquiry but remains stubbornly inscrutable in the face of any particular interpretive scheme. To some degree it shares its mystique with the composer's other late piano miniatures, which, as a group, have been persistently understood as idiosyncratic and introverted. Eduard Hanslick's review of the *Klavierstücke*, Opp. 118 and 119, provides a *locus classicus* in the early reception of these pieces:

> One could entitle these two volumes "monologues at the piano": monologues, as Brahms holds them with and for himself in a solitary evening hour, in sullenly pessimistic rebellion, in brooding meditation, in romantic reminiscences, occasionally also in dreamy melancholy.[1]

This evocative description is surely the most frequently quoted contemporary account of the late piano works.[2] Yet before finding broad readership in one of Hanslick's many collections of critical writings, it originated far more narrowly in a review of a concert featuring the violinist Jenö Hubay and pianist Ignaz Brüll. As a change of pace between overtly virtuosic works for both instruments, Brüll had presented the Vienna premiere of the E♭-minor *Intermezzo* and just three more of Brahms's latest piano pieces (the *Romanze* and *Ballade* from Op. 118 and the *Rhapsody* from Op. 119) on February 8, 1894. He had obtained his copy of the printed score from the composer himself two months prior.[3] Along with a select group of compositions, then, the *Intermezzo* had actually provided the point of entry for an emerging repertoire, making Hanslick's characterization all the more intriguing and specifically apropos.

---

[1] Eduard Hanslick, review of Jenö Hubay and Ignaz Brüll, *Neue Freie Presse,* 10594, February 20, 1894, 1. The review was later reprinted, with minimal changes, in *Fünf Jahre Musik* (Berlin: Allgemeiner Verein für deutschen Literatur, 1896), 258–59.

[2] Among the most sensitive interpretations in recent years occurs in Steven Rings, "The Learned Self," 25–26.

[3] Brahms, *Briefe an Simrock* 4:111. For a detailed account of the program presented by Hubay and Brüll, see the advertisement in the *Neue Freie Presse* 10578 (February 4, 1894), 14.

Subsequent reviews preserve further evidence of perceived obscurity in the *Intermezzo*. An English commentary from five weeks later was more prosaic than Hanslick's but no less emphatic in its attempts to convey the work's melancholic oddity.

> No. 6, Intermezzo, in the mournful key of E-flat minor, is a weird, sad piece; and the sombreness is relieved only for one moment, when the theme in the relative major key enters; loud minor chords are soon heard, followed by a passionate delivery of the principal theme. The composer must indeed have been in sorrowful mood when he penned this piece.[4]

Although refracted through changing music-analytic vocabularies, later reckonings with the *Intermezzo* have continued to reiterate concerns anticipated in these early reviews. A broad array of scholarly literature on the work has charted its obsessive motivic repetition, its juxtaposition of affective extremes, and its air of veiled significance.[5]

These characteristics also shaped the *Intermezzo*'s reception within the composer's own circles. Just after correcting the proofs for the Op. 118 piano pieces in November 1893, Brahms mailed a postcard to Theodor Wilhelm Engelmann, a biologist, physiologist, and amateur cellist. Although Theodor Wilhelm lived in Utrecht, he had now been friendly with Brahms for more than twenty years, ever since they first met at the Schumann festival in Bonn in August 1873.[6] The first sentence of Brahms's postcard incorporated a concise musical diagram (see ex. 10.1). Like several of the many scraps of musical notation in the Engelmann correspondence, the original diagram differs slightly from Julius Röntgen's transcription in the published edition.[7] The g♭" cryptically stood for the *Intermezzo*, which begins on that pitch, and thus for the subject of a sentence with a predicate no less cryptic. Whatever he meant by it, however, the composer's comment clearly reopened an ongoing discussion of the piece. Previous correspondence suggests the possibility of a face-to-face meeting with Theodor Wilhelm in Switzerland during the summer of 1893, just as the *Klavierstücke* were

---

[4] Anonymous, "Clavierstücke. Von Johannes Brahms. Op. 118 and Op. 119," *Musical Times* 35/614 (April 1, 1894): 246.

[5] As representatives of the plethora of music-analytic and stylistic issues embedded in previous scholarship on the E♭-minor *Intermezzo*, one might point to: echoes of the *style hongrois* in Musgrave, *Music of Brahms*, 261–62; voicing and orchestral overtones in MacDonald, *Brahms*, 359–60; and Kalbeck, *Brahms* 4:302–4; the possibility of allusion to music from the Catholic liturgy in Floros, *Frei aber einsam*, 177–78; and "Studien zu Brahms' Klaviermusik," *Brahms-Studien* 5 (1983): 25–63; the tension between motivic uniformity and tonal insecurity in John Rink, "Opposition and Integration in the Piano Music," in Musgrave, *Cambridge Companion to Brahms*, 79–97; and the aesthetics of order and dissolution in Jan Brachmann, *Kunst—Religion—Krise: Der Fall Brahms* (Kassel: Bärenreiter, 2003), 273–82.

[6] Kalbeck, *Brahms* 2:460; and Brahms/Engelmann, *Briefwechsel*, 11n.

[7] Examples in this chapter are based directly on Brahms's original letters, which are currently housed in the Berlin Staatsbibliothek, Preußicher Kulturbesitz, Musikabteilung mit Mendelssohn-Archiv. For Röntgen's subtly inaccurate transcription of the diagram, see Brahms/Engelmann, *Briefwechsel*, 156.

taking shape; at the very least, both men had put considerable effort into their attempts to arrange a rendezvous.[8]

EXAMPLE 10.1   Johannes Brahms to Theodor Wilhelm Engelmann, November 21, 1893. From the autograph (Musikabteilung mit Mendelssohn-Archiv, Staatsbibliothek zu Berlin, Preußischer Kulturbesitz). With kind permission.

Dear friend  will appear to you

still more frequently, and I hope you will not tell others where I get my melodies, but perhaps tell me whether you also like them in my dress.

Atypically direct but frustratingly nonspecific, Brahms's acknowledgment of musical borrowing in the *Intermezzo* remains completely unaddressed in scholarly literature.[9] Taking his postcard in isolation, one might assume he was referring to the oft-remarked resemblance between the work's pervasive initial motive and the familiar chant melody associated with the Requiem sequence, *Dies irae, dies illa* (Day of wrath, day of mourning). Example 10.2 presents the two melodies with the chant transposed to facilitate comparison. The tunes share precise intervallic content for their first four pitches, and, heard against the backdrop of common practice tonality, both trace a larger descent from scale degree 3 to 1. The solemn liturgical origins and grim textual associations of the chant melody certainly fit the dark key and depressive mood of Brahms's piece. On the other hand, the melody was already well known to a broad spectrum of European audiences as a source for musical borrowing and parody in such diverse works as Franz Liszt's *Totentanz*, Charles Gounod's *Faust*, and Hector Berlioz's *Symphonie Fantastique*. This prior popularity makes it unlikely that Brahms could have realistically hoped to suppress speculation concerning potential borrowings from the tune in his *Intermezzo*. If, indeed, it was a resemblance to the Requiem sequence that he sought to conceal through his cautionary note to Theodor Wilhelm, he failed spectacularly, as attested by countless commentators who have described the similarity in the years since the work's publication.[10]

[8] Ibid., 153 and 156.

[9] The second and third clauses in Brahms's remark have provoked a solitary, passing reference in previous scholarship; see *Bruckner-Probleme: internationales Kolloquium 7.–9. Oktober 1996 in Berlin*, ed. Albrecht Riethmüller, 173 (Stuttgart: Steiner, 1999). Here Riethmüller referred to Brahms's words during the discussion session of the conference, as evidence of a general desire on the part of late-nineteenth-century composers to ensure the impression of originality in their works. No author has ever attempted to discern the source from which Brahms "got his melodies."

[10] Among recent commentators to explore the similarity and its implications are MacDonald and Floros (*Brahms*, 360; *Frei aber einsam*, 177–78; and "Studien zu Brahms' Klaviermusik," 54–56). Brachmann has also noted the similarity while expressing concern at its undue influence on the work of other (unnamed) analysts; see *Kunst—Religion—Krise*, 281.

EXAMPLE 10.2   Brahms, *Intermezzo*, Op. 118 No. 6, and Requiem sequence, *Dies irae*.
Head motives.

Read in the context of previous correspondence with the Engelmanns, however, Brahms's postcard hints instead at a far less audible connection between his introspective music and a sprightly piano miniature in A major, titled simply *Stücklein* (Little Piece), from Robert Schumann's *Bunte Blätter*, Op. 99. For more than sixteen years, Brahms had employed the initial melody of this tiny piece in letters to Theodor Wilhelm as musical shorthand for the scientist's wife, Emma. Emma was a diminutive, small-handed pianist who had amassed a dynamic reputation as a teenage virtuoso. Born Emma Vick in 1853, she had adopted her mother's maiden name as a stage name in 1866 and toured as Emma Brandes throughout the late 1860s and early 1870s. She played for Clara Schumann in 1869 and began studying with her in earnest the following summer. Over the ensuing years she gave joint recitals with Clara and with Joseph and Amalie Joachim, and she seems to have met Brahms as well.[11] In July 1870, Clara confided to her diary her mingled feelings of admiration and sadness at encountering a musician so similar to herself:

> I had great joy in her, and she became dearer to me with every passing day. But it was also a very agitated time for me, I relived my earliest youth in her again, and along with the joy that I had in finally, truly seeing a talent rise after my own inclination and also, above all, a female interpreter [*Interpretin*] for Robert's compositions, I was constantly seized by the melancholy thought, now I soon won't need to be there any more—she will relieve me! She will perhaps not have quite all of the enthusiasm and the fire of my playing, but that is also not necessary, there are actually never two individualities precisely alike.... And who knows, when love warms her heart through for the first time, whether the fire won't also come, along with the deep inwardness that only life with its joys and pains brings.[12]

Clara's words actually revealed more about her own expectations than about Emma's aspirations as a performer. Her diction emphasized Emma's gender as an important condition of suitability for Robert's music, and her final clauses hinted at aesthetic priorities directly aligned with her own, highly unconventional decision to continue concertizing in public as a wife and a mother. For

---

[11] Clara informed Brahms of Emma's engagement to Theodor Wilhelm in December 1873 in a matter-of-fact postscript to an unrelated letter. Her tone and diction make it clear that he was already acquainted with both of the affianced (Brahms/Schumann, *Briefe* 2:36).

[12] Litzmann, *Clara Schumann* 3:241.

Clara, at least, true musical and artistic maturity had emerged only through the challenging life experiences inherent in adult womanhood.

By contrast, far from embracing her mentor's model of continued professional engagement, Emma retired from the stage immediately upon her marriage to Engelmann in 1874. To maintain her formidable technique, she relied exclusively upon domestic practice and performances in private venues. As her husband put it shortly after the wedding in a letter to Clara, Emma had to search consciously for ways "not to forget the artist for the housewife."[13] Nevertheless, given Clara's enthusiasm for her playing of Robert's compositions, it is not surprising that Brahms used a quotation from one of those compositions to refer to Emma in correspondence with Theodor Wilhelm. Example 10.3 presents extant samples. Robert's melody surfaced in connection to Emma in June 1877, when Brahms closed a letter with its first four notes, followed by the words "So tenderly I greet the little woman." By November 1877, the same excerpt, minus key signature, simply substituted for Emma's name in the middle of a sentence. In March 1881, the excerpt itself was abbreviated using its first note, f♯", which in July 1888 acquired Schumann's tie and characteristic dynamic hairpin. In turn, that hairpin became the unwritten punch line of a pianists' joke in November 1890, as the imagined player obligingly sought to generate dynamic flux by desperately shifting fingers atop a single depressed key.[14] The ring finger, which initiates and completes this extravaganza, was ostensibly Brahms's preference for the f♯"; its selection placed the hand securely over the first four pitches of Robert's melody in preparation for the shift over the thumb on the ensuing downbeat.

EXAMPLE 10.3   Echoes of Robert Schumann's *Stücklein* in Brahms's letters to the Engelmanns. From the autographs (Musikabteilung mit Mendelssohn-Archiv, Staatsbibliothek zu Berlin, Preußischer Kulturbesitz). With kind permission.

| June 1877 | November 1877 | March 1881 | July 1888 | November 1890 |

And it is the same f♯" that reappeared in Brahms's musical diagram in November 1893, alongside the *Intermezzo*'s g♭". Examples 10.4a, b, and c present the diagram again, accompanied now by the opening measures of each piece, which reveal short-lived but subtly important similarities. Schumann's *Stücklein* begins on the same sounding pitch as the *Intermezzo*. Both works sustain the pitch for the same notated duration and isolate it as the slurred beginning of a quiet,

---

[13] Ibid., 315.
[14] The musical excerpts cited here are transcribed, sometimes inaccurately, in Brahms/Engelmann, *Briefwechsel*, 63, 67, 100, 137, and 146.

sixteenth-note solo for the right hand, against which the left hand then enters, along with sustain pedal. In Brahms's diagram the initial pitches were especially intertwined. They demanded the same fingering, and their durations were notationally inverted: the *Intermezzo*'s g♭" received Schumann's eighth note with tie, while the *Stücklein*'s f♯" received Brahms's dotted eighth. Along with their inverted durations, their order also ensured that they would not be read linearly as separate syntactic elements in a quasi-verbal utterance. Had the f♯" come first, the pair might have been perceived as part of a continuous opening sentence: "Dear Friend [and Emma, the *Intermezzo*] will appear to you still more frequently." Instead, on the surface of the postcard, the two works were made one, fused into a single experience at the moment of their inception in performance.

EXAMPLE 10.4a   Johannes Brahms to Theodor Wilhelm Engelmann, November 21, 1893. From the autograph (Musikabteilung mit Mendelssohn-Archiv, Staatsbibliothek zu Berlin, Preußischer Kulturbesitz). With kind permission.

EXAMPLE 10.4b   Robert Schumann, *Stücklein*, Op. 99 No. 1, mm. 1–2

EXAMPLE 10.4c   Brahms, *Intermezzo*, Op. 118 No. 6, mm. 1–5

Having begun grounded in identical physical acts, however, *Stücklein* and *Intermezzo* then unfolded in disparate directions. Brahms's meter immediately established a marked alternative to Robert's. His tempo and unusual

affect indication placed the *Intermezzo* amid a select group of intensely sor-
rowful works for keyboard or chamber ensemble, including the *Largo e
mesto* and *Adagio molto e mesto* from Beethoven's piano sonata, Op. 10 No. 3,
and string quartet, Op. 59 No. 1, and the *Adagio mesto* from Brahms's own
Horn Trio, Op. 40. Melodic contour and tonal affiliation veered asunder as
well. Robert's tune was broad and dynamic, creating a comfortable sense of
goal-directed motion throughout its initial gesture, whereas Brahms's was
circumscribed and repetitive, awkwardly confining the hand to just three
notes. The shared opening pitch was soon revealed to the ear as a constituent of opposite modes a tritone apart. Whether the distance between them
was measured around the circle of fifths, across the lattice of the *Tonnetz*, or
along the surface of the keyboard, the two works inhabited fundamentally
disjunct harmonic regions. Figuration, too, quickly divided them from each
other. The *Stücklein* maintained a single underlying texture throughout.
Once initiated on the first downbeat, the continuously interlocking alternation of the hands created a steady stream of sixteenth notes in the middle
of the keyboard for the remainder of the work. The *Intermezzo* was texturally diverse and significantly more difficult to play. The straightforward distinction between melody and accompaniment in its opening measures soon
gave way to overlapping counterpoint and hand-crossing far more extreme
than anything demanded by Robert's piece (see ex. 10.5).

EXAMPLE 10.5   Brahms, *Intermezzo*, Op. 118 No. 6, mm. 13–15

Finally, the overarching formal and affective trajectories characteristic of
the two works diverged as well. Example 10.6 provides a score of the entire
Stücklein, based on the Complete Works edition that Clara Schumann edited
and published in 1885. Robert's gently off-tonic beginning resolved unambiguously to A major on the downbeat of the second measure. The characteristic rhythmic profile, melodic contour, and dynamic hairpin of the
work's incipit recurred with predictable regularity, punctuating a series of
two- and four-bar phrases. In turn, a concise, sixteen-measure binary form
confined these phrases within two halves of precisely equal length, each immediately repeated. Crystalline phrase structure supported an incremental

approach to chromatic saturation. Measures 1–2 were purely diatonic, mm.
3–4 introduced a single chromatically altered pitch class, and mm. 5–8 provided three more altered pitch classes, leaving just one pitch class unexplored in the first half of the piece. The first four measures of the second
half then aligned fully a dozen occurrences of that new pitch class, G♮, with
a phrase gently set apart by supertonic harmony, minor mode, and newly
accented leaps in the right hand. Finally, mm. 13–16 cycled through the first
three altered pitches once more, in order, on the way back to the tonic. The

EXAMPLE 10.6   Robert Schumann, *Stücklein*, Op. 99 No. 1, complete

result was a balanced interplay between conventional, sectional form and the larger affective shape articulated by chromatic harmony.

Against the comfortably expressive backdrop of the *Stücklein*, the *Intermezzo*'s oft-remarked idiosyncrasies stood in especially stark relief. Brahms's initial accompaniment eschewed tonal clarity in favor of hazy diminished-seventh chords, and no complete authentic cadence confirmed the tonic until the final measures of the entire work. Like the *Stücklein*, the *Intermezzo* began with a repeated, monothematic section that articulated a shift toward the dominant, but here the repetition was written out and partially obscured by a temporary change in accompanimental figuration (see ex. 10.7). Moreover, half way through the *Intermezzo*, Brahms replaced his initial melody with a craggily punctuated alternative that succeeded, for a time, in jolting the piece out of its baleful wanderings (ex. 10.8). Thematic multiplicity thus opened up the possibility of dramatic conflict and a steepened affective curve. Confronted at its own climax by aggressively reharmonized versions of the melodic incipit, the contrasting theme suddenly vanished utterly, leaving in its wake an enervated and prolonged return to the status quo. Example 10.9 shows this darkly pivotal moment in the unfolding of the *Intermezzo*—a moment for which the *Stücklein* provided no analogue whatsoever.

EXAMPLE 10.7   Brahms, *Intermezzo*, Op. 118 No. 6, mm. 21–24

EXAMPLE 10.8   Brahms, *Intermezzo*, Op. 118 No. 6, mm. 41–42

In fact, the placement and intensity of Brahms's thematic and affective shifts paradoxically undercut straightforward apprehension of the *Intermezzo*'s overriding ternary structure. When Clara Schumann first saw the piece in early September 1893, she surmised that it was a movement from a piano sonata in progress. Her reasoning rested, in part, upon the autograph that

10.9   Brahms, *Intermezzo*, Op. 118 No. 6, mm. 55–66

Brahms had sent her the previous month, along with manuscripts of the other *Klavierstücke* from Opp. 118 and 119. None of the pieces bore any title save their tempo and affect markings, so it must have seemed natural for Clara to categorize the longest among them (the *Intermezzi*, Op. 118 Nos. 2 and 6, and the *Rhapsody*, Op. 119 No. 4) as potential sonata movements.[15] Of these, Op. 118 No. 6 was by far the most likely candidate for a first movement, particularly since a finale in E♭, complete with rondo-like form and Hungarian-tinged motives, stood ready to hand in Op. 119 No. 4. By placing the formal unfolding and affective scope of the E♭-minor *Intermezzo* into implicit dialogue with the expectations associated with sonata form, Clara anticipated the multivalent approaches to structure in Brahms's late *Klavierstücke* adopted by recent scholars.[16] Heard in accordance with such

---

[15] Brahms/Schumann, *Briefe* 2:527. The autograph of Op. 118 No. 6 was continuous with autographs for Op. 118 No. 2 and Op. 118 No. 3. For all three of these pieces, the copy that Brahms made for Clara notated internal repetitions using measure numbers and *dal segno* indications. In the case of Op. 118 No. 6, these indications may have drawn increased attention to the large, repeated A section, thereby accentuating the work's affiliation with sonata form. See McCorkle, *Werkverzeichnis*, 472–73; the autograph comprising Op. 118 Nos. 2, 3, and 6 is preserved today in the Berlin Staatsbibliothek, Preußicher Kulturbesitz, Musikabteilung mit Mendelssohn-Archiv.

[16] The most rigorous and yet flexible of these approaches remains Camilla Cai's, as articulated in "Forms Made Miniature: Three Intermezzi of Brahms," in *The Varieties of Musicology: Essays in Honor of Murray Lefkowitz*, ed. John Daverio and John Ogasapian, 135–50 (Warren, MI: Harmonie Park Press, 2000).

approaches, the collapse into familiar material at the end of the *Intermezzo*'s middle section resonates strikingly against the climactically blurred retransitions and recapitulations characteristic of Brahms's sonata-form movements in small- and large-scale genres from the 1860s through the 1880s. Here in Op. 118 No. 6, a formal juncture that had so often witnessed the triumphant recovery of momentum becomes instead a scene of weariness and loss, its generic associations of renewal pointedly displaced by shades of resignation.

As understood by generations of scholars both musical and literary, the technique of allusion operates by bringing separate works into conscious and interpretively productive proximity during the act of listening, reading, or performing. Even allusive borrowings that ultimately emphasize the friction between disparate works or diverging stylistic traditions depend, all the same, upon imagined contact between the old and the new.[17] Yet these two piano miniatures prove remarkably difficult to keep in mind, or under the fingers, at the same time. Motive, harmony, affect, form—along the spectra established by virtually every musical parameter, Brahms's piece departs so quickly and so decisively from Robert's that their shared initial gesture immediately becomes irrelevant, indeed, almost impossible to recall. For this reason, one might justifiably claim that the *Intermezzo* does not allude to the *Stücklein* at all or even borrow from it in any conventional sense. Instead, it effaces it, calling up the barest traces of its memory in the hands of an informed pianist only to annihilate them so thoroughly and so emphatically that—had Brahms's postcard to Theodor Wilhelm not happened to survive—any attempt to argue on behalf of a deliberate connection between them would seem entirely implausible from a music-analytic standpoint alone.

For the only listeners demonstrably aware of the strange kinship, however, the *Intermezzo* soon fulfilled its potential as a dark and overwhelming antipode to Schumann's model. During Brahms's final illness in 1897, Theodor Wilhelm concluded a letter of encouragement with the postscript shown in example 10.10.[18] Through interwoven words and music, Theodor Wilhelm drew all three musicians close at a time of uncertainty by recalling their privately shared insight into Brahms's music. He also figured his wife's sympathetic concern as an obsession with the *Intermezzo*, which had temporarily banished the *Stücklein* from her rep-

---

[17] Christopher Reynolds has written penetratingly concerning such gestures, which he calls "contrastive allusions," in *Motives for Allusion*, 68–87.

[18] Brahms/Engelmann, *Briefwechsel*, 175.

ertoire and, by implication, compromised her musical identity until the composer's recovery. Of course, even within the charming imaginary of a get-well card, Emma could adopt the *Intermezzo* as an emotionally charged opposite to the *Stücklein* only in proportion to the depth of her ongoing familiarity with Schumann's piece—its melody and harmony, its form and affective trajectory, and, most of all, the kinesthetic demands that it placed upon her fingers. The centrality of prior experience with the *Stücklein* in apprehending and interpreting Brahms's borrowing also provides a point of entry in assessing his appeal for the Engelmanns' help in concealing that borrowing from unidentified "others." With Brahms's reputation for compositional craftsmanship at its height in the early 1890s, learning where he got his melodies would surely have interested many listeners. But for one mutual friend of Brahms and the Engelmanns, Schumann's amiable miniature had long carried personal associations against which the *Intermezzo*'s blurred outlines might reveal a sharper edge.

EXAMPLE 10.10   Theodor Wilhelm Engelmann to Johannes Brahms, January 18, 1897. As transcribed by Julius Röntgen (1918).

By the time Clara Schumann received manuscripts of Brahms's latest piano pieces in August 1893, she had known her late husband's *Stücklein* for nearly fifty-five years. She had first encountered it, too, in autograph form, through the mail. Unlike the *Intermezzo*, however, the autograph of the *Stücklein* brought with it a detailed title and specific connections to a particular occasion. The manuscript bore the heading "Wish, for my beloved bride" and was timed to arrive on Christmas Eve, 1838, along with a remarkable letter.[19] Here, twenty-one months before they could actually hope to wed over her father's objections, Robert shared with his secret fiancée a vision of their first Christmas Eve as husband and wife. He presented that day, two years hence, as the end point in an ongoing reorientation of the shared attitudes embodied in their embraces. The clandestine ardor of the mid-1830s had already found calmer expression as the couple came to trust each other; marriage would complete the process as their passion took its place within the domestic exchange of gifts, kisses, and mutual support. As if in assurance of positive changes to come, Robert's hopeful future tense gradually dissolved into the present at the end of his opening paragraph.

---

[19] For details concerning the autograph and compositional history of the *Stücklein*, see McCorkle, *Schumann Werkverzeichnis*, 428 and 430.

God greet you, my sweet girl. You have made Spring around me, and the tips of golden flowers tremble forth, in other words I have been composing since your last letter, I simply cannot get away from music. Here you have my little Christmas gift. You will understand my wish. Do you still remember how you embraced me three years ago on Christmas Eve? Sometimes it was as if you frightened yourself when you gave yourself to me like that. But now it is different, and you rest quietly and securely against my heart and know what you possess. You my love, my dear companion, my gracious future wife—when I open the door now in two years and show you everything I have given you, a bonnet, many playthings, new compositions, then you will embrace me in yet a different way and cry out again and again "how pretty is she who has a husband and one as excellent as you." And then I won't be able to mar your happiness at all, and you will then lead me into your room, where *you* have dressed up and shared your presents: your portrait in miniature, a slate for composing, a sugar slipper that I eat immediately, and many things; for you give me far more than I you, and I know you by this. Happiness! then we become ever quieter, the Christmas tree burns ever dimmer, and kisses are our prayer that it may ever remain so, that good God will keep us together until the end.[20]

Heard in imagined accompaniment to a quiet evening in front of the Christmas tree, the gentle counterpoint between balanced structure and affective flux in Robert's *Stücklein* clarified his vision of an ordered Biedermeyer intimacy. Once established, connections between present music and future married life could ramify in myriad ways as Clara played through the piece. Major mode, moderate tempo, and subdued dynamics all softened the tone and brightened the colors of the projected scene. The choice of A major as tonic key may even have appealed to her unique preferences as a listener and performer, at least as Robert understood them at the time. One day after he had mailed his gift, Clara sent him a surprise package of her own, which happened to include a pair of slippers and a note asking for "a little spark" from his latest compositional projects.[21] The two packages crossed in the mail, and the coincidental alignment of their contents with desires expressed in the letters delighted Robert, as he explained to Clara when her package arrived ten days later: "I think such things, even though lifeless, converse with each other when they meet each other in the mail. 'How do you do, dear slipper,' my letter said there, and it replied 'You come already expected; she loves A major.'"[22] Joking aside, the comment hints that Robert considered the key of his piece particularly appropriate to its extramusical connotations. Above all, the interlocking of the hands across the center of the keyboard could stand as a musical analogue for harmonious partnership. Clara might even have imagined playing the *Stücklein* as a four-hand

---

[20] Clara Wieck and Robert Schumann, *Clara und Robert Schumann: Briefwechsel. Kritische Gesamtausgabe*, ed. Eva Weissweiler, 1:326 (Basel: Stroemfeld/Roter Stern, 1984). Emphasis in original.
[21] Ibid., 325.
[22] Ibid., 332.

duet, with the *primo* player's left hand and the *secondo*'s right inevitably touching as they alternated in measured rhythm, sharing equal and complementary roles in the binding together of melody and bass line. As Robert had put it in his initial letter, "you will understand my wish."

How, then, might Clara have understood the fleeting hints of Robert's music in the initial tones of the *Intermezzo*, if anyone had revealed them to her? By 1893, she had been Brahms's closest friend for nearly forty years. The extent of their physical intimacy during the months following Robert's breakdown in 1854 will always be debated, but the depth and influence of their long-term relationship after his death is indisputable. As explored in chapter 5, they occasionally and quite predictably found themselves at odds over the nature of Brahms's complicated connection with the Schumann family. Their last and most explicit argument over the issue had come to a head just recently, in September 1892, when Brahms used an ongoing disagreement concerning the publication of Robert's D-minor symphony in its original version as a point of entry into overtly emotional terrain that he had usually striven to avoid, at least in prose. To make matters more uncomfortable, he chose to write on September 13, Clara's birthday. In stark contrast to the many delicate musical offerings he had provided around this date in previous years—among them manuscripts of the F♯-minor *Capriccio* and the two *Regenlieder*—his words now positioned him bluntly as an outcast from her circle, wrongfully rejected and grimly resigned to his fate:

> Permit even a poor outsider to tell you today that he thinks of you with always the same devotion and wishes you, the person most important to him, everything good, dear, and beautiful, from a full heart. Unfortunately, I am an outsider to you more than any other. This I have long perceived and painfully, only had not expected that it would be expressed so bitterly. You know that I cannot acknowledge the completely superficial cause (the publication of the symphony). Years ago already I have perceived exactly the same thing, silently but deeply—when the Schumann piano pieces that I first edited were not accepted in the complete works edition. Both times I could only think that you did not find it congenial to see my name there; much as I would like to, I cannot find or admit another reason....It is harsh, after 40 years of faithful service (or whatever you want to call my relationship with you), to be no more than "one more bad experience." Well, it will be endured, I am used to loneliness and ought to be at the thought of this great emptiness. But I may repeat to you today that you and your husband are for me the most beautiful experience of my life and represent its greatest treasure and its noblest content.[23]

Since it offers unparalleled access to long-simmering tensions, Brahms's outburst has been featured prominently in biographies dating back to Kalbeck's.

---

[23] Brahms/Schumann, *Briefe* 2:476–77. Parentheses original.

Chief among the composer's weapons were Clara's own words, "one more bad experience," which were apparently spoken in frustration at his intractability during their last visit together. Her ensuing response is less frequently quoted but just as revealing. After systematically refuting each of Brahms's complaints, she begged them both, in words that parodied the finale to Beethoven's Ninth Symphony, to put aside their hurt feelings, and she asked him to send her copies of the piano miniatures from Op. 116, about which she had heard rumors from her student Ilona Eibenschütz: "So let us then, dear Johannes, again intone friendlier tones, to which end your beautiful new piano pieces that Ilona wrote me about offer the best opportunity, if you are willing!"[24] The implication was clear: renewed prepublication access to Brahms's piano music was the most fitting recompense for his unusually explicit attack. Brahms obliged, sending autographs of new *Klavierstücke* regularly, as he completed them, over the ensuing year. Yet to an informed connoisseur of Robert's A-major *Stücklein*, the E♭ minor *Intermezzo* was no peace offering. To the contrary, one can easily imagine Clara perceiving in its destruction of its tender predecessor an outsider's bitter commentary on the fraught distance between her marriage, idealized in memory, and the frustrations of their own ongoing interchange. Recognizing the connection between the pieces could well have come to feel like the resumption of a struggle that she thought had already ended, an unprovoked assault made all the more damaging because it would issue forth from beneath her own hands at the keyboard.

For his part, Brahms was most likely familiar with Robert's original autograph of the *Stücklein*. He had advised Clara closely, both in person and via correspondence, throughout her own editing of her late husband's piano music for Breitkopf and Härtel's complete works edition in the late 1870s and early 1880s. A decade later, in the aftermath of their fraught exchange in September 1892, he had gradually convinced her to include several of Robert's more obscure works in a supplemental volume to the complete edition, the selection and editing of which she then left largely to him. Brahms seems to have finished much of the task by January 1893, but it was still on his mind when he visited Clara at her Frankfurt home in February, in part because he had just sent copies of his edited versions to the publisher and in part because Clara had just decided to reject a piece he had hoped to include.[25] In search of alternatives, he may well have pored over her collection of

[24] See ibid., 478.
[25] The piece in question was the duet *Sommerruh*; only in late June 1893 did Brahms convince Clara to change her mind and include it after all. Extant correspondence preserves plentiful evidence of his work on the supplemental volume, from the first glimmerings of the idea in October 1892 to its publication in July 1893. Nearly every letter he and Clara exchanged during those months mentions the volume in one way or another (Brahms/Schumann, *Briefe* 2:478–519). For other relevant letters, see Brahms, Breitkopf & Härtel, et al., *Briefwechsel*, 409–10.

autographs at that time, within months of composing the *Intermezzo*. Moreover, it is absolutely certain that he had done so on numerous earlier occasions. Clara herself had long acknowledged his expertise regarding her family's musical treasures, which at times exceeded her own. In 1878, baffled by an unsigned piano piece that had surfaced among her effects, she had actually recommended to her daughters Marie and Eugenie that they ask Brahms instead. Her explanation was telling: "I believe that Brahms, who knows every scrap of paper I possess and has rummaged through everything, will perhaps know to whom it belongs."[26]

Whether Brahms's rummaging extended beyond musical manuscripts is more difficult to corroborate independently. He and Clara had discussed correspondence dating from her courtship in connection with an edition of Robert's early letters that she released in 1885, with help from Heinrich von Herzogenberg.[27] Clara first informed Brahms of the edition in August 1885 and promised a longer conversation about it in person; unfortunately, none of his replies from this period survive, but the topic did surface again the following July, when her publisher was pressuring her to capitalize on the success of the collection by issuing a sequel.[28] Although Clara never published Robert's extraordinary Christmas letter, Brahms's exposure to either its gist or its specific contents seems probable, given his long access to the family papers and the many opportunities at which it might have come up in conversation. In any case, the date of Robert's original autograph, its title, and its dedication "for my beloved bride" would have been more than enough to allow Brahms to discern the broad contours of her likely attitudes toward Robert's *Stücklein* and, therefore, to predict essential aspects of her possible responses to his own veiled borrowing. Put simply, for Clara Schumann, the *Intermezzo* carried the hidden potential to reopen old wounds, and Brahms most likely knew it.

Yet he ultimately sought to shield her from its effects. The Engelmanns seem to have kept their silence, for surviving documents indicate that the piece brought Clara nothing but enjoyment. Her own diary placed the *Intermezzo* among a group of Brahms's works that she practiced again and again as means of distracting herself from a bout of depression in October 1893. As much as any extant letter, her private, self-directed prose hints at her attachment to the physical act of playing his music: "How I thank him again for this balm that he

---

[26] Eugenie Schumann, *Erinnerungen*, 258. Ironically, the unknown piece was itself one of Brahms's practical jokes: having retained some old manuscript paper with Clara's signature on it, he had written new music in imitation of her youthful style and enlisted her daughters' help in planting the result amid her papers.

[27] Clara Schumann, ed., *Jugendbriefe von Robert Schumann* (Leipzig: Breitkopf & Härtel, 1885). Regarding Heinrich's contributions, see Wiechert, *Heinrich von Herzogenberg*, 54.

[28] Brahms/Schumann, *Briefe* 2:291 and 304–6.

prepares for me in the midst of my deep sadness! How uplifted I always feel, when I can thus forget myself completely for half an hour."[29] Furthermore, every relative who published recollections of Clara's last years accorded the *Intermezzo* pride of place among Brahms's late piano miniatures. In a diary entry from September 1895, her grandson Ferdinand recalled that Clara extolled the work as a special exemplar of the composer's skill, holding it up as proof of his superiority to his contemporaries: "She often calls the Eb-minor Intermezzo from Op. 118 a piece exceptional even for Brahms himself. Often she speaks crabbily when she reads or hears people say that one could place Rubinstein at Brahms's side as a creative personality. 'Brahms has no rivals and stands alone among the living.'"[30] And within four months of moving in with his grandmother in 1894, Ferdinand had already noted that the piece was among her most frequent choices at the keyboard.[31]

Most important, of Brahms's many piano pieces, the *Intermezzo* was the second of two that Clara played for the composer at her home in October 1895, at what turned out to be their final meeting. Her daughter Eugenie described entering the room after hearing music through the door:

> The next morning I heard Mama play: Prelude and Fugue plus Pastoral (both for organ) by Bach, then Romanze in F major and Intermezzo in Eb minor Opus 118 by Brahms. A while after she had stopped playing, I went in the music room. Mama sat sideways at her writing desk; her cheeks were gently reddened and her eye glowed as if with inner light. Brahms sat across from her and looked weak and deeply moved. "Your mother has played magnificently for me," he said.[32]

In Eugenie's account, both musicians are moved, but in opposite directions: blood rushes to her face as it drains from his. Their contrasting physical responses ascribe disparate rhetorical functions to the same music, functions that resonate in tune with my speculations as to Brahms's motives. For Clara, deliberately kept ignorant of his veiled borrowing and its potential implications, the performance is a triumph of skill over the passage of time, a reassurance that her aging fingers could still master her old friend's music and her artistry could still touch his heart. For Brahms, the act of listening acknowledges the cost at which the mind rejects its darker impulses. By placing in her hands a secret talisman of their conflict, he inflicts upon himself emotional injuries once meant for her and thereby achieves a painful détente with his long-standing grievance. Through the desolate tones of his own music, he renegotiates once more the

[29] Litzmann, *Clara Schumann* 3:573.
[30] Ferdinand Schumann, "Erinnerungen an Johannes Brahms, 1894, 1895, 1896," *Neue Zeitschrift für Musik* 82/28 (July 15, 1915): 241.
[31] Ferdinand Schumann, "Erinnerungen an Clara Schumann, Tagebuchblätter ihres Enkels," *Neue Zeitschrift für Musik* 84/10 (March 8, 1917): 77.
[32] Eugenie Schumann, *Erinnerungen*, 271.

inner boundaries of his deepest relationship and recasts his erotic solitude as chivalric self-restraint.

As an interpretation of Brahms's compositional strategy and emotional commitments, this reading of the E♭-minor *Intermezzo* remains, at best, merely plausible. Contrasting scenarios could also account for extant evidence regarding the design of the piece and the contexts in which Brahms discussed its construction. To varying degrees, the same is true of every case study in this book. Documentary evidence as to the precise state of any interpersonal dynamic is inevitably fragmentary, particularly when viewed in retrospect. Moreover, by virtue of the kinds of sources that tend to survive, it is usually far easier to identify the words and music that enflamed tensions within a given milieu than it is to chart the measured acts of sound and silence that brought about reconciliation or maintained the status quo. Yet only amid the give and take of stable, long-term relationships could Brahms's music fully engage the varieties of rhetorical potential instantiated in the minds and bodies of the musicians around him. Where surviving evidence permits even its fragmentary reconstruction, that potential can reshape our understanding of his social sphere and his compositional methods alike.

To reshape is not necessarily to overturn. Taken individually, the analyses presented here rarely necessitate a radical overhaul of our common assumptions regarding Brahms's personality or compositional preferences. Indeed, most chapters either deepen or complement the curve of his biography as it has already been inscribed through more than a century of scholarly debate. Virtually every established facet of his mature personality casts its reflection somewhere among the pages of this volume: craftsman, lover, misogynist, scholar, reluctant pedagogue, frustrated Liberal, gregarious prankster, sympathetic consoler. Sustained patterns of kindness and concern vis-à-vis the Joachims, the Fabers, and the Schumanns find a familiar counterbalance in the fractures and failures endemic in interchange with the Stockhausens, the Herzogenbergs, and Agathe von Siebold. Furthermore, to scholars of his life and oeuvre it will come as no surprise that Brahms's craft was deeply intertwined with his understanding of earlier repertoire, that his music sometimes played important roles in the unfolding drama of his interpersonal relationships, or that he might occasionally have preferred to substitute compositional puzzles for the challenges of face-to-face negotiation.

What emerges from the aggregate mosaic of these studies is therefore an image not of Brahms's circumstances or inclinations per se, but of the specific mechanisms by which circumstance and inclination informed the creation and reception of his music. The clarity of that image fluctuates depending upon the degree to which extant documents can be made to illuminate the potential perspectives of his acquaintances, which have traditionally been construed in significantly less detail than Brahms's own. When approached as historically situated agents in their own right rather than mere foils for their more famous colleague, those acquaintances emerge as crucial figures without whom subsequently canonical repertoire would likely have been constructed differently—if, indeed, it existed at all. In an era before recorded sound, their memories and habits of listening and performance provided the multivalent substrate for a complex and idiosyncratic manner of persuasion and self-evaluation in intimate musical genres. Through the technique of concise, polyphonically imbricated, and kinesthetically marked allusion, Brahms was able to conjure up and manipulate the prior musical experiences and interpretive attitudes characteristic of his various interlocutors, creating finely tuned emotional landscapes within which they and he might vicariously explore issues at the core of their mutual relationships: familial allegiance, religious and political identity, professional collaboration and dysfunction, romantic attachment, joy and depression.

These emotional landscapes were inherently private, foundational to but ultimately separate from the ongoing generic and stylistic conversations that Brahms's music stimulated upon its publication. There is no reason to assume that they pervaded more than a fraction of his output, or that their contours were ever intended to be mapped by any wider group of critics, scholars, or musicians, either in the nineteenth century or today. Once reopened, however, such landscapes suggest a profound reorientation in the historiography of allusion. They appeal to modes of inquiry—rhetorical, tactile, ethnographic— that have long been undervalued in musicological and music-analytic discourse on nineteenth-century music. From those accustomed to cynicism, they demand respect for the power of sentiment and the intricacy of human relations. Most of all, they call us to focus on the particular rather than the general: to ask, first and foremost, not what a given musical gesture "means" or which broader patterns of cultural production it exemplifies but, instead, for whom it might have been designed and how it might have functioned subjectively, for that person alone.

Questions of this kind will not always lead to satisfying answers. Much of Brahms's compositional workshop remains forever inaccessible, concealed even from his most trusted associates and, hence, from those of us today who pore over surviving correspondence, musical manuscripts, and other documents from within his circles. By the same token, his motivations for musical borrowing were manifold and unpredictable. Even if we could somehow differentiate deliberate borrowings from happenstance resemblances using music-analytic criteria alone, the majority of those borrowings probably were not meant to serve allusive ends for any audience, large or small. But given sufficient evidence from both musical and documentary sources, the collection of allusive gestures investigated here offers the chance to plausibly reconstruct and imaginatively inhabit the intersections of aesthetic perception and social praxis among members of a tight-knit musical community increasingly distant from our own. Analogous opportunities may well await us in the works and interpersonal exchanges of other composers who made music amid the claims of friendship.

BIBLIOGRAPHY

Autograph Materials

Anonymous. Copyist's manuscript of Johannes Brahms, *Alte Liebe*, Op. 72 No. 1. Mus. Ms. 1523. Universitäts- und Landesbibliothek, Darmstadt.

Anonymous. Copyist's manuscript of Johannes Brahms, arrangement of Franz Schubert's *Greisen-Gesang*, D. 778, for voice and orchestra. MS. Coll. 97. Rare Book and Manuscript Library, University of Pennsylvania.

Anonymous. Two handwritten partbooks containing repertoire from the Hamburger Frauenchor. Photostats in the Sophie Hutchinson Drinker Papers, Sophia Smith Collection. Smith College, Northampton, MA.

Brahms, Johannes. *Adagio espressivo.* Autograph musical fragment in a letter to Clara Schumann (1879). Bra: A1: 13. Brahms-Institut an der Musikhochschule Lübeck.

Brahms, Johannes. *Allegro con espressione.* Autograph Albumblatt in the scrapbook of Arnold Wehner. Sold at auction by Doyle Auction Galleries, New York. Facsimile available online via www.doylenewyork.com, catalogue for April 20, 2011, Lot 228.

Brahms, Johannes. *Alte Liebe*, Op. 72 No. 1. Autograph. FRKF 870, Friedrich R. Koch Collection. Beinecke Rare Book and Manuscript Library, Yale University, New Haven, CT.

Brahms, Johannes. Arrangement of Franz Schubert's *Greisen-Gesang*, D. 778, for voice and orchestra. Autograph. Private owner. Partial facsimile in *Schubert: Sechs Lieder für Singstimme und Orchester, bearbeitet von Johannes Brahms*, edited by Peter Jost. Leipzig: Breitkopf & Härtel, 2000.

Brahms, Johannes. *Auf dem Kirchhofe*, Op. 105 No. 4. Autograph. Musiksammlung, MH 5500/c. Wienbiblothek im Rathaus, Vienna.

Brahms, Johannes. *Capriccio*, Op. 76 No. 1. Autograph. Music Deposit 17. Gilmore Music Library, Yale University, New Haven, CT.

Brahms, Johannes. *Ein Sonett*, Op. 14 No. 4. Autograph. Bra: A1: 4. Brahms-Institut an der Musikhochschule Lübeck.

Brahms, Johannes. Handwritten inventory of the composer's published music through Opus 79. Handschriftensammlung. Wienbiblothek im Rathaus, Vienna.

Brahms, Johannes. *Intermezzo*, Op. 118 No. 6. Autograph. Preußicher Kulturbesitz, Musikabteilung mit Mendelssohn-Archiv, Mus. ms. autogr. J. Brahms 12. Staatsbibliothek, Berlin.

Brahms, Johannes. Letters to Theodor Wilhelm and Emma Engelmann. Preußicher Kulturbesitz, Musikabteilung mit Mendelssohn-Archiv, Mus. ep. Brahms, J. 27, 68, and 79. Staatsbibliothek, Berlin.

Brahms, Johannes. *Meine Liebe ist grün*, Op. 63 No. 5. Autograph. Private owner, Vienna.

Brahms, Johannes. *O schöne Nacht*, Op. 92 No. 1, initial version (1877). Autograph. Universitätsbibliothek, Leipzig. Partial facsimile in *Johannes Brahms: Neue Ausgabe sämtlicher Werke VI/2: Chorwerke und Vokalquartette mit Klavier oder Orgel. II*, edited by Bernd Wiechert. Munich: Henle, 2008.

Brahms, Johannes. Piano Trio, Op. 87. Autograph. Library of Congress. Facsimile in *Johannes Brahms Autographs: Facsimiles of Eight Manuscripts in the Library of Congress*, edited by George Bozarth. New York: Garland, 1983.

Brahms, Johannes. Pocket Calendars with autograph entries. Handschriftensammlung. Wienbiblothek im Rathaus, Vienna.

Brahms, Johannes. *Regenlied*, Op. 59 No. 3. Autograph. ML96.B813 no. 1, accession no. 1371315. Sibley Music Library at the Eastman School of Music. University of Rochester, Rochester, NY.

Brahms, Johannes. Taschenbücher (autograph collections of song texts). Handschriftensammlung. Wienbiblothek im Rathaus, Vienna.

Brahms, Johannes. Untitled musical fragment. Autograph, in a notebook dated 1854. Musiksammlung, MH 3912/c. Wienbiblothek im Rathaus, Vienna.

Brahms, Johannes. *Unüberwindlich*, Op. 72 No. 5. Autograph. Mus. Ms. 1522. Universitäts- und Landesbibliothek, Darmstadt.

Brahms, Johannes. Violin Sonata, Op. 78. Autograph. Musiksammlung, MH 3908. Wienbibliothek im Rathaus, Vienna.

Brahms, Johannes. *Wenn um den Holunder*, Op. 63 No. 6. Autograph. Autographensammlung Geigy–Hagenbach, 2451. Universitätsbibliothek, Basel.

Faber, Bertha (née Porubsky). Handwritten partbook containing repertoire from the Hamburger Frauenchor. BRA: Af2. Staats- und Universitätsbibliothek, Hamburg.

Graupner, Christoph. *Befiehl du deine Wege*. Autograph. Mus. Ms. 435/24. Universitäts- und Landesbibliothek, Darmstadt.

Groth, Klaus. *Hundert Blätter: Paralipomena zum Quickborn* (Hamburg: Perthes-Besser & Mauke, 1854), with annotations by the author. Brahms Nachlaß. Vienna: Gesellschaft der Musikfreunde.

Herzogenberg, Elisabeth von. *Volkskinderlieder*. Copyist's manuscript (1881) with annotations by the composer. Brahms Nachlaß, VI 36483. Vienna: Gesellschaft der Musikfreunde.

Hlavaczek, Franz. Engraver's model for Johannes Brahms, *Alte Liebe*, Op. 72 No. 1, with annotations by the composer. Bra: A2: 31. Brahms-Institut an der Musikhochschule Lübeck.

Hlavaczek, Franz. Engraver's model for Johannes Brahms, *Es liebt sich so lieblich im Lenze*, Op. 71 No. 1, with annotations by the composer. Bra: A2: 29. Brahms-Institut an der Musikhochschule Lübeck.

Keller, Robert. Engraver's model for Johannes Brahms, *Alte Liebe*, Op. 72 No. 1, transposed for high voice, with annotations by the composer. Bra: A2: 32. Brahms-Institut an der Musikhochschule Lübeck.

Keller, Robert. Engraver's model for Johannes Brahms, *Es liebt sich so lieblich im Lenze*, Op. 71 No. 1, transposed for low voice, with annotations by the composer. Bra: A2: 30. Brahms-Institut an der Musikhochschule Lübeck.

Kupfer, William. Engraver's model for Johannes Brahms, *Geistliches Wiegenlied*, Op. 91 No. 2, with annotations by the composer. Bra: A2: 40. Brahms-Institut an der Musikhochschule Lübeck.

Rückert, Friedrich. *Gesammelte Gedichte*. Erlangen: Carl Heyder, 1837. Vol. 4, with annotations by Johannes Brahms. Brahms Nachlaß. Vienna: Gesellschaft der Musikfreunde.

Schumann, Clara. *Romanze*, Op. 5 No. 3. Autograph (1836). Preußicher Kulturbesitz, Musikabteilung mit Mendelssohn-Archiv, Staatsbibliothek, Berlin. Partial facsimile in Ingrid Bodsch and Gerd Nauhaus, *Clara Schumann 1819–1896 Katalog zur Ausstellung*. Bonn: Stadtmuseum Bonn, 1996.

Schumann, Clara. *Romanze*, Op. 5 No. 3. Autograph (1838). Vienna: Gesellschaft der Musikfreunde. Partial facsimile in Ingrid Bodsch and Gerd Nauhaus, *Clara Schumann 1819–1896 Katalog zur Ausstellung*. Bonn: Stadtmuseum Bonn, 1996.

Schumann, Clara. *Romanze* (WoO, 1856). Vienna: Gesellschaft der Musikfreunde. Partial facsimile in Ingrid Bodsch and Gerd Nauhaus, *Clara Schumann 1819–1896 Katalog zur Ausstellung*. Bonn: Stadtmuseum Bonn, 1996.

Schumann, Robert. *Liederkreis*, Op. 39. 1st ed. Vienna: Haslinger, 1842. With autograph corrections by the composer. Special Collections. Sibley Music Library, Eastman School of Music, Rochester, NY.

Schumann, Robert. Miscellaneous piano works, including *Faschingsschwank aus Wien*, Op. 26. Bound collection of printed scores, signed and annotated by Johannes Brahms. Brahms Nachlaß, VII 48826. Vienna: Gesellschaft der Musikfreunde.

Schumann, Robert. Variations in E♭ major ("Geister-Variationen"), WoO 24. Autograph. Private owner. Facsimile in Walter Beck, *Robert Schumann und seine Geister-Variationen: Ein Lebensbericht mit Notenbild und neuen Dokumenten*. Tutzing: Schneider, 1992.

Völkers, Marie. Handwritten partbook containing repertoire from the Hamburger Frauenchor. Photostat in the Sophie Hutchinson Drinker Papers, Sophia Smith Collection. Smith College, Northampton, MA.

Nineteenth-Century Journals

Berliner allgemeine musikalische Zeitung
Deutsche Rundschau
Die Gegenwart: Wochenschrift für Literatur, Kunst und öffentliches Leben
Die Musik
[Leipziger] Allgemeine musikalische Zeitung
Musical World
Musical Times
Musikalisches Wochenblatt
Neue Freie Presse
Neue Zeitschrift für Musik
Neues Wiener Tagblatt
Sammlung Musikalischer Vorträge
Schweizerische Musikzeitung
Vierteljahrsschrift für Musikwissenschaft
Wiener Zeitung

Digital Archives and Digital Resources

Brahms-Institut an der Musikhochschule Lübeck. "Brahms digital." Accessed August 1, 2013. http://www.brahms–institut.de/web/bihl_digital/archive_index.html.

Doyle New York. "Books, Photographs & Prints—Sale 11BP01—Lot 228" (auction catalogue containing a facsimile of the autograph of Brahms's *Allegro con espressione*). Accessed August 1, 2013. http://www.doylenewyork.com/asp/fullcatalogue.asp?salelot=11BP01+++228+&refno=++802656#.

Loeb Music Library. "Digital Scores and Libretti." Accessed August 1, 2013. http://vc.lib.harvard.edu/vc/deliver/home?_collection=scores.

Österreichische Nationalbibliothek. "ANNO: AustriaN Newspapers Online." Accessed August 1, 2013. http://anno.onb.ac.at/index.htm.

Sibley Music Library at the Eastman School of Music, University of Rochester. "Sibley Digitized Material." Accessed August 1, 2013. https://urresearch.rochester.edu/viewInstitutionalCollection.action?collectionId=25.

Universitäts– und Landesbibliothek Darmstadt. "Digitale Sammlungen, Musikhandschriften." Accessed August 1, 2013. http://tudigit.ulb.tu–darmstadt.de/show/sammlung23.

Published Correspondence

Billroth, Theodor, and Johannes Brahms. *Billroth und Brahms im Briefwechsel: Mit Einleitung, Anmerkungen und 4 Bildtafeln*. Edited by Otto Gottlieb-Billroth. Berlin and Vienna: Urban & Schwarzenberg, 1935.

Brahms, Johannes. *Briefe an Joseph Viktor Widmann, Ellen und Ferdinand Vetter, Adolf Schubring*. Edited by Max Kalbeck. *Johannes Brahms: Briefwechsel, VIII*. Berlin: Deutsche Brahms-Gesellschaft, 1915.

Brahms, Johannes. *Briefe an P. J. Simrock und Fritz Simrock*. 4 vols. Edited by Max Kalbeck. *Johannes Brahms: Briefwechsel, IX–XII*. Berlin: Deutsche Brahms-Gesellschaft, 1917–19.

Brahms, Johannes, and Theodor Wilhelm Engelmann. *Johannes Brahms im Briefwechsel mit Th. Wilhelm Engelmann*. Edited by Julius Röntgen. *Johannes Brahms: Briefwechsel, XIII*. Berlin: Deutsche Brahms-Gesellschaft, 1918.

Brahms, Johannes, and Julius Otto Grimm. *Johannes Brahms im Briefwechsel mit J. O. Grimm*. Edited by Richard Barth. *Johannes Brahms: Briefwechsel, IV*. Berlin: Deutsche Brahms-Gesellschaft, 1908.

Brahms, Johannes, and Klaus Groth. *Briefe der Freundschaft: Johannes Brahms–Klaus Groth*. Edited by Volquart Pauls. Heide, Schleswig-Holstein: Westholsteinische Verlagsdruckerei Boyens & Co., 1956.

Brahms, Johannes, and Elisabeth von Herzogenberg and Heinrich von Herzogenberg. *Johannes Brahms im Briefwechsel mit Heinrich und Elisabet von Herzogenberg*. 2 vols. Edited by Max Kalbeck. *Johannes Brahms: Briefwechsel, I–II*. Berlin: Deutsche Brahms-Gesellschaft, 1907.

Brahms, Johannes, and Joseph Joachim. *Johannes Brahms im Briefwechsel mit Joseph Joachim*. 2 vols. Edited by Andreas Moser. *Johannes Brahms: Briefwechsel, V–VI*. Berlin: Deutsche Brahms-Gesellschaft, 1908.

Brahms, Johannes, and Clara Schumann. *Briefe aus den Jahren 1853–1896: Im Auftrage von Marie Schumann*. 2 vols. Edited by Berthold Litzmann. Leipzig: Breitkopf & Härtel, 1927.

Brahms, Johannes, and Julius Stockhausen. *Johannes Brahms im Briefwechsel mit Julius Stockhausen*. Edited by Renate Hofmann. *Johannes–Brahms–Briefwechsel, Neue Folge, XVIII*, edited by Otto Biba and Kurt and Renate Hofmann. Tutzing: Schneider, 1993.

Brahms, Johannes et al. *Johannes Brahms im Briefwechsel mit Breitkopf und Härtel, Bartolf Senff, J. Rieter-Biedermann, C. F. Peters, E. W. Fritzsch und Robert Lienau*. Edited by Wilhelm Altmann. *Johannes Brahms: Briefwechsel, XIV*. Berlin: Deutsche Brahms-Gesellschaft, 1920.

Brahms, Johannes et al. *Johannes Brahms im Briefwechsel mit Hermann Levi, Friedrich Gernsheim sowie den Familien Hecht und Fellinger*. Edited by Leopold Schmidt. *Johannes Brahms: Briefwechsel, VII*. Berlin: Deutsche Brahms-Gesellschaft, 1910.

Brahms, Johannes et al. *Johannes Brahms im Briefwechsel mit Philipp Spitta und Offo Dessoff*. Edited by Carl Krebs. *Johannes Brahms: Briefwechsel, XVI*. Berlin: Deutsche Brahms-Gesellschaft, 1920.

Brahms, Johannes et al. *Johannes Brahms in seiner Familie: Der Briefwechsel*. Edited by Kurt Stephenson. Hamburg: Dr. Ernst Hauswedell & Co., 1973.

Fontane, Theodor. *Briefe I: Briefe an den Vater, die Mutter, und die Frau*. Edited by Kurt Schreiner and Charlotte Jolles. Berlin: Propyläen, 1968.

Fontane, Theodor et al. *Theodor Fontane und Martha Fontane: ein Familienbriefnetz*. Edited by Regina Dieterle. *Schriften der Theodor–Fontane–Gesellschaft IV*. Berlin: de Gruyter, 2002.

Joachim, Joseph et al. *Briefe von und an Joachim.* 3 vols. Edited by Johannes Joachim and Andreas Moser. Berlin: Julius Bard, 1912.

Simrock, Fritz. *Johannes Brahms und Fritz Simrock: Weg einer Freundschaft. Briefe des Verlegers an den Komponisten. Veröffentlichungen aus der Hamburger Staats– und Universitäts-Bibliothek, VI.* Edited by Kurt Stephenson. Hamburg: J. J. Augustin, 1961.

Schumann, Robert, and Clara Wieck. *Clara und Robert Schumann: Briefwechsel. Kritische Gesamtausgabe.* Edited by Eva Weissweiler. Basel: Stroemfeld/Roter Stern, 1984.

Studies and Scores

Altmann, Wilhelm. "Brahms im Briefwechsel mit dem Ehepaar Herzogenberg." *Die Musik* 6/16 (1907): 228–33.

Altmann, Wilhelm. "Heinrich von Herzogenberg, sein Leben und Schaffen." *Die Musik* 2/19 (1903): 28–47.

Arnim, Achim von, and Clemens Brentano. *Kinderlieder: Anhang zum Wunderhorn.* Heidelberg: Mohr und Zimmer, 1808.

Avins, Styra. *Johannes Brahms: Life and Letters.* Oxford: Oxford University Press, 1997.

Avins, Styra. "Performing Brahms's Music: Clues from His Letters." In *Performing Brahms: Early Evidence of Performance Style,* edited by Michael Musgrave and Bernard D. Sherman, 11–47. Cambridge: Cambridge University Press, 2003.

Balassa, Ottilie von. *Die Brahmsfreundin Ottilie Ebner und ihr Kreis.* Vienna: Franz Bondy, 1933.

Beck, Walter. *Robert Schumann und seine Geister-Variationen: Ein Lebensbericht mit Notenbild und neuen Dokumenten.* Tutzing: Schneider, 1992.

Behr, Johannes. *Johannes Brahms—Vom Ratgeber zum Kompositionslehrer: Eine Untersuchung in Fallstudien.* Kassel: Bärenreiter, 2007.

Bell, A. Craig. *Brahms—The Vocal Music.* London: Associated University Presses, 1996.

Beller-McKenna, Daniel. *Brahms and the German Spirit.* Cambridge, MA: Harvard University Press, 2004.

Beller-McKenna, Daniel. "Distance and Disembodiment: Harps, Horns, and the Requiem Idea in Schumann and Brahms." *Journal of Musicology* 22 (2005): 47–89.

Beller-McKenna, Daniel. "How 'deutsch' a Requiem? Absolute Music, Universality, and the Reception of Brahms's 'Ein Deutsches Requiem,' Op. 45." *19th-Century Music* 22 (1998): 3–19.

Beller-McKenna, Daniel. "*Verlorene Jugend*: The Backwards Glance in Brahms's Late Choral Lieder." Paper presented at the annual meeting of the American Musicological Society, Washington, 2005.

Berger, Anna Maria Busse. *Medieval Music and the Art of Memory.* Berkeley: University of California Press, 2005.

Berry, Paul. "Old Love: Johannes Brahms, Clara Schumann, and the Poetics of Musical Memory." *Journal of Musicology* 24 (2007): 77–112.

Beythien, Jürgen. "Die Violinsonate in G-Dur, Op. 78, von Johannes Brahms—Ein Beitrag zum Verhältnis zwischen Formaler und Inhaltlicher Gestaltung." In *Bericht über den Internationalen Musikwissenschaftlichen Kongress Leipzig 1966*, edited by Carl Dahlhaus et al., 325–32. Kassel: Bärenreiter, 1970.

Bodsch, Ingrid, and Gerd Nauhaus. *Clara Schumann 1819–1896 Katalog zur Ausstellung.* Bonn: Stadtmuseum Bonn, 1996.

Borchard, Beatrix. *Stimme und Geige, Amalie and Joseph Joachim: Biographie und Interpretationsgeschichte.* Vienna: Böhlau, 2005.

Botstein, Leon. "Brahms and Nineteenth-Century Painting." *19th-Century Music* 14 (1990): 154–68.

Botstein, Leon, ed. *The Compleat Brahms.* New York: Norton, 1999.

Botstein, Leon. "Music and Ideology: Thoughts on Bruckner." *Musical Quarterly* 80 (1996): 1–11.

Botstein, Leon. "Time and Memory: Concert Life, Science, and Music in Brahms's Vienna." In *Brahms and His World*, edited by Walter Frisch and Kevin Karnes, 3–26. Rev. ed. Princeton, NJ: Princeton University Press, 2009.

Bottge, Karen. "Brahms's Wiegenlied and the Maternal Voice." *19th-Century Music* 28 (2005): 185–213.

Bozarth, George. "Brahms's Lieder Inventory of 1859–60 and Other Documents of His Life and Work." *Fontes Artis Musicae* 30 (1983): 98–117.

Bozarth, George. "Brahms's *Lieder ohne Worte*: The 'Poetic' Andantes of the Piano Sonatas." In *Brahms Studies: Analytical and Historical Perspectives*, edited by George Bozarth, 345–378. Oxford: Clarendon Press, 1990.

Bozarth, George. "The First Generation of Brahms Manuscript Collections." *Notes* 40 (1983): 239–62.

Bozarth, George, ed. *Johannes Brahms Autographs: Facsimiles of Eight Manuscripts in the Library of Congress.* New York: Garland, 1983.

Bozarth, George. *Johannes Brahms and George Henschel: An Enduring Friendship.* Sterling Heights, Michigan: Harmonie Park Press, 2008.

Bozarth, George. "Johannes Brahms und die Liedersammlungen von David Gregor Corner, Karl Severin Meister und Friedrich Wilhelm Arnold." *Die Musikforschung* 36 (1983): 177–99.

Bozarth, George. "The 'Lieder' of Johannes Brahms—1868–1871: Studies in Chronology and Compositional Process." PhD diss., Princeton University, 1978.

Bozarth, George, and Wiltrud Martin, eds. *The Brahms–Keller Correspondence.* Lincoln: University of Nebraska Press, 1996.

Bloom, Harold. *Anxiety of Influence: A Theory of Poetry.* Oxford: Oxford University Press, 1973.

Bloom, Harold. *A Map of Misreading.* Oxford: Oxford University Press, 1985.

Brachmann, Jan. *Kunst—Religion—Krise: Der Fall Brahms.* Kassel: Bärenreiter, 2003.

Braus, Ira. "Poetic–Musical Rhetoric in Brahms's *Auf dem Kirchhofe.*" *Theory and Practice* 13 (1988): 15–30.

Braus, Ira. "Textual Rhetoric and Harmonic Anomaly in Selected Lieder of Johannes Brahms." PhD diss., Harvard University, 1988.

Brentano, Clemens. *Gedichte: In neuer Auswahl.* 2nd ed. Frankfurt am Main: J. D. Sauer-länder, 1861.

Brinkmann, Reinhold. *Late Idyll: The Second Symphony of Johannes Brahms.* Translated by Peter Palmer. Cambridge, MA: Harvard University Press, 1995.

Brodbeck, David. "Brahms." In *The Nineteenth-Century Symphony*, edited by D. Kern Holoman, 224–72. New York: Schirmer, 1997.

Brodbeck, David. "The Brahms-Joachim Counterpoint Exchange: or, Robert, Clara, and 'the Best Harmony between Jos. and Joh.'" In *Brahms Studies 1*, edited by David Brodbeck, 30–80. Lincoln: University of Nebraska Press, 1994.

Brodbeck, David. *Brahms: Symphony No. 1.* Cambridge: Cambridge University Press, 1997.

Brodbeck, David. "Dvořák's Reception in Liberal Vienna: Language Ordinances, National Property, and the Rhetoric of Deutschtum." *Journal of the American Musi-cological Society* 60 (2007): 71–132.

Brodbeck, David. "Medium and Meaning: New Aspects of the Chamber Music." In *The Cambridge Companion to Brahms*, edited by Michael Musgrave, 98–132. Cambridge: Cambridge University Press, 1999.

Bromen, Stefan. *Studien zu den Klaviertranskriptionen Schumannscher Lieder von Franz Liszt, Clara Schumann, und Carl Reinecke. Schumann-Studien, Sonderband 1.* Edited by Gerd Nauhaus, through the Robert-Schumann-Gesellschaft, Zwickau. Sinzig: Studio, 1997.

Brown, Clive. "Joachim's Violin Playing and the Performance of Brahms's String Music." In *Performing Brahms: Early Evidence of Performance Style*, edited by Michael Mus-grave and Bernard D. Sherman, 48–98. Cambridge: Cambridge University Press, 2003.

Budde, Elmar. "Brahms oder der Versuch, das Ende zu denken." In *Abschied in die Gegenwart: Teleologie und Zustand in der Musik*, edited by Otto Kolleritsch, 267–78. Vienna: Universal, 1998.

Burke, Kenneth. *The Philosophy of Literary Form: Studies in Symbolic Action.* Baton Rouge: Louisiana State University Press, 1941.

Burke, Kenneth. *A Rhetoric of Motives.* Berkeley: University of California Press, 1967.

Byron, George Gordon, and Isaac Nathan. *A Selection of Hebrew Melodies…* London, 1815.

Cai, Camilla. "Forms Made Miniature: Three Intermezzi of Brahms." In *The Varieties of Musicology: Essays in Honor of Murray Lefkowitz*, edited by John Daverio and John Ogasapian, 135–50. Warren, MI: Harmonie Park Press, 2000.

Candidus, Carl. *Vermischte Gedichte.* Leipzig: S. Hirzel, 1869.

Caplin, William. *Classical Form: A Theory of Formal Functions for the Instrumental Music of Haydn, Mozart, and Beethoven.* Oxford: Oxford University Press, 1998.

Clampitt, David. "In Brahms's Workshop: Compositional Modeling in op. 40, *Adagio mesto.*" Paper presented at the annual meeting of the Society for Music Theory, Seattle, 2004.

Clive, Peter. *Brahms and His World: A Biographical Dictionary*. Lanham, MD: The Scarecrow Press, 2006.

Corner, David Gregor. *Groß-Catolisch Gesangbuch*. Nürnberg: Georg Enders der Jüngere, 1631.

Czerny, Carl, ed. *Sämmtliche Werke für das Piano-Forte von Dominic Scarlatti*. Vienna: Tobias Haslinger, 1839.

Daumer, Georg Friedrich. *Polydora, ein weltpoetisches Liederbuch*. Frankfurt am Main: Literarische Anstalt, 1855.

Daverio, John. *Crossing Paths: Schubert, Schumann, and Brahms*. Oxford: Oxford University Press, 2002.

Daverio, John. *Robert Schumann: Herald of a 'New Poetic Age.'* Oxford: Oxford University Press, 1997.

Deiters, Hermann. "Johannes Brahms." *Sammlung Musikalischer Vorträge* 23/24 (1880): 319–74.

Deutsch, Otto Erich. *Franz Schubert: Thematisches Verzeichnis seiner Werke in chronologischer Folge*. Kassel: Bärenreiter, 1978.

Dorfmüller, Joachim, ed. *Jan Albert van Eyken: Sonata Nr. 1 c-moll für die Orgel, op. 13, über den Choral Befiehl Du Deine Wege*. Bonn: Rob. Forberg, 1974.

Drinker, Sophie. *Brahms and his Women's Choruses*. Merion, PA: author, under the auspices of Musurgia Publishers, A. G. Hess, 1952.

Dürr, Walter, ed. *Franz Schubert: Neue Ausgabe sämtlicher Werke, Lieder*. Vol. 3. Kassel: Bärenreiter, 1982.

Ehlert, Louis. "Brahms." *Deutsche Rundschau* 23 (April–June 1880): 341–57.

Ehrlich, Heinrich. *Aus allen Tonarten: Studien über Musik*. Berlin: Brachvogel & Ranft, 1888.

Ehrlich, Heinrich. "Von der Musiksaison." *Die Gegenwart: Wochenschrift für Literatur, Kunst und öffentliches Leben* 10/49 (December 2, 1876): 365–66.

Eichendorff, Joseph Freiherr von. *Gedichte*. 2nd ed. Berlin: M. Simion, 1843.

Eichendorff, Joseph Freiherr von. *Gedichte*. Berlin: Duncker & Humblot, 1837.

Elon, Amos. *The Pity of It All: A History of Jews in Germany, 1742–1933*. New York: Metropolitan Books, 2002.

Evans, Edwin. *Handbook to the Vocal Works of Brahms*. London: W. Reeves, 1912.

Fellinger, Imogen. "Brahms' Sonate für Pianoforte und Violine op. 78: Ein Beitrag zum Schaffensprozeß des Meisters." *Die Musikforschung* 18 (1965): 11–24.

Fellinger, Imogen. "Cyclic Tendencies in Brahms's Song Collections." In *Brahms Studies: Analytical and Historical Perspectives*, edited by George Bozarth, 379–90. Oxford: Clarendon Press, 1990.

Floros, Constantin. *Johannes Brahms, "Frei, aber einsam": Ein Leben für eine poetische Musik*. Hamburg: Arche, 1997.

Floros, Constantin. *Johannes Brahms: Sinfonie Nr. 2 D–Dur, op. 73*. Mainz: Goldmann/Schott, 1986.

Floros, Constantin. "Studien zu Brahms' Klaviermusik." *Brahms–Studien* 5 (1983): 25–63.

Friedländer, Max. *Brahms' Lieder: Einführung in seine Lieder für eine und zwei Stimmen*. Berlin: N. Simrock, 1922.

Frisch, Walter. "Brahms and the Herzogenbergs." *American Brahms Society Newsletter* 4/1 (1986): 1–3.

Frisch, Walter. *Brahms and the Principle of Developing Variation*. Berkeley: University of California Press, 1984.

Frisch, Walter. "'The Brahms Fog': On Tracing Brahmsian Influences." *American Brahms Society Newsletter* 7/1 (1989): 1–3.

Frisch, Walter. *Brahms: The Four Symhonies*. New York: Schirmer, 1996.

Fuller Maitland, John Alexander. *Brahms*. New York: John Lane, 1911.

Geibel, Emmanuel, and Paul Heyse. *Spanisches Liederbuch*. Berlin: Wilhelm Gertz, 1852.

Geiringer, Karl. "Brahms as a Reader and Collector." *Musical Quarterly* 19 (1933): 158–68.

Geiringer, Karl, ed. *Johannes Brahms: Fünf Ophelia-Lieder für eine Sopranstimme und Klavierbegleitung*. Vienna: Schönborn, 1960.

Geiringer, Karl. *Johannes Brahms: Leben und Schaffen eines deutschen Meisters*. Vienna: Rohrer, 1935.

Gennrich, Friedrich. "Glossen zu Johannes Brahms' 'Sonnet' op. 14 Nr. 4: Ach könnt' ich, könnte vergessen sie!" *Zeitschrift für Musikwissenschaft* 10/3 (December 1927): 129–39.

Gerards, Marion. *Frauenliebe—Männerleben: Die Musik von Johannes Brahms und der Geschlechterdiskurs im 19. Jahrhundert*. Vienna: Böhlau, 2010.

Goethe, Johann Wolfgang von. *Reinecke Fuchs in zwölf Gesängen*. Berlin: Johann Friedrich Unger, 1794.

Goldberg, Clemens. "Vergänglichkeit als ästhetische Kategorie und Erlebnis in Liedern von Johannes Brahms." In *Brahms als Liedkomponist: Studien zum Verhältnis von Text und Vertonung*, edited by Peter Jost, 190–211. Stuttgart: Franz Steiner, 1992.

Goldmark, Carl. *Notes from the Life of a Viennese Composer*. Translated by Alice Goldmark Brandeis. New York: Boni, 1927.

Greene, Harry Plunket. *Interpretation in Song*. New York: Macmillan, 1912.

Groth, Klaus. *Hundert Blätter: Paralipomena zum Quickborn*. Hamburg: Perthes-Besser & Mauke, 1854.

Hagen, Friedrich Heinrich von der. *Minnesinger: Deutsche Liederdichter des zwölften, dreizehnten und vierzehnten Jahrhunderts*. Leipzig: Barth, 1838.

Hancock, Virginia. *Brahms's Choral Compositions and His Library of Early Music*. Ann Arbor: UMI Research Press, 1983.

Hancock, Virginia. Review of *Brahms als Liedkomponist: Studien zum Verhältnis von Text und Vertonung*, edited by Peter Jost. *Notes: Quarterly Journal of the Music Library Association* 50 (September 1993): 143–45.

Hancock, Virginia. Review of *The Cambridge Companion to Brahms*, edited by Michael Musgrave. *Music & Letters* 83 (2002): 131–33.

Hanslick, Eduard. *Aus meinem Leben*. 2 vols. Berlin: Allgemeine Verein für Deutsche Literatur, 1894.

Hanslick, Eduard. *Fünf Jahre Musik*. Berlin: Allgemeiner Verein für deutschen Literatur, 1896.

Hanslick, Eduard. *Musikalisches und Literarisches*. Berlin: Allgemeiner Verein für Deutsche Literatur, 1889.

Hanslick, Eduard. *Sämtliche Schriften: Historisch–kritische Ausgabe*. Vol. I:2. Edited by Dietmar Strauß. Vienna: Böhlau, 1994.

Harrison, Max. *The Lieder of Brahms*. New York: Praeger Publishers, 1972.

Hefling, Stephen, ed. *Nineteenth-Century Chamber Music*. New York: Routledge, 2004.

Heine, Heinrich. *Heinrich Heine's Sämtliche Werke. Rechtmäßige Originalausgabe*. 18 vols. Hamburg: Hoffmann und Campe, 1861–63.

Henschel, George. "Personal Recollections of Johannes Brahms." *Century Illustrated Magazine* 66/5 (March 1901): 725–36.

Henschel, George. *Personal Recollections of Johannes Brahms*. Boston: Richard C. Badger, 1907.

Hepokoski, James. "Beethoven Reception: The Symphonic Tradition." In *The Cambridge History of Nineteenth-Century Music*, edited by Jim Samson, 424–59. Cambridge: Cambridge University Press, 2002.

Herder, Johann Gottfried von. *Sämmtliche Werke: Zur schönen Literatur und Kunst*. 20 vols. Stuttgart: J. G. Cotta, 1827–30.

Hertz, Deborah Sadie. *Jewish High Society in Old Regime Berlin*. Syracuse: Syracuse University Press, 2005.

Herzogenberg, Heinrich von. "Tonalität." *Vierteljahrsschrift für Musikwissenschaft* 6 (1890): 553–82.

Hinckel, Hans Otto, ed. *Johannes Brahms: Sonate für Klavier und Violine G-dur Opus 78*. Munich: G. Henle, 2008.

Hirsch, Marjorie. "The Spiral Journey Back Home: Brahms's 'Heimweh' Lieder." *Journal of Musicology* 22 (2005): 454–89.

Hofmann, Kurt. *Die Bibliothek von Johannes Brahms: Bücher- und Musikalienverzeichnis*. Hamburg: Musikalienhandlung Karl Dieter Wagner, 1974.

Hofmann, Renate, and Kurt Hofmann. "Frauen um Johannes Brahms, von einer Freundin im Adressen-Buch des Komponisten vermerkt. Eine erste Bestandsaufnahme." In *Festschrift Rudolf Elvers zum 60. Geburtstag*, edited by Ernst Heinrich and Hans Schneider, 257–70. Tutzing: Schneider, 1985.

Hofmann, Renate, and Kurt Hofmann. *Johannes Brahms als Pianist und Dirigent: Chronologie seines Wirkens als Interpret*. Tutzing: Schneider, 2006.

Hofmann, Renate, and Kurt Hofmann. *Johannes Brahms: Zeittafel zu Leben und Werk*. Tutzing: Schneider, 1983.

Horne, William. "Brahms' Heine-Lieder." In *Brahms als Liedkomponist: Studien zum Verhältnis von Text und Vertonung*, edited by Peter Jost, 93–115. Stuttgart: Franz Steiner, 1992.

Horne, William. "Brahms Variations on a Hungarian Song, op. 21, no. 2: 'Betrachte dann die Beethovenschen und, wenn Du willst, meine.'" In *Brahms Studies 3*, edited by David Brodbeck, 47–127. Lincoln: University of Nebraska Press, 2001.

Horstmann, Angelika. *Untersuchungen zur Brahms-Rezeption der Jahre 1860–1880*. Hamburg: Karl Dieter Wagner, 1986.

Hull, Kenneth. "Allusive Irony in Brahms's Fourth Symphony." In *Brahms Studies 2*, edited by David Brodbeck, 135–68. Lincoln: University of Nebraska 1998.

Hull, Kenneth. "Brahms the Allusive: Extra-Compositional Reference in the Instrumental Music of Johannes Brahms." PhD diss., Princeton University, 1989.

Hussey, William. "Compositional Modeling, Quotation, and Multiple Influence Analysis in the Works of Johannes Brahms: An Application of Harold Bloom's Theory of Influence to Music." PhD diss., University of Texas at Austin, 1997.

Jahn, Otto. *W. A. Mozart.* Vol. 4. Leipzig: Breitkopf & Härtel, 1859.

Jenner, Gustav. *Johannes Brahms als Mensch, Lehrer, und Künstler. Studien und Erlebnisse.* Marburg: N. C. Elevert, 1905.

Jost, Peter. "Brahms und das deutsche Lied." In *Brahms als Liedkomponist: Studien zum Verhältnis von Text und Vertonung*, edited by Peter Jost, 9–37. Stuttgart: Franz Steiner, 1992.

Jost, Peter, ed. *Brahms als Liedkomponist: Studien zum Verhältnis von Text und Vertonung.* Stuttgart: Franz Steiner, 1992.

Jost, Peter. "Lieder und Gesänge." In *Brahms Handbuch*, edited by Wolfgang Sandberger, 208–67. Kassel: Bärenreiter, 2009.

Jost, Peter, ed. *Schubert: Sechs Lieder für Singstimme und Orchester, bearbeitet von Johannes Brahms.* Leipzig: Breitkopf & Härtel, 2000.

Kahler, Otto-Hans. "Brahms' Wiegenlied und die Gebirgs–Bleamln des Alexander Baumann." *Brahms–Studien 6*, edited by Kurt Hofmann and Karl Dieter Wagner, 65–70. Hamburg: Johannes–Brahms–Gesellschaft, 1985.

Kalbeck, Max. *Johannes Brahms.* 4 vols. Berlin: Deutsche Brahms–Gesellschaft, 1915–27.

Kalbeck, Max. "Neues über Brahms, mitgetheilt von Max Kalbeck." *Neues Wiener Tagblatt*, 32/91 and 32/94 (April 2 and 5, 1898).

Kapp, Reinhard, ed. *Robert Schumann. Konzert für Violine und Orchester d–Moll WoO 1, nach der Neuen Robert Schumann Gesamtausgabe.* Mainz: Schott, 2010.

Kerman, Joseph. "Follow the Lieder." *New York Review of Books* 24 (1977): 15–16.

Kirkendale, Warren. *Fuge und Fugato in der Kammermusik des Rokoko und der Klassik.* Tutzing: Schneider, 1966.

Knapp, Raymond. *Brahms and the Challenge of the Symphony.* Stuyvesant: Pendragon Press, 1997.

Knapp, Raymond. Review of *Motives for Allusion*, by Christopher Reynolds. *Journal of the American Musicological Society* 58 (2005): 736–48.

Knapp, Raymond. "The Finale of Brahms's Fourth Symphony: The Tale of the Subject." *19th-Century Music* 13 (1989): 3–17.

Körner, Julius. *Israelitisches Gesänge. Lord Byron's Poesien 1.* Zwickau: Schumann, 1821.

Korsyn, Kevin. "Brahms Research and Aesthetic Ideology." *Music Analysis* 12 (1993): 89–103.

Korsyn, Kevin. *Decentering Music: A Critique of Contemporary Musical Research.* Oxford: Oxford University Press, 2003.

Korsyn, Kevin. "Towards a New Poetics of Musical Influence." *Music Analysis* 10 (1991): 3–72.

Kramer, Richard. *Distant Cycles: Schubert and the Conceiving of Song.* Chicago: University of Chicago Press, 1994.

Kretschmer, Andreas. *Hebräische Gesänge.* Berlin: Magazin für Kunst, Geographie, und Musik, 1822.

Kretschmer, August, and Anton Wilhelm von Zuccalmaglio. *Deutsche Volkslieder mit ihren Original-Weisen.* Berlin: Vereins-Buchhandlung, 1838.

Krones, Hartmut. "Harmonische Symbolik im Vokalschaffen von Johannes Brahms." In *Johannes Brahms: Quellen—Text—Rezeption—Interpretation. Internationaler Brahms–Kongreß, Hamburg 1997,* edited by Friedhelm Krummacher and Michael Strunk, with Constantin Floros and Peter Petersen, 415–37. München: Henle, 1999.

Krummacher, Friedhelm. *Das Streichquartett Teilband 2: Von Mendelssohn bis zur Gegenwart.* Laaber: Laaber-Verlag, 2003.

Krummacher, Friedhelm. "Von 'allerlei Delikatessen': Überlegungen zum Streichquartett op. 67 von Brahms." In *Johannes Brahms: Quellen—Text—Rezeption—Interpretation. Internationaler Brahms–Kongreß, Hamburg 1997,* edited by Friedhelm Krummacher and Michael Strunk, with Constantin Floros and Peter Petersen, 127–41. München: Henle, 1999.

Kühn, Hellmut. "Brahms und sein Epigone Heinrich von Herzogenberg. Zur Musik in der Grunderzeit und im Fin de siècle I." *Musica* 28 (1974): 517–21.

Küntzel, Hans. *"Aber Fesseln tragen kann ich nicht": Johannes Brahms und Agathe von Siebold.* Göttingen: Steidl, 2003.

Küntzel, Hans. *Brahms in Göttingen, mit Erinnerungen von Agathe Schütte, geb. Siebold.* Göttingen: edition herodot, 1985.

Le Guin, Elisabeth. *Boccherini's Body: An Essay in Carnal Musicology.* Berkeley: University of California Press, 2006.

Lewin, David. "Brahms, His Past, and Modes of Theory." In *Brahms Studies: Analytical and Historical Perspectives,* edited by George Bozarth, 13–27. Oxford: Clarendon Press, 1990.

Liliencron, Detlev von. *Adjutantenritte und andere Gedichte.* Leipzig: Wilhelm Friedrich, 1883.

Littlewood, Julian. *The Variations of Johannes Brahms.* London: Plumbago Books, 2004.

Litzmann, Berthold. *Clara Schumann: Ein Künstlerleben, nach Tagebüchern und Briefen.* 3 vols. Leipzig: Breitkopf & Härtel, 1923.

Luther, Martin. *Die gantze Heilige Schrifft Deudsch.* 2 vols. Wittenberg, 1545. Reprint edited by Hanz Volz in collaboration with Heinze Blanke and Friedrich Kur. Munich: Rogner & Bernhard, 1972.

MacDonald, Malcolm. *Brahms.* 2nd ed. Oxford: Oxford University Press, 2001.

Mast, Paul, ed. and trans. "Brahms's study, *Octaven u. Quinten u. A.,* with Schenker's commentary translated." *Music Forum* 5 (1980): 1–196.

May, Florence. *The Life of Johannes Brahms.* 2 vols. London: Edward Arnold, 1905.

McCorkle, Margit L. *Johannes Brahms: Thematisch-bibliographisches Werkverzeichnis.* Edited in collaboration with Donald M. McCorkle†. München: Henle, 1984.

McCorkle, Margit L. *Thematisch-Bibliographisches Werkverzeichnis.* Düsseldorf: Robert-Schumann-Gesellschaft, 2003.

McKay, Elizabeth. "Brahms and Scarlatti." *Musical Times* 130 (1989): 586–88.

Meister, Karl Severin. *Das katholische deutsche Kirchenlied in seinen Singweisen von den frühesten Zeiten bis gegen Ende des siebzehnten Jahrhunderts.* Freiburg im Breisgau: Herder'scheVerlagshandlung, 1862.

Michelmann, Emil. *Agathe von Siebold, Johannes Brahms' Jugendliebe.* Göttingen: Dr. L. Hützchel & Co., 1930.

Minor, Ryan. "Occasions and Nations in Brahms's *Fest- und Gedenksprüche.*" *19th-Century Music* 39 (2006): 261–88.

Moseley, Roger. "Reforming Johannes: Brahms, Kreisler Junior and the Piano Trio in B, Op. 8." *Journal of the Royal Musical Association* 132 (2007): 252–305.

Musgrave, Michael. *A Brahms Reader.* New Haven, CT: Yale University Press, 2000.

Musgrave, Michael, ed. *Brahms 2: Biographical, Documentary and Analytical Studies.* Cambridge: Cambridge University Press, 1987.

Musgrave, Michael, ed. *The Cambridge Companion to Brahms.* Cambridge: Cambridge University Press, 1999.

Musgrave, Michael. *The Music of Brahms.* London: Routledge and Kegan Paul, 1985.

Musgrave, Michael. "Words for Music: the Songs for Solo Voice and Piano." In *The Cambridge Companion to Brahms,* edited by Michael Musgrave, 195–227. Cambridge: Cambridge University Press, 1999.

Musgrave, Michael, and Bernard D. Sherman, eds. *Performing Brahms: Early Evidence of Performance Style.* Cambridge: Cambridge University Press, 2003.

Muxfeldt, Kristina. "*Frauenliebe und Leben* Now and Then." *19th-Century Music* 25 (2001): 27–48.

Muxfeldt, Kristina. "Schubert Song Studies." PhD diss., State University of New York at Stonybrook, 1991.

Notley, Margaret. "Brahms as Liberal: Genre, Style, and Politics in Late Nineteenth-Century Vienna." *19th-Century Music* 17 (1993): 107–23.

Notley, Margaret. "Brahms's Cello Sonata in F major and Its Genesis: A Study in Half-Step Relations." In *Brahms Studies 1,* edited by David Brodbeck, 139–60. Lincoln: University of Nebraska Press, 1994.

Notley, Margaret. "Bruckner Problems in Perpetuity." *19th-Century Music* 30 (2006): 81–93.

Notley, Margaret. "Discourse and Allusion: The Chamber Music of Brahms." In *Nineteenth-Century Chamber Music,* edited by Stephen Hefling, 242–86. New York: Routledge, 2004.

Notley, Margaret. *Lateness and Brahms: Music and Culture in the Twilight of Viennese Liberalism.* Oxford: Oxford University Press, 2006.

Oechsle, Siegfried. "Klaviertrios, Klavierquartette, Klavierquintett." In *Brahms Handbuch,* edited by Wolfgang Sandberger, 408–36. Kassel: Bärenreiter, 2009.

Parmer, Dillon. "Brahms and the Poetic Motto: A Hermeneutic Aid?" *Journal of Musicology* 15 (1997): 353–89.

Parmer, Dillon. "Brahms the Programmatic? A Critical Assessment." PhD diss., Eastman School of Music, 1995.

Parmer, Dillon. "Brahms, Song Quotation, and Secret Programs." *19th-Century Music* 19 (1995): 161–90.

Pascall, Robert. "Brahms und die Kleinmeister." *Hamburger Jahrbuch für Musikwissenschaft* 7 (1984): 199–209.

Pascall, Robert. "Brahms's *Missa Canonica* and its Recomposition in his 'Warum' Op. 74 No. 1." In *Brahms 2: Biographical, Documentary and Analytical Studies*, edited by Michael Musgrave, 111–36. Cambridge: Cambridge University Press, 1987.

Pascall, Robert. "Unknown Gavottes by Brahms." *Music & Letters* 57 (1976): 404–11.

Paulsen, Wolfgang. "Theodor Fontane: The Philosemitic Anti–Semite." *Leo Baeck Institute Yearbook* 26 (1981): 303–22.

Petersen, Peter, ed. *Klavierstücke op. 76: mit der Urfassung des Capriccio fis–moll.* Vienna: Wiener Urtext Edition (Universal Edition), 1992.

Plantinga, Leon. "Design and Unity in Schumann's *Liederkreis*, op. 39?" In *Word and Music Studies: Essays on the Song Cycle and on Defining the Field (proceedings of the Second International Conference on Word and Music Studies at Ann Arbor, MI, 1999)*, edited by Walter Bernhart and Werner Wolf, 141–63. Atlanta: Rodopi, 2001.

Platt, Heather. "2 Gesänge, for Alto, Viola, and Piano, Opus 91." In *The Compleat Brahms*, edited by Leon Botstein, 276. New York: Norton, 1999.

Platt, Heather. "5 Gesänge, Opus 72." In *The Compleat Brahms*, edited by Leon Botstein, 263–66. New York: Norton, 1999.

Platt, Heather. "Text–Music Relationships in the Lieder of Johannes Brahms." PhD diss., City University of New York, 1992.

Platt, Heather, and Peter H. Smith, eds. *Expressive Intersections in Brahms: Essays in Analysis and Meaning.* Bloomington: Indiana University Press, 2012.

Rahden, Till van. "Jews and the Ambivalences of Civil Society in Germany, 1800–1930: Assessment and Reassessment." *Journal of Modern History* 77 (2005): 1024–47.

Ratner, Leonard. *Classic Music: Expression, Form, and Style.* New York: Schirmer, 1980.

Reich, Nancy. *Clara Schumann: The Artist and the Woman.* Rev. ed. Ithaca, NY: Cornell University Press, 2001.

Reik, Theodor. *The Haunting Melody: Psychoanalytic Experiences in Life and Music.* New York: Farrar, Straus, and Young, 1953.

Reynolds, Christopher. "Brahms Rhapsodizing: The Alto Rhapsody and Its Expressive Double." *Journal of Musicology* 29 (2012): 191–238.

Reynolds, Christopher. "A Choral Symphony by Brahms?" *19th-Century Music* 9 (1985): 3–25.

Reynolds, Christopher. *Motives for Allusion: Context and Content in Ninteenth-Century Music.* Cambridge, MA: Harvard University Press, 2003.

Riethmüller, Albrecht, ed. *Bruckner-Probleme: internationales Kolloquium 7.–9. Oktober 1996 in Berlin.* Stuttgart: Steiner, 1999.

Rij, Inge van. *Brahms's Song Collections*. Cambridge: Cambridge University Press, 2006.

Rings, Steven. "The Learned Self: Artifice in Brahms's Late Intermezzi." In *Expressive Intersections in Brahms: Essays in Analysis and Meaning*, edited by Heather Platt and Peter H. Smith, 19–50. Bloomington: Indiana University Press, 2012.

Rink, John. "Opposition and Integration in the Piano Music." In *The Cambridge Companion to Brahms*, edited by Michael Musgrave, 79–97. Cambridge: Cambridge University Press, 1999.

Rosen, Charles. "Brahms: Classicism and the Inspiration of Awkwardness." In *Critical Entertainments: Music Old and New*. Cambridge, MA: Harvard University Press, 2000. 162–97.

Rosen, Charles. "Brahms: Influence, Plagiarism, and Inspiration." In *Critical Entertainments: Music Old and New*. Cambridge, MA: Harvard University Press, 2000. 127–43.

Rosen, Charles. *The Romantic Generation*. Cambridge, MA: Harvard University Press, 1995.

Rückert, Friedrich. *Östliche Rosen: Drei Lesen*. Leipzig: F. A. Brockhaus, 1822.

Rückert, Friedrich. *Gesammelte Gedichte*. Erlangen: Carl Heyder, 1837.

Ruhbaum, Antje. *Elisabeth von Herzogenberg. Salon—Mäzenatentum—Musikforderung*. Kenzingen: Centaurus, 2009.

Russell, Peter. *Johannes Brahms and Klaus Groth: The Biography of a Friendship*. Burlington, VT: Ashgate, 2006.

Sams, Eric. *The Songs of Johannes Brahms*. New Haven, CT: Yale University Press, 2000.

Sandberger, Wolfgang, ed. *Brahms Handbuch*. Brahms-Institut an der Musikhochschule Lübeck. Kassel: Bärenreiter, 2009.

Sandberger, Wolfgang. "Vorwort." In *Johannes Brahms: Sonate für Klavier und Violine G-dur Opus 78*, edited by Hans Otto Hinckel, iii–ix. Munich: G. Henle, 2008.

Schanze, Helmut, and Krischan Schulte. *Robert Schumann. Neue Ausgabe sämtlicher Werke. Supplemente. Literarische Vorlagen der ein- und mehrstimmigen Lieder, Gesängen und Deklamationen*. Mainz: Schott, 2002.

Scheffel, Joseph Victor von. *Frau Aventiure. Lieder aus Heinrich von Osterdingens Zeit*. Stuttgart: J. B. Metzler, 1863.

Scher, Steven Paul, ed. *Music and Text: Critical Inquiries*. New York: Cambridge University Press, 1992.

Scherer, Georg. *Deutsche Volkslieder*. Leipzig: Gustav Mayer, 1851.

Schillemeit, Jost. "Berlin und die Berliner: Neuaufgefundene Fontane–Manuskripte." *Jahrbuch der deutschen Schillergesellschaft* 30 (1986): 34–82.

Schochow, Maximilian, and Lilly Schochow. *Franz Schubert: Die Texte seiner einstimmig komponierten Lieder und ihre Dichter*. 2 vols. Hildesheim: Georg Olms, 1974.

Schubring, Adolf. "Schumanniana Nr. 8. Die Schumann'sche Schule. IV. Johannes Brahms." *Neue Zeitschrift für Musik* 56/12 (March 21, 1862): 93–96; 56/13 (March 28, 1862): 101–4; 56/14 (April 4, 1862): 109–12; 56/15 (April 11, 1862): 117–19; and 56/16 (April 18, 1862): 125–28.

Schubring, Adolf. "Schumanniana Nr. 11. Die Schumann'sche Schule. Schumann und Brahms. Brahms' vierhändige Schumann–Variationen." *Leipziger Allgemeine*

Musikalische Zeitung 3/6 (February 5, 1868): 41–42; and 3/7 (February 12, 1868): 49–51

Schumann, Clara, ed. *Jugendbriefe von Robert Schumann*. Leipzig: Breitkopf & Härtel, 1885.

Schumann, Eugenie. *Erinnerungen*. Stuttgart: J. Engelhorns Nachf., 1925.

Schumann, Eugenie. "Eugenie Schumann. Über das letzte Werk ihres Vaters Robert Schumann." *Schweizerische Musikzeitung* 78/1 (1938): 8–10.

Schumann, Ferdinand. "Erinnerungen an Clara Schumann, Tagebuchblätter ihres Enkels." Neue Zeitschrift für Musik 84 (1917): 69–72, 77–80, 85–88, 93–96, 101–4.

Schumann, Ferdinand. "Erinnerungen an Johannes Brahms, 1894, 1895, 1896." *Neue Zeitschrift für Musik* 82 (1915): 225–28, 233–36, 241–43.

Schumann, Robert. "Ältere Claviermusik." *Neue Zeitschrift für Musik*, 10/39 (1839):153–54.

Seiffert, Wolf-Dieter. ed. *Robert Schumann: Thema mit Variationen "Geistervariationen."* Munich: Henle, 1995.

Seiffert, Wolf-Dieter. "Robert Schumanns Thema mit Variationen Es-Dur, genannt 'Geistervariationen.'" In *Compositionswissenschaft: Festschrift Reinhold und Roswitha Schlötterer zum 70. Geburtstag*, edited by Bernd Edelmann and Sabine Kurth, 189–214. Augsburg: Wißner, 1999.

Sherman, Bernard D. "How Different Was Brahms's Playing Style from Our Own." In *Performing Brahms: Early Evidence of Performance Style*, edited by Michael Musgrave and Bernard D. Sherman, 1–10. Cambridge: Cambridge University Press, 2003.

Sheveloff, Joel Leonard. "The Keyboard Music of Domenico Scarlatti: A Re-Evaluation of the Present State of Knowledge in the Light of the Sources." PhD diss., Brandeis University, 1970.

Sholes, Jacqueline. "Lovelorn Lamentation or Histrionic Historicism? Reconsidering Allusion and Extramusical Meaning in the 1854 Version of Brahms's B-major Trio." *19th-Century Music* 34 (2010): 61–86.

Simrock, Karl, ed. *Die deutschen Sprichwörter*. Vol. 20 (1846), *Die deutschen Volksbücher*. Frankfurt am Main: H. L. Brönner, 1839–1867. Vol. 20 reprinted in Stuttgart: Reclam, 1988. Introduction by Wolfgang Mieder.

Sisman, Elaine. "Brahms and the Variation Canon." *19th-Century Music* 14 (1990): 132–53.

Smyth, Ethyl. *Impressions that Remained: Memoirs*. New York: Knopf, 1946.

Solie, Ruth. "Whose Life? The Gendered Self in Schumann's Frauenliebe songs." In *Music and Text: Critical Inquiries*, edited by Steven Paul Scher, 219–40. Cambridge: Cambridge University Press, 1992.

Specht, Richard. *Johannes Brahms*. Translated by Eric Blom. London: J. M. Dent, 1930.

Spiero, Heinrich. *Detlev von Liliencron: sein Leben und seine Werke*. Berlin: Schuster & Loffler, 1913.

Spies, Minna. *Hermine Spies: Ein Gedenkbuch für ihre Freunde*. 3rd ed. Leipzig: G. J. Göschen, 1905.

Spitta, Philipp. "Ein Lebensbild Robert Schumann's." *Sammlung Musikalischer Vorträge* 4 (1882): 1–102.

Spitta, Philipp. "Robert Schumann." In *Dictionary of Music and Musicians*, edited by George Grove, 3: 384–421. London: Macmillan, 1883.

Sposato, Jeffrey. *Price of Assimilation: Felix Mendelssohn and the Nineteenth-Century Anti-Semitic Tradition*. Oxford: Oxford University Press, 2006.

Stark, Lucien. *A Guide to the Solo Songs of Johannes Brahms*. Bloomington: Indiana University Press, 1995.

Stark, Lucien. *Brahms's Vocal Duets and Quartets with Piano: A Guide with Full Texts and Translations*. Bloomington: Indiana University Press, 1998.

Starobinsky, Georges. "Brahms et la nostalgie de l'enfance: 'Volks-Kinderlieder,' berceuses et 'Klaus–Groth–Lieder.'" *Acta Musicologica* 74 (2002): 141–94.

Struck, Michael. "Dialog über die Variation–präzisiert: Joseph Joachims *Variationen über ein irisches Elfenlied* und Johannes Brahms' Variationenpaar *op. 21* im Licht der gemeinsamen gattungstheoretischen Diskussion." In *Musikkulturgeschichte: Festschrift für Constantin Floros zum 60. Geburtstag*, edited by Peter Petersen, 105–54. Wiesbaden: Breitkopf & Härtel, 1990.

Struck, Michael. *Die umstrittenen späten Instrumentalwerke Schumanns: Untersuchungen zur Entstehung, Struktur und Rezeption*. Hamburger Beiträge zur Musikwissenschaft 29, edited by Constantin Floros. Hamburg: Karl Dieter Wagner, 1984.

Struck, Michael, ed. *Johannes Brahms: Vier Lieder nach Gedichten von Klaus Groth*. Munich: Henle, 1997.

Struck, Michael. "New Evidence on the Genesis of Brahms's G major Violin Sonata, Op. 78." Translated by George Bozarth and Ben Kohn. *American Brahms Society Newsletter* 9/1 (1991): 5–6.

Struck, Michael. "Revisionsbedürftig: Zur gedruckten Korrespondenz von Johannes Brahms und Clara Schumann." *Die Musikforschung* 41 (1988): 235–41.

Struck, Michael. *Robert Schumann. Violinkonzert D–Moll (WoO 23). Meisterwerke der Musik* 47, edited by Stefan Kunze. Munich: Wilhlem Fink, 1988.

Swafford, Jan. *Johannes Brahms: A Biography*. 2nd ed. New York: Vintage Books, 1999.

Szigeti, Joseph. *A Violinist's Notebook: 200 Examples with Notes for Practice and Performance*. London: Gerald Duckworth, 1964.

Tardel, Hermann. *Studien zur Lyrik Chamissos: Beilage zum Programm der Handelsschule (Oberrealschule) zu Bremen, Ostern 1902*. Bremen: A. Guthe, 1902.

Theremin, Franz. *Hebräische Gesänge*. Berlin: Duncker & Humblot, 1820.

Tomlinson, Gary. "The Web of Culture: A Context for Musicology." *19th-Century Music* 7 (1984): 350–62.

Tovey, Donald Francis. "Brahms, Johannes." In *Cobbett's Cyclopedic Survey of Chamber Music*, edited by Walter Wilson Cobbett, 1: 158–82. London: Oxford University Press, 1929.

Vries, Claudia de. *Die Pianistin Clara Wieck-Schumann: Interpretation im Spannungsfeld von Tradition und Individualität. Schumann–Forschungen V*, edited by Akio Meyer and Klaus Wolfgang Niemöller, through the Robert-Schumann-Gesellschaft, Düsseldorf. Mainz: Schott Musik International, 1996.

Wagner, Hans-Dieter. *Johannes Brahms—das Liedschaffen: Ein Wegweiser zum Verständnis und zur Interpretation.* Mannheim: Palatium, 2001.

Walker, Ernest. "Brahms and Heine." *Monthly Musical Record* 63/745 (March–April 1933): 51–52.

Walker, Ernest. *Free Thought and the Musician.* Oxford: Oxford University Press, 1946.

Wander, Karl Friedrich Wilhelm, ed. *Deutsches Sprichwörterlexikon: Ein Hausschatz für das deutsche Volk.* 5 vols. Leipzig: F. A. Brockhaus, 1867–1880.

Wasielewski, Joseph Wilhelm von. *Robert Schumann: Eine Biographie.* Dresden: Rudolf Kunze, 1858.

Wasielewski, Joseph Wilhelm von. *Robert Schumann: Eine Biographie.* 4th ed., posth. Edited by Woldemar von Wasielewksi. Leipzig: Breitkopf & Härtel, 1906.

Webster, James. "The *Alto Rhapsody*: Psychology, Intertextuality, and Brahms's Artistic Development." In *Brahms Studies 3*, edited by David Brodbeck, 19–46. Lincoln: University of Nebraska Press, 2001.

Widmann, Joseph Viktor. *Johannes Brahms in Erinnerungen.* Berlin: Gebrüder Paetel, 1898.

Wiechert, Bernd. *Heinrich von Herzogenberg (1843–1900): Studien zu Leben und Werk.* Göttingen: Vandenhoeck und Ruprecht, 1997.

Wiechert, Bernd, ed. *Johannes Brahms: Neue Ausgabe sämtlicher Werke VI/2: Chorwerke und Vokalquartette mit Klavier oder Orgel. II.* Munich: Henle, 2008.

Winter, Robert. "Paper Studies and the Future of Schubert Research." In *Schubert Studies: Problems of Style and Chronology*, edited by Eva Badura-Skoda and Peter Branscombe, 209–75. Cambridge: Cambridge University Press, 1982.

Wirth, Julia (née Stockhausen). *Julius Stockhausen, der Sänger des deutschen Liedes: Nach Dokumenten seiner Zeit.* Frankfurt am Main: Englert und Schlosser, 1927.

INDEX

Boldface page numbers denote musical examples and translated poems.

SAVING DARWIN

How to Be a Christian and Believe in Evolution

Karl W. Giberson

HarperOne
An Imprint of HarperCollinsPublishers

HarperOne

A Giniger Book
The K.S. Giniger Company
1045 Park Avenue
New York, NY 10028

FIRST HARPERCOLLINS PAPERBACK EDITION PUBLISHED IN 2009

Library of Congress Cataloging-in-Publication Data

Giberson, Karl.
Saving Darwin : how to be a Christian and believe in evolution /
Karl W. Giberson.
p. cm.
Includes bibliographical references (p.) and index.
ISBN 978-0-06-144173-8
1. Evolution (Biology)—Religious aspects—Christianity.
2. Creationism. 3. Darwin, Charles, 1809-1882. I. Title.
BT712.G53 2008
231.7'652—dc22   2007034605

09 10 11 12 13 RRD (H) 10 9 8 7 6 5 4 3 2 1

CONTENTS

FOREWORD

Americans live, according to the lyrics of their national anthem, in the land of the free and the home of the brave. They also live in a land that hosts one of the great paradoxes of our time. Many of its citizens have faith in science and technology to solve society's problems, but many others have faith in a literal interpretation of the book of Genesis that is utterly in conflict with what science tells us about our own origins.

The science-religion conversation is often not a friendly debate. A spate of angry new books denouncing religious faith has appeared, some of them penned by atheist biologists who use evolution as a club to berate believers. On the other side of the great divide, the Intelligent Design (ID) movement presses on with its challenge to evolution's ability to explain "irreducibly complex" structures in living organisms, despite lack of any meaningful support in the scientific community and a recent stunning court defeat of the plan to teach ID as an alternative to evolution in the school system. As perhaps the strangest development of all, a "creation museum" has opened just outside Cincinnati, depicting humans frolicking with dinosaurs, despite overwhelming scientific evidence that they were separated in history by more than sixty million years. What's going on here? How can the most advanced technological country in the world also be home to such antiscientific thinking?

Some have dismissed this as an inevitable consequence of the fact that Americans take their religion seriously. In that context, they say that this is just one more chapter in a perpetual and irreconcilable battle between science and faith, arguing that these worldviews are simply incompatible and that individuals have to make a choice about which to believe in. But, as Karl Giberson ably describes in this much-needed book, that would be a misrepresentation of the facts. In reality, science and religion have generally coexisted quite comfortably until about a century or so ago. Copernicus, Kepler, and Galileo were all firm believers, and Newton wrote more words about biblical interpretation than he did on mathematics and physics. Clearly the greatest threat to that harmony has been the arrival of Darwin's theory of evolution, but even that development was not initially seen by leaders of the Christian church as all that threatening to their worldview after publication of *On the Origin of Species*.

Giberson has provided a critical service by leading us carefully through a series of historical events that began in the late nineteenth century and led to the current culture wars. These events stretch from Ellen White's Seventh-day Adventist visions of creation, to the birth of fundamentalism as a response to a liberal form of Christian theology that actually denied the divinity of Christ, to the human misery wrought by those who misused Darwin's theory to justify oppressive social changes, to the ill-conceived but still widely embraced *The Genesis Flood* of Henry Morris, which proposed a scientific basis for a very young earth.

Giberson's carefully documented history provides a sobering response to the claims of those who think that the current controversy can be quickly resolved. Just as with other great world conflicts, such as the current war in the Middle East, we will be forever doomed to disappointment in an effort to find peace and harmony if we don't understand how we got to this contentious juncture.

C. S. Lewis, the great proponent of a rational approach to Christian faith, led the Socratic Club at Oxford more than half a century ago, and the motto of the group was "to follow the argument wherever it leads." *Saving Darwin* is in that distinguished tradition. We should all be able to agree, believers and nonbelievers alike, that finding the truth is our task. We may disagree about how to interpret some of the facts, of course, but we cannot dismiss them as just inconvenient.

Here are some true statements that cannot be ignored:

Darwin's theory of evolution has been overwhelmingly supported by evidence from a wide variety of sources. Those include the increasingly detailed fossil record, but even more compelling evidence now comes from the study of genomes from many organisms, providing much more proof of common descent (including *Homo sapiens*) than Darwin could have dreamed

of. Given such oddities in our own DNA record as pseudogenes and ancestral chromosome fusions, special creation of humans simply cannot be embraced by those familiar with the data, unless they wish to postulate a God
who intentionally placed misleading clues in our own DNA to test our faith.

Alternatives to evolution such as young- or old-earth creationism and
intelligent design find almost no support in the scientific community. Although many nonscientist Christians have been taught to embrace one or
another of these alternatives as a means of opposing the perception that evolution is godless, the God of all truth is not well served by lies, no matter
how noble the intentions of those who spread them.

On the other hand, a purely naturalistic worldview can be justly criticized as narrow and impoverished. Science must forever remain silent on
questions such as: "What is the meaning of life?" "Is there a God?" "Do
right and wrong have any real meaning?" and "What happens after we die?"
And yet surely those are profoundly important questions that we humans
should be trying to answer. Only a spiritual worldview can help us here.

The good news is that there is a harmonious solution at hand. Many
working scientists, including Giberson and myself, find no conflict in both
embracing the conclusion that evolution is true and seeing this as the means
by which God implemented his majestic creation. In that synthesis of the
natural and spiritual perspectives we have found much joy and peace, where
our increasingly detailed understanding of the molecules of life only adds
to our awe of the Creator. Put in that framework, DNA is essentially the language God used to speak us and all other living things into being.

Yet the culture wars continue. And if some resolution is not found soon,
we will all be the losers. Would that we could return to the exhortations of
theologians like Benjamin Warfield, who wrote these words in the late nineteenth century, fully aware of the significance of Darwin's theory and unafraid of its consequences for the future of the Christian faith:

> We must not, then, as Christians, assume an attitude of antagonism toward
> the truths of reason, or the truths of philosophy, or the truths of science,
> or the truths of history, or the truths of criticism. As children of the light,
> we must be careful to keep ourselves open to every ray of light. Let us, then,
> cultivate an attitude of courage as over against the investigations of the day.
> None should be more zealous in them than we. None should be more quick

to discern truth in every field, more hospitable to receive it, more loyal to follow it, whithersoever it leads. (From B. B. Warfield, *Selected Shorter Writings* [Phillipsburg, NJ: PRR Publishing, 1970, pp. 463–65.])

Saving Darwin is a powerful contribution to this critically important effort to seek an enlightened and worshipful peace. With clearly presented statements of truth like those within these pages, together with a shared confidence that scientific discoveries about nature can hardly threaten nature's Creator, perhaps we have a chance in this century to develop a new Christian theology that celebrates God's awesome creation, unafraid of what science can tell us about the details. Then perhaps we can get beyond these destructive battles to focus on the real meaning of Christianity. That actually has little to do with alternative creation stories and everything to do with God's love as demonstrated most profoundly in the life, death, and resurrection of Jesus Christ.

Francis S. Collins, M.D., Ph.D.

THE DISSOLUTION OF A FUNDAMENTALIST

I n 1975 I left my home in maritime Canada to attend Eastern Nazarene College on Boston's historic south shore. Among my prized possessions, as I nervously traded the potato fields for the big city, were dog-eared copies of Henry Morris's classic texts of scientific creationism and Christian apologetics, *The Genesis Flood* and *Many Infallible Proofs*.[1]

Morris, who passed away in early 2006 as I was writing these words, was one of my boyhood heroes. As Willie Mays had inspired me to play center field, and Gordon Lightfoot the guitar, so Morris inspired me to master the art of Christian apologetics, to be, in the immortal words of St. Paul, "not ashamed of the testimony of our Lord." Morris, a giant of American fundamentalism, profoundly influenced religion in twentieth-century America, an influence that extended undiminished into much of Canada as well.

My childhood experiences in center field convinced me that, although I had mastered Mays's famous basket catch, baseball held no future for me. The great gulf between Gordon Lightfoot's guitar playing and my own confirmed that I would never make a living in folk music. But I was good at math and science—and arguing—and it looked as though I might follow in Morris's footsteps and become a Christian apologist. I was particularly enamored with Morris's eloquent and scientifically informed defense of the Genesis creation story and his clear-headed refutation of Darwinian evolution. I planned to major in physics, get a Ph.D., and go to work at Morris's recently created Institute for Creation Research in San Diego, where I would join those noble fundamentalist warriors as they stormed the ramparts of evolution and rescued the Genesis story of creation.

Like many young people raised in fundamentalist churches, I had been captured by the promise of scientific creationism, which Morris had launched in the early 1960s with the publication of his remarkable book *The Genesis Flood*. In that classic and impressively technical work, Morris and his coauthor, Old Testament scholar John C. Whitcomb, argue persuasively that the Bible and the Book of Nature agree that the earth was created in its present state about ten thousand years ago. The 518-page volume, which has sold over a quarter million copies and is still available in its forty-fourth printing, had enough footnotes, graphs, and pictures to convince any intellectually oriented fundamentalist that there was no reason to take evolution seriously. Readers could rest assured in the knowledge that Darwin's theory was deeply flawed, without empirical support, and on the verge of collapse. A few celebrated and highly publicized defections from the evolutionary camp illustrated the magnitude of the problem and suggested that this was an opportune time to join the war against Darwin's evil theory. In stark contrast to the failing fortunes of evolution, Whitcomb and Morris argued persuasively that the biblical creation story became increasingly credible as scientific evidence accumulated.

My first year at Eastern Nazarene College, which wasn't the fundamentalist haven I had anticipated, was troubling. Away in a strange new city, homesick for the rolling hills of the beautiful St. John River Valley I had left behind in New Brunswick, and without close friends, I struggled in the classroom. My Bible professor assaulted my literalist reading of Genesis, suggesting that Genesis should be read as poetry rather than science, a liberal heresy that Morris had warned me I might encounter. To make matters worse, the science faculty—despite claiming to be Christians—all seemed to accept evolution. Even my fellow students, at least in the science division, had limited interest in the creationist cause to which I had heroically dedicated myself.

These experiences steeled my resolve to stay the course. My extensive reading in fundamentalist apologetics and scientific creationism—and my enthusiasm for arguing—gave me confidence I was right. I could quote credentialed biblical scholars who understood that Genesis was more than poetry and that Christian theology would come apart if Genesis was not read literally. I had books by real scientists refuting evolution with solid arguments that, strangely, many of my professors did not know. The literature buttressing my position was extensive, my authorities were unassailable, and someday I too would have the credentials to speak with authority on this topic.

During my freshman year I attended a creationist event at Boston University, where Duane Gish, the premier and highly polished creationist debater, humiliated his inarticulate and unprepared opponent, who utterly failed to defend evolution. A vision of myself in that same role, perhaps a decade hence, further inspired me. At the end of the year I had the good fortune to meet the grand old man of creationism himself—Henry Morris—at a local church, where he was giving a Saturday seminar on creation. I chatted with him afterwards, and he encouraged me on my course, suggesting that I follow through on my plans to earn a Ph.D. in physics and then contact him at the Institute for Creation Research for a possible research position. He signed my well-worn copy of his manifesto, *Many Infallible Proofs,* inscribing the following biblical reference, 2 Timothy 1:7–9:

> For God hath not given us the spirit of fear; but of power, and of love, and of a sound mind. Be not thou therefore ashamed of the testimony of our Lord, nor of me his prisoner: but be thou partaker of the afflictions of the gospel according to the power of God; who hath saved us, and called *us* with an holy calling, not according to our works, but according to his own purpose and grace, which was given us in Christ Jesus before the world began.[2]

I WAS A TEENAGE FUNDAMENTALIST

Scientific creationism, the idea that the biblical story of creation rests on solid scientific evidence, is an integral part of the fundamentalist worldview that inspired me as a teenager. This understanding of Christianity starts with the assumption that the Bible is completely without error of any kind, having essentially been written by God. Scientific statements in the Bible are completely accurate, and historical references are utterly reliable. All statements on all topics are absolutely trustworthy in all respects. This is the fundamentalist creed, learned at mother's knee, reinforced in Sunday school, to be defended at all costs.

God inspired the biblical authors in such a way that their writings would be indistinguishable from dictation directly from God. God is thus the *author* of the Bible, and the "writers" are little more than scribes. Fundamentalist preachers quote Scripture constantly, rarely introducing it with anything other than "the Bible says" or "God says." This view of Scripture gives the Bible both an extraordinary authority and a complete unity of perspective. It has one author and no errors. Complex arguments can thus be securely developed by lifting bits of text from widely disparate books of the Bible and combining them, just as geometrical proofs can be constructed by combining axioms and theorems. If God wrote the entire Bible, then it is one long coherent message.

God provided the Genesis creation story so that we might understand our origins. In this account we read that God created a perfect world, with no sin, no death, and great harmony between his creatures and himself. Under the temptation of Satan, the first human couple, Adam and Eve, sinned—of their own free will—bringing death, suffering, and destruction into the world. If they had not sinned, they would still be alive, listening to music on their iPods and enjoying millions of great-grandchildren. This is the clear meaning of the text, taken at face value. Any other reading implies that God created an imperfect world and that the evils of death and suffering were part of his original creation.

Such dramatic and deeply counterintuitive elements are common in the fundamentalist reading of the Genesis creation story. The first appearance of sin in a perfect creation was a catastrophic transformation, like a crack in a magnificent glass window or a beautiful vase. Sin completely changed the *physical* as well as the *moral* structure of the world, introducing a major "break" in natural history. Women's bodies were altered so childbirth would be painful. The ecology changed so growing crops would be hard work. Plants developed thorns, and helpful bacteria turned into sinister parasites, inflicting disease on their hosts. Elsewhere in the Bible we read that all of creation "groans" under a universal curse that an enraged God placed on the creation because of the sin of Adam and Eve.[3] Many scientific creationists identify this curse with the physicists' famous second law of thermodynamics, that mysterious statement that nature constantly grows ever more disordered as time passes. What better explanation for the origin of this law than the sin of Adam and Eve?

THE END OF CREATION

At the end of the creation story in Genesis, God rests. Whatever processes were used to "create" shut down on the sixth day of creation and are no longer a part of the natural order. Science thus has no access to these processes and is limited to studying the stable, status-quo, postcreation patterns of nature. It follows that there can really be no "science" of origins, and we should not expect to understand the various mechanisms—all of them supernatural—that God used to create the world. Secular scientists err in attempting to understand origins by inspection of the fossil record and geological history. The record that the geologists and paleontologists are reading to recreate the natural history of our planet is not the story of our origins; it is, in fact, nothing more than the residue of Noah's great flood.

The flood story is a central underpinning of scientific creationism. Genesis says that the human race, about four thousand years ago, had become so wicked it had to be annihilated. God wiped out almost all humanity with a flood—a global cataclysm that completely reshaped the surface of the earth. This flood laid down virtually all the fossil strata we find today and completely contoured the surface features of the earth, from the Grand Canyon to Mt. Everest. Tectonic activity thrust up mountains. Receding floodwaters carved out canyons, both grand and small. The flood scoured off any prior earth history, like a bulldozer removing an ancient forest to make room for a parking lot.

The classic text by Whitcomb and Morris, *The Genesis Flood*, marshals scientific evidence for this biblical story, arguing that it provides a better explanation for the fossil record and the surface geology of the earth than the conventional scientific account arising from the erroneous assumption by misguided scientists that the earth is billions of years old. *The Genesis Flood* also argues effectively that the Bible intends us to take the flood story literally and understand it as a global, rather than local, event. After the floodwaters receded, God promised Noah that he would never again flood the earth. He placed a rainbow, for the first time, in the heavens as a sign of his promise. The laws of physics changed at this time—about four thousand years ago—to enable rainbows.

Whitcomb and Morris argue convincingly that the scientific and biblical witnesses to these historical accounts agree perfectly. So why, I wondered, does such widespread opposition exist within the scientific community? How can it be that the entire academic community of geologists rejects the worldwide flood of Noah and claims the earth is billions of years old? Why are biologists so blind to the simple truth that God created the world in six days? Why do physicists and astronomers propose so many ideas—from radioactive dating to stellar evolution to the big bang—that suggest the universe is ancient? Why do so many biblical scholars—who claim to be

Christians—reject the biblical witness to all of this? Why do theologians say that none of this matters?

Morris's answers to these questions are simple. Human beings, he explains, are fallen, sinful creatures, easily deceived by Satan. Blind to God's truth, secular scientists and liberal scholars of religion are unknowingly doing the will of the devil. The existence of such a widespread conspiracy to destroy the simple truths of Genesis demands nothing less than just such a comprehensive explanation. Satan has deceived the scientific community, and a great many Christians as well.

Apparently, I wasn't the only reader convinced by the arguments of Whitcomb and Morris. A 2004 CBS poll revealed that over half the population of the United States accepts the biblical creation story, many of them embracing the exact version Whitcomb and Morris presented a half century ago.[4] This position is thoroughly at odds with almost *all* the relevant scholarship of the past century. Today I would describe this view as sophomoric in the most literal sense of the word, which it certainly was for me, as I watched it wilt over the course of my sophomore year in college. By the middle of that critical year I was sliding uncontrollably down the slippery slope that has characterized religion since it began the liberalizing process just over a century ago.

THE EVOLUTION OF A FUNDAMENTALIST

An interesting concept in evolutionary theory is the pompous-sounding *ontogeny recapitulates phylogeny*. Originally proposed by the German evolutionist Ernst Haeckel in 1866, this idea claims that the development of the embryo of a species—its *ontogeny*—is a fast-forward version of its entire evolutionary history—its *phylogeny*. The sequence of developmental steps through which an embryo passes as it matures—in mother's womb, for humans—is a mirror of the developmental steps through which the species has passed in the course of its evolution over millions of years.

Scientists today reject much of Haeckel's once influential idea. Nevertheless, the concept provides a marvelous description of the process I went through in my sophomore year of college as I evolved rapidly from the simple intellectual life-form called *Homo fundamentalis* to something more complex, in the process passing rapidly through the various intermediate forms that emerged in the decades since Darwin.

As I studied science and mathematics, I began to doubt that science could have gotten everything as thoroughly wrong as the creationists suggested. The simple physics of radioactivity, widely used to date rocks, provides a characteristic example. Many different ways exist to date the earth, and almost all of them agree that the earth is billions, not thousands, of years old. If the earth was really just a few thousand years old as the Bible seemed to indicate,[5] why would God plant evidence to trick us into thinking it was billions of years old?

Just as my counterparts in the eighteenth and nineteenth centuries struggled to reconcile the new geology of their day with the Bible, I tried at first to play with different, but still literal, readings of Genesis. Maybe I could salvage the Genesis story by reading the "days" of creation as long periods of time. But this didn't seem reasonable. The Bible says, "In the beginning God created the heaven and the earth," while science says the earth appeared some nine billion years *after* the universe began. Furthermore, God created the sun on the fourth day, *after* the vegetation, which presumably needed the sun to survive. If the third day was a billion years long, the vegetation would have been long gone before the photosynthesis of the fourth day ever got started.

Each new question made things more complicated. A billion-year-old earth demands that we reinterpret "the fall." As long as Adam and Eve appeared in the same week as everything else, it was at least possible that their "sin" brought unintended death and suffering into the world. But now it appears that death and suffering had been present for a billion years with entire species going extinct long before humans appeared. Why would God create species only to have them go extinct long before Adam even had time to name them? Was this the same God who would later *preserve* every species on the planet by having Noah build an ark to rescue them from the flood? If extinction was normal, why did we need an ark? What, exactly, were the implications of the fall?

The acceptance of an ancient earth brings other troubles. If we take the geological record seriously, we confront fossils of what look like humans in rock strata more than a hundred thousand years old. And these fossils look as if they belong to a species that evolved from similar, earlier species. If we line up all these species in historical order, we have what certainly looks like a compelling narrative of human evolution from subhuman ancestors. Where in this history do we place Adam and Eve? No logical place appears in the unbroken sequence of human evolution for the famous residents of the Garden of Eden. And where, exactly, *was* the Garden of Eden? The Genesis story says that God placed an angel at the entrance to keep people out, which certainly implies that it was to continue even after Adam and Eve were expelled. We have no record of God closing it down. If God didn't destroy Eden, where is it now?

Doubts about the historicity of Adam and Eve and the Garden of Eden make it hard to read the creation stories without asking additional difficult questions. And fundamentalists in the midst of their theological breakdowns look in vain to contemporary biblical scholarship for help. Al Truesdale, my freshman Bible professor, had offered many helpful suggestions just a year earlier, bless his heart, but I had rejected all of them. They now came rushing back to haunt me. I found myself in an uncomfortable alternate reality that was a strange and darkened mirror image of the fundamentalist world I had inhabited for my entire life.

Fundamentalists find a satisfying harmony between science, as they understand it, and the Bible, as they interpret it. Their "science" is scientific creationism, which gathers evidence for the Genesis creation story. Their approach to the Bible is biblical literalism, which reads the text in the simplest way possible. These approaches reinforce each other and make the whole greater than the sum of the parts. But real science, which I was studying in college, and contemporary biblical scholarship, which religion majors were studying, conspire in such a way that the whole becomes *less* than the parts. The Genesis story of creation loses all contact with natural history and starts to look strangely like an old-fashioned fairy tale that might teach a lesson, but certainly makes no claim to historicity.

I learned, for example, that the word we translate as "Adam" in our English Bibles simply means "man" in Hebrew. And "Eve" means "woman." I began to wonder how an old story about a guy named "Man" in a magical garden who had a mate named "Woman" made from one of his ribs could ever be mistaken for actual history. And yet this was exactly what I had believed just one year earlier. Talking snakes, visits from God in the evening, naming the animals—the story takes on such a different character the moment one applies even the most basic literary analysis. The literalist interpretation I had formerly embraced and defended so vigorously began to look ridiculous, as did the person I had been just one year earlier.

THE JENGA TOWER

I would have liked to find some simple alternative reading of Genesis to re-place the literalist interpretation, but, if one existed, I certainly couldn't find it. I turned with some optimism to religion scholars, but found they had lit-tle to offer. Some of them strangely insisted on the historicity of *some* por-tions of the Genesis story, while allowing that much of it was not historical. The fall, for example, was sometimes an important part of elaborate theo-logical systems, serving the critical function of getting God off the hook for a creation filled with so much suffering. So even though Adam and Eve were not actual characters themselves and Eden was not a real place, they at least represented *something* historical. Once upon a time human beings did *some-thing* to ruin God's perfect creation, and this is where it all went wrong.

I was now wearing scientific spectacles almost all the time, and these ex-planations looked a little too convenient to me. Some theologians, for exam-ple, liked the way that Paul's reference to Jesus as the "second Adam" drew a provocative connection between the fall and redemption (1 Cor. 15:45). The first Adam made the mess; the second Adam cleaned it up. I could never see, though, how theologians could be so comfortable with a mythical interpretation of Eden, but insist on an important historical role for its first resident. Paul's "first Adam" was indeed the original sinner, but he didn't live in the Garden of Eden, he didn't name all the animals, and he may or may not have been married to Eve.

Further complicating my struggles, the religion scholars I consulted were quite accepting of evolution. An Old Testament scholar with a Ph.D. from Boston University assured me that "Genesis was never intended to be read literally." He and his colleagues had made their peace with evolution, appar-ently as toddlers, and had been at peace about this ever since. They were surprisingly disinterested in the struggles of those who, like me, were try-ing to hold on to some version of their childhood faith, while portions of its foundations were slowly removed, like the pieces of a Jenga tower that may or may not come crashing down as once extracts the tiny logs.

THE UNIVERSAL ACID OF DARWINISM

Tufts University philosopher Daniel Dennett describes evolution as a "uni-versal acid." With undisguised glee he outlines how evolution, which he calls

"Darwin's dangerous idea," eats through and dissolves the foundations of religion. The theory of evolution, which he thinks is the greatest idea anyone ever had, destroys the belief that God created everything, including humans. "Darwin's idea," he writes with approval, "eats through just about every traditional concept, and leaves in its wake a revolutionized worldview."[6]

Acid is an appropriate metaphor for the erosion of my fundamentalism, as I slowly lost my confidence in the Genesis story of creation and the scientific creationism that placed this ancient story within the framework of modern science. Dennett's universal acid dissolved Adam and Eve; it ate through the Garden of Eden; it destroyed the historicity of the events of creation week. It etched holes in those parts of Christianity connected to these stories—the fall, "Christ as second Adam," the origins of sin, and nearly everything else that I counted sacred. I discovered, however, that this was about where Dennett's acid ran out of steam (or whatever acid runs out of when it stops dissolving everything). The acid of evolution is not universal, and claims that evolution "revolutionizes" our worldview and dissolves every traditional concept are exaggerated.

For starters, what exactly does evolution have to do with belief in God as creator? It rules out *certain* mechanisms that God might have used to create the world, but others remain. God apparently did not create the entire universe and everything in it over the course of a few busy days ten thousand years ago. Neither Rome nor the universe was built in a day. But saying that Rome was not built in a day does not imply that Rome was not built or that Rome did not have builders. The acid of evolution dissolves the claim that God created the world a few thousand years ago, but does nothing to the claim that God may have taken billions of years to create or that God even continues to work as creator.

Creation, I hasten to point out, is a *secondary* doctrine for Christians. The central idea in Christianity concerns Jesus Christ and the claim that he was the Son of God, truly divine and truly human. This extraordinary idea implies the strange notion that the creator of the entire universe chose to enter the human race in the person of an itinerant preacher from Galilee. From its beginnings Christianity had to defend itself against charges that this was a ridiculous idea. Some of the most influential early church fathers were quite clear that the claims of Christianity were, indeed, absurd, but this did not mean they were not true. A second-century theologian named Tertullian said he believed in the divinity of Jesus partly because it *was* absurd.[7]

Most thoughtful Christians, myself included, wonder about exactly how it could be that God entered the human race in the person of Jesus—the historical event called the Incarnation. Over the centuries many have been simply unable to believe that this claim was even sensible. Today thinking Christians everywhere struggle with this belief and what it means. Many have asked God for more faith, to keep doubt at bay or reestablish a foundation for belief. Darwin's theory of evolution adds *nothing* to the complexities and challenges of believing in the Incarnation. It didn't take Darwin to make Christianity offensive, complex, and intellectually challenging. The arguments against the incarnation have been around for two thousand years, which is why Christianity is described as a *faith*, not as the conclusion of a logical argument.

Christianity merges the Incarnation with the belief that Jesus rose from the dead. Christ's Resurrection offers hope that we too can have eternal life and one day be united with God. Human skepticism regarding these claims is hardly new. The contemporaries of Jesus found this hard to believe, and many of them, including the infamous "doubting Thomas," had to be convinced by more than hearsay. Human beings, including Jesus, may have evolved over billions of years, or they may have been created a few thousand years ago. The Resurrection is equally implausible in either case. Dennett's universal acid of evolution does nothing to eat away at this central Christian belief. The "acid" of logic and reason was hard at work on this before the New Testament was even penned.

Christianity, as its name suggests, is *primarily* about Christ. To be sure, different ideas about Christ exist across the spectrum of Christian belief. But these beliefs, rather than creationist assertions, are the heart and soul of Christianity. And these beliefs are not threatened by Darwin's dangerous idea. Evolution does, however, pose two challenges to *secondary* Christian beliefs: the *fall* of humankind, and the *uniqueness* of humankind.

DISSOLVING THE FALL

Clearly, the historicity of Adam and Eve and their fall from grace are hard to reconcile with natural history. The geological and fossil records make this case compellingly. Nevertheless, scholars have proposed many convoluted and implausible ways to resolve these tensions in the past couple centuries. One could believe, for example, that at some point in evolutionary history

God "chose" two people from a group of evolving "humans," gave them his image, and then put them in Eden, which they promptly corrupted by sinning. But this solution is unsatisfactory, artificial, and certainly not what the writer of Genesis intended. Nor does any historical evidence suggest this interpretation. This modification also does absolutely nothing to support the idea that death did not exist in the world before sin. We must concede that the acid of evolution has indeed eaten away the literal part of this story, but I would argue that the most important part of the story remains untouched.

The idea at the center of the fall is human sinfulness. Human beings are sinful creatures, and many of us are really quite dreadful. Even the best of us dare not lay claim to anything even approaching perfection. G. K. Chesterton once quipped that the sinful nature of humans was the only Christian doctrine that we could confirm empirically.[8] The classic story of the fall is best understood as a powerful statement that we are, when all is said and done, sinful creatures.

But what, exactly, does it mean to be *sinful*? Various theological interpretations exist, some more compelling than others. But when the rubber hits the road, *sinfulness* is mainly *selfishness*. We put ourselves ahead of others and ahead of God. We advance our own agenda as if that is all that matters.

Evolution says some interesting things about selfishness. Selfishness, in fact, drives the evolutionary process. Unselfish creatures died, and their unselfish genes perished with them. Selfish creatures, who attended to their own needs for food, power, and sex, flourished and passed on these genes to their offspring. After many generations selfishness was so fully programmed in our genomes that it was a significant part of what we now call human nature.

But an interesting tension exists in human nature. As incurably selfish as we appear to be, we also possess an innate altruism. Human beings are easily capable of actions that benefit others at their own expense—from taking a pie to a new neighbor, to giving money to charities, to risking one's life to save a child. Although altruism is scientifically harder to understand than selfishness, it remains clear that humans are a powerful mix of selfish and unselfish tendencies.

So where does sin originate? In the traditional picture, sin originates in a free act of the first humans: God gave humans free will and they used it to contaminate the entire creation. That was the risk God took in creation. But now we have a new and better way to understand the origins of sin. We start by enlarging our own troublesome "freedom" to include nature. In the same way that we possess a genuine freedom to explore possibilities, nature has freedom as well, although not a conscious freedom, of course. Physicists enshrine this insight in the Heisenberg Uncertainty Principle, which accords a degree of genuine "freedom" to particles like the electron.

If nature, in all its many processes, is "free" to explore pathways of possibility, then the evolutionary process would predictably lead to creatures with pathological levels of selfishness. Creatures inattentive to their own needs would not have made it. By these lights, God did not "build" sin into the natural order. Rather, God endowed the natural order with the freedom to "become," and the result was an interesting, morally complex, spiritually rich, but ultimately selfish species we call *Homo sapiens*. This is an entirely reasonable theological speculation, at least by my amateur standards. It brings the Christian doctrine of the fall into the larger picture of an extended creation. Humankind did not appear all at once, and neither did sin.

DISSOLVING THE UNIQUENESS OF HUMANKIND

Once we accept the full evolutionary picture of human origins, we face the problem of human uniqueness. The picture of natural history disclosed by modern science reveals human beings evolving slowly and imperceptibly from earlier, simpler creatures. None of our attributes—intelligence, upright posture, moral sense, opposable thumbs, language capacity—emerged suddenly. Every one of our remarkable capacities must have appeared gradually and been present in some partial, anticipatory way in our primate ancestors. This provocatively suggests that animals, especially the higher primates, ought to possess an identifiable moral sense that is only *quantitatively* different from that of humans. Not surprisingly, current research supports this notion.

Scientists who have spent enough time with primates, especially in natural settings, are continually struck by their sophistication. In his remarkable books on primates, Emory University primatologist Frans de Waal describes primate behaviors that, were they associated with humans, would suggest a well-defined sense of right and wrong, cruelty and kindness, loyalty and manipulation. A remarkable bonobo named Kuni, to recount one example, saw a starling hit a glass wall and plummet to the ground. Kuni carefully picked up the stunned bird, set it on its feet, and waited with apparent concern for

it to fly. When it didn't fly off on its own, Kuni picked up the bird and carried it carefully to the top of a large tree. Wrapping her legs around the tree
to free both hands, Kuni spread the wings of the bird and released it, only
to watch it flutter to the ground. Kuni then stood watch over the bird for a
good portion of the day until it finally recovered and flew off on its own.[9]
This story is close enough to that of the good Samaritan to make it hard to
treat morality as a purely human attribute. And we have records of countless
other examples of similar animal behaviors.

Primates have learned enough language to communicate with over a
hundred symbols. They can do simple math, punching a key for "3" when
they see three candies in a bowl. Primate "societies" are home to such typically human behaviors as male competition, the bullying of nerds, and female solidarity. Researchers find traits like loyalty, jealousy, and generosity
among primates and other species as well. Anthropologists have even observed what look like collective spiritual gatherings of primates, in which
a group of chimpanzees will gather to watch, in silence, a beautiful sunset,
dispersing after the event when a leader signals it is time to go. The large
number of human traits that appear in primate societies is intriguing and
sobering, especially as we contemplate the ongoing threat that our activities
pose to them.

Does the "acid" of our evolutionary kinship with the primates dissolve
anything of importance to Christian theology? I am not convinced that it
does.

The tricky issue for Christianity is teasing out which biblical and theological claims derive from a mistaken picture of science and which are central to the ongoing vitality of the faith. Until recently just about everyone in
all cultures perceived a great *qualitative* distinction between humans and
the higher primates. Certainly the biblical writers and the formative thinkers
of the Christian tradition could not have anticipated what we have learned
from primate studies in the past few decades. So we may suppose that they
would frame their religious understanding in exclusively human terms. In
the same way Christian cosmology was developed with the earth at the center of the universe, because that was the best understanding at the time.

Speculations such as these are above my pay grade, of course, and best
left to theologians. Still, I find no compelling reason to think that the central message of Christianity is incompatible with humanity's kinship with
the rest of the animal world. In fact, this continuity with the animal world

may place increasing theological significance on the welfare of animals and ecological responsibility.

THE VIEW FROM OUTSIDE

Many informed and careful Christian thinkers have made their peace with evolution and found ways to incorporate its central insights into their theology. Coming from conservative evangelical traditions are physicist Howard Van Till, in the Reformed tradition, formerly of Calvin College, and biologist Darrel Falk, from the Wesleyan tradition, who currently teaches at Point Loma Nazarene University. These respected thinkers ventured into the troubled waters of evolution and wrote popular books in an effort to bring their respective denominations out of the nineteenth century. [10] Both are committed Christians with stellar records of serving at their respective denominational colleges. Yet powerful, but deeply uninformed fundamentalists who wanted them censured assaulted their works.

Recently the head of the Human Genome Project and one of America's most visible scientists, Francis Collins, has endorsed the idea that evolution is compatible with Christianity. Collins, who converted from atheism to evangelical Christianity after reading C. S. Lewis's *Mere Christianity*, wrote *The Language of God: A Scientist Presents Evidence for Belief*.[11] In that influential book Collins stakes out a middle ground for evolution between the dogmatisms of atheistic materialism and fundamentalist creationism.

The Roman Catholic tradition currently has a significant dialog with science, and the Pontifical Academy of Science numbers many leading scientists, including evolutionists, among its members. This dialog has allowed Catholicism to avoid much of the anti-evolutionary frenzy that rained down on Falk and Van Till. Out of this tradition come Brown University biologist Ken Miller and Georgetown University theologian John Haught. Miller's 1999 *Finding Darwin's God* became something of a classic and its author an important public intellectual and symbol of the integration of evolution and Christianity.[12] Haught has written several books in this area, the most important of which is *God After Darwin*, a tweaking of traditional Catholic theology in response to evolution.[13]

In England, two influential theologians, Alister McGrath and Keith Ward, have penned several popular works apiece integrating evolution and Christian theology. McGrath holds the chair of Professor of Historical

Theology at Oxford University and Ward is the Emeritus Regius Professor of Divinity at Oxford, the most prestigious theological posting in the Anglican Church. McGrath has written the three-volume *Scientific Theology*, inaugurating a major project to reformulate Christian theology in light of recent scientific developments, particularly evolution.[14] Ward's *God, Chance and Necessity* offers helpful ways to reconcile evolution with belief in the doctrine of creation.[15]

Philosopher Michael Ruse has also made an interesting contribution. A prolific author, Ruse has been a fixture in America's creation–evolution controversy since he testified for the American Civil Liberties Union (ACLU) at the Arkansas "Scopes II" trial in 1981. In response to claims that the truth of evolution entails the falsity of Christianity, Ruse, a nonbeliever, wrote *Can a Darwinian Be a Christian?* He looks at every imaginable point of contact between evolution and Christianity and answers yes to the question posed in his title:

> If you are a Darwinian or a Christian or both, remember that we are mere humans and not God. We are middle-range primates with the adaptations to get down out of the trees, and to live on the plains in social groups. We do not have powers which will necessarily allow us to peer into the ultimate mysteries. If nothing else, these reflections should give us a little modesty about what we can and cannot know, and a little humility before the unknown.[16]

LOOKING AHEAD: THE PLAN OF THE BOOK

The creation–evolution controversy in America has become so overheated and loaded with half-truths and nonsense that it is all but impossible to get a clear picture of anything. Mythologies abound on both sides. Darwin's apocryphal deathbed repudiation of evolution is a popular and widely circulated myth comforting the faithful. The imminent collapse of evolutionary theory and the occasional celebrated negative comment about evolution by a leading scientist are others. These offer hope that biblical creation will make a comeback in America. Mirror-image mythologies about evolution are equally plentiful: the theory provides a solid foundation for atheism and assures the ultimate victory of secularization; every intelligent person now believes it; dissenters are "stupid, wicked, or insane."[17] We even hear that evolution will soon explain religion away. Such affirmations assure blinkered secularists that someday religion will go extinct, eaten away by the acid of evolution.

In the pages that follow I offer readers a tour of this troubled battlefield. Darwin, we will see, began his career as a committed Christian. He planned to become a minister and certainly had no intention of undermining religion. That his theory did this kept his stomach in a constant knot. Nevertheless, the responses to his theory, even from religious conservatives, were not uniformly hostile and, almost immediately, thinkers were finding ways to incorporate this new view of origins into their theological understanding of creation. Some even welcomed the theory as a more satisfactory explanation for nature's excessive waste and carnage. The widespread hostility currently leveled at Darwin's theory is a recent development, although it has always been present to some degree.

The most interesting and often unintentionally humorous challenges to Darwinism have not been scientific, but legal. Curiously, a cavalcade of lawyers claiming to have detected logical flaws in evolutionary reasoning starts with one of Darwin's contemporaries and runs through to some prominent lawyers in the present. Some of these lawyers, strangely, actually boast of their ignorance of biology as they flail about in irrelevance.

Moving into the present we encounter "scientific creationism" (also called "creation science") and "intelligent design," sibling perspectives insisting they are unrelated. Despite being largely devoid of scientific content, these movements have captured the hearts and minds of over half the country, although they remain, for the time being at least, banned from America's public schools.

In the current controversy, science has disappeared, and the argument has turned into a culture war, with political allies in smoke-filled back rooms formulating strategies with little regard for truth. Meanwhile, off the front pages of the newspapers, the science of evolution grows increasingly robust and secure, even as America's schools find the topic increasingly harder to teach.

I wish I could promise that the story in the following pages has a happy ending, but it does not. Loud confident voices, including the echo of my own college worldview, assure us that evolution is a false theory being used by Satan to destroy faith in God; equally loud voices counter that evolution is a true theory that is destroying faith in God. Quiet but less confident voices point out the absurdity of both of these claims. This disagreement is not going away anytime soon.

Places exist on which believers can stand, however, in the midst of the controversy. We don't know anywhere near enough about evolution to infer from it that God is not the creator. And we don't know anywhere near enough about God to dismiss the idea that evolution might be a part of God's creative processes. If we can embrace a bit of humility and avoid the temptation to enlarge either evolution or biblical literalism into an entire worldview, we can dismiss this controversy as the irrelevant shouting match that it is.

These insights, of course, were nowhere in sight as I began to wrestle in college with the unwelcome truth that evolution had strong empirical support and could not be dismissed as a satanic delusion. As I look back after three decades of reflection I can see, however, that my sophomoric struggles were nothing more than my personal encounter with Darwin's dangerous idea, an encounter that was hardly original with me. Believers everywhere, especially in America, continue the search for the elusive role that evolution should play in a comprehensive and satisfying understanding of ourselves and our origins.

CHAPTER 1

THE LIE AMONG US

History records three Charles Darwins. The most interesting Darwin is the one who repudiated his theory of evolution on his deathbed. A colorful character named Lady Hope claimed to have visited Darwin on his deathbed, where she found him reading his Bible and recanting his life's work. "I was a young man with unformed ideas," she quotes him as saying. "I threw out queries, suggestions, wondering all the time over everything. And to my astonishment the ideas took like wildfire. People made a religion of them."[1] Lady Hope's winsome story, which historians have shown was a complete fabrication,[2] has been circulating broadly among American evangelicals for the better part of a century and can still be found there.[3]

History's second Darwin is a sinister character in a story even more popular among evangelicals than Lady Hope's fiction. This Darwin was an enthusiastic and committed unbeliever who combed the globe gathering evidence to rationalize his disbelief. Authors and television personalities John Ankerberg and John Weldon present this Darwin in their popular *Darwin's Leap of Faith*. They argue that Darwin himself never even found evolution convincing. Their demonized Darwin rationalized atheism by concocting a preposterous theory whose only saving grace was its demolition of the idea that God created the world. To "soothe his fears," Ankerberg and Weldon write, "Darwin adopted a philosophy convenient to his own rejection of God."[4] This Darwin is also a fabrication, although less entertaining than the Lady Hope myth. Reading any one of the many recent excellent biographies of Darwin will put this to rest.

The third and actual Darwin was neither a deathbed convert nor lifelong crusader against belief in God. He was, in fact, a sincere religious believer who began his career with a strong faith in the Bible and plans to become an Anglican clergyman. He did eventually lose his childhood faith, but it was reluctantly and not until middle age, long after his famous voyage on the *Beagle*. Toward the end of his life he wrote to an old friend about the painful experience of losing his faith: "I was very unwilling to give up my belief." He recalled daydreaming about something that could arrest his slide into disbelief, perhaps the discovery of "old letters between distinguished Romans, and manuscripts being discovered at Pompeii or elsewhere, which confirmed in the most striking manner all that was written in the Gospels." Gradually, though, he found it harder to imagine being rescued in this way, and "disbelief crept over me at a very slow rate, but was at last complete."[5]

THE DEMONIZED DARWIN

Unfortunately, the real Darwin is the only one of no interest to antievolutionary demagogues. Eager to keep the faithful on track, they smear Darwin and his theory unmercifully. In *The Long War Against God: The History and Impact of the Creation/Evolution Controversy*, the late Henry Morris proposed that Darwin actually got his theory indirectly from Satan. Darwin, argues Morris with a perfectly straight face, was simply one in a long line of dupes spreading a sinister gospel of materialism originally delivered to humanity by Satan at the Tower of Babel.

> The very first evolutionist was not Charles Darwin or Lucretius or Thales or Nimrod, but Satan himself. He has not only deceived the whole world with the monstrous lie of evolution but has deceived himself most of all. He still thinks he can defeat God because, like modern "scientific" evolutionists, he refuses to believe that God is really God.[6]

Ken Ham, who heads the popular Answers in Genesis organization and is currently America's leading creationist, sees an apocalyptic dimension to evolution. On the back cover of his book *The Lie: Evolution,* Ham writes: "The Bible prophetically warns that in the last days false teachers will introduce lies among the people. Their purpose is to bring God's Truth into disrepute and to exploit Believers by telling them made-up and imagined stories. Such a Lie is among us. That Lie is Evolution."[7]

And finally, in more careful, restrained, and intentionally secular-sounding prose Phillip Johnson, the leader of the intelligent design movement, says:

"The aim of historical scientists—those who attempt to trace cosmic history from the big bang or before to the present—is to provide a complete naturalistic picture of reality. This enterprise is defined by its determination to push God out of reality."[8] In Johnson's opinion natural science is far too natural.

To the amazement of most Europeans, who made their peace with evolution long ago, these views on Darwin and his theory are widespread in the United States. The majority of children raised in America's evangelical culture encounter them somewhere, often from creationist evangelists like Ham who head organizations dedicated to destroying evolution. Ham's Answers in Genesis organization, for example, has almost two hundred employees and sponsors thousands of events every year, from visits to churches to massive rallies in public arenas with music and multimedia presentations. Sixty thousand people visit his Web site every day, and his books, videos, and tracts sell well. A $27 million creation museum opened in 2007. A glossy magazine, *Answers,* goes out to almost fifty thousand readers.[9] And, although Ham's operation is the most polished and best funded, there are dozens of others like it. Spreading the gospel of anti-evolution, with Darwin as the villain, is a million-dollar industry reaching an eager audience of American evangelicals larger than the population of any country in Europe.

But Charles Darwin is not a villain, and these portraits of him are irresponsible and malicious caricatures distorting him beyond recognition. In their eagerness to turn Darwin into a scary boogeyman, his detractors rewrite history and invent motives to suggest that evolution began as a conspiracy to destroy belief in God.

THE TORMENTED EVOLUTIONIST

Charles Darwin was born in 1809 to a well-to-do British family who, despite having some unorthodox characters listed in the family Bible, raised him in the Anglican Church, educated him at an Anglican school, and put him on the train to Edinburgh to study medicine. When this career ran off the rails, Charles's father, fearing his son might become an "idle sporting man," sent him to Cambridge to study theology in the hopes that he might become a parish priest.[10] Charles obliged, for he took family obligations seriously and was attracted to the genteel life of a "country clergyman." Nevertheless, he did look closely at the affirmations of the Anglican creeds, but since he did not "in the least doubt the strict and literal truth of every word in the Bible," he concluded that the creeds were acceptable, if confusing.[11] Whatever radical genes the young Darwin may have possessed had not yet kicked in.

Darwin's interest in natural history was enriched through his study of both medicine and theology, which were nicely complementary pursuits in nineteenth-century England. Science—which medicine aspired to be—nestled within a framework of natural theology, which uses insights from nature to fashion arguments about God. The most common argument was the traditional claim that design in nature implied the existence of an intelligent creator. Unlike today, when theology and science reside in different buildings on opposite corners of university campuses separated by armed guards and barbed wire, at this time they were in a robust and congenial dialog. Many parish priests were active naturalists, and there was a consensus that the rapidly developing sciences would continue to provide useful theological insights.

While studying theology at Cambridge University, Darwin came under the spell of William Paley, a leading Anglican philosopher and passionate abolitionist. Paley's influential texts, *Natural Theology, The Principles of Moral and Political Philosophy,* and *Evidences of Christianity,*[12] were standard fare for students of Darwin's generation and greatly influenced nineteenth-century British thought. Darwin would later comment that he could probably "have written out the whole of the *Evidences* with perfect correctness."[13] The design in nature, articulated Paley with arguments so clear and compelling they were compared to those of Euclid, implied the existence of a designer, namely, God. Darwin and his generation were taught to see the handiwork of God in nature; its beauty, order, and rich creativity reflected the attributes of its creator.

Darwin's career took a critical turn when Captain Robert Fitzroy, a conservative Anglican, accepted a recommendation that Darwin join him on an epic journey around the globe on a modest ship named the *Beagle.* The primary agenda was a survey of South America, though Fitzroy also intended to return some Fuegians who had trained in England as missionaries to Tierra del Fuego.

Extended journeys at sea were often lonely affairs for captains, typically the only cultured member of a tiny community of illiterate, seafaring philistines, all of them male and living in close quarters for months on end.

Fitzroy's uncle had committed suicide at sea, probably driven to it by intense loneliness. The *Beagle*'s captain needed a companion with whom to eat, talk, and stay sane. The passenger could also function as the ship's naturalist, cataloging the exotic flora and fauna of the globe to the greater glory of God and Great Britain.

Enter twenty-two-year-old Charles Darwin, for whom this posting was custom-made. After some negotiations with his father, Darwin joined the crew of the *Beagle* and set sail from Plymouth harbor two days after Christmas in 1831. The *Beagle* would return five years later with her captain still sane and her famous passenger in a muddle.

Darwin boarded the *Beagle* with his childhood Christian faith intact, although he had begun to wonder about the historicity of the more fanciful Old Testament stories, like the Tower of Babel. He was also starting to wonder about the vengeful, tyrannical God of the ancient Israelites. At one point during the voyage he recalled being "heartily laughed at by several of the officers for quoting the Bible as an unanswerable authority on some point of morality."[14] For the most part, however, Darwin's faith was unruffled, with the exception of his natural theology, which was constantly pierced by troubling observations that defied his expectations.

UNNATURAL THEOLOGY

Naturalists of Darwin's generation, like most scientists before and since, studied nature within the framework of their best understanding of the natural world. It is a popular fallacy that scientists study nature with no expectations, their observations falling on mental blank slates to be organized with perfect objectivity into secure and dispassionate generalizations that do nothing more than summarize the facts. Observations, rather, are gathered to *test* various ideas that are in play. Most often the ideas pass the tests and become more secure as a result, but sometimes the observations raise important questions. Darwin, like all scientists, brought his *expectations* to his observations of the natural world, constantly checking to see if the new facts were *consistent* with the expectations.

The network of expectations guiding scientific research at any given time is called a *paradigm*. It represents the collective wisdom of the scientific community and would have been reflected in the textbooks and lectures that

Darwin encountered at the university. Science advances, in general, by refining the understanding of these paradigms and by bringing more and more observations under the paradigm's explanatory umbrella.[15]

The role played by paradigms in science is paradoxical and can appear suspicious to outsiders. How can it be that a scientist like Darwin can *start* his investigation of nature "with his mind made up," so to speak? Are not these assumptions equivalent to *prejudices* blinding scientists to the truth and preventing them from correctly interpreting their observations? Does this not turn scientific investigation into a simple rationalization of the status quo? Was the Darwin of the *Beagle* simply reading his preconceptions into his observations of nature?

These questions are entirely legitimate. Nevertheless, there is a simple response: this is how the science that cured smallpox, built the atomic bomb, and put a man on the moon works. Centuries of rapid and creative scientific advance have honed the methods of science to the point where most people simply have faith in science. Advertisers exploit this faith when they describe their claims as "scientific" facts, as if some facts are more factual than others. Most people today are quite content to check into a hospital and place their very lives in the hands—one is tempted to say "on the altars"—of this science.

Under normal circumstances paradigms offer helpful guidance. In the century before Darwin, for example, Newton's law of universal gravity was an important guide to understanding the motions of a growing roster of celestial objects. After a few spectacular successes, astronomers stopped wondering if the law was correct. They simply assumed that it was and saw their assumption repeatedly validated.

Paradigms become interesting when they start to fail, which was what Darwin experienced on the *Beagle*. Long-standing assumptions about the natural world, buttressed by the authority of countless experts and integrated into comprehensive visions of reality, are challenged by fresh observations. "Commonsense" views of the world begin to crumble; order descends into chaos and understanding into confusion. These radical, world-shaking developments receive the label "scientific revolutions."

Scientists typically embrace their paradigms with a tenacity bordering on the irrational. In my training as a physicist I was simply taught the laws of physics, with no hint that they were anything other than decrees handed down by God to people like Albert Einstein and Niels Bohr. When it came time to start laboratory work, I did not consider for a moment that my experiments might contradict what I had learned; if I had run into my adviser's office waving a graph I said refuted quantum theory, my adviser would have laughed hysterically and suggested I switch to philosophy. Science is an incredibly conservative enterprise. Nevertheless, practicing scientists are anything but conservative and are quite often eccentric iconoclasts, or "nerds" in popular parlance. Dreams of revolution inspire scientists—of being the next Einstein and laying waste to the status quo—but the great staying power of their paradigms keeps them on course.

The inertia of paradigms is, paradoxically, the very reason we can trust science. New ideas in science are subjected to a withering scrutiny before they are accepted. Old ideas must be thoroughly refuted before they are discarded. If a long-standing and traditional idea, like astrology or a young earth, has been abandoned by science, we can be confident that it was not without compelling reasons.

So how do scientific revolutions occur? They start with observations that don't fit. Initially these "observations" often don't even register, like parents who can't see that their son is a bully. Then they register and become puzzles of great significance that raise questions about the prevailing paradigm. (Why does my son have no friends?) And then they become ho-hum facts that fit into a new paradigm. (My son is a bully, and his peers don't like him!) A classic example from the history of astronomy reveals this pattern.

STAR LIGHT, STAR BRIGHT, THE STAR I CAN'T SEE TONIGHT

In 1054 a brilliant new star appeared brightly in the constellation Taurus. Four times brighter than Venus, it was visible in daylight for several weeks and at night for almost two years. Enthralled Chinese astronomers wrote extensively about it and what it meant for developments on earth. European and Arab astronomers, however, were strangely silent about the new star, as if they did not even see it. They did "see" it, of course, for they were active observers, and the star was not to be missed. The only explanation for their oversight is that a new star was so thoroughly inconsistent with their expectations that they could not accept the testimony of their own eyes. Their astronomical paradigm included an ancient belief that the heavens were unchanging. The appearance of a new star would entail the absurd proposition that God had "restarted" the process of creation that had been completed on the sixth day. And that, of course, was simply ridiculous.

When such "impossible" observations become accepted as real, they "register" and raise deep questions about the veracity of the reigning paradigm. In 1572 Europe's greatest astronomer, Tycho Brahe, observed another new star in the heavens and was dumbfounded:

> Amazed, and as if astonished and stupefied, I stood still, gazing ... intently
> upon it.... When I had satisfied myself that no star of that kind had ever
> shone forth before, I was led into such perplexity by the unbelievability of
> the thing that I began to doubt the faith of my own eyes.... And at length,
> having confirmed that my vision was not deceiving me, but in fact that an
> unusual star existed there ... immediately I got ready my instrument. I began
> to measure its situation and distance from the neighboring stars.[16]

Brahe's new star made no sense within the reigning explanatory paradigm. But there it was, visible in daylight, clearly a new star. In time such observations helped topple the reigning paradigm, and astronomers became comfortable with the idea that new things occasionally appeared in the heavens.

In 1987 another new "star"—Supernova 1987a—appeared and, although it made the cover of *Time* magazine, it occasioned no distress in the scientific community.[17] By 1987 such phenomena had become part of mainstream astronomy, and this time the new star was of interest largely because it confirmed some untested implications of theories of stellar evolution.

DARWIN AND THE PARADIGM OF INTELLIGENT DESIGN

Darwin's observations on the *Beagle* mimic those of astronomers reacting to the appearance of new stars that don't fit into accepted paradigms. When he boarded the *Beagle*, Darwin had a traditional Christian worldview. On a personal level, he trusted the Bible and looked to it for moral guidance. On a philosophical level, he believed strongly in God as the source of the created order and the foundation for belief in salvation and eternal life. And, on a scientific level, he believed that the natural world was intelligently designed and that its design spoke clearly and eloquently of the wisdom, love, and creative power of God. The Darwin of the *Beagle*, like all naturalists of

his generation, looked at the world through the same eyes as the contemporary proponents of intelligent design, who see the handiwork of God in nature's intricate machinery.

Paley and the other natural theologians shaping Darwin's era had created a compelling framework for understanding the world as a collection of
elegantly designed organisms flourishing in custom-made ecological niches.
Hydrodynamically sophisticated fish swam in water, and aerodynamically
sophisticated birds flew in air. Like toddlers on a playground with brightly
colored and unusually safe equipment that is "just their size," the flora and
fauna of planet earth flourish in environments designed for them. The world
and its inhabitants were, quite literally, *made* for each other, and everything
everywhere testified to the glory of God.

It would be hard to overstate the importance of divine design among
British naturalists of Darwin's generation. The patterns of nature were all
attributed to God; the roster of living creatures was organized in a "great
chain of being" that revealed the hierarchical structure of the created order,
progressing from simple to complex; the properties of water and air and soil
and weather reflected God's wisdom and care.

Paley's *Natural Theology,* published in 1802, was one of the most popular texts in the English language. Read by all of Britain's naturalists, it provided the paradigm for understanding the natural world. As Darwin gazed
over the railing of the *Beagle,* he saw the world through spectacles provided
for him by William Paley. The handiwork of God was everywhere visible.
That he was often leaning over the rail being sick did nothing to dissuade
him from his conviction that the world, including his own troubled digestive
system, was a grand machine crafted by the Great Mechanic.

NATURAL THEOLOGY

Creationists have launched a salvo of accusations at Darwin, claiming he
invented evolutionary theory to rationalize his lack of faith. These claims
are so blatantly false and so clearly in opposition to everything we know
about Darwin, that we have to wonder how they arose. The facts are quite
clear: Darwin inherited a worldview that was solidly creationist, although
that term was not in use at that time. The young Darwin could have been a
staff biologist at Henry Morris's Institute for Creation Research or perhaps
a tour guide in Ken Ham's creation museum. Certainly he could have been a

senior fellow at the Discovery Institute, helping Phillip Johnson write op-eds and popular books promoting intelligent design.

Darwin, as we know, eventually abandoned this way of looking at the world. But this transition did not derive from his creeping agnosticism. It resulted from his repeated discoveries that the world was full of things that did not look intelligently designed. Eventually he slowly, and quite reluctantly, began to wonder whether there might be a better explanation for the observations that were his passion.

The young Darwin was, in fact, the equivalent of today's "intelligent design theorist," and perhaps it is as a traitor to this viewpoint that he generates so much hostility from his twenty-first-century counterparts. But there is no historical ambiguity about the central role that ideas about intelligent design played in his thought.

Darwin worked within an intellectual tradition that had been doing science—then called *natural philosophy*—in a theological context for centuries. And, although the term *intelligent design* was not in use at the time, there is little difference between this tradition and what currently bears the label. The only real difference is *political:* contemporary intelligent design is at war with mainstream science, while its precursor was in harmony with science. The drama of Darwin's generation was further reduced by the almost complete absence of polemicists like Richard Dawkins using science as a weapon against religion. Virtually the entire scientific tradition from Galileo to Darwin was deeply religious.

Science before Darwin rarely ran afoul of religion.[18] Galileo is a notable exception, but his conflict with the Roman Catholic Church represents only one aspect of his rich and varied scientific career. Most interactions were less exciting, and many were actually constructive. Not long after Galileo, for example, Newton discovered that the universe ran by a few simple laws. This led to the idea that the universe was like a great clock, implying that there must be a Grand Clockmaker who created it.

In the near perfect circular motion of the planets around the sun, Newton discovered an astonishing balance between the speeds of the planets and the stability of their orbits. Slow them down and they spiral into the sun; speed them up and they spiral away and leave the sun's gravitational embrace. This delicate balance was but one of many impressive features of the Newtonian world machine, exhibiting what mathematicians call beauty. Everywhere Newton looked he saw clear evidence of design. In his most important work, the *Principia Mathematica,* first published in 1687, Newton wrote: "This most beautiful system of the sun, planets, and comets could only proceed from the counsel and dominion of an intelligent and powerful Being." He goes on to mention other examples of God's wisdom, like the placement of the stars at great distances from each other, "lest the systems of the fixed stars should, by their gravity, fall on each other."[19]

Newton lit a fuse that ignited an explosion of scientific knowledge that transformed the following centuries. He modeled a way of using science to support religious belief, an approach rooted in the Middle Ages, when science was known as the "handmaiden" of theology. It was an approach that would carry forward into Darwin's century and even into our own, although with modification.

Across Europe, amid the splintering Christian denominations and even in the emerging deism, science supported natural theology. The marvelous hand of God was readily discerned in creation, as Newton, Paley, and everyone in between made so clear. Scientists were fascinated by a range of mysteries, including the enigmatic character of everyday occurrences like ice. Mysteriously, it is less dense than water and floats, enabling creatures to survive beneath it, protected from the ravages of cold northern winters. Does this not reveal the wisdom of God? Consider the eye. How could so many intricate parts—balls, sockets, lids, lenses, retinas, optic nerves—come together and work so well? Human joints, bats' wings, mother's milk, chicken eggs, roots, leaves, wind, rain—all celebrated the glory of God. Books with titles like *Water Theology* and *Insect Theology* argued directly from the details of creation to the nature and existence of the creator. God's fingerprints were everywhere.

Even those starting to reject Christianity and the Bible found in nature a compelling witness to God as creator. Thomas Paine, who penned the notorious *Age of Reason,* in which he claimed to "detest" the Bible "as I detest everything that is cruel," found in nature a clear revelation of God's power and benevolence.[20] The Bible, Paine contested, was written by men; God wrote the book of nature. The Bible was parochial and recent; nature was ancient and universal, available to all people at all times. Such celebrations of nature were common across Europe and in the New World. Everywhere, science supported belief in God through its revelations of both God's wisdom and concern for creatures. This tradition of natural theology nurtured the young Charles Darwin who set sail on the *Beagle.*

To be sure, there were exceptions. The Scottish skeptic David Hume, for example, challenged any argument claiming to identify divine "design." Perhaps, he suggested, design in nature was illusory or unintended. Glasses sit neatly on one's nose, but who would argue that the nose was made for this purpose? And some design looks stupid, even malevolent. Consider, Hume wrote, the many "curious artifices of nature, in order to embitter the life of every living being."[21] The French satirist Voltaire lampooned the idea that the world was well designed for its inhabitants. Appalled by the Lisbon earthquake, which killed a hundred thousand people, Voltaire ridiculed the popular idea that this was the "best of all possible worlds."[22]

Dissenters like Voltaire, who continued to believe in God, and Hume, who did not, could not hear nature testifying to a wise and benevolent creator. But they were minority voices, remembered as cranky renegades at odds with more traditional notions tucked deep into the hearts of their fellow Europeans. Such naysayers did little to chase natural theology from Britain, where earthquakes of the sort that destroyed Lisbon had never disrupted the blessed and bucolic countryside.

The centerpiece of nineteenth-century natural theology, of course, was William Paley's 1802 classic *Natural Theology, or Evidences of the Existence and Attributes of the Deity Collected from the Appearances of Nature,* where we find his famous watchmaker analogy:

In crossing a heath, suppose I pitched my foot against a stone, and were asked how the stone came to be there; I might possibly answer, that, for anything I knew to the contrary, it had lain there forever.... But suppose I had found a watch upon the ground, and it should be inquired how the watch happened to be in that place; I should hardly think of the answer I had before given.... There must have existed, at some time, and at some place or other, an artificer or artificers, who formed [the watch] for the purpose which we find it actually to answer; who comprehended its construction, and designed its use.... Every indication of contrivance, every manifestation of design, which existed in the watch, exists in the works of nature; with the difference, on the side of nature, of being greater or more, and that in a degree which exceeds all computation.[23]

Paley's watchmaker analogy—a standard part of the early nineteenth-century curriculum in England—bears exactly the same form as arguments that would be made two centuries later by intelligent design proponents. Compare this passage by the organizers of a major intelligent design conference two centuries after Paley:

> The universe and its laws have not always been around in their present state. The data from science also suggest a high degree of complexity throughout the history of life, and such complexity requires explanation that not only includes but also transcends natural processes alone. In addition, the data from science indicates an incredibly high degree of fine-tuning or balance within the structure of the universe at all levels. This also calls for an explanation that transcends natural processes.[24]

This is a critically important part of our story, as it illustrates the vitality of intelligent design thinking at the time of Darwin and, I am arguing, makes the early Darwin a nineteenth-century intelligent design theorist.

Paley's book was an eloquent summary of a broad range of arguments that had been developed over the preceding decades. Here we have an ingeniously fashioned wing; there a clever fin; look at this eye; consider this antenna; marvel at this or that appendage with this or that specific function. In compelling and captivating prose, the prose Darwin could quote by heart, he summarized an impressive range of design in the natural world and how this design pointed with clarity to the existence of a designer, "an intelligent designing mind for the contriving and determining of the forms which organized bodies bear."[25]

As Darwin boarded the *Beagle* the design of the natural world was as clear to him as the design of the boat that would carry him around the planet. Both were obviously the work of intelligent designers who matched form to function, and the *Beagle* lived up to expectations. The natural world, however, repeatedly failed to match Darwin's expectations. Each time the *Beagle* put down its anchor and Darwin inspected the local flora and fauna, he returned with troubling questions. Trained to believe that the natural world revealed a benevolent and wise creator, he began to wonder why so much of the world looked neither wise nor benevolent.

TROUBLING QUESTIONS

Scientific revolutions are three-act plays. In the first act, the status quo is so universally accepted that people have trouble even noticing ill-fitting anomalies. A new star where there is not supposed to be one will be over-looked or dismissed as irrelevant. In the second act, anomalies are noticed but viewed as puzzles to be solved, it is hoped, within the framework of the status quo. The new star creates a crisis forcing examination of the prevailing framework to see if it can be adjusted to accommodate this irregularity. In the final act, the anomalies precipitate the collapse of the status quo and become evidence supporting an entirely new understanding. Here is a "new" star, and it makes perfect sense.

Darwin's thought followed this same trajectory. He started his career as a naturalist viewing the world through the lens of natural theology and seeing intelligent design. But then he began to notice things that didn't fit: here is an animal with webbed feet living on dry land; there is a bee that dies after stinging its prey, its stinger serrated in a way that prevents extraction after insertion; here is a cat apparently torturing a mouse before killing it.

To suggest that these examples manifested God's wisdom and benevolence made a mockery of those terms. Did the loving God of Darwin's youth *really* install instincts in cats that would make them enjoy pummeling mice as if they were feline loan sharks from a barnyard parody of an old gangster movie? Surely not. Like Brahe observing a new star, Darwin made observations that challenged the bedrock assumptions of his paradigm.

The *Beagle* was a small ship, some twenty-four feet wide and ninety feet long. Cramped quarters provided limited room to maneuver, adding to the stress of the long journey. The framework of natural theology within which Darwin worked was similarly cramped and offered little room for intellectual maneuver. The anomalies that bothered Darwin had responses, of course. Maybe we just don't see the big picture; perhaps sin and the fall are responsible for some of the problems; maybe we don't understand the phenomena well enough; and so on. But these responses are woefully inadequate and little more than patches on an ancient ship riddled with holes and taking on water.

BATS, CATS, AND WASPS

As befits one of our species' true revolutionaries, scholars have scrutinized Darwin in detail. Every scribble in his voluminous notebooks and every letter in his vast correspondence have been dissected; every scientific paper has been examined for hints of the revolution to come; every footnote is a possible shaping influence, every acquaintance a possible intellectual accomplice. His modest autobiography, written near the end of his life and based on fragile recollections, has been laid out beside his more historical notebooks and the discrepancies analyzed. Magisterial new biographies appear with regularity, each one updating our unfolding picture of the nineteenth century's greatest scientist. The result is a clear picture of how Darwin came to his theory.

The natural theology of Darwin's training explained the distribution of life on the planet as God's coordinated design of both creatures and their habitats, an explanation that accounted for the many remarkable adaptations. But some things didn't fit. In South America, to take one example, Darwin encountered a new species of rhea, a flightless bird living on the pampas of Patagonia in an area adjacent to that of the common rhea. Each species of rhea had its own territory, but there was a large contested area between them that they shared. The rhea posed puzzles. The most obvious was the idea of a flightless bird. Why would God create a bird with so much unused aerodynamic paraphernalia? Why would God place two virtually identical birds in different habitats? And, finally, what was up with the pointless competition between the two species for control of the borderlands separating them? The humble rhea embodied a set of contradictions that even Paley would have had trouble rationalizing as the handiwork of God.

Similar difficulties cropped up all over the planet. Darwin noted an upland goose that never went in the water, yet was handicapped by webbed feet. If this was the handiwork of God, it was surely a cruel joke, as anyone who has ever tried to walk in flippers knows only too well. There were birds resembling woodpeckers with all the necessary facial reinforcements to pound their heads constantly against a tree, and yet they lived on insects found on the ground. God seemed to be wasting resources in giving these birds such overdesigned beaks.

The geographical distribution of animals puzzled Darwin. Charles Lyell offered one explanation in his influential *Principles of Geology,*[26] which Darwin was reading carefully while aboard the *Beagle.* Lyell was among the emerging "scientific geologists" working to free their new science from "Mosaic geology," which they regarded as "marginal" and "worthy only of derision."[27] These geologists, on scientific grounds, rejected the flood of Noah and its implication that the worldwide distribution of animals derived from their dispersal from Mt. Ararat, where the ark came to rest. Alternative explanations for the distribution of animals still invoked divine creation, of course, but in ways based on empirical, rather than biblical, considerations. In Lyell's view, with which Darwin would wrestle, God had placed individual species in "centers of creation" specifically prepared for them. God created the earth with its various habitats—deserts, meadows, swamps, mountains, rivers, oceans, islands, cold climates, hot climates, and so on—and then created animals to flourish in the different habitats. Darwin thus anticipated that animals indigenous to these centers of creation would have features optimized to the local conditions.

Contrary to expectations, however, Darwin could not explain the distribution of animals he encountered. Why, for example, were certain islands populated by bats but no other mammals of any sort, when they would have provided wonderful habitats for many mammals? Was it just a coincidence that the only mammal on these islands was one that could have flown there on its own? Why did each of the Galapagos Islands have its own species of tortoise, so easily distinguished that the locals could simply look at a tortoise and tell you the island from which it came? If God matched species to their habitats in centers of creation, as Lyell believed, why would identical habitats have different species?

None of these observations ruled out the possibility that God was still the creator of all the life-forms on the earth. But they did raise troubling questions about the mechanisms of creation and the degree to which God was involved in the details. Darwin described such phenomena as "utterly inexplicable on the theory of independent acts of creation."[28] This is the first level of Darwin's concern—the intelligent design paradigm could not explain many of the details of the natural world.

An even stronger conviction that God was not responsible for the details came from Darwin's growing awareness of natural phenomena so horrible it was inconceivable that they embodied plans originating in the mind of God. For example, the way Ichneumonidae wasps feed off the internal organs of their caterpillar hosts appalled Darwin. The mother wasp inserts a paralyzing chemical into the nervous system of the caterpillar and then places her eggs inside the still-living host, where they hatch and then gradually devour the paralyzed caterpillar from the inside. The hatched baby wasps emerge with preprogrammed instincts to consume the internal organs of the caterpillar in a sequence that keeps their caterpillar host alive as long as possible.

Such examples posed disturbing challenges to natural theology. The system by which Ichneumonidae eggs hatch is truly ingenious, although the host caterpillars might prefer a different term. Variations on the theme show up regularly in science fiction movies about aliens that parasitize human hosts. In the classic *Alien* films, aggressive alien parasites take over human bodies by attaching to their faces, inserting tubes down their throats, and planting embryos inside them. When the embryos are mature, they explode out through the chests of their human hosts, killing them and scaring the bejeezus out of the audience.

Nonfictional horror shows like the creepy Ichneumonidae and sadistic cats bothered Darwin. How were they to be reconciled with his belief in creation? On the living-room floor a kitten is entertaining as it plays with a ball of yarn, and it would be easy to see this as simply delightful. But outside in the yard, the kitten's mother, influenced by the same instincts, is beating up a mouse that she may or may not eat after she kills it.

In a letter to the American biologist Asa Gray in 1860, a year after he had published *On the Origin of Species* and twenty-four years after getting off the *Beagle,* Darwin was still wrestling with these issues: "I cannot see, as plainly as others do," he wrote, "evidence of design and beneficence on all sides of us. There seems to be too much misery in the world. I cannot persuade myself that a beneficent and omnipotent God would have designedly created the Ichneumonidae with the express intention of their feeding within the living bodies of caterpillars, or that a cat should play with mice."[29]

ON THE ORIGIN OF SPECIES

Revolutionary ideas in science rarely come roaring down the track with belching smoke, piercing whistles, and squealing brakes. They arrive more like a gathering storm. A cloud appears, here and there, in a blue sky. A drop of rain is felt. More clouds. More rain. The sky becomes partially, then fully, obscured. The sun is blotted out. A bit of thunder and lightning creates drama, the clouds begin to break, and the sun reappears. But it is not the same sun, and everything looks somehow different.

Darwin grew dissatisfied with the prevailing creationist ideas. They made no sense theologically, and they offered almost nothing scientifically. His growing dissatisfaction was a gathering storm; puzzles like the Ichneumonidae, cats, rheas, and flightless birds were its clouds. Eventually the old sun was blotted out, and the landscape became hard to see and impossible to comprehend. It was in the rain and fog of this storm that Darwin developed his theory of evolution.

Darwin circulated his theory privately among close friends for two decades before publishing, nervous about the anticipated controversy. But eventually, prodded by the awareness that a fellow naturalist, Alfred Wallace, had developed an identical theory, Darwin published what turned out to be a most paradoxical theory—one that combined great explanatory power and theoretical simplicity. "Why didn't I think of that?" responded many of his associates.

His theory is disarmingly simple. Darwin begins by noting the great competition in nature. Most species produce far more offspring than can survive. As a child I loved to gather the little "helicopters" dropped by the mighty maple in my yard. One maple can drop up to seven thousand of these twirly seeds in a single year, enough to create a large forest, if they were all to survive. Similarly, one spawning salmon can release five thousand eggs each year, enough to stock a lake.

However, most attempts at reproduction fail. No salmon has five thousand babies that grow to maturity. The ones that succeed, argued Darwin, do so because they are more fit, better able to meet the challenges of the local environment. This enhanced fitness can be passed on to the next generation. In this way, species evolve slowly, imperceptibly, as they become better adapted to their local environments. Fish grow ever more hydrodynamic; hawks get better vision; camels store larger quantities of water.

Sometimes, however, the local environment changes. A river dries up, a peninsula breaks off into an island, a new predator arrives, an earthquake moves a beach up on to the side of a slope, an avalanche covers the mouth of a watery cave. Such changes alter the environment, and previously well-adapted species face new challenges. A goose with webbed feet that evolved to accommodate swimming may be relocated away from the water. Turtles confined to a newly isolated island will evolve independently of their siblings on the mainland. Birds with powerful beaks may no longer find prey in trees. And so on.

Such modifications to the environment pose new challenges. Take the goose with webbed feet, now constrained to make its way on dry land. The webbing between its toes, once useful for moving in the water, is now an encumbrance, making walking slow and awkward. What was useful in one environment is a disadvantage in another. And, although natural selection may gradually minimize the problem of webbed feet, there is no mechanism available to simply remove it. Natural selection tinkers with existing traits relevant to reproduction, making them ever more useful in the existing environment. Natural selection, however, cannot suddenly make wholesale changes or undo developments long in the making.

For Darwin, explanations like these made more sense than supposing that God had placed a goose with webbed feet on dry land or that the goose had walked there after disembarking from Noah's ark. Darwin's explanations illuminated countless oddities across the globe that made no sense within the explanatory paradigm of intelligent design.

Natural selection, operating on tiny changes in organisms over vast periods of time, accounted for much of what Darwin was struggling to understand. Even the Ichneumonidae were less disturbing when viewed as the product of natural selection rather than the direct handiwork of God. By these lights, God no longer seemed like a cruel despot, creating monsters to prey on innocent life; the villain doing the dirty work was now a blind and impersonal process of natural selection. Darwin found this interpretation far more congenial than the theological gymnastics required to fit nature's monstrosities into Paley's framework of natural theology.

Although Darwin rejected the idea that God was responsible for each individual organism, he continued to believe that God played a role in nature. In the same 1860 letter to Asa Gray expressing his disgust at the Ichneumonidae, he noted that he could not be "contented to view this wonderful universe and especially the nature of man, and to conclude that everything is the result of brute force." He preferred instead "to look at everything as resulting from designed laws."[30] God, he suggested, may have created the vast physical framework in which natural history unfolded, charting its own course, sometimes for better and sometimes for worse.

Darwin's critics write as if this suggestion—that nature has its own freedom within a framework of laws designed by God—is an appalling and antireligious stance. This is an odd response. Christian theology has always had a place for freedom, even for the followers of John Calvin, with their predestination; even they can smuggle in a bit of free will for themselves. Christian theology embraces the very human freedom to create or destroy, to choose evil or good, to promote life or death. Darwin's invocation of chance in nature is equivalent to granting the natural order some measure of the very freedom so evident in human experience. Out of this freedom the natural order produces delightful birds, such as the red cardinal that often perches outside my window on the branches of the beautiful dogwood I planted many years ago. But this freedom also gives rise to the disgusting Ichneumonidae and the naughty cat that tortures its lunch before eating it. Why is this freedom, embodied in the natural order, so much more troubling than the freedom that human beings possess—a freedom that has given rise to both hospitals and concentration camps, violins and guillotines, poetry and pornography?

THE SLIDE TO AGNOSTICISM

The Darwin described above was not a crusader against Christianity. Nor was he part of a conspiracy to destroy belief in God. He was, rather, a *reluctant* convert to evolution and ultimately agnosticism. His spiritual journey was at odds with fundamentalism, which holds that true seekers will inevitably find its version of faith. To fail to find this faith can only mean that one is not truly seeking; to *abandon* faith is simply perverted; and to create a theory that might compel people to reject faith is simply evil. In the eyes of these critics, who believe passionately that Satan is everywhere at work trying to turn people from their truth, Darwin is nothing short of an agent of the devil.[31]

Darwin eventually lost his childhood faith, but it was long after his fateful voyage aboard the *Beagle*. And although his faith in the creationist explanation for origins was undermined by his scientific work, the heart of his Christianity was destroyed by concerns much closer to home.

Darwin, like most thoughtful believers, found the Christian concept of hell—a secondary doctrine that even many conservatives reject—difficult to reconcile with the more central concept of God's love. Just as there was something theologically repugnant about God creating cats to torture mice, even briefly, there was something even more appalling about a God creating an eternal torture for those unwilling or, like Darwin, *unable* to believe. When his father died without any religious faith in 1848, Darwin confronted the reality that Christian doctrine taught that his father was now a permanent resident of hell, at the beginning of an endless torture.

Darwin became convinced that an eternal hell was more than simply a troubling and implausible concept, a cosmic parallel to the Ichneumonidae:

"I can indeed hardly see how anyone ought to wish Christianity to be true," he wrote near the end of his career, for "the plain language of the text seems to show that the men who do not believe, and this would include my Father, Brother and almost all of my friends, will be everlastingly punished. And this is a damnable doctrine."[32] Darwin's religious struggles distressed his beloved wife, Emma, as she considered the prospects of being separated eternally from her increasingly unorthodox husband. Darwin respected Emma's consistency in her faith and was troubled by the space his creeping unbelief opened between them.

In the final analysis, however, the event that did the most to destroy Darwin's faith was not his concerns about the legitimacy of hell. It was not the growing implausibility of creationism or his embrace of evolution. It was the death of an innocent and beloved child a brief three years after the death of his father.

Darwin, from birth to death, was a family man, devoted at first to his parents and siblings, then to his wife, and finally and most dramatically to his children. He had ten children, all of whom were raised in the comfortable security of Downe House, just a short distance from the family church at Downe, Kent, where he hoped to be buried. By all accounts Darwin's family life was rich. His children often accompanied him on walks, crawled onto his lap while he was working, and generally filled his home and his life with laughter. One of them, Annie, held a particularly special place in his heart.

In 1851, at the age of eleven, Annie contracted a childhood illness, possibly tuberculosis, and began what was to be a short battle for her life. The local physician dropped by several times, as did the parish priest. Emma spent much time in prayer, asking God to spare Annie's life. Charles struggled mightily. On the one hand, Annie's fight for her life was the struggle for survival that was the way of all biological life. Nobody understood that better than he. But he still believed in God, and hidden beneath the decaying vegetation of his once vibrant faith was the residue of an enduring conviction that a good and beneficent God was in control. This God cared about the fall of sparrows, the hairs on our heads, and the health of our children. "Suffer the little children to come unto me," said Jesus, when his associates would shoo them away.

Little Annie Darwin, the jewel of Charles and Emma's remarkable family, passed away on April 23, 1851. Emma memorialized Annie by creating a box of her special possessions, which she opened when the empty space created by Annie's passing seemed to grow too large. Darwin's great-grandson Randall Keynes has lovingly told this story in *Darwin, His Daughter and Human Evolution*.[33] Darwin, as befits the author of one of the world's most important books, processed his grief through writing: "We have lost the joy of the household, and the solace of our old age," he wrote on April 30, 1851.[34]

THE BODY SNATCHERS

In the final analysis, one of the greatest scientists who ever lived, the architect of the worldview that countless Christians believe was inspired by Satan to destroy their faith, the thinker who did more than anyone to drive natural theology from intellectual discourse, lost his faith when his daughter died. Darwin's belief in God weathered the theological storms brought on by the Ichneumonidae, the sadistic cats, and the webbed feet of the upland geese. He understood that those features of the natural world could be reconciled with belief in God as creator. He is followed in this belief by the majority of theologians who have reflected on these problems and concluded that evolution by natural selection is not incompatible with belief in God as creator.

But Christianity is not fundamentally about how God created the world and its many interesting creatures. Christianity is about the extraordinary claim that God loves those creatures and cares deeply about their welfare. This, alas, is undeniably difficult to square with the death of a child. Darwin's diaries, notebooks, personal correspondence, and other writings reveal the unfolding patterns of his thoughts on religion. The evidence suggests a lifetime of complex wrestling with issues of faith. His belief in God waxed and waned, but took a severe blow when Annie died.

This is not to claim that Darwin's religious faith ever completely died. He had important personal and social reasons to hang on to belief and never joined his contemporaries in their attack on the church. He continued to support his local church financially and helped with parish work, but on Sundays he went for a walk while his family was at worship. He never embraced atheism. And even within his controversial theory he continued to find room for God. In a beautiful and often quoted passage at the end of *On the Origin of Species,* Darwin wrote:

There is grandeur in this view of life, with its several powers, having been originally breathed into a few forms or into one; and that, whilst this planet has gone cycling on according to the fixed law of gravity, from so simple a beginning endless forms most beautiful and most wonderful have been, and are being, evolved.[35]

Darwin's wish was to be buried in St. Mary's churchyard at Downe next to the bodies of his children who had died. It was a place he called "the happiest on earth." But by the time of his passing in April 1882 at the age of seventy-three he had become an international symbol. Reposing in the graveyard of a humble parish would not do. Darwin's allies saw in his work the foundations of a welcome new social order, one in which science replaced religion as the dominant cultural authority and traditional social straitjackets were cast aside. This transition was effectively symbolized by a funeral that was a state occasion and a burial in Westminster Abbey, where other influential—if more orthodox—British luminaries were laid to rest. Darwin's interment in Westminster Abbey, next to the imposing statue marking the grave of the great Isaac Newton, was an emphatic statement that a new order had arrived. "Darwin's body," penned biographers Adrian Desmond and James Moore, "was enshrined to the greater glory of the new professionals who had snatched it."[36]

Society and the world, at least for those who captured Darwin's vision, had been naturalized. Throughout Britain, the power of the clergy continued a decline begun even before Darwin set foot on the *Beagle*. Eventually the church became a minority voice in an increasingly secular, pluralistic society. Throughout nature the explanatory power of theology was in similar decline, as scientific explanations displaced more traditional religious ones. Theology, however, was reeling under the impact of a far more serious crisis that had nothing to do with Darwin, brought on by radically new biblical scholarship coming out of Germany.

CHAPTER 2

A TALE OF TWO BOOKS

D arwin," writes Richard Dawkins, "made it possible to be an intellectually fulfilled atheist."[1] Such claims, by our leading public intellectual,
have earned Dawkins his nickname: "Darwin's rottweiler." The label
is a diplomatic downgrade from one attached to the kinder, gentler Thomas
Huxley a century earlier—"Darwin's bulldog"—and derives from Dawkins's
enthusiastic, in-your-face promotion of all things Darwinian.

Dawkins, the Charles Simonyi Professor for the Public Understanding
of Science at Oxford University, is the world's leading popularizer of evolution. He has written many influential books, starting with the classic *The
Selfish Gene* in 1976, then *The Blind Watchmaker* in 1987, and, two decades
later, his 688-page opus, *The Ancestor's Tale*. One of his staunchest critics
says he is "as articulate as anyone alive."[2]

Although Dawkins's writings are mainly science exposition at its best, he
clearly has an antireligious ax to grind and often concludes his books by musing about how scientific accounts of origins are superior to their religious
counterparts. At the end of *The Ancestor's Tale,* for example, he writes: "My
objection to supernatural beliefs is precisely that they miserably fail to do justice to the sublime grandeur of the real world. They represent a narrowing-
down from reality, an impoverishment of what the real world has to offer."[3]

Not surprisingly, religious believers have been at war with Dawkins for
some time, a conflict escalated by his recent work *The God Delusion,* an aggressive diatribe against religion. His writings and public appearances insult
Christians on two fronts—their cherished beliefs and their intelligence. Responses to Dawkins tend to be more restrained and include *Dawkins' God*
and *The Dawkins Delusion* by an Oxford colleague, theologian Alister Mc-
Grath,[4] and a lengthy chapter in *The Oracles of Science: Celebrity Scientists*

Versus God and Religion.[5] Dawkins's conservative critics consider him a well-defined enemy. Phillip Johnson, speaking for most of them, accuses him of being "scientifically absurd and morally naive."[6] Christians inclined to think evolution is a Satanic conspiracy see him as downright sinister. If in his next public appearance horns suddenly grew out of Dawkins's head and he announced that he was the Antichrist, come to complete the task of destroying religion begun by Charles Darwin a hundred and fifty years ago, some Christians would nod knowingly and say, "I thought so."

Dawkins and his colleagues-in-arms—Steven Pinker, Sam Harris, Peter Atkins, Francis Crick, Steven Weinberg, and Daniel Dennett—fret over the intellectual trajectory of the twenty-first century. Science has not captured the heart and mind of the culture, as they had anticipated, and religion, after a century of steady retreat, has come roaring back with a vengeance, especially in the United States. And the religion roaring back is the worst kind—Bible-reading (or at least Bible-thumping), miracle-believing, born-again, evolution-bashing Christianity. Science finds itself in an uncomfortable and unfamiliar defensive role, reduced to defending hard-won territory against the philistines.

Dawkins, Dennett, and company, who call themselves "brights"[7] to distinguish themselves from "dims," who believe in God, are the contemporary champions of the secularist worldview that captured France in the eighteenth century, invaded England in the nineteenth century, and frightened America in the twentieth. But Dawkins's use of evolution to undermine religion differs from what happened in nineteenth-century England, when Darwin's new theory was first introduced.

GOD'S FUNERAL

In the first place, the nineteenth-century secularism that Dawkins celebrates was not driven primarily by science, but by forces *internal* to religion, especially German biblical scholarship. Science played but a small role, and an ambiguous one at that. Ironically, it was those most familiar with the Christian Scriptures and the history of the early church who initiated and encouraged the move toward secularism. David Friedrich Strauss, for example, produced a critical and scholarly analysis of the Bible titled *The Life of Jesus Critically Examined.* This book raised thundering questions about the reliability of the Bible.[8] Appearing in 1835 in German, while Darwin was measuring finch beaks on the Galapagos Islands, Strauss's monumental work was translated into English by the novelist George Eliot in 1846. Over the next decades the book exerted an unprecedented influence on the study of Jesus's life. Strauss sought to discover the "historical Jesus" using both the gospels and extrabiblical sources. In doing so, he undermined the validity and historical reliability of the gospels, spreading crises of faith across Europe like a plague. In contrast, many of those same readers, as well as scientists and even clergy, were reading *On the Origin of Species* without getting the least bit sick.

In the second place, the nineteenth-century loss of faith was not received as a liberation—an "intellectual fulfillment," to paraphrase Dawkins. The soldiers of doubt that came blasting through the walls of England's many houses of worship, from Westminster Abbey to the humble parish church where the Darwins worshiped, were enemies, not liberators. Most nineteenth-century Christians who lost their faith were deeply troubled by the experience. Some were plagued by apocalyptic visions of a post-Christian Europe. Like Darwin, who fantasized about the discovery of documents corroborating the New Testament stories and chasing away the demons of his doubt, nineteenth-century unbelievers did not enjoy the disintegration of their faith.

The most eloquent of these laments is Matthew Arnold's "Dover Beach," written in 1867. Arnold concludes his poignant masterpiece by comparing the European loss of faith to a tide going out:

> The Sea of Faith
> Was once, too, at the full, and round earth's shore
> Lay like the folds of a bright girdle furled.
> But now I only hear
> Its melancholy, long, withdrawing roar,
> Retreating, to the breath
> Of the night-wind, down the vast edges drear
> And naked shingles of the world.
> Ah, love, let us be true
> To one another! for the world, which seems
> To lie before us like a land of dreams,
> So various, so beautiful, so new,
> Hath really neither joy, nor love, nor light,

> Nor certitude, nor peace, nor help for pain;
> And we are here as on a darkling plain
> Swept with confused alarms of struggle and flight,
> Where ignorant armies clash by night.[9]

The novelist and poet Thomas Hardy penned "God's Funeral" around 1909, even as he was being engulfed by the unwelcome fog of atheism. Like Arnold, Hardy captures the sense of loss and hopelessness brought on by the emerging crisis of faith:

> So, toward our myth's oblivion,
> Darkling, and languid-lipped, we creep and grope
> Sadlier than those who wept in Babylon,
> Whose Zion was still abiding hope.[10]

Hardy, Arnold, and their fellow Victorians who attended God's funeral found no intellectual fulfillment in the ideas that made belief in God optional, redundant, or even unacceptable.[11] It would be decades before people like Dawkins would upend the Victorian sentiments and try to spin the nineteenth-century loss of faith into something wonderful and liberating. Dawkins's lament, of course, is that God, like Jesus in the New Testament, didn't stay dead.

TWO BOOKS

These European intellectual currents traced different courses as they made their way to America. It is instructive to compare the reception of the two great books from Europe, Strauss's *The Life of Jesus Critically Examined* and Darwin's *On the Origin of Species*. Both were destined to exert great influence on Christianity, although in dramatically different ways and on different schedules.

Strauss's work, a part of the movement already under way known as *higher criticism,* generated enormous controversy. Immediately rejected by conservative Christians, it spawned a backlash that split Christianity into two camps—liberals, who accepted it, and fundamentalists, who did not. *On the Origin of Species* produced a more complex and organic reaction. Destined to eventually be at the heart of a national crisis in the public schools, evolution was initially dismissed by many American religious leaders as scientifically absurd and unlikely to endure. Within a decade, however, the scientific community had embraced evolution, muting claims it was absurd and motivating thoughtful Christians, including many conservatives, to make peace with Darwin's new theory. Many concluded that evolution offered no clear threat to faith. Flexibility in interpreting both the theory and the Bible enabled the reduction and even elimination of apparent contradictions.

No such peace was to be found with higher criticism, which appeared to be making a full frontal assault on the reliability of the Bible. Strauss and his colleagues brought an unprecedented historical and literary approach to the Bible, treating it as any other ancient document rather than the sacrosanct "Word of God." The results were disturbing. Serious questions were raised about everything from miracles to the very existence of Jesus.

The gospels, noted the critics, disagree on such basic history as Jesus's resurrection. Matthew places two women at Jesus's tomb, Mark places three, Luke more than three, and John only one. What is going on here? Now that we understand the importance of history, how can readers put faith in the historicity of an event chronicled by such unreliable reporters? And what was the big deal about Christian miracles when miracle stories were so common outside of Christianity? Pythagoras, for example, was said to be the son of Apollo, born of a virgin, and to have calmed storms and visited the dead in Hades.[12] Why do we privilege such claims when we find them inside the Bible and reject them when we find them outside of it?

Strauss's bombshell, despite the author's assurances that his work was in the service of Christ, riled his colleagues in Germany and got him fired from Tübingen University. As his inflammatory text made its way across the Atlantic Ocean to America, religious militias lined up along the coast from Maine to Florida trying to prevent it from coming ashore and taking up residence within evangelicalism. In contrast, Darwin's *On the Origin of Species* disembarked with less fanfare and soon found some evangelical doors open to it—doors that had been slammed in the face of higher criticism.

DARWIN COMES TO AMERICA

On the Origin of Species arrived in America in 1860. Considered an important new scientific work, it was reviewed by leading scientists in influential opinion journals like the *Atlantic Monthly* and the *American Journal of*

Science and Arts. America's leading biologist, Louis Agassiz, of Harvard, described Darwin's theory as "a scientific mistake, untrue in facts, unscientific in its methods, and mischievous in its tendency."[13] Critics like Agassiz empowered Christians, at least initially, to reject Darwin's theory on scientific grounds.

Darwin's book sold well. It slowly began to win the loyalty of biologists and reshape the life sciences, but it did so without apparently disrupting the prior religious commitments of those who embraced it.[14] It would be a half century before William Jennings Bryan and Clarence Darrow would spar about evolution at the Scopes trial, and a full century before America's fundamentalists would be united en masse against it, certain it had been conjured in hell by Satan himself.

The steadily evolving complexity of America's response to Darwin resulted from multiple ambiguities in play.[15] For starters, there was no consensus on exactly how Darwin's theory should be understood. Evolution in several forms was "in the air," and Darwin's contribution was in some ways just a well-documented presentation of ideas that had been bandied about for decades. Darwin's own theory, with the unique role assigned to natural selection, had been circulating quietly for two decades and had even been independently proposed by another naturalist named Alfred Wallace. Most biologists were soon convinced that evolution had occurred, more or less as Darwin described in *On the Origin of Species,* but they were skeptical that the process of natural selection, all by itself, was up to the task of turning an amoeba into a proper Victorian.

Complementary ambiguities attended the interpretations of Genesis and whether evolution was necessarily incompatible with creation. Between multiple explanations for how evolution worked—some of which were congenial to Christianity—and various interpretive schemes for Genesis, there was simply no need for Christians to get alarmed about Darwin's American debut. Earlier developments, in fact, had even prepared the way for evolution through a series of compromises on things like the age of the earth or the extent of Noah's flood. Such compromises had opened space for new ideas. Controversy was also muted by the fact that the great scientific authorities of the day were mostly all Christians and not inclined to put any antireligious spin on new scientific developments.

Prior to Darwin, the influential Swedish farm boy turned botanist Carolus Linnaeus (1707–78), who gave us such delightful labels as *Homo trog-*

lodyte (cave man), had subscribed to a clearly religious concept of origins: God created two of each species, which then dispersed to populate the globe. Species could neither evolve nor go extinct, so Linnaeus's famous labeling exercise simply cataloged what God had done a few thousand years ago. Biblically influenced views like those of Linnaeus were modified under the pressure of accumulating evidence. Charles Lyell (1797–1875), whose *Principles of Geology* had shaped Darwin's views while aboard the *Beagle*, believed the scientific evidence indicated that God had created species at multiple locations and on numerous occasions, a strongly creationist but decidedly unbiblical explanation.[16] Louis Agassiz (1807–73), a world-class ichthyologist and one of America's first great scientists, believed that God had created species in large numbers, repopulating the earth after various divine tantrums like the great flood of Noah. These and other views with meaningful connections to the Christian understanding of creation were endorsed by leading naturalists during a time when biology was still developing. The variety of such theories made it impossible to assess the degree to which new science challenged religious understandings of origins. Furthermore, Darwin did not yet tower over others of the nineteenth century as the key scientist, so his authority was not considerably greater than that of scientists promoting other views.

Confronted with multiple theories about geology, biology, and Genesis and their relevance to each other, scientists and clergy alike were liberated to think creatively about origins. Growing evidence that the earth was ancient pushed the origin of the earth back in time; the discovery of fossils belonging to creatures that went extinct long before humans appeared forced a reinterpretation of the chronology in Genesis. And although such developments put Linnaeus's creationism to rest, there were other options available at the time.

For those who would defend the Genesis creation story as more than a myth, there were two interpretations of it that preserved at least a mutant form of biblical inerrancy: the *day-age* theory and the *gap* theory. Both achieved some currency during the nineteenth century in response to the growing geological evidence for the great age of the earth.

The day-age theory accommodated the great age of the earth by converting the days of creation in Genesis into geological epochs. There was biblical license for making this move. The Hebrew word for "day," *yom,* sometimes referred to a period of time rather than an interval of twenty-four hours. In

Psalm 90:10, which contains the word *yom*, we read: "The days of our life are seventy years" (NRSV). Modern English expressions like "in this day and age" and "your day will come" reflect similar usage. William Jennings Bryan admitted on the Scopes trial witness stand that he subscribed to the day-age theory, to the delight of Clarence Darrow and the chagrin of the more literalist members of his fan club.

A version of the day-age theory appeared in 1778 when a leading French intellectual bearing the ponderous name Georges-Louis Leclerc de Buffon published *Epochs of Nature*. Buffon was one of the first to surmise that the earth had a long, complex evolutionary history and had not been created a few thousand years ago looking much as it does today. He proposed that the earth originated when a comet collided with the sun and ejected material out of which the earth formed. This molten material needed more than a few thousand years to cool to its present temperature, perhaps as much as three million years.[17]

Criticism rained down on Buffon as the guardians of biblical orthodoxy and even Voltaire reacted to this new theory of earth history. To pacify the religious critics Buffon divided the newly extended history of the earth into seven epochs, sequenced in a way that lined up with his proposed evolution of the planet. The seven epochs may have been a charade, but it provided a scheme by which a creative interpretation of Genesis could be reconciled with what was to be a steadily increasing age for the earth.

In the early nineteenth century the day-age scheme became enormously popular through the writings of Hugh Miller, a respected religious leader gifted with "elegance, grace, and wit."[18] This interpretive scheme found broad application as religious believers, including geologists, sought to preserve the historicity of the Genesis account of creation, even as their understanding of that creation underwent cataclysmic change. The day-age theory lives today in the work of several leading fundamentalists, most notably Hugh Ross, who heads up the Christian apologetics ministry Reasons to Believe. Ross, who has a Ph.D. in astronomy, promotes an integration of natural history and the Genesis creation story utilizing the day-age concept to reconcile his literal reading of Genesis with evidence for the great age of the universe. Other creationists view Ross with suspicion, however, and lament his capitulation to a flawed scientific perspective and compromised reading of the Bible.

The second strategy for dealing with the age of the earth was the gap theory, so-called for its insertion of a great historical gap between the first and second verses of Genesis. In the first verse in Genesis we read: "In the beginning God created the heavens and the earth." In the second verse we read: "And the earth was without form and void." The gap theory interprets the first verse in Genesis as referring to a *prior* creation event. The second verse refers to the most recent creation. We thus have an undefined epoch between the two into which almost anything can be inserted. If geologists need a few billion years of history before humans appear, we can insert that history neatly between verses 1 and 2.

Two theologically trained geologists popularized the gap theory at the beginning of the nineteenth century, Thomas Chalmers in Scotland and William Buckland in England. Motivated by geological developments and rationalized with the same sort of scriptural vagaries exploited by the day-age theory, the gap theory provided space for a different creation before the present one. Chalmers and Buckland thus developed a second biblically acceptable way to deal with the emerging geological evidence for an ancient earth. Most practicing geologists at the time took the Bible seriously. But, since they also took geology seriously, they were forced to find space in the Bible's hermeneutical holes for the latest discoveries about the earth.

Textual license exists for the gap theory. The Hebrew grammatical construction does not require that God is creating "out of nothing," but rather allows the translation that God is working with preexisting materials. In the more recent and literal translation of the New Revised Standard Version, Genesis 1:1–2 reads: "In the beginning when God created the heavens and the earth, the earth was a formless void and darkness covered the face of the deep." The most straightforward interpretation of these verses is that there was something in place on which God was working at the time the story begins. We are not told what it was or how it came to be a "formless void," but there is no obvious reason that it could not be the residue of a previous catastrophe along the lines of Noah's flood or the destruction of Sodom and Gomorrah.

The gap theory became very popular and eventually made its way into the influential *Scofield Reference Bible,* first published in 1909, which has since sold over two million copies. The Scofield Bible, still available from Oxford University Press in a revised edition, contains copious study aids prepared by a biblical scholar named Cyrus I. Scofield. This study Bible was the definitive Scripture for many fundamentalists throughout the twentieth century. Oddball interpretations of various biblical passages showed up in the study aids and acquired an almost canonical status by virtue of being included in the volume. One of the more alarming examples of this involves the episode in Genesis that follows the great flood. Noah's son Ham is cursed for improprieties with his naked, drunken father. The curse includes a reference to slavery, and Scofield's notes in the earlier versions suggest that these verses offer a justification for the abuse of black people. The curse on Ham's descendants was supposedly dark skin and a secondary role as servants of white people, an interpretation used to rationalize slavery.

In the notes accompanying the first chapter of Genesis, Scofield references multiple biblical passages that "clearly indicate that the earth had undergone a cataclysmic change as the result of divine judgment."[19] He goes on to say, "The face of the earth bears everywhere the marks of such a catastrophe," and suggests that the catastrophe resulted from "a previous testing and fall of angels." I can remember reading these notes in my father's Bible as a child, impressed that Scofield knew so much about how God had done things and wondering what marvelous events must have attended the testing and fall of angels.

The Scofield Bible also reproduced Bishop James Ussher's seventeenth-century biblical chronology, which stated that the creation week described in Genesis occurred in the year 4004 BCE, but after the gap inserted between the first two verses to accommodate a prior creation. In the early versions of the Scofield Bible that date appears in a column in the center of the first page of Genesis.

The day-age and the gap theory are tools to reconcile the great age of the earth with a literal reading of Genesis, and millions of Christians found them entirely adequate. However, there were reasons why this interpretive strategy might not even be necessary. Multiple elements in the Genesis stories of creation suggest a figurative or symbolic, rather than a literal, reading. The angel with flaming sword guarding Eden's gate, for example, struck many as a mythological element, especially as it implies that the Garden of Eden is still present somewhere on earth. The talking serpent, God strolling through the garden in the evening with Adam, and the rib surgery to make woman all strained the plausibility of a purely literal reading. Even some literalists will concede that these elements are laden with symbolism and allegory.

The history of interpreting Genesis also reveals a diversity of readings, even before there were pressures from science. More than a millennium before Darwin, to take one example, St. Augustine took time off from obsessing about the evils of sex to write a commentary suggesting that the Genesis creation week was not to be taken literally.[20] Augustine saw no reason to suppose that God would organize his work week as humans do and then, when he was done, take a day off to do God knows what.

All these factors were in play in late nineteenth-century America when Darwin arrived. There were several entirely legitimate readings of Genesis available, from Augustine's allegorical approach, to Buffon's geological interpretation, to the traditional six-day creationism. Some of these readings were compatible with evolution, and some were not. Without some galvanizing event or charismatic leader to rally Christians to the cause, there was simply no need for them to take up arms to defend the integrity of the Bible against any imagined assault from evolution.

In addition to the lack of unanimity on how to read the biblical creation stories, America's response to *On the Origin of Species* was further shaped by the ambivalence of biologists toward Darwin's explanation for evolution. Darwin, most agreed by 1870, had amassed compelling evidence that evolution had occurred. That all life was the result of constant change over time from common ancestors became known as the "fact" of evolution. But Darwin's theory purporting to explain *how* this occurred was another matter. There was simply no consensus that natural selection was the mechanism of evolutionary change. Many, in fact, were skeptical that an undirected chance process could account for the astonishing diversity and creativity of the natural world.

Some who accepted evolution suspected that unknown mechanisms were at work, perhaps guided by God. In any event, the historical fact that evolution had occurred was easily separated from any particular theory of how it had occurred. We must keep in mind that the full name of Darwin's book was *On the Origin of Species by Means of Natural Selection, Or the Preservation of Favoured Races in the Struggle for Life*. Darwin's great work must thus be considered from two separate and separable perspectives: common ancestry as an empirical fact, and natural selection as a theoretical explanation for that fact.

Biologists today consider the common ancestry of all life a fact on par with the sphericity of the earth or its motion around the sun. They note the

mountain of evidence that all life came from a common ancestor several billion years ago. Evidence from comparative DNA, the fossil record, the geographical distribution of life, comparative anatomy, and other data point to a
common ancestor. The evidence is so compelling that even some dedicated
anti-evolutionary intelligent design advocates have grudgingly conceded
on this point, even as they reject just about every other aspect of evolution.
Michael Behe, for example, author of the important and readable intelligent design classic *Darwin's Black Box,* suggests that all the life-forms on
the earth may have come from a single common ancestor—an "über-cell"
with all the "designed systems" needed to give rise to the entire panorama
of all the life that has existed.[21] His fellow intelligent design theorist William
Dembski has speculated that maybe God "front-loaded" everything into the
big bang.[22] Belief in a common ancestry for all life, from Darwin's day to our
own, has never entailed accepting any particular mechanism for how that
common ancestor managed to give rise to the great panorama of life that has
graced our planet.

Without the insights of genetics, which were not incorporated into Darwin's theory until well into the twentieth century, there was no knockdown
argument for natural selection as *the* mechanism for evolution. Certainly his
fellow biologists were not knocked down by natural selection as the mechanism to get a Victorian from an amoeba. And although they were convinced
that this was indeed how Victorians had arisen, they were not sure that
something so feeble and obviously purposeless as blind natural selection
could accomplish that remarkable task.

ALTERNATIVE EXPLANATIONS FOR EVOLUTION

Two alternatives challenged natural selection as the driving force of evolution, and both of them nestled comfortably into the worldview of the nineteenth century, with its orientation toward progress and purpose. The first
had a pedigree going back to the French naturalist Jean-Baptiste Lamarck
(1744–1829) and was based on the inheritance of acquired characteristics.
Lamarck was an evolutionary voice in the wilderness, preparing the way
for Darwin. His central idea of evolution, however, despite eventually being proven completely wrong, resonated so well with nineteenth-century intuitions that it would be a century before biologists had fully expunged its
heresy.

Lamarck noted the obvious fact that organisms develop adaptations that help them function. A blacksmith, for example, develops large muscles, which aid him in his work. A concert pianist develops nimble fingers. Giraffes stretch their necks to reach food, and dancers become more graceful as they perform continually on stage. Lamarck proposed that such traits, developed to better negotiate the challenges of life, could be passed on to offspring. If a mother giraffe had been especially industrious in stretching her neck to reach food at inconvenient heights, her offspring would be born with the potential for longer necks than their peers. The son of an industrious blacksmith would be destined to develop a robust physique; the daughter of a nimble ballerina would be born with enhanced grace and agility; a politician who learned how to fool people would have similarly talented children. In this way, lineages could experience genuine progress.

Those of Darwin's generation believed in nothing so much as progress, enamored as they were with the elevated stature of their own culture. Lamarck's theory reinforced Victorians' belief that their achievements—in industry, literature, music, and so on—were the result of diligence and hard work, as each generation benefited from the efforts of the previous one. As an important corollary, such a belief also relieved concerns about caring for the poor, whose unfortunate circumstances could be rationalized as the result of laziness. Generations of lazy slackers had been passing down a deteriorating work ethic for centuries, and now the situation was beyond repair.

Lamarck's theory invested natural history with a moral dimension. Progress was good, the reward for diligence and hard work, whether it be a finch pecking with greater vigor on the Galapagos Islands or a human ancestor showing courage and vigor in the face of life's challenges. The commonsense character of Lamarck's explanation, especially in the decades before the genetic basis for inheritance was understood, was deeply intuitive, and most naturalists, including Darwin, accepted it. Even today we must admit that it is far more appealing than the blind and purposeless selection processes that eventually came to define orthodox Darwinism. Unfortunately, it isn't true.

Another alternative to natural selection available at the end of the nineteenth century was *orthogenesis,* which was about as anti-Darwinian an evolutionary explanation as one can imagine. The term means "evolution in a straight line" and refers to the idea that species evolve along a path specified by something akin to a blueprint. Evolution by these lights has "momentum" and moves species forward according to a plan of some sort, which many were quite happy to ascribe to God, now residing comfortably in deist quarters. There were variations on this basic theme, but the central notion was that evolution is driven by a force independent of the environment or any other conditions associated with species.

Orthogenesis was partially inspired by interesting similarities between evolution and human development, a topic explored at great length by many nineteenth-century thinkers. Human beings, for example, begin as simple one-celled organisms—the fertilized egg—and develop steadily in complexity, first in the womb and then outside of it. They reach adulthood, enter a period of stability, then begin to deteriorate, and finally die. Likewise, species originated with one-celled common ancestors, increased steadily in complexity until they reached a period of stasis, and finally went extinct. The similarities were provocative, to say the least.

Human development was deeply mysterious and poorly understood at the time of Darwin, and is still deeply mysterious in many ways. But there was no denying that it occurs regularly and reliably, driven by mechanisms completely unknown to Darwin's generation and not fully known to ours. The champions of orthogenesis simply and reasonably invoked an analogous mechanism as the driver of evolutionary change. There was ample evidence that could be offered in support.

Consider the many things that have evolved that don't seem remotely adaptive. Some, like the interesting patterns on butterfly wings, seemed pointless. Others, like the gigantic antlers on the Irish elk, were maladaptive and thought to have contributed to the extinction of that species. Such evidence, if legitimate, was difficult to square with evolution by natural selection, which would hardly endow elks with antlers that would hasten their demise. On the other hand, if there was such a thing as "evolutionary momentum," it was easy to see how a developmental process that produced antlers in the first place could "overshoot" and leave the unfortunate elk with an unmanageably large rack. A human parallel might be a person increasing in weight in the movement toward adulthood, but then moving inexorably into a state of great obesity, leading to health problems and ultimately to death.

Orthogenesis was, and is, intuitive. It is such a natural misunderstanding that, when I teach evolution, I make a point of emphasizing that "evolution is not a force like gravity, constantly prodding everything to evolve." Nevertheless, it is inevitable that at least one skeptical student will raise a hand and challenge me by asking: "If we evolved from apes, then why are there still apes?" Or, "If evolution is true, then why are we not still evolving?" Both these questions assume that evolution is some kind of mysterious force that, like gravity, propels species along some evolutionary pathway. Orthogenesis postulated just such a force moving the evolutionary process along, much like the force that drives human development from conception to adulthood.

Both Lamarckism and orthogenesis offered alternatives to natural selection, especially for audiences obsessed with progress. Both theories were compatible with religion, viewed from the right angle. The blueprints guiding orthogenesis *could* be viewed as the handiwork of God. The progress of organisms under Lamarckism *could* be viewed as moral imperatives, with every creature investing in its own creative and purposeful advance, for the good of its offspring.

Historian of evolution Peter Bowler has examined the non-Darwinian options available around 1900 in his book *The Eclipse of Darwinism*. He concludes that the popularity of these alternatives that were eclipsing natural selection "all originated in a long-standing tradition that organic development must be an orderly process controlled by laws inherent in life itself." Identifying and understanding these laws had the potential to transform biology into the same sort of rigorous, mathematical science as physics, which was taken as the ideal. What we now call Darwinism, in contrast, with its emphasis on boring, blind, and lifeless natural selection, seemed "moribund and incapable of furthering biological research."[23]

BACK TO THE TALE OF TWO BOOKS

I have sailed briefly into these non-Darwinian waters to make the point that the Darwin who arrived in America was not the same fellow who had written *On the Origin of Species*. By 1875 evolution as a historical fact had been established to the satisfaction of most scientists as well as educated people who had taken the time to absorb Darwin's argument. The vastness of natural history, both geological and biological, no longer threatened people as it once had. But nobody had a clear idea of how evolution occurred, largely because so little was known of genetics. In the absence of a solid, empirically grounded theory of evolutionary change, speculative hypotheses found a ready audience. And some of these hypotheses were quite congenial to both religion and common sense. No one could argue convincingly yet that the central character in the evolutionary story was that blind and indifferent pruner called natural selection.

Ambiguities about evolution coexisted with ambiguities about biblical interpretation. For evolution to conflict with the Bible, these ambiguities would have to resolve in a specific way that was genuinely incompatible. We can certainly select a biblical interpretation that will conflict with a particular explanation for evolution. But why would we want to do that? Absent a revelation from God commanding such a cantankerous move, there is simply no reason to do this. Blessed are the peacemakers, said Jesus, not those who go around manufacturing controversy.

THE TINY SEED OF CONTROVERSY

Unfortunately, there was one American religious leader who did get a command from God to make just such a fuss about evolution. Her name was Ellen White, and the small anti-evolutionary flame she kindled over a century ago has all but engulfed evangelical science in America.

Ellen White (1827–1915) and her family were part of a cult that followed an apocalyptic preacher named William Miller, who predicted that Jesus would return on October 22, 1844. Needless to say, Jesus did not return as predicted, and the mass gathering of frustrated faithful dispersed. Many returned to their former, more traditional denominations. Shortly after this "Great Disappointment," as it became known, White began to experience vivid religious visions. Many believed that God was speaking to her, and she soon emerged as an important religious leader in a new sect known as the Seventh-day Adventists. In 1863 the Adventist religious group was formally established, with White as one of the founders. Her followers consider her writings to be inspired and treat them with great respect, almost on par with the Bible. One of White's first visions was of the Seventh-day Adventists marching into heaven, unaccompanied by the apostate Christian groups.

In 1864, five years after the publication of *On the Origin of Species*, White wrote that God had given her a vision of the actual creation: "I was then carried back to the creation and was shown that the first week, in which God performed the work of creation in six days and rested on the seventh day, was just like every other week."[24] These and other prophetic writings by White rooted the Adventist movement firmly in the soil of young-earth creationism.

White's influence on American culture was limited, however, by the small size of the Adventist sect, which numbered just 140,000 members early in the twentieth century. (In contrast, there are now 14 million Adventists in 202 countries.) Most Christians view Seventh-day Adventists with suspicion, put off by their apocalypticism, odd dietary laws, and theology of the Sabbath, according to which they worship on Saturday, when they should be mowing their lawns. And many Christians have long considered White somewhere between a false prophet and a mentally deranged person, or perhaps even a mentally deranged false prophet.

Despite Adventism's cultural insignificance in nineteenth-century America, the modern creationist movement was gestating within its eccentric theological womb. By the early twentieth century a self-taught Adventist geologist named George McCready Price would recast White's vision of Noah's flood in scientific terms. The achievement inspired John Whitcomb and Henry Morris to write *The Genesis Flood,* and the rest, as they say, is history.

But flood geology was irrelevant when Darwin arrived in America in the middle of the nineteenth century, and there was limited active opposition. Scientists had various interpretations of evolution, some of which were theologically benign. Likewise, theologians and biblical scholars were not united behind a reading of Genesis incompatible with evolution. With the exception of the marginalized Adventists and a few Protestant conservatives, there was far less fuss than might have been expected. A mass movement opposing evolution was a half century away.

THE BIRTH OF FUNDAMENTALISM

There was, however, a mass movement opposing the other book from Europe, Strauss's *Life of Jesus Critically Examined*. Strauss's controversial book had conservatives wringing their hands, lamenting from pulpits, and feverishly writing refutations.

Segments of American Christianity under the influence of higher critics like Strauss abandoned the Bible as the ultimate authority for faith. Theologians calling themselves "Christian" rejected the New Testament miracles and the divinity of Christ. They treated the Bible as a purely human book. Lyman Abbott (1835–1922), for example, a prolific author and theologian who was for several years a minister in the Congregational Church, in 1892 published *The Evolution of Christianity,* offering an "updated" religion with no heaven, hell, original sin, or divine Christ.[25] Such reformulations of Christianity abandoned so many traditional beliefs that many feared there was no baby left in the tiny puddle of remaining bathwater.

To meet the rising tide of modernism, as it was known, an influential project was launched in 1909 to identify the essential core ideas of Christianity—the fundamentals—and rally Christians to protect those beliefs and keep them from being swept away by the rising tide of modernism. A lively conversation ensued. Which ideas were fundamental to Christianity and which were secondary or even peripheral? What were the issues on which Christians could disagree? Do Christians have to believe that a whale swallowed Jonah? That Job was a real character? That Noah's flood was global? That Jesus was born of a virgin? That God is a trinity? Selection of the contributors, which included many leading Protestant thinkers,[26] required identification of scholars believed to represent the best Christian thinking. The entire fundamentals project entailed engagement with traditional Christianity at all levels. The result was a four-volume set of essays titled *The Fundamentals*.

The primary target of *The Fundamentals* was obvious. Of about ninety articles in the series, fully one-third defended the Bible against Strauss and the higher critics. The rest presented doctrines, laid out apologetic arguments, criticized various "isms," and discussed world evangelism and other practical matters. Some of the essays were personal testimonies written by exemplary Christians.

Evolution in some guise appeared in about 20 percent of the essays. What was remarkable about these discussions of evolution, however, was the almost total absence of the six-day creationist viewpoint. Leading "fundamentalist" thinkers spoke approvingly of progressive creationism, historical linkages between species, and an ancient earth. There were critical comments as well, of course. One author maligned evolution by connecting it to higher criticism and called it an enemy of the Christian faith. More typical, however, were the views expressed by George Frederick Wright of Oberlin College, who claimed that the challenges from philosophy were far more serious than those from science. "Hume," he wrote, "is more dangerous than Darwin."[27]

Clearly, even leaders concerned with defining and protecting the *fundamentals* of Christianity shared no consensus on what Christians should think about evolution. This ambivalence in *The Fundamentals* offers a key insight into the history of this controversy. The fundamentalist movement, today unanimously opposed to evolution, takes its very name from this project. And yet this original generation of authentic fundamentalists was relatively unconcerned about evolution. Modern creationists should reflect on the fact that *The Fundamentals* contains no call to take up arms against evolution.

The Fundamentals succeeded in rescuing Christianity from modernism, largely because two wealthy Christian oilmen donated a small fortune to the project. They underwrote the production of the original twelve pamphlets of essays and then paid to ship almost four million copies free of charge to Christian leaders around the world. A distinct branch of Christianity known as *fundamentalism* resulted.

Much of the opposition to evolution in the early twentieth century came from the marginal and largely irrelevant Adventists, who were not invited to contribute to *The Fundamentals*. Eventually, however, the anti-evolutionary views of the Adventists migrated beyond the borders of their small sect and influenced the larger fundamentalist community, evolving into the movement we now know as *scientific creationism*.

Profound concerns about evolution emerged from a very different source, however. Darwin, it seemed, was gathering an unsavory collection of traveling companions. His central idea that nature improved species by "selecting" the more fit attracted the attention of some shady characters with rather different ideas about exactly what "fit" should mean. Aggressive militarists, particularly in Germany, invoked Darwin to justify assaults on weaker nations. Social planners claimed that programs that forcibly sterilized the "unfit" were simply good science. Empire builders rationalized the extermination of "less advanced" races as a way to improve the human species.

Eventually Darwin's name was on the lips of the architects of Nazism as they rationalized their implementation of the "final solution." As thoughtful Christians observed Darwin's shady and immoral fraternizing, it became increasingly natural for them to recoil from evolution altogether. Many, like William Jennings Bryan, were alarmed to see evolution invoked to justify the German militarism that led to World War I. Closer to home, many Christians wondered if evolution really justified a 1927 Virginia court order to sterilize Carrie Buck against her will for being "feebleminded." The "science" of evolution dropped off the radar as these social agendas loomed ever larger.

Defenders of evolution as a reliable theory of origins worked steadily throughout the twentieth century to detach Darwin's theory from its fraternity of dark companions. They had limited success. Like unwanted ghosts, the dark companions continued to haunt the theory of evolution even as it became the central organizing principle of the entire field of biology.

CHAPTER 3

DARWIN'S DARK COMPANIONS

A crime was committed while I was writing this chapter. My daughter, on a travel course to Rome, had her iPod stolen. This, of course, constituted an emergency, for iPods are as important to American teenagers as kidneys and lungs. The tiny music player had to be replaced immediately.

Apple's iPod and its associated iTunes music store have been wildly successful international consumer products, changing the way music is marketed, redefining "cool" (for the moment, at least), and raking in revenues for Apple shareholders. Apple's business model in this market has been aggressive, designed to destroy competitors. Both the iPod and the iTunes store are best-of-breed products. But neither is especially unique. Less sexy but equally effective models are available, at least for now, from Microsoft, Sansa, Sony, and a host of other market competitors. Online stores can beat the iTune prices as well, with everyone from Microsoft to Wal-Mart selling music online to a growing market of listeners.

Apple, however, knows its iPod is so totally cool that every teenager has to have one, even though there are other similar music players. Apple also knows its iTunes store is by far the most popular place to buy music, even though it is not all that different from the stores run by the competition. But to weaken Microsoft, Sony, and all the other companies who make portable music players, Apple designed iTunes so that they would play only on iPods. If you want to shop at the popular iTunes store, you have to play your music on an iPod.

Apple competes in the tough world of modern capitalism, where, at least in theory, companies making the best products for the lowest price defeat competitors in the quest for consumer dollars. Apple's goal is to kill off the competition in a sort of economic genocide so their "superior race" of products will have the market to itself. And we all benefit from this practice, at least in theory.

The capitalism practiced by Apple is much older than the theory of evolution, but as soon as Darwin's theory came on the scene, with its "selection" and "survival of the fittest" themes, obvious comparisons were invoked. The "free market" was to capitalism what "nature" was to evolution, a competitive environment rewarding excellence and weeding out inferior products. The best music player by these lights—the iPod, at the moment—is the "fittest" and wins the battle, if not the war. The less fit challengers, the Zune and the Walkman, will go extinct if they cannot evolve into something more "fit."

The upside of this competition is better products at lower prices, if everyone plays by the rules. The downside is the trampling of companies—and employees—creating products that don't survive. But because there are "rules" to the game, critics are charging Apple with a crime in response to the company's aggressive business practices. This is a peculiar state of affairs. Apple makes iPods and runs the iTunes online store. Nobody is forced to shop at iTunes—there are other places to purchase music—but if customers want to shop at the popular iTunes store, they have to buy an iPod music player. Critics accuse Apple of breaking the law, however, and argue they should be penalized, just as if they were robbing banks or dumping hazardous waste into a river.

Apple's business practices raise the fascinating question of so-called *social Darwinism,* the application of evolutionary principles to social behaviors. Conventional *biological Darwinism* provides an acceptable explanation for the origin of species: complex "fit" species evolve, survive, and prosper, while less fit competitors stagnate, die, and go extinct. Biological evolution, in its pure form at least, is purely *descriptive.* It tells us, as best it can, what happened, like a video of an event. It does not pass judgment on whether the history it describes was good or bad, just as a video passes no judgment on the event it captures.

Social Darwinism, in contrast, often has a strongly *prescriptive* component, since it applies to human behavior. Moral judgment is passed on behaviors based on how they fit into the overall Darwinian scheme. Apple—or any other corporation—is allowed to destroy the products and companies competing with it, provided it plays by the rules. If people lose their jobs and become homeless, that is acceptable, since the *process* is valued and protected for the *products* it produces. As Andrew Carnegie wrote in 1889, "While the law may be sometimes hard for the individual, it is best for the race, because it insures the survival of the fittest in every department."[1] Carnegie's key phrase, "survival of the fittest," almost universally ascribed to Darwin, actually originated with the influential British philosopher Herbert Spencer. Spencer believed that everything, from the cosmos, to society, to Carnegie's free market where Apple competes with Microsoft, steadily evolves toward some sort of perfection through a process similar to what Lamarck had proposed. Spencer's ideas were in circulation before Darwin published *On the Origin of Species* and are credited with popularizing social Darwinism, although questions exist about exactly how "Darwinian" his ideas actually were.[2]

Social Darwinism remains a controversial topic around which countless questions continue to revolve. What, exactly, does the term mean? What did Darwin think about this supposed extension of his ideas? What is the actual connection between biological evolution and social Darwinism? Do the moral prescriptions of social Darwinism really find support in Darwin's theory? To what degree was biological Darwinism invoked for propaganda purposes to buttress ideas with no connection to evolution? Was there, for example, an *actual* connection between evolution and Nazism, as a recent scholar has argued?[3] Or is this just a propaganda move to make evolution smell bad?

These questions will no doubt occupy scholars for years to come and may never be resolved. Certainly I am not going to resolve them in this brief chapter. But their resolution is not important for my purposes. I simply want to argue that the mere existence of the *concept* of social Darwinism has enormous significance for understanding reactions to evolution. That a connection can be and has been drawn between evolution and Nazism creates a disastrous public relations problem for Darwin. Such connections only further prejudice the millions predisposed to be skeptical about evolution against the theory and play into the hands of already powerful anti-evolutionary pundits.

These and the other controversies that swirl around evolution derive from the theory's great subtlety, ambiguity, and widespread applicability. We encounter evolutionary phenomena at so many levels and apply the term in so many contexts that it is hard to get a clear sense of exactly what the theory does and does not say. Certainly stellar and cosmic evolution, neither of which experience anything resembling natural selection, bear little resemblance to the evolution of species, and yet they share the label "evolution." But even the more narrow, purely biological evolution that occupied Darwin is complex and layered.

Biological evolution, as we understand it today, is like a digital photo composed of tiny square pixels that are normally invisible. If you zoom in too close on a digital photo, all you can see are square pixels, which look nothing like the picture. Zoom in on biological evolution and you encounter a disturbing amount of death and destruction. The majority of the offspring of many organisms simply don't make it to adulthood. Predators kill the slow and stupid; disease and bad luck wipe out many of the rest. To get one robust, fit animal across the finish line to procreation requires that nature start the race with ten animals, nine of which are doomed to a senseless death. That happy goldfinch I am watching now on my feeder has dead relatives scattered throughout my woods. This is survival of the fittest stripped of any charm or romance: the pristine wilderness where the delightful survivors cavort is littered with the bones of the less fortunate. Many of them died painfully and tragically.

Zoom out and look at evolution from farther away, and we see entire species going extinct. The fossil record—all those fascinating bones that attract kids in the science museum—is one long story of *failure*. Dinosaurs couldn't manage climate change effectively, so they went extinct, making room for mammals to rise to dominance. The dodos went extinct in the seventeenth century, unable to handle the arrival of "civilization" on their island homes. "Nature," wrote Alfred Lord Tennyson in *In Memoriam,* is "red in tooth and claw," challenging the pre-Darwinian vision of nature as a sunny meadow full of butterflies, songbirds, and lovers with picnic baskets.

Zoom all the way out, however, to the scale where ape-men are being steadily promoted and fish are scrambling onto tidal flats, and the picture gains some charm. Evolution from this vantage point looks rather glorious, working patiently over millennia to turn sponges into people and a few simple life-forms into the rich diversity that makes the world so interesting. The blood oozing in the picture up close is invisible from far away.

A deep paradox exists here between the *product* of evolution and the *process*. Most of us value life more than nonlife, complex life more than simple life, conscious life more than unconscious life, and people more than other animals. We think nothing about bulldozing ant colonies to make room for our houses; we use herbicides and pesticides with impunity, concerned only about whether they make our dogs sick. We kill mice that come indoors, and we drive owls to extinction. Most of us are fine with slaughtering cattle to make hamburgers and shooting monkeys that get too violent in the zoo. Our concerns are, first and foremost, for ourselves, our families, our communities, and our species, in that order. Those with broader concerns typically have to become a public spectacle to get heard, chaining themselves to trees or lying down in front of bulldozers.

This hierarchy of values has implications for human behavior. It also shapes the way we view evolution. If humans are more valuable than simpler life-forms, then evolution produces *value* over the course of time. This mitigates and, in the eyes of many, justifies the continual bloodletting associated with the evolutionary process. You have to break an egg to make an omelet. Or, as the more philosophically inclined might put it, the ends justify the means.

IS THERE AN END IN SIGHT?

Competition for limited resources, said Darwin, leads to improved competitors. If only the fittest survive to reproduce, then the next generation will be fitter. Darwin developed his theory to explain how species adapt in nature, but the basic idea clearly had broader applications. Any competition that consistently eliminates the weak and advances the best will produce a superior final product. Think of the Olympic athletes with their gold medals. How many lesser athletes were eliminated in their long climb to the top?

Social Darwinism is the idea that selection processes can work on different entities or "social units." People can compete; but so can teams. Towns can compete with each other to attract businesses. Ethnic groups can compete. Corporations compete for consumer dollars. Entire countries compete in everything from the Olympics to the occasional violent conflict. Each one of these social units has its own arena of competition and specific fitness criteria. If fitness is going to improve—a desirable goal—then the stronger players must be able to defeat the weaker ones. The defeat of the weak is the downside, the price paid for the generation of excellence. In the Olympics, the defeats entail personal heartbreak and even humiliation on national television. At the corporate level defeats result in companies going bankrupt and people losing their jobs. Globally they can mean war, with thousands of people losing their lives. In Darwin's theory they mean that some organisms succeed at producing offspring while others fail, often because they die before adulthood. And just as Darwinian bloodletting seemed necessary to enable a process leading to human beings—a necessary evil, so to speak—so every selection process justifies a bit of collateral carnage in the service of something larger.

In the decades after Darwin published his theory, dramatically different agendas invoked his theory as a rationale to justify various ideologies. If "survival of the fittest" was indeed a scientifically established vehicle for "progress," then why restrict it to the production of species? Why not use it, for example, to selectively weed out unfit humans in order to improve the human race? If less fit humans were sterilized by the stronger stock, then wouldn't the human race be stronger? Or perhaps unfit humans should simply be destroyed, suggested the Nazis.

In the marketplace, why not allow strong companies to run roughshod over those less able to compete? If companies compete without regulations, so the strong can drive the weak into bankruptcy, then the surviving companies will be stronger, the economy more productive, and we'll all have better iPods. And what about nations? Why not allow strong nations—with more "fit" societies—to overrun and absorb the less fit? Are not strong nations, with the various superiorities that give them their strength, to be preferred to weak ones? Who can look at the happy Canadians and not conclude that their way of life should be forcibly imposed on the poor Haitians?

Capitalists, nationalists, and racists, of course, promote agendas of self-interest and appeal to whatever rationale seems most helpful. Few of them are interested in any progress other than their own. And none of them are or were inspired by Darwin, for they have been around for ages. Two millennia before Darwin, for example, Plato championed selective breeding of humans as a way to increase the fitness of the race. His fellow Greek, Thrasymachus, preached that "might makes right," justifying the strong trampling the weak as a way to achieve more powerful political structures. The ancient Hebrews, in a campaign of reverse anti-Semitism, thought it appropriate to slaughter the men, women, children, infants, sheep, camels, donkeys, and cattle of the Amalekites, to prevent contamination of their superior religion.[4] You can't have Hebrew cows mating with pagan bulls. Such examples illustrate the countless ways that strength and fitness could be promoted through subordination of the less fit—all without any help from Darwin.

Once Darwin's theory appeared, however, Spencer and like-minded political pundits immediately adapted it to rationalize the crushing of the weak by the strong. Disturbing philosophies of self-interest thus acquired a gloss of scientific respectability, making them even more pernicious. Naïve but horrified biologists tried unsuccessfully to argue that evolution by natural selection was simply a *description* of a historical process, making no moral judgments about the ethics or integrity of this process. The historical fact that volcanoes spew lava over villagers hardly provides license for people to proactively mimic nature with moral impunity. But evolutionary theory provided an extraordinary new worldview that was especially seductive to self-congratulatory Europeans, already convinced that human history was best understood as a steady advance to the exalted plateau on which they found themselves. And much of this plateau, of course, rested on the blood, sweat, and tears of conquered peoples.

Darwinism, for better or worse, but mainly worse, has been continually attached to agendas that have nothing to do with the "origin of species." Right or wrong, but mainly wrong, Darwinism has always looked much larger than biology. And today the opposition to evolution from Christians is driven by a conviction that Darwin's theory undermines traditional values and opens doors to assorted evils. This conviction, although often poorly articulated, has ample historical precedent and should be taken seriously. The same naive and horrified biologists, of course, continue to lament this misapplication of the theory and accuse Darwin's critics of muddled thinking. But the truth is that Darwinism emerged in a socially complex milieu and has been socially embedded ever since. To understand the enduring intensity of America's reaction to Darwinism, we must acknowledge the significance of this history, not dismiss it as a trivial aberration. There is nothing new, uniquely American, or pathologically religious about seeing more in Darwinism than a simple theory to explain the origin of species by means of natural selection.

BLESSED ARE THE POOR–OR NOT

The first and most significant of the many Darwinian social agendas is one that preceded Darwin and played a role in his development of the theory. Darwin's England was caught in a struggle involving the social order. At the top, royalty claimed a divine right to their power. Privileged clergy were protected and paid by the state. There were lords with historical titles and wealthy landowners whose socioeconomic status had dubious origins in the distant past. And there were working classes and unemployed poor. This hierarchy constituted a well-defined social order that the privileged upper classes wanted to protect. But the order was everywhere under attack. Secularists blasted the entrenched power of the clergy. Reformers blasted the persistence of questionably obtained historical affluence and influence, passed down from one undeserving generation to the next. The poor rioted and assaulted the bastions of power, demanding more opportunity.

The problem of the poor was especially vexing. They tended to have larger families and were moving from rural England into the cities to work in the new factories. The industrializing cities were growing crowded and dirty and developing concentrations of these poorer classes, who were demanding attention. Their poverty, living conditions, and poor education made them susceptible to illness, criminality, drunkenness, and other vices. Those who took pity on them demanded housing, hospitals, asylums, education, and laws to protect children from abusive labor practices.

Programs to support the poor, however, inevitably lead to an increase in their numbers. Give them food and fewer will starve; give them medicine and disease will be checked; employ and educate them and they will be less likely to kill each other. Unchecked populations, unfortunately, increase exponentially: one million leads to two million then to four, then eight, sixteen, and so on. If the poor flourish, their numbers will rise faster than the resources necessary to sustain them, leading inevitably to a disastrous imbalance that will ultimately be corrected by widespread starvation. By this logic, programs to support the poor were clearly misguided. Better for half the population to starve when that number is one million, rather than when it is sixteen.

An Anglican clergyman named Thomas Malthus worked out this morbid mathematics in his widely read *An Essay on the Principle of Population*, published in 1798. "The power of population," he wrote, "is so superior to the power of the earth to produce subsistence for man, that premature death must in some shape or other visit the human race." Fortunately, death had a great many conscripts—"extermination, sickly seasons, epidemics, pestilence, and plague"—but should these front-line soldiers prove inadequate to keep overpopulation at bay, "gigantic inevitable famine stalks in the rear, and with one mighty blow levels the population with the food of the world."[5]

Darwin encountered Malthus's essay in 1838 while working on his theory. He recognized that Malthus's insight—unchecked population growth will outstrip increases in the food supply—applied to *all* species, not just humans. Therefore, since most populations are stable, there must be widespread competition for the limited resources. The fittest were winning this competition; the unfit were being weeded out, "selected" by nature for removal.

Incorporated into Darwin's theory, Malthus's principle was promoted from a depressing socioeconomic insight to full partner in the grand creative process that had sponges competing to see who could be the first to turn into a supermodel. Famine and pestilence went upscale, joining chisels and sandpaper as tools that create through destruction. Defenders of the status quo, in love with the idea that their exalted status derived from their competitive prowess, had been accused of being heartless and uncompassionate. They now leaped enthusiastically onto this shiny new Darwinian bandwagon, arguing that it was unnatural and ultimately cruel to enable any swelling of the ranks of the poor. Do nothing and let nature take its course, unless the idea of mass starvation is somehow attractive to you.

Herbert Spencer, who turned the phrase "survival of the fittest" into a household term, mocked the liberal reformers lobbying on behalf of the poor: "'They have no work,' you say. Say rather that they either refuse work or quickly turn themselves out of it. They are simply good-for-nothings, who in one way or other live on the good-for-somethings."[6] Quoting the Bible—"if any would not work neither should he eat"—Spencer argued that it was natural that "a creature not energetic enough to maintain itself must die."[7]

As for Darwin, he barely recognized his theory draped in such dark cloth. Perhaps because of his experience with his daughter Annie's death or perhaps because of the Christian charity he retained throughout his life—a charity he practiced through his family church even after he stopped attending—he was never personally able to get past the simple conviction that people should help each other, even if it meant tolerating legislation that taxed the productive members of society to provide support for the so-called "good-for-nothings." Nevertheless, he struggled with the tensions between his personal feelings and the broader implications of his theory.

EUGENICS

Leaving the poor to their own devices was a *passive* strategy to ensure that productive societies did not become diluted with useless, stupid, or otherwise defective people. Natural selection would do the dirty work as long as nothing—like misguided pie-in-the-sky liberals and their social reform agendas—interfered. But natural selection was slow and, despite the intelligence implied by the word *selection,* the process was really little more than a crapshoot with slightly loaded dice. Breeders, for example, could move tulips and dogs along the happy road of progress much faster using *artificial* rather than *natural* selection. Why not assist Mother Nature by inserting a bit of intelligence?

It was Darwin's cousin, Francis Galton, who suggested that the pestilential growth of the lower classes required something more aggressive than unaided natural selection. Even without social assistance, the downtown slums were filling up with lunatics and criminals, the result of unchecked procreation. In contrast, the superior residents of the uptown penthouses were having fewer children, sensibly moderating their procreation. For anyone who could do the math, the social trajectory looked grim. The human race, at least in England, was deteriorating.

Galton's solution was simple: encourage the more fit members of society to have more children, just as better cattle are bred by mating the stronger members of that species. In an 1865 article in *Macmillan's Magazine* titled "Hereditary Talent and Character," he outlined his vision for the production of a superrace of humans:

> If a twentieth part of the cost and pains were spent in measures for the improvement of the human race that is spent on the improvement of the breed of horses and cattle, what a galaxy of genius might we not create! We might introduce prophets and high priests of civilization into the world, as surely as we can propagate idiots by mating *cretins*.[8]

Galton, like most everyone at the time, including cousin Charles, was deeply racist. His classic treatise, *Hereditary Genius,* is filled with the most natural and straightforward analysis of the quality of England's public figures as well as the races of the world. The chapter titled "The Comparative Worth of Different Races" offers a sobering portrait of nineteenth-century Victorian elitism.[9]

The self-congratulatory Victorian obsession with progress, coupled to the belief that evolution produced "higher" creatures from "lower" ones, had nearly everyone convinced that the various human "races" could be ranked. Not surprisingly, the scale had white Europeans at the top, reciting poetry while eating cooked foods off china with knives and forks rather than plucking bananas from trees like lower primates. If the lower races became extinct, that would represent progress. Galton and his followers were quite animated about the prospects of breeding the best representatives of the most advanced culture to create a superrace. Galton coined the term *eugenics,* meaning "best born," to describe his program. It was a program that soon found itself shrouded in a dark, sinister fog.

THREE GENERATIONS OF IMBECILES

The eugenics movement became popular in most of Europe, Canada, and the United States. In the United States an influential study by a New York social reformer, Richard Dugdale, traced the "Jukes" family through five generations, establishing that most of the 709 relatives examined were "criminals, prostitutes, or destitute."[10] Convinced that such defects were hereditary, reformers enthusiastically promoted legislation to forcibly sterilize such defectives or otherwise prevent them from breeding.

Government offices sprang up to create eugenics policies and track progress. In the United States this was done through the Eugenics Record Office, created in 1910 with donations from wealthy American industrialists. Between 1900 and 1935, thirty-two states enacted laws permitting forced sterilization of defective humans. More than sixty thousand people were sterilized for defects ranging from "feeblemindedness" to epilepsy. Virtually every state in the United States and every country in Europe had some kind of a program to prevent defective humans from passing on their defects.

In 1914 the Eugenics Record Office developed a proposal to sterilize one-tenth of the population of every generation,[11] until fifteen million people had been sterilized. The sarcastic journalist who became famous covering the Scopes trial, H. L. Mencken, suggested that all the sharecroppers in the South should be sterilized.

The public schools taught children to think hard about choosing marriage partners and warned about the drain on society caused by defective humans. In the textbook from which John Scopes was accused of teaching evolution, author George W. Hunter outlines the social disaster of the infamous Jukes family, which produced "24 confirmed drunkards, 3 epileptics, and 143 feebleminded" as well as 33 who were "sexually immoral." Such families, the children read, were "parasites," spreading "disease, immorality, and crime to all parts of the country."[12] In a chapter titled "Heredity and Variation," Hunter continues:

> The cost to society of such families is very severe. Just as certain animals or plants become parasitic on other plants or animals, these families have become parasitic on society. They not only do harm to others by corrupting, stealing, or spreading disease, but they are actually protected and cared for by the state out of public money. Largely for them the poorhouse and the asylum exist. They take from society, but they give nothing in return. They are true parasites.[13]

In both the United States and Britain Protestant clergy floated proposals that would have required certificates of "eugenic fitness" before getting approval for a church wedding.[14] There was no room in their inns for feebleminded children. Only the Catholic Church seemed consistently concerned about these proposals for governmental meddling in human reproduction.

The U.S. Supreme Court, with a lone dissenting voice, ruled in 1927 that mandatory sterilization was constitutional for patients in mental institutions. In a landmark case, plaintiff Carrie Buck was forcibly sterilized for being "feebleminded." At the time she was a patient at the Virginia State Colony for Epileptics and Feebleminded. Her mother, Emma, had also been accused of being "feebleminded," as was her daughter, Vivian, who was sterilized as a child.

Invoking the "public welfare," in 1927 Justice Oliver Wendell Holmes wrote for the court that such "manifestly unfit" people should be prevented from breeding, rather than "waiting to execute degenerate offspring." Claiming that Carrie, her mother, and her daughter were all "feebleminded," the court ruled that the public good was served and the Constitution upheld by forcibly sterilizing Carrie Buck. "Three generations of imbeciles," wrote Holmes in a chilling conclusion, "is enough."

Eventually paroled, Carrie Buck was an avid reader until she died in 1983; the case against her "feeblemindedness" was undermined when it was discovered that a relative of her adopted family had raped her. Carrie had been committed to hide the rape and protect the family's "good name." Her "feebleminded" daughter, Vivian, died at age eight, leaving behind an academic record of modest success, including being on the honor roll.

THE FINAL SOLUTION

Eugenics took a sinister turn in Europe, especially Germany, and subsequently fell so far from grace that it became a concept from which politically savvy people would flee. Galton, we will recall, originally made the benign suggestion that the quality of the human race would be improved if the "fittest" members of society had more children. Even though Galton held a low opinion of the poor, he understood them to be a part of the species that included him and his "fit" colleagues. This diverse group, with its great variation in fitness, would be improved if the less fit had fewer children and the fitter folks had more children. This form of "positive" eugenics is still practiced through the marketing of "superior" eggs and sperm. (I have in my files, for example, a request from a sperm bank for a sample. Apparently I have passed some criteria for "fitness.")

Galton's eugenics strategies would work, at least in principle, on any group of organisms. Applied to a human group—Caucasians, Asians, baseball fans, Trekkies, or even the readers of this book—selective breeding of the "fittest" members would improve group averages. But this was not the only way to understand eugenics.

Nineteenth-century Europeans, after three centuries of global exploration and empire building, were only too aware of the different human "races." And there was general agreement that racial groups were fundamentally unequal, as both the European and American legacy regarding slavery makes painfully clear. It was only natural, argued some, to view biological competition as between entire *races,* rather than between the individual *members* of a specific race. Extending eugenics into the realm of race relations seemed entirely reasonable and logical, based on what they knew at the time. If Malthus was correct that Caucasian England was better off with fewer poor people and that reducing their number should be the goal of social policy, then it followed that the human race as a whole, or any subgroup in it, was better off if the populations of the weaker segments were reduced.

The cold trajectory of this logic is all too easy to see. In its more benign incarnations it resulted in restrictions on immigration. In 1924, for example, the U.S. Congress passed laws restricting immigration from countries and ethnic groups perceived as inferior. Such laws had a glossy scientific veneer, and racist politicians took comfort in the sophistication and wisdom of policies informed by the best science of the day.

More sobering developments in Germany led to a national program of extermination of groups perceived to be inferior. Hitler and his Third Reich viewed Jews, gypsies, Poles, and homosexuals as inferior. Ernst Haeckel nudged the racism of the Third Reich along its malignant road by suggesting that the various human races were like stages in the embryonic development of a fetus. He arrayed the various human races along a ladder with subhuman primates at the bottom and Aryan supermen like him at the top. Black Africans and Tasmanians, in his scheme, were closer to animals than to the advanced European races. It would be hard to imagine a more dangerous articulation of racism than Haeckel's. Not surprisingly, the Nazis eagerly embraced his ideas. Eager to rationalize their calculated genocide to a well-educated and culturally sophisticated populace, the Nazis invoked science whenever it served their interests and ignored it when it did not.

"If you draw a sharp boundary," Haeckel wrote in a popular book published in 1868, "you must draw it between the most highly developed civilized people on the one hand and the crudest primitive people on the other, and unite the latter with the animals."[15] The book contained sketches illustrating Haeckel's imaginative "ranking" based on the shapes of the heads of the various races.

How shocking it is today to acknowledge that virtually every educated person in Western culture at the time, on both sides of the Atlantic, shared Haeckel's ideas. Countless atrocities around the globe were rationalized by the belief that superior races were improving the planet by exterminating defective elements. This expressed itself in a variety of imperial attitudes toward non-Western peoples, lifestyles, religious practices, and ethics. The particular atrocities, of course, were not inspired by this version of social Darwinism, but there can be little doubt that such viewpoints muted voices that would otherwise have been raised in protest.

Empire-building imperialists invoked social Darwinism to rationalize colonial subordination and even organized slaughter of conquered peoples. The enslavement of blacks, the destruction of Native Americans, and the genocidal treatment of aboriginal tribes in Australia were defended as part of a grand Darwinian project to advance humanity. Joseph Le Conte, a respected geologist and president of the American Association for the Advancement of Science, addressed this issue in *The Race Problem in the South,* published in 1892. Le Conte argued that the docile character of the Negroes made them appropriate for enslavement; for races like the "redskin," however, who were more specialized and thus less flexible, "extermination is unavoidable."[16]

Well-meaning Christians, alas, believed they had license to abuse both their horses and their black servants (formerly slaves), since the best science of the day taught that neither was fully human. Racist theories like those of Haeckel produced a moral fog that made it hard for even Christians to show compassion and charity to those in need, if they fell outside certain boundaries. The most frightening incarnation of social Darwinism, of course, was Hitler's eugenics program, which eventually sent twelve million "defective" humans, half of them Jews, to various execution chambers. Nazi anti-Semitism, of course, did not originate with Darwin. In fact, there is more blame to be laid at the feet of Martin Luther than Charles Darwin. Luther had described Jews as "poisonous envenomed worms" and encouraged Christians to destroy them, inaugurating hostilities that continued unabated into the twentieth century.[17]

But German racial politics needed scientific, not religious, rationale and looked eagerly to Darwinism. Many Nazis were, to be sure, dullards and thugs easily manipulated by Hitler, with his peculiar malignant genius. Hitler certainly didn't need Darwin to help him abuse Jews. But there were many sophisticated Nazis, teaching at universities and holding high posts in the government and state churches. They needed something more than the anti-Semitic rants of their deranged führer to get behind the "final solution." Stung by their humiliation after losing World War I, Germans wanted nothing so much as to regain the glory of their past. If eliminating defective elements within their borders could accomplish this, then they were on board. And so much the better that there was a scientific rationale for this project.

I hasten to point out that the connection between Darwinism and movements like Nazism is not causal, as some shrill anti-evolutionary pundits like Ann Coulter claim.[18] Aryan Germans were not happily playing soccer and eating bagels with Jewish Germans until Darwin convinced them this was a bad idea. The connection is, rather, one of *rhetoric* and *rationalization*. It is rhetorical in the sense that dumb ideas play better when dressed in fine clothes. It sounds better to promote "cleansing the human race" than "killing people you don't like," a distinction of no value to Jews en route to Auschwitz. It is rationalization in the sense that conclusions already embraced rest easier on one's conscience if supported by some thread of rational argument, no matter how thin. The relevance of these considerations, however, is not that Darwinism leads somehow to dreadful social policies. The point is, rather, that Darwinism has been, for all of its short life, hanging out in some rather terrible company and has now got a reputation.

There is no shortage of creative rationalizations of Nazi anti-Semitism; for our purposes here one example will suffice. And although this example highlights the victimization of Jews, nearly identical arguments were applied to Negroes, Native Americans, and just about any group outside of Caucasian Europeans.

The following argument comes from Alfred Kirchhoff, a geographer at the University of Leipzig, who posthumously published *Darwinism Applied to Peoples and States* in 1910. Kirchhoff, like many evolutionists, believed that morality had evolved along with the physical and mental structures of organisms. Obviously, primitive life-forms had no morality. What exactly, could a sponge do that was *wrong*? More complex animals, like primates, had a simple morality. "Lower" human races, such as blacks and Native Americans, had a more developed morality. The higher races, which for Kirchhoff meant Europeans, had the most advanced morality. The "average" morality of the entire human race was thus "lowered" by the presence of morally inferior subgroups, just as the performance of an orchestra is compromised by the presence of a few bad musicians. So in a breathtaking application of this logic, an argument was developed that morality would actually *increase* if the morally advanced European races eliminated the morally underdeveloped races. Invoking Darwin, Kirchhoff defended this genocidal agenda, calling it the "righteousness of the struggle for existence." This struggle would lead to "the extermination of the crude, immoral hordes." The diversity of races and the resulting struggle were necessary for the "progress of humanity."[19]

As we've seen repeatedly in our discussion of Darwin and the nineteenth century, educated Europeans were marching in lockstep behind the pied piper of progress. Progress was now a moral crusade, and policies perceived as progressive needed little additional justification. *Might,* as an enabler of progress, slowly, imperceptibly, turned into *right,* in the eyes of far too many of Europe's leading lights. Subtle statements and innuendos, in textbooks like that used by John Scopes, acclimated schoolchildren to this mind-set. Less subtle, deeply political messages appeared in places like *Mein Kampf,* where Hitler waxed eloquent about the triumph of the strong, calling it an "iron law of necessity," justified as the "right of victory of the best." Note the value judgment implied by the word "best." "Whoever will not fight in this world of eternal struggle," Hitler wrote in language eerily reminiscent of Darwin's explanation of natural selection, "does not deserve to live."[20]

A small library of books could be assembled rationalizing the sinister ideas that became incarnate at Auschwitz and Dachau. Educated Germans designed efficient killing machines, over which trained medical personnel presided, for the purpose of advancing the human race through the destruction of the weak. This is a tragic chapter in German history that scholars are still trying to understand. But one thing is crystal clear: the Holocaust would have happened with or without Charles Darwin. There can be no doubt, however, that the Nazi campaign against the Jews was assisted via *rhetoric* and *rationalization* with arguments from social Darwinism.[21]

UNHAPPY BEDFELLOWS

The connection between biological and social Darwinism is complex and troubling, and perhaps even suspicious, but there is no denying that it has always been there, even before evolutionary theory became known as "Darwinism." The arguments and even some of the practices are still in play. Most sperm banks take in account eugenic considerations. Parents routinely test for birth defects, and "defective" embryos are often aborted. William Shockley, who won a Nobel Prize for physics in 1956, used his fame as a platform to warn humanity about "the genetic deterioration of the human race through lack of elimination of the least fit as the basis of continuing evolution."[22] In 1994 two prominent social scientists, Richard Herrnstein and Charles Murray, reignited the controversy with their book *The Bell Curve: Intelligence and Class Structure in American Life.* The authors updated eugenic concerns identical to those that worried Galton: "higher fertility and faster generational cycle among the less intelligent." This has dire social consequences. "Something worth worrying about," they warn, "is happening to the cognitive capacities of the country."[23]

Storms of occasionally violent protest greeted the eugenic agendas of Shockley and *The Bell Curve.* Few ideas upset contemporary sensibilities more than the suggestion that intelligence varies by race. Its association with that idea gives Darwin's theory a stench that many find unbearable. And there are other, equally troubling connections drawn between evolution and unpopular ideas, including philandering, infanticide, violence, and rape. The Harvard linguist Steven Pinker invokes Darwinian principles to explain infanticide, suggesting that killing one's newborn should not be viewed with the same seriousness as killing one's child later in life.[24] The authors of *A Natural History of Rape* invoke Darwin to explain that rape is a consequence of "men's evolved machinery for obtaining a high number of mates."[25] Connecting evolution to racism, rape, infanticide, philandering, and so on makes many people very nervous.

Thoughtful evolutionists hasten to point out that no necessary connection exists between biological evolution, which provides *descriptive* explanations of how nature works, and social Darwinism, which suggests *prescriptive* guidelines for how society *should* behave. It is far from obvious that eugenics, unbridled capitalism, relaxed attitudes about infanticide, or rampant militarism is implied by the theory that species originate through natural selection.

Let us suppose, for the sake of argument, that such extensions are warranted, perhaps in the service of some "greater good." We immediately face a host of ambiguities. How do we actually apply Darwinian principles to social behaviors? Consider the relatively benign world of capitalism, with iPods, Toyotas, and dishwashers. Applying Darwin's "survival of the fittest" to resolve the dispute over Apple's aggressive business practices, for example, is far from straightforward.

For starters, since we are making a *moral* judgment about actions in the free market, we must decide what it is that *should* have its "fitness" protected. Is it the *products* competing in the portable music space? Are they the units of Darwinian selection? Do we want to enable the development of the best and most fit music players and best online music stores? If so, then we should not allow Apple to artificially enhance the market share of either the iPod or the iTunes store by linking them in a way that makes it harder for other products to get into this market space. Such a practice would be anticompetitive and non-Darwinian. But what if, instead of using competition to enhance the fitness of *products,* we look instead at ways to use competition to enhance the fitness of the *companies* that make the products? Maybe the "unit of selection" is Apple Corporation, not the iPod. Certainly when Andrew Carnegie appealed to Darwinism to justify aggressive business practices, he was more interested in the fitness of the corporations than the products they produced. Under this interpretation we should want the *company* to be stronger, and we should allow Apple Computer do whatever it wishes to grow its market share and profits. What should disappear in this competition are not competitors' products but the competitors themselves.

Applying social Darwinism to society creates the same problems. Is the unit of selection the *individual,* for example, or the *society*? Is the competition between *people* or between *countries*? Is the competition *military* or *economic*? And how is success defined? In the United States we hear a lot about the gross national product and how important it is for that to become larger. In dramatic contrast to this, tiny Bhutan calculates a "gross national happiness" and works to increase that index. Which is the better measure of Darwinian fitness?[26]

Social Darwinism turns out to be almost useless when you actually try to do something with it. Many ideologically driven decisions have to be made before you can even apply it. As a result, it ends up being little more than a bogus appeal to science to rationalize an agenda already embraced for other reasons.

CONCLUSIONS

Despite nonstop critique by philosophically sophisticated evolutionists, pundits continue to find, within the science of biological evolution, justification for controversial moral stances on an array of social problems. Right or wrong, but mainly wrong, evolution continues to be connected to far more than the historical origin of species. And these connections exacerbate whatever concerns people might have about whether evolution is actually "true." Believing something is false is much easier when you desperately want it to be false.

These associations are problematic in the context of America's current controversy over evolution. Half the population of America thinks evolution is simply not true. For this vast constituency, God created the species individually; they did not evolve by natural selection or any other method. The evidence is unconvincing, the religious problems overwhelming, and the idea that a sponge could turn into a person is ridiculous. Furthermore, there are noisy "creation scientists" and "intelligent design theorists" highlighting the problems with evolution and offering simplistic alternatives that satisfy the limited curiosity of most Americans about origins.

The morally complex baggage carried by evolution hampers its acceptance. Even if evolutionary theory were true, why would anyone *want* to believe a theory that rationalizes Nazism, infanticide, and rape? The theory's supposed "explanation" of these horrors represents for its detractors further evidence that the theory is really just a secular myth, undermining morality, condoning evil, and destroying religion.

Curiously, surveys of evolution by its many eloquent advocates gloss over social Darwinism as little more than an historical aberration. In the companion volume to the seven-part PBS series on evolution, science writer Carl Zimmer draws no connection whatsoever between evolution and social Darwinism. It appears only in a discussion of religious objections, where it is dismissed as "scientifically baseless."[27] According to Zimmer, people like William Jennings Bryan, the lawyer who prosecuted John Scopes and who despised Darwinism for its apparent evil implications, were simply confused.[28] Presumably the biologists who wrote the textbooks used in the high schools at the time were similarly confused, although Zimmer makes no mention of them. Niles Eldredge, curator at the American Museum of Natural History, comments in *Darwin: Discovering the Tree of Life* only that there is no "neat one-on-one correspondence between evolution and any single system of ethics."[29] Eugenie C. Scott, who heads up the National Center for Science Education, barely mentions it in her encyclopedic *Evolution vs. Creationism*.[30] Ernst Mayr, who until his death in 2005 was the dean of American evolutionists, relegates social Darwinism to a two-line entry in the glossary of his authoritative *What Evolution Is*. The text contains no discussion of it at all.[31]

These recent treatments contrast sharply with the history of evolution. Are social Darwinism and evolutionary theory really as unrelated as today's champions of evolution claim? How, then, did their predecessors get it so thoroughly wrong? It took Nazism, apparently, to deflate the eugenics balloon and two world wars to silence the loudest of the "might makes right" enthusiasts. Yet now we are told that these connections should never have been made and that they derived from "confusion."

Is it not disingenuous for evolutionists to pretend that these historical connections are aberrations? How many times do we see John Scopes held up as a martyr for the noble cause of teaching schoolchildren the truth, and yet we never read a word of criticism about the racism in the text he used? William Jennings Bryan continues to be ridiculed for thinking that social Darwinism contributed to World War I, but American eugenicists who, in the name of Darwin, sterilized thousands of people against their will have strangely disappeared from history. Darwin's dark companions are being written out of history, like characters in George Orwell's novel *1984*.

Popular books disputing evolution, not surprisingly, give plenty of space to Darwin's dark companions. Of course, the goal of this propaganda is to nurture revulsion in their readers against evolution and convince them that it. is truly a Satanic theory, as Ken Ham and Henry Morris claim. Ham's book *The Lie: Evolution* contains a chapter titled "The Evils of Evolution," which opens with a drawing showing evolution as the literal foundation of lawlessness, homosexuality, pornography, and abortion. Parallel section headings in the chapter link the following to evolution: Nazism, racism, drugs, abortion, business methods, and male chauvinism.[32]

Conservatives, by tradition and perhaps by definition, have always lamented the direction and pace of social change. From Plato and Socrates decrying the ruffians of ancient Greece to anti-evolutionary crusaders warning about the misguided youth of today, there has always been hand-wringing about change. And every generation of conservatives needs a scapegoat against which to rally the faithful. Tragically, Darwin plays that role today, as the most preposterous charges are leveled against him. In a slickly produced DVD from Coral Ridge Ministries, the late D. James Kennedy blames Darwin for everything from the Holocaust to the shootings at the Columbine high school.[33] "If evolution is true," Kennedy writes in the foreword to a companion book, "then we are simply the product of time and chance, and there is no morality and no intrinsic worth to human life."[34]

Ann Coulter, Lee Strobel, and other anti-evolutionary culture warriors join Kennedy on the DVD in a disturbing and appalling piece of propaganda dramatically at odds with contemporary scholarship. They can be forgiven, perhaps, since they are neither scientists nor historians of science. But they are so thoroughly and completely wrong that it is hard to imagine that they believe their own rhetoric. Perhaps what they believe themselves is not that important. But, unfortunately, millions of Americans are listening.

These sinister portrayals of Darwin and his dangerous theory frighten millions of ordinary people. True or false, who wants a theory that destroys all that is noble and good about being human? And who would want their taxes supporting the teaching of such dreadful falsehoods to their children? So, when Darwin's dangerous idea began to show up in the public schools, there was an immediate reaction. From Dayton, Tennessee, where John Scopes stood trial for teaching evolution, to Dover, Pennsylvania, where a local school board tried to wriggle intelligent design into the curriculum, evolution has had a nearly permanent home in America's courtrooms.

CHAPTER 4

THE NEVER ENDING CLOSING ARGUMENT

John Scopes, by all accounts, was a nice guy. He taught a variety of subjects, including biology, in the local high school in Dayton, Tennessee. One fateful day, in the middle of a lesson explaining Darwin's theory of evolution to his students, the local sheriff dropped by. The sheriff, with a couple of other prominent local citizens including a clergyman, stood ominously at the rear of the classroom, listening to Scopes's explanation of evolution. Put off by the strange and uninvited visitors, Scopes did the best he could to maintain normalcy in the class and continue the lesson:

> Darwin's theory tells us that man evolved from a lower order of animals: from the first wiggly protozoa here in the sea, to the ape, and finally to man. And some of you fellas out there are probably gonna say that's why some of us act like monkeys ...

The sheriff interrupted Scopes and made a great show of verifying his identity, although they had known each other for years. Reading from a paper, he informed the young biology teacher that he had broken the law that forbade "any teacher of the public school to teach any theory that denies the creation of man as taught in the Bible and to teach instead that man has descended from a lower order of animals." The sheriff arrested Scopes and took him to the local jail. His crime was the teaching of evolution. While he was in jail, the local citizens, seemingly all mean-spirited fundamentalist Christians, burned Scopes in effigy and sang about hanging him "from the sour apple tree."

The subsequent trial was a great media event. The famous politician William Jennings Bryan represented the state of Tennessee, and the equally famous agnostic lawyer Clarence Darrow represented John Scopes. Darrow, representing both Scopes and evolution, humiliated both Bryan and the anti-evolutionary forces. Bryan dropped dead immediately after the verdict. And the anti-evolutionary forces went into hiding.[1]

This is the famous "Monkey Trial," which, apart from Jesus's trial before Pilate, is probably the best-known legal confrontation in history. There is one problem, however. The events outlined above, although at least vaguely familiar to most educated Americans, did not occur.

WILL THE REAL JOHN SCOPES PLEASE STAND UP?

The Scopes trial was a definitive moment in American history. It captured the nation's attention like no trial before or since and now sits in the background of all confrontations between creation and evolution.

The trial contains both more and less than meets the eye. It is less in the sense that the trial was really just a show, and none of the players were interested in the trial itself. The version above, which most people recall as the history of the trial, comes from *Inherit the Wind*, a movie inspired by and *loosely* based on the trial. The play of the same name had also played widely across America before being brought to the big screen. But the Scopes trial is also more than meets the eye, incarnating the inevitable and cataclysmic confrontation of two cultural groups. A new secular America was emerging, with a theory assaulting the traditional story of creation. Traditionally religious Americans opposed secularization, of course. And they were uneasy about a theory that rationalized all manner of social evils from eugenic sterilization of the feebleminded to the invasion of weak countries by the strong.

The legend of the Scopes trial, in popular mythology, makes many conservatives see red. The national reporting of the trial was dominated by H. L. Mencken of the *Baltimore Sun,* probably the most sarcastic journalist who ever worked in the English language. Mencken hated Bryan, the South, small-town America, and fundamentalists, which he saw as something of a stone-age package. He loved Darrow, hyperbole, Northern liberalism, and the sound of his own typewriter. "Fundamentalists," wrote Mencken shortly after the trial, are thick in the mean streets and gas-works. They are everywhere where learning is too heavy a burden for mortal minds to carry, even the vague, pathetic learning on tap in the little red schoolhouses. They march with the Klan, with the Christian Endeavor Society, with the Junior Order of United American Mechanics, with the Epworth League, with all the Rococo bands that poor and unhappy folk organize to bring some new light of purpose into their lives.[2]

The unofficial "history" of the Scopes trial appeared in 1931, six years after the verdict. A leading journalist wrote a lively, sensationalized, simplistic, and best-selling history of the Roaring Twenties. In true journalistic fashion the story became a confrontation between well-defined and polarized opponents, without complexities or middle ground. The loser, conservative Christianity, was led by a political dinosaur named Bryan who went extinct one week after the trial ended. The winner was twentieth-century skepticism, led by a liberal crusader on a white horse named Clarence Darrow.[3]

In giving cinematic life to this drama, *Inherit the Wind* further maligned Bryan, transforming him into a pompous buffoon named Matthew Harrison Brady, played with enthusiasm by Frederic March. The town of Dayton, which Mencken conceded was "full of charm and even beauty,"[4] became a creepy cultural backwater. The townsfolk, mainly just old-fashioned Christians, became narrow-minded bigots, hostile to progress and science. The sedate faith of the real-life Daytonians became dark and sinister and was personified in the Reverend Brown, a vindictive and totally fictional character. The unsympathetic Brown, representing the worst in anti-evolutionary bigotry, calls down God's wrath on his daughter for supporting Bertram Cates, the Scopes character. The controversial American Civil Liberties Union (ACLU) attorney, Darrow, was named William Henry Drummond and played by the beloved Spencer Tracy. *Inherit the Wind* portrays this character as lovable and heroic, a warm grandfatherly figure. This portrayal stands in stark contrast to the real-life Darrow, a notorious lawyer who had just defended two rich Chicago teenagers who had murdered fourteen-year-old Bobby Franks for kicks.

Many view America's creation–evolution controversy as a part of the war between science and religion. Through this lens, science appears to triumph over religion at Dayton. This was not, technically, the verdict, but who cares about the truth when the myth is so interesting? Strangely, however, the true story is actually less plausible than the legend.

JUST THE FACTS, PLEASE

I grew up in a small town like Dayton, Tennessee, where everybody knows everybody else, concerns are mostly local, and the rest of the world seems far away. Such small towns, rendered so faithfully in Sinclair Lewis's novels, have informal meeting places where gossip and town business are always on the agenda. In my boyhood town of Bath, New Brunswick—population one thousand—the location was Abe's barbershop, which always had way more men on its hard wooden benches than needed haircuts. In Dayton, Tennessee—population eighteen hundred—in the 1920s, the place to meet was the soda fountain in Fred Robinson's drugstore. The topic on May 4, 1925, was evolution in the public schools, an unusually weighty subject.

The conversation that led to the Scopes trial started innocently, if ominously, on Friday, March 13, 1923, when the Tennessee Senate made it illegal "to teach any theory that denies the Story of Divine Creation of man as taught in the Bible, and to teach instead that man has descended from a lower order of animal." The Tennessee law was drafted by a farmer and part-time schoolteacher named John Washington Butler, who was also the clerk of the Round Lick Association of Primitive Baptists. It was the second of many such laws that states were passing to keep Darwin's dangerous idea away from their children, who were at last staying in school past the eighth grade.

The ACLU believed the law violated the Fourteenth Amendment, forbidding states from depriving anyone, including public-school teachers like John Scopes, of "life, liberty, or property without due process of law." The Tennessee law clearly restricted what a public-school teacher could teach, and the ACLU had been looking for a case like this. About a month after the law went into effect, the ACLU started running an advertisement in a newspaper in Chattanooga, forty miles from Dayton, looking for a guinea pig who would admit to the crime of teaching evolution to the children of Tennessee. It offered to pay the legal expenses of this criminal.

Everyone knew that the trial the ACLU was orchestrating would be a big show. Probably William Jennings Bryan, whose personal anti-evolutionary crusade had inspired much of the associated legislation, would ride in on his populist bandwagon to defend the law. And certainly the ACLU would import some colorful, arrogant big shot from the North to defend evolution and ridicule those who opposed it. Interested onlookers, probably in the thousands, would pour into whatever town hosted the event.

The locals at Robinson's drugstore thought it would be good for business if all these legal enthusiasts came to Dayton. Hotels would fill up, restaurants would boom, and Robinson would sell lots of sodas. Of course, if Dayton were to host the trial, they would need to find a local criminal who had broken the law against teaching evolution. And tiny Dayton with its handful of conservative Christian high-school teachers had few candidates. But one came to mind.

John Scopes, a general science teacher who taught physics and math and coached football, was one of the few "liberals" in Dayton. He willingly embraced the role proposed by the drugstore conspirators. He had no recollection of having taught evolution, but he had filled in once for a biology teacher in a class that used a textbook, Hunter's *Civic Biology*, which did have a few pages on evolution. As it turned out, that was close enough, and Scopes was "arrested" for breaking the law against teaching theories of origins in conflict with those contained in Genesis. The crime and the arrest were total shams of course, and Scopes worried about being exposed:

> I didn't violate the law.... I never taught that evolution lesson. I skipped it. I was doing something else the day I should have taught it, and I missed the whole lesson about Darwin and never did teach it. Those kids they put on the stand couldn't remember what I taught them three months ago. They were coached by the lawyers.[5]

As expected, William Jennings Bryan, the "Great Commoner," immediately presented himself as attorney for the prosecution. Although courtroom sparring was an unfamiliar game to this lifelong politician, he was arguably the country's greatest orator, and he welcomed the opportunity to bring his anti-evolutionary cause to Dayton. Clarence Darrow, the agnostic lawyer, elbowed his way onto the defense team, looking eagerly past Scopes to Bryan, with whom he had been sparring in print for years.

Also as expected, tiny Dayton was overrun with reporters, spectators, and the occasional expert witness. The hotels filled, and Robinson sold many sodas. The *Baltimore Sun* sent H. L. Mencken, who regaled eager Northern readers with witty, sarcastic, and partially true stories about the great confrontation in Dayton, where the nineteenth century was going head-to-head with the twentieth. The *Courier Journal* of Louisville, Kentucky, ran a headline on July 21, 1925: "3,000 AT TRIAL, GET THRILL."

The "Monkey Trial," as it was known, was peculiar in many ways. The defense brought expert witnesses to testify that evolution was a mainstream biological idea and should be taught in the public schools. The court ruled their testimony inadmissible and irrelevant, since the truth of evolution was not the issue, so these experts sat on the sidelines. The law said simply that human evolution could not be taught. And there was little doubt that Scopes had indeed confessed to teaching that humans had evolved.

The trial roared to life when Darrow called Bryan as an expert witness on the Bible. The judge had frustrated the defense by ruling that its expert scientific witnesses could not testify to the truth of evolution. And its expert theological witnesses did not get to testify to the compatibility of the Bible and evolution. So Darrow resorted to a quixotic, self-aggrandizing, and ultimately brilliant legal maneuver in calling the opposing counsel as an expert witness. Bryan could have refused, of course. What advantage did he perceive in serving as an expert witness for his adversary? But Bryan was a powerful orator who could move crowds with his eloquence. He had a solid layman's familiarity with the Bible, which he could quote to great effect. And there were settings in which audiences would marvel at his command of the Bible. Unfortunately, the witness chair on the lawn outside the Dayton courtroom, where the judge moved the trial, would not prove to be such a setting. Bryan's knowledge of Scripture was almost purely devotional, and he was unfamiliar with the problems that even elementary biblical scholarship was raising.

As a flame draws a moth, the witness stand beckoned to an unprepared Bryan. Years past his prime, he found himself outmatched by the wily Darrow. Sensing Bryan's vulnerability, Darrow circled logically about him, nipping at the Great Commoner's heels with standard village atheist fare: Where did Cain get his wife? Was Jonah swallowed by a whale? Did God really make the sun stand still for Joshua? These were questions Darrow had been lobbing at Bryan for years in print, and now Darrow had him, tethered to a witness stand with the entire world watching. The audience on the lawn grew from five hundred to three thousand, energizing the actors. This was classic theater, and Darrow knew it; even the playwrights who infused so much dramatic fiction into *Inherit the Wind* could scarcely improve on the drama of the actual interrogation. Of course, all of this had nothing to do with whether John Scopes should be convicted for teaching evolution, but it was the epic struggle that put Dayton and the Scopes trial on the national map.

How much Bryan embarrassed himself on the witness stand is hard to say. He died one week after the trial ended, silencing critics uneasy about flogging a national corpse. Transcripts and eyewitness accounts, though, certainly indicate moments of muddle. When Darrow pressed him on the date of Noah's flood, Bryan hedged, saying he had not thought about it much, deferring to unnamed scholars who had written on the topic. Darrow wanted some kind of answer and pressed Bryan further: "What do you think?" he asked, to which Bryan responded, "I do not think about things I don't think about." Darrow came back with, "Do you think about things you do think about?" and Bryan responded "Well, sometimes."[6] The assembled crowd laughed, clearly *at* and not *with* the Great Commoner.

Certainly the media, dominated by the North's low opinion of all things Southern, concluded that Bryan, fundamentalism, and the creationist cause had been thoroughly humiliated. The *New York Times* called the Darrow-Bryan duel "an absurdly pathetic performance."[7] Even Tennessee papers were critical: "Darrow succeeded," wrote a Memphis paper, "in showing that Bryan knows little about the science of the world."[8]

But great men and great causes cannot be reduced to their worst moments. The fires of anti-evolutionary fundamentalism barely flickered at Dayton and soon came roaring back. As for Dayton, it built a college to honor the great hero who fell on its battlefield. William Jennings Bryan College opened for classes on September 18, 1930, in the old school where John Scopes did not break the law against teaching evolution. Bryan College is now a healthy Christian liberal arts college with thousands of graduates, one of whom is my sister, who received her mathematics degree in 1981.

POST-SCOPES

The aftermath of the Scopes trial clarifies an important theme in America's creation–evolution controversy, namely, the great divide that began to separate ordinary religious people from the educated leadership of the country. Bryan saw this only too clearly at Dayton, warning the common people who idolized him not to turn over the education of their children to an elite establishment that did not share their values. Whether evolution was right or wrong, and Bryan clearly believed it was wrong, it conflicted with the religion of most Americans. Ordinary taxpayers, argued Bryan, should be empowered to prohibit public schools from teaching their children things in conflict with what they were learning at home and in their churches. The public schools should serve common, ordinary people, not ivory-tower elites with no appreciation for traditional values. Arguments like these earned Bryan his nickname, the Great Commoner.

America's great divide over creation and evolution is a complex cultural phenomenon, largely because of the way power is distributed in America. The power divide establishes a significant distance between ordinary people, of which there are many, and elite leaders, of which there are few. If I may be forgiven some oversimplification, this can be pictured as a pyramid, with multitudes of ordinary people at the bottom supporting an increasingly smaller number of more educated leaders at the top. Anti-evolutionary sentiments are strongest at the bottom, weakest at the top.

In America's culture war over evolution the base of this pyramid wields its power to fight evolution as consumers, taxpayers, and voters. The top of the pyramid wields its power through control of the government, the courts, the universities, and the media. In that stifling hot courtroom in Dayton, the base of this pyramid was represented by the twelve jurors, all farmers, and the locals who came to watch. The tip of the pyramid was represented by Mencken, Darrow, and the expert witnesses from the universities. Bryan's greatness lay in his ability to support people like the farmers in their struggle against powerful leaders who disrespected their values.

Every time creationism has clashed with evolution, this same tension has been present. Ordinary people concerned about evolution organize on state and local levels and take their concerns to the next level, which is inevitably "higher up" on the pyramid. As concern rises upward from the base, it encounters increased opposition as it ascends farther from its base of support. In the court cases that followed Scopes, we repeatedly encounter this pattern, but often the most important battles are not fought in the courts.

THE RECEDING DARWIN

The Scopes trial ended with a verdict for the prosecution; Darrow had requested this verdict, intent on appealing the conviction to a higher court, he hoped en route to the Supreme Court. Scopes was fined $100, paid by Mencken's paper.

This plan derailed when the Tennessee high court overturned Scopes's conviction on a technicality. No conviction, no appeal. Darrow and the defense team were outraged. Tennessee leadership relaxed, hoping that the Northern papers would cease their barrage of cartoons and articles lampooning their poor state.

Meanwhile, the anti-evolution law in Tennessee remained on the books, joined by a few more passed in other states. Scopes was off the hook, but evolution was not. Concern about grassroots, bottom-of-the-pyramid opposition to evolution motivated textbook publishers to downplay and even remove Darwin from their pages in order to sell more books. This textbook evolution can be seen in the various editions of Truman Moon's *Biology for Beginners*. From 1921 to 1963 this text went through a series of revisions, and each time coverage of Darwin and evolution was reduced. Initially the text had a frontispiece with a picture of Darwin and a meaningful discussion of evolution. Three chapters were removed to accommodate a 1925 Texas anti-evolution law.[9] The 1926 edition dropped Darwin's picture and reduced discussion of evolution, calling it "development." A volume in the 1930s completely removed discussion of human evolution. By the 1950s the word itself had been excised. Each change made the book more popular, and eventually it was the dominant textbook for high-school biology.[10]

In striking contrast to its steady erosion in textbooks, the importance of evolution to the field of biology steadily increased. Within a few decades it was the central organizing principle of the entire discipline. The synthesis of classical Darwinism with the new field of genetics was so compelling that scientific opposition to evolution all but disappeared. A mid-century anniversary essay declared simply: "Biologists one hundred years after Darwin take the *fact* of evolution for granted, as a necessary basis for interpreting the phenomena of life."[11] The tensions that brought Bryan and Darrow to Dayton, however, continued undiminished. They simmered steadily until the 1960s, when they again boiled over, this time in Arkansas.

EQUAL TIME

Separation of church and state is an endless negotiation in America. In 1963 the courts ruled, in a case that would influence the handling of evolution in the public schools, that Bible reading and the Lord's Prayer were not appropriate for public schools. The majority opinion in this case, *Abington School District v. Schempp,* emphasized the importance of a balance in which the public schools would neither advance nor inhibit religion. Critics charged that prohibiting prayer and Bible reading was hostile to religion, serving to establish a "religion of secularism." The court responded that the schools must do nothing to favor "those who believe in no religion over those who do believe."[12]

Evolution returned, invigorated, to the public schools in the 1960s. Cold War competition and a space race with Russia raised concerns about the general weakness of science education in America. Curricular overhaul produced new textbooks across the board. The biology texts were often written in ivory towers by northern academics blissfully unaware that most Americans remained opposed to evolution. Darwin's controversial theory moved onto center stage and became the heart of the entire biology curriculum.

Anti-evolutionists applauded Schempp's demand for neutrality, charging that a curriculum containing only the secular story of origins was far from neutral in that it promoted the "religion" of secularism over traditional Christianity. They demanded "equal time." If a theory of origins *hostile* to Christianity was taught it must be balanced by a *congenial* theory of origins. This was an interesting variation on Bryan's demand at the Scopes trial. Where Bryan wanted balance by teaching *no* theories of origins—a "balance" essentially achieved when textbook publishers all but eliminated coverage of evolution—the new creationist strategy was a balance achieved by equal time for both positions.

Meanwhile, anti-evolution laws remained on the books, remnants of Bryan's populist rampage. The emasculated coverage of evolution made these laws moot, for the most part, but the curricular reform of the 1960s gave birth to textbooks filled with evolutionary biology. Clouds began to appear in the form of concerns that "equal time" needed to advance from an interpretation of the law to mandated practice. The gathering storm grew steadily as evolution took up residence in textbooks, even while the states purchasing those books had legal, if largely ignored, bans on teaching the theory. The past and the present grew increasingly at odds.

Things came to a head in 1968 in a trial eerily reminiscent of the Scopes trial. A young biology teacher, Susan Epperson, challenged Arkansas's law against teaching evolution, claiming, among other things, that it violated her freedom of speech. The years that separated the trials, however, had witnessed dramatic changes in America and things looked very different now.

The Scopes judge considered the issue so simple that he refused to even hear expert witnesses. There was no need for "clarification." In the four decades since Scopes, science had moved steadily forward, while anti-evolutionary sentiment ran in place on a treadmill powered by nineteenth-century arguments. The advances in science displaced the perception that evolution was a speculative theory on the margins of biology. Evolution was now what educated people believed and, of course, children should learn it. Laws against teaching evolution were like the archaic laws still on the books about not leading animals onto the interstate—although there had been no occasion to repeal these legal fossils, their relevance had certainly diminished over the years.

The judge hearing the Epperson case thought the Arkansas statute was ridiculous, reasoning that if evolution was in the biology text, then it should be taught. He scheduled the trial on April Fool's Day to make his point and gave the state just one day to queue up their expert witnesses to make the case against evolution.[13] The exact legal issue was complex, nonetheless. The Epperson lawyers argued the case on the basis of First Amendment freedom: teachers have a constitutionally guaranteed freedom of speech and should not be legally prevented from teaching whatever topics they deem appropriate. This interpretation, of course, is really quite unworkable, at least in theory, for it sets no limits on what a teacher could bring to the classroom. Under this broad freedom astrology, psychic healing, channeling, and alien abductions would all be permitted in public-school classrooms. And, of course, it would be permissible to teach creation science. The defense warned that schools could now be forced to make room for "the haranguing of every soapbox orator with a crackpot theory."[14] Epperson's attorneys responded by asking only that Epperson be allowed to teach what was in the textbook, essentially making their case now identical to that of Scopes. And, just as in Dayton, attempts to engage the truth or falsity of evolution were consistently derailed.

The judge rejected the Arkansas statute as unconstitutional. Epperson and her fellow Arkansas teachers were now free to teach what was in the textbooks, whether or not it offended the religious sensibilities of their students. They were also free to teach creation science, tellingly absent from the textbooks.

ON TO THE ARKANSAS SUPREME COURT

The Arkansas Supreme Court consisted of elected officials in a state where most voters opposed evolution. Biologists from Arkansas did not write Epperson's textbooks, and the Epperson ruling did not sit well with many locals. So perhaps it is not surprising that the court reversed the Epperson ruling a year later, with little reason given, and restored the Scopes interpretation of anti-evolutionary statutes: states should control the public-school curriculum. The obvious motivation was a desire to pass an unpopular buck to the Supreme Court, an act of judicial cowardice that did not go unnoticed by the Supreme Court justices. Even Epperson's concern that she would get in trouble for teaching the evolution in her textbook was viewed with skepticism. Justice Black, intuiting that Epperson was just play-acting in an updated John Scopes role, wrote:

> Now, nearly 40 years after the law has slumbered on the books as though dead, a teacher [Epperson] alleging fear that the State might arouse from its lethargy and try to punish her has asked for a declaratory judgment holding the law unconstitutional.[15]

Fully aware it was playing a game with Arkansas legislators, the Supreme Court struck down the 1928 Arkansas statute in November 1968. Two years later, Mississippi's state Supreme Court struck down its law against teaching evolution. It was the last one standing, and with its departure the legal legacy of Bryan's anti-evolution campaign was finally dismantled. There remained, however, a general enthusiasm in most of the country for the teaching of creationism and an even more widespread conviction that high schools should teach "both sides," giving equal time to both creation and evolution. Anti-evolutionary forces were already at work to create this awkward balance.

UNEASY TRUCE

The 1970s saw great discussion of the *balance* between the teaching of creation and evolution. Most Americans thought creation belonged in the public schools, at least as an option. The scientific community, however, insisted that evolution was the only real science of biological origins. Creationists, searching eagerly for some legal doorway into the public schools, became enthusiastic champions of exposing high-school students to different ideas and then letting them choose. Apparently, they believed that bored sixteen-year-olds, obsessed with dating and their complexions, were better positioned to evaluate theories of origins than the scientific community.

In the early 1970s, the Christian publisher Zondervan produced a polished creationist textbook, *Biology: A Search for Order in Complexity*. Although the text appeared on educational radar screens, it was continually mired in controversy and never became the standard alternative text that its champions hoped. The legal climate was such that this unique text, in principle, could have been widely used. Carefully avoiding mention of biblical ideas, *Biology: A Search for Order in Complexity* was approved for adoption by many state school districts. But when one local district adopted *only* this text, implying that its students would have no evolutionary text at all, the ACLU predictably took the matter to court. Once again the "pyramid problem" worked against the creationists. Although it was approved by a state commission and adopted by a local school board, a judge rejected the text because it "advanced particular religious preferences and entangled the state with religion."[16]

This critique proved to be the Achilles' heel of creationism and its successor, intelligent design. The pattern would repeat. Textbooks, theories, ideas, and even individual scholars that impressed grassroots conservatives would vaporize into irrelevance when confronted with a more sophisticated audience. It would be an enduring challenge to the anti-evolutionary movement—a challenge that would intimidate most, but not all, of the champions of creationism.

One such champion was Yale law student Wendell Bird. In January 1978, Bird published an award-winning article in the *Yale Law Journal* outlining a strategy for getting creationism into America's public schools. Rather than relying on the simple absence of prohibitions to create space for creationism, Bird developed an argument for the mandatory inclusion of both creation and evolution.

Bird dusted off Bryan's old concern that teaching evolution violated many students' religious faith. Government-supported teaching of evolution was an unconstitutional interference in students' religious freedom. Students from traditions that read Genesis literally, in keeping with precedents granted to groups like the Amish and Jehovah's Witnesses, had a right to opt out of instruction incompatible with their faith. But, Bird argued sensibly, opting out of high-school biology was undesirable, and schools should "neutralize" this consequence by teaching creationism alongside evolution. Furthermore, creationism could be recast as pure science, so the "balanced treatment" really amounted to nothing more than a fuller presentation of scientific ideas about origins.

Overnight, Bird became a celebrity in the creationist cause. He was an intellectual heavyweight from the top of the pyramid, taking the torch from Bryan and supported by the same grassroots populism that energized the Great Commoner. Bird joined Henry Morris at the Institute for Creation Research (ICR) and served for a while as its staff attorney. ICR is a multi-pronged, fundamentalist center of anti-evolution, working on many fronts to reverse the "harmful consequences of evolutionary thinking on families and society (abortion, promiscuity, drug abuse, homosexuality, and many others)."[17]

At ICR, Bird drafted a "resolution" promoting a balanced treatment of creation and evolution. The resolution, designed to help interested citizens frame legislation promoting creationism in the public schools, treated both theories as exclusively scientific. Statements based on the resolution circulated broadly, and by 1981 variants had appeared in two dozen state legislatures.[18] The Arkansas Senate passed its version of Bird's resolution by a vote of 22 to 2.[19] The date was Friday, March 13, the same day that the Dayton conspirators in Robinson's drugstore, forty-eight years earlier, had hatched the scheme that led to the Scopes trial.

The ever watchful ACLU took notice and began to move, even as Louisiana passed a similar resolution. It was the beginning of the end of creationism in America's public schools.

THE MIGHTY ACT OF ARKANSAS

Arkansas Act 590 called for a "balanced treatment of creation science and evolution science," defined as follows. *Creation science* means the scientific evidences for creation and inferences from those scientific evidences. Creation science includes the scientific evidences and related inferences that indicate:

1 The sudden creation of the universe, energy, and life from nothing;
2 The insufficiency of mutation and natural selection in bringing about development of all living kinds from a single organism;

3 Changes only within fixed limits of originally created kinds of plants and animals;

4 Separate ancestry for man and apes;

5 An explanation of the earth's geology by catastrophism, including the occurrence of a worldwide flood; and

6 A relatively recent inception of the earth and living kinds.

Evolution science means the scientific evidences for evolution and inferences from those scientific evidences. Evolution science includes the scientific evidences and related inferences that indicate:

1 The emergence by naturalistic processes of the universe from disordered matter and emergence of life from nonlife;

2 The sufficiency of mutation and natural selection in bringing about development of present living kinds from simple earlier kinds;

3 The emergence by mutation and natural selection of present living kinds from simple earlier kinds;

4 The emergence of man from a common ancestor with apes;

5 An explanation of the earth's geology and the evolutionary sequence by uniformitarianism; and

6 An inception several billion years ago of the earth and somewhat later of life.[20]

The Arkansas trial did what Darrow had failed to do at Dayton when his expert witnesses were muted. Arkansas put the creationist *ideas* on trial, exploring whether they were adequately secular for the public schools and scientifically plausible.

As theater the Arkansas trial floundered in the long shadow of Scopes. There was no Bryan-Darrow confrontation, no poor schoolteacher in the dock, no hyperbolic Mencken dressing up the tale for the daily papers, no jury of farmers, and no interesting "North versus South" back story. Reporters called the trial "Scopes II" and made so many references to the original Scopes trial that one journalist commented: "If the readers learned anything, we may assume it is the details of the Scopes Trial."[21]

As an intellectual contest, though, Scopes II made its namesake look like a cartoon. Heavyweights from both sides provided hours of expert testimony, and this time the focus was on the scientific, philosophical, and religious character of creationism and evolution. This case, unlike the charade in Dayton, would not be decided on a technicality.

The intellectual shallowness of the creationist position had pundits on both sides predicting defeat for the statute before the trial even began. Pat Robertson, to whom God apparently speaks directly, accused the Arkansas attorney general, Steven Clark, of being "crooked" and "biased." Robertson suggested that the ACLU had targeted Arkansas because Clark was secretly on its side. The late Jerry Falwell, Robertson's fellow prophet from Virginia, made similar charges.[22] Tellingly, no evidence emerged to support these charges. Clark was simply outgunned by the high-powered legal help that the ACLU brought in from New York.

The expert witnesses fared no better. The stark contrast that results from lining them up side by side makes its own argument for why creationism does not belong in the public schools. To establish whether creation science is religion or science, each side called on testimonies from experts in theology and philosophy. University of Chicago professor of theology Langdon Gilkey testified for the plaintiffs and came across as clever and articulate. At one point he testified that from the perspective of Christian theology, Act 590 contained an egregious heresy. Spectators in the courtroom audibly gasped. In portraying the act as completely secular, Gilkey argued, its supporters had been forced to clarify that the "creator" presupposed in the act and responsible for the "sudden creation of the universe, energy, and life from nothing" was not necessarily "God" as understood in the Judeo-Christian tradition. This, exulted Gilkey, "was precisely the early heresy of Marcion and the Gnostics (about 150 to 200 A.D.), who said that there were in fact two Gods, one a blind, cruel but powerful God of creation ... and the other a good loving God of redemption ... and thus the creator God was *not* the same as the redeemer God."[23]

Gilkey's point had great drama, and he certainly enjoyed its retelling. However, from a legal perspective, his point is irrelevant. The defense was arguing that Act 590 was *not* religious; whether it contained a formal religious heresy should have been of no consequence. But one has to wonder how it was that the fundamentalist Christians who had shepherded this act could have missed this point.

Norman Geisler, then professor of systematic theology at Dallas Theological Seminary, the intellectual heart of American fundamentalism, was

Gilkey's counterpart for the defense. Geisler, a major fundamentalist scholar, has written over fifty books and hundreds of articles. Unfortunately, he embarrassed himself at Arkansas, becoming the brunt of countless jokes in the media about the state's "expert" theological witness. Geisler, like most fundamentalists, believes in a literal devil, the biblical Satan, and in demons. In his deposition for the trial he stated that he had "known personally at least twelve persons who were clearly possessed by the devil." Further evidence for the reality of Satan at work in the world came from UFOs, which Geisler said represented "the Devil's major, in fact, final attack on the earth." And then, to ensure that he completely buried himself, he claimed to know that UFOs were real because he "read it in the *Reader's Digest.*"[24] When he repeated these remarks on the witness stand, the courtroom audience literally laughed out loud; over the next few days newspaper accounts of the trial presented Geisler's remarks as if they were his entire testimony. Lost were his more credible comments about the religious character of evolution and the role of assumptions in science.

The expert witnesses on science were equally mismatched. The plaintiffs had Francisco Ayala, one of the world leading geneticists and a former Dominican priest; Harvard's Stephen Jay Gould, a leading paleontologist and America's greatest science essayist; G. Brent Dalrymple, who had been on the NASA team that investigated moon rocks; Michael Ruse, a leading philosopher of biology; among others. The defense counterparts paled in comparison, a collection of relatively unknown scholars from obscure institutions. There was one major exception, an astronomer named Chandra Wickramasinghe, notorious for proposing that life on earth was "seeded" from outer space rather than developing here:

> The facts as we have them show clearly that life on Earth is derived from what appears to be an all-pervasive galaxy-wide living system. Terrestrial life had its origins in the gas and dust clouds of space, which later became incorporated in and amplified within comets. Life was derived from and continues to be driven by sources outside the Earth, in direct contradiction to the Darwinian theory that everybody is supposed to believe.[25]

Wickramasinghe believed that aspects of evolution were highly implausible. Convinced he had been misled about the credibility of evolution, he supported the general idea that alternative explanations belonged in the public schools. He was, however, hardly in the camp of the creationists and completely rejected almost all the tenets of Act 590. Why the defense called him is curious. Perhaps, in its conviction that there were only two possible positions on origins, the defense inferred that anyone not firmly in the Darwinian camp would necessarily be in the creationist camp. The "two models" approach to origins did, in fact, presume that there were just two models and no others.

The defense attorneys apparently embraced the general and damning creationist confusion that there are only two models of origins. This peculiar oversimplification assumes the two models are in such contradiction that evidence *against* one of them counts as evidence *for* the other. Ayala found it necessary to "educate" attorney David Williams on this elementary point of logic.

"My dear young man," said Ayala, looking at Williams with what Gilkey described as "evident pity," "negative criticisms of evolutionary theory, even if they carried some weight, are utterly irrelevant to the question of the validity or legitimacy of creation science. Sure you realize that *not* being Mr. Williams in no way entails *being* Mr. Ayala!"[26]

With that, Mr. Williams neatly folded his legal tail between his legs and slunk back to his table. "No more questions, your honor."

The creation scientists who were called[27] made it clear that their primary allegiance was to the Bible, not to science. And, although they were confident the two could not conflict, they would set aside scientific findings that disagreed with a literal reading of the Bible.

JUDGE OVERTON'S DECISION

The presiding judge, William Overton, ruled against Arkansas Act 590, finding it religious rather than scientific and likely to harm those students whose education would have been affected by it:

Implementation of Act 590 will have serious and untoward consequences for students, particularly those planning to attend college. Evolution is the cornerstone of modern biology, and many courses in public schools contain subject matter relating to such varied topics as the age of the earth, geology, and relationships among living things. Any student who is deprived of instruction as to the prevailing scientific thought on these topics will be denied a significant part of science education. Such a deprivation through the high school level would undoubtedly have an impact upon the quality of education in the State's colleges and universities, especially including the pre-professional and professional programs in the health sciences.[28]

Overton's decision attracted much attention and was widely reprinted by various publications, including America's leading scientific journal, *Science*.[29] The creationists, of course, were disappointed and disagreed. Duane Gish charged that Overton's decision essentially established that "secular humanism will now be our official state-sanctioned religion."[30] Geisler charged that the decision would have "devastating consequences for the pursuit of truth in the public schools."[31]

Philosophers had mixed reactions. Conservative philosopher J. P. Moreland devoted much of his book *Christianity and the Nature of Science* to a critique of Overton's decision.[32] Secular philosopher Larry Laudan, while agreeing with Overton's conclusion, assaulted his reasoning with words like "specious," "egregious," "dubious," "opaque," "woeful," and "silly."[33] But nobody pays much attention to the hair-splitting commentaries of philosophers, and Overton's decision is still widely quoted with approval.

LAST MAN STANDING

By the time the media finished poking fun at poor Norman Geisler for his views on UFOs, statutes mandating equal time for creationism were almost extinct, save for one lone survivor, hiding from the ACLU in the bayous of Louisiana. Called the "Balanced Treatment Act," it was a clone of the statute that had been defeated in Arkansas. It would be creationism's last attempt to sneak into the public schools.

The act stated that schools "shall give balanced treatment to creation science and to evolution science." This balance applied to lectures, texts, and library materials and required the identification of appropriate creation-science materials. The act further specified: "When creation or evolution is taught, each shall be taught as a theory, rather than as proven scientific fact." Creation science was inadequately described as "the scientific evidences for creation and inferences from those scientific evidences."[34] Evolution science had a correspondingly circular definition.

The Louisiana act, unlike its Arkansas sibling, did not define creation in ways that tied it to the Bible. By leaving creation vague and undefined, the religious connection had to be inferred, which everyone in Louisiana, except Wendell Bird apparently, found easy to do. Bird would later argue the case before the Supreme Court, finally getting a "secularized" creation science the hearing he thought it deserved, but first he had to navigate a complex legal maze that would have deterred anyone with less than total dedication.

A COMEDY OF DETOURS

On behalf of Louisiana senator Bill Keith, Bird launched a campaign to force Louisiana schools to implement the Balanced Treatment Act. Implementation was almost nonexistent, probably because it was impossible to find suitable educational materials. The ACLU, still flushed from its victory in Arkansas, responded the next day. On behalf of Daniel Aguillard, it attacked the Louisiana act as unconstitutional, arguing that the mandated creation science was still the Judeo-Christian creation story despite the careful secularization. Furthermore, the ACLU noted that the act's history revealed consistent support from fundamentalist Christians, further evidence of its religious character. Bird would later challenge this, arguing that a position is not automatically religious just because it has religious roots or religious supporters.

Bird was appointed special assistant attorney general for the state of Louisiana and became the point man in the upcoming trials. He hoped to finally square off against the ACLU on the constitutionality of teaching a secularized creation science. He demanded a trial, but was soon frustrated, as both trials began to mutate, evolve, and stagger toward extinction.

The court looking at the Keith motion to implement the Balanced Treatment Act decided that no constitutional issue was at stake and the Louisiana courts could decide this matter internally. The Keith motion would not lead to a constitutional review of creation science.

The Aguillard court ruled that the Louisiana legislature could not tell the state education board how to run the schools. It insisted on an unusual, and perhaps contrived, autonomy for the state education board. The judge ruled that the education board should decide how, and if, the Balanced Treatment Act would be implemented. A frustrated Bird appealed this decision and won. The trial, which had been a mirage, began to take shape, although not in Louisiana.

Bird built much of his case on five affidavits he had prepared for the elusive earlier trial. Two scientists, a philosopher, a theologian, and a school administrator had prepared briefs arguing for the legality of teaching a religiously neutered version of creation science. Bird intended to present these expert opinions, hoping the judge would find them convincing. The Aguillard judge, however, was not impressed. He ruled that the Balanced Treatment Act was religious despite the claims in the affidavits. Even though the ACLU had not followed standard practice by bringing countering affidavits, the judge was not persuaded to give Bird his trial on the merits of creation science.

Bird, of course, was far more than a lawyer arguing one side of a case. He believed passionately that creation science was a true account of origins, supported by overwhelming scientific evidence. He was equally convinced that evolution rested on flimsy evidence and had a checkered history of false claims and disturbing applications. Like so many creationists, Bird was alarmed that America was not teaching the truth about origins to its children. If God created the earth ten thousand years ago, this event was a *scientific* fact, regardless of what the Bible or any religion might say on the matter.

Bird convinced Louisiana to appeal the decision, and in 1985 the appeals court agreed to hear the case. Bird pointed to the five affidavits that the ACLU had not challenged with countering affidavits. Was this not, inquired Bird, because these affidavits were so compelling there were no effective challenges? Technically, affidavits presented by one side should be accepted as true unless countered by opposing affidavits. The earlier decision declaring the Balanced Treatment Act religious should therefore be overruled.

Bird lost again. The judges were not convinced by the affidavits and ruled the act was religious, with no secular purpose. Bowed but unbeaten, Bird challenged their decision. Invoking a technicality, he demanded a ruling from all fifteen of the judges on the court; if the majority agreed with the full court press, then they would all have to participate. But it was not to be. Eight of fifteen judges disagreed, and Bird lost again, by one vote.

The seven dissenting judges, however, indicated some support for creation science, agreeing it was constitutionally feasible to teach creation science in the public schools. After years of frustration, Bird finally received encouragement that high-level legal opinion might actually come down on the side of creation science. His sights began to set on Washington, D.C., where nine of the nation's leading judges could resolve, once and for all, the constitutionality of teaching creation science in America's public schools.

ON TO THE U.S. SUPREME COURT

Bird's petition for a Supreme Court review referenced the five unchallenged affidavits ignored by the Louisiana judges. The court agreed to hear the case on December 10, 1987.

Despite the years of preparation involved in getting this case to the U.S. Supreme Court, when the legal ball game finally got started, it was Scopes and Arkansas all over again. When the best arguments from both sides were lined up, there was simply no competition. Bird's affidavits and other briefs filed by creationist groups looked like high-school projects alongside the opposing arguments assembled by the ACLU. Bird's affidavits included two by scientists. One was Dean Kenyon, a minor, although competent, scientific figure from San Francisco State University whose reputation was derived almost entirely from his support for creationism. Kenyon argued:

> It is also my conclusion that balanced presentation of creation-science and evolution is educationally valuable, and in fact is more educationally valuable than indoctrination in just the viewpoint of evolution. Presentation of alternate scientific explanations has educational benefit, and balanced presentation of creation-science and evolution does exactly that. Creation-science can indeed be taught in the classroom in a strictly scientific sense, and a textbook can present creation-science in a strictly scientific sense, either as a supplement or as a part of a balanced presentation text.[35]

The other scientist was W. Scott Morrow, who taught chemistry at a small religious college. Like Kenyon, Morrow had little reputation beyond what he acquired as an advocate of creationism. In the Arkansas trial Morrow noted that it would be interesting to teach flat-earth theory in the public schools, so it was not obvious what criteria he was using to endorse school curricula.[36] Morrow also called himself an agnostic and an evolutionist.

Affidavits from prestigious scientific groups in support of the ACLU challenged those of Bird. The National Academy of Sciences wrote one, as did seventeen state academies of science. One ACLU brief was signed by seventy-two Nobel laureates in science. Under the bright lights of this Supreme Court case, this head-to-head battle once again looked like an embarrassing contest.

Bird's presentation didn't fare much better on the religious side. Two of his venerable affidavits were from minor scholars of religion: Terry L. Miethe, then at Liberty University, fundamentalism's most powerful bastion of higher education but without respect in the secular world; and William G. Most, of Loras College, a Catholic school. Miethe and Most both argued that, although they did not themselves accept creation science, it was indeed possible to teach it in fully secular manner.

The Supreme Court case laid out the question exactly as Bird had long wanted. Bird, clutching his briefs and affidavits, argued that creation science met the criteria for science at least as well as evolution. Both dealt with a murky history that was hard to interpret. Both invoked processes, such as the origin of life or the appearance of the universe, that are not presently occurring and thus cannot be studied directly. Both were complex, with elaborate logical and empirical structures.

Addressing religious concerns, Bird argued that creation science could be secularized for the public schools. This, in fact, was precisely the difference between "creation" and "creation science." If the universe originated ten thousand years ago, as creation scientists claim the data indicates, presenting evidence for this in the public schools is not inherently religious. Neither is it religious to note that the fossil record contains fewer intermediate forms than evolutionists would like, and that most new species appear in that record suddenly. This was, in fact, exactly what America's best-known evolutionist, the late Stephen Jay Gould of Harvard, had long been calling paleontology's "dirty little secret."[37] There is nothing religious about noting the absence of any generally accepted theory explaining the origin of life. Scientific claims don't become religious just because religious people like them.

Bird waxed eloquent. There are two different, incompatible models for origins. One suggests that everything evolved slowly from simpler forms; the other asserts that everything appeared suddenly. Why not teach both models in high-school biology, exposing students to a broader range of ideas? Shouldn't we encourage critical thinking on the part of our students? Shouldn't we allow them to weigh the evidence and make up their own minds?

Creation *science,* argued Bird, was not religious. The lower courts in Louisiana had pulled that idea "out of thin air,"[38] and the Supreme Court justices would surely know better. Requiring that evolution be balanced with creation science was Louisiana's way of promoting fairness, giving all sides a place on the chalkboard, and ensuring academic freedom for teachers. The goal here was simply providing the best possible curriculum for the students.

Shortly after the trial, in a massive two-volume survey of the topic, Bird wrote:

> The issue is *not* which explanation of origins is correct, but whether any is so compellingly established and universally accepted that it ought to be taught to the exclusion of other scientific explanations. Because no theory is so unquestionably true, all scientific views should be taught to protect the students' right to receive scientific information and the teachers' right to academic freedom by offering the "whole scientific truth."[39]

BYE-BYE BIRDIE

Mounting a more effective defense for creation science than what Bird presented to the Supreme Court on that Wednesday in Washington, D.C., would be hard. The contours of the legal arguments that had been circulating for the past decade had been outlined in his influential paper at Yale. He understood as well as anyone exactly how the First Amendment applied to this issue. Bird had worked closely with the world's leading creationist organization, the Institute for Creation Research, and knew all the key players. He was familiar with the scandal of the Scopes trial and had watched in horror as the creationists humiliated themselves in Arkansas. And he had nurtured the Louisiana case from infancy to its full maturity before the highest court in the country, where a victory could have transformed the teaching of origins across the country.

Nevertheless, Bird lost.

Bird's arguments were compelling and in a perfect world with no history might have carried the day. The Supreme Court justices certainly did not sneer and laugh, as had their counterparts in Arkansas. William Brennan wrote the majority opinion. Speaking for seven of the nine justices, he rejected Bird's argument that the Louisiana statue was truly secular. Brennan was known for preferring a "high" wall of separation between the state and religion, in part because he believed religion was "too important to be co-opted by the state."[40]

The two justices most interested in religion (and probably most personally religious) disagreed with the majority opinion. William Rehnquist, an active Lutheran, joined Antonin Scalia, a conservative Catholic whose son Paul was a priest, in a dissenting opinion. Scalia accused his fellow justices of being blinkered by the Scopes legacy and argued, echoing Bryan, that the people of Louisiana were entitled "to have whatever evidence there may be against evolution presented in their schools."[41]

Bird's argument, in the final analysis and perhaps even independently of his own understanding of the law, was a Trojan horse. As noble as it might seem to "balance" education, the reality was that creation science was nothing but a tiny intellectual backwater championed by a handful of minor fundamentalist scientists.[42] If every tiny opposing viewpoint received the equal time that Louisiana wanted for creation science, the public schools would be opening their doors to astrology, Holocaust denial, alien visitation, and countless other preposterous topics.

The long history of creation science revealed its thoroughly religious pedigree. Unlike evolution, whose adherents include many Christians of almost every variety as well as agnostics and outspoken atheists, creation-science adherents were almost exclusively fundamentalist Christians. This was not a coincidence and support for creationism has consistently been driven by a particular enthusiasm for biblical literalism, not scientific data. Furthermore, creationism has scant support among educated theologians and biblical scholars.

CREATIONISM EVOLVES

One of my favorite Monty Python skits involves a strange conversation in which a man with many pets named Eric tries to buy a license from a shopkeeper for his fish, Eric. At one point the pet owner states that he has a license for his cat, Eric. The shopkeeper responds that there is no such thing as a cat license. Defending his claim that there is, the eccentric pet owner triumphantly presents written documentation as evidence. Upon examining the documentation, the shopkeeper responds, "This isn't a *cat* license. It's a *dog* license with the word 'dog' crossed out and 'cat' written in, in crayon." The next major trial involving creationism in America's public schools gave new meaning to this absurd skit.

The Supreme Court's ruling in *Edwards v. Aguillard* derailed creationism's ride into the public schools by legal mandate. Creation science could not be decoupled from the Bible to the court's satisfaction, even by clever legal strategists like Bird. However, rather than going extinct, creationism evolved rapidly and before long reappeared in a dramatic new guise known as intelligent design, or "ID" for short.[43] ID's champion was Phillip Johnson, a legal scholar then at Berkeley's prestigious Boalt Hall law school.

Johnson recognized that the most theologically important issue in the origins controversy was not creation versus evolution, but the exclusive reliance of the natural sciences on purely naturalistic explanations. Science had come to the point where, by definition, *nothing* could ever be explained by reference to God. This naturalism, in Johnson's mind, was equivalent to atheism. In a hyperbolic generalization of the sort that came to characterize his polemical style, he rearticulated the traditional anti-evolutionary argument: (1) the institutions of modern society are based on science; (2) science is based on atheism; and (3) a society with atheistic foundations will quickly go to hell in a handbasket, just as Western civilization is presently doing.

Johnson developed a legal strategy for continuing the fight against evolution not unlike what Bird had done a decade earlier. But he used a new tactic, making no reference to creation or a creator and completely avoiding anything even resembling the biblical story of origins. Johnson simply called attention to complex phenomena in nature that posed problems for evolutionary explanations. He argued that these phenomena could be explained only by invoking an outside intelligence. "Intelligent design," as this strategy became known, was defined as the theory that "various forms of life began abruptly through an intelligent agency, with their distinctive features already intact."[44]

Johnson and the enthusiasts who jumped on his bandwagon insisted that by not specifying the identity of the "intelligent agency" they had at last fully secularized their "theory." The movement gathered steam throughout the 1990s and attracted scholars like biochemist Michael Behe, mathematician-philosopher William Dembski, biologist Jonathan Wells, philosopher Stephen Meyer, and biologist Dean Kenyon. Adopting the politically expedient philosophy that "the enemy of my enemy is my friend," the ID tent grew very large, welcoming any and all opponents of evolution. ID embraced creationists of all stripes, young-earth and otherwise, and even welcomed the occasional non-Christian anti-evolutionist. Supporters of ID shared one—and sometimes only one—central belief: there is design in nature that evolution cannot explain. Disagreements like whether the earth is thousands or billions of years old were set aside as unnecessarily divisive.

Johnson's leadership, a handful of surprisingly popular books, and ID's big-tent strategy combined to grow an impressive, popular movement that fanned the waning flames of anti-evolutionary activism. Countless school boards, populated as they were by ordinary citizens, passed initiatives weakening the teaching of evolution, convinced that serious objections to biology's central concept were being established. Some of these initiatives were cancelled democratically, by simply voting out members of the school boards responsible. Other initiatives went to court. The intelligent design movement got its fifteen minutes of fame in late 2005 in Dover, Pennsylvania.

CREATIONISM IN DESIGNER CLOTHING

The Dover trial was something of a replay of the case Bird lost before the Supreme Court. The challenge facing Bird in that trial was establishing that creation science was secular and thus *not* the same collection of ideas that had been ruled religious in the *McLean v. Arkansas Board of Education* trial. Likewise the Dover trial turned on the question of whether ID was a secular concept or a repackaging of creationism.

The Dover story hit the news on November 19, 2004, when the local school district issued a press release stating that, come January, teachers would have to read the following statement to students in ninth-grade biology:

The Pennsylvania Academic Standards require students to learn about Darwin's Theory of Evolution and eventually to take a standardized test of which evolution is a part.

Because Darwin's Theory is a theory, it continues to be tested as new evidence is discovered. The Theory is not a fact. Gaps in the Theory exist for which there is no evidence. A theory is defined as a well-tested explanation that unifies a broad range of observations.

Intelligent Design is an explanation of the origin of life that differs from Darwin's view. The reference book, *Of Pandas and People,* is available for students who might be interested in gaining an understanding of what Intelligent Design actually involves.

With respect to any theory, students are encouraged to keep an open mind. The school leaves the discussion of the Origins of Life to individual students and their families. As a Standards-driven district, class instruction focuses upon preparing students to achieve proficiency on Standards-based assessments.

There were two questions on the table in Dover: Is ID something other than creationism? Is *Of Pandas and People* a creationist book?

Reminiscent of Scopes, Dover attracted big legal guns itching for a fight. Much of the energy behind the Dover initiative came from the Thomas More Law Center, the self-proclaimed "Christian Answer to the ACLU." Thomas More aggressively sought confrontations with the ACLU on all of the standard issues such as gay marriage, pornography, public displays of the Ten Commandments, and nativity scenes. Representatives from Thomas More had been encouraging school districts across the country to teach ID and authorize the *Pandas* book as a supplemental biology text. Knowing that the ACLU would eventually challenge such decisions, Thomas More promised to defend, for free, any school that got sued.

Sure enough, on December 14, 2004, the ACLU filed suit against the Dover school district on behalf of some parents with school-age children. A call went out for a big law firm to provide pro bono legal help. Eric Rothschild, a partner in a major Philadelphia firm, quickly volunteered, saying "I've been waiting for this for fifteen years."[45]

Because of the role played by precedent in the American legal system, the Dover trial was not really about ID per se, but rather turned on the somewhat simpler question of whether ID was, as Leonard Krishtalka, who directs the Natural History Museum at the University of Kansas, put it, "creationism in a cheap tuxedo."[46] The courts had already established that creationism was religious and could not be taught in the public schools. If it could be established that ID was a form of creationism, then precedent mandated that it had no place in the public schools.

Dover was a disaster for ID. The ACLU established in a variety of ways that ID was indeed a dressed-up version of creationism. Adding salt to the already severe wounds, it emerged that key ID people—deeply religious people—in the trial were actually lying and knowingly misrepresenting their case.

The 1989 *Pandas* book, at the center of the Dover controversy, provides an excellent example of this deception. ID pundits claimed that the text was the "first intelligent design textbook,"[47] and *not* a creationist text. Unfortunately, there existed damning early drafts of the book from before the Aguillard ruling that creation science could not be taught in the public schools. These earlier versions revealed that the original plan was for the book to be a creationist text. A 1983 draft was even titled *Creation Biology;* a 1986 draft was titled *Biology and Creation* and contained the following definition: "Creation means that the various forms of life began abruptly through the agency of an intelligent creator with their distinctive features already intact. Fish with fins and scales, birds with feathers, beaks, and wings, etc."[48]

In a Monty Pythonesque editorial move, the post-Aguillard edition of the book replaced "creation" with "intelligent design" and left the rest of the definition virtually unchanged: "Intelligent design means that various forms of life began abruptly through an intelligent agency, with their distinctive features already intact—fish with fins and scales, birds with feathers, beaks, wings, etc."[49]

The defense attorneys then argued that *Pandas* was *not* a creationist book, but rather was about something entirely different. To say the least, this was exceedingly disingenuous. They certainly knew better. If the changes had been made in crayon, Monty Python could have sued them for stealing their skit.

To make matters worse, the writers who had produced *Pandas* had strong connections to creation science. Dean Kenyon, the lead author, had written the foreword to *What Is Creation Science?* in which he proposed "that all students of the sciences … should be taught the major arguments of both the creation and evolutionary views."[50] The second author, Percival Davis, had coauthored *A Case for Creation.*[51] Journalist Nancy Pearcey, who made major contributions to *Pandas*, was a young-earth creationist and editor of the *Bible Science Newsletter*, where portions of *Pandas* had been excerpted.

Witnesses from the Dover school board testified that there had been considerable support for creationism on the board. The chair of the curriculum committee, William Buckingham, denied that he had supported creationism, but multiple witnesses and stories in local papers all reported that he had been arguing that evolution must be balanced with creation. Although he denied it in his deposition, Buckingham was quite passionate about this, convinced he was doing God a favor: "Two thousand years ago, someone died on a cross," he said. "Can't someone take a stand for him?"[52] Though he claimed to have no knowledge of the source of the funds used to purchase and distribute copies of *Pandas*, it turned out he had raised the money himself from his church. Such duplicity plagued the defense to the point that Judge Jones actually got angry and started asking questions. In his decision he made reference to these "flagrant and insulting falsehoods,"[53] noting as "ironic" the contradiction between defendants who "staunchly and proudly touted their religious convictions in public," but then in the trial would "time and again lie to cover their tracks."[54]

The Thomas More lawyers needed to show that the Dover legislation was not motivated by a religious agenda in order to avoid one of the criteria used to label such initiatives unconstitutional. There was, however, no way to hide the local religious enthusiasm for something other than evolution in the schools.

The leaders of the ID movement had also damned themselves on the record. The leading ID think tank, the Seattle-based Discovery Institute, had produced a strategic plan for the widespread promotion of ID. Called the "Wedge Document," the plan stated that the goal of ID was "to replace materialistic explanations with the theistic understanding that nature and human beings are created by God." The ID movement was mainly a populist crusade against evolution, nurtured by the same grass roots that energized Bryan eight decades earlier. ID leaders had all written voluminously for their primary audience, conservative evangelicals. Such writings, usually published by conservative Christian presses, were filled with discussions of how ID supported a biblical worldview, how ID helped prove the existence of God, and how evolution was just atheism in disguise. Now, in a setting where ID had to be secular to survive, its deeply religious character was clearly visible beneath a thin veneer of secular rhetoric.

The defense didn't fare much better on the science side. The Discovery Institute actually got worried that things were going so badly it convinced some of its "fellows" not to participate, lest their reputations go down in the flames they saw being kindled.

Michael Behe testified anyway, as the star witness for the defense. As the author of the best-selling *Darwin's Black Box,* published by the respected and secular Free Press, and one of a small number actively publishing scientists in the ID movement, Behe was something of a celebrity. But his performance on the witness stand was somewhere between ineffective and disastrous. He admitted, for example, that he did not agree with the description of ID in *Pandas,* despite the fact that he was listed as a "critical reviewer" of the book. He admitted being unfamiliar with many major research studies contradicting claims he had made himself in *Darwin's Black Box.* He admitted that neither he nor anyone else had actually developed any "quantitative criteria for determining the degree of complexity,"[55] a critical first step in making ID scientific. Devastatingly, he admitted that changing the definition of science to include ID would also bring astrology into the scientific fold.

The judge quoted extensively from Behe's testimony in his remarks, including the following damning admission: "There are no peer reviewed articles by anyone advocating for intelligent design supported by pertinent experiments or calculations which provide detailed rigorous accounts of how intelligent design of any biological system occurred."[56]

Despite being a respected, competent, and well-published biochemist at a major university, Behe projected a persona in Dover that was of a lone and eccentric outsider with idiosyncratic and occasionally confused notions about science. Even his own department at Lehigh issued a statement of nonsupport for Behe's work on ID. Behe did, of course, have considerable stature within the ID movement itself. ID proponents hoped that at Dover he would appear to be the voice of a growing movement of mainstream scientists dissatisfied with evolution. It didn't happen.

THE DOVER RULING: "BREATHTAKING INANITY"

Judge Jones issued his ruling shortly before Christmas, indicting ID on every front. Any reasonable person would know, he wrote, that the ID strategy was nothing more than a continuation of the failed strategies employed by "earlier forms of creationism." The support for ID in Dover was rooted in local fundamentalist fervor and started not with concern about science in the schools, but concern about the absence of religion. Several board members admitted knowing nothing about ID other than that getting it into the schools would undermine evolution and advance creation. One board member, strongly on the side of the defense, didn't even know what ID stood for, referring to it as "intelligence design."[57] And in the months leading up to the trial the Thomas More law firm was cheering from the sidelines, eager to meet the ACLU in court and confident that that "God was on their side."

The disclaimer the defense wanted read in the classrooms, wrote Jones,

> singled out the theory of evolution for special treatment, misrepresents its status in the scientific community, causes students to doubt its validity without scientific justification, presents students with a religious alternative masquerading as a scientific theory, directs them to consult a creationist text as though it were a science resource, and instructs students to forego scientific inquiry in the public school classroom and instead to seek out religious instruction elsewhere.[58]

As earlier trials had revealed, creationists had no alternative science of their own. *Pandas* was a relabeled creationist text containing little more than a list of things not adequately explained by evolution. It was hopelessly out of date and could only be mistaken for a science text by readers who knew nothing about science. *Pandas* was a religious book with the word *religion* crossed out and the word *science* written in.

Dover was a tragic defeat for ID, the tragedy compounded by the hopeless disorganization of the defense. A naive and uninformed school board, bewitched by a century of anti-Darwinism and cheered on by a zealous law firm, failed to make even its own best case. Completely missing was a new Wendell Bird, who, although he lost at the Supreme Court, had at least made the best possible case for creation science. The judge suggested that the Dover school board's actions constituted "breathtaking inanity" and precipitated a pointless trial that was an "utter waste of monetary and personal resources."[59]

ID could certainly have turned in a more impressive performance. The politically savvy Discovery Institute probably acted wisely in minimizing its involvement, given the debacle it saw developing. Nevertheless, once the damage was done, it tried to contain its impact by publishing aggressive critiques of the judge's decision.[60] These initiatives were clearly disingenuous, given that the institute had refused to cooperate. By refusing to be involved in the trial, the Discovery Institute had forsaken its opportunity to help Judge Jones get the clearest possible picture of ID, or at least their version of the picture.

The Dover decision remained a local ruling, which means that it applies in Dover and nowhere else. But the trial's national publicity, like that of Dayton eight decades earlier, certainly discouraged at least some similar initiatives elsewhere.

THE NEVER ENDING TRIAL

America's creation–evolution trials make for great drama—literally in the case of Scopes, but also on smaller stages with lesser-known protagonists. Each trial offers its own window into the fears and frustrations of ordinary people as they struggle with a science threatening their faith. From William Jennings Bryan in Dayton to William Buckingham in Dover, the trials were never truly about science. Bryan thundered his anti-evolution message across the country because he wanted to protect ordinary Americans from those who "have no other purpose than ridiculing every Christian who believes in the Bible."[61] Buckingham labored to make space for creationism in Dover for similar reasons. Bryan and Buckingham are typical anti-evolutionists. Not scientists, both were enthusiastic Christians concerned about the pernicious effects of evolution steadily eroding traditional American values.

Every one of the trials, and countless smaller episodes that did not make it to trial, had its Bryan or Buckingham. Always in the background were local churches, where people prayed and pastors promoted. The scientists who testified were almost always outsiders to the community in more ways than one; sometimes they were atheists. The creationists were often well-known Christian leaders, "brothers and sisters in Christ." The deliberations inevitably took on an apocalyptic character as the forces of "good" and "evil" locked horns in a conflict that was cosmic, not local. When Clarence Darrow strolled down Main Street in Dayton, two local women called him a "damned infidel."[62] When Cornell sociologist Dorothy Nelkin admitted under oath in the Arkansas trial that she did not believe in a personal God, three spectators in the court fell dramatically to their knees and began to pray audibly for her soul.[63]

Anecdotes like these were enlarged in Mencken's sarcastic reporting, in the enduring presentations of *Inherit the Wind,* and in newspaper accounts of the subsequent trials. Eccentric and extreme players on both sides were juxtaposed as representative, turning the trials into caricatures. Creationists were inevitably portrayed as corny Southern hillbillies, or their Northern equivalent, and freakishly religious; evolutionists were articulate, agnostic, and sometimes antireligious. Pitting them against each other was great journalistic fun.

America's long legal struggle with evolution, however, is anything but a war of religious hillbillies against Ivy League agnostics. It is the ongoing story of a deeply religious nation, with enduring populist and even anti-intellectual sentiments, struggling with an emerging secular science. The trials, when viewed as a whole and separated from the colorful personalities who make them so interesting, reveal a remarkably coherent story.

The Scopes trial culminated Bryan's anti-evolution crusade that had state legislatures across the South outlawing the teaching of evolution. The energy for this crusade, however, did not come from widespread concern that evolution was incompatible with the Bible, although that was certainly a background issue. The energy came from the belief that evolution was the foundation of evil social agendas. In this sense the anti-evolutionary campaign was more like the war on drugs than a war of ideas.

The stakes were smaller the next time evolution went to court, and all that was asked was that creationism be taught alongside evolution. Finally, at Dover, an even more modest proposal went on trial: that evolution be taught with recognition that it was flawed. Each time, evolution, post-Dayton, emerged victorious.

Polls, however, continued to show unwavering support for creationism regardless of what was legally mandated for America's science classrooms. A 2005 survey conducted by *CBS News* revealed that 51 percent of Americans believe that God created humans in present form.[64] The steadily increasing credibility of evolution and its embrace by the educated elite were more than offset by successful grassroots campaigns that maintained the anti-evolutionary fervor whipped up by Bryan decades earlier.

The caricatures of the trials that took up residence in American culture neatly divided the opponents into "science" and "religion" camps. Creationism became the "religious" position, in the eyes of many, and evolution the "scientific" position. But the actual history is much different.

I argued in an earlier chapter that creationism was not, from a religious point of view, particularly important at the beginning of the twentieth century. At Dayton potential religious witnesses sided with Scopes, although their testimony was precluded as irrelevant. The ACLU's strategy included showing that the conflict was not between "religion" and "science," but between a religion that was keeping up with science and one that was not. At Dayton, in Arkansas, at the Supreme Court, in Dover, and on every legal field where creation and evolution met, there were always strong religious voices in support of evolution. Biblical scholars and theologians from all but the most conservative Christian denominations were every bit as opposed to creationism as the scientists from their ivory towers. I have found, for example, after more than two decades as a faculty member at an evangelical college, that the most vigorous opposition to creationism comes from scholars in religion departments rather than in scientific disciplines. As strong as the scientific evidence against creationism has become, the biblical and theological arguments for rejecting it are perhaps even stronger. Expert scholars of religion made this clear in each of the trials.

But Americans have never been eager or even willing to be led by intellectual elites. A simple commonsense argument by someone you trust is worth more than the pompous pronouncements of an entire university of condescending eggheads. America is a nation that loves cowboys, and cowboys don't need experts telling them what to think.

CHAPTER 5

THE EMPEROR'S NEW SCIENCE

Scientists know the moon to be two hundred and forty thousand miles away. How would you react if your neighbor, who was very interested in science, said it was a quarter mile away, closer than the convenience store you can see from your front step? Imagine attending a massive rock concert that broke all attendance records with ten million fans. Your neighbor, who was in attendance, claims there were just ten fans at the concert. Suppose you discussed the age of the earth with your neighbor. In agreement with scientists, you say the earth is five billion years old; your neighbor, however, says that number is a million times too large and the true age of the earth is just over five thousand years. Such extreme disagreements seem laughable and artificial. The last one, however, is a highly animated argument in America as young-earth creationists, a hundred million strong, spar with the scientific community over the age of the earth. Nobody thinks the moon is just above the rooftops, but most people in America have a neighbor who thinks the earth is ten thousand years old.

Creationists disagree with mainstream science on many topics, preferring their own alternative creation science. We hunt in vain, though, to find a more dramatic numerical disagreement on any topic than the one that exists in America today over the age of the earth. If the number of creationists was small, say, comparable to the group claiming abduction by aliens, this would be nothing more than a curious example of human eccentricity. But a 2006 Gallup poll indicated that almost half of all Americans are bona fide creationists, agreeing that "God created man pretty much in his present form at one time within the last 10,000 years."[1]

This disagreement does not result from simple scientific ignorance, as would be the case with a question about Einstein's theory of relativity, which is understood by a small fraction of advanced students. Nor does it derive from an ambiguity of the sort that got Pluto demoted from its prior planetary status. The age of the earth is a topic encountered in geology, astronomy, and biology, which students are already studying in middle school.

In the public high school down the street from my office, there are at least four textbooks in use in earth science alone that discuss the age of the earth. All of them present data from studies of radioactivity indicating the earth is between four and five billion years old.[2] Nowhere in the approved public-school curriculum is there *any* discussion of a ten-thousand-year-old earth. The five-billion-year estimate for the age of the earth is reinforced by science television shows, museum presentations, and plaques in national parks.

If polls reported that people did not know the age of the earth in the same way they don't know why it is colder in the winter than the summer,[3] we could simply and justifiably roll our eyes about the sad state of science education in America. But this is not what the polls indicate. Polling data suggests that half the people in America reject the scientifically determined age of the earth in favor of the age provided by the creationists. That the creationists have managed to spread their message so widely and so effectively makes you wonder if perhaps God isn't on their side, as they claim. They clearly understand how to wage a culture war.

THE "ADVENT" OF SCIENTIFIC CREATIONISM

A century ago creationism was an eddy in the backwaters of an embryonic fundamentalism. Evolutionists contributed to *The Fundamentals* and, although all the contributors affirmed that God was the creator, there was no universal rejection of evolution as a mechanism of creation. The most consistent creationist voice belonged to the new Seventh-day Adventist movement, which looked to the mid-nineteenth-century prophetic writings of Ellen White for guidance.

White was an eccentric prophetess whose writings have been more widely translated than any other American writer. As mentioned in Chapter 2, she experienced the "Great Disappointment" in 1844, when Jesus failed to appear. White nevertheless remained faithful and began receiving her own visions. Before long she was at the heart of an emerging new sect that now boasts more than fourteen million followers in two hundred countries. Her prodigious literary output exceeded five thousand articles and forty books.

Among White's influential writings is *Patriarchs and Prophets* in her series "Conflict of the Ages," first published in 1890. In this fascinating text White offers an expanded vision of Bible stories such as the Genesis creation accounts, the fall, and Noah's great flood. In a curious twist of history, modern creationism can be traced to her expansion of the Genesis flood narrative.

By the middle of the nineteenth century, when White's visions began, geologists, most of them Christian, had concluded that Noah's flood was a local affair confined to the Middle East. Its effects had been erased over time. This interpretation of the story, though not the most literal reading, was uncontroversial and accepted by most educated Christians. White rejected these geologically motivated "compromises" as inconsistent with the plain account given in the Bible. She insisted Noah's flood was worldwide and that it had produced all of the geological layers. The flood completely reshaped the surface of the earth, and the fossils testified to the cataclysmic nature of the flood. Earth history prior to the flood was completely obliterated, but the flood itself left the clearest evidence imaginable. Here is White's vision:

> The entire surface of the earth was changed at the Flood.... As the waters began to subside, the hills and mountains were surrounded by a vast turbid sea. Everywhere were strewn the dead bodies of men and beasts. The Lord would not permit these to remain to decompose and pollute the air, therefore He made of the earth a vast burial ground. A violent wind which was caused to blow for the purpose of drying up the waters, moved them with great force, in some instances even carrying away the tops of the mountains and heaping up trees, rocks, and earth above the bodies of the dead....
>
> At this time immense forests were buried. These have since been changed to coal, forming the extensive coal beds that now exist and yielding large quantities of oil.[4]

White's embellishment of the biblical narrative attracted little interest outside Adventist circles, but within the Adventist tradition her writings acquired a stature comparable to that of Scripture. Loma Linda University near San Bernardino in southern California, for example, was founded in 1905 to educate students in the context of White's visions and other Adventist distinctives.

White's interpretation of the flood became widely known outside Adventist circles through the writings of George McCready Price (1870–1963), who was born in New Brunswick, Canada, not far from my hometown. A self-taught geologist with little education beyond high school, Price was a gifted writer, amateur scientist, and tireless crusader in the cause of anti-evolution. His *The New Geology*,[5] published in 1923, was catapulted into relevance by William Jennings Bryan, who wielded its anti-evolutionary arguments in his crusade against Darwinism. A few decades later respected fundamentalist scholars John Whitcomb and Henry Morris joined forces to mainstream Price's ideas in *The Genesis Flood*. The book launched the modern creationist movement and helped convince half of America that the earth was just a few thousand years old.

Price defended a recent six-day creation, relying on the flood to provide an alternative explanation for the data that serve as the primary evidence for evolution. Evolution is supported by the observation that the fossil record shows increasing complexity over time. If Price could undermine this foundational evidence, the so-called geological column, the evolutionary theory resting on it would collapse.

The New Geology assaulted the concept of the geological column, the sequence of past epochs inferred from the stacking patterns found when layers of rock are exposed. Guides inform tourists traveling into the Grand Canyon, for example, that they can read geological history as they descend. The surface layer records the present and contains indicators such as existing plants, animals, and Coke cans along with Snickers wrappers and tabloids with stories about the travails of current celebrities. Lower rock layers provide information about increasingly older geological eras. At one level we find a fossil that is two million years old; farther down we have fossils that are twenty million years old. The pattern is clear. Traveling down is like going backwards in time, say geologists.

Price disagreed and, over the course of seven hundred pages in *The New Geology*, masterfully gathered every exception, counterexample, and questionable extrapolation used by geologists to argue that the geological column tells a believable historical tale. He says:

This alleged historical order of the fossils is clearly a scientific blunder; for there are many unequivocal evidences to prove that this supposedly historical order must be a mistake. There is no possible way to prove that the Cretaceous dinosaurs were not contemporary with the late Tertiary mammals; no evidence whatever that the trilobites were not living in one part of the ocean at the very same time that the ammonites and the nummulites were living in other parts of the ocean; and no proof whatever that all these marine forms were not contemporary alike with the dinosaurs and the mammals. In short, the only scientific way to look at this matter is to say that we have in the fossils merely *an older state of our world;* and the man who wishes to arrange the various burials of these animals off in some sort of chronological order will have to invent some other scheme than any hitherto considered, for all such schemes of an alleged historical order which have been hitherto proposed are now seen to be wholly unscientific.[6]

We can appreciate the misleading character of this claim by considering how fossils are distributed and why Price disputed the conventional interpretation. The geological column he wants to dismantle doesn't actually exist anywhere. There is no place on the planet where the full geological and fossil history of the earth is neatly displayed in all its glory from primordial beginnings to the present. We would not, however, expect to find such a convenient distribution, as it would require that some local area remained undisturbed for billions of years while one layer of sediment piled atop another. Such an area would have experienced no ice age, no earthquake, no volcano, no flood, no continental drift, no meteorite, no bulldozer, and no major geological activity of any sort. Such a column would only be exposed to the steady entombment of successive generations of fossils buried in place by one unusual event after the other. The geological column is, instead, assembled piecemeal by combining local distributions. For this reason we have an undisturbed record of one epoch at the Grand Canyon, but we have to look a few miles away to see clear evidence of another era. And then we must look in some third place to find a sequence that overlaps both of them. By comparing thousands of partial records around the planet a complete history can be created.

Each partial geological record chronicles a bit of natural history, a "chapter" in the life of the earth. Lower layers typically contain fossils of animals very different from those that exist at present. Upper layers contain fossils similar to those presently existing. And middle layers contain fossils in between. By lining up these partial histories with each other a more complete record can be developed. Often the newest part of an old formation overlaps the oldest part of a newer formation, connecting them. There are many strategies for making these connections, one of which uses "index fossils."

Certain fossils are found often enough in the same geological layer that they can be used as an "index" to date the layer simply by their presence. By analogy, when my mother was young, Newfoundland had not jet joined Canada and was issuing its own postage stamps, some of which I have in the collection she passed on to me. A letter with a Newfoundland stamp on it belongs to that brief era after the establishment of the Canadian post office but before Newfoundland became a part of Canada. Because this history is well understood, historians can use these stamps as historical dividers, like a bookmark slid into the pages of time. In the same way, index fossils point to particular geological periods and, because such fossils have been correlated with other indicators of age, it is possible to infer from the fossil alone the age of the rock in which it appears.

Price rejects all this, highlighting exceptions called "thrust faults." Thrust faults occur when geological material gets knocked out of its normal spot. Sometimes upheavals and earthquakes invert the layers, which makes it look as though the fossils and other age indicators are in the wrong order. Other times material is pushed or "thrust" into the middle of an otherwise organized stack, like the book reviews I sometimes insert into the middle of my books. Identifying thrust faults is pivotal to making sense of data that appear out of order. Price, however, suggests that the "theory of 'thrusts' is a rather pitiful example of the hypnotizing power of a false theory in the presence of the very plainest facts."[7] The reason that faults are invoked at all, he says, is "solely because the fossils are found occurring in the wrong order."[8]

Lay readers, unfamiliar with geology, often find Price's argument convincing. William Jennings Bryan certainly did. But informed readers are appalled. Why would Price make such a big deal about fossils in the wrong order? Only a tiny fraction of the rock formations have this problem. And why would Price say that "fossils ... in the wrong order" is the *only* reason to claim that a section of rock has been overturned? This is as ridiculous as arguing that "tires on top" is the *only* way to tell that a car has rolled over. When a geological formation has been inverted there are *many* indicators. Fossilized animals will be found on their backs, with their feet pointing up, not likely the orientation in which they were buried. Strata with rain and wind marks will have those marks on the underside. An eroded trench might face down rather than up. An inverted formation may contain large objects with their centers of gravity high rather than low. A pyramid-shaped boulder, for example, might be found with its point down. Radioactive dating of the rock layers, which generally correlates almost perfectly with the age of the fossils, will be backward. There are many ways to identify an inverted formation.

Price's book presented many photographs of such formations. He was widely traveled and, for an amateur, well read in geology. How could he make such inexcusable errors in an ambitious textbook he hoped would overturn the entire science of geology? Who, exactly, was he writing for? He certainly was not writing for anyone with geological training; experts would, and did, immediately recognize the falsity of these claims.

In addition to challenging the central concepts of geology, Price offered his own bizarre replacement geology. Prior to the great flood of Noah, he stated with assurance, the earth was a delightful planet-wide greenhouse. He claimed that everywhere the terrestrial "climate was a mantle of springlike loveliness." Although he offered no explanation for how this climate originated, he assured readers that this floral era was, quite simply, "a matter of fact," a claim he hung on the most speculative of threads.[9] Furthermore, this global paradise was the "only" climate that existed anywhere on the earth prior to the flood. During this epoch the plants and animals were "larger and more thrifty-looking than their corresponding modern representatives." Our modern counterparts are "degenerate dwarfs." Unfortunately, we have not discovered a single human fossil from before the flood because God "buried their remains so completely."[10]

Readers may object that I have dug up a dead creationist and flogged him unfairly. Any 1923 geology book is bound to contain problems. The difference is that the successors to other geology books corrected and updated their content. Errors discovered in earlier texts disappeared from later texts, and the content steadily improved. This didn't happen with Price's eccentric "flood geology." It was simply recycled without advancing much beyond where it was when Bryan invoked it in Dayton, Tennessee.

The New Geology, for those who read it, stirred up a vigorous sandstorm across the geological landscape, until the entire science of geology looked obscure and questionable to outsiders. Price's writing style was comfortable and convincing for laypeople; his arguments were logical and easy to follow. The book synergistically combined elements that made it effective and, in so doing, provided a template for the anti-evolutionary work that followed.

These elements, used to great effect in virtually every creationist text since, included:

1 A preference for simple observations laypeople could easily understand and pass on in casual conversation or in speeches and sermons.

2 The use of glib generalizations that, though not false, ignored the nuances that a professional scientist would feel obligated to include. Such pandering to the uninformed came to characterize creationist writings, which were readily critiqued and refuted by specialists. This was to no avail, however, since such refutations occurred in publications that laypeople did not read and often involved subtleties they could not follow. As we shall see later, some peculiar creationist arguments had an enduring presence within fundamentalism and would continue to circulate long after they had been rejected, even by the creationists who first promoted them.

3 A winsome celebration of the commonsense insights of ordinary people over a "scientific establishment" blinded by its need to rationalize its preferred paradigms.

4 A consistent portrayal of the scientific establishment as inappropriately "secular," rhetorically glossed to mean "godless."

5 A pejorative stance toward "theory," implying that a theory is really just a guess based on assumptions, in contrast to observable facts. Price wrote "*a theory put to work is a hypothesis*. And hypotheses are always dangerous things."[11]

6 Nonstop ad hominem attacks on scientists, making them appear so closed-minded that nothing they claim could possibly be legitimate: "They made many and grievous blunders of observation, due to the hypnotic suggestion of their supposedly infallible theory."[12]

Despite Price's emergence as "the principal scientific authority of the Fundamentalists,"[13] he had little formal scientific training, virtually no publications in peer-reviewed journals, and no credentials of any sort beyond an introductory education to which he kept adding. He was not a member of the scientific community and, except for his notoriety as a popular enemy of evolution, was unknown in scientific circles. This was not a problem, however, for Price's audience was uninformed fundamentalists who were content to know that some smart guy had proven that the biblical flood refuted all the geological evidence for evolution, even though they couldn't remember how.

Canadian humorist Stephen Leacock captures this attitude perfectly in his *Sunshine Sketches of a Little Town,* in which he introduces Mallory Tompkins and Mr. Pupkin, who "used to have the most tremendous arguments about creation and evolution." "Tompkins," writes Leacock, "used to show that the flood was contrary to geology, and Pupkin would acknowledge that the point was an excellent one, but that he had read a book—the title of which he ought to have written down—which explained geology away altogether."[14] Pupkin's book that "explained geology away" may have been Price's *Illogical Geology,* which appeared in 1906,[15] six years before Leacock's *Sunshine Sketches.* In any event, a Pupkinesque confidence emerged within American fundamentalism that there was evidence "out there" that refuted evolution.

Price's version of White's young-earth creationism, his "flood geology," did not catch on at first. Evangelical Christians, with notable exceptions, remained content to accept the great age of the earth, inserting the geological ages into the hermeneutical orifices in the Genesis creation story. The scholarly community looked at Price with amusement, a geological Don Quixote heroically tilting at scientific windmills, convinced he could single-handedly overturn two centuries of geological work. His work was riddled with so many simple errors that any consideration he did get from the scholarly community was highly critical.

In the final analysis Price's ideas served little purpose beyond providing an "authority" for fundamentalists to invoke against evolution. Bryan and other leading anti-evolutionists certainly looked to Price as an authority. And for decades he was *the* scientific authority. Most people, however, accepted the great antiquity of the earth, content to believe that the days of Genesis were geological epochs. Leading Protestant thinkers, even within the conservative evangelical camp, were satisfied that the great flood of Noah was a local affair, and not Price's global catastrophe.[16] Evolutionary voices also were quiet in the decades after Scopes, with textbook publishers pandering to the Pupkins to avoid controversy and ensure that their sales were strong.

THE GENESIS FLOOD

On October 4, 1957, the Soviet Union launched the first Sputnik satellite. The event jolted a complacent America that had been resting on its scientific laurels ever since its atomic bombs and radar had won World War II. Immediately alarmed about the state of science and science education, the government poured money into the reform of high-school science teaching, including biology.

These reforms led to a new high-school biology curriculum, the Biological Sciences Curriculum Study, which assigned evolution a prominent role, consistent with what it was playing in the field of biology. For the first time in decades, biology texts had their evolution content driven by *scientific* rather than *commercial* considerations. Dramatically increased coverage of evolution resulted, which generated widespread and negative reactions from fundamentalists. A growing hunger for an anti-evolutionary messiah to replace William Jennings Bryan began to develop.

That messiah came in from the wilderness in 1961 carrying a book under his arm that would come to define creationism in America. In so doing it would establish itself as perhaps the most influential text on any topic in the second half of the twentieth century. This messiah and architect of contemporary creationism was a winsome Southern Baptist named Henry Morris, who got his academic start at Rice University in Houston, Texas, then known officially as Rice Institute and locally as a "hotbed of infidelity."[17] Morris attended Rice because it was free and close enough that he could live at home, his family having come on hard times in the Depression.[18] He was a brilliant engineering student and graduated Phi Beta Kappa in 1939.

Morris loved the Bible, which he studied and read on a daily basis, a practice he continued for his entire life and modeled as an important family activity for his children. He helped the Gideons distribute Bibles. Consistent with his fundamentalist commitments, he believed that God had authored the entire Bible and that all of its statements were true, whether they pertained to history, science, morals, or fishing and farming.

In the 1940s Morris returned to Rice to teach engineering. He grew increasingly committed to reading the biblical stories of the creation, fall, and flood as literal history. He wanted to validate these literal interpretations with scientific models. The important task of developing these models had been neglected because biblical scholars, even those claiming to be evangelicals, had been promoting alternative readings. In particular there were few fundamentalists insisting on a young earth, preferring the gap theory or the day-age interpretation of Genesis. Morris was especially disturbed by the near universal belief that the biblical flood had not been universal, but local, inundating Noah's stomping ground but little else. Why in the world, asked Morris quite sensibly, would Noah labor for a century to build an ark to save his family and the local animals when they could simply have migrated upland? To Morris, such a reading of the flood story was blasphemous, a compromise with a secular science that reflected an unwillingness to take God at his word.

Morris was a new and improved George McCready Price. Whereas Price was self-taught in science, with credentials easily dismissed by his critics, Morris had a stellar and relevant academic pedigree culminating in a Ph.D. in hydraulic engineering from the University of Minnesota. He minored in geology and mathematics. He could hardly have been more qualified to work on flood geology if he had been Noah's first mate. Price taught at Bible schools and other small religious colleges; Morris taught at Rice and later became the head of the engineering department at the respected Virginia Polytechnical Institute. And, perhaps most important, Morris belonged to the Southern Baptists, a mainstream evangelical tradition with none of the baggage of the marginal Seventh-day Adventist tradition to which Price belonged. If Morris was the messiah the creationist movement needed, Price had been his John the Baptist, crying in the wilderness for Christians to prepare.

The book that would launch the creationist movement and move fundamentalism strongly away from its errant and misguided reading of the Bible was *The Genesis Flood: The Biblical Record and Its Scientific Implications.* Published in 1961, the bombshell was coauthored by Morris and John C. Whitcomb, Jr., an Old Testament scholar. Whitcomb, like Morris, was well credentialed, with an honors degree in history from Princeton University and a doctorate from Grace Theological Seminary. In contrast to the gentle and diplomatic Morris, Whitcomb was angry about the deplorable state of biblical interpretation. Much of his wrath was directed at Bernard Ramm, who in 1954 had published the influential *The Christian View of Science and Scripture.*

Ramm had worked with the great Swiss theologian Karl Barth and gained a significant reputation himself. He taught at several evangelical institutions, including Baylor University, and combined a deeply held belief in the inspiration and reliability of the Bible with a respect for science. He rejected fundamentalist claims that a "high" view of Scripture demanded that all its references to the natural world be taken literally.

"Conservative Christianity," he wrote, "is caught between the embarrassments of simple fiat creationism, which is indigestible to modern science, and evolutionism, which is indigestible to much of Fundamentalism." The only way out of this "impasse" is to accept "progressive creationism."[19] Progressive creationism was the idea that God created the world and its life-forms gradually, along the trajectory disclosed in the fossil record and with methods similar to those described by evolution. Ramm took the geological record at face value, rejecting claims by Price and others that it was an artifact of Noah's flood. The earth is ancient, said Ramm, not young; and Noah's flood was local, not global. Ramm labeled fundamentalists who rejected these ideas "hyperorthodox" and accused them of various intellectual crimes from inconsistency to gross and inexcusable ignorance of science.[20] Their "pedantic hyperorthodoxy" caused the "great cleavage between science and evangelicalism" in the nineteenth century. Their continued obstinacy was only widening this gap, guaranteeing that Christianity would continue to be humiliated. Science marches onward, said Ramm, but creationism keeps running in place on its creaky nineteenth-century treadmill.

Ramm's broadsides enraged Whitcomb, who decided to take him on in print. He began revising for publication his dissertation, *The Genesis Flood,* and searching for someone approximating a geologist who would bring scientific credibility to the project. Henry Morris could not have been a better fit. Whitcomb and Morris's classic text has since been through dozens of print runs and sold hundreds of thousands of copies. What it accomplished is nothing short of astonishing and makes it easy to see why the authors claimed that God helped them write it.[21]

At the time the book appeared, most fundamentalists accepted the great age of the earth, in agreement with the scientific community. Now, a half century later, fundamentalists are largely united under the banner of young-earth creationism. In the decades that span this transformation, there were no scientific discoveries undermining the great age of the earth; no new books were added to the Bible; no advances in biblical interpretation suggested more literal readings of Genesis. And yet millions of American fundamentalists changed their minds about the age of the earth.

The Genesis Flood, in a nutshell, is two long arguments woven together, a logical double helix. The first is warmed-over Price, updated, energized, and stripped of its Adventist origins. The second is an assault on Ramm and his school of "compromise" biblical interpretation.

The Price connection is all but invisible unless one reads *The Genesis Flood* alongside *The New Geology.* By the time Whitcomb and Morris began work on their book, Price's public image was that of a geological clown, a strange one-man scientific community combing the planet for evidences to support the bizarre visions of a nineteenth-century prophetess. *The New Geology* had been blasted to bits in the press, and even those who endorsed it, like Bryan, strangely missed the fact that it was not compatible with the prevailing old-earth creationism. One can't help but wonder if its loyal promoters read it carefully. It may be that it was embraced, Pupkin-style, as an "authoritative refutation of evolution," with scant attention paid to exactly how it accomplished that feat.

In Whitcomb's early draft of *The Genesis Flood,* Morris had noted with caution that the geology was "merely a survey of George McCready Price's arguments."[22] Mindful that Price's book had flopped, Morris worried that a recycling might not fare much better. Whitcomb agreed, and they set out to recast Price's work in a way that retained its strengths but hid its origins. When *The Genesis Flood* was finally published, there were but four references to Price in the index and nothing of substance in the text itself. Morris, forever gracious, was concerned about this move and apologized to Price when he asked him to review some of the chapters that drew heavily on his work. Price was not upset, but some of his supporters felt Whitcomb and Morris were disingenuous and unprofessional in concealing their debts to Price.[23]

The Genesis Flood, however, was more than recycled Price. Its extensive discussion of biblical interpretation, for example, had no counterpart in *The New Geology.* And it addressed at least one of the difficulties in Price. Recall Price's flimsy argument that before the flood the earth was a greenhouse of "springlike loveliness."[24] Whitcomb and Morris kept this idea and went on to argue that this greenhouse hypothesis can actually be explained by the presence of a great canopy of water vapor circling the earth. This canopy, they argued, did two things: it protected the earth from harmful radiation from space, enabling preflood earthlings to live for hundreds of years and creatures to grow to gigantic sizes; and it provided the waters for Noah's flood.

The vapor-canopy hypothesis, which has been a critically important fixture in creationist thinking since *The Genesis Flood* was published, hangs on threads connected tenuously to two biblical passages. The existence of the "canopy" is supposedly implied by Genesis 1:6–7, where we read: "And God said, Let there be a firmament in the midst of the waters, and let it divide the waters from the waters. And God made the firmament and divided the waters which were under the firmament from the waters which were above the firmament: and it was so" (KJV). The canopy as a *source* of the waters for the flood comes from Genesis 7:11, where we read that "the windows of heaven were opened" to provide floodwaters.

This improvement on Price "rounded out" the flood geology model of *The Genesis Flood.* An Edenic preflood world, where people lived for centuries (as the first chapters of Genesis record) and animals grew to grand sizes, was destroyed by a global cataclysm. The disaster precipitated a vast water canopy from above and released waters from the "great deep." This flood created the fossil record we study today. The postflood environment is, of course, anything but Edenic, with unhealthy radiation from space and ongoing geological and atmospheric turmoil.

The submerged reworking of Price was accompanied by an unsubmerged assault on Ramm, who was damned on two accounts.[25] In the first place, Ramm had insulted Price, calling his ascendancy to the position of fundamentalism's "leading apologist in the domain of geology" one of the "strangest developments of the early part of the twentieth century."[26] Ramm's argument laments the abandonment of serious intellectual engagement with science in favor of Price and other pseudoscientific cranks. In the second place, Ramm proposes a less literal approach to biblical interpretation, still maintaining that the Bible was fully inspired by God and infallible. Ramm put people like Whitcomb on the defensive. The response needed to be careful and measured and not resemble the anti-intellectual "hyperorthodoxy" that Ramm claimed had come to describe evangelicalism.

History, for better or worse—actually just worse—is on the side of the fundamentalists when it comes to issues of biblical interpretation. This odd reality provided a strategy for Whitcomb and Morris to counterattack Ramm. Ramm's "questionable" views about the Bible arose from *compromises*. Positions Christians had historically held were abandoned or modified in response to secular developments. Nobody, for example, construed the days of creation as geological epochs until scientists uncovered what looked like evidence for the great age of the earth. Nobody thought Noah's flood was local until geologists supposedly found portions of the earth that had never been flooded. Nobody proposed a long developmental process for creation until scientists decided that such a process was clearly disclosed in the fossil record.

The central role of the Bible in Christianity, together with the doctrine of biblical inspiration, makes it hard to simply shrug one's shoulders and say, "I guess the Bible got it wrong there." My favorite example, which I invoke every year when I teach this material, is the Bible verse thrown at Galileo when he argued that the earth was moving around the sun and not vice versa: "The world is firmly established; it cannot be moved" (Ps. 93:1, NIV). I have yet to encounter a Christian who, when confronted with this verse, which is rarely quoted from pulpits, responds: "The guy who wrote that thought that the earth didn't move, but he was wrong. The Bible verse contains an error." (Galileo couldn't find anyone with that response either.) The usual response is to suggest that the Psalmist meant something less immediately obvious like "Human beings cannot move the earth" or "The earth is a secure place for humanity." Such responses emphasize that the text has multiple *interpretations,* and showing that one *interpretation* is wrong is not equivalent to finding a factual error in the Bible. The goal, for conservative readers, is always to look for some *plausible* interpretation of the biblical text that keeps it free from error.

There is an informal pecking order in conservative Christianity when it comes to biblical interpretation. Among people with a conviction that the Bible is without error, the "highest" view of Scripture is the one that reads the text most literally. The "lower" views are those that "compromise" the most literal meaning of the text by developing "interpretations" that, however legitimate, are not the most obvious and certainly not the most literal. Such views are considered to be "compromises." It was precisely on this point that Whitcomb crossed swords with Ramm, despite their shared convictions about the nature of the Bible.

In the introduction to *The Genesis Flood,* Whitcomb and Morris write: "We desire to ascertain exactly what the Scriptures say.... We do this from the perspective of full belief in the complete divine inspiration and perspicuity of Scripture, believing that a true exegesis thereof yields determinative Truth in all matters with which it deals."[27] In the first chapter of *The Christian View of Science and Scripture,* Ramm writes that he "believes in the divine origin of the Bible and therefore in its divine inspiration." He "emphatically rejects any partial theory of inspiration" and anticipates that, through careful scholarship, "science and Scripture will eventually concur."[28]

There is but a subtle difference between these two positions as they played out in practice. Ramm took science seriously and would use its conclusions to modify his interpretations of the Bible, while Whitcomb and Morris regarded the most natural interpretation of the Bible as necessary. They rejected any science in conflict with that interpretation. This disagreement shows up consistently throughout the Bible, but nowhere with more clarity than in the first chapter of Genesis, which describes God's creation of the world in six days, each with an evening and a morning. The most obvious interpretation of this passage is that the "days" refer to ordinary twenty-four-hour days. However, as the science of geology developed, it became clear that the developmental history described in the Genesis creation story was much longer than six days. A "pure" and uncompromising biblical literalist, with the "highest" view of Scripture, would simply reject these conclusions from geology and look to undermine the relevant science. This was the approach of Whitcomb and Morris. Ramm, however, was unwilling to set science aside and preferred instead to look for alternate interpretations. Such an interpretation could be found in the proposal that the "days" of Genesis were long periods. Thus, by choosing a less obvious but still plausible interpretation of Genesis, harmony was achieved between science and the Bible, without acknowledging error in the Bible.

The Genesis Flood is a long argument against Ramm's approach. For Morris and Whitcomb, the Bible is God's revelation to humanity. Science, in contrast, is sinful humankind's fallen and feeble attempt to understand the natural world. How can we possibly use the latter to understand the former? Should we not take God at his word and interpret natural phenomena within the framework of the biblical revelation? If we start compromising the literal meaning of the Bible to bring it into alignment with science, where do we end? Is this not a dangerous slippery slope? Will this approach not ultimately prove corrosive to faith in the Bible and, when we are finished, will we not discover to our dismay that the "acid of compromise" has eaten away the entire Bible?

Whitcomb and Morris declared war on Ramm. And they won. *The Genesis Flood,* a half century after it first appeared, is currently sales-ranked at

30,870 on Amazon.com. Ramm's *The Christian View of Science and Scripture* ranks at 1,168,000 and is technically out of print.

REFLECTIONS ON CREATIONISM

I have dwelt at length on *The Genesis Flood,* tracing its origins to two roots. The first was the flood geology of Ellen White and George McCready Price, which it embraced, albeit sheepishly. The second was the nuanced approach to Scripture of Bernard Ramm, which it rejected. These two sources form the basis for the entire 518 pages of the book.

The argument in *The Genesis Flood* is compelling to a conservative Christian layperson interested in science, precisely the sort of lad I was when I read it in high school. The lengthy footnotes on virtually every page, the constant invocation of authorities from every imaginable discipline, the diagrams and pictures, and the synergistic credentials of the authors all combine to endow the book with authority. The uncompromising respect for the complete truth and accuracy of the Bible is comforting to readers raised in homes where the Bible is read daily, memorized, and applied consistently to daily life. Christians everywhere look to the Bible, and there are no more encouraging champions of its veracity than John Whitcomb and (the late) Henry Morris. The argument itself is both compelling and intriguing: compelling because of the logical rigor and careful reasoning, and intriguing because of the suggestion that the entire scientific community had run off the rails in trying to explain all of creation without acknowledging God. There were even Bible verses alluding to this kind of "last days" intellectual apostasy.[29] Their entire presentation was very believable, which is why the argument won the day and now sits at the center of the evangelical worldview.

The Genesis Flood sold a few hundred thousand copies, which surprised everyone and probably got someone fired at Moody Press. Fundamentalist Moody Press declined the book because its editors thought that the "day-age" interpretation of Genesis was both true and so generally accepted by its target audience that it would be pointless to publish a mammoth book assaulting it. Despite relatively robust sales, however, the numbers indicate that less than 1 percent of American evangelicals actually read *The Genesis Flood*. So how did its central message fare so well?

THE PUPKINIZATION OF AMERICAN EVANGELICALISM

The Genesis Flood was a watershed event in the evangelical engagement with science. It represented the abandonment of a long tradition of taking mainstream science seriously. The founders of modern science—Galileo, Kepler, Newton—had all been deeply religious and invested in the integration of science and faith. The nineteenth-century milieu that gave birth to Darwinism had a similar set of deep Christian thinkers—Faraday, Wallace, Gray, and even the young Darwin. These scientists took seriously the task of integrating evolution with key Christian doctrines. Evangelicals in the first half of the twentieth century, from B. B. Warfield at Princeton to the infamous Bernard Ramm, had continued this task. This was all to end.

The Genesis Flood was intellectually disastrous on two fronts. On the scientific front it convinced far too many evangelicals that there was an "alternative science" out there for them, and that this alternative was consistent with a simple reading of the Bible and required no complex "reinterpretations." On the religious front, *The Genesis Flood* convinced far too many evangelicals that a faithful interpretation of the biblical text required subscribing to a young age for the earth and a worldwide flood. Furthermore, these beliefs were dramatically elevated in importance. For almost two thousand years virtually nobody made a big deal about the age of the earth or the details of the flood. *The Fundamentals,* published at the beginning of the twentieth century, paid scant attention to these topics. Now, suddenly, Christians had to embrace these beliefs in order to be faithful to the Bible they cherished. A broad range of acceptable positions on this topic collapsed into one. "Creationism" lost almost all of its traditional theological meaning and became a political label attached to Christians who reject evolution and embrace a young earth and worldwide flood. Twenty years later, when Isaac Asimov expressed his dismay by saying, "Creationists are stupid, lying people,"[30] everyone knew exactly what he was talking about. The same statement a century earlier would have been deeply ambiguous.

FIVE DECADES OF "FLOODING"

The Genesis Flood became "brand-name creationism" and created the paradigm for almost all subsequent developments in the creation–evolution controversy. When creationism appeared in the courts, it was this brand. When a "creation research" center was started, it was to explore this brand. When a "creation journal" was launched, it was to promote this brand. When a "creation museum" opened up, it was to present this brand. The shelves on Christian bookstores filled up with various presentations of this brand of creationism, from popularizations of the weighty Whitcomb and Morris tome to cartoon books for children showing people and dinosaurs on Noah's ark together. Bible study materials appeared, arguing that this is the only way to interpret the various relevant Bible passages and even that these ideas are essential for Christians.

"Research" centers and organizations emerged to support this surging creationism. The most influential was the Institute for Creation Research (ICR), affiliated with the fundamentalist Christian Heritage College in San Diego. The college had been started by Morris and Tim LaHaye, the latter of whom went on to great fame and wealth as the best-selling coauthor of the wildly popular *Left Behind* series. Morris was proud that Christian Heritage was the "first college in modern times formed in order to provide a liberal arts education based specifically on strict Biblical Creationism and full Bible controls in all courses."[31] He envisioned ICR making important contributions to "creation science" and turning into a major research center. Imagine the impact of qualified Ph.D. scientists working with eager graduate students on sophisticated creation research projects! Morris dreamed of moving the scientific community away from its exclusively old-earth, evolutionary paradigms.

Morris's dream of gaining academic respectability for creation science crashed and burned in the decades following the emergence of ICR and other "research" centers. Creation science proved unable to establish itself and made no inroads into mainstream science. If anything, by becoming better known, it marginalized itself even further and became a sad academic joke to be studied as an example of "pseudoscience,"[32] written about in books with titles like *Why People Believe Weird Things*[33] and lampooned on television shows.[34]

The key "scientific implications" outlined in *The Genesis Flood* proved incapable of inspiring meaningful research, although some efforts were made. The intriguing "vapor canopy" idea received much attention, but nobody could come up with a model to show how it might have developed or been sustained. An ICR physicist created computer models that yielded results even he described as "disappointing for advocates of a vapor canopy."[35] Claims that radiocarbon dating was unreliable led nowhere. A recent study speculatively and hopefully looked for a mechanism tied to the flood that would produce "millions of years' worth of nuclear decay ... in just days."[36]

One of the more intriguing claims in *The Genesis Flood,* accompanied by a photograph, is that human and dinosaur footprints have been discovered together in a riverbed in Texas.[37] This appeared to confirm the provocative claim that dinosaurs were contemporary with humans rather than having gone extinct seventy million years earlier. The photos were circulated broadly and appeared in countless creationist books and even in a film distributed by ICR titled *Footprints in Stone.* The claim turned out to be fraudulent. Some of the footprints had even been chiseled in the stone by a local man who then sold them. ICR eventually withdrew the film from circulation, but not before the argument had taken up residence within fundamentalism, where it is still being trotted out by charlatans and the hopelessly uninformed.

The growing popularity of creationism threatened public education and raised concerns within the scientific community. Many books and articles appeared refuting its pseudoscientific claims and defending the conventional interpretation of earth history. But such claims were lost on rank-and-file evangelicals, who were certainly not going to read books attacking their faith. They knew better than to open the pages of books by godless agnostics like Richard Dawkins and Stephen Jay Gould or even deluded fellow believers like biologists Ken Miller and Darrel Falk.[38] Critics of creationism were often rude and dismissive and appeared to have agendas that went beyond the truth of various claims about the natural history of the earth. I mentioned above that Isaac Asimov called creationists "stupid, lying people." Oxford biologist Richard Dawkins, in similar vein, stated that anyone who rejects evolution is "ignorant, stupid, or insane."[39] Tufts University philosopher Daniel Dennett suggested that creationists should be "quarantined" and their children told that their parents are engaged in the "spreading of falsehoods."[40] Such examples can be endlessly multiplied.

These famous critics failed to grasp that creationists are also committed Christians and many of them are reasonable, generous, and motivated by the noblest of intentions. Thoughtful Christians sense something disingenuous about the mean-spirited lambasting that accompanies what should be a civil argument about science. These diatribes, they reason, must derive either from a great insecurity about one's own beliefs or a sinister spirit working to undermine God's eternal truth. As mentioned earlier, Morris explored this latter thesis in a popular book titled *The Long War Against God,* in which he made the extraordinary claim that evolution came directly from Satan. The passage is worth quoting in full:

> Now if Satan (or Lucifer) is going to believe that God isn't really the Creator, then he has to have some other explanation. That's why I have to say that Satan was the first evolutionist. Evolutionists ridicule me for saying that, but again, I can think of no better explanation for how this worldwide, age-long lie came to be, than through the father of liars, who is the devil. Satan is the deceiver of the whole world, but he has deceived himself most of all!
>
> And he still thinks, apparently—because he's still fighting against God—that somehow he's going to win. So he keeps on fighting. He has to use the same lie with which he deceived himself, that the universe is the ultimate reality, that it's evolving itself into higher and higher systems, and that now men think they can even control its future evolution. Men can develop human beings and other things the way they want them in the future if Satan can just get control of everything.[41]

By these lights it is easy to understand the passions in this ongoing cultural clash. "Lying, stupid, wicked creationists" battle "satanically inspired evolutionists" to see whose version of natural history will win, whose creation story will be embraced by America. The overheated rhetoric is long past communication; it is nearly impossible to find a civil conversation on this topic anywhere. The evolutionists have won the academy, the prize being public schools, courts, and public television. The creationists have won the grass roots and created a self-sustaining (pseudo)scientific subculture with its own standards. They have their own publishing houses, magazines, colleges, and even their own accrediting agency, the Transnational Association of Christian Colleges and Schools (TRACS). TRACS requires member schools to affirm belief in the "special creation of the existing space-time universe and all its basic systems and kinds of organisms in the six literal days of the creation week."[42]

"WHAT A FOOL BELIEVES"

Henry Morris's dream of a creation-science research program gave way to a populist movement repeating anecdotes in the way that Pupkin argued with

Mallory Tompkins. The anecdotes remain sheltered in a subculture where, insulated from peer review, scholarly consideration, and scientific advance, they reproduce and thrive. When I ask my students how many of them have heard that dinosaurs were contemporary with humans, hands go up. How about carbon dating being unreliable? Hands go up. The fossil record full of holes? Hands go up. My colleagues at secular schools in conservative parts of the country report the same phenomena.

I am not surprised by this, for these are the stories of my youth, provided by preachers, Sunday school teachers, and the books I was encouraged to read. It wasn't until I started studying science in earnest that I discovered that these stories were simply rubbish. Many of these stories have even been quietly repudiated by the creationists themselves. There is little evidence, however, that the creationists care how new players come to be on their team. *The Genesis Flood,* after forty-four printings, has never been revised and still contains pictures of fraudulent footprints "proving" that dinosaurs coexisted with humans, despite the authors' appropriate disavowal of that claim.

There is no reason for anyone, Christian or otherwise, to take any of these claims seriously. The key ideas being promoted under the banner of "scientific creationism" originated in Ellen White's "visions." And the ideas might have stayed within the cloisters of the tiny Adventist sect, had not a clever amateur geologist named George McCready Price started to bang the flood-geology drum. Even Price won but few converts, and it wasn't until Whitcomb and Morris produced the masterful *The Genesis Flood* that the argument took off.

CREATION GOES GLOBAL

The popularity of scientific creationism is a fascinating phenomenon, authentically American in many ways and incomprehensible to Europeans. I was recently in Rome to address a conference at the Vatican on America's peculiar attraction to creationism. European Christians remain in dialog with mainstream science, harboring no fears that evolutionary biologists are all possessed by the devil. That half of America maintains allegiance to a set of ideas they discarded a century ago is beyond belief. Nevertheless, creationism appears to be going global and, although its influence abroad is limited, there are indications that it is time for the global scientific community to start preparing a response.[43]

Scientific creationism has climbed onto the radar screens of American intellectual culture only as a bad joke. Creationism's low point would have to be a 2006 episode of *The Simpsons,* "The Monkey Suit," caricaturing the key elements that turned creationism into such an intellectual embarrassment. When the show's popular evangelical character, Ned Flanders, wanders with his children into an evolution display at the local museum, he encounters, to his increasing horror "Man's Early Ancestors," "Indisputable Fossil Records," and "Unisex Bathrooms."

Agitated, Flanders asks the director, "How can you put up an exhibit on the origin of man and not have *one* mention of the Bible?" The director refers him to a display with a huge hand coming down from heaven and poking at the ground, out of which animals and humans pop into existence. The Doobie Brothers song "What a Fool Believes" plays in the background. Flanders seeks counsel from his pastor, who opportunistically sees a controversy that might get people back into his church. Seemingly interested only in celebrity, the pastor blackmails the local school into teaching creation.

A "two-models" video for the public school titled "An Unbiased Comparison of Evolution and Creationism" shows the Bible coming down from heaven on a beam of light, ringed by a halo. A choir sings, and the narrator intones that it was written by "Our Lord." The other book, *On the Origin of Species,* arises in flames, its title written in blood. Heavy metal music replaces the heavenly choir, and the narrator notes that it was written by a "cowardly drunk named Charles Darwin."

Lisa Simpson, the program's voice of reason, responds by teaching evolution in secret and gets arrested, recalling *Inherit the Wind.* A slick witness claiming a Ph.D. in "truthology" from "Christian Tech" testifies against "devolution," calling it "pure hogwash." The locals are impressed with the polished imposter; they boo the ACLU lawyer when they find out she is from New York.

Fifty years ago this humor would not have worked. But the success of Morris's anti-evolution crusade not only consolidated young-earth creationism as the primary option for evangelicals, but also introduced it to America's educated elite as a peculiar cultural phenomenon. That the movement is now so well known for its foibles is a sad commentary on just how completely lost Morris's original vision has become. His movement has utterly failed to provide a vital creation research program or to win back the scientific community. In fact, his flagship project, the ICR, now languishes under the uninspired leadership of his son John. The heart of young-earth creationism is now located at Ken Ham's Answers in Genesis organization, where writing cartoon books and funny songs about dinosaurs has replaced research and graduate education as the top priority for advancing the cause.

The discussion of young-earth creationism is now an in-house conversation, reaching few Americans outside of the evangelical subculture. There is no longer any chance that it will influence the courts, the public schools, or higher education. And, although this restriction will not interfere with book sales, the lecture circuit, or the popularity of creation museums, it does imply that this brand of anti-evolutionism has lost its chance to influence Western culture. It will play no role in reversing the tide of secularism that Christians have been fighting for over a century. It was precisely this recognition that motivated a charismatic law professor named Phillip Johnson to craft a different approach to fighting evolution called intelligent design.

CHAPTER 6

CREATIONISM EVOLVES INTO INTELLIGENT DESIGN

The arrival of *The Genesis Flood* in 1961 energized creationists. They started research institutes; they launched creationist journals; they published a library of books and articles. They created videos, Sunday school literature, and comic books. They built museums. When the Internet arrived, they produced Web sites. Whitcomb and Morris could hardly have envisioned the movement launched by their collaboration. And yet their project, by the most important yardstick of all—their own—has been a complete failure: creationism has had absolutely no impact on science. The flood geology they promoted so enthusiastically in their seminal manifesto never even appeared on the far horizon of mainstream science.

As of this writing, there is not a single scientist at a major university working within the flood-geology paradigm of scientific creationism. Not one. Not a single scientific paper explicitly promoting *any* aspect of this brand of creationism has been published in a scientific journal. Not even one.[1] Every "working" creationist is either at a tiny research center like the ICR or at a fundamentalist Christian school, like Liberty or Bob Jones, which do very little research anyway, even outside the sciences. The vast corpus of creationist literature, for its thousands of pages, consists almost entirely of popular-level books published by evangelical presses. The "scientific" output of creationist scholars is a modest bookcase of unnoticed semitechnical works and articles in "in-house" journals containing little more than miscellaneous sniping at poorly understood details in evolutionary theory.

To make matters worse, a substantial literature demolishing creationism has appeared. A few mainstream scientists, initially certain that something so fanciful and antiquated as flood geology would die on its own, recognized that creationism's grassroots popularity threatened science education. They began looking more closely at creationist claims with an eye toward refuting them and getting them out of the conversation. Unfortunately for the creationists, their assertions were all too easy to refute.[2] Unfortunately for the scientific community, the assertions they so carefully refuted kept appearing in book after book, like a gag candle that keeps reigniting after you blow it out. Apparently, some creationists believe there is no such thing as a wrong argument against evolution.

Geologists noted that there were portions of the planet, such as the polar regions, that clearly had never experienced a flood. If they were flooded four thousand years ago, as creationists claim, there would be some interruption in the seasonal stacking pattern clearly visible in ice cores and extending back for tens of thousands of years. Noah's ark, noted biologists, may have been adequate to carry most of the local animals in Noah's neighborhood, but it was way too small to house the vast menagerie that we now understand to inhabit the earth. So much evidence accumulated for the five-billion-year age for the earth that claims it was six thousand years old sounded no more plausible than the claim that it was flat.[3] The parade of evidence continued, until there was hardly a single creationist claim that retained even a shred of scientific credibility. Creationism's best-educated advocate is Kurt Wise, a geologist who obtained his Ph.D. under Stephen Jay Gould at Harvard University. Even Wise concedes that the scientific evidence was clearly stacked against creationism. Belief in creationism, for Wise, is *in spite of* the scientific evidence, not because of it; he stands with creationists because of his prior commitment to biblical inerrancy.[4] Two other forthright and well-credentialed creationists, Paul Nelson and John Mark Reynolds, share Wise's view and caution their young-earth colleagues to "humbly agree that their view is, at the moment, implausible on purely scientific grounds."[5] Greater intellectual condemnation would be hard to imagine. Needless to say, this is not the future for which Morris and Whitcomb hoped.

Effective critiques of creationism came from Christian scientists who, despite having personal faith in the Bible and fully endorsing the idea that God created the world, considered creationism to be absurd in the light of current science. Evolution, an increasing number of them argued, was, and is, both true and compatible with their Christian faith.[6] Often these scientists, who were surrounded by the people buying creationist literature in droves, had to face derision and even persecution from their own religious traditions. Biblical scholars and theologians were also weighing in critically, charging that the creationists were reading an anti-evolutionary agenda into the Bible, twisting its ancient wisdom to speak to a modern issue it never intended to address.[7]

There was widespread fundamentalist enthusiasm for creationism. The excitement drew opportunists to the cause, like hot-dog vendors to an outdoor concert. Preachers who knew nothing about science began pontificating from pulpits and writing books as if they were trained scientists speaking with authority on subjects like genetics and paleontology. The articulate and influential D. James Kennedy, for example, who heads the huge Coral Ridge Ministries, assured his millions of viewers that evolution is little more than an ill-begotten joke turned into an argument for atheism: "Darwin's ideas, which provoked laughter and lampoons in virtually every newspaper of his own day, and is a theory for which to this day there is virtually no reliable scientific evidence, have become the cornerstone of modern humanism."[8] James Dobson, Pat Robertson, and the late Jerry Falwell all launched attacks on evolution and assured their millions of listeners and readers that there were no reasons to take the theory seriously. Charlatans with virtually no education began to put Ph.D. after their names and claim to be "creation researchers." One of the most bizarre examples of this was "Dr." Carl Baugh, who became, and remains, surprisingly popular even after being exposed as a fraud.[9]

Baugh promotes a peculiar pet theory in which the preflood earth possessed a "firmament consisting of compressed hydrogen taking on near metallic characteristics, in the middle of a solid water formation about eleven miles above the earth." This amazing solid sphere was mysteriously immune to being shattered by incoming meteoroids. With the earth floating exactly in the middle of it, this shield bathed the planet in a "gentle pink glow," which enabled human brains to work at "maximum efficiency."[10] Baugh's claims are pseudoscientific nonsense, on a par with alien abductions, psychic surgery, and spoon bending. Astoundingly, though, it was this crackpot who appeared on a 1989 *Nova* program representing the creationist viewpoint! Baugh has a "museum" and continues to be a fixture on fundamentalist programs like Kenneth Copeland's *Believer's Voice of Victory*. He even has his own weekly show on the Trinity Broadcasting Network, *Creation in the 21st Century*, where he is referred to as the "foremost doctor on creation science."[11]

Comparable gibberish can be found in the writings of "Dr." Ken Hovind, who calls himself "Dr. Dino" and built a theme park in Florida organized around the idea that humans and dinosaurs coexisted. Hovind, an active crusader for creationism, has his own "Hovind Theory," which explains that an ice meteor caused Noah's flood. He claims to carry a $250,000 check for anyone who can show that evolution is the best explanation for origins. His critiques of evolution include such illuminating gems as: "Every farmer on planet Earth counts on evolution not happening. They count on it. It doesn't happen. People can believe whatever they want, but whenever a farmer crossbreeds a cow he expects to get a cow, not a kitten."[12]

Like Baugh, Hovind has bogus educational credentials. And like Baugh his writings are filled with pseudoscientific nonsense, supplemented with a surprising number of spelling and grammatical errors. This tireless crusader for creation has repudiated his American citizenship, refusing to pay taxes, and in 2006 was arrested and indicted in federal court on fifty-eight charges related to his tax problems. As of this writing he is in jail. Baugh and Hovind are but two of the more popular frauds in the creationist movement, which seems capable of generating and supporting an endless number of mountebanks and charlatans who make a mockery of both the religious faith they claim to serve and the science they pretend to understand.

The confident assertions of polemicists like Baugh and Hovind play well on Main Street. The rhetorical power of claims that evolutionists can't defend their own theory, even with a $250,000 incentive, makes it appear that evolution must indeed be dying. Perhaps it never had much life in the first place. It is thus not surprising that creationists love to claim that evolution is gradually being abandoned. In 1963, two years after *The Genesis Flood* began its long cultural tsunami, Morris published *The Twilight of Evolution*, the last chapter of which bore the title "The Death of Evolution."[13] A surprisingly steady stream of books making identical claims followed, even as evolutionary science became stronger and healthier in scientific circles.[14] The growth of this misperception no doubt reflected the steady disengagement from the scientific community of the creationists as they gradually stopped talking to practicing scientists and instead talked only to themselves. They convinced themselves that their position was so obviously superior that the opposition much surely be on its last legs.

By the 1990s creationism had become a scientific joke, consistently providing raw material for television comedies. When Peter Griffin, the lead character on *Family Guy,* was having his intelligence tested, he discovered that he ranked below "retarded" but above "creationist."[15]

This is not to say, of course, that creationism is dying. Far from it. The lampooning on television works only because the ideas are so widely popular. And, as polls, book sales, and the continuing popularity of "creation museums" attest, creationism shows nothing but robust political and economic health. Nevertheless, from a scientific and even broader intellectual perspective, creationism lacks credibility. And there can be no doubt that its ideas are irrelevant within the scientific community.

Furthermore, as a purely practical matter, the defeats suffered by creationism in the courts all but guaranteed that it would be making no comeback through the public schools. The Supreme Court's 1987 expulsion of creation science from America's public-school classrooms hammered the last nail into that coffin.

Had evolution finally won, at least on the legal and academic fronts? Was creationism now forever restricted to a large but purely fundamentalist comfort zone, out of the sight of mainstream science and without influence on American intellectual culture as a whole? Conservative Christian intellectuals, many of whom would admit to being embarrassed by creationism, found this disturbing. If evolution continued to own the academy, they reasoned, its pernicious naturalism would keep seeping into the intellectual foundations of all aspects of American life. After all, almost every leader graduates from a college or university dominated by evolutionary thinking. As these leaders take their places in positions of power, so the evolutionary thinking they imbibed in the academy would inform and control decision making everywhere. The acidic philosophy of evolution was corroding everything in America, from the Supreme Court, to foreign policy, to corporate finance, to the curricula in the public schools, to Hollywood scripts.

REASON IN THE BALANCE

No one was more disturbed about all this than the colorful, opinionated, and theologically conservative law professor Phillip Johnson, who was about to explode onto the scene like a promised messiah to rally the demoralized faithful. Johnson, a tenured professor at Boalt Hall, the law school of the University of California at Berkeley, was convinced that the issue was not evolution per se, but rather the pervasive and dogmatic *naturalism* of science. Johnson objected to the way the scientific community insisted that *all* explanations for *all* phenomena at *all* times present and *all* times past must be purely naturalistic. This effectively ruled out the *possibility* that God might be a relevant part of a comprehensive understanding of the world. Even substantial and compelling evidence would be inadequate to infer that God was involved in the world. Scientific explanations were allowed to invoke only natural laws and ordinary events for their explanation. If the face of Jesus appeared on Mount Rushmore with God's name signed underneath, geologists would still have to explain this curious phenomenon as an improbable byproduct of erosion and tectonics. A choir of heavenly angels singing carols in the sky over the White House would likewise have to be explained as an anomalous weather pattern, a flock of unusual birds, or a publicity stunt by Pat Robertson gearing up to run for president. Invoking God to explain *anything* was simply not allowed in science, *no matter how compelling the reasons for doing so.*

But why, asked Johnson, should an explanation invoking God be ruled out before even being considered? Was this not "stacking the deck" in favor of atheistic naturalism? Are the explanations provided by science really the "best" explanations? Or are they simply the "best that can be had without invoking God"? What kind of twisted logic was this?

Applied to origins, this restrictive naturalism excluded God from any involvement whatsoever in how things came to be the way they are. From the big bang, to the appearance of our solar system, to the origin of life, to the evolution of our complex brains, to the emergence of our sense of morality, God was simply not there. Or, if God was there, he was just watching, cheering from the sidelines like a fan at a football game who, although interested in the game, is irrelevant to the outcome. Everything happened by itself. Johnson found these conclusions unacceptable and began developing a strategy to level this highly sloped playing field. He would rehabilitate the argument from design and give the courts something they could not summarily reject as a breach of the battered but still standing wall between church and state. In so doing, he would single-handedly reenergize anti-evolutionism and breathe life into a new species of creationism, which he labeled *intelligent design.*

THE WEDGE OF NATURALISM

Johnson's career as the leader of this emerging "intelligent design" (ID) movement was both launched and secured with the publication of *Darwin on Trial* in 1991. The book was short, popular, readable, and rhetorically powerful. It assaulted evolution but presented no religious or biblical alternative. And, just as Price and Whitcomb and Morris had launched manifestos that guided and defined anti-evolution earlier, *Darwin on Trial* became the manifesto for the fledgling ID movement.

Johnson's stature as a respected legal scholar and the cleverness of his attack on evolution gained him entry where previous creationists had failed. No less a luminary than the late Stephen Jay Gould reviewed *Darwin on Trial* in the prestigious pages of *Scientific American*.[16] Despite the negativity of Gould's review, its mere appearance signaled the engagement of the scientific community. Gould's review also shone a national spotlight on Johnson, who was only too willing to put evolution and scientific naturalism on trial. Like the Pied Piper marching through the streets of Hamelin with children in tow, Johnson soon found himself at the head of a tiny but determined army of highly disgruntled, newly resurrected, and occasionally brilliant anti-evolutionists.

As befit a lawyer preparing a case, Johnson had a set of strategies to fight evolution. He knew there were many constituencies separately opposing evolution but on different pages regarding the biblical and theological aspects of creationism. Their differences on "minor" questions like the age of the earth or the extent of the flood had them squandering their energies on in-house quibbles or preaching to tiny choirs. They were all fighting their own individual wars against evolution, and in that odd phenomena that Freud called the "narcissism of small differences" they were energetically fighting each other. Under Johnson's leadership, they set aside their differences and joined forces against their common enemy, united in their conviction that evolution was false, while agreeing to disagree on how creationism should be understood.

Johnson's strategy contrasted strongly with that of Whitcomb and Morris, who had intertwined science and religion to great effect. But it was precisely this intertwining that ultimately resulted in the barring of their brand of creationism from the public schools. The young earth, the worldwide flood, the rejection of evolution between "kinds," the separate ancestry for humans and apes—all these ideas connected so tightly to the Genesis story that there was simply no way to "secularize" this creationism for presentation in the public schools. The creationism rejected by the Supreme Court was so obviously based on the Genesis creation story that even the articulate

Wendell Bird could not get the justices to see the science without also seeing the religion.

Johnson highlighted the naturalism of science as a philosophical problem, a bogus antireligious assumption masquerading as a scientific inference. *Darwin on Trial* concludes with sweeping, if undocumented, generalizations offered with breathtaking confidence. The "purpose" of evolution, Johnson writes on the last page, is not to understand the development of life on this planet, but "to persuade the public to believe that there is no purposeful intelligence that transcends the natural world." This assumption creates an intellectual straitjacket that prevents scientists from even *considering* possibilities inconsistent with "strict philosophical naturalism."

"Darwinists," Johnson writes, "took the wrong view of science because they were infected with the craving to be right." They confuse their "pseudoscientific practices" with real science, because they are too dense to even recognize that they have become slaves to the "philosophical program of scientific naturalism." If only Darwinists could see this with the same clarity as Johnson, they could toss off the "dead weight of prejudice" and be free at last to "look for the truth."[17]

Johnson's anti-evolution polemic made him the poster child for ID. Creationists of all stripes joined hands under the big tent he was erecting. This strategy was in evidence at a conference held at Biola College in Los Angeles in November 1996. A beefy anthology titled *Mere Creation: Science, Faith, and Intelligent Design* resulted.[18] Some creationists, of course, are uneasy about the way that ID asserts its independence from the Bible, but are nevertheless happy to join the ID crusaders in their war against evolution. The enemy of my enemy is my friend.

The foreword to *Mere Creation* celebrated contributions from Roman Catholic, Eastern Orthodox, and Jewish scholars, not to mention a spectrum of conservative Protestant thinkers—and even a disciple of Reverend Sun Myung Moon. Some contributors believed the earth was ten thousand years old; others accepted the conventional scientific age of four and a half billion. Some participants rejected evolution completely; others accepted it as long as God was constantly and intimately involved. About a third were practicing scientists or engineers. The others were philosophers, theologians, journalists, and writers. Two convictions united them: conventional evolutionary theory was wrong; and living organisms displayed clear evidence of intelligent design that could not possibly have been produced by natural processes. This was pure, or "mere," creationism, uncontaminated by divisive religious commitments or nuances of biblical interpretation. Johnson's strategy was working.

The rapid emergence of ID as a cultural phenomenon has been nothing less than astonishing. There have been many strong reactions, from sympathetic,[19] neutral,[20] and hostile[21] perspectives. ID was on the front pages of America's leading newspapers and being praised in the White House.

ID, like the creationism it was intentionally replacing, rode the same wave of anti-evolutionism that took creationism to the Supreme Court. This time, however, the energy came from a more intellectually sophisticated demographic. Flakey, fringe creationists like Carl Baugh and Ken Hovind were nowhere in sight.

The Seattle-based Discovery Institute provided generous financial support, embracing ID as a partner in its mission of cultural renewal. Much of the money came from Howard Fieldstead Ahmanson and his wife, whose affiliation with a variety of extreme right-wing causes has made some people nervous about the ultimate agenda of the Discovery Institute.[22] Proponents of ID, some of them fully funded by the Discovery Institute and devoted full-time to the cause, found a ready audience for their books and widespread demand for public appearances. Venues like public television, National Public Radio, the *Wall Street Journal,* and *New York Times* took notice, sometimes favorably. Leading science magazines gave them an occasional, if generally negative, nod. The roster of ID enthusiasts, or at least public figures coming out in support, included important national figures, from politicians like George W. Bush, Bill Frist, and Rick Santorum, to media personalities like Ann Coulter, Pat Buchanan, Chuck Colson, and Bill O'Reilly, to televangelists with huge audiences like the late D. James Kennedy.

ID was, of course, similar in many ways to creationism. As we saw in a previous chapter, the judge in the Dover case ruled that it *was* creationism, deceptively packaged to look like something else. ID's leading lights were all conservative Christians who wrote primarily for Christian audiences arguing that ID was critical for restoring God to the center of the Western worldview. William Dembski, perhaps ID's leading theorist, even titled one of his books *Intelligent Design: The Bridge Between Science and Theology.*[23] And certainly the ID movement's eagerness to join forces with the more credible young-earth creationists like Kurt Wise and Paul Nelson guaranteed that there would be a strong creationist tinge to everything under the ID umbrella.

The central argument of ID, however, was simply that the world had more design in it than could be accounted for by purely natural explanations. Dembski, ID's most prolific author, put it like this: "There exist natural systems that cannot be adequately explained in terms of undirected natural causes and that exhibit features which in any other circumstance we would attribute to intelligence."[24]

THE SEDUCTIVE POWER OF DESIGN ARGUMENTS

So what exactly are the design arguments? And what makes them so compelling? Design arguments are, in fact, logically attractive on many levels, practical, scientific, and even religious. They "feel" right, as if they somehow *have* to be true, and therein lies their attraction. And the ID proponents are indeed correct that people make judgments all the time about design. Why should such inferences be excluded from science?

An all too familiar example is the September 11 attack on the twin towers of the World Trade Center. When American Airlines flight 11 hit the north tower at 8:45, many people concluded that a terrible tragedy had occurred, but that the event was random. Eighteen minutes later United Airlines flight 175 hit the south tower, and everyone immediately *knew* a nefarious plan was being executed: an "intelligent design." Drawing design conclusions like this, as they say, is a "no-brainer," and one hardly needs specialized training to do this. Every day we routinely make such design inferences. A chocolate bar on the sidewalk is a random event; the chocolate bar I put in my daughter's lunchbox is an intentional act. The shape of a river is a random meander; the shape of an *s* is a design, even when they look similar.

Design inferences are also drawn in science. Archaeologists must decide if something they dig up is a human artifact. An interesting arrangement of stones may be simply interesting, or it may be the work of intelligent creatures. Competence in the social sciences requires the ability to distinguish between intelligent causes and purely natural ones. Astronomers listening for extraterrestrial signals believe an intelligent signal will be distinguishable from the background noise in which it is embedded.

Theologically, intelligent design in some form is almost a requirement for Christians. If God created the world, then the creation is the consequence of an intelligent act. Religious language is filled with allusions to the intelligence of God. How often do we hear that "God has a plan for your life" or "God's will be done, on earth as it is in heaven." Countless biblical passages allude to God as the source of order and rational structure. The gospel of John opens with a sort of hymn praising Jesus for being the "logos" of creation. *Logos* is a Greek term with no exact analog in English. It is usually translated "Word," but it embodies the idea of "rationality," "order," or "logic." The imagery in the Genesis creation account is of God hovering over a formless void and bringing order to the chaos. To believe in God is to believe in design.

There are three distinct strands of design: practical, scientific, and religious. These arguments have long been braided together by religious believers into a compelling argument for the existence of God. We saw earlier how William Paley created a powerful apologetic argument based on design in nature. This argument, which haunted Darwin as he gathered his observations, would eventually give way to the theory of evolution.

ID wants to rehabilitate Paley, or at least undermine the arguments that did him in. The claim that complex and interesting natural phenomena reveal the handiwork of God is indeed compelling and perennially attractive. However, although I wish it were true, it must be rejected.

WHY THE ID ARGUMENT FAILS

How can I reject the ID argument, while, paradoxically, wishing it were true? Let me start with the reasons why I, and all Christians for that matter, should wish it were true.

Like so many people, I believe in God and have done so for my entire life. And, like most believers who go on to earn advanced degrees, I have been forced to recognize that belief in God is not a simple matter. Many of the arguments that worked so well for me in high school have since lost their power to persuade. And I have a great appreciation for the counterarguments for God's existence. I understand how honest thinkers and seekers after truth like Daniel Dennett and Michael Ruse can end up rejecting God. Like that of most thinking Christians, my belief in God is tinged with doubts and, in my more reflective moments, I sometimes wonder if I am perhaps simply continuing along the trajectory of a childhood faith that should be abandoned.

As a purely *practical* matter, I have compelling reasons to believe in God. My parents are deeply committed Christians and would be devastated, were I to reject my faith. My wife and children believe in God, and we attend church together regularly. Most of my friends are believers. I have a job I love at a Christian college that would be forced to dismiss me if I were to reject the faith that underpins the mission of the college. Abandoning belief in God would be disruptive, sending my life completely off the rails. I can sympathize with Darwin as he struggled against the unwanted challenges to his faith.

If I could convince myself that ID were true, I would have a solid *argument* to believe in God, to keep those nagging doubts at bay. I would be less controversial at the college where I teach, able to affirm my students in their confident but unexamined beliefs that evolution is untrue. The president of the college would not have to worry about fundamentalist donors who won't support their alma mater because I teach there. I have many solid reasons to embrace ID and have been at times, in the words of that ancient hymn, "almost persuaded." So, when I say that I reject ID, I say it with pangs of regret. I truly wish it were true.

From my perspective, ID must be rejected on two completely separate grounds. In the first place, ID doesn't work scientifically. As I pointed out in the earlier chapter on Darwin, ID was once a viable paradigm in science, accepted by everyone. But it was not abandoned because scientists wanted to get God out of the way, as is so disingenuously claimed by some. ID was discredited because it proved inadequate as an explanation for so many phenomena. In the second place, ID is theologically problematic. To suppose that there are various structures in nature specifically designed by a transcendent intelligence, which we all know is God, is to open a Pandora's box of problems, not the least of which is the problem of bad design. And even when the design is good, what do we make of ingenious designs employed for sinister purposes?

The ID argument is simplicity itself, which accounts for its enduring and widespread popularity. We find something interesting in nature—the eye, the blood-clotting mechanism, the opposable thumb, the immune system, the bat's radar, the brain—that exhibits more complexity than science can explain. The human blood-clotting mechanism, for example, needs more than twenty different proteins to work properly; if some of them are missing, the process doesn't work. How did nature develop this complex process? It is inconceivable that all the parts just randomly came together. But it is also inconceivable that blind evolution, with no sense of where it was "going," slowly tinkered with molecules and ended up with this complex and remarkable process. So are we not then forced to invoke an outside intervention to account for the complex design of the blood-clotting mechanism?

Leading ID theorist William Dembski developed what he calls an "explanatory filter" to determine when "design" should be invoked by ruling out the less interesting alternatives. Applied to the example above, it works like this. We start by asking if the blood-clotting mechanism is something that necessarily *had* to happen, like rocks sinking in a river. The answer, of course, is no, which means that we cannot explain the blood-clotting mechanism as the *necessary* result of a law of nature.

We then ask if the mechanism is too complex to have resulted from chance. If the pattern is simple, like a row of three stones, it can easily be the result of chance. The blood-clotting mechanism, of course, is too complex to be produced by chance. But not all complex patterns require intelligence to explain them. Certain complex patterns, like a cloud resembling Homer Simpson, can indeed be produced by chance, as anyone who has ever watched clouds on a lazy summer day can attest. But even though such patterns are complex and interesting, they are not specified in advance. Given that there are thousands of patterns that would look interesting, it is unremarkable that we find one on occasion.

The final step in the explanatory filter is the question of *specification*. Is the complexity of the mechanism under consideration something that would have to be specified in advance? Certainly a series of typed letters explaining how to assemble a bookcase is highly specified and the same number of letters in a random order is not. The blood-clotting mechanism is not simply complex, but complex in such a highly specific way that, if the explanatory filter is to be trusted, forces us to conclude that the mechanism is the result of design.

Dembski's design-detecting explanatory filter has received much criticism, and Dembski has responded to some of his critics. Readers interested in this discussion will find more than enough of it on the Internet.

My reaction to Dembski's filter, and to the general comments made by other ID people about how science might detect design, is that they seem strangely incompatible with the way that science actually works in practice. When lawyers, mathematicians, philosophers, and theologians start pontificating about how empirical science is supposed to work, they do so as *spectators,* not *practitioners.* Such spectators are easily confused about the so-called rules of science. There really aren't *rules* in science. Rather, there exists an ongoing tradition in which certain productive *approaches* become standard practice because they have proven to be helpful in generating new knowledge. Scientific approaches that are not effective in generating new knowledge are abandoned, but not because they cannot withstand philosophical or logical scrutiny, which scientists don't care about. Scientific theories without effective explanatory power and unproductive scientific approaches are rejected because they are *useless*.

The ID theorists are hung up on the so-called rules of science. But, as anyone who has earned a Ph.D. in a scientific discipline can tell you, there is no course of instruction in the rules of science required for its practitioners. You learn by becoming a part of a tradition, building intuitions, and studying under mentors. In this way, science is different from, say, law, where rules dominate and the prevailing philosophy is that following the rules leads to the truth. That is why the offices of lawyers are lined with expansive bookcases, and the law degree hanging on the wall is the product of just three years of study. Learning rules and reading books are easy. By contrast, a Ph.D. takes, on average, about ten years of specialized study. Mastering a subtle tradition of learning is complex and not something to be understood by simply looking in the window of a research lab or spending a quiet evening curled up with *An Idiot's Guide to the Scientific Method*.

If there were more historians of science in the ID movement, I think this would be better understood. The history of science is, in many ways, the history of the gradual and reluctant abandonment of ID as a helpful approach to understanding the world. Let me offer one of the clearest examples.

Isaac Newton's theory of universal gravity explained many things about the motion of the planets, including the elliptical shape of their orbits and how the size of their orbits related to their speed as they went around the sun. But his remarkable theory offered no insight into why the planets all went around the sun in the same direction. Newton was impressed by this "design." There was no law specifying this order. And it would be a strange and improbable coincidence for this to be the case. So Newton, the greatest scientist of his age, concluded that, as there was no natural explanation for the order in the solar system, it was the work of God. He "filtered out" naturalistic explanations and inferred "design."

At the time Newton made this design inference there was no satisfactory explanation of the origin of the solar system. A century later such a theory was developed and, lo and behold, the theory stated clearly that all the planets should revolve about the sun in the same direction. If Newton had known or discovered this, he would never have attributed the uniformity of the planetary directions to God.

At the time of Newton, science—then called *natural philosophy*—was a small and simple enterprise, still finding its way and fighting to be born. The world was mysterious and, with a few small exceptions, so far beyond the grasp of science that God was regularly invoked in the face of many mysteries. Newton's invocation of God is of interest precisely because of the simple clarity of the reasoning: a solid theory explained many things; the unexplained residue—the explanatory "gaps"—were attributed to God. But then science advanced and a natural explanation was discovered for the phenomena of interest, closing that gap in our knowledge.

As science advances, these gaps close. In fact, the closing of such gaps is what we mean by the advance of science. Gaps are the shadows where ignorance hides from the light of science. Inserting God into these gaps has proven, historically, to be a fool's errand and ultimately both unnecessary and embarrassing. Again and again science has made surprising advances that have allowed us to revisit these gaps in our knowledge and, often to our great surprise, close them. Historians of science know this only too well, which may be why this critically important group is so underrepresented in the ID Movement.

The central role of scientific ignorance is hidden in Dembski's explanatory filter. When theorists decide that some phenomenon is "contingent" (which means there is no law requiring it to be the way it is), what they are really saying is that they don't *know* of any such law. Newton did not *know* that solar systems form with all the planets going in the same direction, so he assumed this phenomenon was contingent and ended up invoking a design explanation.

The proponents of ID are, of course, aware of this basic objection, and they have some elaborate responses that are simply not relevant to the actual practice of real science. I don't think they have a good feel for how the historical practice of science has gradually generated a "conventional wisdom" or "common sense" that leads practicing scientists away from such explanations. When a certain approach has failed so many times, it is not irrational or dogmatic to suspect that it will fail again—it is just prudence.

The naturalism of science is like the naturalism of plumbing. When plumbers seek to understand plumbing phenomena, their experience leads them to pursue certain promising possibilities. They look for leaks, broken valves, and blockages, because this approach has been effective in the past. Why are the ID theorists not calling down the wrath of God on the plumbing community for its blinkered adherence to pure naturalism?

In the final analysis, from a scientific point of view, there is no difference between Newton's unknown mechanism for planetary directions and the currently unknown mechanism for the origin of the blood-clotting mechanism. And, I might add, the plumber's unknown leak. Why would we invoke a supernatural explanation for any of these?

The publicity surrounding the creation–evolution controversy can easily blind us to the reality that the majority of work in science has absolutely nothing to do with origins and thus couldn't make use of ID, even if it wanted to. The naturalism that ID is so quick to condemn actually works quite well, without controversy, and with the blessing of the ID community in most areas of science. Chemists make new molecules; geologists develop models to predict earthquakes; climatologists work on weather. ID enthusiasts with day jobs in science labs work comfortably within a fully naturalistic framework. Even if the ID approach were fully embraced by the entire scientific community and enthusiastically applied wherever possible, almost nothing would change outside of those small areas of biology and cosmology that study origins.

The second reason I reject ID is theological. I think ID makes dangerous and incoherent claims about God that create far more problems than they solve.

We must start by looking at ID's peculiar claim that the identity of the "designer" is of no consequence. This contrasts with the notions of Paley, for whom ID was an argument for the God of Christianity. ID theorists have actually suggested that the inferred designer could be "space aliens from Alpha Centauri; time travelers; or some utterly unknown intelligent being."[25] Although this might be true in the narrow sense that there is no way to refute the claim that a space alien designed the blood-clotting mechanism, nobody is making this claim. In contrast, virtually all of the ID people are on record enthusiastically proclaiming that God is the designer. In the subtitle of one of his books, Dembski calls ID a "bridge" between science and theology, but nowhere has he, or any other ID enthusiast, suggested that ID might be a bridge between science and space aliens.

So, what happens when we open the doors of science to supernatural design explanations? What results when we invoke God as the cause of complex phenomena like the blood-clotting mechanism, our brains, or bat radar? A lot, unfortunately.

In the first place, the God of Christianity has to be way more than just a *designer*. Centuries of Christian reflection on the nature of God have highlighted various characteristics of God: justice, love, goodness, holiness, grace, sovereignty, and so forth. Are not compassion and grace far more central to understanding God than design? Although nobody except TV preachers speaks with too much confidence about the nature of God, there is general agreement among theologians that God must be understood as multifaceted. And, although "designer" can certainly be one of these facets, it takes a backseat to God's other attributes such as love, wisdom, and grace.

Spotlighting design in nature and attributing it to God raises troubling questions. We saw how Darwin wrestled with this as he wondered why God would have endowed creatures with ingenious capacities to inflict pain. Nature, as Tennyson wrote, is "red in tooth and claw." And many of those teeth and claws are extremely well designed. Some of them would make it with flying colors all the way through Dembski's explanatory filter. However, if we run all of nature's marvelous devices through this filter, some uncomfortable results appear. The remarkable blood-clotting mechanism has received much attention and is an example that works well for the ID Movement. We are fortunate that our blood clots and have no difficulty believing that God intelligently designed the process. And we can't use our blood-clotting mechanism to inflict any pain on other creatures. So it seems like a win-win; we get something we need and God gets the credit for designing something truly beautiful as well as complex.

But what about the Ichneumonidae, which troubled Darwin? Its remarkable design would certainly make it through Dembski's explanatory filter, and we would have to conclude that the instincts of the Ichneumonidae meet the criteria for ID. So here we have an insect laying eggs inside a caterpillar. The newly hatched parasites live inside the caterpillar, consuming its internal organs. And, in a most amazing illustration of intelligent design, the Ichneumonidae eat the internal organs in a specified order that keeps their host caterpillar alive as long as possible. The parasites are born knowing

how to do this; they come into the world with a genetically programmed in-
stinct to consume the internal organs of their host caterpillar in a specific
order. Forget blood clotting! This is real design. But it's horrible, as Hollywood directors know only too well. I suspect that if the champions of ID
were to highlight the most revolting examples of design in nature, the evangelical community would lose all interest. Who wants a bridge from theology to a spacecraft filled with hungry parasites?

Nature is a complex web of interconnected systems. Organisms feed on
each other. Parasites live within hosts. There is cruelty and barbaric behavior. There are ingenious devices for stabbing, poisoning, paralyzing, decap-
itating, and biting. Many of these devices appear to be designed. Are we
going to run them all through Dembski's filter and ascribe them to God if
they pass? How can this possibly be theologically helpful? This bridge, as
Darwin figured out a hundred and fifty years ago, is better left unbuilt.

Much of nature exhibits impressive levels of design. But so do torture
chambers, gun factories, and liposuction machines. Design, even intelligent
design, is not automatically desirable. Promoting "design" in isolation from
God's other attributes is a dangerous and ultimately self-defeating way to get
God back into science. Christianity will be far better off if ID fails.

NORENE'S KNEES

Even if we can somehow convince ourselves that "intelligently designed
mechanisms for doing terrible things" should be explained as the handiwork of God, there is an even more serious problem: bad design. As soon as
we begin to "review" nature's many intricate mechanisms, we discover, like
any reviewer, that our subject matter varies greatly in quality. Some things
are designed very well and are so ingenious that we cannot help but marvel
at them. Others are designed so poorly that we can only shake our heads.

Take Norene's knees, for example. Norene is a friend of mine, not yet at
retirement age, who recently had both of her knees replaced. They weren't
damaged by any accident or overuse in some jarring athletic activity; she
wasn't even an occasional jogger. Her knees, like those of so many other humans like her, just wore out through normal usage, and long before she was
through using them. Why does this happen?

Our knees are strangely designed and destined for injury. Below them
are ankles that can move in several directions; above them are hips attached

via "ball joints" that also permit a wide range of motion, as anyone who has ever played with a hula-hoop knows. But the knees themselves bend in only one direction. No engineer would put three joints in a row and constrain the middle one in the way our knee is constrained. The design is so bad that countless athletes have to wear a special brace to help prevent a knee from bending about the wrong axis.

The human body is riddled with design problems. Our spines are mechanically configured for walking on all fours. But we walk upright. The result? Back problems. Our mouth is designed to admit both food and air, which allows food to go "down the wrong pipe," leading to choking. We would fire an engineer who designed a car with a single opening for both oil and gas and a complex valve to keep them from mixing. There is a reason why cars are not designed like that. Why are we?

A standard roster of similar design problems is highlighted in just about any human anatomy text. We have appendices that need to be surgically removed; our mouths are too small for our wisdom teeth; our eye has a blind spot. Women's pelvises are not designed to give birth to babies with standard-size heads. And these are just a few of the specifically *human* problems. There are upland birds with webbed feet that never go in the water. Hens have genes to produce teeth that are never turned on, unless artificially induced. Genes contain meaningless sequences of "junk DNA."

There is a substantial literature looking at these aspects of nature, starting with Darwin's own reflections in *On the Origin of Species*. As the inheritor of a tradition shaped by Paley's natural theology, Darwin expected to find clear evidence of God's providential design everywhere he looked in nature. Instead, he found a globe full of exceptions, many of them quite disturbing.

There is great design in nature, to be sure. And much of it is extraordinary. But there is simply too much *bad* design to infer safely that nature's many contrivances are the handiwork of God. Our blood may indeed clot in remarkable ways, but our poor knees don't bend the way they should. Just ask Norene.

BEWARE THE GAPS

These objections I have raised to ID are far from unique. I would like to come up with a completely original critique and get everyone discussing my new insight, but that isn't going to happen for one obvious reason: this controversy is almost two hundred years old. ID was a "live" question in 1831 when Darwin boarded the *Beagle*. Naturalists at that time were trained to see "intelligent design" everywhere they looked. The Darwin of the *Beagle*, like most religious believers, myself included, had every reason to want ID to be true. After all, it provided solid scientific reasons for believing in God, carrying some of the burden of faith.

The doubts that Darwin developed about God's relationship to the natural world troubled him for his entire career. He wanted the traditional view of God as creator to remain intact because of the security that belief provided. He did not want science to be secularized. In the same way, Phillip Johnson, William Dembski, Michael Behe, and their colleagues in the ID movement desperately want God to retain the traditional role as creator, involved in enough of the details to leave divine fingerprints on nature. Like Darwin and the other Victorian mourners at God's funeral, they don't want science secularized. And so they keep fighting the young Darwin's battle for him, picking holes in this or that argument, struggling heroically and with great ingenuity to find examples in nature for which supernatural explanations can still be invoked.

When fish are removed from water and placed on land, they flail about vigorously, unable to get the oxygen they need. Fish belong in the water. Intelligent design is a nineteenth-century argument, flailing about in a new century where it doesn't belong. What looks like vigor is simply the last gasp of a way of understanding the world that died a hundred and fifty years ago.

The world is a complex place, and there is much about the universe that we still don't understand. We are centuries away from closing the many gaps in our current scientific understanding of the natural world. For a time, perhaps a long time, we may take some comfort in supposing that God hides in those gaps. We can develop ingenious explanatory filters to buttress our confidence that God is in those gaps. But it is the business of science to close gaps, and it has long been the central intuition of theology to find a better place to look for God.

Evolution, however, speaks to that all-important question of what it means to be human. And, although it may indeed be a robust science in the narrow sense of that word, when it speaks about what matters most, it does so with a deeply ambiguous voice. Different people hear different things, and in those differences reside profoundly incompatible worldviews.

CHAPTER 7

**HOW TO BE STUPID,
WICKED, AND INSANE**

Evolution is the most culturally complex and controversial idea in all of science. Nothing else comes close. More than a century after Darwin's *On the Origin of Species,* the theory arouses hostile reactions in everyone from clueless high-school students to TV preachers to the well-educated senior fellows at the Discovery Institute. Less than half the country agrees with the scientific community that evolution is the best explanation for origins.

Courts have had to protect the central role played by evolution in high-school biology. If popular consensus refereed the schools, the embattled theory would be long gone. Teachers in school districts from Oregon to Florida struggle with how to present evolution to their students. Many don't bother, omitting or glossing over the topic to avoid controversy.[1] Some Christian colleges and universities, even accredited ones such as Cedarville College in Cedarville, Ohio, and Liberty University in Lynchburg, Virginia, teach that evolution is false.[2]

Professors at secular universities in conservative parts of the country report that students arrive in their classes with strong creationist sympathies, and many of them graduate without changing their minds. Consider the remarkable case of Kurt Wise, the leading young-earth creationist we met earlier. Wise completed an undergraduate degree in geophysics at the University of Chicago and then went on earn a Ph.D. from Harvard, working for the late Stephen Jay Gould. Wise graduated from Harvard with the same young-earth creationist beliefs he had entered college with. Creationism can be hard to dislodge.

Teaching evolution is almost impossible. In no other subject, even outside of science, is the primary challenge whether the students *believe* what is taught, rather than *understand* what is taught. Despite the simplicity of

Darwin's equation-free theory with its winsome stories of giraffes stretching their necks to reach the top of the fruit trees and peacocks preening to impress the peahens, few high-school students seem able to learn it. Despite its universal presence in high-school and college classrooms, Americans reject evolution with the same enthusiasm today as in previous decades. And despite its increasing relevance to research in biology, well-educated anti-evolutionists continue to oppose it.

The controversy surrounding evolution generates enormous press. Books appear daily attacking the theory or defending it against attack. A secondary literature has emerged analyzing the controversy and tracing its roots. Books arguing that evolution is incompatible with Christianity[3] counter those arguing the opposite.[4] There are magazines devoted to promoting evolution,[5] disputing it,[6] and even dealing with the disputations.[7] Publications nominally covering the intersection of science and religion provide disproportionate coverage of the creation–evolution controversy.[8] Television presents the same coverage. The seven-part PBS series *Evolution* devoted an entire episode titled "What About God?" to the controversy.

The creation–evolution controversy is only, in the most trivial sense, a scientific dispute. It is, instead, a culture war, fought with culture-war weapons by culture warriors. Facts are almost irrelevant. Truth is valued when it serves a purpose and not for its own sake. Name-calling, caricature, cover-up, and hyperbole dominate. Compromise is out of the question. And, in the midst of all this, high-school teachers are supposed to teach evolution to their students, oblivious to the gunfire outside the window.

A TALE OF TWO WORDS

Decades of reflecting on the evolution controversy convinces me that the conflict is only tangentially scientific. Those who would adjudicate this dispute by appealing to science are wasting their time. The conflict is not about determining the proper inferences to draw from fossils, genes, and comparative anatomy. The conflict resides at the much deeper and far more important level of *worldview*. It centers on one simple question: Can there be any role at all for God in our own creation story?

This is a far more important question than whether Darwin's theory is true. The attachment of this question to the creation–evolution controversy raises the stakes. If accepting evolution means abandoning belief in God as creator, then evolution should be opposed. And opposed with the same fervor that animated the great martyrs of the church as they marched serenely to their deaths, confident they were doing the will of God. On the other hand, science has made great strides in explaining the natural world without invoking the supernatural, and those gains must be protected. If conceding a role for God in creation turns back the clock of scientific progress, then that must be opposed in honor of Galileo, Newton, and those who fought so valiantly to create intellectual space for natural explanations of natural phenomena.

Hysterical overreactions to trivia are the signature of conflicts with high stakes. Benefits accruing to one side must be opposed, not because they are wrong or even significant, but simply because anything that strengthens the "enemy" is bad. If shortening shoelaces by a millimeter makes creationists happy, then we must immediately launch a national campaign to keep shoelaces unchanged or perhaps even made longer.

The cartoonlike character of the creation–evolution controversy was all too apparent in 1995, when the National Association of Biology Teachers (NABT) published its "Statement on Teaching Evolution." Nominally motivated by a desire to help high-school teachers navigate the troubled waters of evolution, the document was instead a rhetorical Trojan horse, designed to eliminate whatever tiny role students may have been retaining for God in the process of evolution. The central part of the document contained the following definition: "The diversity of life on earth is the outcome of evolution: an unsupervised, impersonal, unpredictable and natural process of temporal descent with genetic modification that is affected by natural selection, chance, historical contingencies and changing environments."[9]

The NABT supposedly wanted to be helpful in clarifying for high-school teachers just how evolution should be understood. But it's hard to imagine what the NABT was thinking, or if it was thinking at all. The definition is quite inadequate on its own terms and unnecessarily offensive to the very sensibilities that made teaching evolution complex in the first place.

For starters, nobody understands the trajectory of evolution well enough to make *unpredictability* a part of its *definition*. Evolution, as understood by some of its leading and most respected theorists, like Simon Conway Morris of Cambridge University, does have a direction. Taking direct aim at Gould, Morris suggests: "Rerun the tape of life as often as you like, and the end results will be much the same."[10] Conway Morris notes that many interesting properties of organisms, from compound eyes, to the ability of bats and certain birds to echo-locate, to the intricate social structure of ants and bees, have evolved more than once.[11] If evolution was entirely unpredictable, we would not expect this. Robert Wright, in his provocative book *Non-Zero: The Logic of Human Destiny,* argues from game theory that certain evolutionary trajectories are naturally favored over others.[12]

Capabilities like vision and intelligence are so valuable to organisms that many, if not most, biologists believe they would probably arise under any normal evolutionary process. I suspect that the majority of evolutionists, if informed that life had just begun evolving on some distant planet, would anticipate that vision and intelligence would eventually appear. So how can evolution be entirely random, if certain sophisticated end points are predictable? Evolution is like the path of a water molecule making its way down the side of mountain—unpredictable on a small scale but certainly not without a general direction. The NABT's claim that *unpredictability* should be a part of the definition of evolution was, to say the least, misleading.

The definition also states that natural selection, chance, historical contingencies, and changing environments are the factors affecting evolution. This list is presented as apparently exhaustive. How does the NABT *know* that these four factors are the only ones to be considered? Does it know already that no undiscovered laws of biochemistry and no mathematically preferred genetic patterns come into play?

The definition's greatest controversy arose from the words *unsupervised* and *impersonal.* These are peculiar terms in the context of a scientific definition. Since when is "supervision" something that science comments on? If the NABT read the definitions of other concepts in science, it would certainly have noticed that *nobody* uses the descriptor *unsupervised.* Do students learning chemistry or geology have to understand the natural phenomena of those disciplines as "unsupervised"? Similar problems attend the use of the word *impersonal.* The only possible role played by these two words is the expulsion of God from the evolutionary process. Who, exactly, is the "supervisor" who is not there? And what is the "personal" involvement being excluded?

Some distinguished philosophers pointed these problems out to the NABT, arguing that the definition made *theological* claims that went beyond science. Furthermore, they suggested that this definition would boomerang and ultimately prove counterproductive. Anti-evolutionists would eagerly endorse the definition, highlighting its clear incompatibility with religion, thus enlarging the gap between the scientific community and religious believers. The statement, they wrote, "gives aid and comfort to extremists in the religious right for whom it provides a legitimate target." Deleting the two loaded words would "defuse tensions" that were causing "unnecessary problems."[13] Wise counsel, indeed.

It would be nice to report that the NABT was simply careless in creating its inflammatory definition and, once that was pointed out, it happily changed it to reduce the controversy that makes evolution so hard to teach in the first place. However, this is not what happened.

The board of the NABT met in October 1997 to consider the recommendation that the theological terms be removed from the definition. After consideration, it voted *unanimously* to leave the terms in place and the definition unchanged. In pure culture-wars reasoning it explained that modifying the definition would give creationists "aid and comfort."[14] Never mind whether the terms were appropriate or not, the issue at stake was the comfort of the enemy. If doing the right thing comforts the enemy, then we mustn't do the right thing. It might be misconstrued as apologizing.

The NABT eventually made the suggested changes, but only after the level-headed and politically savvy anti-creationist Eugenie Scott convinced that body the offensive definition would come back to haunt it. The words *unsupervised* and *impersonal* were removed; the scientific content of the definition was, of course, unchanged by these deletions. Evolution was now like chemistry, geology, and football. God, if he exists, was allowed to watch.

WAR OF THE WORDS: ROUND TWO

A similar war of words occurred in 2001 when creationist senator Rick Santorum added the following language to an education bill dealing with the "No Child Left Behind" program:

> Good science education should prepare students to distinguish the data or testable theories of science from philosophical or religious claims that are made in the name of science; and ... where biological *evolution* is taught, the curriculum should help students to understand why the subject generates so much continuing controversy, and should prepare the students to be informed participants in public discussions regarding the subject.

At face value, this paragraph looks quite sensible. After all, evolution is constantly in the news and students—and their parents—are certainly going to be interested in why. Evolution is the only topic in the curriculum that is there by court order. Once upon a time it was illegal to teach it in some states. The most famous intellectual contest on American soil was over evolution. Half the country rejects the theory, despite the confident endorsements of the scientific community. Would it not be prudent to help students understand why evolution is so controversial?

The Senate apparently thought so and passed the bill 91 to 8. The version passed by the House, however, did not contain Santorum's amendment, so a committee met to reconcile the two versions of the bill. By now, however, Santorum's amendment was out in the open, and culture warriors on both sides were talking strategy. Because creationists hailed the language as something of a victory, the champions of evolution became alarmed. Anything that makes creationists happy must be bad. The scientific community responded in the form of a letter not unlike the one that the NABT received earlier regarding evolution. The letter outlined objections to Santorum's amendment and, just in case the logic of the letter was not adequately convincing, it was signed by representatives of almost a hundred scientific organizations.

"The apparently innocuous statements in this resolution," they wrote, "mask an anti-evolution agenda that repeatedly has been rejected by the courts." They objected that the language "singles out biological evolution as a controversial subject," even though "from the standpoint of science there is no controversy." Evolution, they said, was like Einstein's theory of relativity—"robust, generally accepted, thoroughly tested and broadly applicable."[15]

Comparing evolution to relativity in this way is ludicrous, and I speak as someone who has taught both topics for years to college students. Relativity is a simple theory and easy to test in a comprehensive way; it deals with a limited range of phenomena and attempts nothing so ambitious as the reconstruction of the history of life on this planet. Virtually all of it was worked out decades ago, and so little remains to do that there is limited activity in the field. I can't recall the last time something significant emerged out of relativity theory, and one can teach the subject from a textbook that is fifty years old.[16]

In contrast, evolution is vibrant and challenging, with tremendous activity and daily breakthroughs. And although it is technically true that the scientific community is reasonably united behind evolutionary theory, there are significant controversies within the field about details. Two of its leading theorists, Dawkins and Gould, both penned massive works within the past few years defending very different explanations of how evolution works.[17] Conway Morris thinks they both got it wrong.[18] Evolution contains plenty of controversy. The combatants agree that evolution is true, but that is not the same as agreeing on how it occurred. But we don't want students to know this, of course, lest it make them vulnerable to creationism. Never mind that the controversy about how evolution works is the single most interesting topic in all of science.

In marked contrast to evolution, opposition to relativity is not constantly—or even occasionally—in the news. No law has ever ruled that it could not be taught in school, or that a competing view must have equal time, or that it, and it alone, must be taught. Most students don't even encounter relativity, since it appears only in advanced physics courses avoided by all but the most elite students. Virtually none of the senators receiving the letter assuring them that evolution was like relativity could have made even an introductory comment about relativity.

There is only one theory in all of science that generates constant controversy. Acknowledging that fact is hardly "singling out" that theory for special consideration. Evolution is already getting plenty of consideration. If a theory generates this much controversy, would it not be appropriate to take note of this in those classes where it comes up?

Despite the obvious problems with the letter, it was signed by the heads of every imaginable scientific society—and some unimaginable ones—most with no vested interest of any sort in the teaching of evolution. The American Astronomical Society signed it, as did its counterparts in chemistry, physics, geology, meteorology, and even mathematics and linguistics. Several psychological societies weighed in, as did the American Political Science Association. Geographers were represented—we can't have the creationists redrawing the coastlines or doing away with latitude. The president of the Freshwater Mollusk Conservation Society signed it. And we must not forget the American Fern or Clay Minerals societies. Even the CEO of "Shape Up America!" signed it.

What was going on here? Why was the president of the Freshwater Mollusk Conservation Society weighing in on this issue? What was at stake? Why were so many mighty soldiers being recruited to fight so tiny a battle?

On the other hand, we must wonder why the creationists were loading this sort of baggage onto an otherwise straightforward education bill, hidden at the back where it was unlikely to be seen. Phillip Johnson, the leader of the ID movement, had actually drafted the language for Santorum, so there clearly was a "conspiracy" of some sort to get this language into the bill. Obviously the creationists and ID supporters believed this bill would crack open some door through which they might smuggle something of interest to them into America's public schools.

The answer is, quite simply, that evolution has become the focal point of a culture war, which means that the goal of the protagonists is to *win,* not to discover the truth. Conceding minor points to your opponents, using inoffensive language, working out compromises, and finding middle ground are simply not allowed. Too much is at stake for such wimpy pussyfooting.

How else can we explain the offensive definition of the NABT? Or Santorum's sneaky insertion of language into an education bill? Or the crazed overreaction to the Santorum amendment, which, by the way, was removed, allowing the president of the Freshwater Mollusk Conservation Society to sleep much better at night.

EVOLUTION'S PERENNIAL CULTURE WAR

When Galileo quarreled with the Roman Catholic Church in the seventeenth century over the motion of the earth, the political dimensions of the conflict were lopsided. The church had the power to put Galileo on trial, sentence him to house arrest, and, if we can trust Catholic theology, excommunicate him and consign his soul to hell; in contrast, Galileo had little more than the strength of his arguments. And, at the time, these were not compelling.

Science in Galileo's century was young. It was both nurtured and constrained by the church. Because later developments vindicated Galileo, the verdict of history—at least popular history—is that the church abused its power in dealing with Galileo. This verdict has haunted the Roman Catholic Church ever since, as every generation has created for itself a new Galileo—a scientific martyr to wave in the face of the church when they disagreed with it.[19]

Two hundred years later, when Darwin published his controversial theory, science was a more substantial cultural force. Nevertheless, the church remained socially and politically powerful, and Darwin had to struggle against far more than simply opposing ideas. On an intensely personal level, this included his wife's theology and strong Christian faith. Darwin's persistent nervous disorders may have resulted from his concern about placing himself at odds with those he loved.

On a larger scale, Victorian society still retained many of the political structures through which the church had historically wielded its power. Ecclesiastical authorities sometimes maligned the champions of evolution for undercutting religion. Social pressures were brought to bear in ways that were deeply resented by honest scientists who simply wanted a fair hearing for their ideas. Like parents who can send children to bed when an argument starts going poorly, religious authorities were resented when they used the power of religion to settle disputes about which they knew nothing. Darwin's clerical contemporaries turned many away from evolution by claiming it was incompatible with the Bible. More recently, on the other side of the Atlantic, Henry Morris convinced millions of Americans that evolution is a satanic theory, at odds with the Bible and the Christian faith. As a political strategy this works wonderfully. No need to engage the scientific issues and open that can of worms—you simply poison the theory, so people will reject it without troubling themselves over whether it is right or wrong.

For all of its history, as we have seen in earlier chapters, evolution has been embedded in larger and often more substantial agendas than simply the history of life on this planet. William Jennings Bryan blamed it for World War I. Hitler's henchmen appealed to it to rationalize their genocide. Andrew Carnegie invoked it to promote unfettered capitalism. Eugenicists used it to justify mandatory sterilization of the "feebleminded."

Hostile creationists continue to blame evolution for everything from pornography to drug abuse. Evolution, in their eyes, is the root of all evil. Likewise, eager evolutionists appeal to the theory to explain rape and infanticide. Bystanders can't help but be nervous, but they dare not disbelieve, lest they turn into buffoons.

Those who oppose evolution, for whatever reason, or suggest that it might not be the full story, or look for some small role for God inevitably find ridicule raining down on their poor benighted heads. Dawkins, the leading public spokesperson for evolution, labels them "ignorant, stupid, or insane (or wicked ...)."[20] You *must* believe ...

EVOLUTION AS RELIGION

The promotion of evolution—both biological and cosmic—by its champions grows ever more evangelical as time goes by. Proponents sound more and more like preachers. Who can forget the priestly image of Carl Sagan standing behind his scientific pulpit on *Cosmos,* with majestic music and inspiring images in the background? The book titles sound increasingly religious—*Darwin's Cathedral, River Out of Eden, The Devil's Chaplain, The Creation, The Demon-Haunted World, The Dragons of Eden, The First Three Minutes, The God Gene, In the Beginning.*

Recently the long arm of evolutionary explanation has reached directly into territory where traditionally religious phenomena reside. Evolutionary theory now provides naturalistic explanations for altruism, morality, our religiosity and predisposition to believe in God, even the love we feel for our children. It explains "sin" and offers explanations for rape, infanticide, and the pervasive genocide that plagues our planet. Evolution now provides a rich and satisfying creation story—a scientific myth displacing the religious origins myth in the Bible. Evolution offers a source of meaning and an explanation for good and evil.

Is it any wonder that evolution and creation are locked in mortal combat? No longer do we seek a peaceful coexistence for science and religion, for the former now insists it has devoured the latter. The creation myth of our time is, as the original NABT definition stated, impersonal and unsupervised.

The obvious objection to all this is, of course, that it isn't true. Few evolutionary biologists think this way, and many are on record arguing that science has no business setting up camp in religious territory. Unfortunately, those who promote this conciliatory arrangement are a silent majority, all but invisible, missing from bookstands and public television.

In contrast, virtually all the leading spokespersons for science—the ones on bookstands and public television—are strongly antireligious. Even though religious belief is common in the scientific community, it is almost nonexistent among scientists who have become public figures. Richard Dawkins, Steven Weinberg, E. O. Wilson, Stephen Jay Gould, Carl Sagan,

Stephen Hawking, Steven Pinker, Francis Crick, Peter Atkins—all have (or had) considerable stature in the scientific community. But they are all hostile to religion and see it as something to be "explained away" by science. Even Gould and Wilson, the diplomats of the group, treat religion in a way that offends most religious people.

These are the scientists who have been setting the agenda, leading the larger cultural discussions of our time, creating the image of science in popular culture. They exert enormous influence on public perceptions of science and play roles in our society similar to those of the oracles of ancient Greece—delivering deep messages about the way things really are.

Dawkins, for example, is probably the leading public intellectual in the English-speaking world and uniquely a member of both scientific and literary societies; Wilson was recognized by *Time* as the seventeenth most influential person of the twentieth century and has won two Pulitzer Prizes; Weinberg and Crick are Nobel laureates. Gould has appeared on *The Simpsons,* in a special episode parodying his suggestion that science and religion should be "nonoverlapping magisteria." (The episode closes with a judge ordering religion to stay five hundred yards away from science at all times.) Hawking packs large auditoriums in his public appearances and has written a runaway best seller. Sagan was once one of the most recognizable people on the planet. Pinker is Harvard's "celebrity professor."

These thinkers—who all endorse fully naturalistic evolution with enthusiasm—are communicators par excellence. Their writings are models of clarity and eloquence; there is no doubt that they take communication seriously, despite being (or having been) active scholars within their fields who also publish in technical journals. Now, if all that Dawkins and company were doing was popularizing science, there would no cause for alarm. But an examination of the writings of this group reveals a larger agenda, one of breathtaking scope and ambition. In addition to lucid expositions of a wide range of scientific concepts from DNA to consciousness, we find suggestions that science should replace religion.

The idea that science should be a religion on its own runs like a subterranean reservoir through the writing of these popularizers, gurgling beneath the surface and bubbling into view every time the conversation gets to the now-here-is-what-it-all-means phase. In the closing paragraphs of long books about science, the exposition suddenly morphs into theology. The scientist is transformed into an oracle, telling us something grand and important that is, surprisingly, so much larger than the story unfolded in the previous pages. Readers are subtly carried to the top of a grand scientific mountain and offered a view of the promised land.

Marvel at the "ancestor's tale," writes Dawkins in a book of the same name, and note how much grander it is than the fairy tales of Genesis. Let science lift you above farce, says Weinberg, and provide some meaning in this pointless universe. Worship the evolutionary epic preaches Wilson. Harness the energy being squandered in traditional religions and redirect it where it might do some good; seek out a theory of everything, says Hawking, for there you find the mind of God. Celebrate the cosmos, says Sagan, for it is "all that is, ever was, or ever will be." Marvel at the luck that brought you here, says Gould, for natural history reveals no purposeful trajectory from simple organisms to us.

When the NABT proposed the controversial definition of evolution discussed above, there was at least a semblance of objectivity and, in the final analysis, it did provide a definition that was certainly less overtly antireligious than it might have been. The problem is that few people, except for high-school biology teachers and scholars following the creation–evolution controversy, have even heard of the NABT. Ordinary Americans are far more likely to encounter discussions of evolution, and science in general, in popular presentations.

Books about evolution, for example, appear on the nonfiction best-seller lists; PBS science programs and radio talk shows often deal with evolution; and leading evolutionary thinkers are often quoted in news stories. In such settings it is rarely advantageous to speak with dispassionate scientific objectivity. Audiences want excitement, hyperbole, and controversy; if you can provide that, you will be quoted. If you say that creationists are "stupid, wicked, or insane," journalists will return to you for commentary on subsequent controversies. The media are no respecters of scientific boundaries, and few journalists will scold a scientist for stepping outside the bounds of science to say something colorful, no matter how irresponsible.

When scientists speak as scientists, as they would when writing for scientific journals or presenting results at conferences, they are scrupulously careful to the point of tedium to maintain a strict silence on questions outside of science. Evolution, when discussed in the prestigious journals

Nature and *Science,* for example, would never be described as "unsupervised" or proposed as a replacement creation story. Critics would never be labeled "wicked" or "insane." But when a scientist writes or speaks to popular audiences, the rules change dramatically.

Dawkins is the worst offender. He has written many popular books on evolution, and in 2004 he published a 614-page opus titled *The Ancestor's Tale.* This magisterial work traces the history of life on this planet from its beginnings to the present, explicating our best understanding of that process. The content is mainstream science popularization carried along by outstanding prose and unencumbered by philosophical and theological asides. In the final three paragraphs of the book, however, as he draws his grand narrative to a close, he reflects on the meaning of what he has done:

> I have not had occasion here to mention my impatience with traditional piety, and my disdain for reverence where the object is anything supernatural. But I make no secret of them. It is not because I wish to limit or circumscribe reverence; not because I want to reduce or downgrade the true reverence with which we are moved to celebrate the universe, once we understand it properly. "On the contrary" would be an understatement. My objection to supernatural beliefs is precisely that they miserably fail to do justice to the sublime grandeur of the real world. They represent a narrowing-down from reality, an impoverishment of what the real world has to offer.[21]

Carl Sagan offered similar reflections in the final paragraph of the 345-page *Cosmos,* on which the television series was based:

> We are the local embodiment of a Cosmos grown to self-awareness. We have begun to contemplate our origins: starstuff pondering the stars; organized assemblages of ten billion billion billion atoms considering the evolution of atoms; tracing the long journey by which, here at least, consciousness arose. Our loyalties are to the species and the planet. *We* speak for Earth. Our obligation to survive is owed not just to ourselves but also to that Cosmos, ancient and vast, from which we spring.[22]

Stephen Jay Gould, who desperately wanted to be a mediator between science and religion, was nevertheless insistent that evolution was purposeless and without direction. Unchecked by the referees that brought the NABT to its senses, he wrote in the final paragraph of the 323-page *Wonderful Life:*

> And so, if you wish to ask the question of the ages—why do humans exist?—a major part of the answer, touching those aspects of the issue that science can treat at all, must be: because *Pikaia* survived the Burgess decimation. This response does not cite a single law of nature; it embodies no statement about predictable evolutionary pathways, no calculation of probabilities based on general rules of anatomy or ecology. The survival of *Pikaia* was a contingency of "just history." I do not think that any "higher" answer can be given, and I cannot imagine that any resolution could be more fascinating. We are the offspring of history, and must establish our own paths in this most diverse and interesting of conceivable universes—one indifferent to our suffering, and therefore offering us maximal freedom to thrive, or to fail, in our own chosen way.[23]

E. O. Wilson is arguably our greatest living scientist, the founder of the field of evolutionary psychology and humanity's most eloquent conservationist. His recent book *The Creation* was written as a series of letters to pastors, encouraging them to join him on his crusade to protect the environment. Nevertheless, despite the value he places on religious communities as partners in care for the planet, he ultimately intends that religion will be explained by science. Near the end of his Pulitzer Prize–winning *On Human Nature,* he writes:

> If religion, including the dogmatic secular ideologies, can be systematically analyzed and explained as a product of the brain's evolution, its power as an external source of morality will be gone forever and the solution of the second dilemma will have become a practical necessity.... What I am suggesting, in the end, is that the evolutionary epic is probably the best myth we will ever have. It can be adjusted until it comes as close to truth as the human mind is constructed to judge the truth. And if that is the case, the mythopoeic requirements of the mind must somehow be met by scientific materialism so as to reinvest our superb energies.[24]

Nobel laureate Steven Weinberg ends his classic *The First Three Minutes* with these widely discussed reflections:

It is very hard to realize that this all is just a tiny part of an overwhelmingly hostile universe. It is even harder to realize that this present universe has evolved from an unspeakably unfamiliar early condition, and faces a future extinction of endless cold or intolerable heat. The more the universe seems comprehensible, the more it also seems pointless.

But if there is no solace in the fruits of our research, there is at least some consolation in the research itself. Men and women are not content to comfort themselves with tales of gods and giants, or to confine their thoughts to the daily affairs of life; they also build telescopes and satellites and accelerators, and sit at their desks for endless hours working out the meaning of the data they gather. The effort to understand the universe is one of the very few things that lifts human life a little above the level of farce, and gives it some of the grace of tragedy.[25]

Identical sentiments can be found in the writings of other leading science popularizers as well. The few mentioned above are simply the best known and most influential.

For better or worse, mainly worse, the content and significance of evolutionary theory is communicated to broad audiences by people like Dawkins. Suppose you wander into a typical bookstore, say Barnes & Noble, and ask the manager for a book that would help you "understand evolution, what it is, and what it all means." The manager may likely point you to Dawkins's *The Blind Watchmaker*. A blurb from the *Economist* on the back cover suggests that the book is "as readable and vigorous a defense of Darwinism as has been published since 1859." E. O. Wilson of Harvard calls it "the best general account of evolution I have read in recent years." The author, a chaired professor at Oxford University, is well credentialed. Nowhere is there so much as a *hint* that *The Blind Watchmaker* is anything other than a superb articulation of Darwin's theory of evolution.

As you read the book, perhaps wondering about the relationship between evolution and your belief that God created everything, or at least was involved in some way, you gradually discover that evolution is absolutely incompatible with the idea that God created the world. *The Blind Watchmaker* presents you with a choice—either accept evolution and be on the side of science, enlightenment, progress, and truth or accept creation and be against science, on the side of superstition, darkness, and irrelevance. Just six pages into the book you encounter the following claim: "Although atheism might have been *logically* tenable before Darwin, Darwin made it possible to be an intellectually fulfilled atheist."[26]

Dawkins's claims might disturb you enough to make you seek a second opinion. Returning to the bookstore, you pick up other popular books by leading biologists and philosophers of biology and discover they agree with Dawkins. The leading spokespersons for evolution almost all say the theory refutes and replaces the traditional belief that God created everything. And many of them write with unbridled glee about this state of affairs, as if replacing belief in creation is the most important feature of evolution.

Now suppose you go to a Christian bookstore looking for another perspective. In a surprising twist, you encounter this identical argument in the writings of the anti-evolutionists. The architect of modern creationism, the late Henry Morris, describes evolution as Satan's "long war against God." And, despite the oddness of that claim, you take note that Morris is a solid academic, with a real Ph.D. and an impressive academic career. He is no fraud posturing with a fake degree and pretending to be a scientist. Morris and his fellow creationists believe that evolution has no supporting evidence and is literally nothing more than an alternative creation story to make atheists happy and fulfilled.

"There is no scientific proof," Morris writes, "that vertically-upward evolution occurs today, has even occurred in the past, or is even possible at all, yet it is widely promoted as a proven fact."[27] Nevertheless, despite evolution being scientifically vacuous, he concludes that "evolutionism is the proximate cause of the world's evils, for it is the basic belief and deceptive tool of Satan."[28]

Creationist Jonathan Sarfati, with a Ph.D. in physical chemistry, makes a similar point at the beginning of *Refuting Evolution:* "The framework behind the evolutionists' interpretation is naturalism—it is assumed that things made themselves, that no divine intervention has happened, and that God has not revealed to us knowledge about the past." "Evolution" Sarfati argues, "is a deduction from this assumption" rather than an inference from observations of the natural world.[29]

Phillip Johnson's strategy is based on his conviction that a blinkered and deluded commitment to naturalism is the reason scientists can't see the weaknesses of evolutionary theory—why they miss the clear evidence for design in DNA, in the blood-clotting mechanism, in the flagella of the bacteria, and elsewhere. In his assault on naturalism, titled *Reason in the Balance,* he writes:

> What is presented to the public as scientific knowledge about evolutionary mechanisms is mostly philosophical speculation and is not even consistent with the evidence once the naturalistic spectacles are removed. If that leaves us without a known mechanism of biological creation, so be it: it is better to admit ignorance than to have confidence in an explanation that is not true.[30]

For those whose worldviews include Satan as an omnipresent evil personality, evolution is precisely the sort of deception that makes sense. Convince people they are the product of a random, purposeless, cruel process, and atheism, moral anarchy, and decadent reality shows about wife swapping won't be far behind. Even without Satan the charges above are damning, although not quite so literally. If evolution starts with the assumption that there is no God and then selectively and deceptively assembles a case to rationalize this starting point, the scientific community is no different than a team of creepy defense lawyers working to free rapists and serial killers they know are guilty.

Such ad hominem attacks on the integrity of science seem unfair. Surely the scientific community that put a man on the moon, wiped out smallpox, and built the iPod is not engaged in this sort of shady enterprise. Significantly, though, some prominent members of the scientific community agree that their enterprise *is* all about making God obsolete. They admit they will defend and even promote preposterous notions, rather than admit that God might have some relevance to understanding the natural world. A leading geneticist, Richard Lewontin, has stated this commitment with impressive, if unrepresentative, candor:

> We take the side of science *in spite* of the patent absurdity of some of its constructs, *in spite* of its failure to fulfill many of its extravagant promises of health and life, *in spite* of the tolerance of the scientific community for unsubstantiated just-so stories, because we have a prior commitment, a commitment to materialism. It is not that the methods and institutions of science somehow compel us to accept a material explanation of the phenomenal world, but, on the contrary, that we are forced by our *a priori* adherence to

material causes to create an apparatus of investigation and a set of concepts that produce material explanations, no matter how counter-intuitive, no matter how mystifying to the uninitiated. Moreover, that materialism is an absolute, for we cannot allow a Divine Foot in the door.[31]

Lewontin's honesty is interesting and, despite what looks like a disturbing admission of the very blindness that Johnson has assaulted, Lewontin's views are echoed by many scientists who have taken the time to describe its inner workings.

Another evolutionary biologist describes science as a "game with one overriding and defining rule," namely, that science "explain the behavior of the physical and material universe in terms of purely physical and material causes, without invoking the supernatural."[32] A leading Cornell University historian of science, William Provine, has written that "biology leads to a wholly mechanistic view of life." This view cannot be reconciled with belief in God: "The frequently made assertion that modern biology and assumptions of the Judeo-Christian tradition are fully compatible is false."[33]

THE CULTURE WAR

Viewed by these lights, the creation–evolution controversy is far more than a debate over the origin and development of life on this planet, the age of the earth, or the relationship between humans and the rest of the animal kingdom. The controversy is about the larger question of who decides what the nature of ultimate reality is. Will Dawkins and his merry band of materialistic naysayers provide the creation story for our culture? Or will it be Johnson and his underdog team of designer Christians? Dawkins and Johnson agree that the choice is a real one, the alternatives are incompatible, and the consequences significant.

In his recent projects, Dawkins clarifies that his agenda is not simply the promotion of evolution, or even the "public understanding of science," as his endowed professorship at Oxford is titled. His agenda is the destruction of religion. He produced a documentary on religion for British television titled "The Root of All Evil." His recent book was called, provocatively, *The God Delusion*. His 2003 Tanner Lectures at Harvard were titled *The Science of Religion and the Religion of Science*. On these occasions he assaulted religion with venom not seen since an angry mob offered Jesus up for crucifixion. Dawkins and his followers, in their Oxbridge and Ivy League professorial robes, lament that the great engine of secularization has stalled and religion is making a comeback. Forget Darwin and widespread cultural confusion about evolution; the troops must be rallied to oppose religion.

Johnson is a mirror image of Dawkins. He sees in naturalism the same pernicious cultural cancer Dawkins sees in religion. His interest in evolution derives entirely from its role as an important part of the foundation for naturalism. His agenda for destroying naturalism is to use weaknesses in evolution as openings into which to insert his "wedge." Everyone knows, however, that if evolution collapsed without also bringing down naturalism, he would keep on fighting.

Dawkins, Gould, Weinberg, Provine, Pinker, Dennett, and Atkins versus Johnson, Morris, Dembski, Wise, Wells, Meyer, and Behe. Atheism versus theism. Evolution versus creation.

Evolution has been embroiled in this kind of controversy since before Darwin published *On the Origin of Species by Means of Natural Selection* in 1859. Enthusiastic polemicists were forever looking into the deep well of its grand story and seeing their reflections. Thomas Huxley saw a weapon to wield against the clerics and their archaic political power. Andrew Carnegie saw a rationalization for unbridled capitalism. Privileged Victorians saw a rationale for ignoring the plight of England's poor. Herbert Spencer saw a "might makes right" moral code. William Jennings Bryan saw the roots of World War I. Nazis saw a rationale for genocide. American social planners saw a rationale for eugenics. Fascists looked at evolution and saw fascism; Marxists saw Marxism; free-market enthusiasts saw capitalism. Now today, Harvard's Steven Pinker sees in evolution an explanation for infanticide; Randy Thornhill and Craig Palmer see an explanation for rape.[34] Evolutionary psychologists see the genetic basis of male philandering and playground bullying. But they also see the genetic basis for brotherly love and sacrificial care for one's children.

Is this Darwin's theory of evolution—this catchall story of origins that can be adapted as the scientific basis of everything from capitalism to brotherly love? For the majority of scientists, excluding the few who write books with titles like *The God Delusion,* evolution is simply the central idea in biology. They would like to see evolution taught in America's high-school biology classes and are frustrated that this poses such a problem.

Darwinism, however, cannot escape its rich, complex, troubling, exhilarating, sobering, and inspiring history. Evolution in the labs, in the field, and in the textbooks may actually be nothing more than a central biological theory of great utility, uniting a broad range of natural phenomena under a single explanatory umbrella. But, in ways that have no analog anywhere else in all of science, evolution is connected to a host of other ideas, some very disturbing. To suppose, as so many do, that evolution can be disconnected from these ideas and taught purely as science is naive. To argue, on the other hand, that evolution derives from these ideas is simply wrong. No wonder the conversation is going nowhere.

CHAPTER 8

EVOLUTION AND PHYSICS ENVY

On September 22, 1919, Albert Einstein received a telegram that said: "Eddington found star displacement at rim of sun." Sir Arthur Eddington was England's greatest astronomer. And he had just determined that light beams from stars in the Hyades cluster deflected as they passed near the sun on their way to earth. The deflection made the stars appear in a different location in the sky, just as a spoon in water will appear to be bent. Eddington's ambitious observation, made during a total eclipse on an island off the coast of West Africa, tested Einstein's theory of general relativity. This theory, destined to overturn Isaac Newton's venerable explanation for gravity, suggested that "empty" space was *warped* by gravitational masses like the sun. As a test of his novel theory, Einstein predicted that light beams passing through this warped space would be deflected.

Einstein's prediction was bold and reckless. If the light had not deflected, his theory would have collapsed and a decade of hard work would have been lost. But when his prediction came true, the theory was confirmed. An oversized *New York Times* headline on November 10 declared, "Lights All Askew in the Heavens," celebrating the arrival of Einstein's theory. The few who understood were deeply impressed. A theory challenging Newton's durable explanation had predicted an exotic physical effect. Eddington observed the effect. Newton, quite literally, had just been eclipsed by Einstein.

The precision and rigor of these tests of Einstein's theory impressed Sir Karl Popper, Europe's greatest philosopher of science. How could a theory so remarkably confirmed *not* be true? And what intellectual courage and confidence Einstein showed in developing such a *risky* prediction—a prediction that could have *falsified* his theory. Surely this was science at its best—

rigorously empirical, testable, objective, and, ultimately, *true*. Should not the generation of such predictions be the hallmark of *all* scientific theories?

Popper developed this idea into an influential definition of science. All genuinely scientific theories, he argued, must make novel predictions about unknown phenomena. These predictions must be articulated so clearly that that they can be conclusively refuted by observation. And if the predictions fail, the theory has been falsified. If a theory *cannot* make such falsifiable predictions, then it cannot claim to be scientific.

Evolutionary theory, however, because of its scope, complexity, and dependence on history, does not lend itself to this kind of simple analysis, which led Popper to reject it initially as a pseudoscience. The scope of evolution's explanatory power is breathtaking, however, and eventually Popper changed his mind. In this chapter I want to spotlight evolutionary theory's remarkable capacity to unite disparate observations of the natural world. Seemingly unrelated patterns in nature become part of a coordinated package when brought under the explanatory umbrella of evolution, although not exactly in the simple and elegant way that Popper would have preferred.

Despite its problems, the falsifiability criterion developed by Popper was broadly admired and promoted as a simple test to distinguish authentically scientific ideas from pseudoscientific imposters. As the twentieth century unfolded, the falsifiability yardstick would be laid alongside many ideas to see how they measured up. In the 1982 creationism trial in Little Rock, Arkansas, for example, Judge William Overton ruled that creationism could not make falsifiable predictions and thus was not science.[1] The creationist claim that an invisible being using processes not now operating created all life on earth could not generate falsifiable predictions. Therefore, it could not claim to be scientific.

Creationists, in a clever response, use Popper's falsifiability criterion to argue that *evolution* is not science.[2] In his autobiography, *Unended Quest,* Popper fanned this particular flame by lumping evolution together with Marxism and Freudian psychology as pseudoscientific metaphysics. He later changed his mind about evolution,[3] a reversal that has escaped the attention of the creationists, who continue to invoke him.[4]

Popper contrasted these pseudosciences with general relativity, noting that the latter made truly falsifiable and thus genuinely scientific claims about the world. The vagueness and unlimited flexibility of Freudian,

Marxist, and, for a time, Darwinian explanations distressed Popper. Marxism, to take one example, predicted the exploitation of workers by bosses, but when counterexamples were found—such as companies that paid good salaries to their workers—Marxists would explain those as a different or subtler form of exploitation. The unexpected counterexamples were strangely incapable of falsifying the theory. Marxism, in fact, couldn't seem to make *any* predictions that, if they failed, would refute the theory.

Creationists—and the early Popper—see the same sort of wishy-washy can't-be-falsified explanations in evolution. Early Darwinists, and Darwin himself, predicted the existence of countless transitional forms in the fossil record. When those were not found, however, the theory was adjusted to accommodate the failed prediction rather than rejected as falsified. This contrasted dramatically with general relativity, which handed an ax to Eddington and then placed its scientific neck firmly on the chopping block of observation.

Pseudosciences, argued Popper, were not science, but *ideology,* and their signature was the blind devotion of their advocates, who forever adjusted their "theory" to square it with anomalous data, rather than subject it to genuine testing. Eventually such false ideologies masquerading as science would be exposed and abandoned.

Popper began his thoughtful and devastating critiques of the theories of Freud, Marx, and Darwin in the early decades of the twentieth century. Subsequent developments proved him partially right. Marxism has indeed all but died except around a small table in North Korea; its central ideas turned out to be anachronistic ideology, and its founder has faded into the canvas of history. Ditto for Freud. Darwinism, in contrast, has not died, but rather has grown steadily stronger and more influential. Few philosophers today would reject it as unscientific. And, of course, even Popper, in a rare act of intellectual humility, reversed his earlier stance on evolution.

Nearly a century later, relativity and evolution are still being juxtaposed. When the National Association of Biology Teachers defended evolution against charges that it was "only a theory," it compared it to relativity. If relativity's claims to truth were not compromised by its status as a theory, then evolution, it argued, can hardly be criticized for being "only" a theory.

But, on the other hand, creationists and intelligent design enthusiasts remind us just how inferior the theory of evolution is to theories in physics. Physical theories present their conclusions in tidy mathematical equations—

think $E = mc^2$. The relevant phenomena can be demonstrated in laboratory experiments and in public displays at science museums. Impressive technological spin-offs bathe the underlying science in the warm glow of credibility. Evolution, alas, offers nothing but vague generalities—"the fittest survive"—and invokes entities like "common ancestors" or processes like "speciation," for which the evidence is often depressingly small and indirect. That slippery and mysterious character named "chance" plays a central, but vague, role in the great drama of evolution. The process is driven by an elusive and all-but-unobservable metaphor called "natural selection" conferring "reproductive advantage" on organisms. Most of the work of evolution is done by mutations that occur in species that go extinct and leave no trace. Species that go extinct without leaving any evidence that they ever existed bear an unfortunate resemblance to fairies and leprechauns.

The theory of evolution, embedded in biology as it is, bears little resemblance to theories in physics. The disciplines are quite different. The phenomena they study have little overlap, and even the scientists in the two fields are different. When Francis Crick, who won the 1962 Nobel Prize for determining the structure of DNA, moved from physics to biology, he found the transition so dramatic that it was "almost as if one had to be born again." Crick recalls having to consciously abandon the physicists' intuition about nature's "elegance and deep simplicity." Physicists, he warned, are apt to "concoct theoretical models that are too neat, too powerful, and too clean."[5]

Crick observed what Popper had noted a few decades earlier. But Popper, like most philosophers of science before and since, had been bewitched by the grandeur of physics, with its elegant laws and imposing mathematical language. He saw it as the paradigm for all of science, setting an unreasonable standard that other sciences could not possibly reach.

THE SIMPLE LIFE

Physics is science at one extreme of simplicity. Physicists study incredibly simple natural phenomena, like the forces between bodies in space or the behavior of electrons orbiting around nuclei—phenomena that can actually be *thoroughly* understood. I earned a Ph.D. by studying helium atoms for three years and understood them very well by the time I graduated. By restricting its focus to simple systems, physics produces seductively elegant explanations. These explanations are expressed in compact mathematical equations making specific quantitative predictions. The simplicity and thoroughness of such explanations, however, are not due to physicists' superior scientific practices, as many have misconstrued, but to physicists' selection of the simplest problems on which to work. It is no accident that physics was the first science to develop historically or that its first major accomplishment—showing that the earth went around the sun rather than vice versa—was both theoretically trivial and mathematically elegant.

Creationists and ID enthusiasts like to argue, in concert with the early Popper, that evolution is not a science because it is not based on rigorous empirical evidence like physics; there are no "evolution in action" shows at the science museum to go with the whiz-bang electricity demonstrations. In contrast, the NABT argued exactly the opposite—that evolution is a science because it *is* like physics. Both arguments are hopelessly flawed.

THE STORY OF EVOLUTION

Evolution is a solid and robust scientific theory, because it explains many things about the world and relates countless otherwise disconnected facts to each other. It is *not* a science because it resembles physics. Evolution is a messy theory, however, with a history of dumb mistakes, serious errors, occasional fraud, and overconfident assertions. When its problems are gathered and packaged by clever polemicists like Phillip Johnson, Ken Ham, or the late Henry Morris, evolution comes off looking rather pale. Such a judgment, however, is uninformed. To be sure, the theory of evolution does indeed have problems, but these are little more than tiny holes in a vast tapestry of compelling explanation.

The fossil record, for starters, shows an unmistakable trajectory from simple to complex as we go from ancient strata to more recent. The distribution of animals around the globe, called biogeography, shows a clear pattern that suggests that closely related species evolved from each other. The universality of DNA as the structural language of every life-form suggests a global relatedness of all species. And the details of specific DNA patterns link different species to common ancestors with the same clarity that DNA evidence in modern courtrooms links criminals to their crimes. Mutations observed in species that are easy to study, like fruit flies, disclose a genetic code perched on the knife edge of predictability and creativity, exactly the kind of balance that enables reliable evolutionary change over time. Studies comparing the anatomy of different species reveal intriguing similarities that make no sense outside evolution. Developing embryos of different species show strange coincidences that make sense only if those species are related. New computer models based on evolution offer interesting explanations for such things as our preference to remember our cousins in our will rather than our neighbors.

These areas of investigation are quite independent of each other. The fossil data, for example, began to accumulate in the eighteenth century, two hundred years before DNA was understood and long before there was an evolutionary interpretation of that data. Biogeography was controversial before Darwin was born, as European naturalists argued with their American counterparts over which continent had the more important species.

The theory of evolution does not claim to be true because of a single dramatic prediction about the natural world, as was the case with relativity. No prediction made by evolution comes close to Einstein's prediction that gravity would bend light and cause stars in the heavens to appear in new locations. But it is precisely the whiz-bang character of relativity that makes it, in the final analysis, a narrow theory explaining a limited range of phenomena. A theory that can be dramatically confirmed by one observation can hardly explain a gigantic roster of disparate phenomena.

Evolution makes up for its lack of precision and mathematical rigor with its astonishing scope. Before Darwin, who could have imagined that the same theory would explain both the fossil record and the peculiar genetic similarities between disparate organisms? Who could have imagined that when genes and DNA were finally understood, they would confirm relationships between species that had already been inferred from other data, such as comparative anatomy? The convergence of so many unrelated lines of investigation is a compelling argument for the truth of evolution.

LIFE'S GRAND STORY

The modern story of evolution, as Richard Dawkins makes so clear, is a grand tale, evoking wonder and mystery. It crackles with surprise and controversy and raises deep questions. I want to outline briefly what evolution claims about the history of life on this planet, and then look at the lines of evidence suggesting that this story is, indeed, true. Evolution, although not without its puzzles and controversies, is now so well supported that it demands our assent. It also demands our rejection of the various alternatives at play in America.

The story begins with the appearance of the first living cell on the earth roughly four billion years ago. This singular event was preceded by ten billion years of cosmic evolution from the big bang, through the origins of the elements in stars, through the appearance of planet earth with its "just right" conditions for life, to the emergence of a chemical environment capable of hosting the first living cell. There is presently no generally accepted theory of how the first life-form arose, but several options have been proposed. The raw materials, of course, were not alive, but were capable of assembling into a complex structure with the capacity to reproduce itself. And once reproduction was initiated, evolution began.

The first cell made copies of itself. A primitive genetic code guided the cellular machinery to gather material from the local environment to enable this copying. Thus one cell became two, two became four, four became eight, and eight became many billion. Single-celled life was simple and robust. It was the only form of life on the planet for over three billion years and flourishes today in the form of the ubiquitous, resilient, and inextinguishable bacteria.

The machinery enabling a single cell to make another version of itself was an intriguing combination of accuracy and flexibility—accurate in that every copy was largely the same, but flexible in that there was room for small changes to occur without disrupting the entire process. Slightly different cells that could copy themselves faster or more often had an advantage. A cell reproducing itself slightly faster than its peers will, over the course of a million years, take over the world and drive its peers to extinction.

About a half billion years ago a change occurred that enabled single cells to clump together. Perhaps the chemical composition of the external membrane was altered so they could stick together, like primordial Velcro. In any event, multicellular life appeared, bringing with it the possibility of greater complexity. A collection of cells can specialize in ways that a single cell cannot. The cells on the outside can learn to monitor the external world and protect the interior cells from threats, like border guards in a country, vigilant about external invaders but undistracted by internal matters. The interior cells can redirect their resources toward other functions, like reproduction. And the whole can become greater than the sum of the parts as specialization takes over.

A complex, specialized, multicellular organism can evolve along many different paths. Reproductive flexibility can lead to exterior changes like hair, scales, or feathers. External light-sensitive cells can become sophisticated and turn into eyes. A central nervous system can become intelligent. Lungs and kidneys can clone backups. And so on. The more complex the organism, the more things there are to change and improve.

Reproductive flexibility means that virtually all of the members of a species will be slightly different from each other. These differences will include variations in just about everything. Variations enhancing the production of offspring will result in more organisms with those variations, until gradually every member of the species has them. Catholics, for example, believe in large families, which is why there are so many Catholics. Variations irrelevant to procreation will turn out to be, not surprisingly, irrelevant. And those that interfere with reproduction—like the Shaker sect's belief that sex is wrong—will gradually disappear.

New species spin off from their parent species, often because a geographical barrier, like a river, slices through their habitat. Separated from parent species and confronting different reproductive challenges, the orphaned group evolves along its own path until eventually it can no longer interbreed with the parent species of which it was once a part. At this point we say that a new species has appeared; the parent species remains the common ancestor of both this new group and any others that spin off.

This is the trajectory of life on this planet; genetic flexibility constantly tosses out novel variations to be challenged by Mother Nature. If they enhance reproduction, they persist and spread; if they don't, they diminish and disappear.

Sometimes dramatic events intrude and alter the normally imperceptible course of evolution. Seventy million years ago evidence indicates a huge asteroid struck the earth, creating a gigantic crater on the edge of the Yucatan Peninsula. The dinosaurs could not handle the accompanying atmospheric disturbance. It interfered with their reproduction, and they went extinct. The departure of the dinosaurs created space for mammals, which at the time were small and insignificant. Gradually they began to prosper and proliferate, and many new species appeared.

A few million years ago, on the rich terrain of Africa, one mammal species—an apelike primate—began to walk upright, and Mother Nature smiled on the innovation. The new bipedalism spread to other species; before long some of these bipeds began to make tools with their newly available "hands." In one species the brain increased dramatically in size and the capacity for speech appeared. And finally, maybe a hundred thousand years ago, humans appeared. From an evolutionary point of view, nothing much has happened since then.

This is the evolutionary story, as developed by thousands of scientists working in countless disciplines from genetics to geology over the past two centuries. Darwin, of course, is the intellectual father of the theory, but his work built on those who went before him and has been extended in significant ways by the countless scientists who came after him.

HAS THE JURY REACHED A VERDICT?

Critics of evolution claim that the story told above is a "just so" story—countless cute and largely imaginary anecdotes strung together to create a naturalistic account of origins. The story is without foundation, they charge, with nothing to commend it beyond its avoidance of supernatural explanations.

Johnson, using Popper, or at least his vocabulary, charges that evolutionary science is filled with "pseudoscientific practices" because the relevant scientists are simply too stupid to understand the difference between the "scientific method of inquiry" and the "philosophical program of scientific naturalism."[6] He claims that scientists' blinkered embrace of "dogmatic metaphysical naturalism" leads them to "disregard some aspect of reality that is virtually staring them in the face.[7] Duane Gish, the venerable creationist debater and critic of the fossil evidence for evolution, describes evolutionary theories as nothing more than "pointless speculation, totally devoid of empirical evidence."[8] The Moonie creationist Jonathan Wells has written an entire book arguing that the most celebrated evidences for evolution—the "icons"—are all "false or misleading" and that evolutionists often don't even know that many of their favored evidences have been conclusively refuted.[9]

What is striking about these unrestrained assaults on evolution is their assumption that evolutionary biologists are too stupid to understand the situation. These dumb biologists confuse philosophy and science; they don't know their own field; they can't see that evolution is their religion and their belief in it a faith; they can't follow a simple argument or identify a preconception. Biology, apparently, is a field filled with morons and knuckleheads.

This conflict becomes ludicrous when we consider the relative credentials of the critics and those of the scientists they are attacking. Johnson is a lawyer—a bright one, to be sure, but without training of any sort in science. He understands so little about science that he actually celebrates his scientific illiteracy as an *asset,* claiming that this issue needs lawyers with rhetorical skills, not scientists who understand biology.[10] Ken Ham, probably the most influential creationist as of this writing, was a high-school teacher before he became a full-time "creation evangelist." There is something bizarre about Ham, who writes books with titles like *D Is for Dinosaur,* and his sweeping criticisms of the entire enterprise of modern science: "Most scientists do not realize that it is the belief (or religion) of evolution that is the basis for the scientific models (the interpretations, or stories) used to attempt an explanation of the present."[11]

The claim that evolution has no facts supporting it is quite ridiculous. We can argue, to be sure, that the facts might be interpreted in some other way; but to claim that there are no such facts is absurd. Books written by those who make such claims should be read for nothing more than their entertainment value.

The theory of evolution is a vast and complicated network of interlocking explanatory concepts tying together everything from the age of fossil bones to similarities between human and chimp DNA. There is, quite simply, a *mountain* of evidence from multiple sources supporting evolution. Organized by evolutionary theory, this mountain of evidence becomes a comprehensible and manageable landscape. Without evolutionary theory, it disappears into the clouds, a hidden and impenetrable mystery of unexplained patterns.

In no less than five distinct areas, patterns have been discovered that point strongly toward evolution. The confidence that biologists have in evolution derives from the way these lines of evidence converge independently to yield the same explanation. The five lines of evidence, each of which we will look at briefly, are:

The fossil record

Biogeography

Comparative anatomy

Developmental similarities

Comparative biochemistry/physiology

THE FOSSIL RECORD

Compelling arguments that the fossil record supports evolution come from history. Nineteenth-century geologists—most of them believers in biblical creation, as we have seen—were forced by discoveries to modify their belief in a recent sudden creation.

It started when the shovels and pickaxes of the industrial revolution unearthed fossils of many extinct species. Initially they were thought to be the residue of Noah's great (and worldwide) flood, but it was soon clear that many of these animals had never coexisted with humans. Not a single human fossil, for example, was ever discovered with that of a dinosaur, suggesting that the dinosaurs must have belonged to a previous era. Challenging this interpretation, Ken Ham shows dinosaurs being marched into Noah's ark in his creation museum, one of the more colorful claims circulating in fundamentalist circles. If Ham is right, then Noah's flood would have destroyed vast numbers of both humans *and* dinosaurs. Why not even *one* of these unfortunate humans managed to get buried in the same strata as a dinosaur is a deep mystery, if they all drowned together.

Decades before Darwin suggested evolution, geologists recognized that the fossil record spoke clearly of a long natural history that preceded the appearance of humans. Committed to the biblical story of creation, these geologists found ways to reinterpret the Genesis story. Perhaps the "days" of creation were geological epochs; maybe there was an earlier creation before the one described in the Bible. None of these creative reinterpretations proved satisfactory, however, and eventually Darwin's theory provided a simpler explanation.

The argument from fossils is particularly compelling when we realize that much of the data was in hand *before* Darwin. This was not a case of data being gathered to support evolution, but rather of data that seemed mysterious and puzzling until evolution came along to explain it. By the end of the eighteenth century geologists had established that stratified rock—such as would be exposed along the sides of a trench dug to carry railroad tracks—contained fossils in a clearly sequential order. But what did this mean?

Stratified rock, we now understand, tells a simple story that lets scientists see into the past. The stratification of rock is like the layering of a cake. Suppose you make a layer cake and you lay down the base of the cake at 2:00. You put some frosting on this first layer at 2:10 and then add another cake layer at 2:20; you frost this layer at 2:30. At 3:00 you write "Happy Birthday" on the top with colored frosting. A slice cut from this sort of layer cake is like a slice cut into the earth, both of which expose a history. The cake slice reveals the history of the cake. The frosting in the middle is older than the frosting on the top. A mosquito embedded in the first cake layer died before the frosting was put on; parmesan cheese dropped from a pasta dish whisked by at 2:45 will be located on the top layer of frosting, but under the "Happy Birthday" greeting.

Stratified rock layers record history in the same way. The dinosaurs in layers under those containing human fossils are there because they died eons before humans appeared. A thin layer of meteoritic dust at the boundary where dinosaurs disappeared indicates that a huge extraterrestrial mass hit the earth at the time the dinosaurs became extinct. The presence of Neanderthal fossils in the same layers as human fossils indicates that they coexisted.

The history displayed in this stratification gradually became clear, as paleontologists discovered that the sequence of fossils revealed a trajectory from simple to complex. Early fossils were simpler than later ones. The durable stone tools fashioned exclusively by the higher primates, for example, are completely missing from older rock strata.

These patterns were not concocted to support evolution. They were a part of the confusing picture painted by nineteenth-century science that eventually strained the credibility of the traditional biblical story until it could no longer be stretched and twisted to accommodate the data. But all this happened *before* Darwin's theory appeared.

The patterns have proven to be remarkably consistent and are now found around the globe. There are exceptions, to be sure, and Duane Gish has them all catalogued in his creationist classic *Evolution: The Fossils Say No!* The exceptions, however, all come with their own explanations. Most missing fossils are missing because those species went extinct before they had a chance to fossilize. The out-of-order fossils occur when a great thrust or fold of the earth's crust occurs, for example, in an earthquake. Such departures from the norm, however, are as obvious as a layer cake run over by a bicycle and then packed by hand back into its original shape.

In the two centuries since these patterns were first discovered the overall sequence noted in the geological record has been amazingly consistent. The discovery and classification of fossils is now a highly active field, and we can only be impressed that Darwin's original explanation has proven to be such a reliable guide, constantly confirmed by new discoveries.

Once Darwin's theory became a serious candidate to explain the history of life, it attracted more attention as scientists pondered its implications. A puzzle arose. All life-forms supposedly originated from a single common ancestor that evolved gradually into other species. It follows that the history of life must have included every imaginable transitional form as one species evolved into another. But the evidence suggested otherwise.

At the time Darwin wrote *On the Origin of Species* in 1859, there were huge gaps in the fossil record. Darwin was both puzzled and bothered by the absence of certain intermediate forms. Major groups of organisms appeared suddenly in the fossil record, looking as if they had been inserted there from outside, as if God were randomly performing piecemeal acts of creation. Creationists, of course, found this state of affairs to their liking, proclaiming confidently that the missing transitional forms were not "missing," but rather had never existed.

Much of Darwin's misapprehension derived from a simple lack of data. Many of the gaps in the fossil record have been filled in by subsequent discovery, and a great many transitional forms that creationists confidently assured us did not exist have been discovered. To be sure, there are still gaps in the fossil record, but enthusiastically pointing them out has become a bit like crying "wolf."

Hundreds of thousands of fossils now demonstrate transitions from one life-form to another. Discovered in precisely dated rock samples, they have filled in many of the gaps that bothered Darwin. Intermediate forms are well established between fish and amphibians, between amphibians and reptiles, and between reptiles and mammals. These are the large-scale transitions. On a finer scale there are less dramatic transitional forms illuminating smaller changes. The human family tree is especially well documented since it is more recent. An impressive fossilized trajectory has been unearthed, showing the evolutionary pathway from *Homo ergaster* to *Homo mauritanicus*, to *Homo heidelbergensis*, and beyond to *Homo sapiens*. Human evolution is so clearly on display in the fossil record now that one paleontologist has called it "the creationists' worst nightmare."[12]

We now have a catalog of fossils beyond Darwin's wildest imagination. The story told by the fossil record is an ever more detailed version of the one that Darwin told a hundred and fifty years ago. The oldest forms of life on earth were microbial. Rocks three and half billion years old contain evidence of bacterial life. The oldest evidence of more advanced and complex eukaryotic cells come from two-billion-year-old rocks. In much younger strata are found multicellular organisms, after which we find plants, fungi, and animals, the latecomers. The genus *Homo* and the species *Homo sapiens* in this story have just arrived.

SPECIES DISTRIBUTION, OR BIOGEOGRAPHY

The second important large-scale pattern pointing to evolution comes from biogeography, which studies the geographical distribution of species. Life is distributed on our planet in a most curious way. Tiny Hawaii, for example, is home to fully one-quarter of the two thousand species of fruit fly. Australia has an odd collection of animals found nowhere else. Darwin's celebrated Galapagos Islands are home to many different species, most of which resemble species on the mainland six hundred miles away.

These patterns make no sense in the absence of evolution. In the creationist picture all these animals descended from the pairs that disembarked from Noah's ark a few thousand years ago in Turkey. Astonishingly rapid speciation at biologically impossible rates would be required to produce all the animals that populate the Galapagos in the short time since Noah's flood.

Bring in the long history of life, however, and things fall nicely into place. Evolution predicts that speciation occurs most naturally and rapidly in small populations that get cut off from their parent species. In the case of the fruit fly, it is likely that a small population of fruit flies made it to Hawaii ages ago and found their new habitat quite congenial. Newly arrived, they had no predators to worry about and many available niches to occupy. These are the conditions for rapid speciation, as small subgroups broke away and found comfortable new homes. On the different Galapagos Islands, which are actually the tops of submerged volcanoes, there are three different species of mockingbirds, each on its own island. Darwin inferred correctly that they evolved from the single parent species on the coast of South America, six hundred miles away. Ages ago some of these mockingbirds relocated to the Galapagos Islands, and the separate populations evolved independently into different species.[13] The similar long isolation of Australia accounts for its peculiar species.

Across the planet the same patterns of speciation are increasingly apparent and explained as the result of evolutionary history. Biogeography has repeatedly led to novel predictions that have been confirmed, such as the existence of North American camels. There are camels today in Asia and Africa; their close relatives, the llamas, are found in South America. If this linkage is due to evolution, there should be camels in North America, which clearly there aren't. This led to the prediction that there should be extinct species of camels in North America, which were eventually found.[14]

Examples like these may seem minor, but there are so many of them that, taken collectively, they strongly and clearly support evolution. In fact, evolution is supported by many small pillars such as these.

COMMON STRUCTURES

Evolution is a process by which nature tinkers with the parts of existing organisms rather than inventing new ones. Because evolution cannot "see" into the future, changes must be of immediate use. Wholesale reinvention of functions is simply not possible. As a result, there are many examples of complex structures that performed one function being gradually modified to do something entirely different. Often it is clear that a brand-new structure might have been better, but natural selection works only on tiny modifications, like a house being endlessly remodeled to accommodate the changing number and lifestyle of its occupants rather than bulldozed and rebuilt. There are thus countless examples of ancestral forms evolving slowly over millions of years into different species, adapted to different habitats. These similarities provide powerful and easily visualized evidence for evolution.

One striking example is the way our hands and feet are so similar to the forelimbs of other mammals. The similarities with the orangutan and other primates are obvious; what is not so obvious are the similarities with the bat and the mouse. When we compare these species, we might expect to discover entirely unrelated mechanical configurations of bones. After all, what we do with our appendages bears little resemblance to what bats do with theirs. What we find, however, is the same configuration modified for different purposes. In all these cases we find creatures with five "fingers" (or toes, if you prefer), each of which is segmented into digits. In bats the digits are dramatically extended to make a frame for a large unfolding wing; in mice they are smaller and closer together, adapted to walking; in humans, they are optimized for complex motor skills. There is nothing magic about the number five and yet all these creatures have the same number of "fingers." One has only to ponder one's little toe to realize that, for many applications, it would have been fine for "one little piggy" to have gone to market and not come back. Evolution offers the compelling explanation that a five-fingered ancestral form passed down this property to a large number of species. Natural selection worked within this constraint to give us the many variations around this common theme that we see today.

The details of such processes are illustrated in the way that the mammalian jaw evolved from its reptilian ancestor. Mammalian jaws have a single bone, whereas reptilian jaws contain several. (This allows them to open their mouths so wide they can eat things almost as large as they are. It also makes them good inspiration for creepy space aliens.) In the path from reptile to mammal, well documented in the fossil record, the "extra" reptilian jaw bones gradually move back in the head and become the hammer, anvil, and stirrup found in the mammalian ear. These connections explain why stretching your jaw often "pops" your ears.

Without the explanation of common ancestry, similarities like these would be deeply mysterious. Why would the bones in our ears resemble those in the jaws of reptiles? Evolution answers this question.

DEVELOPMENTAL SIMILARITY

Two-month-old embryos of chicken, pigs, fish, and humans look similar. They all have gills, webbed hands and feet, and tails. In a few weeks these formations disappear from the human embryo. What is going on? This fascinating puzzle has a simple evolutionary explanation.

The fish is the oldest of these four species and keeps all these formations into adulthood. The human is the most recent and keeps none of them. Pigs keep their tails; chickens hang on to the webbed feet and the tail, but lose the gills. The evolutionary explanation is that the fish is the common ancestor of all three, with genetic instructions to bring these formations into full maturity. But natural selection, as it tinkered with the transitional forms between the ancient fish and the more modern mammal species descended from the fish, found it easier to shut down various formations in the womb (or egg) rather than remove the genetic instructions that give rise to them. Occasionally, however, this shutdown gets derailed and human babies are born with webbed hands and feet.

Obviously, if human babies are sometimes born with webbed feet and hands, the human genome must have instructions for this. It is quite unlikely that a genetic defect could result in the production of webbed feet from nothing in a single generation, as if the entire set of instructions to do this somehow appeared by accident out of nowhere. Far more likely is that a shutdown instruction got disabled, resulting in full production of the undesired webbing.

Embryology studies like these impressed Darwin, even though he knew nothing of the simple genetic explanation that would eventually be provided for the phenomenon: "How, then, can we explain these several facts of embryology,—namely the very general, though not universal, difference in structure between the embryo and the adult;—the various parts in the same individual embryo, which ultimately become very unlike and serve for diverse purposes, being at an early period of growth alike?"[15]

The answer Darwin provided was *common descent*, also known as common ancestry. It is an insight that continues to receive compelling confirmation as the genomes of various species are mapped and compared.

EVIDENCE FROM GENETICS

Because multiple independent lines of evidence support evolution, it is instructive to compare the conclusions on one line of evidence with another. If, for example, the evidence from paleontology doesn't line up with the evidence from genetics or biogeography, then something is wrong. But when *independent* lines of evidence converge, like in a rock-solid court case, the conclusion becomes quite irresistible.

DNA studies are the most recent line of evolutionary investigation and, as such, work within the preexisting framework provided by the other approaches that have been around longer. Not surprisingly, ongoing DNA studies are steadily clarifying and confirming the general evolutionary picture. Embryology, for example, has been powerfully augmented by DNA studies. We now know that the DNA sequences of humans and other species, even nonprimates, are very similar and share many instructions in common. As more and more genomes are mapped, an increasingly clear picture of the trajectory of life will emerge, including the specific genetic changes that gave rise to new species.

The genes we share in common with worms, for example, contain coded instructions about the most primitive structural elements of our bodies, such as basic body segmentation—getting our head at the right end—or orientation—keeping the back and front from getting mixed up. The genes we share with dogs include instructions for spinal formation. The genes we share with more recent ancestors code for more distinctive features, like our complex brains and remarkable hands.

Ongoing research on the genomes of various species is turning up far more commonalities than even the most enthusiastic evolutionist might have predicted. Not long ago it was conventional wisdom that the eye had evolved many times independently.[16] But recent studies indicate that the genetic instructions for the eye are shared by many different species, from fruit flies to humans. Current genome studies are providing dramatic evidence that we share much of our biology with other species.

Recent studies have established that, in addition to sharing genes that do useful things, like making eyes or hemoglobin, we also share nonsense genes with other species. Called pseudogenes, these bits of "misspelled" DNA make such a compelling argument for the reality of common ancestry that one leading evangelical biologist claims they establish common ancestry as a fact.[17]

A pseudogene is a piece of mutant DNA that has no obvious function, often because it sits beside a healthy unmutated version of itself that does the work it is supposed to do. Because pseudogenes don't actually do anything, there are no selection pressures to remove them—they don't interfere with reproduction—and they can pass securely from parent to offspring, from parent species to daughter species, across millions of years.

A pseudogene is like a misspelled word in a book. When I was a college student I worked as a teaching assistant, grading astronomy homework. On one homework set a student wrote about the "protons" that travel to earth from stars. I scrawled something uncharitable in the margin, explaining the difference between "photons," which do come to earth from stars, and "protons," which most certainly do not. I was quite puzzled when the next student made the same mistake, and I suspected cheating. When a third student made the same mistake, I decided that this wasn't a coincidence and, as the number continued to rise, I decided to consult the textbook. Sure enough, there was a typo in the discussion of how stars shine, referring to the production of *protons,* when the word should have been *photons.* The common mistakes in the homework all had a common ancestor in the textbook. Can we possibly conclude otherwise? Likewise, when we find the same pseudo-gene in many different species, how can we conclude that this identical genetic misspelling happened many times?

There are other forms of genetic gibberish that can be handed down as well and used to trace ancestry. Retroposons are strings of nonsense DNA that are readily overlooked when the genes are being read, just as the string of gibberish jkjkjkjkjkjkjjkjkkjj can be easily overlooked in reading this sentence. If this preceding sentence were quoted in twelve otherwise different reviews of this book, we could hardly believe that the identical string of gibberish emerged independently in all twelve cases.

Identification of retroposons has secured the evolutionary inference, based on fossils, that the whale is related to the hippopotamus, cow, sheep, deer, and giraffe, all of which are "even-toed ungulates." An identical piece of genetic gibberish appears in all of them, at exactly the same place in their genomes. There is simply no explanation other than an original appearance of this genetic string in a common ancestor.[18] If the theory of evolution did not exist today, such discoveries would compel scientists to develop it to explain data like this.

The single most dramatic commonality of life on this planet, of course, would have to be the very chemistry of our genome. Without exception, the genomes of every species, from poison ivy to chimpanzees, use the same DNA language, which has just four "letters"—the molecules cytosine, guanine, adenine, and thymine. These four molecules, called nucleotides, are typically referred to by their first letters: C, G, A, and T. There are other nucleotides that would work equally well—perhaps even better—but somehow *every* life-form on the planet has its genetic code written in this particular language.

To appreciate the significance of this, imagine an alien anthropologist studying humans and discovering that, although humans speak many different languages, in every country there are large numbers of people who speak English. The existence of multiple languages establishes that human communication does not have to occur in English, so our alien anthropologist certainly can't infer that English possesses some strange feature ensuring that every time a language is developed, it will be identical to English.

Our alien anthropologist would have to infer that the English spoken in every country is derived from a single source, a linguistic common ancestor.

CONCLUSION

Evolution unites the disparate data surveyed above in ways that creationism simply cannot. If creationism were true, we should be able to explain the facts of biogeography in terms of animals and plants dispersing from Noah's ark or at least radiating out from the Middle East in some way. We cannot. If creationism were true, we should be able to find some explanation for pseudogenes other than common ancestry. If creationism were true, we should be able to explain the sequences in the fossil record without invoking billions of years of natural history. If creationism were true, we should be able to explain why bats, mice, and humans all have five "fingers" on each "hand." We cannot.

Absent evolution, thousands of patterns in nature become completely mysterious, without explanation. Creationism offers virtually no alternative explanations, and most of its "evidence" is nothing more than a catalog of small details that don't fit neatly into the standard evolutionary scenario. Rejecting evolution on the basis of these small details, however, would be like abandoning modern medicine because it can't cure every illness or declaring that meteorology is not a science because weather forecasts are sometimes unreliable.

We must also take note of another major distinction between evolution and creation. The thousands of scientists who work within the broad paradigm of evolution—the geneticists, paleontologists, biogeographers, biologists, biochemists, and so on—all agree on the broad outlines of the theory. They all agree that common ancestry is a fact. They agree that the earth is billions of years old. They agree that many species, like the dinosaurs, went extinct long before human beings appeared. They agree that natural selection is an important process.

In contrast, the much smaller community of anti-evolution creationists and intelligent design proponents has no such shared vision of its alternative "science." Leading young-earth creationists Duane Gish, Ken Ham, and the late Henry Morris agree that the earth is young, humans and dinosaurs lived together, and the fossils were laid down by Noah's flood. They agree that the scientific evidence is solidly on their side. But their junior colleagues, young-earth creationists Kurt Wise, Paul Nelson, and John Mark Reynolds, are candid in their admission that the scientific evidence is *not* solidly on their side and that young-earth creationism is compelling primarily as an implication of biblical literalism. Old-earth creationist Hugh Ross is also a biblical literalist, but he believes both that the Bible and science agree that the earth is billions of years old and that Noah's flood was a local affair. Ross rejects all aspects of evolution, including common ancestry. Intelligent design proponent Behe rejects portions of evolution, but accepts common ancestry and the great age of the earth. In his most recent book he makes a deliberate effort to distance himself from traditional creationists.[19] Johnson, the leader of the anti-evolutionary crusade, has scrupulously avoided taking a clear position on just about anything in order to avoid dissension in the ranks that might weaken the collective assault on evolution.

The differences that separate anti-evolutionists from each other guarantee that they will never actually produce a real "creation hypothesis," as the title of a popular anthology suggests.[20] These differences are so great that there is simply no common ground on which to meet and resolve differences. Wise thinks the earth is ten thousand years old; Ross thinks it is five billion. Differences of this magnitude are not likely to be "ironed out" by simply sitting down together with some charts and a stopwatch. Furthermore, when the various species of creationists write about each other, they can be quite vicious. If they were not united in opposition to evolution, they would be aggressively attacking each other.

Creationism and intelligent design have thus made little progress, despite decades of huffing and puffing and blowing on the house of evolution. They continue to offer little more than a hodgepodge of anti-evolutionary microarguments, many of which date back to the nineteenth century. Were evolutionary theory to suddenly collapse, as creationists have been confidently predicting for over a century, there would be no shared "creation hypothesis" on which to build a scientific research program.

In dramatic contrast, evolutionary scientists have so many shared commitments that finding common ground on which to resolve differences is easy. The history of evolution certainly has its share of controversies, and there have been multiple small revolutions within the field. But the general agreement on the "big picture" has made it possible to negotiate these various controversies and move forward. And this, of course, is why Darwin's theory has made so much progress in the last century and a half. Evolution as an explanation for the history and diversity of life on this planet is, quite simply, true.

In the meantime, thoughtful Christians who have taken the time to reflect on evolution have found ways to make it a part of their understanding of God's creative process. In the same way that Christians made peace with Galileo's astronomy, once they stopped trying to disprove it, many have made peace with Darwin's theory of evolution. Some have even found evolution to be a rich resource for theology, a "disguised friend of faith," in the words of one thoughtful observer.[21]

PILGRIM'S PROGRESS

Every summer for the past three decades, I have made the same modest pilgrimage. In an old handmade wooden canoe I paddle to the far end of Indian Lake, an unsung body of water just outside the middle of nowhere in rural New Brunswick. The lake is long and narrow and curves around at the end, like a finger on a baseball. Because the lake is remote and far from electricity and population centers, it is usually quiet. The few cabins clustered at one end are generally unoccupied, and my canoe typically has the lake to itself.

The trip to the end of the lake takes about an hour, depending on the wind and, most recently, how vigorously my daughter in the back of the canoe is willing to paddle. As the canoe moves around the bend in the lake, the cabins on the other end recede from view and, with their passing, all indications that Indian Lake shares its pristine wilderness with human beings disappear.

Underwater springs and a modest stream cascading down the hillside feed the lake. The height of the water, which varies, is determined by the beavers that dam up the area where the water runs off into a marshy forest. Once, when a particularly industrious family of beavers took up residence there, I had to tear out some of the dam to lower the level and keep the water from encroaching on my cabin.

A tiny population of loons observes my pilgrimages to the end of the lake. Their mournful laugh authenticates that this is true wilderness, for they are threatened by powerboats and waterfront development. Avid swimmers, the loons dive under the water when startled and reappear somewhere else on the water; I am far more interested in them than they are in me.

The goal of my pilgrimage is always the same—to sit quietly and motionless near the beaver dams and hope the beavers come out.

I love listening to the wilderness—the whisper of leaves, the cascading water, the strange harmony of the birds. It's an interesting sound, almost driven to extinction today by cell phones, televisions, iPods, and planes flying overhead. No planes fly over Indian Lake, though, because it is on the way to nowhere.

I feel strangely at home in that canoe with my daughter. I sense some approval of my presence here among the lily pads just outside the beavers' huts. I feel connected to this little bit of landscape that I have visited every summer since before my children were born. I note that the beavers build their primitive dwellings at this end of the lake, while my species build ours at the other. The beavers construct their homes as a protective haven for their offspring; I suspect they feel about their children somewhat as I do about mine, minus the fretting about boyfriends and college expenses. Little beavers count innocently on their parents just as my daughter behind me in the canoe counts on me.

The wilderness experience is therapeutic for reasons we don't understand very well. Human beings prefer a landscape of trees and lakes to skyscrapers and parking lots. Waterfront property commands a huge premium as real estate; homes are consistently situated to take advantage of natural beauty; and properties are landscaped to look as natural as possible. Everyone agrees that a meadow or a pond is more beautiful than a parking lot, and we will pay well to avoid looking at the parking lot. But why? Why do we all agree that brightly colored cars on gray asphalt are unattractive, but colorful flowers in a green meadow are beautiful?

Research shows that people who drive along tree-lined roads arrive at work with lower blood pressure than those who commute along streets lined with buildings. We nurture plants indoors to soften the artificial character of our homes and workplaces. Owning a pet increases our life expectancy.

We are connected to the natural world in so many ways and, though nature is sometimes "red in tooth and claw," often it is not. As Darwin wrote so eloquently at the end of *On the Origin of Species:* "There is grandeur in this view of life, with its several powers, having been originally breathed into a few forms or into one; and that, whilst this planet has gone cycling on according to the fixed law of gravity, from so simple a beginning endless forms most beautiful and most wonderful have been, and are being, evolved."

Darwin joined all of life together in a most magical way and in so doing dismantled the wall that separated humans from the rest of nature. Critics of Darwin warn ominously that he has reduced human beings to the level of the animals and this accounts for our supposedly bad behavior of late. But this is the "glass half empty" perspective. Might we not say instead, and more optimistically, that Darwin has raised the level of the animals? Darwin provides for us a new appreciation and respect for the loyalty of our dogs, the devoted attention of the mother bird, the industry of the beaver, the playful spirit of the otter, the proud countenance of the wolf, the human-like curiosity of the higher primates. Darwin may have closed the gap between humans and animals, but he did that by promoting the other species, not demoting ours.

We met the bonobo Kuni in the Introduction to this book. Kuni demonstrated great compassion and intelligence in caring for a troubled bird. Kuni's attentive kindness went beyond what most humans would have done. When a bird stuns itself by crashing into my window, I do little more than set it at the edge of the woods, if I do anything at all. I certainly don't hover over it to keep predators at bay while it recovers.

Kuni can't do calculus, and I can. Kuni can't play the guitar or write a book. By the yardsticks we typically use I am superior. But we are learning that intelligence should not be measured along a single yardstick. Kuni's demonstration of interspecies compassion inspires me in ways I find provocative.

THE GLASS HALF FULL

Nature is grand on so many levels. Does this grandeur have something to do with the fact that it was created by God? There is an artistic character to nature that has always struck me as redundant from a purely scientific point of view. Although I am a scientist and a great enthusiast for that approach to understanding the world, I often find myself thinking that our scientific understanding is an inadequate abstraction, that only a portion of reality has been captured in its nets. And maybe that portion is smaller than we think.

I am interested in knowing why it is so intriguing to watch the birds outside my window. Why do they sing so much? Why is their song so pleasant for humans to hear? Why, for example, does almost every scene of undeveloped nature seem so beautiful, from mountain lakes to rolling prairies? If the evolution of our species was driven entirely by survival considerations, then where did we get our rich sense of natural aesthetics? Perhaps there are answers to these questions. E. O. Wilson has coined the word *biophilia* to describe our affinity for nature and started some tentative explorations in these directions.[1] But I wonder how far those explorations will take us.

The scientific approach to nature is strongly biased in favor of engineering analogs, the legacy of Newton's mechanical view and the great power of mathematics. We tend to view the eye as an optical device, the brain as computational, and the knee as mechanical. We borrow what understanding we can from these metaphors. Phenomena without engineering analogs, like our sense of humor or great enthusiasm to play in rock bands, seem harder to understand. I worry that scientific progress has bewitched us into thinking that there is nothing more to the world than what we can understand. Science is like the fisherman's net that can't catch small fish because the holes in the net are too large. We must be careful not to conclude that the fish we can catch disprove the existence of those we cannot. Our failure to understand the deep aesthetic of nature must not delude us into thinking that it does not exist or that the meaning we derive from it is illusory.

The challenge for the religious believer is, of course, the claim that God created everything and whether the grand tapestry of nature can be described as God's handiwork. I side with Darwin in rejecting the idea that God is responsible for the details.[2] There are too many things that don't fit into the standard creationist scenario—bad design, instinctual cruelty, pointless waste. On the other hand, anyone who has contemplated nature in any detail comes away with a deep appreciation for its rich creativity. I am attracted to the idea that God's signature is not on the engineering marvels of the natural world, but rather on its marvelous creativity and aesthetic depth.

Scientists are not supposed to talk about God in this way, for it raises questions that can't be answered. And it upsets Richard Dawkins. But I am going to do it anyway. And I know that the intelligent design theorists I have dismissed earlier will accuse me, perhaps with justification, of being a hypocrite for rejecting the way they talk about God, but then offering my own version of God talk.

THROUGH A GLASS DARKLY

Darwin offered us two revolutions. The first was the destruction of the traditional creationist picture, where God created all things via individual supernatural acts more or less as we find them today. This revolution is one we must accept, despite ongoing hostility from conservative Christians. There is simply too much evidence in its favor. Darwin's second revolution was the establishment of random, "purposeless" selection processes, natural and sexual, as the only creative mechanisms at work in natural history. Gould, that most eloquent of evolutionists, put it like this: "We are glorious accidents of an unpredictable process with no drive to complexity, not the expected results of evolutionary principles that yearn to produce a creature capable of understanding the mode of its own necessary construction."[3]

I agree with Gould that we are "glorious," but I am not convinced we are "accidents." And I am certain that we should not be proclaiming confidently that natural history is a meaningless trajectory. Questions about the movements of history, like questions about ultimate origins, are highly speculative. Most who proclaim on such global questions offer nothing more than their personal ideology, for science has little to say about nature on that scale.

The confident assertions of evolutionists can give the misleading impression that we know everything we need to about the historical details of the process. This is simply not true. Evolution is what we call an *underdetermined* theory, which implies that many of the details are missing and have to be filled in by "connecting the dots." This underdetermination provides no argument that evolution is a false theory or so weakly supported that rational people should withhold support. It suggests, rather, that we should be careful about making global generalizations about evolution.

Dawkins, in *The Ancestor's Tale,* compares evolution to a pilgrimage, a suggestive geographical metaphor. Let me use that metaphor in a different way to illustrate the nature of underdetermination. Suppose you have the passport of a world traveler, filled with stamps from various countries and the dates and times of each border crossing. Suppose also that you have no reason to suspect that any of the information is false or created to mislead. Your task is to reconstruct the travel history of this person, using the passport and your general knowledge of how reasonable people travel.

You would naturally begin by lining up the dates and countries. You might discover, for example, that England, France, Belgium, Germany, Canada, Australia, and Brazil were visited in that order. This part of the history would be quite certain, a solid framework on which to hang additional details. Your knowledge of travel would allow you to infer that the trip from England to France was probably by train, based on the times on the stamps. So our traveler must have used the Chunnel. Further analysis of the time stamps might suggest that all the European travel was by train. This inference would be also be supported by your knowledge of Europe's excellent train system. The trip from Germany to Canada, however, was obviously not by train. Since it took one day, you conclude that it must have been by plane, rather than boat. For similar reasons you conclude that the trip from Canada to Australia must have been by boat, since the travel time appears to have been several weeks and there is obviously no train or highway between those countries.

At a certain level of detail this travel history could be confidently constructed and embraced with a high level of confidence, barring some unlikely scenario like our traveler being a spy. Likewise the history of life on this planet can be constructed with a high level of confidence.

Certain questions related to our world traveler, however, would be hard to answer. Based on his passport alone, we can't infer very much about where he traveled inside France. Did he travel by train or taxi? Did he visit Paris? We might know he was in France for four weeks, but that would be it, without additional information. And why is he traveling so much in the first place? The sequence of countries he visited seems almost random, but we are certainly not justified in concluding that our ignorance of his purpose constitutes evidence that he had no purpose. In fact, most reasonable people would suppose that there was an unknown purpose and start looking for it, rather than conclude there was no purpose. Our traveler's itinerary is *underdetermined*. There is a level of detail that we simply cannot access with the information at hand.

The long pilgrimage through time that Dawkins calls the ancestor's tale is similarly underdetermined. The solid evidence from fossils and genes are the stamps in our passports. We know our story began with simple one-celled life-forms. We passed from fish to amphibians to reptiles and birds. We know our most recent history was mammalian, and our last major sojourn was on the grasslands of Africa.

But we don't know all the intermediate species through which we passed in getting from fish to amphibians. Most species appear and go extinct without leaving so much as a single fossil. The fossil record is the story of unusually successful species that lived long enough to leave behind a record of their existence. They are the "border crossings" in our passport, providing definite answers to some questions while leaving others unaddressed.

To claim, with Gould and Dawkins, that our evolutionary history, our ancestor's tale, is a long and glorious accident is to make a statement about details that we don't have. We must resist the tendency to turn our ignorance into a conclusion. Absence of evidence is only rarely evidence of absence.

Gould and Dawkins are smart guys and know way more about evolution than I do. But they are also agnostics and thus have no choice but to deny any overarching purpose to natural history. In their view, there is no traveler, just a globe-trotting passport wafting on the breeze, getting hit with the occasional stamp. They may be right, of course, but let us admit that their guess is no better than mine.

We can agree, perhaps, that the inspection of natural history per se provides no certain indication that we are the "expected results" of some hidden patterns. However, there is another way to look at this. As a believer in God, I am convinced *in advance* that the world is not an accident and that, in some mysterious way, our existence is an "expected" result. Thus, I do not look at natural history as a source of data to determine whether or not the world has purpose. Rather, my approach is to anticipate that the facts of natural history will be compatible with the purpose and meaning I have encountered elsewhere. And my understanding of science does nothing to dissuade me from this conviction.

Religious believers, from spiritual agnostics like Einstein, to people who enjoy canoeing, to enthusiastic missionaries like Mother Teresa, have always found layers of meaning in the world. Einstein in his ivory tower was enthralled by the mystery of the world's rationality and its accessibility to human reason. How can it possibly be that the brain of a creature that evolved on the grasslands of Africa can penetrate the deep secrets of relativity? Mother Teresa, in the gutters of Calcutta, experienced such a powerful compulsion to help the hopeless that she was energized to dedicate her life to bringing dignity to the most destitute of our species. In my annual pilgrimage at Indian Lake I am drawn to experience the pristine wilderness and share it with my family.

The meaning we encounter in the world is deeply mysterious and existential. In a strange way it is just *there*. Meaning is not derived or inferred from our understanding of the world. Nobody inspects evolutionary theory to see whether the world has meaning. Nobody learns Darwin's theory and decides they should have children, or live on a beach, or seek random sexual encounters, or take a safari, because billions of years of natural selection have ensured that these experiences will be meaningful. Many people, in fact, decide *not* to have children and find meaning in the opportunities enabled by avoiding the obligations of parenthood. Most of us choose *not* to live on beaches. We control our sexual urges and watch nature shows when we feel like taking a safari. The meaning we find in the world is simply *encountered* in all its rich mysterious complexity and in the most surprising of places. Meaning is not the conclusion of a scientific investigation.

Our religions are responses to both our need for meaning and our discovery of that meaning. In the construction of worldviews that try to understand the meaning of our experience we draw connections. We gather with others who see those same connections. Religious communities are both the celebration of the meaning we find in community and the expression of our biological need to be in community. The praise we offer for the transcendent beauty of nature is both a response to that beauty and a celebration that we are creatures capable of that response.

The connections we draw between the mysteries of our existence and those parts of the world we understand must be drawn always in pencil, in anticipation of being erased. Once we connected our relevance to a location in the center of the universe. There were observations that supported this cosmology, to be sure, but the enduring power of this view derived from its connection to an exalted view of ourselves. That line had to be erased. For much the same reason we once celebrated a large gap between our species and all others. That line has also been erased.

Science has perhaps gotten as much from the materialistic paradigm as it is going to get. Matter in motion, so elegantly described by Newton and those who followed him, may not be the best way to understand the world. Science has moved into an age of information, a new and productive way of looking at the world and encouraging in many ways. Human beings are the most complex creatures in the known universe, and perhaps, once again, we find ourselves on the top or at the center or on the motherboard or wherever we locate the privileged spot in an age of information.

Charles Darwin challenged the traditional view of creation, to be sure. But the facts of nature were challenging the traditional view long before Darwin came along, if only we had been willing to look more closely. Nature has always been an untidy, bloody affair. Its messiness is not easily reconciled with the traditional idea of a creator, unless one could be satisfied with the odd explanation that cats torture their prey and roses have thorns because Adam and Eve sinned. Many thinkers welcomed Darwin, seeing in evolution a more acceptable role for God as creator.[4] And there continue to be thoughtful Christians today who have made their peace with evolution and are doing creative theology as they explore what it means to be biologically evolved creatures in relationship with God. That so many other Christians are now massed against Darwin has more to do with American culture than biology or Christian theology. From a purely theological perspective there is much in evolution to interest Christians, and if controversy had not driven discourse so quickly off the rails, the voices of reason might today be speaking from the center of American Christianity, rather than the fringes.

THE QUESTION

Today as I was leaving class a thoughtful student approached me and wanted to know if I was going to "come clean" about evolution and let the students know what I believed. I had been lecturing on Darwin, trying to get the students inside the great scientist's head as he wrestled with the observations that eventually led him to the theory of evolution. This student, like me, was raised to believe that Darwin was evil and evolution was a lie. But, also like me at his age, he was having second thoughts as he was becoming better informed (or brainwashed by his professor, depending on your perspective).

When I teach Darwin, I avoid taking a position, partly so students can feel free to reject evolution if that is their choice. More important, though, I want the students to wrestle, as Darwin did and I did when I was their age, with the implications of cruelty in nature and bad design. They need to confront, on their terms, the mass of data that can't be reconciled with the Genesis creation accounts. If I lay my position out too clearly, some students will make their decision based on what they think of me, rather than the issues at stake.

Many college students, and most Americans for that matter, have little interest in evolution as science. Their concern is that science not crowd out their religious beliefs. At some level they fear Daniel Dennett's "universal acid" may actually have the power to dissolve their beliefs. And they don't want to find out if that is true.

Their fear is understandable. Almost everyone who talks about evolution insists that we must make a choice between evolution or creation, materialism or God, naturalism or supernaturalism. Dawkins and Dennett believe this and say, "Choose evolution"; Johnson and Morris believe this and say, "Choose creation." The four of them are grand evangelists for the positions they have chosen. Just as significantly, all four of them are champions of a false dichotomy.

This dichotomy plays well in the press. It's controversial, combative, and simple. There are good guys and bad guys, no matter where you stand. But this dichotomy is *wrong*. These are not the only two options. These are not even the most reasonable options.

COMING CLEAN

I think evolution is true. The process, as I reflect on it, is an expression of God's creativity, although in a way that is not captured by the scientific view of the world. As soon as we start highlighting specific places where we think we glimpse God's handiwork, we open ourselves up to the old "God of the gaps" problem. I think there are ways, though, that we can begin to look at the creation and understand that the scientific view is not all-encompassing. Science provides a partial set of insights that, though powerful, don't answer all the questions.

Intelligent design and scientific creationism seem inadequate to me, because they reduce God to one agent among other agents in natural history. If ID is true, then it implies that the agents of evolution are natural selection, sexual selection, God, mutation, chance, and whatever else you want on the list. Each of these agents makes its own individual contribution. Natural selection made saliva, God made hemoglobin, sexual selection made the peacock's tail, and chance drove the dinosaurs to extinction. God is one of several agents of change. God may be the "big gun" who steps in to do the projects that exceed the capacities of the other agents, perhaps, but God is still just one agent among many. Is this really how we want to think about natural history?

God's creative activity must not be confined to a six-day period "in the beginning" or the occasional intervention along the evolutionary path. God's role in creation must be more universal—so universal that it cannot be circumscribed by the contours of individual phenomena or events. We must resist the temptation to make God into a "superengineer" or "master craftsman" or "grand artist." God may indeed have all of these attributes, but we ought not to suppose that any of them capture more than the tiniest intuition about God's role in creation. It seems to me a more hopeful perspective to step back as far as we can and examine the biggest possible picture in the hopes of getting a glimpse of what it means to say that God created the world.

A BRIEF HISTORY OF EVERYTHING

Natural history is richly layered in surprising ways. At the deepest level of reality the world is so simple it boggles the mind. There are only four kinds of interactions that occur in nature: gravitational, electromagnetic, strong nuclear, and weak nuclear. Every event, from a thought in your head, to the chirp of a bird, to the explosion of a distant star, results from these four interactions.

There are only two kinds of physical objects in the world: quarks and leptons. The familiar protons and neutrons are composed of quarks; the electron is the best-known example of a lepton. Every physical object, from a guitar string, to the Mona Lisa, to Pluto (whatever it is these days), is made from quarks and leptons.

All natural phenomena, no matter how rich or mundane, result from two kinds of particles interacting via four kinds of interactions. Who could possibly conceptualize the extraordinary creativity of a world built like this?

Imagine that we have a film of the entire history of the universe. Titled "Four Forces and Two Particles," the film offers so little promise that you can hardly bring yourself to pay attention. "Boring," you note to yourself, expecting to see nothing but zillions of marbles floating in the blackness of space.

The world you think will be so boring starts to unfold, and you sit back to watch. In no time at all things start to happen. The quarks, which have electrical charges of $2/3$ and $-1/3$, start sticking together under the influence of the strong nuclear force, and soon they are all gathered into protons and neutrons, which have electrical charges of 1 and 0. All the fractionally charged particles in the universe are gone. "Interesting," you think, "but it's still just marbles."

Protons, neutrons, and electrons are now buzzing about in a chaotic but steadily cooling mix as the universe expands. Their electrical interactions are pulling the electrons toward the protons. As the temperature declines across a certain key threshold, the electrons suddenly drop into orbits around the protons and the universe is full of hydrogen atoms. All the particles in the universe are now electrically neutral and you note something rather puzzling you had missed: the universe has a perfect balance between the positive and negative charges. Interesting ...

Now that all the particles are electrically neutral, the powerful electrical force stops dominating and the much weaker gravitational force takes over. The hydrogen atoms are pulled ever so slowly together until they begin to cluster. Steadily growing balls of hydrogen form and, as the balls get bigger, their gravitational pull on other atoms increases until much of the hydrogen collects into huge balls. The balls get steadily larger, surpassing the size of the moon, then the earth, then a large planet like Jupiter. This, of course, is more interesting, but it is still just marbles.

Suddenly, another critical threshold is crossed, and the balls ignite. Like a drawn-out fireworks display, all across the universe great balls of hydrogen turn into stars. Things are certainly more interesting than you had anticipated, but the universe is still boring, composed almost entirely of hydrogen.

The gravity within these newly born stars crushes the hydrogen atoms like eggs under a steamroller. Astonishingly you notice that the strong force cooperates intimately with this gravitational crushing, and the hydrogen atoms combine to become helium atoms. In fact you notice that the very process that emits the light from the stars builds the periodic table. Hydrogens make helium. A helium and a hydrogen make a lithium. Two helium make beryllium. A beryllium and a helium make a carbon. Other combinations make nitrogen, oxygen, neon, sodium, and on down the periodic table. Interesting ...

A large star suddenly explodes with the force of a billion atomic bombs and brings you out of your seat. The explosion fills a massive region of space with the elements created inside the star; the powerful explosion, though, is strangely orderly. Gravity starts gathering the debris back into balls again, and a large chunk at the center becomes another star. This time, however, some of the balls end up orbiting about the second-generation star. These smaller balls have a rich roster of elements, since they formed from the debris of a star that had converted much of its hydrogen into other elements. In particular, many of these smaller balls possess a curious molecular combination of hydrogen and oxygen. In most parts of the universe, these molecules are in the form of a solid. In the others they are a gas. But on balls that are exactly the right distance from the central star, the molecules are liquid, a particular liquid called *water*. Very interesting ...

The universe is now anything but boring. You marvel at the complex structures that have been built from the simplest of raw materials. Water turns out to be especially amazing and surprisingly capable of encouraging the formation of ever more complex molecules like amino acids, proteins, and enzymes. These complex materials build up steadily until, to your astonishment, a particular arrangement actually starts duplicating itself and the waters become filled with this new process. In amazement you realize that the universe now has life. This is not boring at all.

Subtle and highly nuanced interactions between these primitive life-forms, driven by a seemingly endless set of molecular interactions, steadily and mysteriously push the life-forms to greater and greater complexity. Some kind of subtle advantage accompanies increases in complexity. It is almost like a mysterious force calling life—and the universe—to become ever more interesting. And yet you know that all this is simply the way that quarks and leptons combine under the influence of the four interactions. Your earlier fears that the universe was going to be boring and meaningless now seem laughably ill-founded.

The film turns out, upon reflection, to be quite extraordinary. The credits begin to roll, blurred and illegible, as you watch a member of your own species paddle a canoe to the end of a small lake with his daughter and then sit quietly in a pristine wilderness. Somehow a universe that started out so hopelessly boring has turned out to be quite interesting after all.

MORE THAN PARTICLES

The trajectory of natural history leading to human beings is an amazing story. As we look back at the earlier stages of the universe, we cannot help but marvel at how later developments build on previous ones. There is an "unfolding" to the process, as if each stage is both the completion of what has gone before and the anticipation of what is soon to come. Freeman Dyson, one the greatest scientists of the twentieth century, puts it like this: "The more I examine the universe and study the details of its architecture, the more evidence I find that the universe in some sense must have known that we were coming. There are some striking examples in the laws of nuclear physics of numerical accidents that seem to conspire to make the universe habitable."[5]

The tools of science have been effective at illuminating each individual step on this long and winding road. But many things exist in nature that science does not even try to explain. Those are labeled "chance." When a scientist claims that something occurred by "chance," that is an admission that there is no explanation. I hasten to point out that this does not mean that some causal factor is missing and has to be provided by God. What it does mean, though, is that events occur in nature that fall outside the explanatory purview of science. These events are either genuinely without explanation or to be explained from a perspective outside of science. This offers no proof of God's intervention, of course, for it may indeed be that the events are without explanation. But such inexplicable aspects of creation at least erect explanatory boundaries for science and preclude global generalizations about what it all means.

I mentioned above that the story of evolution was underdetermined by virtue of the large portion of the story that is simply missing. In a more profound way, all of nature is underdetermined. The natural order, as disclosed so remarkably by contemporary physics, is not a closed system of interlocking mechanical parts, as the Newtonian worldview mistakenly implied. Rather, events unfold in ways that are not entirely specified by the laws of physics. The most famous statement of this underdetermination is the Heisenberg Uncertainty Principle, a precise mathematical articulation of exactly how much we can and cannot know about the world. In one of the most general laws in all of science, Heisenberg's principle sets clear limits on how accurately we can know the behavior of particles, such as electrons. An electron passing through a small hole, for example, will have its path altered by the interaction with the hole. We can know that the trajectory will bend by a certain amount, say ten degrees. But we cannot know in which direction; whether the electron goes left or right, up or down is determined by "chance."

If reality contains nothing but quarks, leptons, and four interactions, then history is indeed filled with chance events and, as Dawkins and Dennett would have us believe, we are the result of a mindless process. If God exists, however, then other possibilities open up. Perhaps the unfolding of history includes a steady infusion of divine creativity under the scientific radar. Perhaps the meaning we encounter in so many different places and so many different ways is not simply an accident of our biology, but a hint that the universe is more than particles and their interactions.

Anthropologists tell us that our forebears bowed before the mystery of their poorly understood and intimidating world. Mother Nature was capricious and unpredictable, to be worshiped, patronized, and feared. Animals and even children were sacrificed to the gods to hold their wrath in check. We have now explored this world and discovered that we need not fear Mother Nature, at least not in the same way.

In coming to understand the world so much better, however, we have not banished its mystery. We may not cower before the lightning bolt or hide from the thunder. We no longer throw virgins into volcanoes to appease the lava god. Now we bow before different mysteries. We float tenuously on a tiny planet in the immensity of space, humbled by the knowledge that it took ten billion years of cosmic evolution to prepare our planet for life. Four billion years of the most remarkable and creative explosion of life has preceded us on that planet. And now, here we are, at once both a fragile species and, strangely, a danger to other species and even to ourselves. We have learned so much about the inner workings of our world, and yet so little about what we should do with that knowledge. In deep and important ways we have not dispelled the mystery of our existence at all—we have simply established it with greater clarity.

"We shall not cease from exploration," wrote T. S. Eliot in "Little Gidding," "and the end of all our exploring will be to arrive where we started and to know the place for the first time."

ACKNOWLEDGMENTS

This project began with a phone call out of the blue from Ken Giniger, asking if I knew anyone who might be "interested in writing a book on the evolution controversy for HarperOne." Having just completed a book on a related topic and wondering about my next project, I hastened to recommend myself for this task. Ken fast-tracked the approvals and now, less than two years later, the book is finished. I must thank Ken for conceptualizing this project, giving it to me, and then offering many valuable suggestions on the final version.

My editors at HarperOne, Kris Ashley and Mickey Maudlin, provided valuable input that helped me get started on the right foot. And Kris read the entire draft when it was completed and made many useful suggestions for improvements, all of which I sensibly heeded. Despite my careful scrutiny of the manuscript, my copy editor at HarperOne, Ann Moru, identified countless literary faux pas and made many valuable suggestions for improvement.

I owe a special thanks to several of my busy colleagues at Eastern Nazarene College. Eric Severson took the time to read the first draft of the entire manuscript for both style and content. A consummate teacher, Eric couldn't help making countless suggestions, and the finished product is significantly stronger on several levels because of his efforts. Donald Yerxa and Randall Stephens read a later draft and made valuable suggestions. And Karen Henck and Kelsey Towle, who teach writing at my college, read portions of the manuscript and offered helpful advice on style.

Ron Numbers and Jon Roberts, both leading—and very busy—scholars for whom I have enormous respect, graciously agreed to read the entire manuscript for accuracy. Not surprisingly, they uncovered a number of problems that I hope I have addressed adequately. Both Numbers and Roberts have done important work in this field, and it was gratifying—and somewhat intimidating, to be honest—to have them review my manuscript. Watching the Red Sox at Fenway with them, however, was just plain fun.

Francis Collins, who has to be one of the busiest scientists on the planet, read *Saving Darwin* on a plane ride to Singapore and wrote the Foreword to the book. I am humbled by his encouraging words of support and deeply appreciative of his contribution.

I love to surround myself with talented undergraduates, and this project was no exception. For little more than minimum wage they tracked down sources, formatted footnotes, harassed my faculty colleagues with questions, copyedited, fact-checked, and generally reminded me of why it's great to be a college professor. I would like to thank them and wish them well as they begin their careers: Kurtis Biggs, Amanda Egolf, Sara Kern, and Cameron Young.

During most of the writing of this book, I was just down the hall from two exceptional writers, Marc Kaufman and Heather Wax. I would like to thank both of them for many interesting conversations about words and ideas and for helping me become a better writer.

I especially thank the John Templeton Foundation for providing financial support for this project. Its generous support released me from a heavy teaching load at the college where I work and provided resources to hire student assistants and purchase a small library of relevant books from Amazon.com.

Finally, I would like to thank my wife of many years, Myrna, for her patience and willingness to let me live in the corner of our sunroom, next to the dogwoods and the bird feeder, where I did most of the writing.

It would be nice if all this help could guarantee a flawless final product, but alas, an army of advisers can do only so much. The mistakes that remain, as the refrain goes, are mine, and mine alone.

NOTES

INTRODUCTION: THE DISSOLUTION OF A FUNDAMENTALIST

1. John C. Whitcomb and Henry M. Morris, *The Genesis Flood: The Biblical Record and Its Scientific Implications* (Phillipsburg, NJ: Presbyterian and Reformed Publishing, 1961); Henry M. Morris, *Many Infallible Proofs* (Green Forest, AR: Master Books, 1974).

2. All biblical references in this chapter are taken from the King James Version, which has long been the preferred version of the Bible for fundamentalists.

3. Romans 8:22. The King James says, "For we know that the whole creation groaneth and travaileth in pain ..."

4. Poll: "Creation Trumps Evolution," *CBS News,* November 22, 2004, http://www.cbsnews.com/stories/2004/11/22/opinion/polls/main657083.shtml. Because the poll was imprecise, we cannot distinguish between the three strands of literal creationism: the young-earth creationism of Whitcomb and Morris, day-age creationism, and gap creationism, all of which will be discussed in detail in later chapters.

5. Although some claim that the Bible does not, in a technical sense, give a date for the creation, an approximate date can be determined by adding up the "begats." If Adam was created in the same week as "the heavens and the earth," we can then extrapolate from the chronology provided for Adam's children, his children's children, and so on. There is some vagueness in this process, but most who have done this—it takes just a few minutes—come up with a date for the creation of the universe and the earth that is between six and ten thousand years ago.

6. Daniel Dennett, *Darwin's Dangerous Idea: Evolution and the Meaning of Life* (New York: Simon & Schuster, 1995), p. 63.

7. Tertullian, *De Carne Christi* (London: S.P.C.K., 1956), p. 5 (4).

8. G. K. Chesterton, *Orthodoxy* (Ft. Collins, CO: Ignatius, 1995), p. 11.

9. Frans de Waal, *Our Inner Ape* (New York: Riverhead, 2005), p. 2.

10. Howard Van Till, *The Fourth Day* (Grand Rapids, MI: Eerdmans, 1986); Darrel Falk, *Coming to Peace with Science* (Downers Grove, IL: InterVarsity, 2004).

11. Francis Collins, *The Language of God: A Scientist Presents Evidence for Belief* (New York: Free Press, 2006).

12. Ken Miller, *Finding Darwin's God* (London: Harper Perennial, 1999).

13. John Haught, *God After Darwin* (Boulder, CO: Westview, 2000).

14. Alister McGrath, *Scientific Theology: Nature, Reality, and Theory* (Grand Rapids, MI: Eerdmans, 2002–3).

15. Keith Ward, *God, Chance and Necessity* (Oxford: Oneworld, 1996).

16. Michael Ruse, *Can a Darwinian Be a Christian?* (New York: Cambridge University Press, 2001), p. 219.

17. Richard Dawkins, "Science, Religion, and Evolution," *New York Times,* May 21, 1989, sec. 7, late city final edition.

CHAPTER 1: **THE LIE AMONG US**

1. James Moore, *The Darwin Legend* (Grand Rapids, MI: Baker, 1994), p. 93.

2. Moore, *Darwin Legend,* p. 93.

3. See, for example, http://www.forerunner.com/forerunner/X0724_Darwins_Final_ Recant.html (accessed March 17, 2007).

4. John Ankerberg and John Weldon, *Darwin's Leap of Faith: Exposing the False Religion of Evolution* (Eugene, OR: Harvest House, 1998), p. 127.

5. Francis Darwin, ed., *The Life and Letters of Charles Darwin,* vol. 2 (London: John Murray, 1888), p. 308.

6. Henry Morris, *The Long War Against God: The History and Impact of the Creation/ Evolution Controversy* (Green Forest, AR: Master Books, 2000), p. 260.

7. Ken Ham, *The Lie: Evolution* (El Cajon, CA: Creation-Life Publishers, 1987).

8. Phillip E. Johnson, *Reason in the Balance: The Case Against Naturalism in Science, Law and Education* (Downers Grove, IL: InterVarsity, 1995), p. 59.

9. *Answers,* based in Hebron, KY, and edited by Dale T. Mason, is published quarterly by Answers in Genesis.

10. Nora Barlow, ed., *The Autobiography of Charles Darwin: 1809–1882* (New York: Norton, 1958), p. 56.

11. Barlow, ed., *Autobiography of Charles Darwin,* p. 57.

12. William Paley, *Natural Theology* (New York: American Tract Society, 1802); *The Principles of Moral and Political Philosophy* (Dublin: Exshaw, White, H. Whitestone, Byrne, Cash, Marchbank, and McKenzie, 1785); *Evidences of Christianity* (London: Clowes, 1851).

13. Barlow, ed., *Autobiography of Charles Darwin,* p. 59.

14. Barlow, ed., *Autobiography of Charles Darwin,* p. 85.

15. The importance and role of paradigms in science is convincingly articulated by philosopher Thomas Kuhn in his now classic work *The Structure of Scientific Revolutions,* first published in 1962 (3d ed., Chicago: University of Chicago Press, 1996).

16. Francis Reddy, "High-speed Star Flees Tycho's Blast," *Astronomy Magazine,* November 3, 2004, http://astronomy.com/asy/default.aspx?c=a&id=2571 (accessed March 31, 2007).

17. "The Fate of the Sun," *Time,* March 23, 1987.

18. The widespread view that science and religion have always been at odds is a fiction created in the nineteenth century by polemicists like Andrew Dickson White and John William Draper. See John Hedley Brooke, *Science and Religion: Some Historical Perspectives* (Cambridge: Cambridge University Press, 1991).

19. Isaac Newton, *Principia Mathematica* (Los Angeles: University of California Press, 1996), p. 940.

20. Thomas Paine, *The Age of Reason* (New York: Knickerbocker, 1904), p. 34.

21. David Hume, *Dialogues Concerning Natured Religion* (Indianapolis, IN: Bobbs-Merrill, 1947), p. 194.

22. Voltaire, *Candide* (New York: Bantam Dell, 1984), p. 18.

23. William Paley, *Natural Theology* (Cary, NC: Oxford University Press USA, 2006), pp. 7–16.

24. J. P. Moreland, ed., *The Creation Hypothesis: Scientific Evidence for an Intelligent Designer* (Downers Grove, IL: InterVarsity, 1994), pp. 290–91.

25. Paley, *Natural Theology,* p. 225.

26. Charles Lyell, *Principles of Geology,* 3 vols. (London: John Murray, 1830).

27. Martin J. S. Rudwick, "The Shape and Meaning of Earth History," in David C. Lindberg and Ronald L. Numbers, eds., *God and Nature: Historical Essays on the Encounter Between Christianity and Science* (Berkeley: University of California Press, 1986), p. 313.

28. Charles Darwin, *On the Origin of Species by Means of Natural Selection* (New York: Signet Classics, 2003), p. 449.

29. Quoted in Michael Ruse, *Darwin and Design* (Cambridge, MA: Harvard University Press, 2003), p. 127.

30. Quoted in Ruse, *Darwin and Design,* p. 127.

31. As mentioned, this argument is presented with surprising eloquence in Henry Morris's *The Long War Against God.* See especially chap. 4, "The Dark Nursery of Darwinism," in which Morris suggests that Darwin's fellow evolutionist Alfred Wallace was under the influence of evil spirits.

32. Charles Darwin and Francis Darwin, *The Autobiography of Charles Darwin and Selected Letters* (New York: Dover, 1958), p. 87.

33. Randall Keynes, *Darwin, His Daughter and Human Evolution* (New York: Riverhead, 2002).

34. Francis Darwin, ed., *The Life and Letters of Charles Darwin,* 2 vols. (London: John Murray, 1888), p. 56.

35. Darwin, *On the Origin of Species,* p. 459. Scholars debate the degree to which this passage reflects Darwin's true sentiments. Some would argue that this passage is best understood as Darwin playing politics and pandering to his religious critics. It is likely that Darwin's endorsements of these sentiments waxed and waned over the course of his long and tormented struggle with his faith.

36. Adrian Desmond and James Moore, *Darwin: The Life of a Tormented Evolutionist* (New York: Norton, 1991), p. 677.

CHAPTER 2: A TALE OF TWO BOOKS

1. Richard Dawkins, *The Blind Watchmaker* (New York: Norton, 1996), p. 6.

2. Phillip Johnson, *The Wedge of Truth: Splitting the Foundations of Naturalism* (Downers Grove, IL: InterVarsity, 2000), p. 41.

3. Richard Dawkins, *The Ancestor's Tale: A Pilgrimage to the Dawn of Evolution* (Boston: Houghton Mifflin, 2004), pp. 613–14.

4. Alister McGrath, *Dawkins' God: Genes, Memes, and Meaning of Life* (Oxford: Blackwell, 2005); Alister McGrath and Joanna Collecutt McGrath, *The Dawkins Delusion: Atheist Fundamentalism and the Denial of the Divine* (Downers Grove, IL: InterVarsity, 2007).

5. Karl Giberson and Mariano Artigas, *The Oracles of Science: Celebrity Scientists Versus God and Religion* (Oxford: Oxford University Press, 2007), pp. 19–52.

6. Johnson, *Wedge of Truth*, p. 107.

7. See http://www.the-brights.net for a description of this new movement, started in 2003.

8. David Friedrich Strauss, *The Life of Jesus Critically Examined* (London: Chapman, 1846).

9. Matthew Arnold, *New Poems* (London: Macmillan, 1867).

10. James Gibson, ed., *Thomas Hardy: The Complete Poems* (New York: Palgrave Macmillan, 2002), p. 327.

11. A. N. Wilson offers a compelling account of the Victorian loss of faith in his intellectual history *God's Funeral* (New York: Norton, 1999).

12. Christiane L. Joost-Gaugier, *Measuring Heaven: Pythagoras and His Influence on Thought and Art in Antiquity and the Middle Ages* (Ithaca, NY: Cornell University Press. 2006), pp. 48–50.

13. Louis Agassiz, "Professor Agassiz on the Origin of Species," *American Journal of Science and Arts* (June 1860): 143–47.

14. Ronald L. Numbers, *Darwinism Comes to America* (Cambridge, MA: Harvard University Press, 1998), p. 41.

15. Historian Jon Roberts provides a thoughtful analysis in *Darwinism and the Divine in America: Protestant Intellectuals and Organic Evolution, 1859–1900* (Notre Dame, IN: University of Notre Dame Press, 2001). Roberts divides the indicated time interval into two distinct phases: 1859–1875, when religious leaders inclined to reject evolution did so on the basis of its being bad science; and 1875–1900, when religious leaders, taking note of the scientific community's widespread acceptance of evolution, reformulated their objections to evolution on theological grounds, arguing that it must be rejected as incompatible with Christianity.

16. Charles Lyell, *Principles of Geology,* 3 vols. (London: John Murray, 1830).

17. John Hedley Brooke, *Science and Religion: Some Historical Perspectives* (Cambridge: Cambridge University Press, 1991), p. 237.

18. Davis A. Young, *The Biblical Flood: A Case Study of the Church's Response to Extrabiblical Evidence* (Grand Rapids, MI: Eerdmans, 1995), p. 147.

19. *The Scofield Study Bible NKJV* (Oxford: Oxford University Press, 2002), notes on Genesis 1. The Bible passages referenced are Jeremiah 4:23–27; Isaiah 24:1; 45:18.

20. John Hammond Taylor, ed., *St. Augustine: The Literal Meaning of Genesis,* vol. 1 (Mahway, NJ: Paulist, 1982).

21. Michael J. Behe, *Darwin's Black Box* (New York: Touchstone, 1996), p. 228.

22. William A. Dembski, *No Free Lunch: Why Specified Complexity Cannot Be Purchased Without Intelligence* (Lanham, MD: Rowman & Littlefield, 2002), p. 326.

23. Peter Bowler, *The Eclipse of Darwinism* (Baltimore: Johns Hopkins University Press, 1992), p. 180.

24. Ellen G. White, *The Spirit of Prophecy,* 4 vols. (Battle Creek, MI: Seventh-day Adventist Publishing, 1870, 1877, 1878, 1884, 1969), 1:85.

25. Lyman Abbott, *The Evolution of Christianity* (New York: Outlook, 1892).

26. Contributors included C. I. Scofield of the famous *Scofield Reference Bible,* Benjamin B. Warfield of Princeton Theological Seminary, James Orr of the United Free Church College in Scotland, George Frederick Wright of Oberlin College, and academics from many other leading Christian colleges and institutes.

27. George Frederick Wright, "The Passing of Evolution," in R. A. Torrey and A. C. Dixon, eds., *The Fundamentals: A Testimony to the Truth,* 4 vols. (Los Angeles: Bible Institute of Los Angeles, 1917; repr., Grand Rapids, MI: Baker, 2003), 4: 87.

CHAPTER 3: DARWIN'S DARK COMPANIONS

1. Andrew Carnegie, "Wealth," *North American Review* (June): 653, quoted in Eugenie C. Scott, *Evolution vs. Creationism: An Introduction* (Berkeley: University of California Press, 2004), p. 93.

2. Mike Hawkins, *Social Darwinism in European and American Thought: 1860–1945* (Cambridge: Cambridge University Press, 1997), p. 82.

3. Richard Weikart, *From Darwin to Hitler* (New York: Palgrave Macmillan, 2004).

4. This sordid account appears in 1 Samuel; see especially 1:2–3.

5. T. R. Malthus, *An Essay on the Principle of Population* (1798; Oxford: Oxford University Press, 2004), p. 61.

6. Herbert Spencer, *The Man Versus the State, with Six Essays on Government, Society and Freedom* (Indianapolis, IN: Liberty Classics, 1981), p. 32. The essay from which this is taken, "The Coming Slavery," first appeared in 1884.

7. Spencer, *Man Versus the State,* p. 33.

8. Francis Galton, "Hereditary Talent and Character," *Macmillan's Magazine* 12 (1865): 157–66, 318–27, http://psychclassics.yorku.ca/Galton/talent.htm. Also quoted, without reference, in Martin Brookes, *Extreme Measures: The Dark Visions and Bright Ideas of Francis Galton* (New York: Bloomsbury, 2004), p. 144.

9. Francis Galton, *Hereditary Genius* (Amherst, NY: Prometheus, 2006), pp. 305–15.

10. Edward J. Larson, *Evolution: The Remarkable History of a Scientific Theory* (New York: Modern Library, 2004), p. 193.

11. Larson, *Evolution,* p. 194.

12. George Hunter, *A Civic Biology* (New York: American Book, 1914), p. 263.

13. Hunter, *Civic Biology,* p. 263.

14. Larson, *Evolution,* p. 195.

15. Ernst Haeckel, *Natürliche Schöpfungsgeschichte* (Berlin, 1868), quoted in Weikart, *From Darwin to Hitler,* p. 106.

16. Joseph Le Conte, *The Race Problem in the South,* Evolution Series no. 29: *Man and the State* (New York: Appleton, 1892), pp. 360–61, quoted in Hawkins, *Social Darwinism,* p. 201.

17. Martin Luther, "On the Jews and Their Lies," trans. Martin H. Bertram, in *Luther's Works* (Philadelphia: Fortress, 1971).

18. Ann Coulter, *Godless* (New York: Crown Forum, 2006), p. 271.

19. Alfred Kirchhoff, *Darwinismus* (Frankfurt, 1910), pp. 73, 86–87, quoted in Weikart, *From Darwin to Hitler,* p. 184.

20. Adolf Hitler, *Mein Kampf* (Boston: Houghton Mifflin, 1943), p. 289.

21. Nazism scholar Richard J. Evans makes this point in an essay titled "In Search of German Social Darwinism": "The language of social Darwinism helped to remove all restraint from those who directed the terroristic and exterminatory policies of the regime, and it legitimized these policies in the minds of those who practiced them by persuading them that what they were doing was justified by history, science, and nature." Richard J. Evans, "In Search of German Social Darwinism: The History and Historiography of a Concept," in Manfred Berg and Geoffrey Cocks, eds., *Medicine and Modernity* (Washington, DC: German Historical Society; Cambridge: Cambridge University Press, 1997), p. 79, quoted in Weikart, *From Darwin to Hitler,* p. 233.

22. Joel N. Shurkin, *Broken Genius: The Rise and Fall of William Shockley, Creator of the Electronic Age* (New York: Macmillan, 2006), p. 194.

23. Richard J. Herrnstein and Charles Murray, *The Bell Curve: Intelligence and Class Structure in American Life* (New York: Free Press, 1994), p. 364.

24. Steven Pinker, "Why They Kill Their Newborns," *New York Times,* November 2, 1997, http://www.rightgrrl.com/carolyn/pinker.html (accessed March 4, 2007). Pinker's article has been widely criticized, but is actually much more thoughtful and exploratory than his critics would have you believe.

25. Randy Thornhill and Craig T. Palmer, *A Natural History of Rape: Biological Bases of Sexual Coercion* (Cambridge, MA: MIT Press, 2000), p. 190.

26. Nadia Mustafa, "What About Gross National Happiness?" *Time,* Monday, January 10, 2005, http://www.time.com/time/health/article/0,8599,1016266,00.html?promoid=rss_top (accessed May 17, 2007).

27. Carl Zimmer, *Evolution: The Triumph of an Idea* (New York: HarperCollins, 2001), p. 317.

28. Zimmer, *Evolution,* p. 318.

29. Niles Eldredge, *Darwin: Discovering the Tree of Life* (New York: Norton, 2005).

30. Eugenie C. Scott, *Evolution vs. Creationism: An Introduction* (Berkeley: University of California Press, 2004).

31. Ernst Mayr, *What Evolution Is* (New York: Basic Books, 2001), p. 285.

32. Ken Ham, *The Lie: Evolution* (El Cajon, CA: Creation-Life Publishers, 1987), pp. 83–95.

33. "Darwin's Deadly Legacy," television special by Coral Ridge Ministries and James Kennedy, August 26–27, 2006, on the *Coral Ridge Hour.*

34. Tom DeRosa, *Evolution's Fatal Fruit: How Darwin's Tree of Life Brought Death to Millions* (Fort Lauderdale, FL: Coral Ridge Ministries, 2006), p. 7

CHAPTER 4: THE NEVER ENDING CLOSING ARGUMENT

1. *Inherit the Wind,* videocassette, directed by Stanley Kramer, performances by Spencer Tracey, Fredric March, and Gene Kelly (MGM/UA, 1960).

2. H. L. Mencken, *Prejudices: Fifth Series* (New York: Knopf, 1926), p. 74.

3. Fredrick Allen, *Only Yesterday* (New York: Perennial Classics, 2000), pp. 166–78.

4. H. L. Mencken, "'The Monkey Trial': A Reporter's Account," *Famous Trials in American History,* University of Missouri–Kansas City School of Law, http://www.law.umkc.edu/faculty/projects/ftrials/scopes/menk.htm (accessed January 29, 2007).

5. L. Sprague de Camp, *The Great Monkey Trial* (New York: Doubleday, 1968), p. 432.

6. Clarence Darrow, *Attorney for the Damned,* ed. Arthur Weinberg (Chicago: University of Chicago Press, 1989), p. 199.

7. "Big Crowd Watches Trial Under Trees," *New York Times,* July 21, 1925, sec. I.

8. Tracy Sterling, "Darrow Quizzes Bryan; Agnosticism in Clash with Fundamentalism," *Commercial Appeal* (Memphis), July 21, 1925, sec. I, quoted in Edward Larson, *Summer for the Gods* (New York: Basic Books, 1997), pp. 190–91.

9. Edward Larson, *Trial and Error* (New York: Oxford University Press, 2003), p. 87. This chapter draws heavily on the definitive work of Edward Larson, particularly his Pulitzer Prize–winning account of the Scopes trial, *Summer for the Gods* (New York: Basic Books, 1997), and *Trial and Error,* which is the standard history of America's creation-evolution court cases up to the mid-1990s. Larson has several excellent books on the creation-evolution controversy, all of which I can heartily recommend.

10. Judith Grabner and Peter Miller, "Effects of the Scopes Trial: Was it a Victory for Evolutionists?" *Science* 185, no. 4154 (1974): 832–37.

11. Sol Tax and Charles Callender, eds., *Evolution After Darwin: The University of Chicago Centennial,* vol. 3 (Chicago: University of Chicago, 1960), p. 107.

12. *School District of Abington Township, Pennsylvania v. Schempp,* 374 U.S. 225 (1963).

13. S. McBee and J. Neary, "Evolution Revolution in Arkansas," *Life* 65, no. 21 (1968): 89.

14. "Separate Answer to the Intervention of Hubert H. Blanchard, Jr.," in Susan Epperson and Bruce Bennet, "Proceedings," in *Appendix, Epperson v. Arkansas,* 393 U.S. 97 (1968), 40, quoted in Larson, *Trial and Error,* p. 101.

15. *Epperson v. Arkansas,* 393 U.S. 97 (1968).

16. "Memorandum Opinion," *Hendren,* 19–20, quoted in Larson, *Trial and Error,* p. 145.

17. Institute for Creation Research, "The Institute for Creation Research FAQs," http://www.icr.org/home/faq/ (updated February 26, 2007).

18. Alex Heard, "Creationist Movement Appears to Be Slowed by Loss in Arkansas," *Education Week,* February 17, 1982.

19. Brenda Tirey, "Senate Approves Bill to Distribute Tax on Premiums to Fire Fighter Pension Fund," *Arkansas Gazette,* March 13, 1981, p. 10-A, quoted in Larson, *Trial and Error,* p. 151.

20. I will have more to say about these ideas in a later chapter when I look at the conceptual rather than legal history of creationism, but for now suffice it to say that this description of the creation position represented the thinking of the creationist movement.

21. Marcel La Follette, "Creationism in the News: Mass Media Coverage of the Arkansas Trial," in Marcel La Follette, *Creationism, Science, and the Law: The Arkansas Case* (Cambridge, MA: MIT Press, 1983), p. 194.

22. Norman Geisler, *The Creator in the Courtroom: "Scopes II"* (Milford: Mott Media, 1982), p. 208.

23. Langdon Gilkey, *Creationism on Trial: God and Science at Little Rock* (Charlottesville: University Press of Virginia, 1985), p. 104. Gilkey notes in his account that "Reading over that record of my own testimony, competently as it was done considering the difficulties of reporting and then transcribing often complex and frequently esoteric matters, I realize how much of what was actually said is inevitably omitted from such an official record" (p. 244).

24. Gilkey, *Creationism on Trial,* p. 76.

25. Brig Klyce, "Chandra Wickramasinghe in Arkansas," http://www.panspermia.org/chandra.htm (accessed February 26, 2007).

26. Gilkey, *Creationism on Trial,* p. 141.

27. Robert Gentry and Donald Chittick.

28. *McLean v. Arkansas Board of Education,* Judge William Overton (U.S. Dis. Ct. 1982), quoted in Michael Ruse, ed., *But Is It Science? The Philosophical Question in the Creation/Evolution Controversy* (Amherst, NY: Prometheus, 1996), p. 326.

29. "Creationism in Schools: The Decision in *McLean Versus the Arkansas Board of Education,*" *Science* 215, no. 4535 (1982): 934–43.

30. Duane Gish, Introduction, in Geisler, *Creator in the Courtroom,* p. 1.

31. Geisler, *Creator in the Courtroom,* p. x.

32. J. P. Moreland, *Christianity and the Nature of Science: A Philosophical Investigation* (Grand Rapids, MI: Baker, 1989).

33. Larry Laudan, "Science at the Bar—Cause for Concern," in Ruse, ed., *But Is It Science?* pp. 351–55.

34. *Edwards v. Aguillard* 482 U.S. 578 (5th Cir. Ct. App. 1987).

35. Affidavit of Dr. Dean H. Kenyon, filed in *Edwards v. Aguillard* 482 U.S. 578 (5th Cir. Ct. App. 1987), http://www.talkorigins.org/faqs/edwards-v-aguillard/kenyon.html (accessed February 16, 2007).

36. Joel Cracraft, "Reflections on the Arkansas Creation Trial," *Paleobiology* 8, no. 2 (Spring 1982): 83–89.

37. Stephen Jay Gould, "Evolution's Erratic Pace," *Natural History* 86, no. 5 (May 1977): 14.

38. Larson, *Trial and Error,* p. 177.

39. Wendell Bird, *The Origin of Species Revisited* (Nashville, TN: Philosophical Library, 1991), p. 447.

40. Joan Biskupic, "Justice Brennan, Voice of Court's Social Revolution, Dies," *Washington Post,* July 25, 1997.

41. *Edwards v. Aguillard,* 482 U.S. 578 (1987).

42. One curious feature of twentieth-century creationism, which relies heavily on flood geology, is the nearly total absence of Ph.D. geologists from the ranks of the creationists. Ronald Numbers reports on the challenges the creationists have faced in trying to get a geology student to complete a doctorate without abandoning the central tenets of creationism. See "Flood Geology Without Flood Geologists," in *The Creationists: From Scientific Creationism to Intelligent Design,* expanded ed. (Cambridge, MA: Harvard University Press, 2006), pp. 301–11.

43. Though I outline the conceptual origins of this movement in a later chapter, this is a good place to discuss the legal implications of this new face of creationism. I also note here that some scholars, including the nonpartisan historian Jon Roberts, whom I respect enormously, disagree with me that ID is simply a new face on the old creationism. My equation of the two derives from my conviction that both of them are, when all is said and done, really little more than a catalog of minor challenges to evolutionary theory.

44. Percival Davis and Dean H. Kenyon, *Of Pandas and People,* ed. Charles B. Thaxton (Dallas: Haughton, 1993), pp. 99–100.

45. Burt Humburg and Ed Brayton, "Kitzmiller et al. versus Dover Area School Disctrict," *eSkeptic,* December 20, 2005, http://www.skeptic.com/eskeptic/05-12-20.html (accessed February 26, 2007).

46. Peter Slevin, "Teachers, Scientists Vow to Fight Challenge to Evolution," *Washington Post,* May 5, 2005, p. A03.

47. Nick Matzke, "*Of Pandas and People,* the Foundational Work of the 'Intelligent Design' Movement," National Center for Science Education, November 23, 2004, http://www.ncseweb.org/resources/articles/8442_1_introduction_iof_pandas__11_23_2004.asp.

48. Humburg and Brayton, "Kitzmiller et al. versus Dover Area School District."

49. Davis and Kenyon, *Of Pandas and People,* pp. 99–100.

50. Dean Kenyon, Foreword, in Henry Morris and Gary Parker, *What Is Creation Science?* (Green Forest, AR: Master Books, 1997), p. 2.

51. Wayne Frair and Percival Davis, *A Case for Creation,* 3d ed. (Kansas City, MO: Creation Research Society Books, 1983).

52. Lauri Lebo, "In the Judge's Hands," *York Daily Record/Sunday News Online,* November 5, 2005, http://www.ydr.com/search/ci_3219243 (February 26, 2007). Some board members testified the reporters made up the quotations.

53. *Kitzmiller v. Dover,* case no. 04cv2688132, 132 (Pa. District Ct. 2005).

54. *Kitzmiller v. Dover,* case no. 04cv2688132, 137 (Pa. District Ct. 2005).

55. *Kitzmiller v. Dover,* case no. 04cv2688132, 82 (Pa. District Ct. 2005).

56. *Kitzmiller v. Dover,* case no. 04cv2688132, 88 (Pa. District Ct. 2005).

57. "Weblog: Dover Board Lied! Intelligent Design Died!" *Christianity Today,* http://ctlibrary.com/34400 (accessed March 4, 2007).

58. *Kitzmiller v. Dover,* case no. 04cv2688132, 49 (Pa. District Ct. 2005).

59. *Kitzmiller v. Dover,* case no. 04cv2688132, 138 (Pa. District Ct. 2005).

60. David Dewolf et al., *Traipsing into Evolution* (Seattle: Discovery Institute, 2006).

61. Clarence Darrow, *Attorney for the Damned,* ed. Arthur Weinberg (New York: Simon & Shuster, 1989), pp. 217–18.

62. Irving Stone, *Clarence Darrow for the Defense* (New York: Doubleday, 1941), p. 498.

63. Gilkey, *Creationism on Trial,* p. 93.

64. Poll: Majority Reject Evolution, *CBS News,* October 23, 2005, http://www.cbsnews.com/stories/2005/10/22/opinion/polls/main965223.shtml.

CHAPTER 5: THE EMPEROR'S NEW SCIENCE

1. Jennifer Harper, "Americans Still Hold Faith in Divine Creation," *Washington Times,* June 9, 2006, http://washingtontimes.com/national/20060608-111826-4947r.htm (accessed February 10, 2007). What is not clear from the poll is exactly how many Americans might still hold to the gap theory or some other creation model in which the earth itself might be much older than the human race. My experience suggests, however, that most creationists are young-earth creationists.

2. A typical example is Robert Snyder, Barbara L. Mann, et al., *Earth Science: The Challenge of Discovery* (Lexington, MA: Heath, 1991), p. 377.

3. Most people think winter is colder than summer because the earth is farther from the sun during the winter, a particularly dumb mistake, considering that the Southern Hemisphere experiences summer while the Northern Hemisphere is in winter.

4. Ellen Gould White, *Patriarchs and Prophets* (Hagerstown, MD: Review and Herald Publishing, 1958), pp. 107–8.

5. George McCready Price, *The New Geology* (Mountain View, CA: Pacific Press, 1923).

6. Price, *New Geology*, pp. 676–77.

7. Price, *New Geology*, pp. 627–29.

8. Martin Gardner, *In the Name of Science* (New York: Putnam, 1952), p. 129.

9. Price, *New Geology*, p. 652. A preflood paradisial climate, which he called the "eternal spring," was a staple in Price's writings, inferred from fossils of some non-Arctic organisms found at the poles. Geological evidence for prehistoric ice at the poles is dismissed as ambiguous. See his *Evolutionary Geology and the New Catastrophism* (Mountain View, CA: Pacific Press, 1926), pp. 258–61. The same argument also appears in his *The Fundamentals of Geology* (Mountain View, CA: Pacific Press, 1913), pp. 195–98.

10. Price, *New Geology*, pp. 655–56, 706.

11. Price, *New Geology*, p. 661.

12. Price, *New Geology*, p. 594.

13. George McCready Price, "Letter to the Editor of *Science* from the Principle Scientific Authority of the Fundamentalists," *Science* 63, no. 1627 (March 5, 1926): 259.

14. Stephen Leacock, *Sunshine Sketches of a Little Town* (UK: Echo Library, 2006), p.71.

15. George McCready Price, *Illogical Geology: The Weakest Point in the Evolutionary Theory* (Los Angeles: Modern Heretic Company, 1906).

16. The most influential of these authorities was perhaps Bernard Ramm, a leading theologian and author of many books on Christian theology. His *The Christian View of Science and Scripture* (Grand Rapids, MI: Eerdmans, 1954) was widely viewed as a definitive. It argued that Christians should accept both the great age of the earth and the nonuniversality of Noah's flood on both biblical and scientific grounds.

17. Ronald Numbers, *The Creationists: From Scientific Creationism to Intelligent Design,* expanded ed. (Cambridge, MA: Harvard University Press, 2006), p. 218.

18. Rice University, as it is now known, was founded by William Marsh Rice in 1912 with an endowment so generous that the university did not have to charge tuition until 1965.

19. Ramm, *Christian View of Science and Scripture*, p. 117.

20. Ramm, *Christian View of Science and Scripture*, p. 28.

21. In his chapter on *The Genesis Flood* in *A History of Modern Creationism* (San Diego: Master Books, 1984), Henry Morris writes: "The Lord marvelously led in the necessary research and writing of the book. Time and again, after encountering a difficult geological (or other) problem, I would pray about it, and then a reasonable solution would somehow quickly come to mind" (p. 153).

22. Morris, *History of Modern Creationism*, p. 150.

23. Numbers, *The Creationists*, pp. 198–99.

24. Price, *New Geology*, p. 706.

25. The index to *The Genesis Flood* has four entries for Price and forty for Ramm, despite the fact that the book draws more heavily on Price than Ramm. Ramm's ideas, of course, are being critiqued, while Price's are being repackaged.

26. Ramm, *Christian View of Science and Scripture*, p. 180.

27. John C. Whitcomb and Henry M. Morris, *The Genesis Flood: The Biblical Record and Its Scientific Implications* (Phillipsburg, NJ: Presbyterian and Reformed Publishing, 1961), p. xx.

28. Ramm, *Christian View of Science and Scripture,* pp. 41–42.

29. Romans 1:22 (KJV), obtained at http://bible.cc/romans/1-22.htm.

30. Isaac Asimov, "Is Big Brother Watching?" *The Humanist* 44.4 (July/August 1984): 6–10, 33.

31. Whitcomb and Morris, *Genesis Flood,* p. 222.

32. Daisie Radner and Michael Radner, *Science and Unreason* (Belmont, CA: Wadsworth, 1982). This book looks at pseudoscience and fringe ideas using case studies on flat-earth cosmology, ancient astronauts, biorhythms, creationism, Velikovsky, the bicameral mind, and parapsychology.

33. Michael Shermer, *Why People Believe Weird Things: Pseudoscience, Superstition, and Other Confusions of Our Time* (New York: Holt, 2002).

34. "The Monkey Suit," *The Simpsons,* FOX, May 14, 2006; "The Untitled Griffin Family History," *Family Guy,* FOX, May 14, 2006. On *Saturday Night Live,* NBC, October 29, 2005, Tina Fey read the following "news" item: "The latest Gallup poll found that 66 percent of Americans think President Bush is doing a poor job in Iraq. The remaining 34 percent believe that Adam and Eve rode to church on dinosaurs."

35. Larry Vardiman, "Sensitivity Studies on Vapor Canopy Temperature Profiles," Proceedings of the 4th International Conference on Creationism (Pittsburg: Creation Science Fellowship, 1998), pp. 607–18, 616.

36. Don DeYoung, *Thousands, Not Billions: Challenging an Icon of Evolution: Questioning the Age of the Earth* (Green Forest, AR: Master Books, 2005), p. 60.

37. Whitcomb and Morris, *The Genesis Flood,* p. 167.

38. Richard Dawkins, *The Blind Watchmaker* (New York: Norton, 1986); Stephen Jay Gould, *Wonderful Life: The Burgess Shale and the Nature of History* (New York: Norton, 1990); Ken Miller, *Finding Darwin's God* (London: Harper Perennial, 2000); Darrel Falk, *Coming to Peace with Science* (Downers Grove, IL: InterVarsity, 2004).

39. Richard Dawkins, "Put Your Money on Evolution," *New York Times,* April 9, 1989, accessed via http://proquest.umi.com.

40. Daniel Dennett, *Darwin's Dangerous Idea: Evolution and the Meaning of Life* (New York: Simon & Schuster, 1995) p. 519.

41. Henry Morris, *The Long War Against God: The History and Impact of the Creation/ Evolution Controversy* (Green Forest, AR: Master Books, 2000), p. 260.

42. Transnational Association of Christian Colleges and Schools, "Accreditation Standards," http://www.tracs.org/standards.htm (accessed March 1, 2007).

43. Numbers, *The Creationists,* pp. 399–431.

CHAPTER 6: **CREATIONISM EVOLVES INTO INTELLIGENT DESIGN**

1. I am excluding Stephen Meyer's controversial 2004 publication in *Proceedings of the Biological Society of Washington,* a peer-reviewed scientific journal. The paper, titled "The Origin of Biological Information and the Higher Taxonomic Categories" (117 [2]: 213–39), was later withdrawn by the publisher. The editor of *Proceedings,* a known supporter

of intelligent design, was accused of going outside the usual review procedures in order to get Meyer's paper published. The editor was fired. In any case, Meyer was not advocating flood geology; he is, in fact, a historian and philosopher of science, not a scientist.

2. Rank-and-file creationists typically did not read the "secular" literature critiquing their position, and unscrupulous polemicists would often keep repeating claims, even after their fellow creationists had withdrawn them. This odd state of affairs has led to the publication of books like Mark Isaak's *The Counter-Creation Handbook* (Berkeley: University of California Press, 2007), which simply lists all the standard claims of the creationists with their standard refutation. There are hundreds of claims organized under the headings of philosophy, biology, paleontology, geology, astronomy and cosmology, physics and mathematics, biblical creationism, and intelligent design. Most of the claims continue to appear with regularity in popular anti-evolutionary books.

3. See, for example, Davis Young, *Christianity and the Age of the Earth* (Grand Rapids, MI: Zondervan, 1982). At the time he wrote the book, Young was a fully credentialed professor of geology at Calvin College, one of America's leading liberal arts colleges, and strongly in the evangelical tradition. Young's credentials, affiliation, and strong public Christian faith should have made him an authority on this topic, but his book fell stillborn from the press and was ignored by young-earth creationists.

4. Robert Schadewald, "The 1998 International Conference on Creationism," *NCSE Reports,* www.ncseweb.org/resources/rncse_content/vol18/9954_the_1998_international_confere_12_30_1899.asp (accessed February 13, 2007). Wise's ruthless honesty is shared by fellow creationists Paul Nelson and John Mark Reynolds. See Paul Nelson and John Mark Reynolds, "Young Earth Creationism," in Paul Nelson, Robert C. Newman, and Howard J. Van Till, eds., *Three Views on Creation and Evolution* (Grand Rapids, MI: Zondervan, 1999), pp. 41–75.

5. Nelson and Reynolds, "Young Earth Creationism," p. 51.

6. Ken Miller, *Finding Darwin's God* (London: Harper Perennial, 2000); Howard Van Till, *The Fourth Day* (Grand Rapids, MI: Eerdmans, 1986); Davis Young, *Christianity and the Age of the Earth* (Thousand Oaks, CA: Artisan, 1988); Darrel Falk, *Coming to Peace with Science* (Downers Grove, IL: InterVarsity, 2004); Karl Giberson, *Worlds Apart: The Unholy War Between Science and Religion* (Kansas City: Beacon Hill Press of Kansas City, 1993).

7. M. Conrad Hyers, *The Meaning of Creation: Genesis and Modern Science* (Louisville, KY: Westminster/John Knox, 1984); John Haught, *God After Darwin* (Boulder, CO: Westview, 2000).

8. Taken from a sermon at Coral Ridge Presbyterian Church, http://www.leaderu.com/issues/fabric/chap05.html (accessed February 17, 2007).

9. Glen Kuban, "A Matter of Degree: An Examination of Carl Baugh's Alleged Credentials," *NCSE Reports* 9, no. 6 (November–December 1989), http://paleo.cc/paluxy/degrees.htm (accessed February 17, 2007).

10. Carl E. Baugh, *Panorama of Creation* (Oklahoma City, OK: Creation Evidences Museum, 1989), pp. 49, 51.

11. http://www.tbn.org/index.php/2/4/p/3.html (accessed February 17, 2007).

12. http://www.kent-hovind.com (accessed February 17, 2007).

13. Henry Morris, *The Twilight of Evolution* (Philadelphia: Presbyterian and Reformed Publishing, 1963).

14. Tom McIver's encyclopedic *Anti-Evolution: A Reader's Guide to Writings Before and After Darwin* (Baltimore: Johns Hopkins University Press, 1988) lists many titles announcing the end of evolution. There are three alone titled *The Collapse of Evolution,* the most recent and substantial of which is Scott Huse, *The Collapse of Evolution* (Grand Rapids, MI: Baker, 1997). For an Islamic perspective, but one drawing heavily on Christian creationism, see Harun Yahya, *The Evolution Deceit: The Scientific Collapse of Darwinism and Its Ideological Background* (New York: Global, 2001).

15. "The Untitled Griffin Family History," *Family Guy,* FOX, May 14, 2006.

16. Stephen Jay Gould, "Impeaching a Self-Appointed Judge," *Scientific American* 267 (July 1992): 118–21.

17. Phillip Johnson, *Darwin on Trial* (Washington, DC: Regnery Gateway, 1991), p. 154.

18. William Dembski. *Mere Creation: Science, Faith, and Intelligent Design* (Downers Grove, IL: InterVarsity, 1998).

19. Thomas Woodward, *Doubts About Darwin: A History of ID* (Grand Rapids, MI: Baker, 2003); see also his *Darwin Strikes Back: Defending the Science of ID* (Grand Rapids, MI: Baker, 2006).

20. K. W. Giberson and D. A. Yerxa, *Species of Origins: America's Search for a Creation Story* (New York: Rowman & Littlefield, 2002), pp. 193–233.

21. Barbara Forrest and Paul R. Gross, *Creationism's Trojan Horse: The Wedge of Intelligent Design* (Oxford: Oxford University Press, 2004); Robert Pennock, *Tower of Babel: The Evidence Against the New Creationism* (Cambridge, MA: MIT Press, 1999).

22. Ahmanson has served for years on the board of R. J. Rushdoony's Chalcedon Foundation, a "Christian Reconstructionist" organization seeking to impose Old Testament law on America. Reconstructionists, to take one example, propose capital punishment for "crimes" like blasphemy, heresy, adultery, and homosexuality. See Forrest and Gross, *Creationism's Trojan Horse,* pp. 264–67.

23. William Dembski, *Intelligent Design: The Bridge Between Science and Theology* (Downers Grove, IL: InterVarsity, 1999).

24. William Dembski, *The Design Revolution: Answering the Toughest Questions About Intelligent Design* (Downers Grove, IL: InterVarsity, 2004), p. 45.

25. Michael Behe, "The Modern Intelligent Design Hypothesis," *Philosophia Christi,* series 2, vol. 3, no. 1 (2001): 165.

CHAPTER 7: HOW TO BE STUPID, WICKED, AND INSANE

1. Cornelia Dean, "Evolution Takes a Back Seat in U.S. Classes," *New York Times,* February 1, 2005.

2. Cedarville College, for example, publishes the following statement on its college Web site: "We believe that the universe, solar system, earth, and life were all created recently by an omnipotent, omniscient God during six literal 24 hour days, as described in Genesis Chapters 1 and 2"; see http://www.cedarville.edu/academics/sciencemath/origins.htm (accessed May 17, 2007). Cedarville was accredited in 1975 and is consistently ranked in the top tier of Midwest colleges by *U.S. News & World Report.* Liberty University proudly displays its accreditation by the anti-evolutionary Transnational Association of Christian

Colleges and Schools (TRACS) above its conventional accreditation by the Southern Association of Colleges and Schools; see http://www.liberty.edu/index.cfm?PID=284 (accessed May 18, 2007).

3. Daniel Dennett, *Darwin's Dangerous Idea: Evolution and the Meaning of Life* (New York: Simon & Schuster, 1995); Richard Dawkins, *The God Delusion* (Boston: Houghton Mifflin, 2006); Phillip Johnson, *Defeating Darwin by Opening Minds* (Downers Grove, IL: InterVarsity, 1997); Henry Morris, *The Long War Against God: The History and Impact of the Creation/Evolution Controversy* (Green Forest, AR: Master Books, 2000).

4. Ken Miller, *Finding Darwin's God* (London: Harper Perennial, 2000); John Haught, *God After Darwin* (Boulder, CO: Westview, 2000); Darrel Falk, *Coming to Peace with Science* (Downers Grove, IL: InterVarsity, 2004); Francis Collins, *The Language of God: A Scientist Presents Evidence for Belief* (New York: Free Press, 2006).

5. *Evolution: International Journal of Organic Evolution.*

6. *Answers; Origins & Design; Creation Ex Nihilo; Creation Research Society Quarterly.*

7. *NCSE Reports.*

8. *Perspectives on Science & Faith.*

9. "Statement on Teaching Evolution," National Association of Biology Teachers, March 15, 1995, http://darwin.eeb.uconn.edu/Documents/NABT.htm (accessed March 30, 2007).

10. Simon Conway Morris, *Life's Solution: Inevitable Humans in a Lonely Universe* (Cambridge: Cambridge University Press, 2003), p. 282.

11. Conway Morris, *Life's Solution,* pp. 284–85.

12. Robert Wright, *Non-Zero: The Logic of Human Destiny* (New York: Pantheon, 2000).

13. Phillip Johnson, *Objections Sustained: Subversive Essays on Evolution, Law and Culture* (Downers Grove, IL: InterVarsity, 1995), p. 86.

14. Johnson, *Objections Sustained,* p. 91.

15. Louise Lamphere et al., *August 2001 Joint Letter from Scientific and Educational Leaders on Evolution in H.R.1.,* Letter to House Committee on Education and the Workforce, October 9, 2001, AGI Government Affairs Program, http://www.agiweb.org/gap/legis107/evolutionletter.html (accessed March 6, 2007).

16. My relativity professor at Rice University, where I did my doctoral work in the early 1980s, used Einstein's book *The Meaning of Relativity,* written in 1922. The text was entirely adequate and pedagogically superior to many more recent treatments. A 1922 textbook on evolution, by contrast, would be hopelessly out-of-date if used today, even though, in 1922, evolution was decades older than relativity.

17. Stephen Jay Gould, *The Structure of Evolutionary Theory* (Cambridge, MA: Harvard University Press, Belknap Press, 2002); Richard Dawkins, *The Ancestor's Tale: A Pilgrimage to the Dawn of Evolution* (Boston: Houghton Mifflin, 2004).

18. Conway Morris, *Life's Solution,* pp. 4–5.

19. For an excellent survey of Galileo propaganda, see William R. Shea. and Mariano Artigas, *Galileo Observed: Science and the Politics of Belief* (Sagamore Beach, MA: Science History Publications, 2006).

20. Richard Dawkins, review of Donald Johanson and Maitland Edey, *Blueprints: Solving the Mystery of Evolution, New York Times,* April 9, 1989, sec 7.

21. Dawkins, *The Ancestor's Tale,* pp. 613–14.

22. Carl Sagan, *Cosmos* (New York: Ballantine, 1985), p. 345.

23. Stephen Jay Gould, *Wonderful Life: The Burgess Shale and the Nature of History* (New York: Norton, 1990), p. 323.

24. Edward O. Wilson, *On Human Nature* (Cambridge, MA: Harvard University Press, 1978), p. 201.

25. Steven Weinberg, *The First Three Minutes: A Modern View of the Origin of the Universe,* updated ed. (New York: Basic Books, 1993), pp. 154–55.

26. Richard Dawkins, *The Blind Watchmaker* (New York: Norton, 1986), p. 6.

27. Morris, *The Long War Against God,* p. 25.

28. Morris, *The Long War Against God,* p. 327.

29. Jonathan Sarfati, *Refuting Evolution: A Response to the National Academy of Sciences' Teaching About Evolution and the Nature of Science* (Green Forest, AR: Master Books, 1999), p. 16.

30. Phillip Johnson, *Reason in the Balance: The Case Against Naturalism in Science, Law and Education* (Downers Grove, IL: InterVarsity, 1995), p. 12.

31. Richard Lewontin, "Billions and Billions of Demons," *New York Review,* January 9, 1997, p. 31 (emphases in original).

32. Richard E. Dickerson, "Random Walking," *Journal of Molecular Evolution* 34 (April 1992): 277.

33. William B. Provine, "Influence of Darwin's Ideas on the Study of Evolution," *BioScience* 32 (June 1982): 506.

34. Randy Thornhill and Craig T. Palmer, *A Natural History of Rape: Biological Bases of Sexual Coercion* (Cambridge, MA: MIT Press, 2000).

CHAPTER 8: EVOLUTION AND PHYSICS ENVY

1. William R. Overton, United States District Court Opinion, *McLean v. Arkansas Board of Education,* in Michael Ruse, ed., *But Is It Science? The Philosophical Question in the Creation/Evolution Controversy* (Amherst, NY: Prometheus, 1996), pp. 307–31.

2. Phillip Johnson, *Darwin on Trial* (Washington, DC: Regnery Gateway, 1991), pp. 145–54; Henry M. Morris, *Scientific Creationism* (Green Forest, AR: Master Books, 1985), pp. 6–7.

3. "I have changed my mind about the testability and logical status of the theory of natural selection; and I am glad to have an opportunity to make a recantation." "Natural Selection and the Emergence of Mind," *Dialectica* 32, no. 3–4 (1978): 339–55, http://www.geocities.com/criticalrationalist/popperevolution.htm.

4. Both Johnson and Morris (see n. 2) wrote their remarks years after Popper changed his mind about evolution being falsifiable.

5. Francis Crick, *What Mad Pursuit: A Personal View of Scientific Discovery* (New York: Basic Books, 1988), pp. 138–39.

6. Johnson, *Darwin on Trial,* p. 154.

7. Phillip Johnson, *Reason in the Balance: The Case Against Naturalism in Science, Law and Education* (Downers Grove, IL: InterVarsity, 1995), p. 90.

8. Duane Gish, *Evolution: The Fossils Still Say No!* (San Diego, CA: Master Books, 1995), pp. 81–82.

9. Jonathan Wells, *Icons of Evolution: Science or Myth?* (Washington, DC: Regnery, 2000), p. 8.

10. Johnson, *Darwin on Trial,* p. 13. Johnson has such a poor grasp of science that he can't see the illogic in his claim that "a scientist outside his field of expertise is just another layman" (p. 13). Does he really believe that a chemist or physicist is no more qualified to speak about biology than a bricklayer or novelist?

11. Ken Ham, *The Lie: Evolution* (El Cajon, CA: Creation-Life Publishers, 1987), p. 21.

12. Niles Eldredge, *Darwin: Discovering the Tree of Life* (New York: Norton, 2005), p. 228.

13. Ernst Mayr, *What Evolution Is* (New York: Basic Books, 2001), p. 21.

14. Mayr, *What Evolution Is,* p. 31.

15. Charles Darwin, *On the Origin of Species by Means of Natural Selection* (New York: Avenel, 1979), p. 422.

16. Richard Dawkins, *River Out of Eden: A Darwinian View of Life* (New York: Basic Books, 1995), p. 78.

17. Darrel Falk, *Coming to Peace with Science* (Downers Grove, IL: InterVarsity, 2004), pp. 171–98.

18. M. Shimamura et al., "Molecular Evidence from Retroposons That Whales Form a Clade Within Even-Toed Ungulates," *Nature* 388 (1997): 666–68. The authors note that their conclusions confirm data from paleontological, morphological, and molecular studies (p. 666).

19. Michael J. Behe, *The Edge of Evolution: The Search for the Limits of Darwinism* (New York: Free Press, 2007).

20. J. P. Moreland, ed., *The Creation Hypothesis: Scientific Evidence for an Intelligent Designer* (Downers Grove, IL: InterVarsity, 1994).

21. Arthur Peacocke, *Evolution: The Disguised Friend of Faith?* (Philadelphia: Templeton Foundation Press, 2004)

CONCLUSION: PILGRIM'S PROGRESS

1. E. O. Wilson, *Biophilia* (Cambridge, MA: Harvard University Press, 1984).

2. This view of God's creative involvement does nothing, in principle, to compromise the traditional biblical affirmation that God "numbers the hairs on our heads" or "cares about the sparrow's fall." There is no reason why God cannot be intimately concerned about such details, just because God is the not the immediate creative agent behind those details.

3. Stephen Jay Gould, *Full House: The Spread of Excellence from Plato to Darwin* (New York: Harmony, 1996), p. 216.

4. Mariano Artigas, Thomas F. Glick, and Rafael A. Martinez, *Negotiating Darwin: The Vatican Confronts Evolution, 1877–1902* (Baltimore: Johns Hopkins University Press, 2006); David N. Livingstone, *Darwin's Forgotten Defenders: The Encounter Between Evangelical Theology and Evolutionary Thought* (Grand Rapids, MI: Eerdmans, 1987).

5. Freeman Dyson, *Disturbing the Universe* (New York: Basic Books, 1979), p. 250.

INDEX